C. Henkel

THE
Frugal Gourmet's
Culinary Handbook

ALSO BY JEFF SMITH

The Frugal Gourmet (1984)

The Frugal Gourmet Cooks with Wine (1986)

The Frugal Gourmet Cooks American (1987)

The Frugal Gourmet Cooks Three Ancient Cuisines (1989)

The Frugal Gourmet on Our Immigrant Ancestors (1990)

T H E
Frugal
Gourmet's
Culinary Handbook

**An Updated Version of
an American Classic on Food and Cooking**

**ADAPTED FROM THE ORIGINAL TEXT
BY CHARLES FELLOWS**

*Including revised recipes from
the turn of the century*

JEFF SMITH
CRAIG WOLLAM

D. C. Smith
Research Assistant

William Morrow and Company, Inc.
New York

It is the policy of William Morrow and Company, Inc., and its imprints
and affiliates, recognizing the importance of preserving what has been
written, to print the books we publish on acid-free paper, and we exert
our best efforts to that end.

LIBRARY OF CONGRESS CATALOGING-IN-PUBLICATION DATA

The Frugal Gourmet's culinary handbook : an updated version of an
    American classic on food and cooking / by Jeff Smith and
Craig Wollam.
        p. cm.
    ISBN 0-688-09071-0
    1. Frugal Gourmet (Television program) 2. Cookery—Dictionar-
ies. 3. Food—Dictionaries.   I. Smith, Jeff.   II. Wollam, Craig.
TX349.F78 1991
641'.03—dc20   91-11671
                                                        CIP

Printed in the United States of America

First Edition

1 2 3 4 5 6 7 8 9 10

BOOK DESIGN BY RICHARD ORIOLO

To all of the line cooks
in our fine American restaurants:
heroes of the fire and flame,
heroes we seldom see.

This book is dedicated to them.

Thanks to all of you.

J.S.
C.W.

CONTENTS

ACKNOWLEDGMENTS
ix

INTRODUCTION
xi

About the Original Author
xxi

How to Use This Book
xxv

The Frugal Gourmet's List of Recipes
xxvii

A WORKING CHARLES FELLOWS LEXICON
1

THE CULINARY HANDBOOK
9

INDEX
483

ACKNOWLEDGMENTS

We must again thank Maria Guarnaschelli, our editor. Her enthusiasm for our projects is beyond belief. Once we get going on an idea, we are almost reluctant to tell her of it since she becomes so involved and supportive that she pushes us to insights that we really cannot claim as our own.

Bill Adler, our book agent in New York, sometimes says no to us, but it is usually while we are looking at a menu in a restaurant. The rest of the time Bill is only positive. He says yes to our ideas and dreams, and he seems to be able to pull off almost anything.

Al Marchioni, our publisher at William Morrow, continues to offer affectionate support. Fine man, that one!

D. C. Smith, our research assistant, has been invaluable in this current effort, having spent many hours on the original text. Our secretary, Dawn Sparks, and our business manager, James Paddleford, are so good that they make us look good. Jason Lynch and Heidi Kemper have been our faithful kitchen assistants. So what if they didn't like the parsnip fritters! They have been great helpers.

Finally, we must acknowledge the American restaurant workers, particularly the line cooks to whom this book is dedicated. Since Mr. Fellows was such a lover of the restaurant business, we are sure that he would approve.

JEFF SMITH
CRAIG WOLLAM

INTRODUCTION

This is not the usual kind of cookbook. It is more like a slice of fascinating food history, about which most Americans seem to know little. Still, it remains a fine cookbook.

This book was first published in 1904, the turn of the century, and certainly one of the most important periods in America's culinary history. I read about those times now and I wonder how we could have gotten ourselves into this nouvelle, healthy, and sprout-covered boring current cuisine. When this book was first published, Americans were eating like we had never eaten before . . . or since. How can I long for something that I never really witnessed? Let me tell you.

We are currently experiencing a new camp of cooking that says "Go back to the old cooking." What this usually means is a call to the cooking of World War II—meat loaf and mashed potatoes with overcooked peas—and I don't think this was a particularly fine time in American culinary history. Rather, it was at the turn of the century that our cuisine was really outstanding, though some present-day health experts are also wont to call it terribly unhealthy. Perhaps so, but it was fun!

I have found little joy in the nouvelle cuisine food fad. The plate may have looked like an artistic presentation, but there was so little to eat and enjoy. Now we claim we want to go back to the basics, and this very book, originally published for the "catering fraternity" of the early 1900s, will help us do that. Let's go back to really good times, and then clean up the recipes a bit.

I am going to credit the railroad with the birthing of America's fine restaurants. Prior to the railroad, our cuisine was strictly local, provincial, and certainly seasonal. With the flourishing of the railroad, foods from all over the country could be rushed into our major cities and placed upon our restaurant tables.

It is no coincidence that the greatest New York restaurant of the last century opened its doors in the same year that the first regularly scheduled steam-powered train service in the nation began. It was in the year 1831, and the restaurant was Delmonico's. This was also about the time of the invention of mechanical refrigeration. Couple this with the railroad and you could have anything you wanted from great distances away. By the time that the transcontinental railroad was completed in 1869, Delmonico's had three restaurants and was soon to expand.

The menus that were offered in such places as Delmonico's make a first-class restaurant in our time look like a snack bar. In a fine American restaurant at the turn of the century you could enjoy a greater variety of fresh food than could have been commissioned by any king only a few decades before. And Americans ate like kings. Even in 1838, just a few years after the railroads began, Delmonico's offered a bill of fare that ran to twelve pages and offered the customer no fewer than 371 dishes from which to choose. The consumption was outlandish. And by 1900 it was even wilder!

"With the new century came the greatest prosperity the country had ever known, and with prosperity, wining and dining changed from a subtly tempered art to a gross display of gorging and gourmandizing. The epicurean passed; the exhibitionist entered.

"Spend more money! Eat bigger meals! People tumbled over each other in their efforts to jam into the restaurants and pile their tables high with more food than they could possibly use. They had heard that it was the mark of social distinction to be able to order a 'good' dinner. It became unfashionable to clean one's plate."*

There were some legendary eaters during this time. The railroad had brought in the food and the variations, and the big railroad man was ready to consume same. James Buchanan Brady (1856–1917) was a first-class peddler of railroad equipment, and the railroad itself, for that matter. He became enormously wealthy from his business and just plain enormous due to his eating habits. His penchant for wearing diamonds while consuming whole dining rooms gave rise to his famous nickname, "Diamond Jim" Brady. And, since I am claiming in this article that it was really the railroads that gave us "American" cuisine, we might just as well look into the big boy's eating habits.

"Jim started things off in the morning with a light breakfast of beefsteak, a few chops, eggs, flapjacks, fried potatoes, hominy, corn bread,

*Parker Morrell, *Diamond Jim* (New York: Simon & Schuster, 1934), p. 154.

a few muffins, and a huge beaker of milk. He never touched tea or coffee. Then, about eleven-thirty, when he had finished swimming, he strolled up to the tables that were on the porch of the hotel and as slightly premature hors d'oeuvres, consumed two or three dozen oysters and clams. The waiters at Manhattan Beach knew of his fondness for seafood, and when they saw him coming out of the water, looking for all the world like a Loch Ness sea monster, they promptly scurried around to have a huge platter of chilled, freshly opened oysters ready by the time he would set foot on the porch.

"Luncheon was apt to be a bit heavier than breakfast. It generally consisted of more oysters and clams, a deviled crab or two, or three, perhaps a pair of broiled lobsters, then a joint of beef or another steak, a salad, and several kinds of fruit pie. Jim also liked to finish off this meal with the better part of a box of chocolate candies. It made the food sit better, he figured.

"There was a snack in the afternoon after the races, usually sea food of some sort, perhaps a dozen oysters and two or three bottles of lemon soda, while the rest of the party drank champagne and highballs. (Diamond Jim drank no alcohol.) And, after lying down for an hour or two to gather his forces together for a further assault upon the groaning board, Jim went down for dinner."*

Very often during these eating festivals Mr. Brady would be accompanied by the lovely and famous singer and actress of the time, Lillian Russell. She became so famous for eating in excess with Diamond Jim that as her girth grew so did her reputation. Diamond Lil, they called her.

Now, at last, to the original author of this *Culinary Handbook*. Mr. Charles Fellows was not one to put down the joys of excessive eating during this time, but he was down on pretension. We must realize that the entire menu offered at Delmonico's, the restaurant that set the standards for the New York area, was French. Mr. Fellows, a longtime restaurateur and chef, decried this preference for French cuisine and called for a serious evaluation of American cuisine, which, as I now contend, was possible because of the railroads. Fellows still used a few French terms and a little of the French cooking style here and there, but he was of the Midwest, of Chicago, and he disliked the New York manner of placing French cuisine over that of his country, particularly the Midwest.

A menu from Delmonico's during the early 1900s looked like the one that follows on pages xiv to xv.

Wonderful French dishes and American dishes influenced by French cuisine. However, when Fellows published a menu for his Midwest restaurants during the same time, it looked like the one that follows on pages xvi to xviii.

*Morrell, p. 42.

DELMONICO'S

DINNER.*

MAY.

Clams

SOUPS.

Consommé Carême   Rice à la Rudini   Sherman
Bisque of crawfish à la Batelière   Cream of sorrel with stuffed eggs
Julienne Mogul   Pea purée with croûtons   Croûte au pot
Chicken okra   Chicken okra strained   Small individual soup pots

SIDE DISHES—COLD.

Radishes   Olives   Caviare   Sardines in oil   Lyons sausages
Marinated tunny   Gherkins   Mortadella
Stuffed olives with anchovy butter   Mackerel in oil

SIDE DISH—HOT.

Cromesquis of sweetbread, Babanine

FISH.

Mussels with shallot   Eels broiled tartar sauce   Planked shad ravigote butter
Spotted fish Livournaise   Weakfish à la Brighton   Fried soft shell crabs
Blackfish à la Sandford   Lobster à la Camille   Sheepshead, Buena Vista

REMOVES.

Roast sirloin of beef with brain patties
Rump of beef Boucicault   Pullet in surprise

ENTRÉES.

Mutton pie Canadian style   Sautéd chicken florentine style
Mushrooms crust with truffles   Minions of tenderloin of beef à la Stanley
Hot plover pie   Breasts of turkey Donovan   Squabs à la Crispi
Frog shells   Sweetbread à la St. Cloud
SORBETS: Lalla Rookh   Kirsch   Maraschino   Rum

ROAST.

Leg of mutton à la Roederer   Leg of yearling lamb with gravy
Beef ribs, American style   Squabs
Duckling   Partridge broiled, English style   Chicken in the saucepan

*Charles Ranhofer, *The Epicurean* (Chicago: The Hotel Monthly Press, 1920), p. 167.

COLD.

Galantine of chicken Trout, tartar sauce Terrine of duck livers à l'Aquitaine
SALADS: Lettuce   Water-cress   Macédoine   Chicory

VEGETABLES.

Purslain à la Brabançon   Lima beans thickened maître-d'hôtel
Potatoes Parisienne   Potatoes, Anna   Potatoes half glaze
Green peas, English style   String beans with butter
Boiled asparagus with Hollandaise sauce
Succotash Cèpes baked with cream Stuffed cauliflower à la béchamel, baked
Risot à la Francatelli Tomatoes à la Boquillon Cardoons with half glaze
Fried eggplant   Spaghetti macaroni à la Lawrence
Asparagus tops à la Maintenon Corn on the cob Spinach with cream
Macaroni à la Brignoli   Whole artichoke boiled with white sauce
Macédoine à la Montigny   Sweet potatoes roasted

SWEET ENTREMETS.

HOT: Pancakes with brown sugar   Glazed apple marmalade
COLD: Blanc mange with strawberries   Bain marie cream molded
Charlotte Russe   Cream Malakoff

DESSERT.

FANCY CREAMS: Biscuit, Excelsior   Basket filled with oranges
Nesselrode pudding with candied chestnuts   Biscuit glacé
Neapolitan   Plombière with chestnuts
CREAMS: Vanilla   White coffee   Pistachio
WATER ICE: Lemon   Raspberry   Pineapple
Assorted cakes
Preserved fruits: greengages, peaches, pineapple, quinces
Marmalade: jelly, Dundee, peaches, ginger, Guava, Bar-le-duc
Stewed fruits: pineapple, peaches, pears, prunes, apples, with jelly, bananas,
cherries, chestnuts, oranges, orange salad, strawberries, raspberries.
Brandy fruits: greengages, pears, oranges, strawberries with cream.
CHEESE: Stilton, Brie, Strachino, Gorgonzola, Gruyère, Chester, Gervais,
Port Salut, Holland
French coffee   Turkish coffee

FELLOWS' MENU MAKER

DINNER.*

OYSTERS AND CLAMS.

Rockaways, half dozen 35

Rockaways, Shell Roast with Minced Bacon 40–75

Boston Pan Roast 50   Blue Points 23

Plain or Milk Stew 35   Cream Stew 50

Creamed Oysters, Chafing Dish 1.00

SOUPS.

Tomato with Rice 35–20

Mock Turtle 35–20   Ox Tail 35–20

Puree Mongole 35–20   St. Germain 35–20

Chicken à la Reine 35–20   Chicken Gumbo 35–20

Consommé, Macedoine 35–20

Consommé en Tasse 15   Giblet Gumbo 35–20

Clear Green Turtle 35–20

RELISHES.

Stuffed, Ripe of Queen Olives 25

C. & B. Chow-Chow or Pickled Walnuts 25

Celery 25   Melon Mangoes 25   Radishes 10

Mixed Shelled Nuts 25

New Astrakhan Caviar 1.25

FISH.

Broiled Shad 75–40   Planked Shad 1.10–60

Broiled Live Lobster, Chili Sauce 1 10 60

Broiled Black Bass 75–40

Broiled Fresh Mackerel 75–40

Broiled Jumbo Whitefish 75–40

Planked Jumbo Whitefish 1.10–60

Pompano, Sauté, Trianon Sauce, Long Branch

Potatoes 60–35

ENTREES.

Broiled Lamb Fries with Bacon, Tartar Sauce, 75–40

Tenderloin of Beef, Larded, Mushroom Sauce 75–40

---

*Charles Fellows, *Fellows' Menu Maker* (Chicago: The Hotel Monthly Press, 1910), pp. 2–3.

Fried Spring Chicken, Corn Fritters 90–50
Braised Fowl, à la Creole 90–50
Pineapple Fritters, au Marasquin 25

ROASTS.

Prime Ribs of Beef, au Jus 75–40
Virginia Peanut Ham au Xeres 75–40

POULTRY.

Broiled Spring Chicken 1.10–60

VEGETABLES.

Fried Oyster Plant 20   Cauliflower 20
New Bermuda Potatoes 20   Boiled Potatoes 15
Mashed Potatoes 15   Baked Potatoes 15
Artichokes, Hollandaise 40
French Peas 25   Succotash 20   Green Peas 20
American Asparagus 60–35
Lima Beans 20   Stringless Beans 20
Fried Egg Plant 20   Grilled Tomato 40–25
Fried or Grilled Sweet Potatoes 20

SALADS.

(Mayonnaise or French Dressing)
Imported French Endive 60–35
Lettuce, Romaine, Chicory or Escarole 40–25, with
Grape Fruit, Oranges or Pineapple 60–35
Celery, Apple and Nuts 60–35   Chiffonade 75–40
Grapes and Celery 60–35
Pears and Pineapple 60–35
Artichokes, Vinaigrette 60–35
Combination Lettuce and Tomatoes or Cucumbers 50–30
Tomato Stuffed with Chicken or Sweetbreads (1) 35

DESSERT.

Hot Mince Pie 10   Apple Pie 10   Pumpkin Pie 10
Pie à la Mode 20
English Plum Pudding, Hard and Brandy Sauce 20
Chocolate Eclairs 15   Chocolate Mousse 25
Chocolate Sundae 20   Lady Fingers 15
Macaroons 20   Assorted Cake 20

Frozen Egg Nog 25

Chocolate Ice Cream 15   Neapolitan Ice Cream 20

Tutti-Fruitti Ice Cream 20   Vanilla Ice Cream 15

Strawberry Ice Cream 20   Roman Punch 15

Bisquit Glace 25   Charlotte Russe 20

Port or Sherry Wine Jelly 20

FRUIT.

Strawberries with Cream 40

Apple Butter 10   Malaga Grapes 25

Arkansaw Black Apples 10   Stewed Rhubarb 15

Grape Fruit in glass (1) 35

Figs or Peaches au Cognac 25

Spitzenberg Apples (1) 15

Orange (1) 10   Bananas (2) 15

CHEESE.

Brie 25–15   Roquefort 25–15   Gorgonzola 25–15

English Sage 25–15   Edam 25–15   Cream 25–15

Camembert 25–15   Holland Gouda 25–15

Neufchatel 25–15   Swiss 25–15

American 10

Bar-le-Duc Jelly 50   Cuba Guava Jelly 35

COFFEE, TEA, ETC.

Pot of Coffee (for 1) 15   (for 2) 25

Coffee, per Cup 10   Demi-Tasse 10

Tea—Oolong, Green, English Breakfast, Uncolored Japan or Ceylon 25–15

Cocoa or Chocolate 25–15   Turkish Coffee 25

Milk, per Glass 10   Cream, per Glass 20

And look at the prices. Those numbers are in cents!

Most of us in the food fraternity in our time give our beloved James Beard the credit for calling us to look at a real and existing American cuisine. I think we have to point to Fellows as an earlier pioneer in this field of naming American food, cuisine, and style.

Fellows's book was originally written for the Chicago restaurant trade. Remember that at the time Chicago was the center of the railroad for America, and, as far as Fellows was concerned, the center for American food. By that time the country was taking Chicago and the food of the Midwest for granted, but remember, too, that it was the railroad that moved us from an agrarian culture to an industrialized society. Food could be moved about easily from the farm to the city and fewer people were needed in the production of food and its transport. And everything moved through Chicago! The railroad probably marked the death of Tom Jefferson's American dream in which the vast majority of our men were to be "gentlemen farmers," but the rails certainly convinced us that Americans could celebrate a wider variety of fresh food, even in the city, than had ever been possible anywhere.

Thus this handbook. It calls us to style in preparation, to freshness, to basic ingredients, to very little froufrou, and to good American food carefully prepared and served with concern for the comfort of our guests.

The recipes, ingredients, and preparations to be found in his original volume are basic to American history and thinking. His comments and concerns are far superior to the glib remarks about a new movement to "cook like Grandma did." Grandma cooked during tough times, but Fellows urges us to celebrate good times in this great land, the land of grain, meat, and vegetables, food that cannot be surpassed anywhere.

Mr. Charles Fellows was a serious American cook.

JEFF SMITH

ABOUT THE ORIGINAL AUTHOR

When Jeff and I discovered this book in an out-of-print bookstore, we realized right away that the author was passionate about food. Born in Australia in 1866, Charles Fellows wrote three cookbooks: *The Chef's Reminder, The Culinary Handbook,* and *Fellows' Menu Maker.* All were published by The Hotel Monthly Press in Chicago, which has been defunct since 1933. These books are not really cookbooks in the normal sense in that they are reference books aimed at the professional cook working in a restaurant or hotel during the very early 1900s. The recipes are actually descriptions of dishes, but the skilled home cook can cook from it successfully and come up with variations of one's own.

Charles Fellows began his career working several years as a chef on ocean liners. He arrived in Chicago around the time of the World's Exposition in 1893. In 1895, while working as a chef in a Chicago hotel, he began writing *The Chef's Reminder.* In the months prior to publication excerpts from the book that appeared in *The Hotel Monthly* magazine created enormous excitement throughout the culinary field. Once published, this manual quickly became popular with chefs, stewards, and professional cooks across the country. Its success prompted a re-release, with the addition of hundreds of recipes. The new book, *A Selection of Dishes and the Chef's Reminder,* was said to be the first thoroughly up-to-date culinary reference book. John Willy, publisher of The Hotel Monthly Press, took it a step further and called it "the most popular ready reference book in the world." It was vest-pocket size for convenient reference amid the hustle and bustle of a hotel kitchen.

Fellows was a man who had several pots simmering away at a time.

He went to Pittsburgh to assume the position of steward at a restaurant called Goettman's. While working there, he made friends with Frank Biggers, the head waiter. Together they invented a state-of-the-art dishwashing machine for restaurant use in 1897. It was based on an idea Fellows came up with five years earlier. The design was later manufactured under the name The Fearless Dishwasher. On the application for the patent, the following claims were made: "Uses less hot water than any other machine"; "The most simple of all machines and the most effective"; "Even a child could operate it with no danger attached." The Fearless of course found a ready nationwide market.

In 1889 our chef/author/entrepreneur left his new home in Cleveland, Ohio, and sailed to London to open a butcher business. Before his departure, a friendship was formed among Fellows and three other men in the food business. This fraternity of four was known as the "Cleveland Afternoon Quartet." They met every day at a favorite Bohemian pub called the Rathskeller, owned by William Buse, one of the gentlemen. It was a time for them to socialize, drink a pint or two, and, we are sure, engage in some long conversations about the "biz."

Charles Fellows returned to America when his London butcher business failed, and by 1904 had completed *The Culinary Handbook*. He then went on to write what would be his last work, *Fellows' Menu Maker*, released in 1910. Like his first cookbook, this was also very popular.

The Culinary Handbook was considered the most valuable of his three volumes. Its original selling price was two dollars, and the word was, "Everyone interested in culinary matters will want a copy." Jeff and I were lucky to find a copy, and in reading it and researching the author, we found him to be a most interesting man. So, in an effort to describe his character better, let's look inside his book.

First of all, we must congratulate the author. Anybody who would write a cookbook composed of four thousand recipes must have been a person possessed of enormous patience, dedication, and perseverance. Admirable qualities indeed. However, Mr. Fellows did contradict himself on a few occasions, and in a somewhat amusing and charming way. He stated that in writing this book he refrained from using French terminology. After all, this was to be "an American culinary handbook for Americans." He then slipped into the habit of using French cooking terms throughout the book. We should be fair, however, and admit that it is hard to talk about cuisine without using French terms. Even *cuisine* is a French word. And so is consommé. Fellows offers more than seventy consommé recipes! Only his list of forty recipes for sausage can come near to that number.

I have no doubt, after reading this book, that Mr. Fellows was a concerned cook. In a recipe for mutton stew he recommended: "Do not just dish it out onto the platter simply because it is stew; place the meat neatly on a dish, then garnish it with care. It then appeals to the eye and its savoriness to the palate." He knew the true meaning of hospitality! It would have felt good to have been a patron in his restaurant.

Charles Fellows died in 1921 in Covington, Kentucky. In his fifty-five years he lived a life devoted to the hospitality business and the culinary arts. And in the announcement of his passing the obituary began, "Charles Fellows, well-known culinary author, ..."

CRAIG WOLLAM

HOW TO USE THIS BOOK

W e have made two assumptions in bringing this book to you. The first is that you like to cook. The second is that in preparing these recipes from the turn of the century you intend to offer a meal as the event of the evening, not as a event prior to something like the theater or a concert. In the days when these recipes were used in hotels and restaurants the preparation took a good deal of time, and we do not want your guests to run off after a properly prepared meal.

As this book was originally prepared for serious cooks, you might be surprised by the lack of detail in the instructions or the use of unfamiliar terms. Not to worry. Consult the Charles Fellows Lexicon and read the little paragraph describing the dish and tackle it. It will be great fun.

We have detailed some dishes that we think were typical of the time and yet certainly in step with our current return to basic good food. Just remember that we are talking about old-fashioned, heavy-handed, first-class cooking. The list of the recipes that we have fully developed can be found on page xxvii.

In every case the original text of the book is given, although we have expanded upon many of the definitions and entries. Some of our notes are simply updates. Our added commentary is designated by black type.

We are sure that you will enjoy this book, although you will certainly not turn to it when you have to prepare a full meal for four in 35 minutes. Everything in this volume is from the kitchen of 1904, and that should pretty much say it. The food is delicious, rich, and to be enjoyed both as nourishment and entertainment. Your great-grandmother would be proud of you.

Enjoy!

J.S.
C.W.

THE FRUGAL GOURMET'S
LIST OF RECIPES

Apple Roly Poly	20	Hot Slaw	85
Baked Cabbage with Cheese	83	Kidney Beans, French Style	36
Basic White Sauce	427	Lamb Chops with Mushroom	
Bavarian Sauce	428	Purée	317
Beef Filets with Oysters	54	Lemon Marmalade	286
Beef Soup, English Style	47	Lemon Trifle	287
Beef Stock	48	Macaroni with Oysters,	
Carrot Sauce	430	Milan Style	297
Chantilly Soup	121	Minced Pork with Fried	
Cheese Straws	126	Apples	379
Chicken Broth with Custards	156	Oxtail Soup	49
Chicken Gumbo	154	Parsnip Fritters	234
Chicken Soufflé	147	Peach Ice	358
Chicken Stock	153	Pickled Cauliflower	114
Chili Sauce	432	Poivrade Sauce	443
Chocolate Custard Cups	160	Pork Tenderloin with Sweet	
Clam Chowder	165	Potatoes	376
Corn Fritters	187	Salmon Salad	421
Corn Gems (Muffins)	184	Scalloped Mussels	311
Crab Canapés	190	Scalloped Potatoes	392
Duck Stewed with Chestnuts	210	Smoked Tongue with	
Eggs with Brown Butter	221	Sauerkraut	55
Epping Sausage	387	Spinach and Sausage	
Fricassée of Rabbit	404	Timbales	454
Gardener's Salad	417	Stuffed Eggplant	225
Giblet and Potato Pie	150	Tomato Sauce	447
Golden Buck	125	Turkey Hash with Poached	
Halibut Fried with Bacon	260	Eggs	469
Horseradish Butter	266	Veal (or Pork) Timbales	478
Hot Pot or Hotch Potch	267	Velouté Sauce	448

T H E
Frugal Gourmet's
Culinary Handbook

A WORKING
CHARLES FELLOWS LEXICON

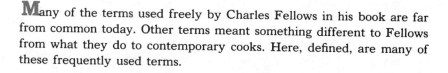

Many of the terms used freely by Charles Fellows in his book are far from common today. Other terms meant something different to Fellows from what they do to contemporary cooks. Here, defined, are many of these frequently used terms.

AIGRETTE—*Aigrette* is a French word used to describe savory deep-fried morsels, usually served as appetizers.

AITCHBONE—Aitchbone or edgebone is an English term for the bone of the rump, or the cut of beef lying over it.

ALLEMANDE GARNISHES—Fellows used *allemande* to describe a variety of garnishes with little in common besides strong flavors. Traditionally, the term referred to recipes of German origin.

ANGLAISE GARNISHES—Anglaise garnishes are another assortment of Fellows's garnishes not grouped together in contemporary cooking.

ASPIC—The name given to a clear savory jelly made from meat, and is used to decorate entrées, pies, hams, tongues, game, pigs' heads, salads, prawns, vegetables, fish, etc.

ASPIC—Aspic jelly, a well-reduced stock that, thanks to its high proportion of natural gelatin, holds a molded form when chilled, was once enormously popular as a medium for presenting meats and fish and as a garnish for pâtés and terrines. It is best when made with an assortment of meats (as in Fellows's recipes), with a calf's foot or two included to ensure adequate gelatin and flavored with aromatic herbs and vegetables. Aspic can also be made by adding powdered gelatin to any stock, but the flavor is far less intense.

Aspic has fallen into disfavor in recent years, probably because its elaborate preparation and old-fashioned appearance clash with the simplicity and bright presentations of the new cuisine. But it is a relatively fat-free method of dressing up meat and fish, and will likely make a comeback.

ATELETTE—Is a skewer generally made of silver or plated metal, and is used to decorate hot and cold pieces for banquet tables; combinations on the skewer according to the dish and the fancy of the cook can be made of cockscombs, button mushrooms, crayfish, prawns, animelles (lamb-fries) carrots, turnips, green peas, parsley, truffles, sweetbreads, crystallized fruits, preserved violets, cherries, strawberries, sweet jelly, aspic jelly, etc., etc.

ATELETTE—These ornamental skewers occasionally can be found in antique shops.

ATTEREAUX—Is a skewer generally used for cooking dishes en brochette (see BROCHETTE).

ATTEREAUX—Not only a skewer, attereaux is also the name of many *dishes* cooked en brochette, usually battered and fried.

BAIN-MARIE—A foreign culinary term for a hot water bath in which are kept the pots or saucepans containing sauces, garnitures, entrées, soups, etc., that require to be kept hot without reaching the boiling point.

BAIN-MARIE—A bain-marie differs from a double boiler in that the pot containing the cooking food actually sits in the hot-water bath. In addition to keeping foods warm, the bain-marie is used whenever extremely gentle and even oven heat is desired, such as in baking pâté, custard, baked eggs, mousse, and cheesecake. The water in a bain-marie must never be allowed to boil; this would create condensation that might enter the pot containing the food.

BLANCH OR BLANCHED—Foods placed to boil in cold water, removed after coming to the boil, poured into a colander and well washed; and in the case of almonds, etc., the skins are then easily removed.

BOUCHÉE—A French word which means "mouthful"; it is used to designate certain specimens of cookery, both savory and sweet, that are filled into puff paste and sponge cake patty cases, hence, a bouchée is a small patty.

BOUCHÉE—Note that what all bouchées have in common is that they are prebaked puff pastry shells that are filled after cooling.

BROCHETTE—A skewer on which are threaded small delicate meats, etc., to be cooked, and served with or without the skewer; also used by confectioners to thread fruit on before candying them.

CASSAREEP—A liquid seasoning made from cassava in South America.

CHASSEUR—Is the French word for "hunter"; à la Chasseur means hunter's style, sauce Chasseur, hunter's sauce, made from the proceeds of the hunt.

CHAUD-FROID—Literally means hot-cold, and is applied to dishes that are prepared hot, then made into a form more suitable to eat cold, such as chaud-froid of game, fowl, partridge, woodcocks, larks, reedbirds, pheasants, plovers, quail and turkey, for recipes of which see the subheading of the articles mentioned.

CHIFFONADE—French term for a mixture of shredded sorrel, lettuce, chervil and parsley that is used to put in soups a few minutes before serving them.

CHIFFONADE—A chiffonade of greens most often consists of sorrel and lettuce, cut into thin ribbons and used as a garnish, usually for soups. They may be sautéed in butter before use.

CHIPOLATA—Name of an Italian garnish composed of little veal sausages, glazed balls of carrot and turnip, roasted and peeled chestnuts, pieces of broiled bacon and button mushrooms, all mixed into a rich brown sauce flavored with sherry wine.

COLLOP—An Americanization, from the French escaloper ("to slice thinly"), this word refers to any thin slice of meat, vegetable, or fish. Like a scallop (as in veal scallop or scaloppine), the slice is often breaded and sautéed.

COMPOTE—A term used in cookery to signify something whole in a sauce. Hence a compote of fruit is the fruit either whole, or split and the stone or core removed, dropped into a thick boiling syrup till cooked without breaking, cooled, served with the syrup. A compote of birds such as larks, reedbirds, ortolans, etc. are the birds boned and stuffed, then lightly roasted, then finished cooking in a bright sauce; served with the sauce.

COTELETTES—The French word for our cutlets, but is generally applied to rib chops of mutton, lamb and veal.

CRAPAUDINE—A French term applied to small birds that are split down the back, then trussed out resembling a frog, such as spring chickens, squabs, quails, partridges, etc., hence a squab "à la crapaudine" would be a squab split, spread out and trussed like a frog, broiled and served with Crapaudine sauce.

CRAPAUDINE—Split and flattened birds *do* resemble toads, which explains the name of this preparation: *Crapaud* is French for "toad."

CROMESKIES—Also spelled "kromeskies," are a sort of fritter made of fish, flesh, game and fowl. The meats are made into a form of salpiçon or croquette mixture, when cold formed into cork shapes, then either rolled in a thin short paste, or fritter batter, fried crisp, garnished, sauced and served. An oyster cromesky is an oyster dried with a cloth, wrapped with a thin slice of parboiled bacon, pinned with a toothpick, dipped in batter and fried; when cooked, the toothpick removed before serving.

CROMESKIES—Here's something you just don't see anymore, at least by this name. To make a cromesky (or cromesqui), any combination of chopped meats or fish was bound together with a sauce (making a *salpicon*), shaped, dipped in batter (they were sometimes wrapped in salt pork or caul before battering), and deep-fried. Note that cromeskies are in reality not much different from croquettes.

CROQUETTES—A mince of some cooked food, such as beef, lamb, mutton, veal, pork, sweetbreads, lobster, ham, all kinds of game, poultry etc., blended with a high seasoning, and a sauce to bind it with; when cold, it is made into forms, such as cones, rolls, balls, cutlets, etc., rolled in flour, then breaded, fried in hot fat a golden color; served with sauces and garnitures that are appropriate to the food used.

CROÛSTADES—Are hollow crusts made with bread, pastry, or a mixture of flour, eggs and watergrain; they are used as receptacles for savories and sweets, such as oysters, oyster crabs, lobster, frogs, terrapin, sweetbreads, lamb, chicken livers, fresh mushrooms, all kinds of garnitures, macedoine of vegetables, green peas; also sherbets, frozen punches, whipped cream, ice cream forms, fruit and wine jellies, etc.

DARNE—Name sometimes seen on "bills of fare." It is the French word for slice, and is generally used in the term "Darne de saumon" which is a salmon steak.

DARNE—A darne is any thick slice of raw fish.

EPIGRAMME—A term used in cookery to denote one kind of meat served in two forms on the same dish, such as, two chops, one breaded and fried, the other broiled; served resting on each other. See headings of respective meats.

FORCEMEAT—Name given to a highly seasoned mince that has been rubbed through a sieve; used in making quenelles, lining pies, etc.

FORCEMEAT—Forcemeat is a synonym for a meat stuffing.

FRITTERS—Are either a mixture of fruits, vegetables, meat or poultry combined with flour and eggs to form a batter; or the article enclosed within a batter, then fried crisp, or baked as for eclairs, etc.

FRIZZLE—To fry or bake until crisp and curled at the edges.

HAIR SIEVE—A fine-meshed sieve used for straining lumps from custards, residue from stock, and so on.

JARDINIERE—Name applied to a garnish of small cut mixed vegetables, such as carrots, turnips, asparagus tips, cauliflower, stringless beans and some green peas, cooked in seasoned broth, drained; served plain or tossed with half glaze or meat gravy.

LARDING—This technique, much employed by Fellows, has largely fallen into disuse. But most experienced cooks have used it, and all should be aware of it. Quite simply, it involves threading pieces of fat (*lardons,* or lardoons, since the fat most frequently used is lard) through meat deemed to be too lean to remain moist during cooking. A larding needle, still available at good kitchen supply stores, is the tool of choice for this task.

MACEDOINE—A French term used to indicate a mixture of fancy cut vegetables or fruits; the former either plain or mixed with sauce is used in soups or as a garnish, the latter generally in sweet jellies.

MACEDOINE—Any mixture of fruit or vegetables, cooked or raw, hot or cold, can qualify as a macedoine.

MATELOTE—Name of a fish stew or garnish for fish (à la Matelote means in sailor's style). See GARNISHES.

MIROTON—A dish of sliced meat (usually boiled beef or leftovers) that has been previously cooked, usually in a meat sauce that includes sliced onions and pickles. It is generally served as a stew.

PANADA—Or *panade.* A paste of flour, bread, bread crumbs, rice, and so on, mixed with milk, water, or stock and used for binding forcemeats. Also the name of a bread soup.

PATTYPAN—Not unlike a muffin tin, this was used for baking small, filled puff pastries. Pattypan is also the name of a SQUASH.

PAUPIETTE—Name given to a thin slice of meat spread with forcemeat, rolled up, tied at each end, stewed with meat gravy; the household name for them is "meat olives."

POUNDED TO A PASTE—When Fellows instructs cooks to "pound to a paste," he undoubtedly meant to use a rather large mortar and pestle. Those contemporary cooks with access to food processors should use them to produce pastes, taking care not to overprocess.

QUENELLES—A fancy word for dumpling, a quenelle is usually made with fish but sometimes with meat, poultry, or game. Eggs are used for binding; and quenelles are almost always poached in liquid.

RISSOLES—Another form of savory croquette; but instead of being breaded and fried, the croquette mixture is divided into even sized pieces, and laid on a sheet of pie paste, covered with another sheet (thin), then stamped out with a fluted biscuit cutter, then fried like croquettes in deep hot lard.

RISSOLETTES—Same as rissoles, but made much smaller and used for garnishing.

ROULADE—Name given to savory rolls of steak. Take thin steaks, spread with a forcemeat, roll up, tie the ends with twine, arrange them in a sautoir with some bacon fat, brown them, then add a little flour, moisten with stock, then let them simmer in the gravy till tender, take up, serve with the twine removed, and garnished with vegetables, mushrooms, etc.

ROULADE—A roulade can be veal, pork, lamb, or even chicken, stuffed, rolled, and tied before cooking.

SALAMANDER—Name given to a heated iron plate used for quickly browning the gratinated surface of certain dishes of escalloped foods, etc. In some kitchens the dish is placed on the ashes under the hot bars of the grate; in others a small shovel is made hot. Where there is a gas oven with a top cooking surface the dish may be placed under the grill. All tend to the same purpose—that of quickly obtaining a brown surface without further cooking the interior.

SALAMANDER—In current parlance the term *salamander* is usually used to refer to the eye-level gas broilers present in almost every professional kitchen.

SALMI (SALMIS)—These two words each signify a form of stew, and seldom are they properly used. It is always applied to game. SALMIS is used when the stew is made from cold cooked game that has been left over from a previous meal. SALMI is a stew made from fresh cooked game specially roasted at the time required to make the stew for the coming meal.

SALPICON—Used freely throughout this book, the word *salpicon* can refer to any diced ingredient bound by a sauce.

SARATOGA CUTTER—Potato chips were originally Saratoga Chips. Thus a Saratoga cutter is a potato-chip cutter.

SAÛTOIR—The French word for sauté pan.

SINGED AND DRAWN—Singeing is the process of removing the remaining feathers or hair from a bird or animal by exposing it to a flame or hot iron made especially for the purpose. Drawing is process of removing the entrails.

SPITCHCOCKED—The *Oxford English Dictionary* lists *spatchcock* as "a fowl, split open and grilled" and *spitchcock* as "an eel split and grilled." Modern cookbook parlance would seem to relate the process to butterflying.

TAMIS—A fine sieve, once made of cloth, now of wire mesh, used for straining stocks, sauces, custards, and so on.

TIMBALE—A round mold designed to hold pastry crusts, which in turn are filled with savory mixtures. *Timbale* can also refer to a small molded mixture that is crustless.

VOL-AU-VENT—A small hollow form of puff pastry, used as a receptacle to viands.

VOL-AU-VENT—Larger than a *bouchée,* the vol-au-vent is a puff pastry shell filled with a savory mixture. It should be extremely light, as befits its name, which was bestowed on it by the famed French chef Careme, who said the pastry *"s'envola au vent"* ("flew away with the wind").

THE CULINARY HANDBOOK

ABSINTHE—A liqueur made principally from wormwood, anise, angelica, coriander seeds and alcohol, sometimes adulterated with aromatic resins and dangerous colorings; its uses are chiefly as a drink diluted with water, and in making many of the American mixed drinks.

ABSINTHE—Absinthe is the familiar name given to a plant (*Artemisia absinthium,* also known as wormwood), as well as the ANISE-flavored liqueur made from that plant. From the Middle Ages to the early twentieth century absinthe was used medicinally; during that period it became increasingly popular as an aperitif, especially in France. In fact, absinthe is a powerful poison, responsible for the deaths of countless Frenchmen during the nineteenth century. (Wrote Alexandre Dumas, "Absinthe has killed more Frenchmen in Africa than . . . the guns of the Arabs. . . .") In the mid-

dle of that century absinthe was banned in French military barracks and, in 1915, its production was made illegal. Pernod and Ricard, two anise liqueurs, took its place in the local cafés and remain popular in France to this day.

ACETIC ACID—The foundation of all vinegars; used by confectioners when making icing from whites of eggs, to facilitate the beating.

ACETIC ACID—Acetic acid is present in every vinegar (although it is *not* itself vinegar; it can be produced industrially, and in far greater strengths than the 5 to 8 percent found in vinegar). It is also found in spoiled wine (once wine is exposed to air, it is attacked by bacteria that produce acetic acid and turn the wine gradually into vinegar); yogurt (which becomes more sour as the days go by and the acid content rises); and cheese (it is one of the components that contribute to "sharpness"). Acetic acid is an effective preservative—vinegar is used extensively in pickle making—and, in a mild solution, such as that found in distilled vinegar, makes a superior household cleaner.

AERATED WATERS—Such as Vichy, Apollinaris, Carlsbad water, Friedrichshall bitter, etc., are obtained from the springs of nature and recommended for the relief and cure of different complaints of the human system. Imitation aerated waters mostly contain sugar, and are sold as pop, such as ginger ale, sarsaparilla, etc. The artificial waters are simply pure waters sweetened, flavored and charged with carbonic acid gas. In Paris oyster shells are washed, and broken into small pieces, and, under the action of vitriol, yield the carbonic acid gas.

AERATED WATERS—Sparkling waters, as aerated waters are now more commonly called, are rarely recommended as medicinal these days, but they have never been more popular ("imitation" aerated waters, as Fellows called soda pop, have become America's most frequently consumed beverage). Consumption of plain sparkling waters, domestic and imported, now tops four hundred million gallons a year in the United States and—with the continuing decline in alcoholic-beverage consumption—it should grow further. The brands mentioned by Fellows, which still exist, are in the European tradition of strongly flavored mineral waters. Americans, it appears, prefer waters such as Perrier, Saratoga, and Poland Springs, all of which have clean, neutral flavors.

ALBUMEN—An opaque fluid found plentifully in eggs, meats, fish and succulent vegetables, especially asparagus. It is the most nourishing substance known; used in its raw state from whites of eggs by cooks chiefly in clarifying purposes.

ALBUMEN—Nowadays, more often spelled *albumin,* this liquid protein is found in all seeds, where it provides an embryo with food. In an egg it is the major component of the white, which surrounds the yolk. In addition to its use as a clarifying agent, the albumen in egg whites also gives them their ability to coagulate, or harden, when heated or beaten.

ALCOHOL—A colorless liquid obtained from fermenting sugar; is found in all wines and spirits and is the intoxicating quality of them. It is largely used in making flavoring extracts, by diluting the oil of the flavor required with the alcohol. Wood alcohol obtained at any drug store is the best and cleanest material to be used in singeing poultry and game.

ALLIGATOR PEAR—A fruit found in the West Indies and Mexico, but can be bought at most of the fruit stores in season; the large green ones are the best; they are served the same as canteloupes, or sliced into a salad seasoned with pepper, salt and the juice of a lime.

ALLIGATOR PEAR—The exotic-sounding alligator pear is the familiar avocado (*Persea americana*). Although it is indigenous to Mexico, Central America, and many Caribbean islands, several hundred varieties are now grown in subtropical climates throughout the world. High in protein, fat, vitamin C, niacin, and fiber, the avocado—a fruit, not a vegetable—is delicious served simply, as described by Fellows.

ALLSPICE—The product of the pimento shrub, used as a food flavoring. When ground it has a graining of a ruby coloring; purchased in its ground state, is often adulterated with mustard husks.

ALLSPICE—In Jamaica, where most allspice is grown, it is generally called pimento. This confuses visitors, but is nevertheless true to the Latin name of the tree upon which it grows (*Pimenta dioica*). In the United States it is most frequently used in spice cakes. This is a shame; try it in meat marinades, pickles, stews, and spice mixtures such as curry.

ALMONDS—The best for culinary purposes is the Jordan; it is about an inch long, flat with a clear brown skin, sweet and rather tough. In making almond soup seven-eighths sweet and one-eighth bitter almonds should be used.

ALMONDS—Closely related to the apricot—its almost inedible fruit vaguely resembles one—the almond is an important part of many of the world's great cuisines. Indigenous to the eastern Mediterranean, the almond tree (*Prunus amygdalus,* or tonsil plum) is now grown almost anywhere the climate replicates that of its homeland, with California being responsible for more than half the world's crop.

There are both sweet and bitter almonds. The latter, which are smaller, are occasionally used in (mostly Italian) confections; but, due to their high prussic-acid content, they are poisonous in fairly small amounts when consumed raw, and consequently are banned from the United States. Still, many traditional recipes call for a small percentage of the highly flavorful bitter almond. The almond with which we are familiar is the sweet almond and, from Fellows's day until now, the Jordan (undoubtedly from the French *jardin,* or "garden") is the most widespread variety.

SALTED ALMONDS—Made by blanching, skinning, and frying them in butter oil till nicely browned, then dusting with salt; make a nice appetizer, or hors d'oeuvre.

DEVILLED ALMONDS—Made like salted almonds, but after salting, well dusted with cayenne pepper.

ALUM—A white astringent salt, often used to whiten flour, to quickly clear gin, to improve the color of inferior red wines.

ANCHOVIES—The Dutch are always cleaned of their scales. The French are not, and are larger. Anchovy paste bought on the markets is often adulterated with red-ochre and Venitian red.

ANCHOVIES—Almost every Mediterranean and northern European country has its "anchovy," although it is not always the same fish. All, or most, are members of the Engraulidae family, and all have one thing in common: They are rarely eaten fresh, when their distinctive flavor is actually quite muted. Rather, they are salted, canned, smoked, pounded into paste, or distilled to make "fish sauce" such as the *nuoc mam* of Vietnam. They once formed the basis for *garum,* the ancient Greco-Roman dipping sauce.

Today, the most common use for anchovies is in Italian and Provençal cooking. Look for salted anchovies, sold in large cans in many Italian food stores. To use them, rinse under cold running water, peel off one fillet, remove the bone and tail from the other fillet, and rinse again. Canned anchovies are a reliable substitute but come packed in oil, an ingredient that may not be necessary in the dish you are preparing. If too salty, soak the fillets in a little milk before using.

ANCHOVY CANAPÉS—Slices of fried bread, one-quarter inch thick, spread with anchovy paste or butter, a filleted anchovy on top, the edges decorated with minced whites of hard boiled egg.

ANCHOVY AIGRETTES—Filleted anchovies washed, then laid for three hours in a pickle of olive oil, vinegar and red pepper; taken up, drained, dipped in batter and fried a light color in very hot fat; served garnished with lobster coral and sprigs of parsley.

ANCHOVY TOAST—Slices of toast spread with a mixture made of three-fifths essence of anchovies, one-fifth grated Parmesan cheese, and one-fifth minced filleted anchovies and chopped parsley.

ANCHOVY ALUMETTES—Preserved anchovies in oil, drained, rolled in very thin pie paste, fried; served garnished with fried parsley.

ANCHOVY TARTINES—Circles of brown bread spread with anchovy paste, decorated with thinly sliced gherkins alternately with white of hard boiled egg.

ANCHOVY FRITTERS—Filleted anchovies coiled up, dipped in batter and fried a light color in hot fat; served garnished with fried parsley.

ANCHOVY BASKETS—Hard boiled eggs, part of the white cut away to form an oval basket, yolks removed and pounded to a paste with anchovy essence, seasoned with lemon juice and cayenne pepper, colored lightly with carmine or cochineal, baskets refilled; served garnished with watercress.

ANCHOVY CROÛTONS—A paste of three-fifths anchovy essence, one-fifth grated cheese and one-fifth melted butter and lemon juice, the paste spread on fancy cut slices of fried bread; served with a coiled anchovy on top.

ANCHOVY SANDWICH—Thin slices of bread cut into shape of circles, spread with the preceding mixture, and filleted anchovies laid between.

ANCHOVIES WITH OLIVES—Anchovy toast garnished with slices of stuffed olives.

ANCHOVY CANAPÉS, BERNE—Triangle shaped pieces of fried bread, spread with anchovy paste or butter, the edges garnished with minced whites of hard boiled eggs, minced yolks, and minced green pickles, with a stuffed olive in the center.

ANCHOVY BUTTER—Two parts of butter to one part of anchovy essence, a little grated Parmesan cheese and nutmeg, thoroughly mixed together.

ANCHOVY PASTE—Anchovies filleted, the fillets rubbed through a fine sieve, the head and bones boiled with a little water and thickened with flour, strained into the paste obtained from the rubbing, mixed; when cooled, a little cochineal, walnut catsup, and vinegar added to give the required color and consistency.

ANCHOVY SAUCE—Anchovy paste or butter worked into a rich brown sauce, or some pounded filleted anchovies, or anchovy essence, lemon juice and cayenne pepper worked into a cream or butter sauce.

ANCHOVY CREAM—Anchovy paste worked into a butter sauce, and finished with whipped cream.

ANCHOVY STUFFING—Used very often for stuffing olives and small game birds. One cupful of breadcrumbs squeezed out of milk, one tablespoonful of minced fried onions, four minced fillets of anchovies, one teaspoonful each of minced capers and chopped parsley, the whole mixed; if used for stuffing birds, add the birds liver minced.

ANCHOVIES POTTED—Anchovy fillets pounded and rubbed through a sieve, mixed with ground allspice and cayenne pepper to taste, placed into small jars, pressed down, and one-eighth of an inch of melted lard poured over the top, to seal the contents.

ANCHOVY SALAD—Shredded fillets of salted anchovies garnished with small white pickled onions, capers and hard boiled eggs; tarragon vinegar sprinkled over the anchovies. Also shredded lettuce and shredded anchovies, a few minced shallots, all mixed together dry, then sprinkled with equal parts of olive oil and caper vinegar beaten together.

ANCHOVY CATSUP—Anchovies, onions, whole cloves, mace, peppers and ginger, sugar and old ale, brought to a quick boil, then slowly simmered till done, strained through a hair sieve, cooled, walnut catsup added; bottled for use.

ANCHOVY FRITTERS—Thin flour pancakes spread with chicken forcemeat, cut in strips twice the size of anchovy fillet, which is laid on one-half of the strip, the other half folded over, then breaded and fried; served garnished with fried parsley.

ANCHOVY OMELET—Beaten eggs seasoned with salt, pepper and chopped parsley, made into an omelet, the center enclosing some cooked fillets of anchovies; served with equal parts of tomato and Espagnole sauces mixed together.

ANGEL FOOD—A light, white, kind of sponge cake.

ANGELICA—A green preserved stalk resembling rhubarb, used to decorate cakes, also in iced puddings, ice creams, etc.

ANGELICA—Its stalks may resemble rhubarb, but angelica is a member of the Umbelliferae family, closely related to PARSLEY. Traditionally angelica, which is rarely seen in this country, was used in making candy, medicine, and wine.

ANILINE—A chemical product of petroleum; the red is the cheapest and best for culinary purposes, besides being perfectly harmless.

ANILINE—A coal-tar derivative, aniline is no longer sold over the counter as a food coloring. Although far from deadly, it is no longer considered "perfectly harmless."

ANISE—An herb, from the seeds of which is extracted the oil of anise; a liqueur called anisette is made from the oil; a small proportion of oil of anise mixed with alcohol, produces essence of aniseed, used in flavoring cakes and confectionery.

ANISE—There are two unrelated plants called anise. Aniseed comes from *Pimpinella anisum,* a member of the parsley family, also known as European anise or sweet cumin. We get the more intensely flavored star anise from *Illicium verum,* a magnolialike tree. Star anise is used by the French to make the licorice-flavored pastis, and is one of the ingredients in five-spice powder.

Other uses for anise are limited. It was a popular ingredient in cakes in Rome, and was popular in Asia before Rome existed, but its strong flavor finds few companions. Now, while it is obviously essential in anise-flavored cookies, it is only an occasional component of spice cakes, although it remains one of the few spices used in Chinese cooking.

ANTELOPE—A species of deer; the young are best for culinary purposes, as the meat, besides being treated in all the same ways as venison, is light enough in color to allow of being larded, which cannot be done to venison. Red meats should never be larded, on account of their loss of blood and gravy in cooking.

APPLES—About twelve really good kinds are obtainable by the steward, for hotel purposes—Pound sweets, King, Baldwins, Spitzenbergs, Northern spy, Rhode Island greenings, Golden pippins, Johnathans, Wine saps, Snow, Shiawasse beauty, Roxbury russets, Wageners. There are others, but these are among the first rank.

APPLES—The "steward" should still choose from a small group of apples, but the apples making up that group have changed entirely since 1904. The new hybrids ship and store better than the old apples, retaining good flavor and crispness over an extended period of time. Although excellent heirloom varieties are grown throughout the United States—including some of Charles Fellows's favorites—the following all-purpose apples have the longest seasons and the most widespread availability: Empire and Jonamac, which most experts believe will soon surpass Red Delicious and McIntosh as this country's best sellers; the crisp, yellow, sweet-tart Golden Delicious; Granny Smith; and the crunchy Asian newcomers Mutsu (also known as Crispin) and Fuji. New apple varieties, many of them quite appealing, appear every year.

Most apples become overripe at room temperature in just a day or two, so, after purchase, put them in the vegetable bin of your refrigerator. Stored this way, many varieties will remain crisp for a month or more. And, if you don't plan to eat them immediately when you peel and slice apples, drop them into a bowl of weakly acidulated water (use vinegar or, better still, lemon juice) to prevent discoloring—or even better, use Fruit-Fresh, a product that works very well.

APPLE BAVAROISE—Apple sauce, flavored with sherry wine and lemon juice, with enough gelatine added to set it, the whole passed through a hair sieve, whipped cream stirred in according to quantity liked, then poured into molds and allowed to set till firm; served with whipped cream.

APPLE BUTTER—Peeled apples boiled down in cider to a pulp with a flavor of allspice, the pulp then passed through a fine strainer.

APPLES BAKED—Good firm apples cored, the core hole filled with a mixture of butter and sugar flavored with nutmeg, then placed into a pan containing a little water, and baked till done.

APPLE CAKE—Apple sauce and an equal quantity of batter of the consistency of cream, made of flour, milk, eggs and sugar, mixed together and baked slowly till done; when nearly done, the top dusted with sugar, returned to oven to get a glazed appearance.

APPLE CHEESECAKES—Patty pans lined with puff paste, filled with apple marmalade containing a little grated lemon rind and enough yolks of eggs to set.

APPLE CHARLOTTE—The bottom and sides of a pan or mold lined with thin slices of buttered bread, the interior filled with thick apple marmalade, the top covered with slices of buttered bread half an inch thick dipped in a mixture of milk and eggs, the charlotte then baked a fine color, turned out and served with whipped cream.

APPLE CHUTNEY—A pint and a half of vinegar, two ounces of whole ginger bruised, one ounce of chillies, one ounce of mustard seed, two ounces of salt, twelve ounces of sugar, boiled slowly for forty-five minutes, then strained through a hair sieve; when cooled the vinegar thus flavored put on again with a large onion minced, one and one-half ounces of minced shallots, two ounces of sultana raisins, and two and one-half pounds of peeled and sliced apples, the whole boiled till apples are pulpy, then placed into stone jars and tied down with skin.

APPLE CREAM—Sweet applesauce, containing a little butter and whipped whites of egg.

APPLE CROQUETTES—Thick apple marmalade containing soft breadcrumbs and egg yolks baked till set. When cold, cut in strips two inches long and one inch thick, breaded, fried, and served with orange sauce.

APPLE CUSTARD—Apple marmalade mixed with beaten eggs and cream, poured into a pan or dish, and baked till set.

APPLE DUMPLINGS—Cored and peeled apples enclosed in pie paste, baked, boiled or steamed till done, served with a sauce or with cream.

APPLE FLOAT—Cream sweetened and flavored with nutmeg poured in a dish or pan; apple marmalade containing whipped whites of egg, poured in the centre; baked till set.

APPLE FRITTERS—Slices of cored apples, dipped in batter and fried till done; served with a syrup or wine sauce.

APPLE PIE—Thin slices of apples, sweetened and spiced, enclosed between an upper and lower crust of pie paste; baked till done.

APPLE ICE—Apple marmalade flavored with orange juice, thinned with water, sweetened to taste, poured into a freezer and frozen.

APPLE CUSTARD PIE—A pie dish lined with puff paste, filled with apple marmalade mixed with cream and yolks of eggs; baked till set.

APPLE CUSTARD FRITTERS—Apple marmalade mixed with custard, baked till set; when cooled, cut in slices, breaded, fried and served with a sauce.

APPLES, PORTUGESE STYLE—Firm apples cored, peeled and simmered in a thin syrup till barely done, taken out, drained, the core hole filled with apricot jam, placed on a dish, the syrup then reduced to a glaze, and poured over them.

APPLE MERINGUE—Apple pulp in a dish, a layer of fruit marmalade spread on it, whipped whites of egg and sugar, tastefully spread over all, then placed in oven till of a light fawn color.

APPLE TART—A pie plate lined with puff paste with a raised fancy edge to it; filled two-thirds full with apple marmalade and baked; when done, filled up with a boiled custard, the interior edge piped round with meringue, also a fancy centre;

returned to oven till of a fawn color.

APPLE SOUP—Minced cooking apples, grated breadcrumbs, and water each one part, a piece of lemon rind and a flavoring of cinnamon, boiled till thoroughly done, the whole then passed through a fine strainer, and enough white wine added to form a soup consistency.

APPLE PANCAKES—Minced apples worked into an ordinary wheat pancake mixture, the pancakes baked in the usual way, and served with butter and sugar.

APPLE SHORTCAKE—Two layers of cooked shortpaste spread between with apple marmalade, the top ornamented with whipped cream; served with sweetened and flavored cream.

APPLE COMPOTE—Cored and pared apples simmered in a boiling syrup till thoroughly done, remaining whole.

APPLE ROLY POLY—A biscuit dough containing a little sugar, rolled out thin, spread with minced apples, seasoned with grated lemon rind, cinnamon, or ground cloves according to taste, rolled up, the ends tucked in, tied in a cloth for boiling (in a mold for steaming) (in a pan for baking); served with a sauce, or with sweetened cream.

APPLES FRIED—Good firm apples, peeled, cored, cut in slices half an inch thick, then dipped in milk, rolled in flour, and fried in very hot lard.

APPLE JOHNNY CAKE—Slices of peeled and cored apples in a buttered baking dish, sweetened and flavored, a pancake batter poured over them; baked till done and served with or without currant jelly.

APPLE MARMALADE—Sweetened apple sauce boiled down till thick enough to cling to a spoon.

APPLE PUDDING—Basins or molds lined with a suet crust, filled with slices of apples, sweetened and flavored to taste, top crust put on, the basin tied over with a cloth, or mold cover placed on and tied, boiled rapidly till done.

APPLE PUFFS—Minced apples fried a little so as not to break, flavored with cinnamon and sugar, placed on squares of puff paste, the edges brought to a top centre and pinched together, brushed over with beaten egg and baked.

APPLE COBBLER—A pan one and a half inches deep lined with a pie paste, filled with apple marmalade, top crust put on, baked and glazed, served with sweetened and flavored cream, or with whipped cream.

APPLE TIMBALE—A timbale mold lined with strips of short paste, filled with apple marmalade, cov-

APPLE ROLY POLY

•

Serves 8 to 10

This dish has an attractive pinwheel pattern when sliced and is a tasty breakfast item or dessert.

For the apples

3 Red Delicious apples, peeled and cut into $1/4$-inch dice

4 tablespoons butter

$1/2$ teaspoon ground cinnamon

Pinch of ground cloves

$2^1/2$ tablespoons sugar

1 teaspoon grated lemon peel

Pinch of salt

For the biscuit dough

$2^1/2$ cups all-purpose flour

2 teaspoons baking powder

$1/2$ teaspoon baking soda

1 tablespoon sugar

1 teaspoon ground cinnamon

$1/4$ cup Crisco

1 cup buttermilk

Garnish

Whipped cream

In a frying pan, sauté the diced apples in the butter, cinnamon, and cloves until just tender. Add the sugar, lemon peel, and salt. Sauté 1 minute more and set aside to cool.

In a mixing bowl, combine $2^1/4$ cups of the flour with the other dry ingredients. Add the Crisco and mix with a pastry blender until coarse and grainy. Stir in the buttermilk and mix to form a dough.

Place the dough on the counter and knead the dough, incorporating the remaining $1/4$ cup flour. Let the dough relax a couple of minutes and roll out a square 15 inches by 15 inches. The dough should be about $1/8$ inch thick. Dust the counter and rolling pin with flour to prevent sticking. Spread the apple mixture over the entire surface of the dough. Roll up the dough into a coil and trim off the ends.

Place the dough on a nonstick baking sheet and bake in a preheated 400°F. oven for 35 minutes. Cool a bit, slice, and serve with whipped cream.

Try chilling the roll, slicing, and toasting, to make a delicious breakfast treat.

C.W.

ered with a crust, baked or steamed till paste is set, turned out, served with apricot sauce, and garnished with preserved cherries.

APPLES GLAZED—Cored and peeled apples of an even size simmered in lemon syrup till just done, taken out, placed on a dish, the syrup reduced till thick, then poured over the apples; when cooled, decorated with angelica and cherries.

APPLE FLORENTINE—Apples cored and simmered till half done, in syrup, taken out, drained, the core hole filled with sweetened rice, the outside coated with a vanilla flavored chestnut purée; made hot again in oven and served with a sprinkling of chopped pistachio nuts.

APRICOTS ON TOAST—Stewed apricots on sweetened toast, garnished with whipped cream (called Apricots au Croûton).

APRICOTS AND RICE FRITTERS— Half an apricot, the other half formed of rice croquette mixture, put together, breaded, fried and served with apricot sauce (called Apricots à la Colbert).

APRICOTS WITH RICE—Stewed or canned apricots in syrup, bordered with sweetened rice, whipped cream over the apricots, sprinkled with chopped pistachio nuts (called Apricots à la Condé).

APRICOT BAVAROISE—Stiff apricot marmalade with whipped cream

containing a little gelatine mixed in, filled into molds, set till firm, turned out on a dish, and the edge piped around with whipped cream.

APRICOT CHARLOTTE—A pan or mold lined with lady fingers, strips of buttered bread or toast, filled with stewed apricots, covered with the same material as the lining, baked, turned out, and served with a fruit sauce.

APRICOT COBBLER—(Sometimes called "Apricots D'Artois.") Two sheets of puff paste baked, one spread with apricot marmalade, the other laid on top, then cut in squares, diamonds or with a fancy shaped cutter, the edge ornamented with piped meringue, dried in the oven to a straw color, the centre of top decorated with jelly.

APRICOT COMPOTE—Apricots simmered in thick syrup till done, served with the syrup they were cooked in.

APRICOT CHARTREUSE—A centre jelly mold decorated at bottom with stiffened cream, sides coated with jelly, halves of cooked apricots fancifully placed around the mold, these again coated with jelly, the mold then filled with jelly, set, turned out, and the centre filled with Bavarian cream.

APRICOTS IN CASES—Fresh apricots halved, stoned, simmered in raspberry syrup, served in rice cases with angelica sauce.

APRICOT FRITTERS—Halves of apricots or spoonfuls of apricot marmalade laid on a thin circle of paste, another circle placed on top, edges pinched together, trimmed, fried till done. Also halves of apricots laid in diluted brandy and sugar for half an hour, then dipped in batter, fried, dusted with sugar, and served with a syrup sauce.

APRICOT PATTIES OR VOL-AU-VENTS—Very light patty shells, nearly filled with apricot marmalade, finished by filling and decorating with whipped cream.

APRICOT MARMALADE OR JAM—Raw apricots stoned and rubbed through a sieve. To every pound of the pulp is added ten ounces of sugar with a few of the kernels blanched and skinned; boiled till thick enough to coat a spoon.

APRICOT SHERBET—Apricots boiled in syrup; when done rubbed through a fine sieve, the syrup and pulp then poured into a freezer and frozen; when nearly done, a flavoring of maraschino and some whipped whites of eggs are added, then frozen five minutes.

APRICOT SAUCE—Water, sugar, apricots, lemon juice and a little grated orange rind, boiled, thickened with corn starch, then rubbed through a fine strainer.

APRICOT TARTLETTES—Small tartlette molds lined with puff paste, filled with apricot marmalade, baked; when done, the edges decorated with crystalized cherries, and the centre piped with whipped cream.

APRICOT OMELET—Beaten eggs with a flavoring of vanilla made into an omelet, the inside enclosing some apricot marmalade or compote, omelet then placed on dish, dusted with sugar, marked with a hot wire, or glazed under a salamander.

ARTICHOKES—Are of two kinds, the green or globe, and the Jerusalem. The globe is sometimes used for salads, and served with a French dressing hot with pepper; also boiled plain and served with any of the sauces appropriate to cauliflower. The Jerusalem resembles a rough knobbly potato.

ARTICHOKES—Globe artichokes are undeveloped thistle flowers that are indigenous to the Mediterranean; their culinary heights are reached in Italy. They are cultivated, and grow like crazy, in Castroville, California, the self-proclaimed Artichoke Capital of the World, which is responsible for 95 percent of this country's artichoke production. Popular since the Renaissance, artichokes remain an integral part of many leisurely meals; enjoying them requires some work in preparation as well as care and thoughtfulness in eating. The prize—the uniquely flavored, silken heart—makes all the effort worthwhile.

Look for bright, glossy leaves when buying artichokes; avoid those that are discolored or shriveled.

By now almost every food lover knows what Charles Fellows did not: that, in fact, a JERUSALEM ARTI-

CHOKE is not an artichoke, nor is it from Jerusalem. The name, however, persists.

ARTICHOKE BOTTOMS BRAISED—Artichoke bottoms filled with chicken forcemeat, braised, served on a croûton, with a rich brown or mushroom sauce poured around.

ARTICHOKE BOTTOMS WITH FORCEMEAT—Artichoke bottoms spread with a purée of onions and rice mixed together, filled up with forcemeat, sprinkled with grated cheese and breadcrumbs, arranged in a pan, moistened with consommé and browned in the oven. Served with cream onion sauce around (called Artichokes à la Soûbise).

ARTICHOKES BOTTOMS WITH FOIE GRAS—Artichoke bottoms spread with a mixture of foie-gras and minced truffles, covered with a reduced white mushroom sauce, grated breadcrumbs sprinkled over, then browned in the oven; served with a truffle sauce poured around (called Fonds d'Artichauts à la Strasbourg).

ARTICHOKE FRITTERS—Cooked artichoke bottoms seasoned, breaded, or dipped in batter and fried in very hot lard; or mashed Jerusalem artichokes mixed with egg yolks, and seasoned with nutmeg, taken up by spoonfuls and fried.

ARTICHOKE CHIPS—Jerusalem artichokes peeled and cut into very thin slices with a Saratoga chip cutter, placed in cold salted water for an hour, taken up a few at a time, dried, then fried in very hot fat, drained, sprinkled with salt.

ARTICHOKES AU GRATIN—Same as artichokes scalloped. Artichoke bottoms cut in slices and mixed with Béchamel sauce, may be used.

ARTICHOKE BOTTOMS WITH RAGOUT—Artichoke bottoms filled with a mixture of diced truffles, mushrooms, tongue and breast of chicken, all mixed with Allemande sauce, a thin layer of chicken forcemeat placed on top, sprinkled with grated breadcrumbs and cheese, then browned (called Fonds d'Artichauts à la Montglas).

GLOBE ARTICHOKES, COLBERT SAUCE—Globe artichokes trimmed and the choke removed, parboiled in salted water, drained, cooled, then arranged in a sauce pan with a little butter, white wine and consommé; simmered till done and glazy; served with Colbert sauce poured around (called Artichokes à la Lyonnaise).

GLOBE ARTICHOKES STUFFED—Globe artichokes trimmed and the choke removed, the bottoms fried quickly in olive oil for three minutes, turned over and the leaves fried a minute, taken up and drained, the interior filled with a savory stuffing of meat, herbs and breadcrumbs; arranged in a saûtoir, then covered with thin slices of bacon, equal parts of white wine and consommé, simmered till tender, taken up, drained, the braise reduced to a glaze, skimmed and added to an Italian sauce; served with the sauce poured around (called Artichokes à la Barigoule).

ARTICHOKE BOTTOMS WITH ONIONS—Artichoke bottoms filled with a mixture of fried onions, breadcrumbs, and Parmesan cheese, sprinkled with lemon juice, then browned in the oven; served with a brown sauce poured around (called Fonds d'Artichauts à l'Italienne).

SCALLOPED ARTICHOKES—Jerusalem artichokes cut to shape of oysters, boiled in salted water till tender, taken up and drained, then put in scallop shells or dishes, covered with anchovy sauce, sprinkled with grated cheese and breadcrumbs, then browned in the oven.

ARTICHOKE BOTTOMS STUFFED—Artichoke bottoms filled with forcemeat, covered with supreme sauce, sprinkled with grated cheese and breadcrumbs, browned in the oven, and served with sauce Suprême (called Fonds d'Artichauts à la Suprême).

ARTICHOKE OMELET—Thin strips of the tender part of the globe artichoke seasoned with salt and pepper, lightly fried in butter, drained, added to beaten eggs containing chopped parsley, made into an omelet; served with cream sauce poured around the omelet.

ARTICHOKES WITH EGG—Artichoke bottoms boiled, served on toast, garnished with quartered hard boiled eggs, and mâitre

d'hôtel butter poured over the artichokes.

ARTICHOKES BOILED—Globe artichokes, the tips of the leaves cut and the bottoms rounded, the stalk removed and the under leaves trimmed away; well washed and soaked in salted water for an hour, placed in boiling salted water, and boiled rapidly till tender, taken up, drained, the choke removed, served with melted butter, or sauces appropriate to cauliflower.

ARTICHOKES, FAMILY STYLE—Jerusalem artichokes peeled and trimmed to the shape of pears with a flat bottom, boiled in salted water till tender; a dish of mashed potatoes, artichokes placed around it point upwards, and a boiled Brussels sprout placed between each artichoke.

ARTICHOKE SOUP—Globe artichokes parboiled in salted water, the choke, edible part and leaves rubbed through a sieve, the purée thus obtained one part; cream of chicken soup, one part; onion cream sauce one part, all incorporated, and boiling milk added to obtain the desired consistency of thin cream.

ARTICHOKE AND ONION SALAD—Artichoke bottoms and onions, both cooked and sliced, dished alternately, garnished with cooked beets and carrots cut with a fancy cutter; served either with French dressing or salad cream.

ARTICHOKE AND TOMATO SALAD—Cooked artichoke bottoms and

raw sliced peeled tomatoes, same size as the bottoms, arranged alternately on dish, sprinkled with French dressing containing chopped chervil.

ASPARAGUS—Is of two kinds, the red and green; the red is large, thick and full; the green is smaller, with a whitish stalk and green head, of delicate flavor.

ASPARAGUS—Like the ARTICHOKE, the asparagus, which was cultivated before the birth of Jesus, is one of our oldest vegetables, and it remains one of the best. Long prized in Mediterranean countries, it is routinely sold in open-air markets, where several different colors (green, purple, and white) and sizes (from string bean–thin to the thickness of a beefy thumb) stand together, all neatly tied in bunches.

Although it is now available year-round, prime asparagus is found in early spring and, with STRAWBERRIES, is a harbinger of the great produce to come. Look for crisp, bright green stalks, with no wrinkling and a short base. When ready to cook, break off the fibrous white bottom section. Steam them standing, tied in bunches, or lying down in water to cover, for just a few minutes. If you do not plan to serve the asparagus immediately, rinse them in cold water to keep lingering heat from overcooking them.

ASPARAGUS STEWED—Asparagus heads, also the tender part of the stalks cut into inch lengths, blanched, drained, then simmered till tender in a butter sauce, finished by adding a liaison of egg yolks and cream.

ASPARAGUS, SAUCE HOLLANDAISE—Asparagus heads with all the tender part of the stalk attached, boiled in boiling water containing a small piece of common washing soda and salt till done, a piece of toast placed on a dish, the asparagus stalks resting on the toast with the heads in the dish, Hollandaise sauce poured over the heads.

ASPARAGUS—Cooked like the preceding may also be served with plain melted butter, cream, Velouté, Mousseline or Béchamel sauce; also, after cooking, allowed to become cold, and served without toast, but with either Tartare, Vinaigrette or mayonnaise sauce.

ASPARAGUS OMELET—Asparagus tips blanched and drained, then fried lightly in butter, surplus butter poured off and a little cream sauce added; omelet mixture containing chopped parsley formed, enclosing a spoonful of the asparagus, placed on a dish and a spoonful of asparagus placed at each end.

ASPARAGUS POINTS WITH QUENELLES—Asparagus points and about two inches of the stalk boiled, drained, laid on toast, bordered with small quenelles of chicken, and Hollandaise sauce poured over the tips.

ASPARAGUS SOUP—Asparagus heads blanched, drained and lightly fried with minced shallots in butter, then laid aside, the stalks boiled in veal or chicken broth till tender, a little white roux added, then rubbed through a sieve and mixed with equal parts of Velouté and cream sauce, brought to a simmer, the heads now added and served.

ASPARAGUS PURÉE—Asparagus points and the tender part of the stalks blanched and drained, lightly fried in butter with some minced shallots, green onions, parsley and a little sugar, turned into chicken broth, brought to a boil, thickened with white roux, the whole rubbed through a sieve, spinach juice added to help give a greenish color, seasoned and served.

ASPARAGUS SALAD—Two inch lengths with the head of cold boiled asparagus served on a leaf of lettuce with a cream salad dressing.

ASPARAGUS AND SALMON SALAD— A spoonful of ice cold salmon en mayonnaise garnished with asparagus tips in French dressing.

ASPARAGUS AND CAULIFLOWER SALAD—Cooked cauliflower in flowerets garnished with asparagus tips, served sprinkled with chopped capers and cream salad dressing.

ASPARAGUS PATTIES—Cooked asparagus heads and mushrooms in equal parts mixed with Velouté sauce, patty shells filled with the mixture, tops placed on; served with a sauce Mousseline poured around the base.

ASPARAGUS WITH CHEESE— Cooked asparagus heads seasoned with salt and pepper, placed in a vegetable dish, equal parts of butter and grated Parmesan cheese pounded together with a seasoning of cayenne pepper and lemon juice, the asparagus covered with the cheese and butter, browned in the oven and served.

ASPIC JELLY—Plenty of veal knuckles, calf's feet boned and blanched, and a fowl or two are covered with clear water, fetched slowly to a boil, skimmed, a little cold water then added, again brought to the boil and skimmed, carrots, onions, celery, parsley, a little garlic, bay leaves, thyme, mace and whole peppers are then added and simmered slowly for six hours, fat taken off, then strained through a consommé towel, allowed to become quite cold and all fat removed, then placed over a quick fire, brought to the boil, skimmed, removed to cool off a little; while cooling, gelatine at the rate of two ounces to the gallon is added; some lean veal is now chopped fine and mixed with some whipped whites of eggs and egg shells, also a bottle of white wine, this mixture poured into the cooling stock and allowed to come to a slow boil; when just at boiling point a little ice water containing lemon juice is put in, and as soon as coagulation takes place it is drawn to one side and allowed to simmer slowly for an hour longer, then strained through a jelly bag and set away for use.

AVOCADO—See ALLIGATOR PEAR.

B

BABA—A light yeast raised cake containing fruit and almonds, generally served as dessert with a rum sauce.

BABA—Baba is also known as babka, and is a cake usually steeped in rum or syrup.

BACON—Is known as salted and dried. The salted is generally used as boiling bacon, and the dried, which is subsequently smoked, is generally used for frying and broiling. In selecting bacon discard any with yellow fat. Good bacon is red in the lean and the fat is white and firm. *** Bacon fat is better than butter for many things that have to be fried, such as liver, veal chops, onions for curry, etc., is also used instead of olive oil with potato salad, lettuce salad, combination salad, etc. *** Bacon is appropriate boiled with cabbage, kraut and string, wax and haricot beans; it is an improvement to an omelet, and is the proper thing to eat with liver, eggs and fowls.

BACON—Bacon, from the old French for HAM, *bakko*, once referred to almost any part of the pig that was cured and smoked. Now it most often refers to cured and smoked pork belly. (There are exceptions, including Canadian bacon, which comes from the loin, and pancetta, the unsmoked, rolled Italian bacon that is an integral part of spaghetti carbonara and many other pasta dishes.)

In England, where bacon remains a popular food if not a staple, different cuts and cures can be found in every town and city. But, distressingly, most of our bacon now comes in plastic-wrapped packages of thin-sliced, oversugared, artificially smoked meat. If you have the energy to search for superior slab bacon, you can find it; some is available by mail, and there are several national brands in which smokiness dominates over sweetness.

The health aspects of bacon need not be mentioned, except to acknowledge that you probably don't want to make it a daily habit. Note, however, that bacon is used sparingly in most of the dishes to which it lends its wonderful flavor. Furthermore, well-made bacon contains less salt than it once did (thanks to refrigeration) and a higher ratio of lean to fat (thanks to selective breeding).

When buying bacon, check the use-by dates printed on vacuum-packed bacon; these are usually accurate. Once opened, bacon will keep for a week or so, as long as it is well wrapped. Slab bacon also keeps well in the refrigerator, but it does not freeze as well as unsmoked meats; the fat will begin to turn rancid in a couple of months.

BAGRATION—The name applied through a foreign medium to a few dishes, principally soups that are composed of a medley of fish and vegetables.

BAKING POWDER—Is better made than bought; the following receipt is cheap and effective; five pounds of tartaric acid, eight pounds of bicarbonate of soda, sixteen pounds of potato flour, mixed and rubbed through a fine sieve. By the addition of a quarter of an ounce of turmeric to eight pounds of baking powder you produce EGG POWDER, which saves eggs and gives richness of color.

BAKING POWDER—It is unlikely that anyone reading these words has ever made, or will ever make, his or her own baking powder. As you can see from Fellows's recipe, baking powder is a combination of acidic (tartaric, in this case) and basic, or alkaline (bicarbonate of soda, or baking sôda), substances. Today's commercially made baking powder actually contains two acids, one that reacts primarily to moisture, the other to heat; thus the adjective *double-acting*.

Mixed together with moist ingredients, such as milk or eggs, especially in the presence of heat, baking powder produces carbon dioxide gas. Trapped by the liquid and glutinous flour present in most batters, the gas causes the batter to rise. Baking soda has the identical effect, but it works only when it is added to a batter already containing an acidic substance, such as vinegar, buttermilk, or lemon juice.

BALLOTTINE—Is the name given to a chaud-froid of poultry, game, foie-gras, spring lamb, etc., is made by mincing the flesh and forming it into forcemeat, then stuffing small boned birds such as larks, quails, snipe, woodcock, squabs, etc., cooking them and serving them cold. Sometimes the forcemeat is stuffed into the skin of a turkey leg, sewn up, cooked, shaped like a ham; when cold, one end is masked with a brown sauce, the other with a white sauce, imitating a ham skin; they are then ornamented with aspic jelly, atelettes, etc.

BALLOTTINE—Ballottine is another name for a galantine—meat, poultry, or game birds stuffed with a sausagelike mixture, then rolled, tied, and poached. It is served warm or cold.

BANANA—Semi-tropical fruit that grow in bunches sometimes six feet in length and containing four to five hundred bananas, that, when ripe, change either to a bright yellow or purple red color. The yellow are esteemed for their flavor, while the red are best for cooking, as they are more firm. The merchants in selling the fruit, fix the price according to the number of HANDS the bunch contains. A hand is a section on the stalk and contains, according to the size of the fruit, from ten to twenty bananas. Bananas may be bought in a green state much cheaper than when ripe. When bought green, the way of ripening is to hang the bunches up in a dark room, and subject them to a steady heat of seventy-five degrees.

BANANA—Probably our most reliable year-round fruit, the banana was a luxury in Fellows's time. But throughout the world, the four hundred or so varieties of the Musaceau family are an important staple: Some are cooked (see PLANTAIN); the leaves of some are used as wrappers in some dishes from the Far East; some are cultivated for rope making; and some are used for wine.

Generally we eat bananas raw, out of hand, or—when they become too ripe—baked in bread or muffins. However, the continuing influx of Latin American and Caribbean immigrants to our country is making itself felt: Not only are plantains found in most supermarkets, but so are a wider variety of sweet bananas, including the small yellow honey and squat red types.

BANANA FRITTERS—Bananas cut slantwise in halves, laid for a while in diluted brandy and sugar, then dipped in batter and fried in plenty of hot fat, taken up, drained, rolled in powdered sugar, and served with a fruit sauce.

BANANAS BAKED—Bananas split in halves lengthwise, laid in a buttered pan, dusted with powdered sugar, browned quickly in the oven; served with a cocoanut syrup sauce.

BANANAS FRIED—Bananas split in halves lengthwise, dipped in milk, then rolled in flour, fried in clear butter to a golden brown; served with currant jelly.

BANANA COMPOTE—Bananas cut in quarters slantwise, simmered in syrup till done; served on a bed of sweetened rice, with the syrup poured over them.

BANANA ICE CREAM—Bananas peeled and rubbed through a fine sieve; added to the cream to be frozen at the rate of one pound of pulp to the gallon.

BANANA SALAD—Alternate slices of bananas, peeled oranges, and dessicated cocoanut are placed in a fruit dish till full, over which is poured enough brandy and rum mixed with sugar to just moisten the salad.

BARAQUILLE—Is the foreign culinary term for a patty or vol-au-vent filled with a mince of veal, chicken, partridge, truffles, small game, fresh mushrooms, sweetbreads, etc.

BARAQUILLE—Baked or deep-fried, these puff-pastry appetizers are rarely made in such an elaborate fashion as Fellows described. They are, however, closely related to the meat pastries made by a wide variety of ethnic groups.

BARBECUE—Means an animal roasted whole; although in recent years the word has been applied to gatherings at places where an animal roasted whole and served to the guests is the principal feature of the party.

BARBECUE—This could be the most ill-defined word in the English language. Rarely these days is barbecue used to mean "an animal roasted whole," although inviting someone "to a barbecue" remains legitimate. Cooking over an open fire, frequently called barbecuing, is better termed *grilling*.

What, then, is barbecue? Its far-from-firm definition varies from one practitioner to another. But it is, most often, pork shoulder, ribs, or beef brisket that has been indirectly slow-cooked—typically upward of 8 hours—with smoke from an oak, hickory, or other hardwood fire. The result, of course, is meat that is smoky-tasting and fall-off-the-bone tender.

True barbecue needs little adornment; but barbecue "sauce" is any sauce served with barbecue.

BARON OF BEEF—One of the olden-time dishes of Great Britain's banquet tables, the term applied to two short loins of beef left whole, resembling a saddle of mutton.

BARLEY—A grain used by brewers in malting; generally found on the market in two sizes or qualities known as Scotch and Pearl. The Scotch is larger and has the inner husk left on; the Pearl is smaller and completely freed from husk, which makes it better adapted for culinary use; chiefly used in soups and gruels.

BARLEY—Fellows's is rather curt treatment for *Hordeum vulgare*, when you consider that barley is probably our oldest cultivated grain. Easy to grow—it flourishes in the high mountain country of Tibet—easy to cook, easy to eat, and easy to digest, barley is sorrowfully underrated. Yes, its primary use is in making first-rate beer (no other grain performs nearly as well in that role). But even when it is boiled for a simple side dish, the flavor of barley is sweeter and more complex than that of RICE; and when ground into flour, it is nearly as versatile as wheat.

BASIL—The name of a favorite herb used in seasoning turtle soup. Cloves resemble it in taste and flavor, and since the herb is as a rule hard to procure, even in the large cities, the clove does duty for it in a very creditable manner.

BASIL—Few of us would ever dream of substituting CLOVES for basil, although many people describe the aroma of basil as being similar to that of MINT or licorice. These days, however, basil is generally considered irreplaceable. In fact, it is one of the few herbs that really should be used only if fresh; dried basil has about as much in common with the fresh variety as, well, cloves.

Basil became the herb of the moment in the 1980s: Pesto (an uncooked sauce made from basil leaves, pine nuts, Parmesan cheese, garlic, and olive oil) was everywhere, and gardeners raved about their basil-and-tomato sandwiches. Soon, it wasn't enough to say "basil"; you had to specify which variety: lemon, opal, lettuce, anise-scented, purple, green ruffles, sacred, bush . . . the list goes on. The basic is sweet basil (*Ocimum basilicum*), which is related to mint and is now widely available, fresh and cheap, all summer long (and reasonably fresh, if not so cheap, in the winter).

BASS—A well known species of fish, especially adapted for culinary purposes on account of its shape and size as well as its firm meat and delicate flavor. There are four or five principal kinds chiefly used, the Black, Striped, Sea, Silver, and Spotted, of which the Black stands first.

BASS—The word *bass* covers, and always has, a wide assortment of unrelated fish. Freshwater bass (also called black bass), including largemouth, smallmouth, shoal, redeye, spotted, and others, is America's favorite inland game fish. But it is rarely found on restaurant menus or in fish markets.

Striped bass and black sea bass are the most commonly found saltwater bass. Black sea bass is a relatively small fish, rarely larger than three pounds, that remains plentiful in the North Atlantic. Its firm flesh makes it especially suitable for Chinese cooking, since a whole fish can stand up to deep-frying or steaming without loss of texture or flavor.

During the 1980s the Northeast's depleted and endangered striped bass population was protected. But

as of this writing, the fish has recovered sufficiently to allow sport fishing; commercial fishing may resume in this decade. A hybrid of striped and white bass is being farmed commercially in southern California and elsewhere. It is expensive, with a less-pronounced flavor and somewhat mushier texture than the wild fish; nevertheless, this product of aquaculture has been well received by chefs and consumers.

BASS BROILED—The fish is chosen of as near a pound in weight as possible, if for club or restaurant use: scaled, trimmed, seasoned, scored slantwise, rolled in flour, brushed with melted butter or olive oil, broiled; served with a slice of broiled bacon, a spoonful of melted butter, slice of lemon, and a garnish of parsley. If used as a course of a dinner, before broiling it is filleted into portion pieces.

BASS FRIED—Prepared as the preceding, except it is not scored; fried a golden brown, and served as if broiled, or with tomato, anchovy or Genevoise sauces.

BASS BOILED—Scaled, trimmed, cut into portion pieces, placed into boiling water containing slices of carrot and onion, bay leaves, whole peppers, salt and a dash of vinegar; served with either butter, cream, parsley, shrimp, anchovy, oyster or Hollandaise sauces; sometimes served with green peas.

BASS BAKED—Scaled, trimmed, (left whole for restaurant and cut in portions if for hotel use), placed in pan, seasoned with wine, broth, oil, salt, pepper and minced shallots, sheet of oiled paper put over, baked; when nearly done, equal quantities of parsley and Espagnole sauces added to the pan; the fish served with the sauce (called Bass à la Condé).

BASS BRAISED—Prepared as the preceding, placed in pan or saûtoir containing slices of carrot, onion, celery and parsley, with enough Bordelaise sauce to moisten the fish, braised slowly till done; served with the sauce and garnished with shrimps (called Bass à la Bordelaise).

BASS BRAISED—The fish cut into fillets, larded, braised in equal parts of tomato and Béchamel sauces; when cooked, the sauce poured into saucepan, and added to it some purée of mushrooms, lobster roe, sliced truffles and Saûterne wine; the fish served with the sauce, and garnished with fish quenelles (called Bass à la Chambord).

BASS SAUTÉ—The fish prepared as for frying, rolled in flour, and fried plain; a little gravy made in the pan the fish was fried in with flour and fish broth, and served with the fish, garnished with fancy potatoes (called Bass à la Meunière).

BASS CROQUETTES—Cold cooked bass with the skin and bones removed, then picked and put in a thick fish cream sauce, seasoned with anchovy essence, salt, pepper and grated nutmeg, allowed to become cold, shaped into croquettes, breaded, fried, and served with either tomato, Bordelaise, Genoise or anchovy sauces, garnished with parsley and sliced lemon.

BATTER—A consistency of flour and liquids used to dip foods in before frying; also a pancake and pudding mixture. The following fritter batter is used for frying any foods of a plain nature: a pound of flour is gradually moistened with a half pint each of milk and water, added to which is the whipped whites of four eggs and half a cup of melted butter.

BATTER—For frying sweet foods and fruits is made of a pound of flour, a heaping teaspoonful of baking powder and half cup of sugar mixed together dry, then moistened with a cup and a half of milk and two beaten eggs.

BATTER—For frying vegetables is made of a pound of flour seasoned with salt, moistened with a pint of milk, one beaten egg, and a spoonful of olive oil.

BATTER—For French pancakes is made of a pound of flour very gradually moistened with a quart of milk and sixteen beaten eggs, the grated rind and juice of one lemon and a seasoning of salt. This batter is fried in small HOT frying pans, very thin, tossed over, spread with preserves, rolled up and sprinkled with powdered sugar. They are also called Jenny Lind Pancakes.

BATTER—For Swiss pancakes is made of six ounces of flour gradually moistened with six beaten eggs and a quart of milk with a seasoning of salt; they are fried like the preceding, but prior to tossing them over they are strewn with steamed currants. Served currant side up with powdered sugar, not rolled.

BATTER—For Yorkshire pudding is made of three quarters of a pound of flour gradually moistened with three pints of milk, nine beaten eggs, and half a cup of melted butter; one teaspoonful of salt and two of baking powder is beaten in just before putting into oven.

BATTER—For wheat griddle cakes is made of a pound of flour, one ounce of baking powder, two beaten eggs, three cups of milk, a little melted butter, sugar and salt.

BATTER—For corn griddle cakes is made of half a pound each of wheat flour and corn meal mixed dry with a little salt and one ounce of baking powder, then moistened with a pint each of milk and water, two beaten eggs, a little syrup and two table-spoonfuls of melted butter.

BATTER—For flannel griddle cakes is made of a pound of flour, a quart of water and a small cake of yeast, this is set to rise; when risen, two eggs, two ounces of melted lard, a little salt and syrup are beaten in, allowed to rise again before baking.

BATTER—For graham griddle cakes is made the same as for corn, except using graham flour for the corn meal.

BATTER—For rice griddle cakes is made of a pint each of sifted flour and dry boiled rice mixed together with a little salt, one teaspoonful of baking powder, moistened with half a pint of milk, three eggs and a little syrup.

BATTER—For buckwheat cakes is made of self-raising buckwheat flour prepared according to the directions given on the package; or one pound of buckwheat flour moistened with a pint and a half of warm water with enough yeast added to raise it; when risen, a little salt, syrup and melted lard or butter is beaten into it, and sometimes a little corn meal is appreciated.

BAY LEAVES—The leaf of the laurel tree dried and used in seasoning soups, sauces, etc.; they resemble in taste and flavor, bitter almonds.

BAY LEAVES—A strong-flavored herb, bay is the leaf of a Mediterranean laurel bush (*Laurus nobilis*). Its importance cannot be overstated: It is an integral part of the bouquet garni, and it has a particular affinity to pork. There are few Italian pork dishes without at least one bay leaf, and French cooking, especially stews, relies heavily on laurel as well. Many Italian cooks use a few bay leaves when rendering pork fat to make lard, which is used even in sweet dishes.

California and Mediterranean bay leaves are equally flavorful, although those from California are larger. Bay leaves are usually used whole and discarded before serving, but they may be well crumbled and left in the preparation. Avoid ground bay; it lacks flavor.

BEANS—One of the most nutritious foods that can be used; the varieties most used are the lima or butter bean, the white haricot or navy bean, the red and the black haricot, the flageolet or kidney bean.

BEANS—Fellows's description is accurate but strictly American. There are several major types of beans, all of which are prehistoric. The haricot (*Phaseolus*), indigenous to the New World, is the most numerous: There are several thousand varieties, some of which are mentioned by Fellows. Black, pinto, and cannellini are a few others.

The broad bean (also called fava, Windsor, round, and a half dozen other names) was the only bean known to Europeans until the late fifteenth century. It is eaten raw when young and cooked when ripe. As it ages, it becomes too tough to eat and so is dried and saved for winter use.

America is the world's largest producer of soybeans, but Americans eat few of them. Some soybeans are fed to livestock—a less than ingenious use of high-quality protein in an underfed world, some argue—and others are shipped to China, the world's largest consumer of soybeans. There, as here, they are eaten more as tofu (best described as soy cheese) than fresh.

PEAS are also beans, as are mung beans, chick-peas, lentils, split peas, green beans, snap peas, and so on, almost indefinitely.

When fresh, beans are easy to cook. When dried, this most economical and healthy food can be tricky. Most are best when soaked overnight; not only does this reduce cooking time and help keep the skin from splitting during cooking, it breaks down the indigestible substances in beans that cause flatulence. (If you forget to soak beans overnight, boil them for 2 minutes and soak for an hour or two before cooking.) Cook beans with meat, spices, vegetables, or whatever else you like, but do not add salt, which prevents their softening, until they become tender. Cooking time varies from bean to bean, and also from season to season; older beans take longer to cook.

LIMA BEANS—A New World bean, the sweet-tasting lima (*Phaseolus limensis*) is grown only in warm climates and is eaten fresh or dried for storage. It is also known as a butter bean in some parts of the United States.

LIMA BEANS BOILED—The dried beans are soaked in water for a few hours, then boiled till tender, drained, seasoned with salt, pepper and butter, or mixed with cream sauce. If canned beans are used they are first washed from their can liquor, then heated and seasoned as above; if fresh beans are used, they are put to boil in boiling water containing salt and a small piece of common washing soda; when done, drained, and seasoned as above.

LIMA BEANS SAUTÉ—The beans either dried, fresh or canned are prepared up to the seasoning point of the preceding receipt, then placed in pan containing either small pieces of cooked bacon or salt pork, or just plain melted butter, then thoroughly tossed and heated in the pan, seasoned; sometimes they are sprinkled with finely chopped parsley before serving.

LIMA BEANS SALAD—Either dried, fresh or canned beans boiled till tender; when cold they are mixed with a cream, Hollandaise or mayonnaise salad dressing and served on a bed of lettuce.

LIMA BEANS PURÉE—Soaked dried beans put to boil with a piece of salt pork in white stock containing onions, carrots, parsley, and whole mace; when cooked the pork and vegetables removed, the beans and stock rubbed through a fine sieve, then placed in a clean saucepan, brought to the boil, seasoned, a little flour and water thickening added to prevent coagulation; served with small toast.

LIMA BEANS, CREAM OF—Equal parts of the finished purée of the preceding, and cream or Velouté sauce, made hot separate, then thoroughly mixed without further boiling.

FLAGEOLETS—Or kidney beans are obtainable in cans or in the dried state. The average patron does not know what a flageolet is, hence the call for them at table is small; but most people know what a kidney bean is, and if put on the bill of fare as such, the demand will be gratifying to the cook.

KIDNEY BEANS IN CREAM—Poulette, Espagnole or Velouté sauces. The beans if canned, washed from the can liquor; if dried they are soaked, then boiled tender, drained and reheated in any of the four sauces above mentioned.

KIDNEY BEANS, GERMAN STYLE— Soaked, boiled and drained dried beans, or canned ones washed off, then heated and tossed in butter, seasoned with salt and pepper with a little summer savoury; a few salted herrings skinned, boned and cut into small pieces, either mixed with the beans, or served as a garnish to them.

KIDNEY BEANS, FRENCH STYLE— Soaked, boiled and drained dried beans, or canned ones washed off, a little minced onion and garlic lightly fried in olive oil to a golden brown color, oil poured off, beans put in with some chopped parsley, tossed together with the onions, then moistened with Velouté sauce, brought to the boil, seasoned and served.

KIDNEY BEANS, ENGLISH STYLE— The cooked beans, seasoned with salt, pepper and butter, sprinkled with chopped parsley and served.

KIDNEY BEANS, PANACHES—The word panaches means mixed. Cold cooked kidney beans mixed with equal parts of cold cooked navy or lima beans, are heated with a little butter, and seasoned with salt, pepper, chopped parsley and served. Another mixture is made of equal parts of cold cooked string beans (green) and wax beans (yellow).

HARICOT—As a general term, *haricot* applies to the beans of the New World—kidney, navy, pinto, black, and so on—that we often group together in the category of dried beans. The term also refers to very thin fresh beans.

HARICOT BEANS, BOSTON STYLE— More often placed on the bill of

KIDNEY BEANS, FRENCH STYLE

▪

Serves 6 as a side dish

Kidney beans are basic and delicious, and certainly they were common on the table in 1904. This recipe is a very flavorful way to prepare them.

2 cups dried red kidney beans	2 tablespoons chopped parsley
5¹/₂ cups cold water	¹/₄ teaspoon dried thyme, whole
2 tablespoons olive oil	
2 tablespoons butter	¹/₂ cup dry white wine
3 cloves garlic, peeled and minced	1¹/₂ cups Velouté Sauce (page 448)
1 medium yellow onion, peeled and diced	Salt and freshly ground black pepper to taste

Place the beans in a 2-quart pot with 4 cups of the cold water. Cover and bring to a boil. Turn off the heat and let stand, covered, for 1 hour. Drain and return the beans to the pot, along with enough fresh water just to cover the beans. Bring to a boil and simmer gently, covered, for 25 minutes. Drain the beans again.

Heat a large frying pan and add the oil, butter, garlic, and onions. Sauté until the onions are tender. Add the drained beans, parsley, thyme, wine, Velouté Sauce, and 1¹/₂ cups more water. Cover and simmer for 30 minutes. Salt and pepper to taste.

C.W.

---

fare as "baked pork and beans." The beans are washed and soaked over night; into the bean jar is put some black molasses, salt, pepper and dry mustard, these are well mixed, cold water is then added to thin the mixture; the soaked beans now placed into the jar filling it two-thirds full, a piece of scored, or slices of salt pork is placed on top of the beans, jar filled with water, lid placed on, and put in a slow oven and baked till done; should be served with steamed brown bread. The more common way, however, that pork and beans are cooked, is to soak them over night, place them on to boil in the morning, when at boiling point they are skimmed, and the salt pork put to boil with them, when done the pork removed and cut in slices, the beans put into pans, seasoned, sometimes colored with caramel, the slices of pork arranged on top of the beans, sprinkled with sugar and placed in the oven till browned.

HARICOT BEANS WITH BACON— The cold beans are nicely fried with butter or bacon fat, seasoned with salt and pepper with a little sage, then served with a slice of broiled bacon.

HARICOT BEANS PURÉE—Soaked beans put to boil with salt pork in white stock containing carrots, onions, celery or celery seed or salt, parsley and whole mace; when done the pork and vegetables removed, the beans and stock rubbed through a fine sieve, then placed in a clean saucepan, seasoned, a little flour and water thickening added to prevent coagulation, served with small toast.

HARICOT SOUP, FAMILY STYLE— Prepared same as the preceding, but instead of the beans being rubbed through a sieve, they are left whole in the soup, and the vegetables and pork cut up very small, returned to the soup and served with it, along with small toast.

BEAN PURÉE WITH ONIONS—Is the purée above but considerable onions boiled in the stock, and rubbed through the sieve with the beans (called Purée of Beans, à la Soûbise).

HARICOT BEANS, CREAM SAUCE— Cold boiled haricot beans with a flavoring of salt pork, mixed into a white cream onion sauce, seasoned

with nutmeg, made hot, but not re-boiled.

RED HARICOT BEANS—Are mostly used as a garniture to salt leg of boiled pork. They are soaked, boiled with the pork, drained, placed in a saucepan, white wine added, then reduced to a glaze with a ladle of consommé; served with the pork in conjunction with small glazed onions.

BLACK BEANS WITH RIS-SOTO—The beans soaked and boiled with bacon; when done, the bacon cut up small and mixed with the drained beans, then moistened with Spanish sauce, seasoned with anchovy butter, made hot again and served garnished with rissoto.

GREEN AND WAX BEANS—Are best suited for culinary use when served as a plain vegetable boiled in salted water with the cover of the saucepan OFF. The beans have the strings removed, then shred or cut across; when boiled, drained, moistened with a little consommé, and seasoned with salt, pepper and butter (time of boiling 15 to 35 minutes according to age).

BEARNAISE—Name of a sauce used with steaks and entrées, composed of minced shallots braised with tarragon vinegar, to which is added a thin Velouté sauce, then some beaten yolks of eggs, continually stirred over the fire till like custard, removed, melted butter then beaten in at the rate of three ounces to the pint, seasoned with lemon juice and red pepper, strained, finished by adding chopped parsley and tarragon leaves. Some cooks omit the Velouté sauce, and use only butter and egg yolks, thus making a kind of butter mayonnaise, that will very readily disintegrate if allowed to keep hot.

BÉARNAISE—These days a typical béarnaise sauce (still a good accompaniment for steak) is made by Fellows's second method, without the velouté sauce.

BÉCHAMEL—Name of a white sauce composed of reduced chicken broth with some essence of mushrooms, an equal quantity of rich milk or cream, boiled up, thickened with flour and butter, seasoned with salt, lemon juice and grated nutmeg, then strained for use.

BÉCHAMEL—One of the simplest and most basic of sauces, today béchamel is usually made with no more than butter and flour, melted and cooked together, and warm milk, added and stirred until thickened.

BEEF—For culinary purposes is of two kinds, the steer and the cow. Steer beef is superior and the flesh should be of a bright red marble with yellow fat, and a thick outside layer of fat under a fine grained skin; the lean should be firm and elastic when pressed with the fingers; the suet should be dry and crumble easily. Cow beef is of closer grain, the fat is white instead of yellow, and the flesh of a darker red. BULL beef is sometimes worked off on the unwary by the packing houses when shipping to distant cities, especially so in the form of tenderloins; it is large, coarse, very dark in color, and unfit for table use.

BEEF—Steer beef has become so superior to cow's beef that it is virtually impossible for anyone without access to a dairy farm to sample cow's beef. In recent years beef has become leaner and leaner; this, combined with a tendency to sell young, unaged beef, has made it difficult to find a good steak or roast. Most often your best bet is to use beef for sauces, stews, hamburgers, stir-fries, and the like.

In the United States beef is divided into eight or nine primal cuts (depending on how you count them), each of which provides the cuts with which we are more or less familiar (European butchering is different).

Short loin: Contains the best meat for eating rare—that is, the most naturally tender—and for grilling, broiling, and dry roasting. Different sections are called porterhouse, tenderloin (filet mignon), and strip.

Sirloin: Almost as tender as the short loin, and eminently suitable for grilling.

Rib: Prime rib comes only from prime beef, which is rarely sold in supermarkets. But even choice rib makes a fine rib roast. The rib eye, sold as steaks and roasts, is also tender and tasty. Rib bones, commonly called beef ribs, are an underrated grill item.

Round: With the chuck, the largest of the primal cuts. These are working muscles, and consequently less tender. The top round, however, when cut into steaks and cooked rare, is tasty if a bit chewy. It is better suited, however, for stir-frying, and bottom round should be reserved exclusively for this. Round

CUTS OF BEEF
and where they come from

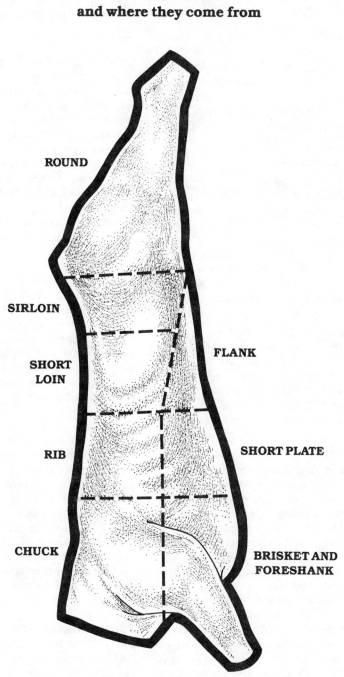

ROUND

SIRLOIN

SHORT
LOIN

FLANK

RIB

SHORT PLATE

CHUCK

BRISKET AND
FORESHANK

roasts, frequently sold in supermarkets, are too lean for pot roasts and too tough for dry roasts; avoid them.

Flank: The only cut we see regularly from the flank is the flank steak, which has two major uses. One, it can be marinated and grilled or broiled, as long as it is sliced thin; this is the familiar London broil. And two, it is excellent in stir-fries.

Plate: Generally sold as stew meat or ground.

Foreshank/Brisket: Actually two cuts, but usually treated as one. The veal foreshank is tender and delicious when braised, and wonderful for ossobuco; but in older steer it is too tough to eat and reserved for stock, soup, and stew. The brisket—which is used for corned beef—makes superior pot roast, especially the fatty point cut.

Chuck: The shoulder, another large, hard-working muscle. Although chuck steaks are sold, they are invariably tough and disappointing. But chuck meat is flavorful: Use large cuts for pot roast, smaller ones or pieces for stews.

BEEF À LA MODE—Any piece of solid beef, preferably the silverside of the round, is larded with seasoned strips of larding pork, then laid in dilute vinegar containing slices of carrot, turnips and onions with whole spices, for several hours. It is then taken out and quickly roasted in oven to get the outside seared, then placed in saucepan, covered with a piquante sauce, lid of saucepan put on, then gently simmered till tender; served in slices with a garnish of braised vegetables and some of the sauce it was cooked in (also called "pot roast" and "sour pot roast").

BEEF STEW, GERMAN STYLE—Cold beef à la mode is cut into small pieces and heated in a sour sauce; served garnished with potato pancakes.

BEEF ROAST—Preferably the set, or seven ribs from the shoulder to the loin is for hotel use. The lower end of the ribs, called shortribs, should be roasted with another pan over the top, so as to become more juicy and tender than by roasting them open. The usual accompaniment to roast beef is some of the pan or dish gravy with a slice of Yorkshire pudding, while for the shortribs a little grated horseradish and browned potatoes is best.

BOILED BEEF—The best pieces for boiling are the flank, brisket, and short ribs; they should be boiled tender with a flavoring of vegetables, and served with horseradish sauce, cream sauce and carrots or suet dumplings, or mixed vegetables such as carrot, turnip, onion, cabbage and potato.

CORNED BEEF—Flank, short ribs, brisket or rump of beef is put to soak in brine made of twenty-five pounds of salt, twelve ounces of rock saltpetre, two pounds of sugar and fifteen gallons of water, all boiled together, skimmed, cooled, the beef then put in with a cover on and a weight on that to keep the beef under the brine (ready for use in a week to ten days).

BOILED CORNED BEEF—The meat put to boil in cold water, scum taken off as it rises, then allowed to simmer till tender (about four hours) served in slices with cabbage, parsnips, carrots, sometimes with all three vegetables; also with suet dumplings; sometimes with a brown sauce and garnished with brussels sprouts.

SPICED BEEF—A whole flank of beef with bones, gristle and inner skin removed, laid out flat, outside skin downwards, then rubbed with a mixture of salt, ground pepper, mace, allspice, cloves and ginger; rolled up and tied, then put to soak for ten days with some pickle from the corned beef brine to which is added whole cloves, peppers, allspice and bay leaves. When to be cooked, it is taken from the pickle, wiped dry, dipped in fat that is near cool so as to take on a good coating, then rolled in a dough made of plain flour and water, placed in a medium oven and slowly baked (five to six hours). If to be served hot, cut in slices and serve with Piquante sauce and garnish with small cut vegetables. If to be served cold, as is generally done, the dough is left on till thoroughly cold, or till to be served; even for a month it will not spoil if the dough is not disturbed. Served cold in thin slices garnished with pickles.

ALL SALT, CORNED OR SMOKED MEATS IF SIMMERED TILL DONE, INSTEAD OF QUICK BOILING, and allowed to cool in the water they were simmered in, will be found always more juicy and tender, and capable of longer keeping.

DRIED BEEF—The thick flank is the part generally used; divided lengthwise in its natural section, it is put in a pickle of salt, saltpetre, sugar and molasses for two weeks, then hung up and smoked like hams (also called Smoked Beef).

CHIPPED BEEF IN CREAM—Very thin slices or shavings of dried beef, blanched, drained, and mixed into cream sauce or reduced cream.

SCRAMBLED BEEF WITH EGGS—Very thin slices of dried beef, again cut into strips like short matches, blanched, drained, mixed with beaten eggs and a little milk, scrambled around in a pan with a little butter till eggs are set, served either plain, or on toast.

FRIZZLED BEEF ON TOAST—Very thin slices of dried beef, blanched, drained, then tossed with frothing butter over a quick fire; served on toast.

SMOKED BEEF WITH SPINACH—Dried beef put to boil in cold water, scum taken off as it rises, then simmered till tender; served in slices on a bed of spinach.

SMOKED BEEF SANDWICHES—Very thin slices of dried beef placed on thin slices of buttered brown bread, rolled up like fingers.

BRISKET OF BEEF WITH VEGETABLES—Lean brisket of beef boned, placed in saucepan with carrot, onions, turnip, celery, parsley, thyme, bay leaves, whole cloves and mace, covered with stock, saucepan cover put on, simmered till tender, taken up and placed on baking pan, little gravy poured over, put in quick oven till gravy has glazed the meat; served in slices with glazed vegetables and brown sauce.

FLANK OF BEEF, ENGLISH STYLE— Lean flank of beef that has been in corned beef brine for a few days, is washed, then put to boil in cold water with carrots, onions, and celery; after coming to the boil, skimmed, then simmered till tender, taken up and glazed in oven like the preceding, served in slices with a suet dumpling, brussels sprouts, shaped piece of carrot and turnip, a boiled onion, and some Piquante sauce poured around.

GLAZED RIBS OF BEEF WITH MACARONI—Lean short ribs of beef larded through the lean with seasoned strips of larding pork; put in sauce pan with carrot, onion, celery, parsley, whole cloves and mace with a little garlic, covered with consommé and sherry wine, cover put on, then simmered till tender, meat then taken up, the liquor strained, skimmed, and reduced, half of which is taken to moisten some boiled and drained macaroni, mixed with grated Parmesan cheese. The beef served in portions, garnished with the macaroni, and a spoonful of the remaining glaze poured over the meat (called Braised Beef à la Piemontaise).

GLAZED RIBS OF BEEF WITH VEGETABLES—The lean short ribs of beef cooked same as in the preceding receipt, served in portion pieces, garnished with glazed shapes of carrot, turnip, onions and artichokes, with a little of the glaze poured over the meat (called Braised Beef à la Bourgeoise).

GLAZED RIBS OF BEEF WITH POTATO CROQUETTES—Lean short ribs of beef larded through the lean with strips of seasoned larding pork; put in a saucepan with a few shallots, half a cup of fresh grated horseradish, parsley and green onions, the meat barely covered with consommé to which is added a bottle of Rhine wine, then simmered till tender and glazy; when done, meat taken up, the liquor strained and skimmed, little red currant jelly and grated orange rind added to it and reduced; the meat served in portion cuts, with a little of the glaze poured over, and garnished with potato croquette mixture rolled into small balls, dipped in beaten eggs, then in flour and fried very quickly in hot fat (called Braised Beef à la Baden-Baden).

BRAISED BEEF, GERMAN STYLE—A top sirloin of beef larded slantwise with strips of seasoned larding pork, put in saucepan with carrot, onions, celery, parsley, bay leaves and a few caraway seeds, barely covered with stock and simmered till tender and glazy, then taken up, the liquor strained, skimmed and reduced to glaze, the meat served in slices with a little of the glaze and garnished with sauerkraut and small shaped potatoes boiled and sprinkled with parsley butter (called Braised Beef à l'Allemande).

BRAISED SIRLOIN OF BEEF, GARNISHED—The braised sirloin of the preceding, but the caraway seeds omitted in the seasonings; when done is served in slices and garnished with stoned olives, mushrooms, truffles, cockscombs and kernels, green peas and small pieces of sweetbreads, all made hot in the glaze with the addition of a little Espagnole sauce (called Braised Beef à la Financière).

BRAISED BEEF WITH RAVIOLIS—Top sirloin of beef larded, put in saucepan with carrot, onions, celery, thyme, bay leaves, cloves, allspice, garlic, claret wine and enough consommé to barely cover the meat, simmered till tender and glazy, taken up, liquor strained, skimmed and reduced to a glaze; meat served in slices with some of the glaze and garnished with small molds of boiled macaroni sprinkled with Parmesan cheese and small raviolis (called Braised Beef à la Milanaise).

BRAISED SIRLOIN OF BEEF WITH QUENELLES—Top sirloin larded and braised with vegetables, spices and consommé; served in slices and garnished with a ragout of small quenelles of poultry or game, cockscombs and kernels, and slices of braised poultry livers (called Braised Beef à la Richelieu).

BRAISED SIRLOIN OF BEEF WITH MUSHROOMS—Top sirloin larded and braised with vegetables, spices and consommé; meat taken up when done, the liquor strained and skimmed, sherry wine and Espagnole sauce added to it; meat served in slices, garnished with fried mushrooms, and sauce poured around.

BRAISED SIRLOIN OF BEEF WITH TRUFFLES—Top sirloin larded and braised, meat taken up when done, the liquor strained, skimmed, Madeira wine added to it and reduced; meat served in slices, garnished with a ragout of truffles, diced sweetbreads, and small veal quenelles (called Braised Beef à la Godard).

BRAISED SIRLOIN WITH RICE CROQUETTES—Top sirloin larded and braised, meat taken up, liquor strained and reduced to a glaze, meat served in slices with some of the glaze poured around, and garnished with small croquettes of rice that have been seasoned with savory herbs and meat glaze (called Braised Beef à l'Orsini).

BRAISED SIRLOIN WITH SPRING VEGETABLES—Top sirloin larded and braised, taken up when done, liquor strained, skimmed and reduced to a glaze; meat served in slices with it, and garnished with glazed carrot, onion, brussels sprouts and red or green cabbage (called Braised Beef à la Flamande).

BRAISED SIRLOIN WITH STUFFED POTATOES—Top sirloin larded and braised, taken up when done, liquor strained, skimmed, and reduced to a glaze; meat served in slices with it, and garnished with potatoes that have been cut out with the largest size potato scoop, centre taken out of the potatoes with a column cutter, blanched, drained, the holes filled with a savory forcemeat, then baked till done and brown with butter (called Braised Beef à la Bignonne).

BRAISED SIRLOIN WITH HORSERADISH—Top sirloin larded and braised, taken up when done, the liquor strained, skimmed and added to it is Espagnole sauce, red currant jelly, horseradish, grated lean ham, port wine and Harvey sauce; it is then rapidly boiled down to glaze; meat served in slices with some of the sauce, and garnished with steamed artichoke bottoms, filled with grated fresh horseradish (called Braised Beef à la Napolitaine).

BRAISED SIRLOIN WITH STUFFED TOMATOES—Top sirloin larded and braised, taken up when done, the liquor strained, skimmed, and mixed with Espagnole sauce, minced fried mushrooms and sherry wine, then rapidly reduced to a glaze; the meat served in slices with some of the sauce, and garnished with stuffed tomatoes and stuffed glazed onions (called Braised Beef à la Provençale).

TENDERLOIN OF BEEF WITH MUSHROOMS—Tenderloin roasted with some sliced vegetables in the pan, mushrooms lightly fried in butter, then put into a rich brown sauce containing sherry wine; the meat served in slices and garnished with the mushrooms in sauce.

TENDERLOIN OF BEEF WITH VEGETABLES—Tenderloin trimmed, larded and braised, the liquor strained, skimmed and mixed with a rich brown sauce containing sherry or Madeira wine, reduced to a half glaze; carrots, turnips and celery are cut into neat pieces, boiled separately in white consommé with a little sugar and butter, when done strained and mixed together with some French peas; meat served in slices with some of the sauce and garnished with the vegetables (called Fillet of Beef à la Jardinière).

When the vegetables are cut into minute squares and diamonds it is (called à la Printanière). When the vegetables are scooped out with a medium sized scoop it is (called à la Parisienne). When taken out of cans or cut in very small fancy shapes and mixed with French string beans cut small and flageolets it is (called à la Macedoine). When carrots, turnips, celery, leeks and onions are cut in strips like matches, it is (called à la Julienne). When the Julienne vegetables are mixed with a Hollandaise, Allemande or yellow cream sauce it is (called à la Nivernaise).

[It is optional with the cook whether he adds asparagus points and small flowerets of cauliflower to the above groups of vegetables, it is still a simple garniture of vegetables, appropriate to either braised or roasted tenderloin, understood by the guest when written in plain English, and often uncalled for and consequently left over when the "à la" is attached. Any of the foregoing garnitures given to braised sirloins, apply equally to braised tenderloins of beef and need not be repeated under the heading of tenderloin; also the vegetable garnitures above given are equally appropriate to braised sirloins of beef.]

TENDERLOIN OF BEEF, SAUCE BEARNAISE—Tenderloin trimmed and larded is either braised or roasted with vegetables; served in slices with Bearnaise sauce.

TENDERLOIN OF BEEF WITH CUSTARDS—Tenderloin larded and either braised or roasted with vegetables, served in slices with a half glaze containing Madeira or Malaga wine. Garnished with slices or small molds of custards made of stirred yolks of eggs mixed with very small cut vegetables of various colors and a little consommé; this vegetable custard is then poured into a pan or small mold and placed in a pan containing water, then, with a sheet of buttered paper over the mold, the pan is put in the oven and the custard cooked (called Filet à la Talleyrand).

TENDERLOIN OF BEEF WITH CÈPES—Tenderloin trimmed, larded, and either braised or roasted with vegetables; the cèpes drained from the oil in the cans, cut into slices, lightly fried in butter, taken up and added to a rich brown sauce, served with slices of the meat.

TENDERLOIN OF BEEF WITH ARTICHOKES—Tenderloin trimmed, larded, and either braised or roasted with vegetables, served in slices, garnished with artichoke bottoms filled with a ragout of truffles, mushrooms and strips of smoked tongue (called Fillet of Beef à la Bayard).

TENDERLOIN OF BEEF WITH STUFFED PEPPERS—Tenderloin larded and roasted, served in slices with a little Andalusian sauce poured around, and garnished with a stuffed tomato at one end, and a stuffed green pepper at the other (called Fillet of Beef à l'Andalouse).

TENDERLOIN STEAK, BORDELAISE —Steak broiled and served with a brown Bordelaise sauce, or with some finely minced shallots, garlic and parsley fried in oil and butter,

with lemon juice added at the finish; garnished with chips.

TENDERLOIN STEAK, PARISIAN POTATOES—Steak broiled and served with some maître d'hôtel butter poured over it and garnished with Parisian potatoes.

TENDERLOIN STEAK, SAUCE BEARNAISE—Steak broiled and served with Bearnaise sauce at one end, and Julienne potatoes with a sprig of parsley at the other.

FILLETS OF BEEF WITH STRING BEANS—Tenderloin steaks larded on one side, broiled, served with French string beans made hot in maître d'hôtel butter at one end, and a slice of fancy toast at the other.

FILLETS OF BEEF, SAUCE PROVENÇALE—Tenderloin steaks larded on one side, broiled, served with some provençale sauce poured around the steak, and a small stuffed tomato at each end.

TENDERLOIN STEAK SAUTÉED, WITH PEPPERS—Steak sautéed in butter; minced green peppers fried in butter, drained, mixed into brown sauce, served around the steak with a stuffed green pepper at each end, and some neat slices of pimentoes decorating the top of the steak.

TENDERLOIN STEAK, SAUCE PERIGUEUX—Steak broiled, served with sauce Perigueux poured around it, top of steak decorated with slices of truffles, a few chip potatoes at one end of the dish, and a fancy croûton with a sprig of parsley at the other end.

HAMBURG STEAK WITH ONIONS—Minced raw beef and onions seasoned with salt and pepper, mixed thoroughly and formed into flat balls or steaks, fried in butter till done, served either plain or with a sauce.

TOMATOED HAMBURG STEAK—Minced raw beef and solid meat of the tomatoes seasoned with salt and pepper, thoroughly mixed and formed into steaks; either broiled or fried in butter; served with tomato sauce poured around.

SALISBURY STEAK WITH GRILLED TOMATOES—Minced raw beef seasoned with salt and pepper made into form of steaks, either broiled, or fried in butter; served garnished with sliced broiled potatoes (plain or sweet) and some mâitre d'hôtel butter on the steak.

SALISBURY STEAK WITH MUSHROOMS—Prepared and cooked same as the preceding; served with some fried mushrooms at one end of the dish, and chip potatoes at the other.

ENGLISH BEEF SOUP—Pieces of raw beef cut small, with carrots, turnips, onions and celery cut in dice, placed in soup pot with butter and lightly fried, flour then added and stirred to form a roux, moistened with boiling beef stock; when about half done, pearl barley is washed and added to the soup, also some whole allspice, peppers, cloves, thyme and bay leaves tied in a piece of muslin; when the soup is finished, the spices removed, seasoned with Worcestershire sauce and chopped parsley. SOME COOKS ARE IN THE HABIT OF PUTTING TOMATOES IN THIS SOUP, WHICH IS DECIDEDLY WRONG.

BEEF BROTH WITH CELERY—Into the soup pot is placed plenty of roast beef bones and clear gravy with slices of carrot, onions, roots and trimmings of celery; filled up with strong beef stock, simmered till done, strained and skimmed; meanwhile celery cut in inch strips like matches is fried lightly in butter, then simmered till tender and added to the soup.

SCOTCH BEEF SOUP—Prepared exactly the same as "English beef soup" above, except using Scotch oatmeal (procurable anywhere) instead of pearl barley, and adding Madeira wine at the finish.

BEEF BROTH WITH RICE—Prepared as for "beef broth with celery," but after the broth is strained and skimmed, allowed to boil up again, thickened lightly with corn starch, and well washed boiled rice added with a seasoning of walnut catsup.

BEEF BOUILLON WITH CRUSTS—Plenty of cold roast beef bones and clear gravy put into the soup pot with some chopped fresh beef, NO SPICES, but a carrot and onion; filled up with good beef stock, simmered for several hours, then strained through a consommé

BEEF SOUP, ENGLISH STYLE

•

Serves 6

A rich barley soup that will warm your insides. Nothing more need be said!

2 tablespoons butter	2 cups water
2 cloves garlic, peeled and chopped	1/2 cup pearl barley
3/4 pound beef stew meat, cut into 1/2-inch cubes	1 cup peeled and diced turnips
1 medium yellow onion, peeled and chopped	1/2 teaspoons dried thyme, whole
1 1/2 cups carrots, cut into 1/4-inch dice	2 tablespoons Worcestershire sauce
3 stalks celery, chopped	Pinch of ground allspice
6 cups Beef Stock (page 48)	Pinch of ground cloves
1 bay leaf	Salt and freshly ground black pepper to taste

Heat a 4- to 6-quart pot and add the butter, garlic, and beef. Brown the beef lightly. Add the onions, carrots, celery, Beef Stock, and bay leaf. Bring to a boil, cover, and simmer gently for 1 hour.

In a small saucepan, bring the water to a boil. Add the barley, cover, and simmer for 10 minutes. Drain and set aside.

After the pot of beef and vegetables has simmered for 1 hour, add the drained barley, cover, and simmer for 20 minutes more. Add the remaining ingredients and simmer an additional 15 minutes. Very rich!

C.W.

cloth, skimmed, seasoned with salt and pepper, served with small toast. Also served plain in cups with a thin slice of lemon.

OX TAIL, CLEAR—Prepare the "bouillon" above and place it on the fire with some trimmings of carrot, turnip, onions and celery, also the thick and thin ends of the tails that have been previously browned in the oven, simmered till done, then strained and clarified, the middle part of the ox tails cut

BEEF STOCK

▪

Makes 5 quarts

It is impossible to think of running a kitchen in 1904 without this basic stock. It is to be used in soups, sauces, glacés—in short, it is *the* kitchen fluid.

*Bare rendering bones,
    sawed into 2-inch
    pieces*

*Carrots, unpeeled and
    chopped*

*Yellow onions, unpeeled
    and chopped*

Celery, chopped

Tell your butcher that you need bare rendering bones. They should not have any meat on them at all, so they should be cheap. Have him saw them up into 2-inch pieces.

Roast the bones in an uncovered pan at 400°F. for 2 hours. Be careful with this, because your oven may be a bit too hot. Watch the bones, which you want to be toasty brown, not black.

Place the roasted bones in a soup pot and add 1 quart water for each pound of bones. For 5 pounds bones, add 1 bunch carrots, 1 head celery, and 3 yellow onions, chopped with peel and all. (The peel will give lovely color to the stock.)

Bring to a simmer, uncovered, and cook for 12 hours. You may need to add water to keep the soup up to the same level. Do not salt the stock.

Strain the stock and store in the refrigerator. Allow the fat to stay on the top of the stock when you refrigerate it; the fat will seal the stock and allow you to keep it for several days.

J.S.

in slices with carrot and turnip to match, boiled separately in consommé till tender and glazy, added to the clarified broth with sherry wine

OX TAIL, THICK—Prepare the "bouillon" above; ox tails cut in slices half inch thick, carrots and turnips cored out with large sized column cutter and sliced to resemble the tails but thinner, all placed with sliced onions in soup pot and fried lightly with butter or beef drippings, flour added to form a roux, moistened with the boiling bouillon, simmered till done,

OXTAIL SOUP

.

Serves 4 to 6

Mr. Fellows's original recipe calls for this to be a clear soup. The clarification process for soups or consommés requires hours of additional cooking time. After tasting the soup as prepared here, I decided that neither you nor I had the time to cook it 1903 restaurant style. You will enjoy the recipe as it is, a recipe for "not so clear" oxtail soup.

2½ pounds oxtails (if some
  of the pieces are very
  large, have the
  butcher cut them in
  half)

¾ cup peeled and chopped
  turnips

¾ cup peeled and chopped
  carrots

1 stalk celery, chopped

¾ cup peeled and chopped
  yellow onions

1 bay leaf

6 whole black peppercorns

3½ cups Beef Stock
  (page 48)

1 tablespoon chopped
  parsley

1 cup julienned carrots

½ cup julienned yellow
  onions

½ cup julienned turnips

¼ cup dry sherry

Salt and freshly ground
  black pepper to taste

In a large nonstick frying pan, brown the oxtails (no oil is needed). Place the meat in a 4-quart pot and add the chopped turnips, carrots, celery, yellow onions, the bay leaf, and peppercorns. Add just enough water to cover the contents (about 1 quart). Simmer, covered, for 2¼ hours. Remove the meat from the soup. Strain the vegetables, reserving the broth. Discard the vegetables and return the meat and broth to the pot. Add the remaining ingredients, except the salt and pepper. Simmer for 15 minutes. Season with salt and pepper.

C.W.

skimmed, seasoned with salt, pepper, Worcestershire sauce and sherry wine.

BEEF CROQUETTES WITH PEAS—A strong roast beef gravy thickened with roux and seasoned with Worcestershire sauce is then reduced till thick, cold roast or other cooked beef is cut very small and stirred into the boiling sauce; when thoroughly heated through it is turned into a pan about an inch deep, smoothed with a knife, covered with a sheet of buttered paper and allowed to become cold, then divided into pieces of the size required, rolled into finger lengths, breaded and fried, served in twos laid slantwise across the dish, seasoned green peas placed between them, and mushroom sauce at each end, with croquette frills stuck in the croquettes if used.

BEEF COLLOPS WITH MUSH-ROOMS—Cold cooked beef is trimmed and cut in circles size of a dollar but thicker, made hot in a thick rich beef gravy; served overlapping each other down the centre of the dish, with some fried mushrooms in sauce down both sides, and a fancy croûton at each end. This dish may also be served with a garnish of green peas, kidney beans, French string beans, mixed vegetables, small quenelles or fancy potatoes.

BEEF CAKES WITH EGG—Cold cooked beef minced and seasoned with salt and powdered savory, moistened slightly with roast beef gravy, made into cakes like Hamburg steaks, placed in pan with a glazy gravy poured over them; when thoroughly heated, served with a poached egg on top, and some thick roast beef gravy poured around.

BEEF CUTLETS WITH PIQUANTE SAUCE—The "beef croquette" mixture above, when cold formed in the shape of veal chops, using a piece of macaroni to imitate the bone; when shaped, rolled in flour, then dipped in beaten egg and fried

in hot dripping; served with Piquante sauce poured around.

BEEF RISSOLES—Cold cooked beef minced three parts, grated bread crumbs one part, mixed and seasoned with herbs, grated lemon rind, salt and pepper, bound with raw yolks of eggs, made into shapes and size of eggs, breaded and fried; served with a mound of mashed potatoes in the centre of dish, a rissole at each end and side, with some thickened roast beef gravy poured around, and a sprig of parsley put into the potatoes. This dish may also be served with kidney beans, green peas, French string beans or mixed vegetables instead of the potatoes.

BEEF RISSOLETTES—Same as the preceding but made smaller, served and garnished the same way.

BEEF PATTIES WITH MUSH-ROOMS—Cold cooked tender beef cut into small dice, mixed and made hot in a rich brown mushroom sauce, filled into patty shells; served with some fried mushrooms in sauce poured around.

BEEF STEAK AND MUSHROOM PIE—Pieces of raw beef cut about an inch square three parts, button mushrooms (fresh or canned) one part, mixed; baking dish lined on the sides with short paste, meat and mushrooms put in with a little flour, salt, pepper, a minced onion and savory herbs, filled up with water to just cover the meat, top crust put on, brushed over with beaten egg and milk, put in slow oven and gently baked.

BEEF STEAK AND OYSTER PIE—
Same as the preceding, but omitting the mushrooms and using
scalded oyster liquor instead of water; when to be served, a few
blanched oysters kept hot in a
brown sauce placed with each
portion.

BEEF STEAK AND KIDNEY
PIE—Same as "beef steak and
mushroom pie" but using pieces of
blanched beef kidney instead of the
mushrooms.

BEEF POT PIE—A rich beef stew
(white or brown) with vegetables,
served with a dumpling and sprinkled with parsley; or the stew
placed in a pan, soft dumpling mixture dropped in pieces all over it,
put in oven and baked; or the stew
left in the saucepan, dumplings put
in, cover put on, then gently simmered till dumplings are cooked.

BEEF PAUPIETTES, MUSHROOM
SAUCE—Thin slices of cold cooked
beef, trimmed to shape of envelope
with the flap open, spread with a
cooked forcemeat composed of
minced bacon, chopped parsley,
grated lemon rind, salt, pepper and
savory herbs, rolled up from the
broad end to the point, this pinned
with a toothpick, dipped in a thin
batter and fried, toothpick then removed; served with a rich mushroom sauce poured around.

SCALLOPED BEEF WITH OYS-
TERS—Small pieces of beef already
made tender in a brown stew seasoned with anchovy essence;
oysters scalded and mixed with the
stew, placed in scallop shells or

dishes, sprinkled with bread
crumbs and Parmesan cheese,
baked in oven and served.

DEVILLED BEEF WITH OYSTERS—
Cold cooked tender beef cut in
finger lengths an inch wide and
half inch thick, laid in a mixture of
salt, pepper, olive oil and Worcestershire sauce for an hour, then
lightly fried in butter, sprinkled
with parsley; served on slices of
buttered toast same size as the
meat alternately with broiled
oysters, and Diable sauce poured
around.

CURRIED BEEF WITH RICE—Either
raw or cooked beef rolled in flour,
then fried in butter with minced
onions; when lightly browned, put
in saucepan with butter, flour and
curry powder, stirred and moistened with white stock, boiled up,
skimmed, then simmered with the
addition of a grated green apple,
lemon juice and a little chutney;
when done, the meat removed to
another saucepan, and the sauce
strained over it; served with a border of dry boiled rice.

MINCED BEEF WITH EGG—Either
minced or finely cut cold cooked
beef seasoned with savory herbs,
salt and pepper is made hot in rich
roast beef gravy, just enough to
moisten the meat only being used;
served with a fancy border of
mashed potatoes, the mince in the
centre, and a poached egg on top of
the mince.

ROAST BEEF HASH—Minced onion
lightly fried in butter added to
finely cut roast beef two parts, and

minced cold potatoes one part, mixed together, seasoned with salt, pepper and powdered marjoram with a very little roast beef gravy; the whole then tossed together, placed in a pan and baked; or kept in a saucepan over a slow fire till thoroughly heated; or portions put into a frying pan, browned on both sides, then formed into shape of an omelet; served either with or without a fried or poached egg, and with a croûton at ends of dish.

CORNED BEEF HASH—Prepared (onion optional), cooked, and served the same way as "roast beef hash" above, but omitting the herb, and using corned instead of roast beef.

SPICED JELLIED BEEF—Leg of beef freed from all bone, cut up in two inch pieces, put to boil in cold water, all scum taken off as it rises, then gently simmered till the meat falls to pieces; the liquor then strained from the meat, put to boil again for half an hour with savory herbs, salt and pepper, then strained, skimmed from all fat, and while cooling a very little gelatine dissolved in it, the meat shredded and added to it, poured into molds to get perfectly cold and firm; served in slices garnished with thinly sliced green pickles.

POTTED BEEF FOR SAND-WICHES—Lean roast or other cold cooked beef trimmings three parts, cold corned lean beef one part, minced fine, then pounded to a paste with two ounces of cold boiled bacon to each pound of beef, seasoned with salt, pepper, ground mace and a very little an-

chovy essence; when in paste form, weigh it, then work in melted butter at the rate of two ounces to the pound; after thoroughly mixing, the paste is put away in jars with a one-quarter of an inch of melted butter poured over the top to seal them from air (this mixture kept sealed will keep many weeks without spoiling).

TOURNEDOS OF BEEF WITH OLIVES—Cold cooked beef tenderloin trimmed to a pear shape, slices of stale bread trimmed the same way, both cut in slices half an inch thick, the bread fried, the meat made hot in a Piquante sauce; served on the toast, garnished with slices of stoned olives, and the sauce poured around.

MIROTON OF BEEF WITH VEGETABLES—Cold cooked tender beef cut in circular pieces two inches in diameter and half an inch thick, sliced onions par-boiled, then fried a golden color in butter, the meat arranged in a pan and just covered with a brown Italian sauce, the onions spread over the whole, placed in oven and baked till the sauce is reduced to a glaze with a buttered paper over the onions; the circles, with the onions still on them, served garnished with a mixture of small cut cooked vegetables in brown sauce, and a fancy croûton at each end of the dish.

EMINCE OF BEEF WITH PEAS—Thin slices of tender cooked beef about the size of half dollars, made hot in a rich thickened roast beef gravy, served overlapping each other down the centre of the dish and the green peas as a border.

SCALLOPS OF BEEF, SAUCE TRIA-NON—Evenly cut thin slices of cold cooked beef tenderloin sautéed with minced shallots in butter; served overlapping each other down the centre of dish, with a sauce Trianon down each side, and a fancy croûton at each end of the dish.

TENDERLOIN WITH BLOOD GRAVY—Thick tenderloin steak placed between two inferior steaks, then broiled till done, the tenderloin served on a hot dish with the gravy of the other two squeezed over it, garnished with fancy potatoes, parsley, and lemon slices (called Filet à la Chateaubriand).

SAUTÉ OF BEEF, TRUFFLE SAUCE—Small tenderloin steaks, seasoned, then fried in butter, served garnished with a croûton at each end of dish, and truffle sauce poured around the steak, with some slices of truffles on top (called Mignons de Boeuf aux Truffes).

SMALL FILLETS OF BEEF WITH OYSTERS—Small tenderloin steaks, seasoned, then fried in butter, large oysters scalded, then tossed quickly over a fire in maître d'hôtel butter containing a little anchovy essence; the fillets served in the centre of the dish garnished with the oysters, and their sauce poured around.

SMALL FILLETS OF BEEF, MAÎTRE D'HÔTEL—Small tenderloin steaks, seasoned, then fried in butter, served garnished with fancy fried potatoes, and maître d'hôtel butter poured over the steak. These may also be garnished with a mixture of small cut vegetables.

RAGOUT OF BEEF, CREOLE SAUCE—Small pieces of beef simmered till tender in tomato sauce containing chopped sweet peppers, minced shallots, and a small quantity of Madeira wine and Madeira sauce; served with the sauce around, and croûtons at end of the dish.

BRAISED BEEF TONGUE WITH TO-MATOES—Fresh tongue soaked in cold water over night, put on in boiling water and blanched for ten minutes, taken up, root and superfluous fat trimmed away, placed in saûtoir with carrot, onions, celery, parsley, whole cloves and mace, covered with stock, and gently simmered till tender, then taken up and placed in another saucepan, the braise strained, skimmed, reduced to a glaze with the addition of some Madeira sauce, this poured over the tongue; served in slices with some sauce poured around, and a stuffed tomato at each end.

SMOKED TONGUE WITH SPIN-ACH—The tongue soaked over night, put on to boil in cold water and simmered for an hour, taken up, placed in a saûtoir with some vegetables and covered with stock, then simmered till tender; served in slices on a bed of spinach, with Madeira sauce poured around.

SMOKED TONGUE WITH SAUER-KRAUT—The tongue soaked over night, put on to boil in cold water and simmered for an hour, taken up, placed in saucepan with some well washed sauerkraut, an onion stuck with cloves, carrot, and a bunch of parsley, moistened with stock to cover the whole, then simmered till tender; served in slices

BEEF FILETS WITH OYSTERS

·

Serves 4

Normally, beef and seafood are cooked separately, not together. However, the oysters complement the meat in this dish. This recipe may sound strange to you at first, but it does make an elegant entrée. No added salt is needed because the oysters will provide salt naturally.

4 (6-ounce) beef filet
mignons

Freshly ground black
pepper to taste

2 tablespoons olive oil

$^1/_2$ cup dry white wine

2 cloves garlic, peeled and
sliced

2 tablespoons butter

1 tablespoon fresh lemon
juice

$^1/_2$ tablespoon chopped
parsley

16 large oysters, freshly
shucked, with their
juices

Pepper the steaks to taste (no salt).

Heat a large frying pan and add the oil. Pan-fry the steaks in the oil to taste (3 to 4 minutes per side for medium rare). Remove the meat to four individual plates and hold in a warm oven.

Deglaze the pan with the wine and add the garlic and butter. Briefly sauté the garlic and add the lemon juice, parsley, and oysters with their juices. Simmer until the oysters are just barely poached. Remove four of the oysters for each of the warming steaks and place on top of the steaks.

Return the pan to the burner. Reduce the sauce until it begins to thicken a bit, about 2 minutes. Pour the sauce over each plate and serve.

C.W.

on a bed of the kraut, and garnished with glazed young carrots, with some Poivrade sauce around.

CORNED BEEF TONGUE WITH SPINACH—The tongue put to boil in cold water and simmered till tender, taken up, skinned, and kept in hot broth; served in slices on a bed of spinach with some Espagnole sauce poured around. Brussels sprouts, or a jardiniere or macedoine of vegetables, form an appropriate garniture to boiled corned tongue; also the tongue

SMOKED TONGUE WITH SAUERKRAUT
·
Serves 6

Does this not sound like a dish from the turn of the century? A smoked tongue that you buy in a good butcher shop has been pickled, like corned beef, and then smoked. That will give you some idea of the flavor. After you taste this recipe, you will then know that tongue and "kraut" belong together. Delicious!

2¹/₂ pounds smoked beef tongue

10 whole black peppercorns

1 bay leaf

4 sprigs parsley

2 tablespoons olive oil

1 medium yellow onion, peeled and thinly sliced

6 cups sauerkraut, rinsed and squeezed dry (I prefer sauerkraut packed in glass, not in a can)

2 tablespoons brown sugar

¹/₂ cup dry white wine

Freshly ground black pepper to taste

Place the tongue in a pot large enough to fit comfortably. Add the peppercorns, bay leaf, and parsley. Add enough water just to cover the tongue. Bring to a boil and simmer, covered, for 3 hours.

Remove the tongue, reserving the broth. When cool enough to handle, peel off the tough skin (peeling the tongue is easy if it is still warm). Trim any cartilage or excessive fat. Slice the tongue in ¹/₄-inch-thick slices. Place the slices on a plate, cover, and set aside.

Heat a 6-quart pot and add the oil and onions. Sauté until the onions are almost clear. Add the sauerkraut, brown sugar, wine, 1 cup of reserved broth, and pepper to taste. Stir to incorporate. Shingle the tongue slices on top of the sauerkraut. Bring to a boil, cover, and simmer for 1 hour.

It is ready to serve as is or accompanied with Poivrade Sauce (page 443).

C.W.

served plain with either raisin or Hollandaise sauce.

BOILED BEEF HEART WITH HORSERADISH—The heart washed and freed from blood, boiled till tender in white stock with whole mace, carrot and onions; served in slices with horseradish sauce poured around, and garnished with a small white turnip hollowed out, steamed, and filled with grated horseradish, or the turnip may be boiled with a little carmine in the water, giving it a reddish color.

ROAST BEEF HEART, STUFFED— The heart prepared and boiled till tender, as above; taken up, drained, the cavities cut out and the space filled with a sage and onion stuffing, placed in pan with brown sauce poured over it and baked till glazy; served in slices on a bed of the stuffing with some sauce poured around, and garnished with potato balls at one end and French beans at the other.

BEEF KIDNEY SAUTÉ—The kidneys cut in small pieces, put to boil in cold water, when blanched, poured into colander, washed and drained, then lightly fried in butter, sprinkled with flour, moistened with stock, simmered till tender, seasoned with salt, pepper and lemon juice; served with a border of potatoes on the dish, kidneys in the centre, sprinkled with chopped parsley.

BEEF KIDNEY SOUP—The kidneys cut small and prepared the same way as "kidney sauté." The soup made of thin Espagnole, the kidneys and their sauce added at the finish; served with small toast.

BRAISED OX TAILS WITH KIDNEY BEANS—The thick end of the tail is cut into portion pieces and placed in saucepan with carrot, onions, celery, bay leaves, thyme and parsley, covered with stock and simmered till tender and glazy, then taken up, the liquor strained, skimmed and added to a Madeira sauce, poured over the tails; served with a border of green kidney beans, and a fancy croûton at each end of dish.

HARICOT OF OX TAILS—The tails cut into pieces at the natural joints, fried with onions in a saucepan till onions are of a golden color, flour added to form a roux, moistened with stock, allowed to simmer for an hour, skimmed, turnips and carrots cut about size of the joints are then added, and simmered another hour, then small potatoes of an even size are added; when they are done, season with salt, pepper and walnut catsup; served, the tails in the centre of the dish, garnished alternately with the vegetables, the whole sprinkled with chopped parsley.

CURRIED OX TAILS WITH SPAGHETTI—The tails cut into sections at the joints, fried with onions in a saucepan till onions are of a golden color, flour and curry powder added, shaken together, then moistened with stock, simmered till tender, meanwhile adding to the sauce a grated green apple, juice of a lemon and some chutney; when done, the tails taken up into another saucepan and the sauce strained over them; served with a border of boiled spaghetti cut in inch pieces, seasoned with Parmesan cheese.

BEEF SAUSAGES—Lean and fat raw beef trimmings two-thirds, soaked stale bread that is squeezed dry one-third, the meat is put through the chopping machine, then mixed with the bread and seasoned with salt, pepper, sage, thyme and a little farina, the whole is then put through the machine again; when it has all passed through cold water is added to the desired stiffness, the knife taken from the machine, filler screwed on; the salted skins having been softened in water, are blown and drawn on to the filler, meat placed in the machine, the skins filled and tied.

SAUSAGE CAKES WITH POTATOES—The sausage meat purchased or made as in the preceding recipe, formed into round cakes, and either fried or arranged in a baking pan and baked till done; served on a bed of mashed potatoes with a little brown gravy poured around.

BEETS—Are of three colors and kinds, red, white and yellow; the white is mostly used in producing beet sugar, the red for culinary purposes, and the yellow for feeding cattle.

BEET GREENS—The leaves of the young beets are washed, put to boil in boiling salted water, containing a small piece of common washing soda; when done, they are strained, pressed, cut up fine, seasoned with

salt, pepper and butter; served as a vegetable, or after being pressed they may be rubbed through a fine sieve, and the purée thus obtained, seasoned and served the same as spinach.

PICKLED BEETS—The small smooth beets washed and boiled till tender, skinned, cut in thin slices, placed in a crock, seasoned with salt, pepper, sugar, bay leaves, and covered with vinegar.

BOILED BEETS IN BUTTER SAUCE—Small new beets washed and boiled till done, skinned, cut in sections like those of an orange, placed into the serving crock, and a sauce composed of water, butter, salt, white pepper and vinegar, thickened with flour poured over them.

BEETS FOR GARNISHING—The pickled beets above left whole and cut into the form of flowers, etc., or the slices cut or stamped with fancy cutters.

BEET AND POTATO SALAD—Small balls of cooked beets placed in tarragon vinegar; small balls of boiled potatoes placed in Ravigote sauce; served by arranging them alternately on the dish.

BEET AND EGG SALAD—Slices of pickled beetroot and hard boiled eggs, arranged alternately around a dish, with some pickled white onions in the centre; served with cream salad dressing.

BENEDICTINE—The name of a liqueur used as a cordial, as a flavoring to sauces and confectionery, in making punches and other drinks; it resembles "yellow chartreuse" in flavor and appearance, is made principally at the Abbey of Fécamp in Europe.

BENEDICTINE—One of the oldest of the secret concoctions—no one except its producers knows the recipe—Benedictine is still made at the abbey and still sold around the world.

BISQUE—The French term given to soups made of a thick purée principally of shellfish and game.

BISQUE OF CRABS—Half a pound of rice boiled to each gallon of soup; when done add half a pound of crab meat to each gallon (good crab meat is obtainable any time of the year in the form of "McMenamin's canned deviled crab meat"), then rub the whole through a fine sieve adding a little melted butter and a seasoning of nutmeg. Make the stock of thin Velouté, add the rice and crab purée, bring to a simmer, then add sliced okras, minced red and green peppers, sliced tomatoes, season with marjoram, thyme, red pepper and lemon juice, simmer slowly for one hour and serve.

BISQUE OF CRAYFISH—Use all crayfish if you can get them; if not, get a dozen or two, which boil in a little water containing salt, whole peppers, parsley and onions, cook them twenty minutes, drain, cool, pick out meat from tails and claws, throw away the intestines, pound the rest, shells and head, also some boiled fish, lobster and yolks of hard boiled eggs to a paste, adding some melted butter; boil this paste with a little veal stock for an hour till dry, then rub it through a sieve, add to it the required amount of good white broth, bring to a boil, add the meat cut up from the tails and claws, a little lobster coral and serve with small toast.

BISQUE OF HERRING—Equal parts of fresh and smoked herrings are boned, skinned and boiled with fresh or canned lobster in seasoned fish stock; when done, it is rubbed through a sieve; the purée then added to a clarified fish broth; served with small quenelles of fish and small toast.

BISQUE OF PRAWNS (OR SHRIMPS)—Made the same as "Bisque of crayfish" except using all prawns or shrimps.

BISQUE OF LOBSTER—Meat of fresh boiled lobsters cut into small squares, the tough parts with the shells and claws boiled for twenty minutes longer, the coral dried in a slow oven, the stock made of Béchamel sauce thinned with the water the fish were boiled in, the coral then rubbed through a sieve and added to the soup giving it a pinkish appearance; finished by adding the squares of meat and some small quenelles of lobster.

BISQUE OF OYSTERS—Scalded oysters and boiled rice in equal bulk rubbed through a sieve, added to a thin cream of oyster soup, flavored with mace and bay leaves.

BISQUE OF SALMON—Cooked salmon rubbed through a sieve added

to stock composed of equal parts of court-bouillon and Velouté sauce, boiled up, seasoned, finished with chopped parsley and Sauterne wine.

BISQUE OF PLOVERS—The plovers braised for an hour in Madeira sauce, taken up and pounded, then rubbed through a sieve; boiled farina, enough to thicken the quantity of the soup, is rubbed through a sieve, the two purées then added to a game stock, boiled up, skimmed, seasoned, finished with port wine.

BISQUE OF PARTRIDGE—Braised or roast partridge meat pounded and rubbed through a sieve with white bread crumbs and a purée of chestnuts, the whole then added to a game-flavored stock, boiled up, skimmed, seasoned, finished with port wine.

BISQUE OF TERRAPIN—Terrapin shells, heads and trimmings simmered in consommé for four hours, strained, the meat rubbed through a sieve and put back into the strained stock with some parsley, thyme, cloves, mace, bay leaves, whole peppers and minced onions, all tied in a muslin bag, brought to a boil, skimmed, an equal quantity of Velouté sauce added, simmered for a few minutes, finished by the addition of some boiling cream.

BISQUE OF JACK RABBIT—The rabbit cut up and braised with spices and vegetables in consommé till tender, then pounded and rubbed through a sieve, the braise

strained, the purée put back into it, boiled up, skimmed, equal volume of thin Velouté sauce added to it, seasoned, finished with sherry wine, and served with some small quenelles of rabbit.

BLACKBERRIES—Also called "dewberries," a fruit of the raspberry species, used as a table fruit, preserves, made into brandies and cordials.

BLACKBERRIES—Hundreds of kinds of blackberries grow all over the United States, all members of the enormous genus *Rubus,* of the rose family. Most have three things in common: thorns, which make them difficult to pick; a distressing tendency to begin to decompose almost immediately after picking, which makes them difficult to cultivate and therefore buy; and unpleasantly hard seeds, which make them difficult to eat. So—unlike their close cousin the RASPBERRY—blackberries are perhaps better suited for jams and jellies than for fresh eating—which is not to say you shouldn't eat your fill whenever you stumble upon a patch.

BLACKBERRIES WITH CREAM—The berries picked over, served in dishes with cream and powdered sugar.

BLACKBERRY PUDDING—Picked over blackberries 3 quarts, flour 2 pounds, baking soda one ounce, New Orleans molasses one quart, little salt, the whole mixed together without water, put into molds, cover tied on, boiled three hours. Served with sauce DORÉE composed of half pound of butter beaten till creamy with half pound of powdered sugar, placed over the fire and two beaten yolks of eggs stirred in; when thick, work in half a pint of brandy, and season with grated nutmeg.

BLACKBERRY CHARLOTTE—Molds or pans lined with slices of buttered bread, sides and bottoms, then filled with picked over berries, seasoned with sugar, covered with slices of buttered bread, sprinkled with sugar, slowly baked till brown and glazy; served with fruit sauce.

BLACKBERRY TARTLETTES—Small fancy molds lined with puff paste with a crimped edge, filled with a dry compote of blackberries; baked; when done, the centre decorated with piped meringue.

BLACKBERRY COMPOTE—The picked over berries put into a boiling syrup and simmered till tender; served in small croustades of sweetened rice.

BLACKBERRY PIE—Pie plates lined with pie paste, berries mixed with sugar and a dusting of flour, the plates filled, little baking soda sprinkled over the fruit to prevent the juice running out, top cover placed on, washed over with pie wash, baked, served with small pieces of cheese.

BLACKBERRY SHORTCAKE—Two sheets of short paste, spread between with the fruit taken from a compote, the upper sheet spread with whipped cream and decorated with some fresh berries.

BLACKBERRY JAM—Fresh picked over berries mixed with ten ounces of sugar to each pound of fruit, gradually brought to a simmer, then allowed to cook till fairly thick, or till it sets when dropped on a cold dish.

BLACKBIRDS—Can be obtained nearly all the year round of the New York and Chicago game and poultry merchants; they are very cheap and make useful entrées.

BLACKBIRDS—Things have changed. The blackbird—similar in size and shape to the thrush (and, you will remember, small enough to fit four and twenty in a pie)—is no longer available at markets in this country, although the French still feature it in pâté and pies. If you are lucky enough to acquire some blackbirds, cook them in a pâté, follow any quail recipe, or try one of Fellows's recipes.

BLACKBIRDS BROILED ON SKEWERS (EN BROCHETTE)—The birds drawn, wiped, picked, and wrapped round with a very thin slice of bacon, run on skewers, broiled, served on toast, garnished with parsley and slices of lemon.

COMPOTE OF BLACKBIRDS—The blackbirds picked, drawn, wiped and trussed, then quickly browned with butter in a hot oven, taken up, placed in a game sauce and simmered till tender; served in croustades with some sauce poured around.

SALMIS OF BLACKBIRDS—The blackbirds picked, drawn, wiped and trussed, quickly roasted, then placed in a game sauce with some mushrooms and stoned olives; when done, served with a fancy croûton at ends of the dish, and the sauce poured over the birds; garnish with the mushrooms and olives.

BLACKBIRD PIE—The blackbirds picked, drawn, wiped and stuffed with breadcrumbs mixed with salt, pepper, chopped parsley, nutmeg, and eggs, trussed, quickly made brown in the oven, placed in pie dish, covered with game sauce and some sliced hard boiled eggs, covered with pie paste and baked.

BLACKBIRDS IN POTATOES—The blackbird picked, drawn, wiped and an oyster placed inside, trussed, quickly browned in the oven with butter. Evenly peeled potatoes (Irish or sweet) split in halves lengthwise, hollowed out, the bird placed in, tied with string, baked and basted with butter; when the potato is done, so is the bird; served with game sauce poured around, and fancy croûtons at ends.

BLACK COCK—Often seen on "bills of fare" as Coq de Bruyere, Heath fowl, Black game and Black grouse.

BLACK COCK—This is nothing more exotic than a male black grouse. Fellows's recipes are suitable for most medium-sized game birds.

BRAISED BLACK GROUSE—The bird picked, singed, drawn and wiped, the breast larded with thin strips of seasoned larding pork; placed in a saucepan with some bacon trimmings, carrot, onions, whole cloves and peppers, moistened with a game sauce and a dash of tarragon vinegar, simmered in the oven till tender; when done, taken up, the braise strained, Burgundy wine added to it, then reduced; the bird served with some of the sauce poured over it, and garnished with small sausage balls.

BROILED BLACK COCK WITH JELLY—The young birds picked, singed, drawn and wiped, split down the back, backbone and breast bone removed, seasoned with salt and pepper, brushed with butter, broiled; served on toast with a sauce made of jelly and butter melted and beaten together, poured over the bird, a little currant jelly served separate, garnished with chip potatoes, and a sprig of parsley.

SALMIS OF HEATH FOWL—The birds picked, drawn, singed and wiped, disjointed, roasted lightly; placed in a saucepan with game sauce, made from the head, feet, liver, heart, neck and gizzard; simmered till tender, seasoned with sherry wine and essence of mushrooms; served with some of the sauce poured over the bird, and garnished with fried button mushrooms.

ROAST BLACK GAME, BREAD SAUCE—The bird picked, drawn, singed, wiped and trussed, roasted with a slice of bacon tied over the breast, when nearly done, the bacon removed, the breast dredged with flour and melted butter, then browned; served with bread sauce, and some of the gravy poured around.

BLACKDIVER—Name of a wild duck held in great esteem by epicures, is at its best in the form of salmis, or braised and served with a little grated chocolate dissolved in the sauce.

BLACKFISH—A black skinned fish of the perch species, found plentifully South.

BLACKFISH—Without a Latin name, it is difficult to know just what Fellows means by a blackfish, but given his description, the type of recipes he supplies, and the information that it is "found plentifully South," I believe he is referring to the black GROUPER (*Mycteroperca bonaci*). In any case, try these recipes with any firm, mild-flavored, white-fleshed fish.

FRIED BLACKFISH WITH BACON—The fish scaled, trimmed, seasoned, rolled in flour; the bacon fried; the fish then fried in the bacon fat; served with a slice of the bacon, garnished with chip potatoes, parsley, and a slice of lemon.

BROILED BLACKFISH WITH PARSLEY BUTTER—The fish scaled, trimmed, scored, brushed with melted butter, seasoned, rolled in flour, brushed again with butter and broiled; served with mâitre d'hôtel butter poured over the fish, and garnished with Julienne potatoes.

BLACKFISH SAUTÉ WITH FINE HERBS—The fish scaled, trimmed, seasoned, rolled in flour, sautéd in butter, then placed in another saûtoir containing fines herbes sauce, simmered for a few minutes, served with some of the sauce poured around, and garnished with Parisienne potatoes.

BAKED BLACKFISH, OYSTER SAUCE—The fish scaled, trimmed, seasoned, placed in a baking pan, brown oyster sauce strained over the fish, baked to a glazy appearance; served with a brown oyster sauce poured over the fish, and garnished with small potato croquettes.

BOILED BLACKFISH, ITALIAN SAUCE—The fish scaled, trimmed and put to boil in boiling water containing an onion stuck with cloves, slices of carrots, salt, bay leaves and a little vinegar, simmered till done; served with a white Italian sauce, and garnished with quarters of small potatoes sprinkled with parsley.

BLACK PUDDING—Often seen on the bill of fare as "Boudin Noir," they are made of sheep's, or pigs' blood and chopped suet, seasoned, filled into intestines, smoked, boiled, and when cold, served in thin slices as an appetizer.

BLANC MANGE—Milk put to boil, containing sugar, grated orange rind, and a few bitter almonds; when boiled, strain into another saucepan, boiled up again, then thickened with corn starch, and poured into molds, the bottoms and sides of which may be decorated with crystallized fruits. After the blanc mange is made it may be made into "ribbon cream" by separating it into four vessels, coloring one green and flavoring it with pistachios, another red with a rose flavor, another with some boiling chocolate; when filling the molds, the white is placed first and the chocolate last.

BLANQUETTE—A term often used in describing a white fricassee of white meats, such as sweetbreads, veal, animal brains, spring lamb, rabbit, chicken, etc., etc.

BLOATERS—Are smoked herrings, and the best are imported from "YARMOUTH," a sea port city of England, which city has never found an equal rival in this production.

BLOATERS—Indispensable at high tea, bloaters never enjoyed the same popularity in the United States that they did in England. You can sometimes find smoked HERRING at good fish markets; more often than not it is from Canada's Maritime Provinces, where it was once a staple.

TOASTED BLOATERS—The head removed with the entrails without opening the fish, which is done by cutting the neck across the back and drawing the entrails with the gills, they are then washed in cold water, wiped dry and slowly broiled; served with melted butter, garnished with lemon and parsley.

BAKED YARMOUTH BLOATERS IN SAUCE—The fish drawn, then blanched, taken up and skinned, the flesh lifted off in fillets free from bone, then laid in pan, and covered with a thick anchovy sauce containing a little bloater paste, sprinkled with grated cheese and breadcrumbs, baked; served garnished with fancy potatoes.

YARMOUTH BLOATERS SAUTÉS—The fillets prepared as in the preceding, then lightly fried in butter, seasoned with red pepper, sprinkled with chopped parsley; served on toast garnished with lemon and parsley.

BLUEFISH—A great favorite and in good demand in any form on the bill of fare, although baked or broiled have the most calls; a six pound fish cuts to best advantage for restaurant use, cutting five good portions; a four to five pound fish being too thin for restaurants, but just the thing for a course dinner.

BLUEFISH—One of the East Coast's most important game fish, the blue, as it is affectionately called by those who hunt it, is one of the few fish with greater sport than market value. Shaped like a tuna, with flesh not unlike that of a mackerel, the bluefish (*Pomatomus saltatrix*) has a strong, delicious, almost sweet flavor, but only when it is absolutely fresh. Smaller fish (under three pounds) are best eaten whole; those of medium size (up to six pounds) can be filleted; larger bluefish—which are generally quite strong-tasting and soft-fleshed—should be steaked and grilled. Bluefish does not keep well in the refrigerator or freezer, although it is spectacular when smoked (and makes excellent pâté).

BLUEFISH STUFFED AND BAKED—
The fish scaled, trimmed, wiped dry
and filled with a stuffing composed
of cooked veal two parts, boiled
bacon one part, and grated bread
crumbs one part, the meat chopped
fine, then mixed with the bread
crumbs, seasoned with salt, pepper, marjoram, thyme, mace, and
lemon juice, mixed thoroughly and
slightly moistened with fish broth;
when filled, the opening sewn up,
the fish dredged with flour and put
in a pan with carrot, turnip, onion,
a few cloves, claret wine and consommé; baked; when done, taken
up, and to the pan is added some
Espagnole sauce; boiled up,
strained; served with some of the
sauce, and garnished with Duchesse potatoes.

BLUEFISH STEAKS, ITALIAN SAUCE—
The fish cut into steaks, and arranged in a buttered pan containing some minced shallots,
white wine and mushroom liquor,
covered with a sheet of buttered
paper, baked; when done, taken up,
some Italian sauce strained into
the pan, boiled up, and strained
back into a rich Italian sauce;
served with some of the sauce
poured over, and garnished with
Hollandaise potatoes.

BAKED BLUEFISH WITH TOMA-
TOES—The fish cut in portions, seasoned, dredged with flour, placed in a
buttered pan, to which is added
minced onions, tomato sauce, and a
can of tomatoes that have been
strained from their juice; baked;
when done, served with some of the
tomatoes poured around, and garnished with small potato croquettes.

BOILED BLUEFISH, SHRIMP
SAUCE—The fish cut in portions, put
to boil in boiling fish broth containing salt, peppers, cloves, carrot
and onion in slices, with a dash of
vinegar; when done, served with a
shrimp sauce poured around, and
garnished with quartered steamed
potatoes sprinkled with mâitre
d'hôtel butter.

BROILED BLUEFISH WITH AN-
CHOVY BUTTER—The fish cut in
portions, seasoned, dredged with
flour, brushed with butter, broiled;
when done, served with some anchovy butter on top of the fish, and
garnished with chip potatoes, parsley, and a slice of lemon.

BAKED BLUEFISH WITH FINE
HERBS—The fish cut in steaks,
seasoned, dredged with flour, arranged in buttered baking pan, covered with a fines-herbes sauce,
baked; served with some of the
sauce poured around, and garnished with potatoes chateau.
Bluefish prepared as in the recipe
just given, may also be served and
baked with Piquante, Bordelaise
and tomato sauces.

BLUEFISH SAUTÉ, ADMIRAL SAUCE—
The fish cut in steaks, seasoned,
dredged with flour, fried in butter;
when done, taken up, and into the
pan they were fried in, some butter
sauce is added, boiled up, and
strained into another saûtoir containing minced fried shallots, capers, grated lemon rind, and
pounded anchovies; boiled,
skimmed, the fish served with the
sauce poured around, and garnished with Condé potatoes.

BLUEFISH SAUTÉ WITH ANCHO-VIES—The fish cut into portions, seasoned, dredged with flour, fried in butter, taken up; into the pan is then put some minced shallots; when browned, anchovy paste and lemon juice added, with a little Bordelaise sauce, boiled up, strained; served with some of the sauce, and garnished with Hollandaise potatoes.

STUFFED FILLETS OF BLUEFISH—The fish filleted and cut in portions, seasoned, dredged with flour, quickly broiled on the cut side, the broiled part spread with a thick Velouté sauce containing grated ham, minced fried shallots, mushrooms and chopped parsley; when all are spread, placed skin side down in a buttered baking pan, with a little white wine, baked; served with parsley sauce poured around and garnished with potato quenelles.

BAKED BLUEFISH IN CRUMBS—The fish cut into portion pieces, seasoned, arranged in a buttered baking pan, moistened with anchovy sauce, sprinkled with grated bread crumbs and melted butter, baked; served with anchovy sauce, and garnished with Parisienne potatoes.

BAKED BLUEFISH, MATELOTE SAUCE—The fish cut in steaks, seasoned, brushed with butter, arranged in pan, moistened with claret wine, baked; when done on one side, turned over and browned on the other, then taken up, and to the wine in the pan is added some Espagnole sauce and mushroom liquor, boiled up, strained, skimmed, finished with grated nutmeg and anchovy butter, the fish served with some of the sauce poured around, and garnished with Victoria potatoes.

BORDEAUX—See CLARET.

BOUCHÉE OF OYSTERS—Oysters scalded, the liquor made into a sauce, oysters cut into dice, added to the finished sauce, seasoned with lemon juice and anchovy essence, filled into puff paste patty shells, and served.

BOUCHÉE OF CHICKEN—Breast of chicken (cooked) cut into dice, mixed into a rich Velouté sauce, made hot, filled into patty shells and served.

BOUCHÉE OF GAME—Any cold cooked game may be used, and if desired can be so named instead of the word "game," the meat cut in small squares, and made hot in a sauce appropriate to the game used, filled into small patty shells and served.

BOUCHÉE OF FOIE-GRAS—This is served cold. The foie-gras is cut into small pieces, put into patty shells with limpid aspic jelly, and served when set.

BOUCHÉE OF SWEETBREADS—The sweetbreads broiled, cut into small squares, made hot in a white Italian sauce, the warm patty shells filled and served.

BOUCHÉE OF LOBSTERS—Fresh boiled lobster meat cut in dice,

made hot in a Suprême sauce, filled into the patty shells and served.

BOUCHÉE WITH RAGOUT—The patty shells filled with a mixture of smoked tongue, breast of chicken, truffles and mushrooms; all cut small and made hot in a Suprême sauce, cover put on and served (called Bouchées à la Reine).

BOUCHÉE WITH MARROW—The spinal marrow of beef cut in pieces, cooked in a sauce Albert, filled into the patty shells and served.

BOUCHÉE WITH GAME PURÉE—The patty shells filled with a rich purée of any form of game, highly seasoned (called Bouchées à la St. Hubert).

BOUCHÉE OF CRAYFISH TAILS—The meat from the tails of fresh boiled crayfish, cut up and made hot in a cream parsley sauce, filled into the patty shells and served.

BOUCHÉE WITH SALPICON—Cooked poultry or game cut small, made hot in a rich sauce, filled into the patty shells and served.

BOUCHÉE WITH OX PALATES—The patty shell filled with a mixture of small cut pieces of braised ox palate and mushrooms, made hot in Allemande sauce.

BOUCHÉE OF SARDINES—The sardines made into a paste with Gruyere cheese, salt, pepper and chili vinegar, mix with a few scalded oysters cut small, the patty shells filled and served, garnished with hard boiled yolks of eggs rubbed through a sieve, resembling vermicelli.

BOUCHÉE WITH MUSHROOMS—Slices of button mushrooms lightly fried in butter, then put into a rich Madeira sauce, made hot, filled into the patty shells, and the opening filled with a cork made of a mushroom nicely glazed.

BOUCHÉE OF REEDBIRD—The reedbird boned, stuffed, braised with wine, taken up, glazed, jointed, put in the patty shells, some Perigueux sauce poured in and served.

BOUCHÉE OF WOODCOCK—Snipe, Larks, Ricebirds and Ortolans, may be prepared and served same as the preceding.

BOUCHÉE OF ANCHOVIES—Coiled anchovies in oil, taken out and drained, mayonnaise sauce beaten with stiff aspic jelly and a dash of tarragon vinegar, the anchovies dipped into it, and filled into cold patty shells, the top then decorated with a cover made of aspic jelly, and served.

BOUCHÉE OF SOLE—The sole filleted and braised, cut in small pieces, when cold, put into the patty shells, limpid fish jelly poured in, the top decorated with Montpelier butter and served.

BOUCHÉE OF SALMON—Cold cooked salmon in flakes, mixed with Ravigote sauce, filled into the patty shells, the top decorated with mayonnaise and studded with capers.

BOUCHÉE OF ORANGES—The patty shell used for sweet bouchées is made of a rich stiff "lady finger mixture" forced out of a pastry bag in rings one on top of the other to the desired height, sprinkled with pink sugar, baked and glazed, the oranges peeled and separated in sections, then simmered in an orange syrup; when done, taken up and drained, put into the bouchées, the top decorated with a flavored water icing (called Bouchées à la Seville).

BOUCHÉE OF PLUMS—The shell made as in the preceding, the plums peeled, stoned and cut in slices, simmered in syrup, taken up and drained, put into the bouchées, limpid sweet jelly poured in; when the jelly is set, the top decorated and served.

BOUCHÉE OF PEACHES—Prepared the same as the preceding, substituting peaches for plums. Strawberries, cherries and red raspberries may also be treated this way.

BOUDIN—The French name for a pudding made of meats, game, poultry and fish, in the form of cakes or sausages.

BOUDIN—The French *boudin* (pronounced boo-DAH) seen most frequently in this country are boudin blanc and boudin noir. But there is also the New Orleans boudin, a soft, super-spicy pork and rice sausage that is eaten out of hand by squeezing the casing so that the hot contents flows directly into the mouth. (You don't see that in France!)

BOUDIN NOIR—Or black pudding; see BLACK PUDDING.

BOUDIN OF VEAL—Finely minced veal and bacon seasoned with aromatic herbs, then made into small sausage shapes, poached in white stock, served with a sauce Perigueux (called Boudin de Veau).

BOUDIN OF RABBIT—Same as the preceding, substituting rabbit for the veal; served with a light game sauce (called Boudin de Lapin).

BOUDIN OF HARE—Same as the preceding, substituting hare for rabbit (called Boudin de Lievre).

BOUDIN OF FOWL—Cold white chicken or turkey meat pounded to a paste with a seasoning of nutmeg, salt, red pepper, lemon juice and herbs, the paste forced into a skin, plunged into boiling white stock till thoroughly heated through, taken up, served cold in slices alternately with slices of black pudding (called Boudin Blanc).

BOULETTES OF GAME—The word boulette signifies "ball" and is used very seldom, except to describe a garnish. "Boulettes of potatoes" are what is better known as potatoes Victoria. Boulettes of game are made of a highly seasoned mince of cold game, breaded and fried.

BOULETTES—The simplest way to think of boulettes—which may be made from almost any fish or meat—is as round croquettes. Like CROQUETTES, boulettes make quick work of leftovers.

BOUILLABAISSE—A national soup of the Latin race, composed of pieces of fish (boned and skinned), garlic, chopped parsley, bay leaves, tomatoes, leeks, onions, lobster, savory herbs, potatoes, olive oil and saffron, fried, then simmered till done; served in platefuls with slices of toast dried in the oven.

BRAINS—Of animals are esteemed by the cook in producing delicate entrées, and are remunerative to the proprietor on account of their small cost. They must, before cooking, be thoroughly cleansed of the skin and blood that covers them; they are easily digested, and fairly nutritious.

BRAINS—It is a shame that we do not appreciate brains (or any organ meats). Most of our ancestors did, and not only because they couldn't afford muscle meat. Brains have a mild flavor and a superb, silky texture.

Veal brains are most common today; they weigh about eight ounces each and are pale in color with a pink tinge. Brains should be rinsed and their membranes and large blood vessels removed before cooking, but they need not be given a preliminary poaching.

The classic preparation—given here as Scrambled Brains—is an odd combination of two similar textures. But fried brains—whether breaded, as below, or simply dredged in flour before frying—is an unsurpassed luxury. Serve with lemon; tartar sauce is too heavy for this delicacy.

SCRAMBLED BRAINS—Pigs, sheep, calf or beef brains, as there is scarcely any difference in the flavor, being all composed of the same material, are cleansed, parboiled in salted water with a dash of vinegar, taken up, drained, cut into small pieces, added to an equal volume of beaten eggs, seasoned with salt, pepper and nutmeg, poured into a pan containing butter, and scrambled around till set. Served on toast (optional), garnished with croûtons and parsley.

BRAIN FORCEMEAT—Cold boiled brains minced, then pounded to a paste with flour, egg yolks; seasoned with nutmeg, salt, pepper and chopped parsley.

BRAIN CROQUETTES WITH PEAS— The croquettes formed in cone shapes of "brain forcemeat" breaded, fried, served with a frill stuck into the croquette, and garnished with green peas at the ends of the dish, with Allemande sauce at side.

BRAIN CUTLETS, VILLEROI SAUCE— The cutlets size and shape of small lamb chops made of "brain forcemeat" with a piece of macaroni to represent the bone, breaded, fried; served with Villeroi sauce poured around.

BRAIN CAKES WITH BACON—The cakes size and shape of small codfish cakes, made of "brain forcemeat" breaded, fried, served with a slice of broiled bacon and Béchamel sauce poured around.

ROAST BRAINS WITH FORCEMEAT BALLS—Calf's brains par-boiled and trimmed, seasoned with salt and pepper, dipped in melted butter, then rolled in flour, quickly roasted and basted with butter; served garnished with fried balls of "brain forcemeat" and fines herbes sauce poured around.

SCALLOPED BRAINS IN SHELL—Cold cooked brains in slices, mixed with a white Italian sauce, filled into scallop shells, sprinkled with grated cheese and breadcrumbs, baked, served in the shells (called Cerveaux en Coquille au Gratin).

BRAINS AND MUSHROOMS IN CASES—Cold cooked brains and button mushrooms cut in neat pieces, tossed in butter over a quick fire to color lightly, then moistened with Suprême sauce; served in fancy paper cases.

CALF'S BRAINS AND TONGUE, MUSHROOM SAUCE—The brains par-boiled and trimmed, the tongues boiled, skinned, trimmed and cut lengthwise, dipped in cooling Piquante sauce; when cold, both breaded and fried; served with mushroom sauce.

FRIED BRAINS WITH BROWN BUTTER—The brains blanched and trimmed, seasoned, brushed with butter, rolled in flour, dipped in beaten eggs, then fried; served with brown butter poured over them,

made by melting butter over a quick fire till it froths and browns, then adding to it the juice of a lemon and some finely chopped parsley (called Cerveaux au Beurre Noir).

FRIED BRAINS BREADED, TARTAR SAUCE—The brains blanched, trimmed, and masked with Tartar sauce, then breaded and fried; served with Tartar sauce at the ends of the dish, and Parisienne potatoes down the sides.

CALF'S BRAINS, SAUCE VINAIGRETTE—The brains blanched, trimmed, and boiled till done in white stock, served with Vinaigrette sauce, and garnished with parsley.

BRAISED BRAINS WITH STUFFED TOMATOES—The brains blanched, trimmed, and arranged in a saûtoir with carrot, onion, parsley, bay leaves and cloves, moistened with white stock, covered with a sheet of buttered paper, braised till done, taken up, the liquor skimmed and strained into a Velouté sauce, reduced, the brains served with some of the sauce poured over them, and garnished with small stuffed tomatoes.

BRAISED BRAINS, SAUCE REMOULADE—The brains prepared and cooked the same way as in the preceding recipe, with the addition of a little white wine to the moistening stock; when done, the braise skimmed, strained and reduced to a glaze, then mixed into a hot Remoulade sauce; served with the sauce poured over the brains, and garnished with fancy croûtons.

BRAISED BRAINS WITH MUSH-ROOMS—The brains blanched, trimmed, and arranged in a saûtoir with slices of bacon, vegetables and spices, moistened with white stock and juice of a lemon, covered with thin slices of bacon, braised till done, taken up, the bacon cut in pieces, the braise reduced to a glaze, and strained over some button mushrooms and small glazed onions, the brains sprinkled with fried breadcrumbs, and garnished with the bacon, mushrooms and onions alternately.

BRAINS IN SAUCE POULETTE WITH RICE—The brains blanched, trimmed and simmered in Poulette sauce, served with the sauce poured over them and garnished with small timbales of rice, with a small sprig of parsley stuck in them.

BRAINS WITH SORREL, SAUCE RA-VIGOTE—The brains blanched, trimmed and simmered till tender in white stock with the juice of a lemon. Served on a bed of purée of sorrel, the brains masked with Ra-vigote sauce.

CREAMED BRAINS WITH KIDNEY BEANS—The brains blanched, trimmed and simmered in cream sauce till done; served masked with the sauce and garnished with kidney beans (flageolets) that have been sautéed in butter.

CROUSTADES OF BRAINS WITH AR-TICHOKES—The brains prepared

and cooked the same way as given for "braised brains with stuffed to-matoes"; when done, the brains cut in slices, mixed with the Velouté sauce, filled into paste croustades; served garnished with artichoke bottoms spread with "brain force-meat" and filled with small pieces of glazed calf's tongue.

BROCHETTE OF CALF'S BRAINS— See brochette dishes.

BRAINS WITH RICE, TURKISH STYLE—Cold cooked brains worked into a creamy paste with cream, seasoned with salt, pepper, lemon juice and nutmeg; the rice boiled in white stock with salt, butter, pepper and cinnamon; served, the rice in small molds, turned out onto the dish, and masked over with brains, sprinkled with finely chopped parsley or chervil.

BRAIN PATTIES OR VOL-AU-VENTS —Cold cooked brains cut in small dice with mushrooms, made hot in Suprême sauce, filled into patty shells, cover placed on and served.

SAVORY OMELET OF CALF'S BRAINS—The brains prepared as in the preceding, the omelet mixture made of beaten eggs, finely cut chives, parsley, salt, pepper and nutmeg, the omelet formed, enclosing some of the mixture; served with more of the brains in sauce poured around.

CALF'S BRAINS, PARSLEY SAUCE— The brains blanched, trimmed, and boiled till done in white stock; served on a slice of toast, parsley sauce poured over the brains and garnished with Hollandaise potatoes.

BRAIN KROMESKIES, MADEIRA SAUCE—Slices of cold cooked brains dipped in glaze, encircled with a very thin strip of cold boiled bacon, pinned with a toothpick, dipped in batter and fried, the toothpick removed; served with Madeira sauce poured around.

BROILED BRAINS WITH PARSLEY BUTTER—The brains blanched, trimmed and cut in slices, seasoned, broiled; served on toast with mâitre d'hôtel butter poured over them and garnished with Julienne potatoes.

BRAISE AND BRAISING—A term applied to foods that are cooked by a top and bottom heat. The pot or braiser has a cover that fits tightly and a receptacle to hold lighted charcoal or coke, so that the heat descends on top of the foods. The general way of the average establishment, however, who, as a rule, are not supplied with a braiser, is to take a shallow saucepan or saûtoir, into which is placed the foods, together with onion, carrot, parsley, bay leaves and whole cloves (and according to the food, with other accessories, but the five mentioned spices and vegetables are always included in a braise) and moistened with stock or sauces, as the recipe may require; the cover of the saûtoir is then put on and placed in the oven, so that it gives an even heat, top, bottom and sides. When the foods are cooked to requirement they are taken up and the remaining liquor is called braise. Braising, besides imparting delicate flavors to the foods thus cooked, is also an exceptional good way of making tough meats tender, as the toughest parts of beef can be made into fine entrées by braising them. See braised dishes under heading of "BEEF."

BRANDY—A spirit distilled from wines, is clear and sparkling. In the year 1878 the vineyards of the Charente were devastated by the phylloxera, causing the annual production, which averaged 170,000,000 gallons, to fall in 1898 to only 11,000,000; consequently, since 1878, only a very small quantity of genuine brandy has been shipped to this country, the bulk being a blend of grain spirit flavored with brandy. An oil distilled from brandy is used with a spirit in producing an imitation that is sold as cooking brandy.

BRANDY SAUCE—Water, lemon juice, sugar and grated nutmeg brought to the boil, butter and flour sizzling in another saucepan, the flavored water strained into it, stirring at the same time, allowed to simmer for a few minutes, taken from the fire, and brandy to the desired flavor added.

BRAWN—The traditional English name for head cheese, made by simmering a pig's head with seasonings. The cooked meat is chopped and set in aspic made from the gelatinous juices.

BREAD—A combination of flour, salt, sugar, water and yeast, mixed, set to rise, kneaded, risen again, molded, proved and baked. The different kinds of bread on the market is legion, and with all sorts of claims, principally for the benefit of health and digestion, such as "whole meal," "gluten," "aerated," "steamed," "dietitic," "diabetic," "butter milk," "dyspepsia," etc., which argument may be based on sound doctrine or not; at least, doctors, chemists and analists, are continually arguing the pro. and con. of the different claimants as the following quotation will show for itself.

White Versus Brown Bread— There appeared in the St. Bartholomew's Hospital report a very interesting communication on the relative digestibilty of white and brown bread by Drs. Lauder, Brunton and Tunnicliffe. While the authors admit that, regarded from a purely chemical point of view, the nutritive value of brown bread is greater than white, they maintain that this is not so when considered from the physiological side. The authors point out that it is absurd to take the mere chemical composition as an index of the value of food stuff, as a stick of charcoal, the atmospheric air, a little water, some sea salt, contain all the elements of a typical diet. Hence, the greatest importance attaches not only to the composition, but to the ways in which the various constituents are combined so that they can be readily and easily assimilated. The conclusion that the authors come to is mainly that, although brown bread, both on account of its large percentage of mineral matters and fat forming constituents, is chemically superior to white bread, yet these constituents do not so readily pass into the blood as in the case of white bread, and that, weight for weight, white bread is more nutritious than brown. In special cases where there is a deficiency of mineral matter, and especially in cases of growing children, when large quantities of these are required for produc-

tion of bone and tissue, brown bread may be useful, but even in these cases, if these mineral salts, and especially salts of calcium, are supplied by other means, white bread is preferable to brown.

BREAD—The most astonishing element of Fellows's entry is how relevant it remains. The debate about whether the added nutrients of whole wheat flour are in fact absorbed as readily as are the more limited components of white flour continues to rage. Fortunately—although bread is not the staple it was at the turn of the century—we are able to enjoy a wide variety of breads, and still more if we bake our own. Fellows evidently did not believe that the professional chef would bother to make bread: That would be left to the baker.

BRIE—Name of a very rich cream cheese made near Paris, France, is of a circular form, an inch thick, wrapped in parchment paper, put into thin wooden boxes and imported to this country; it is, however, very much, and fairly well imitated by our own cheese manufacturers.

BRINE—A preserving and flavoring mixture of salt, spices, saltpetre and water—is the best thing to put meats into that are just on the turn; after first washing them and rubbing them over with powdered charcoal or borax, and again thoroughly washing them. For mixture see "CORNED BEEF."

BROCCOLI—Like its close cousin CAULIFLOWER, broccoli (*Brassica oleracea italica*) is a superb food. It continually reveals new health-giving properties (recent discoveries indicate it is a powerful anticarcinogen, and it has long been valued for its high content of vitamins A and C), and—despite its assertive flavor—it is as versatile a vegetable as you can find.

There are probably hundreds of varieties of broccoli, ranging from purple to yellow, in many different shapes. Broccoli rabe, also known as rapini, is a long-stemmed, small-flowered version that is far more bitter than common broccoli, and is favored in Italian cuisine. It is not unlike common field mustard, which, when its flower buds are tight, produces mustard-flavored broccoli when cooked. Broccoli Romanesco is a rediscovered heirloom form, a light, pale-green pyramid that is more known for its striking appearance than for anything unusual about its flavor. And, as of this writing, broccoflower—essentially a green cauliflower—is making its appearance in supermarkets all over the country.

All of these can be steamed, sautéed, fried, cooked au gratin, stir-fried, or even grilled. Broccoli is best complemented by Italian and Asian seasonings: garlic, soy, ginger, lemon. It can also be served topped with a variety of sauces.

BROCHETTE OF OYSTERS—Oysters, bacon and sweetbreads (optional), the bacon and sweetbreads cut in slices same length as the oysters, seasoned with salt, pepper, powdered thyme and chopped parsley, the oysters and sweetbreads dipped in beaten eggs, then rolled in fresh grated breadcrumbs, threaded alternately on the skewer with the bacon; when full, fried in hot fat, served with some heated tomato catsup, that is seasoned with anchovy essence poured around, and garnished with lemon and parsley.

BROCHETTE OF LAMB KIDNEYS—The kidneys with the skin removed and split in two without quite severing, threaded on the skewer flat, quickly broiled for an instant over a hot fire, then taken off and seasoned with salt, pepper and ground mint, dipped in Velouté sauce, then fresh grated breadcrumbs, brushed with melted butter and broiled over a slow fire till done; served with a Colbert sauce poured around.

BROCHETTE OF SPRING LAMB—Circular steaks of the leg of raw lamb, one cutlet of the leg making about three steaks, laid for an hour in a mixture of minced shallots, chives, mint, garlic, lemon juice, nutmeg, melted butter, salt and pepper, then taken up, rolled in fresh grated breadcrumbs, threaded on the skewer, broiled till done and served with Colbert sauce poured around.

BROCHETTE OF VEAL—Cold cooked veal and boiled ham cut into even sized pieces, the veal seasoned with salt, pepper and powdered marjoram, threaded alternately on the skewer, breaded, fried, served with white Italian sauce poured around, and garnished with watercress.

BROCHETTE OF DUCK LIVERS—The liver is par-boiled, then prepared and cooked the same way as "chicken livers" following; served with Bigarrade sauce poured around, and garnished with watercress and lemon.

BROCHETTE OF CHICKEN LIVERS—The livers washed and dried, seasoned with salt and pepper, slices of bacon lightly broiled, then cut in pieces same size as the livers, the skewer threaded with them alternately; when all on, rolled in melted butter or olive oil, then in fresh grated breadcrumbs, broiled, served on a slice of narrow toast with mâitre d'hôtel butter poured over, and garnished with watercress.

BROCHETTE OF GEESE LIVERS—The livers boiled in stock till done, then cut into slices; smoked cooked tongue the tip end cut in slices same size as the livers; both dipped in cooling Perigueux sauce; when cold, threaded alternately on the skewer, rolled in grated breadcrumbs, then breaded and fried, served with Perigueux sauce poured around, and garnished with watercress and lemon.

BROCHETTE OF TURKEY LIVERS—The livers blanched, cut in slices, lightly sautéed with finely minced shallots, garlic and chives, taken up, drained, seasoned with salt, pepper and lemon juice, threaded alternately on skewer with pieces of half broiled bacon, dipped in melted butter, then breadcrumbs, beaten eggs and breadcrumbs again, broiled, served with Hanover sauce poured around, and garnished with watercress.

BROCHETTE OF EELS—The eels skinned and cut into inch pieces, steeped for an hour in equal quantities of olive oil and vinegar, with salt, pepper, chopped parsley and thyme, then placed on skewer alternately with bacon, arranged on a baking pan with some of the marinade poured over them; roasted for ten minutes, taken up, drained, breaded, fried and served with Tartar sauce.

BROCHETTE OF PIGS' KIDNEYS—The kidneys par-boiled, cut in slices, seasoned with salt, pepper and powdered sage; cold boiled pickled pork cut in slices same size as the kidneys, threaded alternately on skewer, rolled in olive oil, then breaded and fried; served with Robert sauce containing a dash of anchovy essence poured around, and garnished with a small baked and glazed apple.

BROCHETTE OF MUSSELS—Prepared and served the same way as the recipe given for "brochette of oysters."

BROCHETTE OF MUTTON—Cutlets from the leg or loin, cut into even sized pieces, seasoned with a mixture of salt, pepper, cinnamon and powdered savory, threaded on skewer, arranged in baking pan, moistened with a thin tomato sauce, roasted and basted with it; served with tomato sauce poured around, and garnished with chip potatoes.

BROCHETTE OF SWEETBREADS—The sweetbreads soaked, blanched, then boiled till tender with vegetables and spices, taken up, drained, skinned, pressed till cold, cut in pieces, then cut circular with the largest sized column cutter; slices of cold cooked tongue the same way; both dipped in cooling white Italian sauce; when cold, rolled in fresh grated breadcrumbs, then threaded alternately on the skewer; when full, breaded, fried, served with white Italian sauce poured around.

BROCHETTE OF SMELTS—A judicious way of using up the small smelts; the fish wiped, after entrails are drawn, seasoned with salt and pepper, rolled in flour, then in beaten eggs and fresh breadcrumbs, threaded on the skewer through the gills, fried in hot fat, taken up, drained; served with or without Tartar or tomato sauce, garnished with lemon and parsley.

BROCHETTE OF CALF'S BRAINS—The brains soaked, skinned, washed, blanched in boiling water containing a little vinegar, taken up, drained, cut in even sized pieces; also bacon cut the same size; the brains seasoned with salt, pepper, nutmeg, powdered thyme and chopped parsley, threaded on the skewer alternately with the bacon, rolled in melted butter, then in breadcrumbs, broiled, served with Ravigote sauce, and garnished with watercress and lemon.

BROCHETTE OF LOBSTER—Cold boiled lobster meat cut in pieces and marinaded in a mixture of salt, pepper, nutmeg and Worcestershire sauce for an hour, then threaded on skewer alternately with the large head of a button mushroom, rolled in butter, then in fresh breadcrumbs, broiled, served with mâitre d'hôtel butter mixed with anchovy essence

poured around, and garnished with parsley and lemon.

BROCHETTE OF RABBIT—Raw young rabbit meat and cold boiled salt pork cut in even sized pieces, the rabbit sautéed in butter with fine herbs, taken up and threaded alternately on the skewer with the salt pork, seasoned with a mixture of salt, pepper and powdered herbs, breaded, fried, and served with brown Italian sauce poured around.

BROCHETTE OF TURKEY—Slices of light and dark meat of cold cooked turkey, seasoned with salt, pepper and nutmeg, dipped in cooling Suprême sauce; when cold, rolled in breadcrumbs, then breaded and fried; served with sauce Suprême.

BROCHETTE OF LAMB FRIES—Prepared, cooked, and served the same way as the recipe given for "brochette of calf's brains," tomato sauce to be used instead of Ravigote.

BROCHETTE OF SCALLOPS—The scallops drained, seasoned with salt, pepper and chopped parsley, breaded, placed alternately on skewer with pieces of bacon fried, served, with Allemande sauce containing a little lobster coral.

BROCHETTE OF REED BIRDS—The birds picked, drawn, wiped, and trussed with the head tucked under the wing, a small ball of mâitre d'hôtel butter and the liver of the bird minced and put inside, threaded alternately on the skewer with a piece of cold boiled bacon, seasoned, broiled, served on toast and garnished with parsley and lemon.

BROCHETTE OF CRAYFISH TAILS— The fresh boiled meat of the cray-fish tails, prepared and served the same way as the recipe given for "brochette of lobster."

BRUNOISE—Name given to a con-sommé with small cut vegetables. See CONSOMMÉ.

BRUSSELS SPROUTS—Called Choux de Bruxelles are small sprouts that grow on the stalks of cabbages. They are very green and about the size of large olives when trimmed. They make an excellent accompaniment to boiled beef and form a part of many garnitures.

BRUSSELS SPROUTS BOILED—As a vegetable, trimmed, thoroughly washed, thrown into boiling water containing salt and a small piece of common washing soda, boiled till tender with the saucepan lid OFF about fifteen minutes, then turned into a colander, drained, tossed with a little melted butter and served.

BRUSSELS SPROUTS SAUTÉES— Prepared, boiled and drained as in the preceding, then placed in a saûtoir with butter and lightly fried, seasoned with salt and pep-per; served either as a garnish or vegetable.

BRUSSELS SPROUTS WITH PARS-LEY BUTTER—Same as the preced-ing, but served with maître d'hôtel butter poured over them.

BRUSSELS SPROUTS IN CREAM— Prepared and cooked the same as for "boiled" above, then reheated in a good reduced cream (not cream sauce); served as a vege-table.

OMELET WITH BRUSSELS SPROUTS—The above sprouts in cream, enclosed in a savory om-elet; served garnished with some of the sprouts around the omelet and the cream poured over them.

PURÉE OF BRUSSELS SPROUTS— The sprouts prepared as for "brus-sels sprouts sautées"; after sautée-ing they are rubbed through a fine sieve, mixed with egg yolks and butter, seasoned with salt and pep-per; used as a garnish or in a soup; if in soup, as follows; the stock of good veal or chicken, seasoned with salt pork and vegetables, thickened lightly with roux, strained, the purée then worked into it. Served with small toast.

BUCK—The male deer. For dishes of Buck, see VENISON.

BUCKWHEAT—A meal ground from the seeds of buckwheat, principally used in culinary forms for making batter cakes. For recipes, see head-ing of BATTER.

BUCKWHEAT—Buckwheat (*Fagopy-rum esculentum*) is not a grain; rather, it is the seed of a plant that is related to RHUBARB. When ground, however, it behaves exactly like other cereals. It is easy to grow in harsh climates and so is a staple of much of northern Europe, especially the northern provinces of France, Poland, Prussia, and the Ukraine. There, its flour is made into porridge and noodles, and its groats are treated like rice. Pancakes, blinis, and varnishkes are made of buckwheat flour. The Japanese use buckwheat to make soba, thin brown noodles that are often served cold or in broth.

BUISSON—A form resembling a bush; may be made by taking two circular pieces of wood one-half the diameter of the other, used for top and bottom, then nailing strips of laths the desired height, about half an inch apart, screwing small hooks into the laths, the spaces between filled up with bunches of parsley and boiled crayfish or lobsters hanging by the tails from the hooks.

BUISSON—We have never seen one of these massive shellfish cookers, and wonder if any are in use anywhere. However, the term is still used today to describe the method of arranging food such as crayfish in the fashion of a pyramid.

BURGUNDY—There are, arguably, four great wines of France. One sparkles (CHAMPAGNE), one is red, and one, mysteriously missing from these pages, can be red or white. Only the spectacular Côte d'Or ("Slope of Gold"), a skinny strip of thirty miles or so that runs from near Dijon southwest through Beaune, makes red and white wines that rank with the world's best. Unfortunately, Burgundies are made in such small quantities—in a great year, there may be only five hundred cases of Romanée-Conti, for example—that their cost is always high.

The grapes are Pinot Noir (for the reds) and Chardonnay (for the whites), both of which are now grown elsewhere in the world (especially on the West Coast of this country and in Australia), but nowhere with as much success as in Burgundy. Choosing Burgundies is not simple; but those wines labeled *grand cru* or *premier* (or *1er*) *cru* are the most reliable (and the most reliably expensive).

BUTTER—Takes a very prominent part in culinary matters, forms some special butters used for garnishing and scarcely enters at all into what are now known as BUTTER CAKES.

BUTTER—We worry less now about adulterated butter than about butter itself. Although butter has about the same amount of calories and fat as margarine, the latter contains no cholesterol, the scourge of the contemporary eater. (Of course the health aspects of the hydrogenation process that brings liquid oils to a semisolid state so they can be sold as margarine also remain in question.) Margarine, however, adds nothing positive to foods, whereas butter is the foundation of many great dishes. We prefer butter!

The real tragedy about butter is not its cholesterol content, but the fact that few of us ever have a chance to sample fresh-from-the-farm butter, with its deep, earthy flavor that varies, as does cheese, from region to region and even season to season. But even our mass-produced, homogeneous butter is usually preferable to the alternatives.

Except for those on restricted diets, butter should be used when its flavor is irreplaceable, or when the silky texture it adds to sauces cannot be achieved by other means. There are times in cooking when olive or other high-quality oil may be substituted without affecting the quality of a dish, but there will always be a change in flavor.

BUTTER CAKES—Composed of ten pounds of flour, one ounce of soda, one ounce of salt mixed together dry, then moistened with three egg yolks, two ounces of melted butter and two quarts of buttermilk; this is mixed and well broken, then is added three quarts of buttermilk and one quart of sweet milk, this brings it to the consistency of biscuit dough; spread out on table, let rest half an hour, then rolled out, let rest another half hour; again rolled out, cut out with biscuit cutter, allowed to raise or proof and baked on a griddle.

ANCHOVY BUTTER—Two parts of butter to one part of anchovy essence, thoroughly mixed with a little grated Parmesan cheese and seasoned with nutmeg, red pepper and a dash of lemon juice.

CRAYFISH BUTTER—Crayfish shells and claws slowly dried in the oven with a little lobster coral, pounded to a paste, then put with butter and simmered for a few minutes, rubbed through a fine sieve into cold water, then gathered for use.

LOBSTER BUTTER—The head and coral of boiled lobster with its equal weight of butter pounded to a paste with a dash of anchovy essence and a little dry mustard, then rubbed through a fine sieve; gathered for use.

MONTPELIER BUTTER—Blanched watercress, chervil, tarragon and parsley, with hard boiled egg yolks, a few anchovies, gherkins, capers and a clove of garlic are pounded to a paste with their equal weight of butter, a little tarragon vinegar and lemon juice; when smooth, rubbed through a fine sieve and gathered for use.

MAÎTRE D'HÔTEL BUTTER—To each cup of melted butter is added a large spoonful of chopped parsley, juice of two lemons, seasoned with salt, red pepper and nutmeg.

PEPPER BUTTER—Three medium sized green peppers pounded to a paste with one pound of butter, then rubbed through a fine sieve and gathered for use.

RAVIGOTE BUTTER—Blanched chives, parsley, tarragon and shallots, pounded to a paste with butter, lemon juice and a dash of anchovy essence, then rubbed through a fine sieve and gathered for use.

GARLIC BUTTER—A few cloves of garlic are pounded to a paste with olive oil and butter; when smooth, rubbed through a fine sieve; gathered for use.

HORSERADISH BUTTER—Four ounces of fine grated horseradish to each pound of butter pounded to a paste, then rubbed through a sieve and gathered for use. Many people like this on broiled steaks instead of mâitre d'hôtel butter.

SHRIMP BUTTER—Equal weight of shrimp meat (canned or fresh), pounded to a paste with butter, then rubbed through a sieve and gathered for use.

DRAWN BUTTER—Half a pound of clear melted butter, put on fire in a saucepan with two ounces of flour, mixed together, pint of boiling water stirred into it, simmered for a minute, then ready for use.

BUTTER ADULTERATIONS—Although on account of the strict pure food laws are rare, still country butter as is often to be purchased by the steward on the open market is sometimes adulterated with wheat, pea, potato flours, chalk, potato starch, and variously colored with yellow chrome, carrot juice, saffron, alkanet, marigold flowers and celandine juice.

BUTTERINE OR MARGARINE—Is a preparation of animal fats, made by working the fats at the natural heat of the animal, then pressing it by hydraulic pressure, the oil thus obtained is then churned with diluted milk or water.

BUTTER BALL DUCK—A small wild duck of American origin. For recipes see DUCK.

CABBAGE—As sold in our markets are of three colors, white, green and red; appreciated by the average guest in any of the forms following.

CABBAGE—Perhaps by green cabbage Fellows meant Savoy, the crinkle-leaved cabbage that is superior in flavor and texture to the more-familiar smooth, almost white type, which is probably best reserved for sauerkraut or coleslaw. In any case, there are now literally dozens of cabbages—all members of the Cruciferae family, which includes TURNIPS, mustard cabbage, broccoli, KALE, and more—available to the home gardener. Several of these, such as Napa and bok choy, are sold regularly in good supermarkets; almost all are preferable to white cabbage.

BOILED CABBAGE—If young require about fifteen minutes, if old twenty to thirty minutes are required for boiling. They should be cut in quarters, the stalks removed, and then the leaves be separated. It is quite a common thing for the cooks to boil them simply in quarters without separating the leaves; not only is this a dirty way, but seldom is the inner part done till the outer leaves are cooked too much and rendered tasteless. After the leaves are separated they should be soaked in cold water to which is added salt; if this precaution is neglected slugs and various small insects may be retained in the leaves. When thoroughly washed put to boil in boiling salted water with a small piece of common washing soda; cook them with the saucepan lid OFF. As the smell of boiling cabbage often reaches the guests' rooms over the kitchen, a piece of stale bread crust or charcoal tied in a piece of muslin boiled with the cabbage will be found to obviate the smell. When done they should be turned into a colander and the water pressed out, then seasoned with salt, pepper and butter. The too common way of sending cabbage to the table floating in the water it was boiled in cannot be condemned too strongly.

BAKED CABBAGE WITH HAM— Fresh boiled cabbage with the water pressed out, mixed with drawn butter, placed in a baking pan, sprinkled with grated cheese and ham, baked, served with a slice of roast ham on top.

STEWED CABBAGE—Fresh boiled and pressed cabbage cut fine, then sautéed in butter, surplus butter poured off, covered with cream sauce, simmered for a few minutes and served.

CREAMED CABBAGE—Coarsely shred cabbage, thoroughly washed, boiled, drained, then mixed with cream sauce.

STUFFED CABBAGE—Whole cabbage parboiled, the heart removed, its place filled with a stuffing of finely chopped cooked meat and sausage meat mixed together, the aperture covered with a slice of salt pork, tied, placed in a saucepan with white stock and a little sherry wine, cover put on, and simmered till done; served with a good brown gravy poured around.

BRAISED CABBAGE—Cabbage cut in halves, thoroughly picked over and washed, boiled not quite done, taken up and drained, the stalk then removed and the two halves put together and tied, resembling the whole cabbage, braised with white stock for an hour, then taken up, drained; served as a vegetable or cut in shapes to be used as a garniture.

FRIED CABBAGE WITH BACON— Fresh boiled, pressed, and seasoned cabbage cut fine, fried in bacon fat; served with a slice of boiled bacon on top.

CABBAGE TIMBALES—Cabbage prepared and cooked the same as for "boiled cabbage"; then well pressed, finely chopped and mixed with lightly fried minced onion, put in a saûtoir with a little butter and simmered with the lid on for fifteen minutes, then allowed to cool; while cooling, equal parts of sausage meat and fresh breadcrumbs with a few beaten eggs and chopped parsley are thoroughly mixed together; the timbale molds are then buttered, a piece of bacon put in, the sides lined with blanched cabbage leaves, the cabbage and stuffing then filled in the molds in alternate layers till full, another piece of bacon put on the top, the timbales then baked in a moderate oven for about an hour, the bacon removed, cabbage turned out and the inner piece of bacon removed; served with a good brown gravy poured over and around.

BAKED CABBAGE WITH CHEESE— Fresh boiled and pressed cabbage seasoned with salt, pepper and butter, arranged in layers in baking pan, each layer sprinkled with grated cheese, top layer with grated cheese and breadcrumbs mixed, sprinkled with butter, baked and served (called Cabbage au Gratin).

BAKED CABBAGE WITH CHEESE

·

Serves 8 to 10

This recipe makes a very good dish out of one of the most basic
vegetables. It is very rich!

2 (2-pound) heads green cabbage	1 cup grated Parmesan cheese
3 tablespoons olive oil	Salt and freshly ground black pepper to taste
2 cloves garlic, peeled and chopped	2 cups plain breadcrumbs
3 medium yellow onions, peeled and chopped	$^1/_4$ pound butter, melted
1$^1/_2$ pounds sharp white cheddar cheese, grated	

Core the cabbages without cutting them in half. Bring a large pot
of water to a boil. Add the whole cabbages. Pull the cabbage leaves
off the heads as they begin to loosen in the hot water. Remove the
leaves to drain and cool. Trim out the thick part of the leaves where
they were attached to the core.

Heat a large frying pan and sauté the oil, garlic, and onions
until the onions are clear. Set aside.

In the bottom of a large baking dish (about 14 inches by 10
inches), place a layer of cabbage leaves. Make additional layers by
using some of the sautéed onion mixture, cheddar cheese, Parmesan, and salt and pepper between the cabbage leaves. Mix the
breadcrumbs with the melted butter and sprinkle on top of the cabbage. Bake at 350° F. for 1 hour. Allow to cool a bit. Cut into
squares and serve.

C.W.

PAUPIETTES OF CABBAGE—
Blanched cabbage leaves, taken
about four thick, the outer one being the largest, the inner one
spread with sausage meat mixed
with boiled rice, shallots, chopped
parsley and chives, then rolled up
and tied, arranged in a saûtoir till
full, little broth added, cover put
on and simmered till done; served
with brown gravy or as a garniture.

BOILED CABBAGE, GERMAN
STYLE—The cabbage boiled and
pressed, chopped, then mixed with

small pieces of boiled bacon and Allemande sauce.

CABBAGE WITH EGGS—Fresh boiled and pressed cabbage finely chopped, placed in a saûtoir with a little drawn butter and vinegar, stirred over a quick fire for a few minutes till smooth and creamy; served garnished with quartered hard boiled eggs and sprinkled with finely chopped eggs.

STEWED RED CABBAGE WITH SAUSAGES—Shred the cabbage as for cole slaw, wash, drain, place it in a saucepan with butter and simmer it with the lid on for half an hour, then put in some slices of salt pork and white stock and cook till done; take up and drain; serve with fried or boiled sausages on top, and a brown gravy poured around.

COLE SLAW—Finely shred cabbage mixed with pepper, salt, sugar, oil and vinegar; also the plain shred cabbage served as an adjunct to fried or stewed oysters.

COLE SLAW—Here Fellows gave us the classic ingredients for coleslaw. It is frequently made with mayonnaise in place of oil and vinegar, and may also contain a variety of spices. Carrots and red cabbage can also be added for improved color.

CABBAGE SALAD—Finely shred cabbage, some bacon cut in dice and fried; while still in the pan, equal parts of water and vinegar, with a seasoning of salt and pepper added to it, boiled, cooled, then mixed with the cabbage.

RED CABBAGE SALAD—The cabbage finely washed, drained, then covered with vinegar, dredged with salt and pepper and steeped for a few hours, then drained and mixed with French dressing; served garnished with shred celery in mayonnaise.

HOT SLAW—Finely shred cabbage washed and drained, put in saucepan with butter, lid put on and simmered till nearly done, water, vinegar, salt, pepper, and a little sugar then added, and finish cooking till tender; finished by working in some beaten eggs till smooth, yellow and creamy.

PICKLED CABBAGE—Finely shred red cabbage thoroughly dredged with salt and placed in large colander or sieve to drain for several hours, then washed, drained, and packed in jars with a few whole peppers, bay leaves and a little thyme, the jar then filled up with white wine vinegar containing beet juice (or a boiled beet may be put in with the cabbage), cover of jar put on, kept in a cold place; ready for use in about a month.

PICKLED CABBAGE—Two gallons of finely chopped cabbage, one pound of chopped onions, half pound each of red and green peppers cut in shreds, mixed together, with one pound of salt, placed in a crock and stood over night; then taken out, put in colander and well pressed; then put in crock in layers, and on each layer sprinkle mustard seeds and a few cloves till all in, covered with cider vinegar; when vinegar sinks, the next day,

HOT SLAW

·

Serves 6 to 8

A tasty vegetable side dish. Do not overcook the final product as the eggs in this slaw will curdle. You will enjoy cabbage in this form.

2½ pounds green cabbage, cored and thinly sliced

4 tablespoons olive oil

½ cup (1 stick) butter

¾ cup white wine vinegar

1½ tablespoons sugar

¾ cup water

3 eggs

Salt to taste

Garnish

Plenty of freshly ground black pepper

Chopped parsley

In a large frying pan, sauté the cabbage in oil and butter. Cook for about 10 to 15 minutes, or just until tender.

In a small saucepan, combine the vinegar, sugar, and water and simmer until the sugar dissolves.

In a small bowl, beat the eggs. Stir in ½ cup of the hot liquid. Pour the mixture into the saucepan with the remaining liquid. Add to the cabbage and heat, tossing the cabbage about. A sauce will begin to form and coat the cabbage. Salt to taste. Serve immediately with garnishes.

C.W.

fill it up so that the cabbage is covered; ready for use in two days.

SAUERKRAUT—This is finely shred cabbage packed in barrels in layers with salt and allowed to sour. It is a nasty smelling troublesome thing to attend to in hotel life, and can really be bought better and cheaper than by home preparation. When to be cooked, it is thoroughly washed and slowly boiled for two or three hours with carrot, onion stuck with cloves and a piece of ham or bacon.

If to be served with frankfurters, or sausages, they are boiled in it.

CAFÉ—Pronounced KAFFAY. The name used to signify a restaurant or place where coffee is to be obtained. It is the French word for coffee, often seen on the bill of fare as "café noir," which means black coffee or strong coffee.

CAILLES—French name for "quails"; when spoken the two "ells" are silent.

CALF—Is the name given to parts of the young of the cow (in a culinary way) such as the head, feet, liver, tail, heart, brains, kidneys and sweetbreads; the other parts or meat is called veal, for recipes of which see VEAL.

CALF'S HEAD—The head as purchased should be left entire with simply the hair cleaned off, and, if in the country towns or resorts, the cook has to clean it himself, plunge it into boiling water containing common washing soda, let it remain for a few minutes, then scrape it perfectly clean with a fish scaler or curry-comb, then singe it like poultry; the head is then split in halves, the brains removed, washed, put to boil in cold water with salt and vegetables, scum removed as it rises, simmered till tender, taken up and put into a pan of cold water, and all bones removed which come away easily; then skin the roof of the mouth, and put the head and tongue between two boards with a weight on top, and press till cold. The stock which the head was boiled in is good to use for soups and white sauces. The pressed meat will be called "calf's head meat" for the recipes following.

CALF'S HEAD BAKED WITH CHIPOLATA GARNISH—Calf's head meat cut in portions, seasoned with salt, pepper, nutmeg and powdered thyme, arranged in baking pan with small onions, mushrooms, small veal sausages, pieces of ham and chicken, blanched and peeled chestnuts, and small balls of carrots and turnips, the whole covered with a rich brown sauce, baked till the garnish is done and the head glazy; served with a little of the sauce poured over and surrounded with the garnish.

CALF'S HEAD BAKED, ENGLISH STYLE—Calf's head meat cut in slices, arranged in baking pan with a seasoning of salt, pepper, nutmeg, an onion stuck with cloves, covered with a white sauce made from the stock the head was boiled in, baked for half an hour; served with some of the sauce poured over, sprinkled with parsley and garnished with quenelles of brain forcemeat and quartered eggs.

CALF'S HEAD BAKED, GERMAN STYLE—Calf's head meat cut in portion pieces, seasoned, arranged in pan with mushrooms, pieces of sweetbreads, and the tongue cut in thin slices, covered with a sauce Bourgignotte and a sprinkling of Parmesan cheese, baked half an hour; served with some of the sauce poured over, decorated with the slices of tongue, sprinkled with minced truffle peelings and parsley, garnished with sautéed oysters and the mushrooms.

BAKED CALF'S HEAD, SAUCE MAINTENON—Calf's head meat cut in slices, dipped in D'Uxelles sauce, then in cracker crumbs, then breaded and arranged in a buttered baking pan, brushed over with butter, baked till brown, served with a Maintenon sauce poured over. See SAUCES.

CALF'S HEAD WITH BACON AND PARSLEY SAUCE—Calf's head meat cut in slices and made hot in Velouté sauce containing chopped parsley; served with some of the sauce poured over, and garnished with two thin slices of boiled bacon or pork.

CALF'S HEAD AND TONGUE, PIQUANTE SAUCE—Slices of calf's head meat made hot in Piquante sauce; served with some of the sauce poured over, decorated with scallops of the tongue, and garnished with pieces of the brain breaded and fried.

CALF'S HEAD WITH FINANCIÈRE RAGOUT—Slices of calf's head meat arranged in a saûtoir with carrot, onion, parsley, bay leaves and cloves, moistened with consommé and sherry wine, quickly braised for an hour, meat taken up, the braise strained, skimmed and reduced to a glaze, then strained over the meat; served with a fancy croûton at ends of the dish, and garnished with cocks-combs and kernels, pieces of sweetbreads, mushrooms and small quenelles made hot in Madeira sauce.

CALF'S HEAD, SAUCE ITALIENNE—Calf's head meat in slices, made hot in brown Italian sauce; served with the sauce poured over, and garnished with fancy potatoes.

CALF'S HEAD AND BRAINS, MUSHROOM SAUCE—Slices of calf's head meat made hot in mushroom sauce; served with a slice of boiled brains on top, the brains decorated with slices of green pickles, garnished with button mushrooms, and sauce poured around.

CALF'S HEAD, SAUCE POULETTE—Slices of calf's head meat made hot in Poulette sauce; served garnished with balls of potatoes sprinkled with parsley and button mushrooms.

CALF'S HEAD, TURTLE STYLE—Calf's head meat cut in squares, made hot with stoned olives, button mushrooms, small forcemeat balls, and hard boiled yolks of eggs in equal parts of tomato and Madeira sauces; served surrounded with the garnish.

BRAISED CALF'S HEAD WITH VEAL QUENELLES—The meat prepared and braised the same as given for "with financière garnish"; served dipped in the glaze, and garnished with small quenelles of veal dipped in Ravigote sauce alternately with scallops of the tongue.

CALF'S HEAD FRIED, TOMATO SAUCE—Calf's head meat seasoned with salt, pepper and nutmeg, dipped in a mixture of four beaten eggs, yolks of two hard boiled eggs rubbed through a sieve or grater, and half a cup of melted butter, then breaded with grated fresh crumbs, or dipped in batter and fried; served with tomato sauce poured under.

CALF'S HEAD AND BRAINS, SAUCE POIVRADE—Prepared and fried same as the preceding in crumbs, Poivrade sauce poured under, and the ends of dish garnished with the brains cut small and mixed in a thick Ravigote sauce.

FRICASSÉE OF CALF'S HEAD WITH VEGETABLES—Calf's head meat

cut in slices with the tongue, made hot in a rich Allemande sauce, served with the sauce poured over and garnished with balls of carrot, turnip, potatoes and green peas that have been boiled separately in consommé with a little sugar.

BOILED CALF'S HEAD, SAUCE VINAIGRETTE—The meat and tongue cut in slices, made hot in white stock; served alternately with Vinaigrette sauce poured over and garnished with Hollandaise potatoes.

CALF'S HEAD WITH OLIVES, TOMATO SAUCE—Slices of calf's head meat simmered in tomato sauce; served with it, and garnished with stoned olives that have been blanched in consommé.

STUFFED CALF'S HEAD, SAUCE PAPILOTTE—Calf's head meat cut in portion pieces diamond shape, thickly spread with brain forcemeat (see BRAINS), arranged in a buttered baking pan, sprinkled with fresh breadcrumbs and butter, slightly moistened with stock, baked slowly till brown; served with a sauce Papilotte poured around the base.

RAGOUT OF CALF'S HEAD AND TONGUE—Same as "calf's head, turtle style," adding the tongue cut in scallops, and garnishing the ends of the dish with croûtons.

CALF'S HEAD CURRIED WITH RICE—Slices of the meat made hot in a good curry sauce, made either of the stock the head was boiled in, or veal, or chicken stock, a border of dry boiled rice arranged as a border on the dish, with the curried meat in the center.

OMELET WITH CALF'S HEAD—Four-fifths of beaten eggs, one-fifth of cold consommé, and the brains of the head cleaned, beaten to a pulp, little chopped parsley, salt, pepper and nutmeg, all mixed together; small squares of calf's head meat made hot in Madeira sauce; the omelet mixture fried in form, enclosing some of the meat in sauce, turned on to the dish, slit made in the top of the omelet, more meat put in; served with some of the meat and sauce poured around.

CALF'S HEAD SOUP WITH QUENELLES—The stock the head was boiled in and an equal quantity of chicken stock mixed, rice boiled in it till soft, then all rubbed through a purée sieve, the purée thus obtained mixed with an equal quantity of Suprême sauce and brought to the boil, calf's head meat in small squares, and some small quenelles of brain forcemeat added to the soup and served.

CALF'S HEAD SOUP, PORTUGUESE STYLE—The stock the head was boiled in strained into a good veal stock, in which is boiled a jardiniere of vegetables, some tomatoes and barley, thickened with roux; when nearly done, the calf's head meat and tongue with a little calf's liver blanched, all cut in small squares, added to the soup and served.

MOCK TURTLE SOUP, THICK—Sliced carrots, turnips, onions and

shallots sautéed in butter, then put in a saucepan with some browned veal and beef bones, a little vinegar, sweet basil, thyme, bay leaves, mace and whole cloves, fill up with stock, boil up, skimmed, then add a calf's head and boil it till tender; take it out when done, put it in cold water and remove the bones; thicken the stock with roux; into the soup tureen put the calf's head cut up small, some yolks of hard boiled eggs, slices of the white of egg, small quenelles of brain forcemeat, salt, pepper, lemon juice, chopped parsley and sherry wine, then strain the thickened stock into it and serve.

CLEAR MOCK TURTLE—A consommé made of veal and chicken stock in which has been boiled a calf's head and feet, the consommé flavored with essence of anchovies, sweet basil, mushroom catsup, a little curry powder and lemon peel; serve with small quenelles of brain forcemeat, the calf's head cut in dice, and finish with a little brandy.

CALF'S EARS BOILED, SAUCE VILLEROI—The ears cut off close to the head before the head is split for boiling, thoroughly washed, and boiled in white stock with vegetables and spices, taken up; served with Villeroi sauce poured over.

CALF'S EARS FRIED, TOMATO SAUCE—The ears boiled as above, then breaded and fried, retaining their shape as much as possible; served with tomato sauce poured around and garnished with slices of broiled tomatoes that have been sprinkled with cheese while broiling.

CALF'S EARS STUFFED, SAUCE BORDELAISE—The ears boiled not quite done, taken up, stuffed with a veal stuffing, smoothing the face from the opening to the tip, arranged in a saûtoir, moistened with consommé and simmered till done; served with Bordelaise sauce poured over and around.

CALF'S EARS, TURTLE STYLE—The ears boiled and left whole, then made hot with whole-stoned olives, button mushrooms, small forcemeat balls of the brains, and hard boiled yolks of eggs in equal parts of tomato and Madeira sauces; served, the yolk of egg in the opening of the ear, and surrounded with the garnish.

RAGOUT OF CALF'S EARS IN CROÛSTADES—Calf's ears boiled till tender, cut in small squares, sautéed in butter with mushrooms, stoned olives, pieces of brains and tongue, but the ears predominating; when colored, surplus butter drained off, moistened with Madeira sauce, filled into paste croûstades and served.

CALF'S EARS WITH TRUFFLES, SAUCE TRIANON—The ears boiled and left whole, the part just below the tip studded with pieces of diamond-shaped truffle and the opening of the ear with a whole glazed truffle; arranged in a saûtoir with a very little consommé, the ears brushed over with glaze, made hot, and served with a Trianon sauce poured around.

CALF'S BRAINS—For the several recipes of which see heading of BRAINS.

CALF'S FEET—The hoof is split with a knife, then treated the same as calf's head; when done, the bones removed, and the meat pressed between boards.

FRICASSÉE OF CALF'S FEET—The cold meat cut in neat shaped pieces, made hot in Pascaline sauce; served garnished with button mushrooms and small Victoria potatoes.

CALF'S FEET BOILED, POIVRADE SAUCE—Neatly trimmed pieces of the cold meat made hot in white stock; served with Poivrade sauce poured over and garnished with fancy croûtons.

FRIED CALF'S FEET IN BATTER, ITALIAN SAUCE—Cold cooked feet, seasoned with salt, pepper and lemon juice, dipped in plain batter, fried; served with brown Italian sauce poured around, and garnished with small potato croquettes.

CALF'S FEET STEAMED, SAUCE REMOULADE—Slices of the cold meat steamed; served with Remoulade sauce poured over and garnished with Hollandaise potatoes.

CALF'S FEET WITH MUSHROOMS, SAUCE POULETTE—Squares of cold meat made hot in Poulette sauce; served with the sauce, and garnished with button mushrooms that have been lightly fried in butter.

CROÛSTADES OF CALF'S FEET—Small squares of the cold meat made hot in a sauce prepared from the stock they were boiled in, brought to a simmer, then is added some finely minced yolks of eggs, a little dry mustard, salt, red pepper, white wine and lemon juice, quickly reduced, filled into paste croûstades and served.

CALF'S FEET CREPINETTES, SAUCE PROVENÇALE—The cold meat of the feet cut up small, seasoned with salt, pepper, lemon juice and nutmeg, mixed with an equal quantity of veal or pork sausage meat, made into shapes of small Hamburg steaks, broiled; served with Provençale sauce poured around.

CALF'S FEET JELLY—Raw cleaned calf's feet chopped up, put to boil in cold water with a stick of cinnamon and the rind of a lemon, boiled till soft, and the liquor well reduced, strain, allowed to get cold, then all fat and skimmings removed, the liquor which should have become like jelly then put back into a bright kettle with some beaten whites of eggs, sugar to taste, little white wine and lemon juice, brought slowly to the boil without stirring, then allowed to simmer till the coagulation turns a grey color, about twenty minutes, then strained and re-strained through a jelly bag; when nearly cool, filled into glasses or molds, and served when set and cold.

CALF'S HEART STUFFED, MADEIRA SAUCE—The hearts soaked and the veins cut away, put in boiling water and simmered for ten minutes, then refreshed in cold water, taken up and wiped dry, the cavity made and filled with a poultry stuffing, crust of bread tied over the opening to keep the stuffing in, roasted and basted with gravy till done; served split in halves, dressing side up, with Madeira sauce poured around and garnished with croûtons.

CALF'S HEART STUFFED AND BRAISED—Prepare, and stuffed as above, but the opening covered and tied with a slice of salt pork; arranged in a saûtoir with slices of carrot, onions, parsley, bay leaves and whole cloves, moistened with stock, braised and basted till tender, taken up, the braise strained, skimmed and added to a Madeira sauce, reduced to a half glaze; the heart served cut in halves with some of the glaze poured round the edges, and garnished with Parisienne potatoes.

CALF'S HEART LARDED, SAUCE ANDALOUSE—The top of the heart larded with strips of seasoned larding pork, then prepared and stuffed, arranged in a saûtoir and braised as in the preceding recipe; served, the whole heart, point upwards with Andalusian sauce poured over, and garnished at the ends with a macedoine of vegetables.

CALF'S KIDNEYS LARDED, MADEIRA SAUCE—The kidneys blanched for a few minutes, then freshened in cold water and afterwards wiped dry, larded with seasoned strips of pork, arranged in a saûtoir with a dash of tarragon vinegar, powdered mixed herbs, melted butter and consommé, quickly braised and glazed; served on a bed of mashed potatoes with Madeira sauce poured around.

BROCHETTE OF CALF'S KIDNEYS— See receipe under head of BROCHETTE.

CALF'S KIDNEYS BROILED, PARSLEY BUTTER—The kidneys blanched and cooled, then cut in two lengthwise, seasoned with salt and pepper, dipped in melted butter, rolled in fresh breadcrumbs, broiled till done; served on toast with maître d'hôtel butter poured over them, and garnished with cress and lemon.

CALF'S KIDNEYS SAUTÉED WITH MUSHROOMS—The kidneys lightly blanched and refreshed, cut in small slices, sautéed with minced onion and sliced button mushrooms; when done, sprinkled with parsley, salt, pepper and a dash of tarragon vinegar, moistened with a little Colbert sauce and served on a toast garnished with fancy croûtons.

PATTIES OF CALF'S KIDNEYS—Puff paste patty shells filled with the preceding, sauté, but having the kidneys cut in very small dice.

RAGOUT OF CALF'S KIDNEYS—Kidneys cut about the same size as button mushrooms, sautéed in butter with mushrooms and minced shallots with a clove of garlic; when browned, put into a Bordelaise sauce and simmered for a few minutes; served, a border of potato croquette mixture forced through a fancy tube, sprinkled with chopped parsley, and the ragout in the center.

CALF'S KIDNEYS CROQUETTES WITH PEAS—Cold braised kidneys (see CALF'S KIDNEYS LARDED, MADEIRA SAUCE), minced and seasoned, made hot in a thick Madeira sauce, turned into a pan to cool, smoothed with a knife, covered with a buttered paper; when cold, cut in pieces, formed into croquettes of the desired shape, breaded, fried, and served with green peas at the ends of the dish and Madeira sauce poured around, the croquettes decorated with a frill.

CALF'S KIDNEYS FRIED, SAUCE COLBERT—The kidneys split lengthwise and seasoned with salt and pepper, rolled in flour, then fried in butter; served on toast with Colbert sauce poured over; garnished with croûtons.

CALF'S KIDNEYS IN CROÛSTADES—Broiled kidneys and cold boiled ham both cut into small dice; minced mushrooms fried in butter, then drained and added to the meats with a little chopped parsley, all mixed, moistened with Béchamel sauce, made hot, filled into croûstades and served.

CALF'S KIDNEY OMELET—The mixture given for "Patties of Calf's Kidneys," the omelet made of beaten eggs, chopped chives, parsley, salt, pepper and nutmeg, enclosing some of the kidneys, and served with more of the meat in sauce poured around.

CALF'S LIVER WITH CRISPED ONIONS—The liver trimmed from veins, larded through with seasoned strips of bacon, placed in a saûtoir with bacon trimmings, little consommé and sherry wine, cover put on, and roasted till done and glazy, liver taken up, brown sauce added to the residue of the saûtoir, boiled, skimmed and strained, liver served in slices with the gravy and garnished with rings of onions that have been dipped in milk, rolled in flour and fried in hot fat.

CALF'S LIVER SAUTÉ WITH BACON—Slices of liver and bacon, the bacon fried first, then the liver seasoned and rolled in flour, fried in bacon fat; when done, flour added to the pan, stirred, and moistened with stock, boiled up, strained, skimmed, juice of lemon added; the liver served with some of the gravy and garnished with the bacon.

CALF'S LIVER STEWED WITH ONIONS—Green spring onions chopped and fried in bacon fat in a saûtoir, liver cut small and put with the onions and tossed over a quick fire till set, superfluous fat then poured off, flour stirred in, moistened with stock, seasoned with salt and pepper, simmered till tender; served garnished with a border of Victoria potatoes.

BRAISED CALF'S LIVER WITH VEGETABLES—The liver trimmed from veins, larded with seasoned strips of bacon, placed in a saûtoir with some bacon trimmings, carrot, onion, parsley, bay leaves and whole cloves, moistened with consommé and sherry wine, covered with a sheet of buttered paper, lid put on, braised till tender, taken up, sauce added to the braise, boiled up, strained and skimmed; the liver served in slices and garnished with balls of carrot, turnip and small glazed onions.

CALF'S LIVER FRIED WITH FINE HERBS—Slices of the liver seasoned with salt and pepper, rolled in flour, fried in bacon fat with minced chives and shallots, taken up, grease poured off, fines herbes sauce added to the pan, boiled up, served with the liver.

CALF'S LIVER BROILED, ITALIAN SAUCE—Slices of liver seasoned with salt and pepper, rolled in flour, dipped in melted butter, broiled till done; served with brown Italian sauce poured around and garnished with chip potatoes.

SCALLOPS OF CALF'S LIVER WITH MUSHROOMS—Small pieces of liver seasoned and fried in bacon fat, taken up and put into a brown Italian sauce, simmered for a few minutes, served with a border of fried button mushrooms.

CALF'S LIVER AND BACON WITH SPINACH—The liver larded and braised, the bacon boiled tender, the spinach boiled in the bacon water, drained, pressed, chopped fine and seasoned with salt and pepper; served, the spinach as a bed, the liver and bacon in slices alternately on top, with some of the gravy from the braising poured around.

BROCHETTE OF CALF'S LIVER WITH BACON—See recipe under heading of BROCHETTE.

CALF'S LIVER WITH SMOTHERED ONIONS—The liver in slices, sea-soned, floured and fried, the onions sliced and steamed for a few minutes, then put in a sautoir with bacon fat and smothered a light brown over a quick fire; the liver served garnished with the onions.

LIVER CHEESE, ITALIAN STYLE—Calf's liver four-fifths, salt pork one-fifth, finely minced with a few shallots, seasoned with salt and pepper, nutmeg, powdered thyme and sherry wine; bread pans lined with thin slices of bacon, the liver mince filled in, with slices of bacon and bay leaves on top, covered with buttered paper and slowly baked till done (about three hours); served either cold in slices, or between bread as sandwiches, or in slices hot, with Italian sauce poured over.

LIVER FORCEMEAT BALLS—Made the same as "liver cheese" above, but adding some breadcrumbs, raw yolks of eggs and chopped parsley; when thoroughly mixed, made into balls and poached till done in white stock; served with a Hollandaise sauce. The Germans call this dish Liver Klosse.

TIMBALE OF CALF'S LIVER, PI-QUANT SAUCE—The "liver cheese" above filled into timbale molds, and steamed or baked till done; served with Piquant sauce poured over.

CALF'S LIVER QUENELLES IN CRUMBS—The "forcemeat" mixture above, shaped like eggs between two spoons, poached, taken up, and rolled in fried breadcrumbs; served garnished with parsley and lemon, and Allemande sauce served separately.

POTTED CALF'S LIVER WITH ASPIC JELLY—Slices of liver fried in bacon fat with minced onions and mushrooms, taken up and pounded to a paste with wine, powdered mixed herbs, salt, pepper and nutmeg, then rubbed through a fine sieve with its equal weight of fat bacon; into this purée is then mixed a minced clove of garlic, some ham and bacon fat cut in small dice; when thoroughly incorporated, filled into bread pans, covered with thick buttered paper, the filled pans put into roasting pans containing cold water half way up, put in oven and slowly baked till done (about two hours), taken out, allowed to partly cool, then turned out, trimmed; served cold in slices, decorated with aspic jelly.

CALF'S TONGUE BRAISED, TOMATO SAUCE—The tongues blanched and freshened, then larded with strips of seasoned larding pork, arranged in saûtoir with carrot, onion, parsley, bay leaves and whole cloves, moistened with stock, braised and glazed; served in slices cut lengthwise, with tomato sauce.

CALF'S TONGUE SAUTÉ, VINAIGRETTE—The tongues blanched, freshened and skinned, then cut lengthwise in slices, sautéed in butter with minced shallots; served with sauce Vinaigrette.

CALF'S TONGUE, SAUCE TARTARE—The braised tongues above, allowed to become cold; served in slices with Tartar sauce, garnished with strips of pickles.

CALF'S TONGUE FRIED, SAUCE ROBERT—The tongue boiled with vegetables, herbs and spices, skinned, cut lengthwise in slices, breaded, fried; served with a Robert sauce poured under.

CALF'S TONGUE WITH POTATOES, MUSHROOM SAUCE—The tongues boiled and skinned as in the preceding recipe, then cut in long slices, dipped in glaze, arranged on a bed of mashed potatoes, with mushroom sauce poured around.

CALF'S SWEETBREADS BROILED, SAUCE COLBERT—The sweetbreads soaked in cold salted water for a few hours, then boiled with a few whole spices, bay leaves, vegetables and a dash of vinegar till tender, taken up, put into cold water and all rough fat and skin removed, then pressed between boards till cold (for the following recipes the above directions will be called "prepared"), when cold split in slices, dipped in melted butter, then in seasoned breadcrumbs, broiled; served with Colbert sauce poured around. They may also be served with maître d'hôtel butter, and garnished with fancy potatoes.

CALF'S SWEETBREADS SAUTÉED WITH PEAS—Prepared sweetbreads split and sautéed in butter; served on a bed of mashed potatoes, with green peas in sauce poured around.

CALF'S SWEETBREADS IN CREAM, ON TOAST—Prepared sweetbreads

cut in slices crosswise, made hot in reduced cream; served on toast, sprinkled with finely chopped parsley, with some of the cream poured around.

CALF'S SWEETBREADS FRIED, SAUCE PERIGUEUX—Prepared sweetbreads split, seasoned with salt, pepper and nutmeg, dipped in flour, then in beaten eggs, fried a golden color; served with Perigueux sauce, and garnished with fancy croûtons.

CALF'S SWEETBREADS WITH BROWN BUTTER—Prepared sweetbreads split, seasoned with salt, pepper and powdered herbs rolled in flour, fried in butter; served with brown butter, made by melting butter to the frothing point, then adding lemon juice and chopped parsley; poured over the sweetbreads on hot dish.

CALF'S SWEETBREAD CROQUETTES WITH PEAS—Prepared sweetbreads cut into small dice, mixed with half the amount of grated boiled ham, a few minced sautéed shallots and mushrooms, thoroughly heated in a thick Velouté sauce, seasoned with lemon juice and nutmeg, poured into a buttered shallow pan, smoothed with a knife, covered with buttered paper; when cold, cut into pieces of an equal size, shaped, breaded, fried, served with green peas in white sauce or half glaze as a border, with frills in the croquettes.

RISSOLES OF CALF'S SWEETBREADS WITH VEGETABLES—The croquette mixture above, when cold, cut out and formed into balls, size of small egg; two sheets of puff paste rolled out, the balls put in sections all over one, covered with the other, edges pressed down, then stamped out with a fancy cutter, arranged on a baking sheet, washed over, baked; served garnished with a macedoine of vegetables in brown sauce.

RISSOLETTES—The same as rissoles, but smaller.

CALF'S SWEETBREADS IN SHELL—The croquette mixture above, filled into buttered scallop shells, sprinkled with grated breadcrumbs and melted butter, browned in the oven and served, (called Sweetbreads en Coquille).

SCALLOPED CALF'S SWEETBREADS—The same as the preceding, with the addition of grated Parmesan cheese mixed with the breadcrumbs; served in the shell (called Sweetbreads en Coquille au Gratin).

PATTIES OF SCRAMBLED CALF'S SWEETBREADS—Prepared sweetbreads cut into small dice, seasoned with salt, pepper, lemon juice and chopped parsley, mixed into beaten eggs with a little cream, scrambled in butter but kept soft (best when scrambled to order), filled into hot patty shells and served with a little Velouté sauce poured around.

CUTLETS OF CALF'S SWEETBREADS WITH VEGETABLES—The croquette mixture (see Calf's Sweetbread Croquettes with Peas) when cold, cut out and shaped like small lamb chops, with a piece of macaroni to represent the bone, breaded and fried; served with a border of Julienne vegetables mixed into Hollandaise sauce (called Sweetbread Cutlets à la Nivernaise).

CALF'S SWEETBREADS WITH FINANCIÈRE RAGOUT—Prepared sweetbreads split and seasoned with salt, pepper and nutmeg, rolled in flour, sautéed in butter, taken up, kept hot in glaze, served on fancy croûtons surrounded with a garnish of cock's combs and kernels, button mushrooms, small quenelles and truffles, all made hot in a rich Madeira sauce (called Sweetbread Sauté à la Financière).

CALF'S SWEETBREADS IN CASES—Prepared sweetbreads cut in small dice, seasoned with salt and red pepper, made hot in Velouté sauce, filled into paper cases, sprinkled with fresh breadcrumbs and melted butter, arranged on a baking sheet and very quickly browned in the oven or with a salamander and served.

VOL-AU-VENT OF SWEETBREADS AND MUSHROOMS—The preceding with the addition of an equal quantity of cut and sautéed mushrooms, filled into a good sized puff paste patty shell with a cover placed on and served.

TIMBALE OF CALF'S SWEETBREADS—Prepared sweetbreads larded and braised, allowed to become cold, then cut in thin slices. A rich forcemeat of cooked chicken and mushrooms well seasoned, the sweetbreads and forcemeat filled into timbale molds in alternate layers; when full, moistened with the reduced and strained braise, the opening covered with the same short paste as the molds are lined with, baked, turned out; served with a Madeira sauce containing a little chopped parsley and some mushroom tops, poured over and around.

BOUCHÉES OF CALF'S SWEETBREADS—For recipe see heading of BOUCHÉES.

BROCHETTE OR ATTEREAUX OF CALF'S SWEETBREADS—For recipe see BROCHETTE.

BRAISED CALF'S SWEETBREADS, GARNISHED—Prepared sweetbreads larded with seasoned strips of bacon, then arranged in a saûtoir on a bed of thinly sliced vegetables, with bay leaves and one or two cloves, covered with thin slices of bacon, moistened with stock, covered with buttered paper, lid put on and braised quickly for half an hour with frequent basting; when done, the lid, paper and bacon removed, then put back into the oven to dry the glaze on top of the sweetbreads, taken up, the braise strained and skimmed, then poured to a mixture of diced red tongue, truffles, mushrooms and chicken breast, little Madeira wine and sauce then added; the sweetbreads served on toast surrounded with the garnish (called Sweetbreads Braised à la Montglas).

GLAZED CALF'S SWEETBREADS WITH FRENCH BEANS—Prepared sweetbreads larded and braised as in the preceding, the braise strained, skimmed and mixed with green French beans (haricot verts), the sweetbreads served surrounded with the beans.

CALF'S SWEETBREADS WITH DEMIGLACÉ—Prepared sweetbreads larded and braised as (see Braised Calf's Sweetbreads, Garnished), when done the braise strained over them, reduced with a little Madeira sauce and wine; served on toast rolled in glaze, and garnished.

CALF'S SWEETBREADS LARDED AND BRAISED, MUSHROOM SAUCE—Same as "Braised Calf's Sweetbreads Garnished," the braise strained into a rich mushroom sauce, the sweetbreads served surrounded with the mushrooms in sauce.

CALF'S SWEETBREADS LARDED, SAUCE TOULOUSE—Prepared sweetbreads larded and braised, served with asparagus points at one end, green peas at the other end of the dish, with Toulouse sauce at the sides.

BLANQUETTE OF CALF'S SWEETBREADS—Slices of prepared sweetbreads made hot in a light colored Allemande sauce, served with it and decorated on the top with slices of truffles.

CASSEROLE OF CALF'S SWEETBREADS—Slices of prepared sweetbreads and mushrooms made hot in Velouté sauce, the serving dish containing a high border of potato croquette mixture glazed and browned, the sweetbreads filled

into the centre, sprinkled with minced truffle peelings and served.

FRICANDEAU OF SWEETBREADS WITH CHICORY—Prepared sweetbreads larded and braised as in "Braised Calf's Sweetbreads, Garnished," when done the braise strained, skimmed, then poured over the sweetbreads and reduced to a glaze; served on a bed of purée of chicory or spinach, with a rich Madeira sauce poured around.

CROÛSTADE OF CURRIED CALF'S SWEETBREADS—Prepared sweetbreads split and then sliced, made hot in a good curry sauce prepared from the stock they were boiled in, filled into paste croûstade cases, served two cases full alternately with small turned-out molds of dry boiled rice.

CALF'S SWEETBREADS FRIED, MUSHROOM SAUCE—Prepared sweetbreads split, seasoned with salt, pepper and nutmeg, rolled in flour, dipped into beaten eggs, fried in hot fat, served surrounded with button mushrooms in a Madeira sauce.

RAGOUT OF CALF'S SWEETBREADS ON TOAST—Prepared sweetbreads split and then cut in slices, mixed with half the amount of sliced mushrooms, made hot in a Madeira sauce, served piled on toast with the sauce around, garnished with fancy croûtons whose ends are dipped in sauce, then in chopped parsley.

SWEETBREADS AND TRUFFLES IN SHELL—Prepared sweetbreads cut

in slices, mixed with slices of truffles and mushrooms, made hot in a thick Allemande sauce, filled into scallop shells, sprinkled with breadcrumbs and melted butter, browned in the oven or with a salamander, and served.

STEWED CALF'S SWEETBREADS WITH KIDNEY BEANS—Prepared sweetbreads split, and made hot in Velouté sauce containing minced shallots, whole mace, pieces of bacon and sweet herbs for half an hour, taken up, a liaison of egg yolks and cream then beaten into the sauce and strained over the sweetbreads; served garnished with sautéed kidney beans (flageolets) at ends, sauce at the sides.

CALF'S SWEETBREADS WITH CREAMED MUSHROOMS—Prepared sweetbreads cut in slices and sautéed in butter piled on toast; served surrounded with sliced mushrooms boiled down in reduced cream.

RAGOUT OF CALF'S SWEETBREADS WITH MORELS—Prepared sweetbreads cut in slices and sautéed in butter, then mixed into a rich Madeira sauce; served on toast, surrounded with sliced morels that have been fried in their own oil.

BRAISED CALF'S SWEETBREADS WITH SORREL—Prepared sweetbreads larded and braised as in "Braised Calf's Sweetbreads, Garnished"; served on a bed of purée of sorrel, with some of the strained and skimmed glaze poured over and around.

KROMESKIES OF CALF'S SWEET-BREADS—The croquette mixture (see Calf's Sweetbread Croquettes with Peas) when cold, cut out and shaped like long corks, then rolled into a thin slice of cold boiled bacon, pinned with a toothpick, dipped into a plain batter and fried, toothpick then removed; served with a rich Velouté sauce poured around.

CALF'S SWEETBREADS FRIED, SAUCE VILLEROI—Prepared sweetbreads split and coated with cold Villeroi sauce, then rolled in breadcrumbs, beaten eggs and again breadcrumbs, fried; served with Villeroi sauce poured around, and the ends of dish garnished with green peas that have been sautéed in butter.

FRICASSÉE OF SWEETBREADS AND MUSHROOMS—Prepared sweetbreads split and simmered in sauce Albert, served with it, and garnished with button mushrooms that have been lightly fried in butter and sprinkled with chopped parsley.

BRAISED SWEETBREADS, SAUCE BEARNAISE—Prepared sweetbreads larded and braised (as in Braised Calf's Sweetbreads, Garnished); served decorated at the ends and sides with slices of truffles, and with Bearnaise sauce poured around.

SAUTÉ OF CALF'S SWEETBREADS WITH BAKED TOMATOES—Prepared sweetbreads split, rolled in flour, sautéed in butter with minced shallots, strips of green peppers and a crushed clove of garlic; when browned, equal parts of tomato and Napolitaine sauces added, simmered ten minutes, taken up, sauce strained over them. Served with some of the sauce and garnished with small stuffed and baked tomatoes.

SWEETBREADS BREADED, SAUCE TARTARE—Prepared sweetbreads split and spread on both sides with Tartar sauce, rolled in crumbs, then breaded and fried; served with Tartar sauce served separately, and garnished with lemon and parsley.

EPIGRAMME OF SWEETBREADS, SAUCE BÉCHAMEL—Prepared sweetbreads split and trimmed to a cutlet shape, half of them dipped in cooling Béchamel sauce and when cold rolled in breadcrumbs, then breaded and fried, the other half made hot in rich white stock, then taken up and dipped in glaze, then coated with Béchamel sauce; served, one of each, surrounded with scallops of red tongue and sliced mushrooms in Béchamel sauce.

SCALLOPS OF SWEETBREADS WITH TOULOUSE RAGOUT—Prepared sweetbreads cut in slices, then cut circular with large sized column cutter, dipped in cooling Allemande sauce, then in breadcrumbs, afterwards breaded and fried a golden color in butter; served overlapping each other round the dish, the centre filled with cocks combs and kernels, truffles cut in small squares, the trimmings of the sweetbreads, and button mushrooms all made hot in Allemande sauce.

SCALLOPS OF SWEETBREADS WITH POTATO CROQUETTES—The sweet-

breads cut and fried as in the preceding recipe, served overlapping each other around the dish, the centre filled with small potato cone-shaped croquettes, the points being dipped in white sauce, then in chopped parsley, with a sauce Poulette around their base.

LARDED SWEETBREADS WITH TOULOUSE RAGOUT—Prepared sweetbreads larded through from top to bottom with alternate strips of red tongue and truffles, so that they resemble a studding; braised as in "Braised Calf's Sweetbreads, Garnished"; served surrounded with a Toulouse ragout as given in "Scallops of Sweetbreads with Toulouse Ragout."

SWEETBREAD SALAD—Slices of prepared sweetbread dipped in flour and fried in butter, allowed to become cold, shredded lettuce in centre of the dish with cream salad dressing, sweetbreads masked with mayonnaise arranged around the lettuce, the lettuce decorated with alternate slices of radishes and stamped pieces of pickled beet.

SWEETBREAD SOUP—Minced ham and onions with prepared sweetbreads and a bunch of sweet herbs slowly sautéed in butter for an hour, then flour added to form a paste, this then rubbed through a fine sieve, the purée then worked into a good veal or chicken stock, boiled up and skimmed, seasoned with salt, pepper, and a little sugar; served with small croûtons browned in the oven (called Potage à la Comtesse).

CALIPEE AND CALIPASH—The first is the name given to the meat attached to the lower, and the last to the meat attached to upper shells of a turtle.

CAMEMBERT—Name of an imported cheese, put up in round flat boxes like brie. Is in its prime when just soft and creamy with an inclination to run; served in small quantities with toasted crackers.

CAMEMBERT—All of the above is true (but see BRIE). Camembert is a relatively new creation, said to have been invented at the time of the French Revolution by an enterprising Norman woman who lived in the village of Camembert and combined the cheese-making techniques of Normandy with those of Brie, a town in the Île-de-France. As with almost all cheeses, the authentic farmhouse type of Camembert (*Camembert fermier*) is best; it is made only in Normandy and is best bought there.

Commercial Camembert, on the other hand, is manufactured all over the world. Its texture should be firm, but the middle of the cheese should yield to light pressure. The aroma should be slightly moldy but completely devoid of ammonia, a sure sign of an overripe cheese, as is an excessively sagging center or a reddish-brown rind.

CANAPÉS—A French term literally meaning a "couch," used in a culinary sense as a bed or something to rest savory foods on, usually in the form of bread or toast covered with minces, pastes, etc., then decorated.

CANAPÉS—Anything spread upon crustless toast (or bread) that has been cut into shapes qualifies as a canapé.

ANCHOVY CANAPÉS—Hard boiled eggs and anchovies finely minced and spread on buttered toast. Also, very shallow gem pans lined with pie paste and baked, then filled when cold with anchovies pounded to a paste with Gruyère cheese, inverted on a circle of buttered toast and garnished with minced gherkins. Also, a mixture of chopped anchovies, grated ham, truffles and gherkins mixed and moistened with salad oil and caper vinegar, then filled into very small patty cases; served garnished with pieces of toast and aspic jelly.

CANAPÉS BERNE, OR SWISS CANAPÉS—Triangle-shaped pieces of toast spread with anchovy butter, decorated with minced whites of eggs down one side, yolks on the other, and the third with minced green gherkins, and a stuffed olive in the centre.

CANAPÉS OF CRAB—Circles of toast spread with deviled crab meat, sprinkled with Parmesan cheese and browned in the oven (called Canapé Lorenzo).

CANAPÉS OF SMOKED SALMON—Strips of toast spread with anchovy butter, a thin circle of smoked salmon on top, the edges decorated with hard boiled eggs minced and mixed with chopped parsley.

CANAPÉS OF CHICKEN LIVERS—Chicken livers sautéed with an onion till tender, then pounded to a paste with a dash of anchovy essence, salt, red pepper and butter, piled in pyramid form on fried shapes of bread, smoothed with a knife and made hot in the oven; served decorated with slices of pimentoes and rings of red chillies.

CANAPÉS OF SHRIMPS—Fancy shaped slices of toast spread with shrimp paste and decorated with coiled shrimps.

CANAPÉS OF POTTED TONGUE—Circles of brown bread toast spread with potted tongue and decorated in lattice form with strips of red cooked tongue.

INDIAN CANAPÉS—Circles of bread fried in butter, spread first with potted ham, then with chutney, strewed with Parmesan cheese, browned in the oven and served.

CANAPÉS OF POTTED HAM—Strips of toast spread with potted ham, then sprinkled with grated ham, decorated with thin slices of green gherkins.

SARDINE CANAPÉS — Triangle-shaped pieces of toast spread with a mixture of equal parts of boiled egg yolks and sardines pounded to a paste and seasoned with red pepper and lemon juice, decorated with a coiled anchovy out of oil in the centre.

CANAPÉS OF CAVIAR—Circles of toast, the edges spread with anchovy butter, with an onion ring as its base, the ring filled with Russian caviar.

OLIVE CANAPÉS—Circles of buttered toast with a coiled anchovy on them, and a stuffed olive in the centre of the coil. Also circles of toast fried in butter, then spread with anchovy paste, minced olives and capers on top.

CANAPÉ CHASSEUR — Triangle shaped pieces of toast spread with a game forcemeat, the edges decorated with another forcemeat of game but of different color.

CANAPÉS OF OYSTERS—Strips of toast spread with blanched and minced oysters mixed into a Hollandaise sauce, sprinkled with parsley dust. Clams may be treated the same way and named accordingly.

SAVORY CANAPÉS—Strips of toast spread with a mixture of grated ham, cheese, cream sauce and scrambled eggs, the edges decorated with lobster coral.

CANAPÉ MADISON—Slices of toast on which is laid a thin slice of lean ham spread with French mustard, this again is spread with a cold white sauce containing minced cooked onions, garlic, and cheese; Parmesan cheese is then dredged on top, sprinkled with fine breadcrumbs, baked and served.

CHICKEN CANAPÉS — Circles of toast spread with chicken forcemeat in which is worked cream and butter, dredged with Parmesan cheese and baked, then decorated in the centre with a stamped piece of white of egg.

CREOLE CANAPÉS—Grated lean ham, onion, garlic and chopped parsley with pieces of peeled tomatoes and minced green peppers, seasoned with salt and pepper, stewed down dry, then spread on strips of buttered toast, dredged with Parmesan cheese and baked.

SCOTCH CANAPÉS — Breast of chicken, red tongue and lean ham all cut into very small dice, seasoned with nutmeg and a little curry powder, then worked into a thick Velouté sauce, spread on slices of toast, dredged with Parmesan cheese and baked (also called Canapé Aberdeen).

CANAPÉ WINDSOR—Strips of toast spread with a forcemeat of any kind of white fleshed fish, seasoned with mustard and Worcestershire sauce, dredged with Parmesan cheese and baked.

CANAPÉ CABILLAUD — Triangle shaped pieces of toast spread with a forcemeat made of boiled salt codfish, mixed with minced green peppers and spring onions seasoned with tarragon vinegar, decorated with capers.

MADRAS CANAPÉS — Circles of toast spread with a mixture of finely minced white fleshed fish, Madras chutney and sweet pickles, moistened with Hollandaise sauce, dredged with Parmesan cheese and baked (also called Canapé Winchester).

CHEESE CANAPÉS—Strips of bread hollowed out half their thickness, then toasted, the inner part sprayed with Worcestershire sauce, the cavity then fitted with a slice of Swiss cheese, baked, and served very hot.

CANARD—French name for wild duck. Caneton for domestic duck or duckling.

CANNED GOODS—The following quotation clipped from *The Sanitarian* is given for the reader to form his own views:

"Under one heading we may consider several groups of foodstuffs, which, while different in composition, are alike in the form of adulteration which is resorted to. These groups include the varieties of canned vegetables, fruit butters, jellies, preserves and catsups. The forms of adulterations, common to all of these, consist in the use of coloring matter, of imperfect vegetables or fruits, of other vegetables and fruits than those called for of preservatives. In the case of canned vegetables, there is an accidental adulteration from the ingredients of the can, such as lead and tin, and which may, as a rule, be attributed to a lack of care in canning. In all the groups mentioned, the adulteration practised is one of the most flagrant and extensive kind. Catsups are made of skins and cores instead of the pure vegetables, then colored with a coal tar product and loaded with salicylic acid to prevent fermentation. Fruit butters are nothing but parings and scrapings of fruit, to which glucose, starch and colorings have been added, with salicylic acid as a preservative. Jellies are made from glucose, flavored with essential oils and colored, to which salicylic acid is added. Some fruit jellies marked as pure, have never seen a trace of fruit. What is true of jellies is true of preserves. Put together refuse material, the cheapest sort of glucose, some coloring and salicylic acid, and you have the composition of some of the cheaper forms of preserves that are to be found on the shelves of some of our grocery stores. Of these coarser forms of adulterations it will be unnecessary to say even a word; they are universally recognized as being unfit for use and every honest dealer is of the opinion that the sooner they are driven out of the market the better it will be for trade."

CANNED GOODS—Presumably, the unmentionable "coarser forms of adulterations" of canned goods have been discontinued, for the most part at least. In recent years there have been increasing numbers of first-rate canned goods—most notably condiments such as jams, vinegars, mustards, and the like—appearing on the shelves of specialty stores and even supermarkets. Thankfully, the universal use of refrigerator and freezer, and the year-round availability of many foods that once were available for only a short time each year, have made this country far less dependent upon canned goods than it was in Charles Fellows's time.

CANNELONS—Name given to hollow lengths of noodle or puff paste made by twining strips of the paste around a piece of pipe or tubing, then either baked or fried, the pipe removed, the cannelons may then be filled with forcemeats, croquette mixtures, creams, preserves, etc.

CANTELOUPES—Are of different kinds in our markets; although the

"Nutmeg" is pronounced the best, many have a distinct fancy for the "Osage" with its thick yellow fruit. In selecting the nutmegs, those which have a thick broad cording on the rind, and with the section marks inclined to a yellow color, will be found the best fruit. To be served they are first kept on ice, then scrubbed or washed, split in halves lengthwise, pith and seeds removed, and the cavity filled with small broken ice; eaten by some with powdered sugar, by others with salt and pepper.

CANTALOUPES—Some Americans still *do* eat cantaloupes (technically known as muskmelon, and closely related to cucumbers and squash) with salt and pepper or sugar; lemon, cottage cheese, and ice cream are more common adornments. But most people choose to eat melon plain or in fruit salads. Few of us consider the variety of cantaloupe we are eating, however, since we tend to buy them in the supermarket and worry more about their ripeness and their price.

The supermarket cantaloupe is no more than a commercial representation of the glorious group of fruit that is the reserve of the home gardener. For, like the tomato, the vine-ripened melon is in every way superior to that that is picked before it is mature. Ambrosia, Charentais, and Old-time Tennessee are all cantaloupes that are terrific options for gardeners, and should not be passed up when seen at summer fruit stands.

CAPERCAILZIE—A game bird of the grouse species, the male bird differing greatly from the hen in that it attains to twice the size, has dark brown wings, and a dark greeny gold neck, while the hen in appearance and plumage is very like a prairie hen. This bird must always be hung for a week or so to become tender; it may then be cooked in all the ways of prairie chickens.

CAPERS—Are a berry of a plant cultivated in Europe and not in America; are spoken of in the bible as "hyssop." They are imported here in five sizes: "Nonpareils," "Capotes," "Capuchins," "Seconds" and "Thirds," in bottles and in bulk, the latter way being the cheapest for hotel use. Capers, however, are often mixed by unscrupulous dealers with "nasturtium" berries which resemble them in size and appearance. The caper is only used for making sauces, or in garnishing.

CAPERS—In fact, capers are not berries but the immature flower buds of the *Capparis spinosa,* a gangly, roselike bush that grows wild all over the Mediterranean. Eaten fresh off the bush, capers are not especially flavorful. But picked daily—they must be harvested at just the proper size—dried in the sun, and packed in salty vinegar, their pungent, barnyard flavor is not only enjoyable but unique. Traditionally capers were served with boiled mutton, but today they are perhaps better appreciated in salad dressings and with meat and fish dishes, whether poached or sautéed.

CAPONS—Are young fowls that have been sterilized, secluded and fattened, which improves the delicacy and flavor of their flesh, and also allows them to grow to a much larger size. They are best in the fall of the year. The city of Philadel-phia seems to have got the name of producing the best, and when placed on the bill of fare, no matter what part of the country, are generally designated, "Philadelphia Capon."

CAPONS—A capon is a rooster that has been surgically castrated, an unappealing-sounding process with a fortuitous result. The hormonal change in the young bird causes it to deposit layers of fat within its muscles, in effect "marbling" the meat in a way that is found in no other poultry.

There was a time when capons were sterilized with hormones; such treatment is no longer legal. Beware of the butcher who sells a large roasting chicken as a capon, however. Real capons, which are on the expensive side and most frequently found frozen these days, should be labeled as such. They can be cooked in the same manner as chicken and are at their best roasted.

ROAST CAPON STUFFED WITH RICE—Draw, singe and wash the birds, wiped dry, the inside filled with rice that has been boiled in stock; seasoned with salt, pepper, nutmeg and a few herbs; when filled, trussed, breast covered with bacon and tied with string, roasted and basted; when nearly done, the bacon removed, the breast browned; served garnished with watercress, and some Velouté sauce.

ROAST CAPONS WITH NOODLES—The birds drawn, singed, washed and trussed, the breast filled with a savory stuffing, bacon tied over the breast, then roasted;

served with some boiled noodles that are mixed into Allemande sauce, with a little Parmesan cheese at one end, and Allemande sauce at the other.

BRAISED CAPON WITH CHIPOLATA GARNISH—Capons drawn, singed, washed, wiped, larded on the breast, trussed, put in saucepan with vegetables, herbs and spices, moistened half way up with white stock and a glass of white wine, covered with buttered paper, braised till done and glazy. Served garnished with small sausages, blanched and peeled chestnuts, button mushrooms, small glazed onions and pieces of cooked bacon all made hot in a good roast fowl gravy.

BRAISED CAPONS, SAUCE SU-PRÊME—Prepared and braised as in the preceding; served with Suprême sauce poured around, and decorated with strips of cooked tongue and watercress.

ROAST CAPON STUFFED, GIBLET SAUCE—The birds prepared, then filled with a savory stuffing, trussed, bacon tied over the breast, roasted and basted till done, bacon then removed, and the breast quickly browned; served with a sauce made from the residue of the roasting pan, with minced and sautéed giblets worked into it; garnished with watercress.

BOILED CAPON WITH SALT PORK—The capon prepared and the breast filled with chicken forcemeat, then trussed, boiled in white stock with a piece of salt pork,

served with a sauce poured around, made from the stock it was boiled in, to which is added chopped parsley and flanked with thin slices of pork.

BRAISED CAPONS WITH TOMA-TOED RICE—The birds prepared, the breast covered with bacon, braised with vegetables and spices; when done, taken up, and the braise strained, skimmed, and added to a Velouté sauce. Rice boiled in chicken stock till done, drained, mixed with a tomato purée; served with a small mold of the rice turned out on end of dish with some of the sauce poured around.

BRAISED CAPONS WITH QUE-NELLES, SAUCE PERIGUEUX—Prepared and braised as in the preceding, the braise strained, skimmed, reduced to glaze, then mixed into a Perigueux sauce; served with the sauce poured around, and garnished with small quenelles of chicken dipped into parsley sauce.

BOILED CAPON, MUSHROOM SAUCE—The birds drawn, washed, singed and trussed, bacon tied over the breast, boiled in white stock, sauce made from the stock, some mushroom purée worked into it, also some whole button mushrooms that have been sautéed in butter; served surrounded with the mushrooms in sauce.

STEWED CAPON WITH VEGETA-BLES—The birds prepared, then disjointed into portion pieces, lightly fried in butter, then arranged in a saûtoir with slices of carrot, onions and a bunch of sweet herbs, moistened with stock and a glass of Madeira wine, stewed slowly till tender; served garnished with a macedoine of vegetables made hot in Madeira sauce.

BOILED CAPON WITH TONGUE AND CAULIFLOWER — The birds prepared and boiled as in Boiled Capon, Mushroom Sauce; served with a slice of braised smoked tongue, and garnished with flowerets of cauliflower in Béchamel sauce.

BOILED CAPON WITH MILANAISE GARNISH—Prepared and boiled as above, and served surrounded with a garnish of boiled macaroni in inch lengths, with strips of cooked tongue, sliced mushrooms and minced truffle peelings made hot in a Velouté sauce.

BOILED STUFFED CAPON, CELERY SAUCE—The birds prepared, then stuffed with celery, the skin rubbed with lemon juice, bacon tied over the breast, boiled in white stock, sauce made from it, into which is worked strips of blanched celery about an inch long, the celery then simmered in the sauce till tender; served with the sauce poured around, and garnished with green celery tops.

CAPSICUMS—Are better known as chillies or peppers; they are of two shapes, the long thin dark red, which is used in vinegars, pickles, and to grind into red pepper; and the round green bell shaped, which is generally stuffed and baked, or cut up into many sauces, soups and garnitures.

CAPSICUMS—Clearly, we have come a long way in our understanding of *Capsicum,* the highly flavorful genus also known as peppers or chiles, which has literally thousands of members. Although bell and other mild peppers fall in this group, current interest is in the hotter, more flavorful chiles, all of which get their potency from the compound *capsaicin.* This fiery substance primarily is found in the veins and seeds of the fruit, which are usually removed before cooking.

Recent research has led to the development of the Scoville scale, which assigns heat units to peppers in order to allow for ostensibly scientific comparisons. But the different varieties of each chile vary significantly, and even one cayenne pepper, for example, may be far hotter than another taken off a neighboring plant. Since it is all relative, it's enough to learn a little about the major chiles and their uses.

Anaheim: Long, green, and usually very mild; good for stuffing; also known as California, New Mexico, Rio Grande, and Colorado.

Ancho: When dried, the dark-green poblano pepper becomes the more widely used, brick-red ancho; four to five inches long, two to three inches wide at the "shoulders"; quite hot; common in Mexico.

Mulato: Similar in looks to the ancho only darker.

Pasilla: A dried chilaca chile that is blackish in color and weighs about a third of an ounce.

Negro: The regional name for the pasilla chile.

New Mexico: Fresh, this is a chile we call chile verde ("green chile").

Dried, it is long and dark red in color.

Banana: Popular with gardeners; long and yellow; usually mild, but Hungarian wax variety is hot.

Cayenne: Also called red chili and Thai pepper; chile de árbol and bird pepper are similar; three inches long and very thin; used in many red-pepper sauces; fiery hot.

Jalapeño: Small, green, and smooth; medium-hot to hot; smoked, the jalapeño becomes a chipotle, a delicious hot chile with a unique flavor.

Serrano: Thin, green to red, very short (one inch), and super-hot; favored in the American Southwest when heat is needed.

CARAMEL—Is a term used by cooks for burnt sugar thinned with water, and used to color soups, sauces, gravies, syrups, ice creams, etc., that require a brown tint without a pronounced flavoring.

CARAMEL—Caramelization occurs when sugar is heated past a certain point (about 300° F.) and sugar molecules break down into as many as a hundred different compounds. Making caramel is a somewhat delicate process; the goal is not to burn the sugar—which results in a bitter taste—but to melt it to one of the many stages short of that point.

Caramelization may also mean browning foods, sometimes with some added sugar, until a glaze is formed. Caramel sauce is made from nothing more than sugar and water. Caramel candies are made by carefully melting sugar together with butter and milk.

CARAWAY—Name of seeds of a wild plant used in distilling, for cordial and cake flavoring.

CARAWAY—The uses of this spice, which comes from a plant (*Carum carvi*) that grows wild on all the northern continents and is related to PARSLEY and CARROTS, are not extensive, but they are greater than those mentioned by Fellows. Central European cooking, for example, would not be the same without it. The cordial mentioned by Fellows, incidentally, is undoubtedly the Swedish aquavit, the caraway-flavored liquor that is downed cold and neat.

CARBONADE—A French term applied to denote a stew composed of cold meats, generally seasoned with onions and garlic, such as carbonade of beef, mutton, etc.

CARBONADE—Carbonade is actually a Flemish dish—a beef stew almost always cooked with beer. It is served hot.

CARDINAL—Name applied to foods, sauces and drinks that are colored a bright red.

CARDOONS—A vegetable resembling sea-kale, but the stalks are feathery. Plentifully grown in Canada; may be treated the same as sea-kale.

CARDOONS—A thistle related to the ARTICHOKE, the cardoon· (*Cynara cardunculus*) is used for its stalk, which is best eaten young, peeled, and braised. It is not unlike celery in texture and has a flavor similar to that of the artichoke.

CARMINE—A red coloring used for syrups, sauces, cakes, etc., obtained from the cochineal insect;

made by bruising four ounces of cochineal insects and soaking for a few minutes in three pints of cold water, then put to boil with two ounces of common washing soda; when boiling, removed to where it simmers only, then slowly is added two ounces of rock alum, then four ounces of cream of tartar, boiled up for two minutes, strained, and when cold, bottled for use.

CARP—A fresh water fish, in season from September to May; is highly esteemed, and its roe is nearly equal to that of the shad.

CARP—It is a shame that we do not make better use of carp—a good freshwater fish of which there are literally hundreds of species—but I have a feeling that we will be seeing more of it in the coming years. For one thing, it is remarkably easy to farm; the Chinese began cultivating it before the birth of Christ. For another, it is extremely hardy.

BAKED CARP, SAUCE MATELOTE—The fish scaled and trimmed, filled with savory stuffing, sewn up, scored into cutting portions, the back dipped in beaten eggs, then in breadcrumbs, laid in pan, back sprinkled with melted butter, moistened with a little red wine and consommé, a few slices of onions added, slowly baked till done, taken up, the residue of the pan strained into a Matelote sauce, the fish served with it, and garnished with Duchesse potatoes.

BAKED CARP, SAUCE GENOISE— The fish scaled, trimmed and stuffed as above, sewn up, scored, baked in Genoise sauce, served with it, and garnished with potatoes Bignonne.

BRAISED STUFFED CARP, SAUCE ALLEMANDE—The fish scaled, trimmed, stuffed with fish forcemeat, sewn up, the skin then spread with more forcemeat, placed in a saûtoir with vegetables and spices, moistened with fish stock and white wine, covered with buttered paper, slowly braised till done, taken up, braise strained, skimmed, and added to an Allemande sauce, served with it, and garnished with Hollandaise potatoes.

BOILED CARP, CAPER SAUCE—The fish scaled and trimmed, either left whole, or cut into portions, placed in saûtoir with an onion stuck with cloves and a bunch of herbs, covered with good beef gravy and a little port wine, boiled slowly till done, sauce made from the liquor it was boiled in; when done, capers and caper vinegar added to it; served with the fish, garnished with Condé potatoes.

BROILED CARP, LEMON PARSLEY BUTTER—The fish scaled, trimmed, washed, dried and filleted, scored across the skin, seasoned with salt and pepper, rolled in flour, then dipped in olive oil, broiled, served with maître d'hôtel butter poured over and garnished with chip potatoes, lemon and parsley.

BROILED STUFFED CARP, FINES HERBES SAUCE—Fish a pound each in weight; scaled, trimmed and washed, filled with a forcemeat made of minced mushrooms, small pieces of cooked fish, chopped parsley, hard boiled eggs, minced chives and shallots, seasoned with salt, pepper and nutmeg; sewn up, scored, rolled in oil paper, and slowly broiled till done through; served with fines herbes sauce poured over and garnished with Julienne potatoes.

FRIED CARP, PIQUANTE SAUCE— The fish scaled, trimmed, washed, dried, rubbed with lemon juice, seasoned with salt and pepper, rolled in flour, dipped in beaten eggs, fried; served with Piquante sauce poured around, garnished with lemon and parsley, and surrounded with Parisienne potatoes.

BOILED CARP ROES, SAUCE SUPRÊME— The roes washed, then steeped for an hour in cold water with vinegar, slowly boiled in light consommé with lemon juice in it; served with Suprême sauce poured over, and garnished with potatoes Anglaise.

FRIED CARP ROES, SAUCE TARTARE— The roes washed and steeped as above, then blanched in salted vinegar water, taken out and wiped dry, seasoned with salt, pepper and lemon juice, breaded, fried; served with Tartare sauce poured around, garnished with lemon, parsley and chip potatoes.

SCALLOPED CARP ROES IN SHELL —The roes cleansed, steeped and blanched, then boiled in salted vinegar water till done; taken up, cut into dice with mushrooms, put into a Velouté sauce with a little lobster coral, then filled into scallop shells, sprinkled with breadcrumbs and melted butter, baked and served.

PATTIES OF CARP ROES— The preceding mixture filled into patty shells; served with the top sprinkled with lobster coral, and Velouté sauce poured around.

CARP SAUTÉ, ADMIRAL SAUCE— The fish a pound each in weight, scaled, trimmed, washed, dried, scored, seasoned with salt and pepper, rolled in flour, slowly fried in butter till done; served surrounded with Admiral sauce, garnished with parsley, lemon and Victoria potatoes.

CARROTS— A vegetable that in this country enters into almost every soup, sauce, ragout, etc., for its flavor, and in the early summer when new and about two inches long, are relished as an accompaniment to fresh boiled beef, New England dinner, etc.

CARROTS— Carrots have an interesting history: Although they have been around for fifteen hundred years or so (they are thought to have originated in Afghanistan), they became popular only in the last century. That is, popular as food; ladies of the court wore carrot leaves to adorn their hats three hundred years ago. In fact, carrots were not even orange until the last century; they started out purple and became white, yellow, and, finally, orange as a result of selective breeding. It was then that they became part of the cure taken with the waters at Vichy. Even then the carrot (*Daucus carota*) was not considered an elegant food.

Today we have dozens of varieties of carrots, all shapes and sizes (and almost all orange). Few northern cuisines ignore them, and some are downright dependent on them. Now carrots can be considered the second most important vegetable in France (after the POTATO), and most American refrigerators contain a pound or two year-round. For good reason: The carrot is sweet and aromatic on its own, and contributes mightily to soups, stews, and even desserts.

NEW CARROTS IN CREAM—The carrots washed and scraped, then boiled tender in boiling salted water, taken up and drained, then simmered in reduced cream or thin cream sauce; served as a vegetable.

SAUTÉ OF NEW CARROTS—Washed, scraped and boiled as above, then sautéed in butter, taken up, and mixed into maitre d'hôtel butter; served as a garnish.

BRAISED NEW CARROTS, PARSLEY SAUCE—The carrots washed and scraped, then braised in consommé to a glaze, taken up; served on small platters with some parsley sauce, served as a vegetable.

GLAZED NEW CARROTS WITH BUTTER—Prepared and glazed as in the preceding, taken up, dipped in melted butter and used as a garnish.

NEW CARROTS IN BROWN GRAVY—Glazed as above, taken up, put into a rich brown gravy; served as a garnish sprinkled with parsley, or as a vegetable.

STEWED CARROTS WITH GREEN PEAS—New carrots cored with a column cutter, then cut in thin slices, stewed in consommé till tender; green peas boiled in salted water with a bunch of fresh mint, strained off when done, and mixed with the carrots; served as a vegetable.

NEW CARROTS IN POULETTE SAUCE—Washed and scraped, then boiled in boiling salted water till tender, drained off and then mixed into Poulette sauce and served as a vegetable.

CURRIED CARROTS WITH RICE—Vegetarian entrée—The carrots prepared and cooked (as in Braised New Carrots, Parsley Sauce), then taken up and mixed into a good curry sauce made of cream; served in the centre of a border of dry boiled rice.

CARROT SALAD WITH ASPARAGUS TIPS—The carrots glazed and when cold the tips dipped into Ravigote sauce, arranged alternately on dish with points of asparagus sprinkled with Vinaigrette sauce, and garnished with shred lettuce.

CARROT SOUP—Plenty of carrots with a few soup vegetables boiled in stock with a piece of corned beef; when meat is done, taken up, the soup then made thick with roux, then rubbed through a fine sieve, boiled up again, seasoned and skimmed; served with croûtons (called Purée Crecy).

CARVING—To carve a LOIN OF MUT- TON OR VEAL, begin at the small end and cut between the ribs. A FILLET OF VEAL should be cut first from the top, and in a BREAST OF VEAL, the breast and brisket should first be separated, then cut across. A SIR- LOIN OF BEEF should be placed with the tenderloin down, thin cut slices should be cut from the side next the carver, then turn over the roast and carve from underneath; a slice of both should be served. In res- taurants the sirloin is generally all used up in Porterhouse steaks. A RIB ROAST should be put on the carving table thick end down and standing upright, the first two ribs cut off to be used for well done or- ders, the chine removed, and broad level thin slices served, with gravy poured under. SHORT RIBS should be served with the bone left in. A LEG OF MUTTON should be carved across the middle of the bone first and then from the thickest part till the gristle is reached. A few nice slices can be cut from the smaller end, but it is usually hard and stringy. A HAM can be served in several ways: by cutting long delicate slices through the thick fat down to the bone; by running the point of the knife in a circle in the middle and cutting thin circular slices, thus keeping the ham moist; or, by be- ginning at the knuckle end and slicing upwards; the latter is the most economical. A TONGUE should be carved in very thin slices, its delicacy depending upon this; the slices from the centre are consid- ered the most tempting, and should be cut across and the slices taken from both sides with a portion of the fat from the root. In carving

FISH, practice is required in order to prevent the flakes from breaking; the choicest morsels of all large fish are near the head, the thin parts come next; the flavor nearest the bone is never equal to that on the upper part; a fish knife should always be used. FOWLS should be placed breast up, the fork put into the breast to steady the bird, then cut off the wings and legs, cut out the breast bone so as to leave a well browned skin over it and the white meat, cut off the side bones and di- vide what is left in two from the neck down, remove the second joint from the leg and wing. TENDER- LOINS should have the tip cut off and then cut in medium thick slices across. HEARTS should be cut wedge shaped with some of the dressing. FOREQUARTERS OF LAMB should have the shoulder lifted off, and a slice of the shoulder and rib served together. GOOSE should be carved lengthwise of the breast from the point downwards. DUCK- LINGS should simply be cut into four quarters. DUCKS carved same as goose. PARTRIDGE and PHEASANTS same as fowls if large; if small par- tridge, split lengthwise in three, re- moving the backbone of the centre cut. SQUABS, PLOVERS and QUAIL split lengthwise in halves. All SMALL GAME left whole.

CASES—Are fanciful shaped pieces of paper made to hold and serve delicate foods; also made by the cook of rice, potatoes, turnips, etc.; most often seen on the bill of fare as en caisse.

CASSEROLE—French name for a saucepan. It is also the name of a metal or earthenware tureen with a flat bottom, fitted with lid and handles. Various entrées are cooked and served "en casserole," thus forming a pot roast or kind of braise.

CASSOLETTE—Are small cups formed of rice croquette mixture either sweet or savory; when formed, either rolled in flour only, or else breaded and fried; made to hold entrées, jellies, fruits, etc.

CASSIA—Is the name of a small tree which yields a bark that has less aroma, but is hard otherwise to detect from cinnamon; it is ground and made into oils and extracts, and passed off for cinnamon generally without detection.

CATFISH—Are of two kinds or main varieties, the "sea catfish" and "river catfish." Both are good for food, yet they are not of the same species. They are seldom, if ever, put on hotel bills of fare other than as "Fried catfish," "Catfish sauté," "Braised catfish with tomatoes," etc., or as "Catfish chowder."

CATFISH—Sea catfish, one assumes, is the same as ocean catfish (*Anarhichas lupus*), also known as wolffish (it has fangs), a delicious, firm-fleshed fish that should become increasingly available in our markets (the Norwegians have begun farming operations).

There are dozens of varieties of freshwater catfish, the most important being the channel catfish (*Ictalurus punctatus*). In midwestern states as recently as ten years ago all catfish came straight from the great rivers and were usually dipped in cornmeal and deep-fried.

The annual catch was about five thousand tons.

Now catfish farming is Mississippi's biggest industry—it surpassed cotton a couple of years ago—with annual production surpassing one hundred fifty thousand tons. And catfish is turning up on menus in the finest restaurants. Although its white flesh is usually delicate and firm (it can be, on occasion, a bit muddy), the fish does not measure up to the top-notch white-fleshed fish such as red snapper and, indeed, wolffish. But it is still worth eating.

CAULIFLOWER—The name means "flower cabbage" (*cavolfiore*), it probably originated in Asia (where the biggest ones, sometimes two feet across, are still grown), and it remains one of the finest vegetables you can buy. Cauliflower (*Brassica oleracea botrytis*) is closely related to broccoli (*Brassica oleracea italica*), and, with purple, broccoli-shaped cauliflower and light-green pyramid broccoli, the distinctions are becoming more obscure.

A good cauliflower, however, is more subtly flavored than broccoli, and its color—which ranges from creamy to green to purple to stark white ("As white as a cloud on a blue, propitious day," wrote English food writer Jane Grigson)—and tight, firm texture make it more attractive and less likely to become waterlogged.

Trim off brown spots, if any, before cooking cauliflower. Whether you steam it or boil it, cook cauliflower whole whenever possible. And do not overcook: It should be just tender. Dunk it in ice water to arrest its cooking if you are serving it cold or reheating it later.

BOILED CAULIFLOWER, HOLLANDAISE SAUCE—The cauliflower

trimmed, laid in salted water for an hour, then boiled in salted boiling water with a dash of vinegar in it till tender, taken up and drained; served with Hollandaise sauce poured around; may also be served this way with tomato sauce.

STEWED CAULIFLOWER—The cauliflower prepared and boiled as above, then taken up and sectioned, arranged in a saûtoir, covered with butter sauce and simmered; served as a vegetable.

BAKED CAULIFLOWER—Stewed as in the preceding, then placed into baking dish, covered with breadcrumbs and grated cheese, sprinkled with butter and baked.

SCALLOPED CAULIFLOWER—Same as the preceding, but filled into scallop shells instead of baking dish; served in the shells.

FRIED CAULIFLOWER, ALLEMANDE SAUCE—The stewed cauliflower above, taken up, dipped into batter and fried; served with Allemande sauce poured around.

CAULIFLOWER WITH MAYONNAISE —Cold boiled cauliflower in flowerets, marinaded in French dressing, arranged on a leaf of lettuce around the dish, with mayonnaise in the centre.

CAULIFLOWER SALAD—Cold boiled cauliflowerets covered with cream salad dressing, arranged in center of dish, garnished with small balls of beets.

PURÉE OF CAULIFLOWER—One-third Velouté sauce, one-third chicken stock, mixed and brought to the boil, minced cauliflower stalks and roots boiled in it till tender with a little thyme and parsley; when done, rubbed through a fine sieve, brought to the boil again and one-third of the whole of cream sauce then added; served with croûtons.

CREAM OF CAULIFLOWER—Same as the preceding, but when finished, very small flowerets added before serving.

CAULIFLOWER SAUCE—Into a good butter sauce is worked some very small flowerets of boiled cauliflower with a little purée (good for boiled poultry).

PICKLED CAULIFLOWER—Cauliflowers boiled till tender in flowerets, then put into jars, and covered with the following pickle: One pound of dry mustard mixed with one ounce of turmeric, then moistened with vinegar. One gallon of vinegar brought to the boil, the mustard and turmeric paste stirred into it, brought to the simmer and when beginning to thicken, one pound of sugar, half a pint of olive oil, and two ounces of mustard seed successively added to it, simmered for a few minutes, then poured boiling hot over the cauliflowers in the jars.

CAVIAR—Is a preparation made from the roes of sturgeon, can be bought at the grocery stores in cans; it is considered by epicures

PICKLED CAULIFLOWER

•

Makes about 3 quarts

The turmeric in this dish colors the cauliflower a bright yellow. Serve a small bowl of these pickles on your buffet table, but plan ahead—it takes one week to make this recipe.

2 (1½-pound) heads
    cauliflower

1 medium yellow onion,
    peeled and sliced

1 tablespoon dry mustard
    (Colman's from
    England)

1 teaspoon ground turmeric

1 quart distilled white
    vinegar

1 cup sugar

1 tablespoon mustard seeds

¼ cup olive oil

1½ teaspoons salt

Core the cauliflowers and break into flowerets. Blanch the flowerets in boiling water for 2 minutes, drain, and cool. Layer the cauliflower and onions in three 1-quart canning jars.

Stir together the dry mustard and turmeric with 1 tablespoon of the vinegar to make a paste.

In a small saucepan, combine the paste and the remaining ingredients and bring to a boil. Simmer gently for 10 minutes.

Divide the hot brine among the three jars of layered cauliflower and onions. Seal the jars and refrigerate for at least 1 week. Turn the jars over a few times so that all of the contents have a chance to be submerged in the brine.

C.W.

to be one of the finest of appetizers.

CAVIAR—Anyone who says, "Ugh! Fish eggs," cannot have tasted good caviar. It's a mysterious food, one the origins and processing of which are cloaked in secrecy. After all, the two countries surrounding the Caspian Sea, from whence all true caviar originates, are Russia and Iran.

There huge sturgeon are hauled onto land and gutted, their eggs immediately and very carefully salted by highly skilled caviar makers. (For consumption in the United States, the preservative boric acid is also added; it accentuates the flavor and reduces the amount of salt necessary for preserving.)

The caviar is then packed into cans that are wrapped with a distinctively thick rubber band and sold for exorbitant prices. Beluga caviar, the large, grayish pearls taken from eponymous fish that can live to be one hundred years old and grow to weigh a ton or more, is considered to be the best; it sells for sixty dollars an ounce and more; sevruga and ossetra caviars fetch somewhat less. Generally, caviar labeled *malossol* ("little salt") is thought to be the best, but no caviar has "little salt," and each batch is different. If you ever have occasion to buy expensive caviar in quantity, make sure you are offered a taste before you write the check.

Increasingly, good salted fish eggs (usually, if incorrectly, labeled *caviar*) are available. There are American breeds of sturgeon whose caviar can be quite tasty (at an appealing two dollars an ounce); the Chinese keluga also shows promise.

CAVIAR ON TOAST WITH OLIVES—One part each of Russian caviar, soft breadcrumbs, and blanched and peeled Jordan almonds mixed together and minced into a paste, spread on strips of toast, the edges garnished with slices of stoned olives.

CAVIAR TARTINES—Russian caviar spread on toast, and the edges decorated with finely chopped green gherkins, parsley and sweet peppers mixed together.

CANAPÉS OF CAVIAR—Circles of toast, the edges spread with anchovy paste, with an onion ring as its base, the ring filled with Russian caviar.

EGGS STUFFED WITH CAVIAR—Cut slices of hard boiled eggs, the yolks removed, its place filled with Russian caviar; served on thin slices of buttered brown bread.

CAVIAR WITH EGG—Slices of toast, the edges piped with beaten whites of eggs, caviar sprinkled on top, whole yolk of raw egg dropped in the centre, baked till set and served hot.

CAVIAR CROÛSTADES—Very small paste croûstades half an inch deep filled with caviar, on it placed a freshly opened blue point oyster; served garnished with lemon and watercress.

CELERIAC—A form of celery with a bulbous root, used as a salad and for flavoring, but little used in hotel work.

CELERIAC—It is ugly, it is difficult to peel, there's a fair amount of waste, and few people know what to do with it. Still, celeriac (*Apium graveolens rapaceum,* or celery root) is one of our most underrated vegetables. Choose the smoothest, firmest celeriac you can find (it will be easier to peel), and serve it, julienned, in a biting mustard mayonnaise (the classic rémoulade), or use it as you would a turnip. It is really at its best raw, with any acidic dressing.

CELERY—Is an aromatic plant cultivated largely as a flavoring vegetable and for uses of salads. It is generally sent to table in a raw condition, is the one and proper thing to eat with "canvas back duck." Kalamazoo, Michigan, is the great celery raising spot in this country.

When the celery industry was started in Kalamazoo, it was not for several years that the enterprising pioneers in this industry discovered that the thousands of acres of river bottom lands surrounding the city were especially adapted in the raising of celery to the pinnacle of esteem and popular favor it now holds. Visitors to Kalamazoo ate it, and carried away marvelous tales of its delicacy, orders to purchase and forward were sent back to friends and express agents, and the industry that was destined to make Kalamazoo famous as the celery city was born. At the present time there are thousands of acres under cultivation, and celery finds its way from Kalamazoo to every part of the United States and special shipments have been sent by steamer to Liverpool and London. In raising celery the seed is first sown during the winter months in specially prepared hot houses, of which there are acres under glass, the plants are transplanted, thinned out, and about the first of May are again transplanted to the fields, being planted in specially prepared trenches in double rows. There it is carefully looked after, cultivated and irrigated, and when of the proper size, the rich black soil is drawn up around the plants from both sides, until it forms a bank reaching nearly to the top of the leaves. About fourteen days is required for the plant to acquire that silvery whiteness and delicate crispness so enjoyed by every lover of celery. The shipping season then commences, and celery is taken from the fields to the packing rooms, carefully washed and tied in bunches of twelve heads each, packed and delivered to the express company for shipment. The fall crop, which is abundant later, is taken from the fields about the first of November, and is placed in specially constructed houses for preservation during the cold weather months. The season usually commences about the first of July and closes about February. From its start as the appetizer, in front of a good dinner, its rare beauty as a table ornament, etc., the rise of celery to popular appreciation was rapid. The use of celery and its adaptability in the preparation of table condiments is well seen on the grocers' shelves. There is canned celery for cooking only; chopped celery put up in such a manner as to retain its crispness and good quality for use at any time in the preparation of salads; celery pickles, celery mustard, celery salt, celery pepper, celery extracts and tonic, in fact everything that can be manufactured from it in any way. Chopped and canned celery are especially adapted to the wants of the "Chef" as they are always ready at any season of the year, and particularly useful are they at the season when good celery is not obtainable. There is also manufactured a prepared salad ready for the table, whose flavor and excellence is as surprising as it is delicious.

CELERY—Our current uses for celery pale before those described by Charles Fellows. We see it chiefly as a dipping vegetable and as an aromatic addition to soups and stews. Obviously it excels in those roles, but this limitation is unfortunate. Try some of Fellows's terrific recipes.

CREAM OF CELERY—Into a good veal or chicken stock is put a knuckle of ham, a few onions, plenty of outside stalks of celery, and a few blades of mace; boiled till celery is soft, ham then taken out and the soup thickened with roux and rubbed through a fine sieve, boiled up again with the addition of an equal quantity of Béchamel sauce, seasoned and served (also called purée).

PURÉE OF CELERY AND ONIONS—Same as the preceding, but using a purée of onions or sauce Soubise to add with the celery purée, instead of Béchamel.

CELERY CONSOMMÉ—The vegetables in the consommé stock composed mostly of celery, to give it a pronounced flavor; when strained and skimmed, Julienne strips of boiled celery added to it, seasoned and served.

STEWED CELERY ON TOAST—Celery stalks all cut about the same size like asparagus, boiled tender in salted water, taken up and arranged in a saûtoir, moistened with Velouté sauce, simmered; served with one end resting on toast, with some of the sauce poured over the ends.

CELERY PATTIES—The hearts of eight heads of celery boiled till tender, drained, then pounded to a paste with a cupful each of grated ham, cream, and fine breadcrumbs, seasoned with salt, pepper and a little butter, the mixture steamed till it thickens, then filled into patty cases and served hot.

BAKED CELERY WITH CHEESE—The celery cut into inch lengths

like macaroni, boiled in salted water till tender, drained, mixed with a little grated ham and chopped green celery leaves, arranged in layers in baking dish, each layer sprinkled with grated cheese; when full, moistened with Velouté sauce, sprinkled with grated breadcrumbs mixed with cheese, then with melted butter and baked.

CELERY WITH MARROW—The stewed celery (as in Stewed Celery on Toast) served on toast spread with marrow; served garnished with slices of cooked marrow.

FRIED CELERY, SAUCE VILLEROI—Three-inch lengths of celery stalk boiled not quite done in salted water, drained, seasoned with salt and pepper, breaded and fried; served with Villeroi sauce poured around.

BOILED CELERY WITH ONIONS—Stalks of celery about three inches long, small onions of an even size, both boiled together in veal stock till tender; served, the celery on toast masked with Béchamel sauce, garnished with onions.

CELERY FRITTERS—Celery stalks three inches long, tied in bundles three stalks thick, boiled till tender in salted water, taken up and drained, seasoned with salt, pepper and Parmesan cheese, string removed, dipped in batter and fried; served as a vegetable.

BRAISED CELERY ON TOAST—Celery stalks all of an even size, boiled not quite done in salted water, then arranged in a saûtoir, and moistened with strong chicken stock and a piece of glaze, stewed down rich; served on toast with the glaze poured over it.

CELERY SAUTÉ—Celery stalks of an even size, blanched, then arranged in a saûtoir with some bacon trimmings and a minced shallot, heated thoroughly, then moistened with equal parts of tomato and Espagnole sauces, simmered till done; served on toast with the sauce poured over.

MAYONNAISE OF CELERY—The tender parts only should be used by cutting them into pencil strips an inch long, washing thoroughly, then drained and mixed with mayonnaise; served on a leaf of lettuce.

CÈPES—A strongly flavored flat headed mushroom, imported in cans, preserved in olive oil.

CÈPES—We rarely see canned cèpes, which are officially *Boletus edulis,* and also known as porcini. During the summer months when they are in season cèpes can be found fresh in specialty stores. The rest of the year they are sold dried and frozen (the latter also can be difficult to find). Although fresh mushrooms are always best, cèpes dry and reconstitute extremely well, and a small package should be in every pantry, for cèpes are among the most delicious of all mushrooms.

SAUTÉ OF CÈPES ON TOAST—Drained from their oil, lightly fried in pan, when thoroughly heated, sprinkled with lemon juice and chopped parsley, arranged on toast, and served very hot.

STEWED CÈPES ON TOAST—The cèpes drained from their oil and then cut in slices, arranged in a saûtoir with chopped parsley, minced onions and garlic, moistened with Espagnole sauce, simmered; served on toast with sauce around.

BROILED CÈPES ON TOAST—Drained from their oil, seasoned with salt and pepper, rolled in fresh breadcrumbs, broiled; served on toast with maître d'hôtel butter poured over them, and garnished with lemon and parsley.

OMELET WITH CÈPES—The cèpes drained, cut in slices, fried in butter with a crushed clove of garlic, taken up and mixed with a little Colbert sauce; served enclosed in a savory omelet, with more of the cèpes in sauce poured around.

CERCELLES—The French name sometimes seen on bills of fare for "Teal."

CEREALINE—A white flaky pudding material prepared from Indian corn; also boiled plain and eaten with cream as a breakfast cereal; made into puddings according to the various recipes of the vendors, printed on the sides of the packets in which it is sold.

CERVELAS—The French name for a highly spiced small sausage of the bologna order; can be purchased at the Italian and delicatessen stores.

CERVELLES—French name for animal brains, for recipes, see BRAINS.

CHABLIS—The name of a white French wine, principally used for cooking purposes, but some of the brands of the genuine article are highly prized for their digestive and health giving qualities, such as Montrachet, Clos, Blanchot and Moutonne.

CHABLIS—Here Fellows confused Chablis with other white wines from central Burgundy. Both are made with the Chardonnay grape; Chablis is generally more austere, and is often described as "flinty" in character. Burgundy is richer, more generous, and, at its best, "buttery." Only French wines labeled Chablis are, in fact, Chablis, although the name is often used to describe generic white wines made in this country; these are always inferior to the real thing.

CHAFING DISH—A vessel heated from the underneath by a spirit lamp, also by electricity; is used for keeping and serving foods hot, or cooking on the table.

CHAMPAGNE—A wine prepared from grapes; the best varieties are manufactured at Epernay, Rheims and Mareuil in France, but the vintages of each year are vastly different, and sometimes the grape crop is a dismal failure. Hence champagne drinkers in Europe and Great Britain are versed on the merits and demerits of the various vintages. While in the United States, but very little attention has thus far been paid to the matter; the clipping on page 120 from the *Hotel World* of London, England, will doubtless be of interest.

CHAMPAGNE—"A wine prepared from grapes," indeed! In our time there is no wine more symbolic of good times—and celebrating them —than Champagne. And Champagne has one other notable asset: It is the easiest wine to pair with food, complementing almost everything from caviar to chocolate.

Legally (in every country but the United States), only true Champagne, sparkling wine made in the Champagne region of France, can be called Champagne. But good sparkling wines are made elsewhere in France, and in California, Spain, Italy, and Germany. Most sparklers, including Champagne, are made in much the same manner as still wine, but undergo a secondary fermentation in closed bottles, which produces carbonation.

The classic Champagne grapes, and indisputably the best, are Chardonnay and Pinot Noir, usually used together in varying proportions. The white Chardonnay grape contributes elegance, freshness, and clean, spicy fruit; the Pinot Noir brings body, smoothness, strength, and depth.

When buying Champagne, consider the relatively inexpensive nonvintage types; they are no less enjoyable than the pricey, more rare, and usually only marginally more complex vintage wines. *Brut* Champagne is usually the most dry variety; extra dry is somewhat less so; *sec, demi-sec,* and *doux* (rarely made by the old Champagne houses) all are increasingly sweet.

YEAR	YIELD IN GALLONS	CHARACTER OF THE WINES
1891	3,548,292	Passable, but very dear.
1890	5,573,656	Ordinary quality,
1889	6,109,994	Very good, price excessively high.
1888	4,639,098	Passable.
1887	10,409,278	Fairly good, light.
1886	6,525,398	Some good wines, with abundance of vinosity; but for the most part the vintage is under suspicion, which time has not so far lessened.
1885	8,199,070	Mediocre, resembling the 1883's.
1884	11,528,946	Fine elegant wines, highly prized by connoisseurs.
1883	9,051,460	Mediocre and dear; acid.
1882	7,058,568	Mediocre; acid; immature.
1881	14,627,140	Passable.
1880	2,423,236	Very good; lighter than the 1874's, excessively dear.
1879	2,008,776	Complete failure, yield small, fortunately.
1878	11,898,546	Good; fine; light.
1877	10,407,694	Mediocre; acid.
1876	16,120,786	Mediocre.
1875	21,710,346	Passable.
1874	8,178,544	Very fine, both as to vinosity and color, has been greatly sought after.
1873	3,138,718	Bad; acid, and notwithstanding that, dear.
1872	4,480,960	Fairly good.
1871	5,465,306	Mediocre.
1870	4,960,010	Good.
1869	8,542,886	Passable.
1868	12,316,700	Very good, elegant, and lighter than the 1865's.
1867	3,889,356	Mediocre.
1868	19,449,870	Bad.
1865	14,314,542	Wine of superior quality; very vinous.

CHANTILLY—Is the title given by confectioners to a form of basket made of cakes, choux paste, candied peels, almond paste, etc., filled with whipped cream. Chantilly cream is simply whipped cream.

CHANTILLY SOUP—Fresh green peas, a bunch of fresh mint, some green onion tops and a piece of salt pork boiled together in good chicken stock; when done the pork removed, the stock thickened with roux, then rubbed through a sieve, the purée boiled up again and seasoned; served with croûtons.

CHARCOAL—One of the kitchen essentials for good broiling, should be kept dry in a good cellar; often times bought by the load, the load presumed to contain so many bushels; when happening to be delivered as many things are in bulk, during the steward's absence, the following capacities of cribs and boxes for potatoes and other root vegetables, coal, charcoal, etc., will be found reliable and useful [see above]:

[The United States standard (Winchester) bushel, 18½ inches in diameter, and 8 inches deep, contains 2150.42 cubic inches.]

One cubic foot equals four-fifths of a bushel.
A box 3 × 3 × 3
— 27 cubic feet and holds 21⅗ bushels
A box 5 × 3 × 2
— 30 " " " " 24 "
A box 5 × 3 × 3
— 45 " " " " 36 "
A box 5 × 3 × 4
— 60 " " " " 48 "
A box 7 × 5 × 3.9
—131¼ " " " " 104⅓ "

CHANTILLY SOUP

·

Serves 6

A simple but elegant soup. Do not add too much black pepper or mint garnish as you will want to taste the delicate flavor of the peas. The name of the soup comes from a very delicate type of lacework called Chantilly.

2 quarts Chicken Stock
  (page 153)

1/2 cup fresh mint leaves

6 green onions, chopped

1 (2-ounce) piece salt pork

2 tablespoons chopped
  parsley

3 (10-ounce) packages
  frozen peas

Salt and freshly ground
  black pepper to taste

Garnish

Freshly chopped mint
  leaves

In a 4-quart pot, place the Chicken Stock, mint leaves, green onions, salt pork, and parsley. Cover and simmer gently for 1 hour. Remove the salt pork and save for another use. Add the peas, cover, and simmer for 10 minutes.

Pour the soup into a food processor a bit at a time, purée, and place in another pot. Bring the soup back to a simmer; salt and pepper to taste.

Garnish with freshly chopped mint and serve.

C.W.

A box 7 × 7 × 7
  — 343 " " " " 274²/₅ "
A box 8 × 8 × 8
  — 512 " " " " 409³/₅ "
A box 10 × 10 × 10
  — 1000 " " " " 800 "

CHARCOAL—Charcoal is a product that has changed completely since Charles Fellows first wrote *The Culinary Handbook*. At the end of World War II, looking for a way to profitably dispose of the scrap wood that remained after building auto bodies, Henry Ford contacted his friend Charles Kingsford, and together they developed charcoal briquettes. At the same time the United States became a suburban society, and backyard grilling became a widespread phenomenon.

Briquettes, a combination of wood, sawdust, chemicals, fillers, and other ingredients, now dominate the market. True hardwood charcoal (sometimes called lump charcoal), is still made, as it has been for centuries, by smoldering hardwood for several days. Ten years ago it barely existed; today it is widely available. Hardwood charcoal produces a cleaner flame than do briquettes, and is easy to light. But it also burns hotter, so it takes some getting used to.

CHARLOTTE—Is the name given to what might be called a shell of bread, cake, lady fingers, etc., cut to fit into a mold or pan, which is then filled with fruits, creams, custards, etc.

CHARTREUSE—Is the name of a liqueur made in three colors, green, yellow and white; originally made by the monks of a French monastery at Dauphine, in the Alps mountains. There are, however, dishes dedicated to these monks, called "chartreuses"; they are made of various rich foods, such as prairie hens, fish, partridges, larks, snipe, squabs, chickens, fruits, etc., enclosed in a mold or shell of a much more common material, being a disguise, inasmuch as the monks were under severe dicipline, and were supposed to be very frugal. Recipes for chartreuses will be found under the respective food which demands it.

CHATEAUBRIAND—Is the name given to a style of cooking a tenderloin steak between two others of inferior cuts and then pressing the juice of the two outside ones over the fillet. But some cooks simply take a fillet steak, split, stuff and broil it, serve it with a maître d'hôtel butter mixed with beef glaze, and call that "chateaubriand." History says the first is right.

CHATEAUBRIAND—Regardless of Fellows's dogmatism, chateaubriand is generally taken to mean a thick slice taken from the center portion of a filet (or tenderloin) of beef.

CHEESE—A most nutritious food, forming many excellent dishes; it is of various kinds, of which the following are to be found in good hotels: Skim, cream, full cream, cheddar, stilton, roquefort, camembert, brie, neufchatel, parmesan, edam, gorgonzola, gruyère, port-du-salut, sage, sap-sago, and sometimes on the bar and in German clubs may be found Limburger, to describe which the following story will aid without further comment:

LIMBURGER CHEESE—Ma sent me to pay a bill at the grocers last Saturday. The boss behind the counter made me a present of something wrapped in a piece of silver paper, which he told me was a piece of Limburger cheese. When I got outside the shop I opened the paper, and when I smelt what was inside I felt tired. I took it home and put it in the coal shed. In the morning I went to it again. It was still there. Nobody had taken it. I wondered what I could do with it. Father and mother were getting ready to go to church. I put a piece in the back pocket of father's pants, and another piece in the lining of ma's muff. I walked behind when we started for church. It was beginning to get warm. When we got in church, father looked anxious and mother looked as if something had happened. After the first hymn, mother told father not to sing again, but to keep his mouth shut, and breathe through his nose. After the prayer, perspiration stood on father's face, and the people in the next row to ours got up and went out. After the next hymn father whispered to mother that he thought she had better go out and air herself. After the second lesson, some of the church wardens came round to see if there were any stray rats in the church. Some more people near our pew got up and went out, putting their handkerchiefs to their noses as they went. The parson said they had better close the service, and hold a meeting outside to discuss the sanitary condition of the church. Father told mother they had better go home one at a time. Mother told father to go the nearest way home and disinfect himself before she came. When they got home, they both went into the front room, but did not speak for some time. Mother spoke first, and told father to put the cat out of the room, as she thought it was going to be sick. It was sick before father could get it out. Mother then turned round, and noticed that the canary was dead. Mother told father not to sit so near to the fire, as it made matters worse. Father told mother to go and smother herself. Mother said she thought she was smothered already. Just then the servant came in, and asked if she should open the windows, as the room felt very close. Father went upstairs and changed his clothes, and had a hot bath. Mother took father's clothes and offered them to a tramp, who said, "Thanks, kind lady, they are a bit too high for me." Mother threw them over the back fence into the canal. Father was summoned afterwards for poisoning the fish. Mother went to bed. Father asked her if she had been fumigated. Just then father had a note sent him. Father came to wish me "Good Night" at 10 o'clock in the evening, with a note in one hand and a razor strop in the other. I got under the bed. The people next door thought we were beating carpets in the house. I cannot sit down comfortably yet. I have given my little sister what I had left of that Limburger cheese. I thought it a pity to waste it.

CHEESE—Today we can choose from a greater selection of cheeses than ever before. The great cheese-making nations—France, Switzerland, and Italy—eagerly export their products for American consumption. They are joined by other countries also known for their expertise, such as England and Holland. In addition, increasing quantities of good cheese are being made in the United States.

Serious students of cheese know and admire hundreds of varieties, and can distinguish among them despite the usually subtle differences. But the good cook and eater can get along just fine by choosing the best from among a dozen or so cheeses, all of which fall into a few categories. Although the following list is incomplete, it does cover most of the essentials; if you become a cheese fanatic, you can go on from here.

Hard Cheeses

Parmesan: Always buy true Parmigiano-Reggiano imported from Italy, regardless of how expensive it seems relative to the domestic or Argentinian stuff. It is incomparable. Excellent for eating, and one of the best grating cheeses there is.

Pecorino Romano: Sheep's milk cheese, stronger than Parmesan, less expensive, and less subtle. Good for grating and, especially when young, nibbling.

Dry Monterey Jack: At its best, the closest domestic cheese to Parmesan.

Semihard Cheeses

Cheddar: Traditionally, the finest domestic cheese. The best producers are in Wisconsin, Vermont, and New York.

Emmentaler: True Swiss cheese. Nutty and delicious, excellent for melting and eating.

Gruyère: From France and Switzerland. Slightly harder than Emmentaler, with a stronger flavor. Equally enjoyable.

Semisoft to Soft Cheeses

Camembert and **Brie:** See separate entries

Blue-mold cheeses: Each country has a great one. There are three considered superior: Gorgonzola (from Italy; do not buy domestic); Stilton (from England); Roquefort (from France, made of sheep's milk).

Fontina: One of the great cheeses of Italy, this has been copied so many times that the original is hard to find. But look for it: It will be labeled *Fontina Val d'Aosta,* and it is incomparable. The best copy, Fontal, is also from Italy.

Washed-rind cheeses: Most of these—including Limburger, maligned above—have an off-putting smell. But their strong flavors are delicious. Try Pont l'Evêque, Livarot, Chaumes, or Muenster (*not* the domestic Muenster), all from France.

WELSH RAREBIT—A little butter placed in a small shallow saûtoir; when melted, finely cut cheese added to it, seasoned with salt, red pepper, dry mustard and Worcestershire sauce; as it begins to melt, ale added till it becomes of a creamy nature; a hot dish with slices of hot toast, the cheese poured over it and served.

GOLDEN BUCK—Is the preceding with a poached egg on top.

YORKSHIRE RAREBIT—Is a Golden Buck with a strip of broiled bacon on each side of the egg.

OLD FASHIONED YORKSHIRE BUCK —A slice of bread half inch thick thinly spread with mustard, placed in hot oven till brown, moistened with half a glass of ale, covered with a slice of cheese quarter inch thick, two thin slices of bacon placed on the cheese, returned to oven and cooked till the cheese is melted and the bacon done; served very hot.

COTTAGE CHEESE—A good way to use up sour milk; let the milk sour to clotness, boiling water then poured to it, stirred, turned into a colander, little cold water poured over it, salt added and again stirred, then placed into a muslin bag and drained dry; served either plain or mixed with cream. Sometimes a little cream and finely chopped chives are added to it before serving, especially for the bar lunch.

COTTAGE CHEESE—Fellows's is an accurate (and, to most people, surprisingly simple) method for preparing fresh cottage cheese, something that is virtually never done in the home since the advent of large-scale production in commercial dairies.

CHEESE SCALLOPS—Individual patty pans buttered, then lined

GOLDEN BUCK

•

Serves 4

This dish seems to have been quite popular at the turn of the century. It is simply Welsh rarebit with poached eggs. It is terrific, if you do not overpoach the eggs.

1/2 pound medium-sharp cheddar cheese, grated

1 teaspoon butter

1 tablespoon Worcester-shire sauce

2 teaspoons all-purpose flour

1 teaspoon dry mustard (Colman's from England)

1/4 cup heavy cream

1/4 cup beer

Salt and freshly ground black pepper

8 eggs

4 slices buttered toast (sourdough is best)

Garnish

Chopped parsley

In a double boiler, heat everything but the salt, pepper, eggs, toast, and parsley. Using a wire whisk, whip until a smooth sauce is achieved. Add salt and pepper to taste.

Poach the eggs to your liking and place 2 eggs on a piece of buttered toast for each person. Top with the sauce and garnish with parsley.

C.W.

with slices of cheese, an egg then broke into the centre, seasoned with pepper, a tablespoonful of milk or cream poured over the egg, then dredged with grated cheese and slowly baked for twenty minutes, turned out and served on dry or fried toast.

CHEESE STRAWS—One pound of flour, three-quarter pound of grated cheese, four raw yolks of eggs, seasoned with salt and red pepper, made into a paste, rolled out thin, cut into strips and baked a straw color.

CHEESE SAVORIES—Water crackers split, and the open side thinly spread with anchovy butter; then, with a paste made of two parts of

CHEESE STRAWS

·

Makes dozens, depending on shapes and sizes

These are great for the hors d'oeuvres table or just as a snack. You can also form them into fancy shapes using small cookie cutters, thus making cheese crackers.

2 cups all-purpose flour	1¹/₂ teaspoons salt
¹/₂ cup grated Parmesan cheese	1¹/₂ teaspoons cayenne pepper or to taste
³/₄ pound sharp cheddar cheese, grated	¹/₃ cup cold water
	4 egg yolks

Preheat oven to 350° F.

Place all the ingredients, except the water and egg yolks, in the mixing bowl of an electric mixer (a KitchenAid mixer is great for this). Blend until grainy. Add the water and egg yolks, and knead (either by hand or in the mixer) into a smooth dough. Knead with additional flour if too sticky.

Roll the dough out to ¹/₈-inch thickness on a lightly floured surface. Cut into long strips like bread sticks. Or use a cookie cutter to make cheese crackers.

Place on a nonstick cookie sheet and bake for 10 to 15 minutes. Do not brown too much.

C.W.

roquefort cheese to one part of butter, seasoned with salt, red pepper and a dash of sherry wine; served garnished with thin slices of green gherkins.

CHEESE BISCUITS—Half a pound each of butter and flour, four raw egg yolks, ten ounces of grated Swiss cheese, one tablespoonful of dry mustard and a little red pepper,

the butter beaten to a cream, the eggs and dry ingredients then added, made into a stiff dough, rolled out, cut in square biscuits, baked twenty minutes in a rather slow oven and served.

CHEESE RAMEQUINS—Half a pound each of roquefort and Swiss cheeses, one pound of butter, sixteen raw yolks of eggs, and the insides of four breakfast rolls boiled in cream till soft, the whole then made into a paste, and then mixed lightly with the beaten whites of sixteen eggs; filled into fancy paper cases and baked a fine brown; served very hot.

CHEESE BOMBE—Into a choux paste made of three-quarter pound of flour, one-half pound of butter and a quart of water, work in one at a time twelve raw yolks and eight whites of eggs, then three-quarter pound of grated Swiss cheese; cooked by frying small spoonfuls in not too hot fat; when done, served with Montpelier butter.

CHEESE BOMBE—These cheese fritters are also called *gougères,* and need no sauce to make a wonderful hors d'oeuvre.

CHEESE FLANS—Scalloped circles of puff paste, on one half of it is spread a paste made of twelve ounces of Parmesan cheese, eight ounces of butter, eight yolks and four beaten whites of eggs, the other half turned on to it, edges pinched down, arranged on baking sheet, brushed over with egg wash, baked, served with watercress.

CHEESE CASSEROLES—Slices of bread one and a half inches thick, trimmed circular, a center then cut out with column cutter leaving a bottom, dipped in milk, then breaded and fried, taken up and the center filled with a mixture made of two parts breadcrumbs, one part grated cheese, and half a part each of melted butter and milk; seasoned with salt and red pepper,

baked quickly till cheese is melted and served very hot.

CHEESE CUSTARD—Grated cheese, beaten raw eggs, dry mustard, salt and pepper beaten into milk at the rate of three eggs and four ounces of cheese to the quart; poured into hot buttered scallop dishes and baked; served in the dish.

CHEESE PUDDING—Is the same mixture as the preceding, but the scallop dish fitted with a slice of buttered toast, and the mixture poured over it before baking.

CHEESE SOUFFLÉS—Another name for "Cheese Ramequins" (which see).

CHEESE FRITTERS—Half a pound of grated Parmesan cheese seasoned with salt and red pepper worked into the beaten whites of eight eggs; cooked by frying small spoonfuls in hot fat, then taken up and rolled into grated cheese mixed with finely chopped parsley; served very hot.

POTTED CHEESE—Grated cheese, to every pound of which is added four ounces of melted butter and a tablespoonful of brandy, with a seasoning of dry mustard and red pepper, pressed into jars, covered with parchment paper and kept for use. This is also called "Club cheese" and can be bought in small jars.

CHEESE CONES—The paste given for "Cheese Straws" (which see), cut in squares and baked, then a cone of whipped cream and mixed with grated Parmesan cheese forced on top with a bag and fancy tube.

CHEESE OMELET—Beaten eggs with a little cream seasoned with salt and red pepper, fried in omelet form, but before being rolled dredged with grated cheese; served with a dredging of cheese on top, melted in the oven.

CHEESE FINGERS—Strips of puff paste finger lengths; with each fold of the paste, grated cheese is rolled in, then cut in strips, egg washed and baked.

CHEESE SANDWICHES—Thin slices of buttered bread with a thin slice of cheese between, or spread with "Potted Cheese" (which see).

CHEMISE—A French term used to designate potatoes boiled in their skins, which they call "pommes de terre, en chemise."

CHERRIES—California produces our best table cherries, while most all of the states produce the red and black sour cooking cherries. The following clipping from the San Francisco *Wave* will show how an immense crop is handled at a California ranch: "Probably there is no better known and cetainly there are few larger ranches in the state of California than that owned by the Meek estate. It is situated a little way outside the city of Oakland, and it covers a huge tract of land between San Lorenzo and Haywards. It is spread over 3,300 acres of some of the finest fruit bearing country on the Pacific coast. A thousand acres of this extent is in fruit, for the most part cherries. The season's cherry picking goes on at a great rate, and a little army of pickers toil from tree to tree, stripping the branches like a swarm of locusts. The sight is picturesque, for the pickers come by families and live in the cherry orchard in a small village of tents. At the height of the season nearly 150 pickers are employed. They are of all ages and both sexes, as the work is of such a nature that it can be performed as well by women as by men; as well by a ten year old girl as by a grown man. The pickers are boarded at the expense of the ranch, and besides receive from 75 cents to $1 per day, so that a wife and two or three children can make as much during the few weeks of the season as the head of the house in an entire year. After the picking, the cherries are taken over to the packing house and handled at once; the riper cherries are sorted out and put upon the local markets, while the more backward are shipped East. The force of packers can dispose of 420 boxes per day. Two thousand boxes go to the carload, and must be hurried to their destination as speedily as possible, for there is no fruit that loses its flavor quicker by overkeeping than the cherry. For the same reason the boxes must be rapidly marketed, for they will not keep many hours in the heat of an Eastern summer. There are plenty of difficulties in the way of getting the California cherry upon the tables of the Eastern consumer, but with ordinary care and a fair season the prices obtainable are not bad. In Chicago a ten-pound box of California cherries can be made to bring a dollar if properly handled, while in New York, though the Eastern local market comes into competition, the same quality will sometimes fetch 12 cents per pound.

CHERRIES—When their fragile blossoms signal the true end of winter, cherries come to mind. And later, at the height of summer, we treasure these highly perishable, exquisitely delicate, and incomparably delicious fruits, the season of which always has been too short. From the Middle Ages until just a few decades ago that brevity was marked and even celebrated by a cherry fair, a festive time when people wandered through the orchards harvesting cherries, eating them, and feeling that life was fine.

If cherries are somewhat less precious, they are no less delicious. They are still picked by hand, too, although we won't get into the "idyllic" life of the pickers, as depicted by Fellows. California grows a great number of our cherries, but the best come from the Pacific Northwest.

Given their fleeting peak, the best cherries come from whatever orchard is nearest to where you live. Although bing cherries travel well enough to make it to your supermarket, there is nothing as good as a cherry straight from the tree.

Bing cherries are just one of the thousand or so varieties of cherries under cultivation around the world, all members of the huge fruit genus *Prunus*. We eat sweet cherries (*Prunus avium*) and cook with, or should cook with, sour cherries such as the morello (*Prunus cerasus*). Dried cherries, found until recently only in Middle Eastern stores, are beginning to become more common in

this country; they make a great snack and are a suitable stew or sauce ingredient. Maraschino cherries were once the product of an elaborate process that included crushing the pit, fermenting the juice with honey, and adding a bit of extract of bitter almond; now, alas, they are merely sugared and chemically colored.

CHERRY COMPÔTE—Sound, large sweet cherries scalded for three minutes in a boiling syrup made of two pounds of sugar to the quart of water, the cherries then removed; the syrup flavored with noyeau, and when cold added to the cherries; served cold in sauce dishes, or hot as a sweet entrée with a border of sweetened rice.

BRANDIED CHERRIES—Round, large, sweet cherries scalded for two or three minutes in a boiling syrup composed of one pound of sugar to each quart of water, then taken up and laid on dishes to cool, afterwards filled into wide mouthed bottles. The syrup they were scalded in then boiled up again with another pound of sugar added to each quart, scum removed as it rises; when clear, taken off the stove and allowed to become cold, then an equal quantity of brandy added. The brandied syrup then poured over the cherries in the bottles, which are hermetically sealed and put away for use.

BOUCHÉES OF CHERRIES—For recipes of fruit bouchées see "Bouchées."

GLAZED CHERRIES WITH WHIPPED CREAM—Brandied cherries, the

syrup poured off and boiled down till thick and grainy, then flavored with Kirschen wasser, allowed to become cold, then poured over the cherries; served around a dome of whipped cream forced through a bag with fancy tube (called Cerises Glacés, à la Chantilly).

CHERRY JELLY—Five pounds of stoned cherry meat, juice of eight lemons, one pound of red currant jelly and some bruised cherry kernels mixed and brought to the boil in a gallon of syrup, simmered and skimmed, removed from the fire and four ounces of dissolved gelatine added, then strained and restrained through a jelly bag till clear, filled into molds or glasses; served when set.

CHERRY PIE—Stoned red sour cherries slightly flavored with noyeau, mixed with sugar, filled into a pie plate lined with pie paste, the fruit then sprinkled with carbonate of soda to prevent the juice running over, covered with a top crust, edges pressed and crimped, brushed with egg wash and baked.

DEEP CHERRY PIE—Sound red or black sour cherries mixed with sugar, filled into a deep lined pie dish, heaped high in the center, covered with top crust, egg washed, and baked.

CHERRY PUDDING—Molds of bowls lined with shortpaste, filled with cherry meat mixed with sugar, covered with top crust, boiled or steamed till done; served with cherry sauce.

CHERRY ROLY-POLY—Sweet biscuit dough rolled out thin, spread with cherry meat mixed with sugar, rolled up, ends tucked in, put in pans and steamed or baked, or tied in wet floured cloths and plunged into boiling water, kept boiling till done; serve with cherry sauce.

CHERRY TARTS—Tart molds lined with puff paste, filled with cherry meat mixed with sugar, baked, then meringued, browned and served.

CHERRIES IN CROÛSTADES—The croûstades made of sweetened rice croquette mixture, the edges decorated; served hot, filled with cherry compôte.

CHERRY CHARLOTTE—Small pans lined with lady fingers, filled with cherry marmalade, covered with fingers, baked and glazed; served with cherry sauce.

CHERRY MARMALADE—Stoned cherries with some of their kernels boiled to a pulp with a very little water and twelve ounces of sugar to each pound of fruit; when smooth and stiff poured into crocks for future use.

CHERRY COBBLER—Shallow baking pans lined with short paste, sides and bottom, filled with cherry meat mixed with sugar, covered with short paste, egg washed and baked; served with cherry sauce.

CHERRY TRIFLE—Pieces of stale sponge cake moistened with equal parts of the syrup of brandied cherries and sherry wine, smoothed down into a dish, then spread with cherry marmalade, over which is poured a boiled custard flavored with noyeau, the custard decorated with brandied cherries.

CHERRY FRITTERS—Thin slices of fresh bread spread between with cherry marmalade, the sandwich then neatly trimmed, dipped into a thin batter and fried, taken up, rolled in powdered sugar; served with cherry sauce.

CHERRY FLAWN—A flawn mold lined with puff paste, filled with cherry meat mixed with sugar, baked in slack oven till done.

CHERRY WATER ICE—One pound of stoned cherries and half pound of sugar to each quart of water, with a dash of lemon juice and a flavor of bitter almonds, the stoned cherries, bruised kernels and sugar mixed and rubbed through a fine sieve into the flavored water; then frozen.

CHERRY SHERBET—The water ice of the preceding recipe, but when nearly frozen, whipped whites of eggs, two to the quart, are added, then frozen till done.

CHERRY MERINGUE—Sheet of sponge cake spread thickly with cherry marmalade, then spread fancifully with meringue, dotted with brandied cherries, baked a straw color, cut in shapes, served with cream or whipped cream.

CHERVIL—A garden herb with a combined flavor of parsley and fennel.

CHERVIL—One of those herbs that is so fragile that it can be enjoyed only when fresh, chervil (*Anthriscus cerefolium*) is inevitably described as a cross between PARSLEY (to which it is related) and FENNEL (or ANISE). Its fleeting but assertive flavor can tolerate neither drying nor much heat, so it is almost always added to dishes just before serving. Chervil is an integral part of the French mixture known as FINES HERBES.

CHESTNUTS—The large ones obtainable at most Italian stores are the best suited for culinary purposes, the small ones seen at the fruit stalls being far too tedious. They should be first cut through the shell in the form of a cross, so as to strip the shell off easily, then placed in a baking pan, put into a slack oven till done; or they may be boiled till done, and then husked. Some people like to eat boiled chestnuts, the water being flavored with aniseed; when husked, made hot again in a little melted butter.

CHESTNUTS—From sometime after the end of the last ice age until the turn of the century "boundless chestnut woods," as Thoreau described them, dominated the forests of the eastern United States, from Maine to Florida and as far west as Ohio and Arkansas. But, just as Charles Fellows was putting the finishing touches on his book, a group of Asian chestnut saplings was planted on Long Island. Thus began a blight that destroyed nearly every chestnut tree in America, a blight from which we are only beginning to recover.

Consequently, we do not eat the American chestnut (*Castanea dentata*), but the sweet chestnut (*Castanea sativa*), which is imported from Italy and other places. From all reports they are of about equal quality. There are several other varieties of chestnuts from all over the world; all undoubtedly were among the first foods eaten by humans, since they fall to the ground when ripe and can be eaten raw.

Chestnuts are usually boiled, baked, or roasted before eating. Cut an X at the pointed end of each nut, or simply make a single cut along the chestnut's flat side and place in a 350° F. oven for 10 minutes or so, or boil for about 5 minutes. Then peel off the tough outer skin and use in recipes or eat. (For recipes, you can also begin with dried chestnuts, which are already peeled but must be soaked overnight before using.)

The best way to enjoy chestnuts, though, is to roast them over an open fire. Make sure you make a cut in the skin or they will explode. Then hold them over the fire—there are special chestnut pans with holes in the bottom—until softened. Chestnuts can also be parboiled before roasting, which hastens the process and decreases the chances of burning.

CHESTNUT FORCEMEAT—Chestnuts boiled and husked, pounded to a paste with butter, mixed with a little grated ham, breadcrumbs, minced onion, grated lemon rind, yolks of eggs, seasoned with salt and pepper; used to stuff poultry and suckling pigs.

DEVILLED CHESTNUTS—Boiled, peeled, fried brown in butter oil, taken up and sprinkled with salt and red pepper.

PURÉE OF CHESTNUTS—Boiled, peeled, pounded, then rubbed through a fine sieve.

CHESTNUT SOUP—A thin cream of chicken stock thickened with a purée of chestnuts, seasoned and served.

CHIANTI—A low priced yet good Italian wine with a Burgundy flavor.

CHIANTI—Chianti, which has little more than color in common with Burgundy, remains favorably priced, although the days of the three-dollar straw-covered bottle (the *fiasco*) are gone. This Tuscan wine has become steadily more distinctive and enjoyable in recent years. It is usually drunk young, although the best examples (usually labeled *Chianti Classico*) can be aged for some time.

CHICORY—A plant, the leaves of which are used for salads. The root is ground and used to mix with coffee, giving it a sweetish taste and dark color. Chicory should be discarded from coffee. Eminent physicians claim it has a debilitating effect, and a tendency to excite looseness of the bowels. Stewards who buy cheap ground coffee will invariably find it adulterated with chicory, and the chicory adulterated with Venitian red, acorns, beans, peas, coffee husks, rye, parsnips, damaged wheat, dried coffee grounds, sawdust, bark, logwood dust, etc. MORAL: do not handle it at all, buy whole coffee and see it ground yourself.

CHICORY—There are those people —especially in New Orleans—who still enjoy the extra bitterness roasted chicory root provides when blended with coffee, despite its avowed debilitating effects. But our primary interest is in chicory as a green. Closely related to ENDIVE (*Cichorium endivia*), and virtually interchangeable with it in recipes, chicory (*Chichorium intybus*) is an extremely bitter green that is often blanched by storing it in a dark place before harvesting. Although they look like lettuces, chicory and endive are best used only sparingly in salads; they perform equally well in cooked dishes, especially soups, where cooking tames their extreme bitterness.

There are scores of plants in this family, including the now-popular red chicory of northern Italy, radicchio di Treviso (*radicchio* means "chicory"), and Belgian endive (also called witloof, or white leaf), the forced and fully blanched pointed heart that is mild enough to star in a salad on its own. Salsify (also known as OYSTER PLANT) is also a kind of chicory.

CHICKEN—Chicken, first domesticated in India about four thousand years ago, was important in Fellows's day (why else would he include ten pages of recipes?), but it is an even more integral part of our diet now. We cook more chicken than any other meat, as do the people of many other countries. And with good reason: It is inexpensive, reasonably low in fat, and readily absorbs the flavors of an infinite number of herbs, spices, meats, vegetables, and fruits.

Unfortunately, chicken is not as tasty as it once was; the mass production that brought down its cost also reduced its character. If you have the chance to get a just-killed, farm-raised chicken, do so.

Bear in mind that the lean nature of chicken makes cooking it not quite as simple as it might appear. Unless care is taken, the breasts are always cooked through long before the legs and are easily dried out.

Finally, don't allow yourself to become confused by the old-fashioned terms *broiler, fryer,* and *roaster.* Technically, a broiler weighs fewer than two and a half pounds; a fryer, between two and a half and four pounds, and a roaster, anything more than that. But you can roast a fryer without penalty, and these days most chicken is so tender you can broil a roaster.

BROILED CHICKEN—Spring chickens cleaned, split, the breast and backbone removed, thigh bone snapped, seasoned with salt and pepper, brushed with butter, broiled well done; served on buttered toast, garnished with lemon and watercress, using frills on leg and wing bones.

FRIED CHICKEN—Spring chickens cleaned, split down the back, breast and backbone removed, thigh bone snapped, rolled in butter, then in flour, fried in skillet with a cover on; it may also be breaded, or dipped in batter, and fried in hot fat; the first way tastes the best.

SMOTHERED CHICKEN—Spring chickens split in halves, breast and backbone removed, thigh bone snapped, seasoned with salt and pepper, dipped in melted butter, rolled in flour, arranged in a baking pan with bacon fat, sliced vegetables and sweet herbs, moistened with a little chicken gravy, another pan put over as a lid, baked, basted and turned till done and brown, taken up; gravy made in the pan they were cooked in, strained, skimmed and served with the chickens.

CHICKEN CROQUETTES—Cold roast chicken cut into very small dice mixed with minced mushrooms, seasoned with lemon juice, salt and nutmeg, boiled down thick in Velouté sauce, turned into a shallow buttered pan, smoothed with a knife, covered with buttered paper; when cold, cut into even sized pieces, formed into cone shapes, breaded, fried, served with mushroom sauce poured around and garnished with croquette frills.

MINCED CHICKEN CUTLETS, SAUCE BORDELAISE—The croquette mixture preceding with the addition of a seasoning of minced fried shallots, thyme and chopped parsley; when cold, cut into even sized pieces, shaped like small lamb chops, using a piece of macaroni to represent the bone; breaded and fried; served with Bordelaise sauce poured around, and garnished with heart shaped croûtons dipped in tomato sauce and sprinkled with chopped parsley.

FRICASSÉE OF CHICKEN—Tender chickens cut into joints, seasoned with salt, pepper and lemon juice, rolled in flour, lightly fried in butter, then put into Velouté sauce and simmered till tender; Par-isienne potatoes steamed, then plunged into boiling fat and lightly browned; button mushrooms sautéed in butter; the sauce the chickens were stewed in finished with a liaison of egg yolks and cream. Served, the chicken with sauce poured over, and surrounded with alternate potatoes and mushrooms. Fricassée of chicken may also be made of boiled chickens the same way, or using cold boiled ones; the garnish may also be omitted or changed to the fancy of the cook.

CHICKEN PIE—Chickens boiled whole till tender with an onion and piece of salt pork; when done, taken up, the breasts and legs pulled off, the backbones thrown into the stock, the legs cut in halves, the under breast separated, and if the upper breast is large, cut in two, if small left whole; the pork cut into dice, the chicken then put into baking dishes with the pork sliced hard boiled eggs, raw Par-isienne potatoes and some chopped parsley; covered with a sauce made from the stock they were boiled in, reserving some of it, the pie then covered with short paste, egg washed and baked. In serving give liberally of the gravy, using the re-served sauce to replenish the pie.

CHICKEN POT PIE—Chickens boiled with salt pork and a few vegetables till tender, taken up and cut as for chicken pie preceding, put into a pan; sauce made of the stock, seasoned with salt, pepper, nutmeg, lemon juice and chopped parsley, poured over the chickens; spoonfuls of dumpling mixture dropped close together all over it; baked and served. Or the chicken when cut up, may be put into another saucepan, covered with the sauce, dumplings put all over it, lid put on, and the dumplings cooked by thus having the sauce boiled round them.

CHICKEN SAUTÉ WITH RIS-SOTO—Young chickens fried in joints, of a light color with mushrooms, taken up, gravy made in the pan they were fried in, strained over the chicken in a saûtoir, simmered till done, seasoned with salt, pepper and a glass of sherry wine. Rissoto made by cutting some ham fat into small dice and frying it with minced onion in a saûtoir, little curry powder added, then rice, moistened with white stock, lid put on and simmered till rice is well cooked, adding more stock if required. Served, the chicken in sauce in the centre of the dish, flanked with small domes of rissoto formed by filling small molds and turning them out for each order.

SMALL CHICKEN PIES, FRENCH STYLE—Boiled tender chickens, the stock well reduced till of a full flavor, meat taken from the chickens, cut into flakes of an even size; thick sauce made of the stock, seasoned with salt, pepper, nutmeg and chopped parsley, poured to the chicken. Puff paste cut out with large circular cutter, egg washed and baked; when done the paste split, the lower half covered with the chicken meat in sauce, top put on; served surrounded with- small balls of potatoes steamed, then moistened with mâitre d'hôtel butter.

CUTLETS OF CHICKEN WITH VEGE-TABLES—Spring chickens should be used boiled not quite done in white stock, then allowed to become cold, the breasts and legs then taken off, making four cutlets to each chicken, leaving the leg and wing bones a little long and scraping the same, so that it resembles a chop bone; seasoned with salt and pepper, breaded and fried; served surrounded with Julienne vegetables mixed into Hollandaise sauce.

FRIED FRICASSÉE OF CHICKEN—Neat shaped pieces of cold fricasséed chicken with the sauce adhering, rolled in breadcrumbs, then breaded and fried; served with a white Italian sauce poured around.

STEWED CHICKEN WITH TOMA-TOES—The chickens jointed, seasoned with salt and pepper, placed in a saûtoir with olive oil, parsley, some small onions and a clove of garlic, lid placed on and fried or simmered in their own steam till tender, taken up and gravy made in the saûtoir they were stewed in; served, the chicken with some gravy over it, garnished with fried slices of tomatoes sprinkled with parsley dust.

SUPRÊME OF CHICKEN WITH TOU-LOUSE RAGOUT—Breasts of young chickens that have been boiled whole, so that their shape is retained; skinned and trimmed to a pear shape, then sautéed lightly in butter, taken up and placed into a Suprême sauce and simmered gently for a few minutes; slices of cooked smoked tongue trimmed to a pear shape and heated with a little butter; served, the chicken breast resting on a fancy croûton flanked with a slice of the tongue,

Suprême sauce poured over the chicken, garnished with button mushrooms, turned truffles, cocks combs and kernels.

SUPRÊME OF CHICKEN WITH RICE, SAUCE PERIGUEUX—The suprême prepared as in the preceding; served, a bed of dry boiled rice, breast of chicken masked with Suprême sauce on top, flanked with two slices of the tongue, and Perigueux sauce poured around.

STEWED CHICKEN, TURKISH STYLE —Young chickens boiled whole with a rack of mutton (the part that is under the shoulder) in white stock; when the chicken is not quite done it is taken up and drained, placed in a saûtoir with butter and sliced onions and fried a golden color, then taken up and cut into joints, the onions removed and washed rice put into the saûtoir, moistened with the stock the chicken and mutton was boiled in, cooked till dry and tender, sauce made of the remaining stock seasoned with a little cinnamon; served, a bed of the rice, a chop and joint of the chicken resting on it, with the sauce poured over and around.

CHICKEN WITH RICE, MALTESE STYLE—Young chickens roasted whole not quite done, then jointed, then braised for a few minutes with minced onions, garlic, and a few cloves, then one part of tomato sauce and two parts of white stock is added to the chickens, and when boiled up, washed rice is added and the whole simmered till the rice is tender; served, a bed of rice with

joint of chicken on top and sauce Trianon poured around.

ROAST CHICKEN, OYSTER SAUCE —Young chickens drawn, singed, washed, wiped dry, filled with a stuffing made of blanched and chopped oysters, chopped parsley, fresh breadcrumbs, salt, pepper, nutmeg and a dash of anchovy essence, trussed, roasted and basted till tender; served with some of the stuffing underneath and oyster sauce poured around; made by blanching the oysters, then cutting them into neat pieces, sautéeing them with butter and fine herbs; sauce made of the liquor from the blanching, seasoned with salt, pepper and a dash of anchovy essence, the sautéed oysters and herbs then added.

STEWED CHICKEN, SPANISH STYLE —Cold boiled chicken cut into joints, seasoned with salt, pepper and mixed ground spices, sautéed in olive oil with minced shallots, garlic and chopped parsley; when colored, the surplus oil poured off, and Espagnole sauce added, simmered a few minutes; served with the sauce and garnished with slices of hard boiled (hot) eggs.

CHICKEN STUFFED WITH CHESTNUTS, MADEIRA SAUCE—Chickens drawn, singed and washed, then boiled till tender in white stock, taken up, cooled, stuffed with chestnut forcemeat, trussed, roasted quickly, being basted with butter and flour, served with a rich Madeira sauce poured around.

CHICKEN WITH CHESTNUT PURÉE AND VEGETABLES—Cold roast

chickens cut into joints and trimmed, bone removed and its place filled with a stiff purée of chestnuts moistened with a little cream, together with the grated rind of a lemon, the stuffed joints then dipped in limpid aspic jelly and allowed to set, then decorated with a piping of Ravigote butter; served, a cold dish covered with crisp lettuce leaves, at the ends a triangular shape of macedoine of vegetables mixed with salad cream, and chicken joints resting on the salad, and Tartar sauce in the center.

ROASTED CHICKEN WITH MUSH-ROOMS AND BREAD SAUCE—Young chickens drawn, singed, washed, trussed with slices of bacon tied over the breast, roasted and basted, and when nearly done the bacon removed and the breast browned; served with bread sauce at one end of the dish, sautéed mushrooms in sauce as a border, also a garnish of fresh crisp watercress.

CHICKENS, MARYLAND STYLE— Spring chickens singed, split down the back, the breastbone and back-bone removed, left in halves for restaurant, and the leg and breast separated for hotel orders, making four portions of each chicken; sea-soned with salt and pepper, dipped in beaten eggs, then fresh bread-crumbs, arranged in baking pan with slices of bacon, brushed with melted butter, roasted and basted with the bacon fat till done; served, the chicken resting on a corn frit-ter, flanked with two slices of the bacon, and a ladle of Béchamel sauce poured around.

BOILED CHICKEN WITH SALT PORK, PARSLEY SAUCE—Small chickens about two pounds each in weight, singed, drawn, washed and put to boil with a piece of salt pork, an onion stuck with cloves, carrot and celery; when tender, taken up, the breasts and legs carefully re-moved, backbone and trimmings thrown back into the stock, the joints kept hot in white stock, the sauce made of the liquor they were boiled in; served, a breast or leg and under breast flanked with a slice of the pork, and the sauce poured around.

FRIED CHICKEN IN BATTER, TO-MATO SAUCE—Spring chickens blanched whole, then separated (not cut) into four joints, steeped for an hour in a mixture of chopped parsley, salt, pepper, minced shallots, lemon juice and olive oil, then taken up and wiped, dipped into a batter, fried in hot fat; served with tomato sauce poured around.

HARICOT OF CHICKEN WITH VEGE-TABLES—Chickens singed, drawn and washed, then boiled whole with carrots, turnips and onions; when nearly done taken up and cut into joints, seasoned with salt and pepper, rolled in flour, fried a golden brown with butter, placed into a saûtoir, brown sauce made of the stock they were boiled in, strained over the fried chicken, simmered till tender, the cooked vegetables cut into large dice, mixed with cooked green peas, moistened with gravy and kept hot in it; served, the chicken in sauce surrounded with the vegetables.

BRAISED CHICKEN WITH MACA-
RONI—Old fowls singed, drawn,
washed and wiped, then steamed
for an hour, taken up, cut into
joints, placed in a saûtoir with vegetables and spices, moistened with
Madeira sauce, lid put on, saûtoir
placed in hot oven and the chicken
braised till tender, then taken up
into another saûtoir and the braise
strained over them; macaroni in
inch lengths boiled in stock with
an onion; when done, drained,
sprinkled with Parmesan cheese
and chopped parsley; served, the
chicken in sauce surrounded with
the macaroni.

BROILED CHICKEN, HUNTER'S
STYLE—Spring chickens singed,
split down the back, backbone and
breastbone removed, steeped for
an hour in a mixture of olive oil,
minced onions, chopped parsley,
salt, pepper and lemon juice, taken
up, rolled in fresh breadcrumbs,
broiled well done; served with
sauce Chasseur poured around,
and garnished with lemon and
parsley.

EPIGRAMME OF CHICKEN, TO-
MATO SAUCE—Young chickens
singed, drawn, washed and wiped,
blanched, taken up and separated
into four joints, the breast and under breast seasoned with salt and
pepper, then breaded, arranged in a
buttered saûtoir, roasted and
basted till tender and brown, the
legs boned, then filled with chicken
forcemeat, braised and glazed;
served, a fancy croûton in center of
dish with a glazed leg and browned
breast resting on either side, and a
rich tomato sauce poured around.

BLANCHED CHICKEN WITH VE-
LOUTÉ SAUCE—Young white fleshed
chickens singed drawn, washed,
trussed with a piece of butter size of
an egg mixed with the juice of a
lemon and a seasoning of salt and
pepper in the inside of each; arranged in a saûtoir with slices of
lemon and fat bacon, moistened with
a little white stock, lid put on,
steamed in this way till tender;
served, masked with Velouté sauce,
and garnished with Hollandaise potatoes.

MATELOTE OF CHICKEN—Young
chickens singed, drawn, washed,
simmered for half an hour in white
stock, taken up, jointed, put into
Velouté sauce with a glass of white
wine, simmered till tender, then is
added small white onions, balls of
carrot and turnip (some use parsnip) each of which has been boiled
in consommé with a pinch of
sugar; served, the chicken in
sauce, garnished with vegetables.

CHICKEN SAUTÉ WITH MUSH-
ROOMS—Young chickens singed,
drawn, washed, cut into joints, seasoned with salt and pepper, fried in
oil with herbs and garlic, when
brown, taken up and placed into a
saûtoir, button mushrooms then
fried in the oil, taken up and put
with the chickens, surplus oil then
poured off, flour added to the pan,
stirred, moistened with chicken
stock and Madeira wine, boiled up,
skimmed, strained over the chickens, which are then simmered till
tender; served garnished with the
mushrooms (called Chicken à la
Marengo).

CHICKEN STUFFED AND STEWED,
SAUCE MILANAISE—Young chick-

ens singed, drawn, washed, filled with a stuffing made of grated lean ham, chopped hard boiled eggs, fresh breadcrumbs, chopped parsley, minced shallots, juice of a lemon, and a seasoning of thyme, trussed, arranged in a saûtoir, covered with white stock, lid placed on, simmered and basted till tender; served in joints with some of the stuffing underneath, and Milanaise sauce poured around.

FRIED CHICKEN WITH CUCUMBER PURÉE—Spring chickens singed, split down the back, separated into four joints, backbone and breastbone removed, blanched in white stock for a few minutes, then taken up and coated with thick cucumber sauce, rolled in breadcrumbs, then breaded, fried; served surrounded with a purée of cucumbers.

STEWED CHICKEN WITH DUMPLINGS—Young chickens singed, drawn, washed and jointed, arranged in saucepan with carrot, onion, celery and turnip, moistened with white stock, simmered till tender, taken up, sauce made of the stock, the vegetables rubbed through a sieve into the finished sauce, dumplings steamed; served, the chicken in centre of dish, dumpling at each end, sauce poured over the whole, sprinkled with parsley dust.

FRIED CHICKEN, INDIAN STYLE—Spring chickens blanched whole, then jointed, seasoned with salt, pepper and rubbed with curry powder, fried brown in butter; served with a garnish of stewed onions.

BRAISED FILLETS OF CHICKEN, HANOVER SAUCE—Old fowls singed, drawn, washed, steamed for an hour, then cut into fillets, arranged in a saûtoir with spices and vegetables, moistened with consommé, braised till tender and the consommé has reduced to half glaze, fillets taken up into another saûtoir, the braise strained into an Hanover sauce and poured over the chicken; served with it and garnished with fancy croûtons.

CHICKEN CURRIED, WITH RICE—Young chickens singed, drawn, washed, boiled for an hour in white stock, taken up, drained, cut into joints, seasoned with salt, rolled in flour, fried brown in butter with sliced onions and a clove of garlic, chicken then taken up and placed into a saûtoir, sprinkled with curry powder and flour, shook together, moistened with the strained stock they were boiled in, simmered till tender, with the addition of a grated green apple and the juice of a lemon; served in the centre of a border of dry boiled rice.

BLANQUETTE OF CHICKEN WITH TRUFFLES—Young white chickens singed, drawn, washed, arranged in a saûtoir with slices of fat bacon and some lemon juice, moistened with white stock, lid put on and simmered till tender, taken up and cut into joints, placed into another saûtoir, bacon and grease removed, Béchamel sauce then poured in, boiled up, skimmed, strained over the chickens; served with it, sprinkled with minced truffle peelings.

SPITCHCOCKED CHICKEN, CRAPAUDINE SAUCE—Spring chickens singed, split, washed, backbone and breastbone removed, trussed out like a frog, seasoned with salt and pepper, rolled in olive oil. broiled well done; served on toast with Crapaudine sauce poured around, garnished with parsley and lemon.

STEWED CHICKEN WITH RICE—Young chickens singed, split, jointed, fried with olive oil in a saûtoir; when brown, surplus oil poured off, minced green peppers and onions with a clove of garlic (crushed) then added and fried a little more, lightly sprinkled with flour, shook together, moistened with consommé, lid placed on and simmered till tender and glazy, then is added some slices of pimentoes and chutney with a glass of Madeira wine, boiled up; served within a border of dry boiled rice that has been very slightly flavored and colored with curry.

STEWED CHICKEN, MEXICAN STYLE—Young chickens singed, split, jointed, fried with olive oil in a saûtoir till brown, taken up in another saûtoir, ham and garlic then fried in the oil of a light color, surplus oil poured off the onions, etc., then moistened with equal parts of tomato and Espagnole sauces, seasoned with thyme, sage, marjoram and sweet pepper, simmered for half an hour, skimmed, strained over the chickens which are then simmered till tender; raw tomatoes peeled and the seeds removed, cut into pieces and stewed down thick with chili sauce; served, the chicken in sauce with fancy croûtons at ends of dish, garnished at the sides with the tomato and chili mixture.

BRAISED CHICKENS WITH GREEN PEPPERS—Young chickens singed, drawn, washed, filled with a stuffing made by boiling yellow corn meal with chicken stock to mush; when done, mixed with fresh grated breadcrumbs, Parmesan cheese, butter, salt and pepper, trussed with slices of bacon tied over the breast, arranged in a saûtoir with onions, carrot, parsley, bay leaves, cloves and a crushed clove of garlic, moistened with consommé, braised till tender and glazy, taken up, braise strained and skimmed, then added to some Espagnole sauce containing green peppers sliced, and a seasoning of curry powder; served, the chickens in portions with stuffing underneath, sauce poured over, garnished with the peppers.

BOILED CHICKEN WITH VEGETABLES, ALLEMANDE SAUCE—Old fowls singed, drawn, washed and trussed, put into saucepan with carrot, celery and onions, covered with salted water, lid put on, saucepan then placed in hot oven, chickens simmered till tender (about three hours), taken up, Allemande sauce made from the remaining stock; small balls of carrot simmered in consommé till tender, a can each of lima beans and flageolets opened and washed, then mixed with the carrot balls, seasoned with salt, sugar and red pepper; served, the chicken in joints with sauce poured over, and garnished with the mixed vegetables drained out of the consommé.

BOILED LARDED CHICKEN WITH MACARONI—Old fowls singed, drawn, washed, the breasts larded, trussed, arranged in saucepan with carrot, onions and celery, covered with salted water, lid put on, simmered in hot oven till tender; a rich yellow sauce made from the reduced liquor, macaroni broken in inch lengths and boiled in salted water till done, taken up, drained, seasoned with paprika, Parmesan cheese and a little of the sauce for the chickens; served, the birds in joints with the sauce poured over and sprinkled with parsley dust, garnished with the macaroni.

STEWED CHICKENS WITH ESTRAGON—Old fowls singed, drawn, jointed, washed, put into a saûtoir with some fat from the top of the stock pot, a few veal trimmings, a bunch of tarragon and some sherry wine, covered with white stock, lid put on and simmered in a hot oven till tender, then taken up into another saûtoir, the remaining stock strained, skimmed, and added to a rich Poulette sauce containing chopped tarragon leaves; served, the chicken covered with the sauce and garnished with slices of hard boiled (hot) eggs.

BRAISED CHICKENS WITH VEGETABLES—Old fowls singed, drawn, washed, the breasts larded, trussed, arranged in saucepan with some bacon trimmings, spices and vegetables, moistened with white stock and Madeira sauce in equal parts, lid put on, simmered in hot oven till tender, taken up, the braise strained and skimmed, then poured over the chickens; cans of macedoines opened and washed, then kept hot in consommé; served, the chickens in joints with the sauce over, garnished with the vegetables drained from the consommé.

BRAISED CHICKENS WITH MUSHROOMS—Old fowls prepared, bacon tied over the breast, arranged in a saûtoir with vegetables and spices, moistened with consommé, lid put on, then braised till tender and glazy, taken up, braise skimmed, strained and added to button mushrooms that have been sautéed with butter and then mixed into Béchamel sauce; served, the glazed pieces of chicken resting on neat shaped pieces of toast surrounded with the mushrooms in sauce.

CHAUD-FROID OF CHICKEN—Spring chickens a pound and a half each in weight, singed, drawn, washed, trussed, wrapped in buttered paper, roasted without browning, taken up and allowed to cool in the paper, then separated into four joints, neatly trimmed; equal parts of aspic jelly and Poulette sauce made warm enough to mix, then stirred surrounded with broken ice till thick, the chicken then dipped into it, then arranged on a baking sheet to set; when set, decorate them with slices of truffles; the remaining sauce filled into timbale molds that have been lined with aspic jelly and set; served, the chicken joint resting on a croûton of aspic jelly, with the timbale turned out on the end of the chicken, the other end garnished with watercress.

CHARTREUSE OF CHICKEN WITH STRING BEANS—Cold cooked chicken three-fifths; lean cooked ham and fresh grated breadcrumbs each one-fifth; the meats cut into very small squares, mixed with the crumbs together with some chopped chervil, capers and a seasoning of tarragon vinegar, salt and red pepper; moistened with stock and beaten raw eggs; filled into buttered molds within half an inch of the top, lids put on and steamed for an hour; allow them to slightly cool before turning out; served, in slices surrounded with French string beans (haricots verts) taken from the cans; washed, then heated in Velouté sauce.

DEVILLED CHICKEN LEGS WITH BACON—Skinned tender chicken legs, scored, laid for an hour in a mixture of olive oil, Worcestershire sauce, lemon juice, red pepper and anchovy essence, then taken up and slowly broiled; served resting on a croûton, garnished with strips of bacon, and some sauce Diable.

CHICKEN FORCEMEAT—White meat of cooked chicken three parts; white bread soaked in chicken stock, then squeezed dry, one part; pounded together to a paste with two ounces of butter to each pound of meat, seasoned with salt, pepper, nutmeg and a little lemon juice, then rubbed through a fine sieve and mixed to a stiff consistency with egg yolks and cold Velouté sauce.

CHICKEN FORCEMEAT BALLS CURRIED, WITH RICE—Balls of the preceding forcemeat poached in a good curry sauce; served with it, being arranged on the serving dish alternately with small molds of dry boiled rice.

FILLETS OF CHICKEN WITH ASPARAGUS POINTS—Spring chickens one and a half pounds each in weight, singed, drawn, washed, boiled just done, taken up, cooled, skinned, separated into four joints neatly trimmed, reheated in a rich Villeroi sauce; served masked with it, garnished with asparagus points seasoned with butter.

CHICKEN CUTLETS WITH GREEN PEAS—Spring chickens singed, drawn, washed, steamed not quite done, taken up, cooled, skinned, separated into four joints, seasoned with salt, pepper and nutmeg, dipped in cooling Villeroi sauce, then in breadcrumbs, then breaded and arranged in a buttered baking pan, roasted and basted till brown and frothy; served surrounded with green peas moistened with consommé and butter.

SCALLOPED CHICKEN—Cold cooked chicken meat cut into thin slices, moistened with Allemande sauce, filled into scallop shells or oval deep dishes, sprinkled with fresh breadcrumbs mixed with Parmesan cheese, salt, red pepper and nutmeg, then with melted butter, arranged on a baking sheet, heated and browned; served in the shell or dish, garnished with watercress.

CHICKEN KROMESKIES, SAUCE PERIGUEUX—Cooked chicken and tongue, button mushrooms and truffles all cut into very small squares and boiled down thick in a rich Velouté sauce, a liaison of egg yolks and cream added just at the finish, then turned into a buttered shallow pan, smoothed with a palette knife, covered with buttered paper and allowed to become cold, then cut into even sized pieces, formed to the shape of long corks, wrapped round with a thin slice of cold boiled bacon or udder, pinned with a toothpick, dipped into batter and fried, toothpick then removed; served with Perigueux sauce.

SALPIÇON OF CHICKEN WITH PO-
TATOES—Cooked chicken, tongue,
mushrooms and truffles cut into
small squares and made hot in a
rich Poulette sauce; served, the
serving dish bordered with mashed
potatoes forced from a bag and
fancy tube, sprinkled with parsley
dust, the salpiçon in the centre.

CHICKEN PATTIES, SAUCE SU-
PRÊME—The preceding salpiçon,
but cut smaller, filled into patty
shells; served with Suprême sauce
poured around.

STEWED CHICKEN, GERMAN
STYLE—Old fowls singed, drawn,
washed and trussed, arranged in a
saucepan with grated green apples
and onions, covered with stock,
simmered in hot oven till tender,
Allemande sauce made from the reduced liquor, noodles boiled in
stock till tender, taken up and
drained, then mixed with some of
the sauce; served, the chicken
masked with sauce, surrounded
with noodles.

CHICKEN QUENELLE FORCE-
MEAT—Raw skinless chicken meat
with a little beef suet minced,
pounded together to a paste,
rubbed through a fine sieve with
some bread that has been soaked in
milk and squeezed dry, seasoned
with finely chopped parsley, grated
lemon rind, salt, red pepper and
nutmeg, worked to a stiff consistency with raw egg yolks beaten
with a little cream.

CHICKEN QUENELLES WITH MUSH-
ROOMS—The forcemeat preceding
made into balls or shaped like eggs

between two dessert spoons;
poached in white stock till they
float, taken up and rolled in fried
sifted breadcrumbs; served surrounded with button mushrooms
in Velouté sauce.

RISSOLES OF CHICKEN—The salpiçon as given for "Kromeskies"
when cold, cut out with a circular
cutter, two sheets of puff paste
rolled out thin, the chicken placed
over one sheet, covered with the
other, stamped out with a fancy
edged cutter, arranged on a baking
sheet, brushed over with egg wash
and baked.

SAUTÉ OF CHICKEN WITH BOU-
CHÉES—Spring chickens singed,
drawn, washed, then steamed for
five minutes, then separated into
four joints neatly trimmed, scraping the little meat off the wing and
leg shanks to form handles; seasoned with salt, pepper and powdered thyme, fried brown with
butter, then put into Madeira sauce
and simmered till tender; served,
resting against a croûton with frills
on the shanks, sauce poured over
the meat, garnished with very small
patties filled with salpiçon.

VOL-AU-VENT OF CHICKEN WITH
QUENELLES—Large patty shells
with separate covers filled with a
salpiçon of chicken, cover then
placed on, served with Madeira
sauce poured under, and garnished
with small poached chicken quenelles.

ROAST BONED CHICKEN—Large
old fowls and young hens singed,
skin laid open down the back and

all bones removed, the old ones then laid out flat skin side down, seasoned with salt, pepper, nutmeg and powdered thyme, alternate strips of larding pork and red cooked tongue then placed lengthwise down the center, then covered with forcemeat, the young hen without skin laid on top of it so that the white meat covers the dark meat of the fowl, outer skin of the fowl then drawn together and sewn close, leaving no apertures; again sewn up into a cloth, steamed for an hour, cloth then removed, roasted and basted till well done and tender, taken up, pressed; when cold, string removed, glazed; served cold in slices with salad.

BOILED BONED CHICKEN—Same as the preceding, but instead of steaming, it is simmered till tender in white stock containing vegetables; when done, taken up, pressed in the cloth; when cold, cloth and string removed, all adhering grease removed with a hot cloth, it is then glazed; served cold in slices with salad.

GALANTINE OF CHICKEN—Galantine molds placed in a pan of broken ice, salt and water, limpid aspic jelly poured in to coat the sides, which is then decorated with peas, strips of tongue, stamped slices of truffle and whites of hard boiled eggs, etc., the decorations then coated with more limpid jelly and allowed to set, the interior then filled with slices of boned chicken and limpid jelly till full (always see that the slices of chicken are placed on edge, NOT LAID FLAT! so that when it is turned out, the slices may be removed with the jelly adhering merely by the use of

a fork). When set, the mold is slightly warmed with a hot cloth, then turned out, the dish garnished with croûtons of aspic jelly, cress, crisp shred lettuce, fancy slices of pickled beet, or variations at the cook's fancy.

FRIED BREAST OF CHICKEN WITH CORN FRITTERS—Spring chickens singed, drawn, washed and simmered barely done, taken up, cooled, skinned, breasts removed, seasoned with salt, pepper, nutmeg and powdered thyme, rolled in melted butter, then in flour, then in beaten eggs and fried in hot fat, taken up and drained; served with sauce Suprême poured under, and garnished with small corn fritters and watercress.

BREAST OF CHICKEN STEAMED, SAUCE SUPRÊME—Spring chickens singed, drawn, washed, trussed and steamed till done, taken up, breasts removed and skinned, then put into Suprême sauce and served with it, garnished with kidney beans (flageolets).

BROILED CHICKEN LEGS WITH GREEN PEAS—The steamed legs of the preceding recipe, skinned, then laid for an hour in a mixture of olive oil, lemon juice, red pepper, salt and Worcestershire sauce, then broiled slowly to a golden color; served with a frill on the shank, resting on a slice of buttered toast, garnished with French peas made hot in tomato sauce.

FRIED SPRING CHICKEN WITH ARTICHOKE BOTTOMS—Spring chickens singed, split down the back, breastbone and backbone removed, seasoned with salt and pepper, rolled in flour, then in beaten eggs and fried in hot fat till done; artichoke bottoms spread with chicken forcemeat arranged in a saûtoir, moistened with a very little consommé, reduced and glazed, the chicken served with a little Colbert sauce, and garnished with the bottoms.

FRIED SPRING CHICKEN WITH HOMINY FRITTERS—The chickens prepared and fried as in the preceding; fine hominy boiled down to mush, cooled, cut in shapes, then breaded and fried, the chicken served with cream sauce and a strip of broiled bacon, garnished with the fritters.

FRIED CHICKEN WITH RICE AND OKRAS—Cold joints of cooked chicken dipped in thick cold tomato sauce, then in breadcrumbs, then breaded and arranged in a buttered baking pan, roasted and basted with butter till brown and frothy; rice boiled dry, then mixed with boiled fresh or canned okras and a little tomato sauce, the chicken served with a little tomato sauce, and garnished with small mounds of the rice and okras turned out of a timbale mold.

DEVILLED SPRING CHICKEN WITH GREEN PEAS—Spring chickens singed, split down the back, breastbone and backbone removed, thigh bone snapped, seasoned, laid for an hour in Worcestershire sauce, olive oil, tarragon vinegar, chopped chives and chervil, taken up, rolled in flour, then in melted butter and slowly broiled well done; served

with Diable sauce, and garnished with French peas that have been washed, drained and sautéed in butter.

FILLETS OF CHICKEN WITH CARDINAL SAUCE—Spring chickens singed, split, breastbone and backbone removed, thigh bone snapped, seasoned with salt and pepper, rolled in flour and fried a golden brown with butter; served with Cardinal sauce poured under and around, garnished with slices of truffles that have been stewed in sherry wine.

STUFFED BREAST OF CHICKEN, PERIGUEUX SAUCE—Breasts of young chickens split open and filled with quenelle forcemeat, arranged in a saûtoir with slices of salt pork, white stock and butter, simmered till tender; served resting on fancy croûtons with Perigueux sauce.

STEWED CHICKEN, SAUCE RAVIGOTE—Old fowls singed, drawn, washed, jointed, then arranged in a saûtoir with nutmeg, lemon, celery and sliced onions, moistened with white stock, lid put on, simmered in hot oven till tender. Chives, parsley, shallots, chervil and tarragon shred and blanched, onion rings steamed till tender; served, the chicken with Ravigote sauce poured around, garnished with rings of onions filled with the blanched herbs.

STEWED CHICKEN, SAUCE PROVENÇALE—Young chickens singed, drawn, washed, jointed, seasoned with salt and pepper, rolled in flour, sautéed in olive oil with minced shallots and garlic, taken up into another saûtoir with sliced tomatoes, moistened with claret wine and Espagnole sauce, simmered till tender, finished with lemon juice and chopped parsley; served with the sauce and tomatoes.

SPRING CHICKEN IN BATTER WITH FRIED ONIONS—Spring chickens singed, split, backbone and breastbone removed, thigh bone snapped, blanched in white stock a few minutes, taken up and drained, seasoned with salt, pepper, nutmeg and powdered thyme, then dipped in batter and slowly fried in hot fat; rings of onions steamed for a few minutes, then dipped in milk, then flour, fried crisp in hot fat; served as a garnish to the chicken.

STUFFED BREAST OF CHICKEN WITH CUCUMBERS—Breasts of spring chickens that have been steamed whole not quite done, trimmed, spread with chicken forcemeat, then dipped in beaten eggs, then sprinkled with grated lean cooked ham, minced truffle peelings and breadcrumbs, arranged in a baking pan, moistened with a little melted butter, slowly heated and browned; served garnished with a purée of cucumbers.

CHICKEN SAUSAGES, SAUCE HOLLANDAISE—Raw chicken meat without skin three-fifths, cooked chicken meat one-fifth, cooked tongue and mushrooms mixed one-fifth, all minced together, seasoned with salt, pepper, nutmeg and powdered thyme, formed into sausage shapes, lightly breaded, arranged in baking pan with bacon trimmings and butter, slowly roasted and basted till done; served with Hollandaise sauce.

SOUFFLÉS OF CHICKEN—Breast of raw chicken pounded to a paste, then rubbed through a fine sieve and mixed with separately beaten whites and yolks of eggs, seasoned with butter, cream, salt, red pepper, nutmeg and lemon juice, filled into fancy paper cases, the top sprinkled with sifted breadcrumbs and melted butter, slowly baked, then served immediately.

CHICKEN QUENELLES WITH TRUFFLES, SAUCE SUPRÊME—Chicken quenelle forcemeat shaped like eggs between two spoons, poached in seasoned white stock, taken up and drained, then dipped in Suprême sauce; served with it, arranged on serving dish in fours, two of them sprinkled with minced truffle peelings.

CANNELON OF CHICKEN, TARTAR SAUCE—Cannelon case made of puff paste (see CANNELONS) filled with chicken forcemeat, slowly heated through; served with Tartar sauce, garnished with watercress.

CHICKEN FORCEMEAT FRIED, TOMATO SAUCE—Chicken forcemeat rolled with pointed ends size of a finger, resembling a cigar in shape, breaded, fried; served with tomato sauce.

SAUTÉ OF CHICKEN WITH RICE AND LEEKS—Young chickens singed, drawn, washed, jointed, seasoned with salt and pepper,

CHICKEN SOUFFLÉ

•

Serves 6 to 8

This dish is more like a chicken loaf than a regular soufflé. Nonetheless, it is delicious, and especially easy to make if you own a good food processor.

4 tablespoons butter	2 teaspoons salt
2 cloves garlic, peeled and chopped	Juice of half a lemon
2 medium yellow onions, peeled and sliced	3 teaspoons Worcestershire sauce
1¼ pounds chicken thighs	½ teaspoon cayenne pepper
1 pound chicken breasts	5 egg whites at room temperature
6 egg yolks	
⅔ cup heavy cream	

Preheat the oven to 400° F.

In a large frying pan, sauté the butter, garlic, and onions until tender. Set aside.

Skin the chicken, saving the skin. Debone the chicken pieces and trim out any major cartilage. In a large food processor, grind the chicken skin very fine. Add the chicken meat and grind to make a paste. Add the sautéed garlic and onions and the remaining ingredients, except the egg whites. Purée until very smooth. Pour into a large bowl.

Whip the egg whites until they hold soft peaks. Fold the egg whites into the puréed chicken.

Pour into a greased 9-inch by 4-inch soufflé dish. Fill to 1 inch from the top of the dish. If there is any remaining soufflé batter, it can go into another dish. Bake for 35 minutes. The soufflé should rise considerably and be nicely browned on the top.

If there is any leftover soufflé, refrigerate it. The next day slice and pan-fry it in butter.

C.W.

then lightly sautéed with minced onions and ham in butter, taken up into a saûtoir, sauce made in the pan they were fried in, strained over the chickens, simmered till tender, rice boiled dry; then mixed with some of the sauce; served as a border to the chicken, which is further garnished with fried shredded leeks.

CHICKEN SAUTÉ WITH POTATO BALLS—Spring chickens singed, drawn, washed, steamed for five minutes, then taken up and separated into four neat joints, seasoned with salt and pepper, fried with butter to a golden color; balls scooped out of raw potatoes steamed nearly done, then fried in butter like the chickens, both of which are then sprinkled with fine parsley; served, the joints dipped in hot Colbert sauce surrounded with the potatoes.

CROÛSTADES OF CHICKEN—Fancy croûstades made of paste filled with a salpiçon of chicken; garnished with watercress.

CHICKEN HASH WITH PEPPERS ON TOAST—Cold cooked chicken without skin cut into very small squares, green peppers shred and blanched, both mixed and simmered in a rich Velouté sauce; served on toast.

MINCED CHICKEN WITH POACHED EGG—Cold cooked chicken without skin cut into very small squares, mixed into and heated with Béchamel sauce; served on toast with a trimmed poached egg on top, the yolk sprinkled with parsley dust.

CHICKEN HASH WITH STUFFED PEPPERS—Small green peppers split, cleaned and blanched, filled with chicken forcemeat, arranged in a saûtoir, moistened with a little consommé, lid put on and simmered till done; the minced chicken on toast of the preceding recipe served garnished with the stuffed peppers.

CHICKEN FRITTERS, PIQUANTE SAUCE—Cold roast tender chicken in joints, laid for an hour in vinegar with chopped chives, taken up, breaded and fried; served with Piquante sauce.

CHICKEN PANADA WITH EGGS ON TOAST—Cold cooked chicken without skin minced and pounded to a paste, then rubbed through a fine sieve, seasoned with salt, pepper and nutmeg, mixed with an equal quantity of fresh breadcrumbs, moistened with cream, made hot; served heaped high on toast with a trimmed poached egg on top.

POTTED CHICKEN FOR SANDWICHES—Two parts of cold cooked chicken meat without skin, one part cooked ham, one part butter, the meat minced and pounded to a paste with the butter, then rubbed through a fine sieve, seasoned with mace, salt, red pepper and nutmeg, packed into small jars, sealed with melted butter, and stored away in ice box for use.

TIMBALES OF CHICKEN WITH FORCEMEAT BALLS—Timbale molds lined with a quenelle forcemeat, then filled with scallops of braised chicken and slices of mushrooms and truffles, the bottom then covered with forcemeat, molds arranged in a baking pan containing a little water, baked till set; served turned out with sauce Bressoise poured around, and garnished with small balls of poached forcemeat.

CHICKEN SAUTÉ WITH OYSTERS—Large oysters blanched and drained; young chickens singed, drawn, blanched, jointed, seasoned with salt and pepper, rolled in flour, fried in butter, taken up into a saûtoir, gravy made in the pan they were fried in, using stock and the strained oyster liquor, boiled up and skimmed, then strained over the chicken, which is now simmered till tender; the oysters sprinkled with parsley and sautéed in butter for each order; served, the chicken in joints garnished with the oysters sautées.

CAPILOTADE OF CHICKEN—Cold roast chickens cut into neatly trimmed joints, arranged in a saû-toir, covered with a brown Italian sauce, simmered in it for fifteen minutes then served garnished with fancy croûtons.

COLLOPS OF CHICKEN WITH MAC-ARONI—Cold cooked chicken without skin cut into thin slices about the size of a quarter of a dollar, made hot in a rich Béchamel sauce; macaroni broken into inch lengths, boiled in boiling salted water, taken up and drained, then mixed with Parmesan cheese and a little Béchamel sauce; served, the maca-roni as a border sprinkled with parsley dust, the chicken piled high in the center, garnished with strips of cooked red tongue.

HASHED CHICKEN AND HAM WITH RICE—Chicken cut the same as in the preceding recipe, thin slices of lean cooked ham cut out with a column cutter, both mixed and made hot in Velouté sauce. Rice washed and then boiled in chicken broth till moisture is all gone and the grains soft, then mixed with a liaison of egg yolks and Velouté sauce, seasoned with red pepper and nutmeg; served, the rice as a border, the ham and chicken in sauce piled high in the center.

GIBLET AND POTATO PIE—Giz-zards, hearts, livers, necks and sec-ond joints of the wings of chickens stewed tender with pieces of salt pork, then put in a baking pan with slices of hard boiled eggs, chopped parsley and a glass of sherry wine, (having plenty of sauce) the pie then covered three-quarters of an inch thick with mashed potatoes, edges crimped, washed over with beaten egg and baked.

GIBLET PIE—Pie pans lined on the sides with thin short paste, filled with the stewed giblets of the pre-ceding recipe, covered with short paste, egg washed and baked.

GIBLET POT PIE—The preceding stewed giblets either kept hot in the saûtoir and dumplings dropped over it, lid put on and simmered till dumplings are done; or the stew turned into a baking pan, the dumplings dropped close together all over it, then put in oven till dumplings are done.

STEWED CHICKEN GIBLETS WITH RICE—Hearts, gizzards, livers, necks and second joints of the wings of chickens, also small

GIBLET AND POTATO PIE

.

Serves 6

This dish is very much like the Irish shepherd's pie. The use of rich giblets, however, make this much more flavorful.

1³/₄ pounds chicken giblets
(hearts, livers,
gizzards)

2 ounces salt pork,
chopped

¹/₂ tablespoon dried sage,
whole

5 cups water

1 pound chicken wings

¹/₄ cup dry sherry

2 tablespoons olive oil

2 cloves garlic, peeled and
chopped

1 medium yellow onion,
peeled and chopped

¹/₂ teaspoon dried thyme,
whole

Salt and freshly ground
black pepper to taste

3 hard-boiled eggs, shelled
and sliced

6 cups cooked mashed
potatoes

Preheat the oven to 375° F.

In a 4-quart pot, combine the giblets, salt pork, and sage. Add the water and simmer, covered, for 3 hours. Add the chicken wings to the pot and simmer, covered, for 30 minutes more. Strain the meat from the pot, reserving the broth. Allow to cool.

Debone the chicken wings. Chop the giblets and chicken meat coarsely and mix with the sherry and ¹/₂ cup of reserved broth.

Heat a frying pan and sauté the oil, garlic, onions, and thyme until the onions are tender. Add to the giblet mixture and salt and pepper to taste.

Spread the meat mixture in the bottom of a deep 9-inch pie dish. Top with hard-boiled egg slices. Spread the potatoes over all. Bake for 45 minutes, until golden brown on top.

C.W.

pieces of raw salt pork and minced onions, all fried lightly with butter, then sprinkled with flour, shook together, moistened with stock, simmered till tender, seasoned with salt, pepper and a bunch of sweet herbs (which are to be removed when done); served in the centre of a border of dry boiled rice, or barley, or oatmeal.

SAUTÉ OF CHICKEN LIVERS ON TOAST—The livers with gall removed, washed and wiped, then sautéed with minced onions in butter, taken up into a saûtoir, seasoned with salt, pepper and lemon juice, moistened with Madeira wine and Espagnole sauce, simmered for a few minutes; served on toast garnished with croûtons.

STEWED CHICKEN LIVERS WITH MUSHROOMS—The preceding stew placed in the centre of dish without toast, and served surrounded with button mushrooms that have been sautéed in butter and sprinkled with chopped chervil.

CHICKEN LIVERS IN CASES—The livers sautéed above cut in dice, filled into fancy paper cases, that have been lined with chicken forcemeat and heated; mushrooms and truffles in dice to be added to the livers.

CHICKEN LIVER FORCEMEAT—Equal weight of blanched chicken livers and lean cooked ham with two ounces of butter to each pound of meat the meat minced, pounded to a paste, rubbed through a fine sieve, then thoroughly incorporated with the butter, together with a little purée of mushrooms and truffles, seasoned with salt, pepper, nutmeg and chopped parsley, then stored for use.

BROCHETTE OR CROÛTADES OF CHICKEN LIVERS—For recipes of which see BROCHETTE and CROUSTADE.

OMELET OF CHICKEN LIVERS—The livers blanched then cut in slices with mushrooms, sautéed in butter, moistened with wine and brown sauce, seasoned with salt, pepper and lemon juice, sprinkled with chopped parsley, enclosed within a savory omelet; served with more of the livers in sauce poured around.

ROAST CHICKEN LIVERS ON TOAST—Blanched chicken livers masked all over with "chicken liver forcemeat" then wrapped in buttered paper, arranged in a baking pan and baked for fifteen minutes, taken up, paper removed; served on toast with Madeira sauce poured around.

RAGOUT OF CHICKEN GIBLETS WITH POTATO CROQUETTES—Livers, hearts, gizzards, pieces of salt pork and button mushrooms sautéed, then mixed with Madeira sauce, placed in center of dish garnished with small potato croquettes.

GIBLET SAUCE—Gizzards, hearts and necks boiled till tender with an onion, livers blanched, then sautéed with butter, taken up, sauce made in the pan they were sautéed in with the stock from the giblets; livers, hearts and meat from the gizzards then cut fine and mixed into the sauce, seasoned with salt, pepper and nutmeg, finished with sherry wine and chopped parsley.

CHICKEN GIBLET SOUP—Gizzards, hearts, necks and wings boiled till tender with some roast fowl bones in chicken stock, hearts and gizzards then taken up and cut into dice together with some sautéed livers, roux made and moistened with the stock, boiled up and skimmed; washed rice, finely cut carrots, turnips, and onions then boiled in the soup till tender, then is added the cut meats; finished by seasoning with Worcestershire sauce, sherry wine, salt, pepper and nutmeg.

PURÉE OF CHICKEN—Roux made and moistened with chicken stock, cream and almond milk, when boiling, further thickened with some cooked chicken meat that has been pounded and rubbed through a fine sieve, seasoned with salt, nutmeg and red pepper; small squares of cooked breast of chicken then added; served with small croûtons.

CHICKEN SOUP WITH VEGETABLES—Cold roast fowl bones and gravy with some vegetable trimmings boiled in stock till well flavored, roux made and moistened with the strained stock, boiled up and skimmed, shredded cooked vegetables and shreds of chicken then added and served.

CHICKEN CONSOMMÉ—A few veal bones and chopped veal trimmings, slices of carrot, onions, celery, with whole mace, salt, red pepper, broken egg shells and beaten whites of eggs, stirred together with a little broken clean ice, then moistened with skimmed and strained poultry stock that has had a piece of salt pork boiled in it, brought slowly to the boil, then simmered till clear, strained through a towel; small squares of breast of cooked chicken then added, seasoned (but use no wine) and served.

CHICKEN BROTH WITH RICE—The strained and skimmed stock in which fowls and a piece of salt pork and some vegetables have been boiled, is slightly thickened with corn starch, dry boiled rice, and pieces of chicken meat then added, seasoned and served.

CHICKEN GUMBO—Roast chicken bones, minced onion and some ham knuckle meat fried in butter with a few bay leaves and a pod of red pepper, flour then added, moistened with poultry stock, boiled up and skimmed, a half roasted chicken then added and simmered till tender; chicken then taken up and the stock strained into another saucepan in which is either canned okra, okra powder, or fresh okra sliced, also some boiled rice and pieces of chicken meat; boiled up till greeny and gelatinous; seasoned and served.

CREAM OF CHICKEN—Some veal bones and trimmings with a little whole mace, celery and onions are boiled in poultry stock, cold cooked chicken meat pounded, then rubbed through a sieve, moistened with the skimmed and strained stock, boiled up, seasoned with salt, red pepper and nutmeg, then finished with some boiling cream.

CREAM OF CHICKEN WITH RICE— Roux made and moistened with strong poultry stock, boiled up and skimmed, little boiling cream then added together with pieces of

CHICKEN STOCK

·

Makes about 4 quarts

This is the other soup stock, along with beef, that you must have on hand to do the cooking typical of the early 1900s. Yes, you can buy canned, but it has nowhere near the flavor that this stock has. And don't ever, ever, use bouillon cubes!

*3 pounds chicken necks and
   backs*

*4 stalks celery, chopped into
   large pieces*

*6 carrots, chopped into large
   pieces*

*2 large yellow onions, peeled
   and chopped into large
   pieces*

*Salt and freshly ground
   black pepper to taste*

In a large pot, place the chicken necks and backs in water to cover. Bring to a boil, uncovered. Add the celery, carrots, and onions. Add salt and pepper to taste. Reduce the heat and simmer for 2 hours. Strain and refrigerate.

J.S.

---

chicken meat and dry boiled rice; seasoned with salt and red pepper.

CREAM OF CHICKEN WITH QUE-NELLES—Roux made and moistened with poultry stock, boiled up and skimmed, then is worked into it a liaison of egg yolks and cream; seasoned with salt and red pepper, then strained into another saucepan, containing flowerets of cooked cauliflower, balls of cooked carrot, pieces of chicken meat, and some poached quenelles of chicken forcemeat, half of them to be colored green.

PURÉE OF CHICKEN WITH TOMA-TOED QUENELLES—A purée of chicken soup strained into another saucepan containing poached quenelles that have had a stiff tomato purée worked into the forcemeat; seasoned and served.

CHICKEN SOUP WITH RICE AND LEEKS—Poultry stock slightly thickened with roux, plenty of shredded leeks boiled in it with some rice; when done and seasoned, pieces of chicken meat added. (The Scotch call this soup "Cock-a-Leekie.")

CHICKEN SOUP, CREOLE STYLE—Raw chicken meat cut into small pieces and fried with minced onions

CHICKEN GUMBO

▪

Serves 8

Gumbo is strictly an American dish from the Cajun country. Do not be intimidated by the number of ingredients, because this soup is easy to prepare and delicious!

2 pounds chicken thighs

2 cloves garlic, peeled and
　crushed

1 tablespoon olive oil

Salt and freshly ground
　black pepper to taste

1 pound smoked pork hock,
　sawed into 1-inch
　pieces

2 bay leaves

1 medium yellow onion,
　peeled and diced

1 medium green sweet bell
　pepper, cored and
　diced

1 medium red sweet bell
　pepper, cored and
　diced

1 stalk celery, chopped

3 cloves garlic, peeled and
　chopped

1¹/₂ cups chopped ripe
　tomatoes

1 teaspoon dried thyme,
　whole

¹/₄ cup chopped parsley

6¹/₂ cups Chicken Stock
　(page 153)

2 teaspoons filé powder
　(find in any spice shop)

4 tablespoons
　Worcestershire sauce

2 teaspoons Tabasco sauce

2 (10-ounce) packages
　frozen cut okra, thawed

2 cups cooked Uncle Ben's
　Converted Rice
　(cooked as directed on
　the box)

Salt and freshly ground
　black pepper to taste

Rub the chicken thighs with the crushed garlic, oil, salt, and pepper to taste. Roast the chicken in a preheated 375°F. oven for 35 minutes. Cool the chicken and debone it. Chop the chicken meat with the skin and set aside. Save the bones to make Chicken Stock at another time.

In a 4- to 6-quart pot, place the pork hocks, bay leaves, onions, red and green peppers, celery, chopped garlic, tomatoes, thyme, parsley, and Chicken Stock. Bring to a boil, cover, and simmer for 1¹/₂ hours, until the pork hocks are tender. Remove the meat and chop. Return the meat to the pot and discard the bones. Add the reserved chicken meat, filé powder, Worcestershire sauce, Tabasco sauce, and okra. Simmer, covered, for 10 minutes. Add the cooked rice and simmer 5 minutes more. Salt and pepper to taste.

C.W.

in olive oil, then little flour added, stirred, moistened with consommé, boiled up and skimmed, then is added shred lean ham and green peppers, simmered for half an hour, then raw peeled and sliced tomatoes together with well washed rice and a bunch of soup herbs is simmered in it till done.

CHICKEN SOUP, PORTUGUESE STYLE—Raw chicken meat cut small together with minced onions fried in butter, flour added and stirred, moistened with poultry stock, boiled up and skimmed, then is added a Julienne of vegetables and a little well washed rice, simmered till done, seasoned and served.

CHICKEN SOUP, SOUTHERN STYLE—Raw chicken meat cut small, minced onions, shredded green peppers all fried together with butter, little flour then added and stirred, moistened with poultry stock, seasoned lightly with curry powder, salt and red pepper, boiled up and skimmed, then is added equal quantities of lima beans and sugar corn together with half their bulk of okras; simmered till done.

CHICKEN SOUP, TURKISH STYLE—Shredded raw chicken meat, ham and green peppers with sliced onions fried together with butter, little flour added and stirred, moistened with consommé, boiled up and skimmed, seasoned with salt, red pepper and a dash of curry powder, then is added washed rice and tomato purée equaling half the bulk of the stock; when rice is done, served.

CHICKEN SOUP, ENGLISH STYLE—Roux made, moistened with poul-try stock, boiled up and skimmed, then is added a liaison of egg yolks and cream, when thickened, strained into a tureen containing squares of cooked chicken meat and chopped chervil, seasoned and served.

CHICKEN BROTH WITH CUSTARDS—Good poultry stock seasoned; then lightly thickened with corn starch, strained into a tureen containing a macedoine of vegetables and shapes of custard made by taking twelve yolks of eggs and a pint of cold chicken broth seasoned with salt and red pepper, thoroughly mixed without beating, then poured into buttered pans, steamed till set, cut into shapes when cold.

CHICKEN BROTH WITH ASPARAGUS TIPS—Same as the preceding, using the shapes of custards but substituting asparagus tips for the macedoine of vegetables.

CHICKEN BROTH WITH SPRING VEGETABLES—Strong poultry stock thickened very lightly with corn starch, seasoned, boiled up and skimmed, then further thickened with young tender carrots, turnips, green onions, leeks and green cabbage all cut into small dice boiled in the stock with a handful of rice till done, then is added squares of chicken meat; seasoned and served.

CHICKEN BROTH WITH ARTICHOKES—Strong poultry stock thickened lightly with corn starch, seasoned, boiled up and skimmed, then further thickened with a liaison of egg yolks and cream,

CHICKEN BROTH WITH CUSTARDS

·

Serves 6 to 8

This is an elegant broth with julienned vegetables and floating custards. So nice and warming.

8 eggs, beaten	Salt and freshly ground white pepper to taste
3/4 cup milk	
1 teaspoon salt	2 carrots, peeled and julienned
Pinch of cayenne pepper	
2 1/2 quarts Chicken Stock (page 153)	2 stalks celery, julienned
	1 medium yellow onion, peeled and julienned
2 bay leaves	
1/4 cup cornstarch	**Garnish**
1/4 cup cold water	Chopped parsley
2 teaspoons Worcestershire sauce	

In a mixing bowl, combine the beaten eggs with the milk, salt, and cayenne pepper. Pour the mixture into a greased 8-inch by 8-inch baking dish and cover with aluminum foil. Bake at 375°F. for 20 to 25 minutes, until set. Set aside to cool.

In a 6-quart pot, heat the Chicken Stock and bay leaves. Mix together the cornstarch and water until smooth. Stir the cornstarch mixture into the pot and bring it all to a boil. Simmer for 5 minutes, stirring until smooth and lump free. Add the Worcestershire sauce, salt, and white pepper. Stir in the carrots, celery, and onions, and simmer, covered, for 20 minutes. Remove the bay leaves.

Remove the cooked egg mixture from the baking dish. Cut into fancy shapes with a small cookie cutter or cut into squares with a knife. Add to the soup and heat for a minute or two.

Serve garnished with parsley.

C.W.

strained into a tureen with chicken meat and diced artichokes.

CHICKEN BROTH WITH POACHED EGG—Same as "Chicken Broth with Custards" but substituting a soft poached egg for each plate.

CHICKEN BROTH WITH SORREL—Strong poultry stock thickened with a liaison of egg yolks and cream, seasoned, strained into a tureen containing boiled vermicelli and stewed sorrel.

CHICKEN SOUP WITH NOODLES— Strong poultry stock thickened with flour and butter, seasoned with salt, red pepper and nutmeg, straining it afterwards into a tureen containing boiled noodles, chopped chervil and pieces of chicken meat.

CHICKEN BROTH WITH ONIONS— Thickened poultry stock seasoned, then strained into a tureen containing very small boiled onions and green peas.

CHICKEN SOUP WITH PEAS PU-RÉE— Fresh green peas boiled with a bunch of green mint in chicken stock, thickened lightly with roux, mint then removed, and the soup rubbed through a fine sieve, boiled up again and skimmed, seasoned, then strained into a tureen containing chopped chervil and shred lettuce.

CHICKEN SALAD—Tender, juicy cold cooked chicken cut into small dice, with an equal quantity of hearts of celery, mixed, seasoned with salt, red pepper, mayonnaise and a dash of tarragon vinegar; a cold serving dish rubbed with garlic, covered with crisp, tender lettuce leaves, salad placed in the center masked with mayonnaise, smoothed, decorated with capers, beetroot and hard boiled egg.

CHICKEN SALAD—Round croquettes made of chicken, ham, tongue, mushrooms and truffles, breaded and fried, allowed to become cold, then split in halves and set around a bed of mixed shredded lettuce and endive, seasoned with French dressing.

CHICKEN SALAD—Two parts of mayonnaise and one part of limpid aspic jelly beaten together, individual patty pans or timbale molds decorated and lined with the beaten mixture, then filled with scallops of chicken dressed with Remoulade sauce, a few capers and slices of stoned olives, covered with some of the beaten mixture, set till firm, then turned out on to a bed of shredded lettuce garnished with shredded anchovies and gherkins.

CHICKEN MAYONNAISE—Cold roast chickens cut into joints, steeped for an hour in a mixture of salt, pepper, olive oil and tarragon vinegar, then taken up and masked with mayonnaise sauce, served on shred lettuce, garnished with quartered hard boiled eggs, pickled beets and stoned olives or pimentoes.

CHICKEN MAYONNAISE—Boned roasted chicken, pressed, sliced, coated with mayonnaise, served garnished with green peas and asparagus points that are dressed with French dressing, and cubes of savory jelly.

CHILE OR CHILI—See CAPSICUMS.

CHIVES—A flavoring herb of the onion species, grows like the tops of spring onions, deep green in color and very strong in flavor;

such dishes as "Civet of Rabbit," "Ragout of Hare," etc., are strongly impregnated with chives.

CHIVES—Gardeners would grow chives for their flavoring alone, lovely lavender spheres that appear in the spring atop elegant, grasslike leaves. The flowers are edible too, although they are not as tasty as the chopped bits of leaf that are one of the mildest members of the onion family. The flavor of chives (*Allium schoenoprasum*) is distinct and assertive, however, and a useful addition to omelets, soups, salads, sauces, and cream or cottage cheeses.

CHOCOLATE—A wholesome, nutritive flesh forming article of food, greatly used in confectionery, icings, cakes, etc.; when served as a drink it is made into a paste with milk, then boiling milk added to the consistency of thin cream, allowed to simmer for a few minutes before serving.

CHOCOLATE—"Flesh forming article of food . . ." Chocolate is much more than that. The cocoa tree, from whence the chief ingredient of chocolate comes, is called *Theobroma* (which is Greek for "food of the gods") *cacao*. That gives you a sense of how long chocoholics have been around! Now Americans eat $5 billion—that's right, *billion*— worth of chocolate each year; it's a number that grows in spite of every other dietary craze.

Chocolate begins with the cocoa bean, the best of which come from the Criollo cacao trees grown mainly in Central and South America. Unfortunately, those provide only 10 percent of the world's crop; the rest is from the easier-to-

grow and far more abundant Forastero. All cocoa trees live within twenty degrees of the equator.

Cocoa pods are picked from the trees by hand, then split, fermented (a nine-day process), dried, packed, and shipped to manufacturers, mostly in Europe and the United States. There they are cleaned, blended, roasted, and ground. The result is chocolate liquor, which can be made into unsweetened chocolate or pressed to extract cocoa butter, the fat contained therein.

But enough procedure. There are several forms of chocolate.

Unsweetened chocolate: Pure chocolate liquor, cooled and molded; 53 percent cocoa butter. For cooking.

Bittersweet, semisweet, or **dark chocolate:** Chocolate liquor with added cocoa butter and sweeteners. At least 35 percent liquor, and as much as 50 percent sugar. For cooking or eating.

Sweet chocolate: About 15 percent liquor. For cooking or eating.

Milk chocolate: Invented in Switzerland in 1876, a combination of chocolate liquor (at least 10 percent), cocoa butter, milk, and flavorings. For eating only.

Cocoa powder: Partially defatted liquor treated with flavor-robbing alkali. For cooking only.

White chocolate: A combination of cocoa butter, milk, sugar, lecithin, and (usually) vanilla. For eating or cooking.

Couverture: Used in candy making, this has a high percentage (at least 35 percent) of cocoa butter. For cooking only.

Chocolate is useful not only in sweet foods. For example, it is frequently added to chile and is an essential ingredient in Mexican mole sauces.

CHOCOLATE BLANC-MANGE—Milk and sugar brought to the boil in two separate saucepans, then corn starch mixed with milk beaten into both, one to be flavored with vanilla, the other to have melted chocolate and a little butter beaten into it, molds dipped into cold water, the chocolate mixture poured in half way up, then the vanilla used to fill with, set to cool, turned out, served with sweetened and vanilla flavored cream.

CHOCOLATE CREAM FRITTERS— The chocolate part of the preceding recipe made a little stiffer than for blanc-mange, turned into shallow pans, allowed to set till firm and cold, then cut into shapes, double breaded and fried, served dusted with powdered sugar and with apricot marmalade or sauce poured around.

CHOCOLATE CAKE—One pound each of buttered, powdered sugar and grated chocolate, sugar and butter creamed together, chocolate dissolved in a pint of milk, then worked into the cream with eight yolks of eggs, three-quarters of a pound of flour and two teaspoonfuls of baking powder and the whipped whites of eight eggs then lightly stirred in, poured into buttered and papered pans, slowly baked till done, about one hour.

CHOCOLATE CREAM—Three pints of double cream whipped stiff, to which is then added sugar to taste, one ounce of gelatine, juice of a lemon, and half a pound of melted chocolate, poured into molds, and set on ice; the tops of molds may be decorated before pouring in the cream.

CHOCOLATE ICE CREAM—Pure cream sugared to taste, half a pound of chocolate to the gallon, the chocolate dissolved and mixed into some LUKEWARM cream, then strained into the sweetened cream, flavored slightly with vanilla, strained into a freezer and frozen.

CHOCOLATE CUP CUSTARDS—Two quarts of milk, four ounces of chocolate and one pound of sugar mixed and brought to the boil, six yolks of eggs and two ounces of corn starch worked together with a little milk, the boiling mixture stirred into it, put back on the range and stirred till it just thickens, then flavored with vanilla, poured through a conical strainer into cups; when all filled, the cups arranged into a baking pan containing a little water baked slowly till done, served cold with cream poured around.

CHOCOLATE ICING—One pound of sifted sugar (powdered) and six whites of eggs thoroughly beaten till stiff, then flavored with vanilla and four ounces of melted chocolate.

CHOCOLATE PUDDING—Same mixture as given for "Chocolate Cup Custards" baked in a pan, served cold with whipped cream, or sweetened and flavored plain cream.

CHOCOLATE CUSTARD CUPS

•

Serves 6

These custards are so rich that I doubt you could eat more than one, although you may want to. I have offered three serving suggestions for this wonderful dessert.

1 tablespoon cornstarch	1 teaspoon vanilla
2 cups half-and-half	**Optional**
1/3 cup sugar	4 tablespoons sugar
4 ounces Baker's semisweet chocolate	1 tablespoon grated orange peel
5 egg yolks	

Preheat the oven to 350°F.

In a small saucepan, mix the cornstarch with 1/4 cup of the half-and-half over low heat. Add the remaining half-and-half and stir until smooth. Add the sugar and chocolate and bring to a simmer. Cook gently until the sugar is dissolved and the chocolate is melted. Remove from the heat and cool to room temperature. When cool, using a wire whisk, whip in the egg yolks and vanilla.

Pour the mixture into 6 ramekins, approximately 1³/₄ inches by 3 inches. Place the filled cups in a baking pan. Add enough hot water to reach a quarter of the way up the sides of the cups. Bake for 35 minutes. Remove the custards from the baking pan and allow to cool a bit.

Serve warm or cool completely and top custards with a mixture of sugar and orange peel. Place the ramekins under the broiler and broil until the sugar melts and caramelizes. Remove and allow to cool to form an orange-sugar coating. These are also good plain and chilled.

C.W.

CHOCOLATE PUDDING—One pound each of butter and sugar creamed together, ten eggs worked into the cream one at a time, fourteen ounces of sifted flour and two ounces of grated chocolate then lightly stirred in, flavored with vanilla, poured into buttered molds, steamed till done, served hot with sauce.

CHOCOLATE FLOAT—Small cold "Chocolate Cup Custards" turned

out into deep sauce dish, surrounded with a piping of whipped cream the cream then decorated with colored win, jelly chopped fine.

CHOUX-PASTE—Is the name of a batter made of a pint of water, eight ounces of lard or butter, nine ounces of flour and ten eggs. Water and lard is brought to the boil, flour then added all at once and worked over the fire till it is cooked into a smooth paste, allowed then to slightly cool, the eggs then beaten in one at a time; its consistency must be so that it will just fall off from a spoon; from it is prepared "Bell Fritters," "Queen Fritters," "Cream Puffs and Eclairs," "Spanish Puffs," "Pralines," "Croquenbouchées," "Choux Croutons," etc., etc.

CHOW CHOW—One gallon each of cut stringless beans, very small white onions, green gherkins and flowerets of cauliflower, two pounds of dry mustard, two gallons of white wine vinegar, two ounces each of turmeric and mustard seed, two pounds of sugar and one pint of olive oil. The cauliflower, beans and onions boiled separately till tender, the gherkins soaked in strong salted water for one day, then mixed together and filled into crocks; the vinegar brought to the boil, mustard and turmeric mixed and moistened with a little vinegar, then stirred into the boiling vinegar; when it begins to thicken, the mustard seed, sugar and oil are stirred in, poured boiling hot over the vegetables in the crocks, then put away for use.

CHOW CHOW—This long-standing American pickle recipe has been applied to almost every variety of vegetable (fruits have also been preserved this way, but rarely). It is inevitably sweet and hot, and mustard is usually the dominant seasoning, as it is here.

CHUTNEY—A table condiment imported from the East Indies, and purchasable at the grocery stores in bottles, may be made as follows: One and a half pints of vinegar, two ounces of whole ginger bruised, one ounce each of chilies and mustard seed, two ounces of salt and twelve ounces of sugar all boiled together for three quarters of an hour, then strained through a hair sieve. Put the strained vinegar to boil again with one large onion shredded, one crushed clove of garlic, six shallots, two ounces of seedless raisins and two pounds of peeled and sliced apples, boil until they are quite soft, then put into stone jars, tie over with skin or parchment paper and keep for use.

CHUTNEY—The sweet-hot-sour jam described by Fellows is but one of the kinds of foods referred to as chutneys by Indians and Pakistanis. Other kinds are as simple as grated cucumber mixed with lemon, salt, and pepper. In essence, a chutney is a moist, refreshing condiment, based on herbs (mint, for example), vegetables (cucumber), or fruits (apples or mango), usually mixed with spices and served as a pleasant counterbalance to a main dish.

CIDER—Apple juice obtained by pressure, then fermented and matured.

CIDER—Cider is to apples what wine is to grapes. Until quite recently most cider was alcoholic and, in the last century, it was one of the two standard drinks of the British and American populations (beer, which eventually took over, was the other). Like wine, there are levels of cider: that which might be better used as paint remover and that which makes for an elegant, pleasant drink (although no fermented apple juice could ever attain the stature of fermented grape juice). Sweet cider—cider with no alcohol—is simply cider that is served (or, these days, pasteurized) before it is allowed to ferment. Applejack, or apple brandy, called Calvados, is made by distilling cider.

CINNAMON—A spice which may be purchased ground or in stick form, used as a flavoring for cakes, puddings, liqueurs, cordials, syrups, sauces, etc.

CINNAMON—One of the world's exotic flavors, cinnamon (*Cinnamomum zeylanicum*) is the dried bark of a laurellike tree native to Sri Lanka and now grown throughout the tropics. Its close relative CASSIA (*Cinnamomum cassia*), also known as Chinese cinnamon, is less delicately flavored; once the two were interchangeable, but laws were passed prohibiting their substitution.

In Western cooking cinnamon is used almost exclusively in desserts: puddings, custards, cookies, fruit compotes, cakes, and so on (one delightful exception is cinnamon toast, but that is a dessert posing as breakfast.) But it is one ingredient in Chinese five-spice powder and is used extensively in savory dishes throughout the Arab world.

If you want the best flavor of cinnamon, keep cinnamon sticks on hand and grind them in an old coffee grinder as needed, or add them to liquid-based preparations as they simmer, discarding the stick before serving.

CISCO—One of the small fish of the lakes, resembling in size and appearance the fresh water herring.

CISCO—A number of small freshwater fish native to the northern United States and southern Canada. It is also known as baby whitefish, chub, or Lake Superior herring. Frequently cured with smoke in the same manner as whitefish, it is used often in Jewish cooking. Cisco may also be cooked whole, in the manner of trout.

FILLETS OF CISCO IN BATTER—The fish scaled and filleted free from bone, seasoned with salt and pepper, dipped into a thin batter, fried; served with or without tomato sauce and garnished with parsley and lemon.

BROILED CISCO, LEMON PARSLEY SAUCE—The fish scaled, drawn, washed, wiped and the sides scored, seasoned with salt and pepper, rolled in olive oil, then in flour, broiled and basted till done; served with maître d'hôtel butter poured over, and garnished with lemon and chip potatoes.

CISCO SAUTÉ, JULIENNE POTATOES—Prepared as in the preceding recipe, rolled in flour, slowly fried a delicate brown with butter, served with some of the butter over it, garnished with Julienne potatoes, lemon and parsley.

CITRIC ACID—A crystal obtained from acid fruits; used by confectioners and caterers, pop and soda water manufacturers. Street vendors at the fairs simply dissolve it in water, sweeten it, fill it into glasses, place a thin slice of lemon in and sell it for lemonade; also flavor it with a little oil of raspberry, strawberry, etc., adding a drop or two of carmine, and sell it as raspberryade, strawberryade, etc.

CITRIC ACID—High in vitamin C, citric acid is one of the few food additives that is not only harmless but beneficial. It adds a pronounced sour flavor wherever it is used, although it has none of the complexity of lemon or other citrus fruits.

CITRON—A large fruit of the lemon species, the peel is blanched, then boiled in syrup and subsequently dried; used in cakes, puddings, ices, jellies, cordials, liqueurs, etc.

CITRON—One other notable fact about citron (*Citrus medica*), a lumpy, thick-skinned, lemonlike fruit that is rarely seen fresh and, indeed, is most frequently used for its candied peel: It was the first citrus fruit to be eaten—and grown— by Europeans.

CITRON CAKE—One pound each of butter and sugar creamed together, ten eggs then worked in one at a time, then a wine glass of brandy, one pound of sifted flour, and half a pound of shredded citron.

CLAMS—A favorite American shellfish, the "Little Neck" clams being the favored kind for eating from the shell, the large hard clams for soups and chowders, and the soft clam for broiling and frying.

CLAMS—Let's be a tad more precise. Americans recognize two broad categories of clams: hard-shell and soft-shell (although there are more than twenty thousand species worldwide, since the term is used to apply to almost every bivalve). The latter have a thin, brittle shell and, because they are inevitably quite sandy, are reserved for steaming and chowder. The former are excellent raw, on the half shell, or they may be steamed or used in simple but delicious preparations such as pasta with fresh clam sauce. Hardshell clams are classified by size: littlenecks, which are the smallest, have shells from about one to two inches across; cherrystones, up to two and a half or even three inches across; and QUAHOGS (as they are called in New England) are larger (they must be cooked before they are tender enough to eat).

Those who do not like raw clams may be interested to know that both littlenecks and cherrystones can be grilled successfully; thus cooked, they provide as much flavor as raw clams. Simply place them on a hot grill and serve when the shells pop open. They need nothing more than a squirt of lemon.

CLAM BROTH—May be made to order at restaurants by simply chopping some large clams and scalding them in clam liquor, then straining into the serving bowl or cup.

PHILADELPHIA CLAM CHOWDER— Like the preceding but substituting tomatoes and tomato sauce for the white sauce and adding a flavor of thyme.

CLAM CHOWDER—Salt pork cut into dice and fried till light brown. Fish broth and clam liquor in equal parts brought to the boil, skimmed, sliced onions and potatoes then put in and boiled till barely done, then is added the fried salt pork and scalded clams cut in dice; seasoned with pepper, ground mace and salt; brought to the boil again, and poured to an equal quantity of thin white sauce; finished with a few rolled crackers and chopped parsley.

CLAM STEW—Plain or with milk or cream; generally sold in restaurants by the half or dozen (it is customary to give seven and fourteen to the half or dozen); scald the clams with clam liquor, take off the scum, pour into a bowl, add a piece of butter and serve, if for plain; if for a milk or cream stew, scald the milk or cream separately, pour the clams and liquor into the bowl first, then add an equal quantity of the milk, season with butter and serve with crackers.

ROAST CLAMS—May be either served in the shell or on toast. Large clams washed, arranged on baking sheet, put in hot oven till they open. If served in the shell the top shell is removed, the clam separated from the lower, little melted butter then placed in each and served. If to be served on toast, the toast should be cut in strips, buttered, the clams placed neatly on it, melted butter brushed over them; served with lemon and crackers.

BROILED CLAMS—The soft clam is best for this dish, but the ordinary large clam is serviceable; they should be drained, seasoned with salt and pepper, dipped in melted butter then rolled in fresh sifted breadcrumbs, broiled; served on toast, garnished with lemon and watercress.

FRIED CLAMS—Drained, seasoned, dipped in melted butter, rolled in sifted breadcrumbs, then in beaten eggs and again in crumbs; fried in clear butter or in hot fat; served garnished with lemon and watercress.

STEAMED CLAMS—Large clams scrubbed, arranged on the wire false bottom of a fish kettle with a little water under them, lid then put on, placed over a quick fire; when the upper shell is loosened, it is removed, the clam separated from the lower, little melted butter put in each, served very hot with lemon and crackers.

CLAM FRITTERS—Soft clams seasoned, then dipped in batter and fried; or large clams chopped, then mixed in batter and fried by spoonfuls in hot fat; served with a cream sauce made with clam liquor.

SCALLOPED CLAMS—Clams scalded and cut into neat pieces, sauce made of their liquor, the clams mixed in, and either filled into large clam or scallop shells, the tops sprinkled with sifted crumbs and melted butter, then browned in the oven; served in the shell.

CLAM CROQUETTES—Scalded clams cut into small neat pieces (not

CLAM CHOWDER

.

Serves 6

A noted columnist in Seattle asked me to develop a chowder recipe for one of his weekly newspaper articles. "It is to be clammy, with an essence of the ocean, perhaps a little seawater right in it!" We named it Tide Flats Chowder. Since Diamond Jim Brady practically lived on seafood, he would have loved this. It is rich and has no additional thickeners.

4 pounds fresh clams

¹/₂ pound salt pork, diced

1 large yellow onion,
    peeled and chopped

2 stalks celery, chopped

1³/₄ pounds russet potatoes,
    peeled and coarsely
    chopped

1 teaspoon dried thyme,
    whole

2 cloves garlic, peeled and
    minced

1 cup dry white wine

2 (8-ounce) bottles clam
    juice

Ground red pepper flakes
    and/or Tabasco sauce
    to taste

Milk to taste (only if you
    have to!)

Garnish

Chopped parsley

Rinse the clams, place in a large bowl, and cover with plenty of cold water. Set aside for 1 hour; drain.

Heat an 8-quart pot, add the salt pork, and sauté until browned but not crispy. Drain off 2 tablespoons of the fat into a separate 6-quart pot; set aside. In the pot with the browned salt pork, add the onions and celery and sauté for 10 minutes. Add the potatoes and thyme and sauté for 10 minutes more.

Heat the 6-quart pot with the reserved fat and add the garlic. Sauté a couple of minutes and add the clams and ¹/₂ cup of the wine. Turn the heat to high, bring to a boil, cover, and simmer for 7 to 10 minutes, until the clams open. Strain and return the broth to the pot. Remove the meat from the clams and set aside. Return the shells to the pot of broth or "nectar." Add the clam juice to the pot of shells and nectar. Cover and simmer for 30 minutes.

Strain the nectar into the pot of vegetables, discarding the shells and any sand in the bottom of the pot. Add the remaining ¹/₂ cup of wine and bring to a boil. Cover and simmer for about 20 minutes, until the potatoes are tender and the chowder begins to thicken slightly. Add the reserved clam meat and simmer for 1 minute more.

Stir in the ground red pepper flakes or Tabasco sauce to taste. Garnish with chopped parsley. Milk can be added if you're one of those people who won't enjoy the intense richness of this chowder.

C.W.

chopped). Thick sauce made of the liquor, the cut clams put back into it; when thoroughly reheated, poured into a buttered shallow pan, smoothed with a knife, covered with a sheet of greased paper and allowed to become cold and set, then cut in even sized pieces, shaped, breaded, fried; served with a clam sauce poured around.

CLAM FORCEMEAT—Scalded clams finely minced with an equal quantity of canned mushrooms, a little minced onion fried in butter, flour added, moistened with the clam and mushroom liquor, boiled up, seasoned with salt, pepper, little dry mustard, a suspicion of garlic, and some chopped parsley; then is added the clams and mushrooms, boiled up slowly for ten minutes, remove and work in a few beaten egg yolks till of a stiff consistency, put away to cool for use.

FRICASSÉE OF CLAMS—The clams scalded in their own liquor, then strained, equal amount of milk and liquor boiled separately, flour and butter in a saucepan seasoned with red pepper and a little nutmeg moistened with the liquor, then finished to the desired consistency with the boiling milk; when boiled up, finished with a few beaten yolks of eggs, the clams cut either in halves if small, or in neat pieces if large, added to the sauce; served either on toast, or with a border of fancy mashed potatoes, or in scallop shells.

CLAM SOUP OR CREAM OF CLAMS—Same as the preceding recipe, but having the soup of the consistency of thin cream; when serving, a sprinkling of chopped parsley or celery leaves put into each plate. BE CAREFUL NOT TO LET THE SOUP OR FRICASSÉE BOIL AFTER THE EGGS ARE IN OR IT WILL CURDLE, AND YOU CANNOT BRING IT BACK TO SMOOTHNESS WITHOUT YOU SPOIL THE FLAVOR.

CLARET—Name of a Southern French wine so called abroad on account of its color which is distinctive. Used generally as a common dinner wine, although its best brands cannot be too well eulogised. Its use in cookery is largely for flavoring sauces, soups, braising meats and fish, and for ices and jellies.

CLARET—Claret, of course, is the red wine of Bordeaux, about which volumes have been written. Until recent years only the best wines from Bordeaux were exported, and generalizations about aging patterns, vintages, and styles could be made. Now, however, the Bordelaise have entered the competitive world market with a vengeance, and a bottle of Bordeaux wine can just as easily cost six dollars as six hundred.

Still, it is the top wines—the so-called *crus classés* (classed growths) and *crus bourgeois*—that get most of the attention. These are primarily from the subregions of the Haut-Médoc and Graves (where the Cabernet Sauvignon grape is dominant) and Saint-Emilion and Pomerol (where Merlot is most frequently used).

The most expensive wines are usually from Château Margaux, Château Pétrus, and other well-known estates. But, in a good vintage, of which there are several each decade, exceptional wines are made at literally dozens of châteaux. And, unlike the red wines of BURGUNDY, there is sufficient quantity of claret so that excellent wines are actually affordable, at least for special occasions. (Further guidance for consumers is available in books and newspaper columns about wine.)

When properly aged from five to twenty-five years, clarets are the world's most complex wines, with bouquets and flavors regularly described as being reminiscent of leather, tobacco, and cedar. They are a pleasure to drink, but their dedicated adherents are usually found studying and collecting them. If you are offered a good claret, enjoy it.

CLOVES—Name of a valuable spice obtained from the buds of the tree. Used in its whole form for seasoning many stews, sauces, soups, especially turtle soup, where it takes the place of the herb BASIL. It is a valuable addition to apple dumplings, pies and sauces; in its ground state is often adulterated with pimentos and other inferior spices. The word clove is also used to designate a clove or section of garlic.

CLOVES—Although many older cookbooks rank cloves as one of the most important spices in the world, cloves' use has declined, at least in American cooking. The powerful flavor of the clove—the flower bud of a tropical tree (*Eugenia aromatica*), which is indigenous to the Spice Islands near Indonesia—was perhaps better suited to cooking in the days when fresh flavors were not as prevalent as they are now. The Romans relied heavily on cloves to season their sour wine and other drinks, and to disguise the strong and often rancid flavors of their meats. Eugenol, an essential oil also known as oil of cloves, has been used as an antiseptic and preservative since at least the Middle Ages.

Today we use cloves in pies and spiced cakes, in spice mixtures for pickles and curries, to season and garnish hams, and in certain soups and stews (where, typically, a few are stuck into an onion). But they are hardly in daily use, even in the kitchens of the most active cooks.

COBBLER—Name used in cookery to designate a kind of pie used as a sweet entrée; also in the bartenders' guide to designate certain mixed drinks.

COCOA—Name of a bean obtained from the cocoa tree, from which is manufactured the cocoa of commerce; used in cookery as a breakfast and supper beverage; also the expressed oil of the nut is used as cocoa butter, chiefly by confectioners.

COCOA—See CHOCOLATE.

COCOANUT—As generally seen in this country is in shell form devoid of its fibrous husk. The shell when broken shows the enclosed nut; this is used in cookery (after having its dark skin removed) chiefly by confectioners in making cakes, puddings, ices, macaroons, etc.; can be purchased for such work in desiccated form. The milk of the cocoanut as the liquid is called, is a valuable flavoring for curries, mulligatawny soup, almond soup, etc.

COCOANUT—Now spelled *coconut,* the fruit of the *Cocos nucifera* palm is harvested on nearly every tropical beach in the world and on plantations inland. Do not make the mistake—as Fellows evidently did—of substituting coconut *juice,* the naturally occurring liquid contained within the coconut, for coconut *milk,* a liquid made by pouring boiling water over dried (not sweetened) coconut, letting the mixture cool a bit, whirring it in a blender, and then passing it through a fine strainer or cheesecloth. (The difference between coconut milk and coconut cream is simply the ratio of water used to coconut; two to one makes milk, one to one makes cream.)

We tend to think of coconut as a fun food that is an occasional baking ingredient. But coconut milk is indispensable in equatorial cookery, and it is by far the most valuable product of the fruit. Sweetened coconut milk can be bought in cans in most Asian and Latino markets, and is also useful in recipes.

COCOTTE—Name used in cookery to designate a way of cooking eggs. The cocotte cups have been recently placed on the market; they are in cup form without handles and with screw covers; the cups when to be used are slightly buttered, the eggs broken in (keeping the yolks whole) a spoonful of cream poured carefully over them, the lid screwed on, the cups then placed into boiling water or into a steamer; they require two minutes longer than is required for boiled eggs; they are sent to the table in the cup and the lid is simply loosened, so as to be removed by the guest at his or her pleasure, or by the waiter at the request of the guest. The foreign term for this method of cooking eggs is Oeufs à la Cocotte.

COCOTTE—The egg cup, which had a popular phase since Fellows wrote this entry and has once again fallen into relative obscurity, is known in French as a *coquetier.*

COCHINEAL—Name of an insect obtained chiefly from the shores of Phonoecia; used in cookery as a red coloring. For recipe see CARMINE.

COCHINEAL—The red dye made from *Dactylopius coccus,* a scale insect that lives on certain oak trees, is one of the oldest coloring agents. Rarely used anymore, it is also known as kermes.

COCHON—A term used sometimes on bills of fare to designate PIG, such as "pied de cochon," pigs' feet; "cochon de lait," suckling pig, etc.

COCKIE-LEEKIE—Name given by the Scotch people for a soup in which a cock fowl and leeks form the principal ingredients.

COCKIE-LEEKIE SOUP—Young fowls (cocks or hens) washed, trussed and lightly roasted, then put into a white stock of veal or chicken with some white parts of shredded leeks, salt, and a few whole peppers; when the fowls are nearly done, they are taken up, the meat picked into shreds and placed into another saucepan with an equal quantity of fresh shredded leeks, the stock the fowls were boiled in being then strained over; this is then brought to the boil, skimmed, then simmered till the leeks are tender (about half an hour), seasoned with salt and pepper, then served.

COCKS COMBS—Called by the French "Cretes de coq" are the crests of the male domestic fowl cut off and blanched; used in cookery as parts of certain garnitures; are of no value as a flavor, but are valuable as pleasing the eye while the sauce tickles the palate; may be purchased at the large groceries already for use in bottles, generally mixed with the cocks kernels (Spanish fries).

COCKS KERNELS—The testicles of the male domestic fowl, situated in the middle of the back of the bird; when to be cooked, they are washed, blanched, skinned, and made into fricassées, suprêmes, breaded and fried, component parts of garnitures, etc. Often called by gourmets "Spanish fries"; purchasable in bottles combined generally with cocks combs.

COCKS COMBS, COCKS KERNELS—Neither of these rather odd foods is available without a search these days, although they were once quite common. You will frequently see them mentioned in older cookbooks, such as Fellows's.

COCKLES—Name of an English shellfish similar in shape and flavor to the "little neck clam" are imported into this country in small flat cans (cooked). To be used they are taken from the can and thoroughly washed in cold water to rid them of a sandy sediment, they can then be frizzled in butter and served very hot on toast garnished with lemon and parsley, or mixed into cream, Hollandaise, Suprême or Normande sauces and served either on toast or in croûstades, paper cases, with rice, or border of shrimps, or they may be curried and served with a border of rice. They are practically new to the American public, and unless well washed from their sediment will not be much called for.

COCKLES—Like many other bivalves falling in the general category of CLAMS, cockles come in dozens of varieties. And they are not exclusively English; our coastline boasts several species, including the spiny, prickly, and giant Atlantic cockles (one of the best in the world). Unfortunately, cockles, which were sold on street corners in London just a century ago, have lost their popularity and are seen only rarely in U.S. fish markets.

COCKTAILS—Name of a mixed drink; also applied in cookery to oysters and clams.

OYSTER COCKTAIL—Half a dozen freshly opened small oysters dropped into a sherbet glass, seasoned with a dash each of tabasco, Worcestershire, tomato and Harvey sauces.

CLAM COCKTAIL—Same as the preceding, using clams for oysters and omitting the Harvey sauce on account of its saline flavor.

NEPTUNE COCKTAIL—Three each freshly opened small oysters and clams dropped into a sherbet glass, seasoned with a few shreds of fresh horseradish, a dash each of tomato and walnut catsups, and a dash each of Worcestershire and tabasco sauces.

CODFISH—A staple salt water fish fit for hotel use all the year round; caught on the New England coast and in vast numbers off the shores of Newfoundland. The Newfoundland fisheries make a specialty of salting, drying and smoking it, besides making "caviar" of its roe and extracting the oil from its liver.

CODFISH—Codfish was once the staple of New England, doubly valuable because it could be salted and dried. This meant not only that cod could be caught far offshore, but that it could be kept for months before using. So Cape Cod was named after it, and a wooden cod hangs above the entry to the Massachusetts State House in Boston. No food was more important, and it was so plentiful that the air bladders of the fish—called cod sounds—were stewed in milk as a popular breakfast item. Fellows, in fact, had no problem listing three recipes for codfish tongues (try buying those in the local supermarket!).

Now, however, the true Atlantic cod (*Gadus morrhua*), while not an endangered species, is what the experts call a depleted fishery, one that can no longer be profitably caught and sold for widespread distribution. (The Norwegians have begun farming the fish, and it may be available in greater numbers in years to come.) HADDOCK (*Melanogrammus aeglefinus*), often sold as cod, is not much more plentiful. But hake (*Merluccius merluccius*), pollack (*Pollachius virens*), and whiting (*Merlangus merlangus*), are all abundant on both coasts and are good substitutes for cod in most recipes.

Unless and until Americans learn to like strong-flavored fish, cod and its cousins will remain popular. They are stark white and mild-flavored, with almost no odor when fresh; are very lean and soft but with definite "flake"; and are adaptable to virtually every cooking method save grilling. Salt cod also remains popular in Italian, Portuguese, Puerto Rican, and other ethnic cooking. It also makes excellent fish cakes.

BAKED CODFISH, CAPER SAUCE—On account of its size the fish after cleansing is best cut into portion pieces, seasoned with salt and pepper, rolled in flour, then dipped into melted bacon fat or olive oil, arranged on a baking pan, baked and browned on both sides, the head boiled with an onion and grated carrot; butter sauce made from the liquor, into which is then added capers and caper vinegar; fish served garnished with lemon and parsley, with the sauce at one end of the fish.

BAKED CODFISH, STUFFED WITH OYSTERS—Small cod about six pounds each, heads and fins removed, inside filled with an oyster stuffing, sewn up, the back and sides scored into portions, arranged in pan with a few shredded vegetables, moistened with a little fish broth, brushed over with butter, baked and basted till done and glazy; served garnished with a potato croquette and oyster sauce poured around.

BAKED CODFISH, BREADCRUMBED—Slices of the fish free

from bones, laid for an hour in a mixture of olive oil, vinegar, salt and pepper, then taken up and drained, dipped in butter, breadcrumbs, beaten eggs and again breadcrumbs, arranged in baking pan, moistened with a little white wine and oyster liquor, baked a golden brown; served garnished with Duchesse potatoes and lemon, with Hollandaise sauce poured around.

BOILED CODFISH, EGG SAUCE—The fish cut into portion pieces, washed, then laid in salted water for an hour, taken up and put to boil in cold salted water and milk; as soon as the flesh is firm it is done, take up, drain, serve garnished with boiled small potatoes and egg sauce poured around. Other good sauces to serve with boiled cod are oyster, Béchamel and Hollandaise.

BOILED COD STEAK WITH ANCHOVIES—Sells well in restaurants. Cod steaks about three-quarters of a pound in weight, laid in salted water for an hour, then boiled in salted water and milk, taken up and drained well; served garnished with Hollandaise potatoes, butter sauce containing plenty of shredded salt anchovies poured over the steak. (Flemish and Aurora sauces also go well with a boiled cod steak.)

FRIED COD STEAK, TOMATO SAUCE—The steaks laid in salted water for an hour, then taken up and wiped dry; dipped in melted butter, then flour, then in beaten eggs, fried a golden color in oil; served garnished with Julienne potatoes and tomato sauce poured around.

COD STEAK BREADCRUMBED, PARSLEY SAUCE—The steaks laid in salted water for an hour, then taken up and wiped dry, sprinkled with a little lemon juice, dipped in beaten eggs and fresh breadcrumbs, arranged in a buttered pan, brushed over with melted butter or bacon fat, baked and turned so that both sides are brown; served with parsley sauce at end of dish, and garnished with Parisienne potatoes.

FRIED COD CUTLET, PIQUANTE SAUCE—Steaks cut from the middle of the fish, seasoned with salt and pepper, dipped in melted butter, rolled in flour, fried in pan with bacon fat, served with Piquante sauce at one end, Saratoga chips, lemon and parsley at the other.

BROILED COD STEAK, COLBERT SAUCE—The steaks seasoned with salt and pepper, dipped in melted butter, rolled in flour, slowly broiled till done; served with Colbert sauce poured around and garnished with lemon and parsley, also some fancy fried potatoes.

CURRIED COD STEAK WITH RISSOTO—Good way to use the tail steaks; cut them half an inch thick, fry them a golden brown with a little minced onion, then place them in a saucepan, flour and curry then added to the butter and onions they were fried with, stirred, moistened with equal parts of fish broth and cream, boil up, skim, add a little anchovy essence, strain the sauce over the steaks, put on range and simmer for a few minutes; serve with the sauce over and garnish with small molds of rissoto.

CREAMED FRESH COD ON TOAST—
Shoulders and tails of cod are often
bought up cheap; boil them with an
onion in salted water and milk,
when cool, remove all skin and
bones, keeping the flakes whole;
cream sauce made from the liquor
they were boiled in, finished with a
few beaten eggs, the fish flakes
then reheated but not boiled;
served on toast sprinkled with
chopped parsley, and garnished
with strips of toast.

SCALLOPED FRESH CODFISH—The
preceding recipe filled into scallop
shells or oval deep dishes, the top
sprinkled with mixed grated cheese
and sifted breadcrumbs, then with
melted butter, baked a delicate
brown and served.

CRIMPED COD, SHRIMP SAUCE—
To crimp a cod it must be fresh
caught, then instantly killed, cut
and notched with a knife, then
boiled in salt water and milk;
served with shrimp sauce poured
around and garnished with quartered hard boiled eggs, and small
potatoes sprinkled with mâitre
d'hôtel butter.

COD STEAK SAUTÉ, CLUB STYLE—
Steaks cut from the middle of the
fish, seasoned with salt and pepper,
dipped in melted butter, rolled in
flour, fried a pale color in clear
melted butter, taken up and
drained, placed on serving dish,
the outer edge of the top garnished
with fine parsley dust forming a
horse shoe, lobster coral placed
down the centre, and Trianon
sauce poured around.

BOILED CODFISH TONGUES, EGG
SAUCE—The tongues steeped for a

whole day, then blanched for ten
minutes, taken up, masked with
egg sauce; served on toast.

SCALLOPED FRESH CODFISH
TONGUES—The steeped tongues
blanched for ten minutes, a thick
Poulette sauce made from the
blanching stock, tongues then
mixed into it, filled into scallop
shells or deep oval dishes, the top
strewn with mixed chopped parsley, grated cheese and breadcrumbs, browned and served.

FRICASSÉE OF COD'S SOUNDS WITH
OYSTERS—The sounds blanched till
nearly done in salted milk and water,
taken up and drained, the oyster then
blanched in the strained stock; cut
the sounds after blanching to the size
of the oysters; Poulette sauce made
from the blanching stock, to which is
then added the fish; served on toast
with a dusting of finely chopped
parsley.

STUFFED COD'S SOUNDS, OYSTER
SAUCE—The sounds blanched and
allowed to cool, then spread with
an oyster forcemeat (see OYSTERS);
when spread, coiled around and
pinned with a small skewer, rolled
in flour, then in melted butter and
then in sifted breadcrumbs, arranged in a buttered baking pan,
roasted and basted with butter till
brown and frothy; served very hot
with oyster sauce.

BOILED COD'S ROES, BUTTER
SAUCE—The roes blanched and
skinned, then simmered till done
in hot water with a dash of vinegar;
served with a good butter sauce

containing a little anchovy essence and chopped parsley.

BROILED COD'S ROES, BUTTER SAUCE—The roes blanched and skinned, then rolled in flour and fried in butter; served with the sauce of the preceding recipe with an addition of chopped capers.

FRIED COD'S ROES, CAPER SAUCE—The roes blanched and skinned, then rolled in flour and fried in butter; served with a strained Piquante sauce well reduced with caper vinegar and then add chopped capers.

SMOKED COD'S ROES—Are best either split and broiled, or split and fried in butter; served with maître d'hôtel butter poured over, garnished with lemon.

BOILED SALT COD, CREAM SAUCE—Boneless codfish steeped over night, boiled up, water thrown away, again boiled up using cold water; when done, taken up and drained; served with cream sauce poured over, garnished with plain boiled potatoes or with potatoes in their skins.

SALT COD SHREDDED AND CREAMED—The fish prepared as in the preceding, then pulled into shreds, mixed into a reduced cream or cream sauce; served on very hot toast, with a dusting of chopped parsley.

CODFISH BALLS OR CODFISH CAKES—The shredded codfish of the preceding and an equal quantity of well mashed fresh boiled potatoes, seasoned with salt, pepper and nutmeg, bound with a few yolks of eggs, mixed well, made into small flattened cakes, rolled in flour, fried brown in bacon fat; served with a slice of bacon, and a little cream sauce poured around.

SCRAMBLED SALT COD ON TOAST—The cod steeped, double blanched, shred, lightly fried in butter, seasoned with red pepper, equal quantity of cream and beaten eggs then mixed and stirred into the fish, scrambled lightly; served very hot on buttered toast.

SCALLOPED SALT COD (COD AU GRATIN)—The shredded and creamed cod filled into scallop shells or deep oval dishes, sprinkled with mixed grated cheese and sifted breadcrumbs, browned in the oven or under a salamander.

CODFISH CHOWDER—Can be made with either fresh or salt fish; if the salt soak it over night, blanch it twice so as to extract the salt, fry some small pieces of salt pork with an onion minced, when of a light color, remove from the fire, add the fish in flakes (freed from bone), some raw peeled potatoes cut in squares, a seasoning of thyme, marjoram, pepper and a can of tomatoes, fill the saucepan half full with fish broth, put on the lid, place in oven and let it simmer for an hour, take out, and work in without breaking the potatoes an equal quantity of thin cream sauce, add a little chopped parsley and served. (After the cream sauce is in it must not be allowed to boil again or it will curdle.)

COD AND OYSTER PIE, FRENCH STYLE—Fresh boiled cod in flakes, scalded oysters added, mixed with Aurora sauce, kept hot in bain-marie, platter shaped pieces of puff paste split, cod and oysters in sauce placed on the lower crust, covered with the upper crust and served very hot.

CODFISH TONGUE PATTIES—The tongues steeped and blanched, then fried with butter, drained, mixed with tomato sauce, filled into hot patty shells and served.

SALT CODFISH HASH, NEW ENGLAND STYLE—The shredded and creamed cod previously mentioned mixed with an equal quantity of potatoes cut in thin strips like matches, which are then boiled in cream; when done and well reduced, mixed with the fish and served very hot on toast.

COFFEE—The national breakfast beverage; to be well made use a high grade of coffee, perfectly roasted, properly ground, twelve ounces to the gallon of water for morning coffee, while for after dinner coffee (which is generally served in small cups) sixteen ounces to the gallon is required; fresh boiling water the moment it reaches the bubbling point, then only a little at first to open the pores of the coffee and get it ready to receive the remainder, which is to be put on a little at a time until ALL the good and NONE of the bitterness (tannin) is extracted, for if it be too strong for some, it can easily be diluted with boiling water when in the cups; HOT cups first, then the sugar, then warmed milk (not boiled), then the coffee, and if afforded, put on the top a teaspoonful of whipped cream, then you have a veritable nectar; the cream cleaves to the roof of the mouth, and the coffee slips down "like the oil down Aaron's beard."

COFFEE—The description above sounds as though it was written by a true addict, which is what "dedicated" coffee drinkers are. We love being enslaved by the bean of the *Coffea arabica* tree (and that of its lesser cousin *Coffea canephora*, also known as robustica) no less than our grandparents did. The aroma of brewing coffee is enticing, the flavor of well-made coffee is luxuriously delicious, and the kick of caffeine encourages many of us to go about our daily affairs.

It wasn't always so. Coffee, probably indigenous to Ethiopia, where some of the best is still grown, made it to Europe only in the seventeenth century. It almost immediately became the trendy drink of both London and Paris, and its popularity has only increased in the ensuing three-hundred-plus years. It has only recently had a role in cooking.

One hears a great deal about the specialty coffees of different countries—Colombian, for example, and the exorbitantly priced Jamaican Blue Mountain. Different coffees have different assets: One contributes aroma, one strength, one flavor, one acidity, and so on. Find a blend you like and a roast you like (the darker the roast, the stronger the coffee, with the darkest roasts being reserved for espresso coffees), and stick with it.

Once roasted, coffee is perishable (the majority of beans used to be roasted at home). Store beans in the freezer, and by all means grind them yourself. Once ground, coffee begins to lose its flavor immediately and, in an hour or two, the loss will be noticeable.

COFFEE ICE CREAM—One quart of fresh made and cooled coffee, with three pounds of powdered and sifted sugar to each gallon of pure cream, mixed, strained into the freezer and frozen.

COGNAC—Pronounced KONEYAK. The term used by the French for brandy.

COGNAC—Well, cognac is a bit more complicated than Fellows makes out, as is always the case in French wine and spirits making. Cognac is a legally defined geographical area just north of Bordeaux. Strictly speaking, only brandy made in Cognac can be called cognac. There are other French brandies—most notably Armagnac—known collectively as eau de vie.

Brandy has been made in France for five hundred years, but cognac has existed a mere three hundred years. It has always been aged and, like most wine and spirits, older cognac is generally considered better cognac. Three-star cognac is two years old; V.S.O.P. is at least three years old; and the term *Napoleon* is reserved for cognac that is at least six years old. No other descriptions printed on cognac labels (reserve, extra, etc.) have any legal meaning.

COLBERT—Name given to a sauce and a soup. Sauce made of a pint of good Espagnole, into which is mixed a little meat glaze, lemon juice, chopped parsley, and red pepper, made very hot without being boiled, then very gradually beaten in a half pint of clear melted butter. The soup is made with a rich consommé and contains shredded celery and lettuce blanched, diced artichoke bottoms and small button onions.

COLBERT SOUP—Another way is to make a rich cream soup lightly thickened with a liaison of egg yolks and cream, into which is then worked a purée of blanched hearts of endive, a fresh soft poached egg being served with each portion.

CONDÉ—Pronounced KONDAY. Term applied to a dish of stewed apricots served with rice; also to a soup of pureé of red haricot beans, which dishes it is said the "Prince of Condé" originated.

CONSOMMÉ—Name applied in cookery to a strong clarified soup, the different consommés seen on bills of fare, called Consommé à la this and à la that, simply terrorizes the guests as well as the young cooks, and are merely significant of the different garnitures that are placed in the soup or plate before being served, or else the flavor of the principal meat of which the consommé was made. The ingredients for a good general every day consommé is here given.

CONSOMMÉ INGREDIENTS—To make five gallons (which quantity should serve 100 guests) take fifteen pounds of LEAN beef trimmings, six medium sized peeled carrots, same of onions, twelve leeks, two heads of celery, a bunch of parsley and a gallon of tomatoes all chopped fine, mix with them after chopping, one tablespoonful of whole peppers, twelve cloves, six bay leaves, eighteen beaten whites of eggs and their shells, a little salt, then add stirring all the time, eight gallons of good stock free from fat, COLD, or if hot, place a chunk of ice in the saucepan before pouring in the hot stock. Next, place saucepan on the range, add three hens (they can be used as salads after), fetch to a slow simmer and reduce to about five gallons in four hours, then strain through a consommé towel (double cheese cloth).

In the following numerous consommés there will be stated certain flavors such as "veal," "chicken," "game," "mutton," "vegetable," "fish," etc. When the recipe has this statement, it means that the stock besides containing the ingredients mentioned for making consommé should have an extra supply of the flavor called for, so that it will be distinct from the ordinary flavor of plain consommé.

CONSOMMÉ AFRICAINE—Cooked artichoke bottoms and egg plant cut in small squares, kept hot in consommé, spoonful placed in each plate at time of serving; a teaspoonful of curry powder to each gallon of stock should be mixed with the ingredients before boiling so as to give the soup a light curry flavor.

CONSOMMÉ ANDALOUSE—After the plain consommé is strained and seasoned, some well washed pearl tapioca is simmered in it till perfectly clear; small poached quenelles of forcemeat are kept hot in a little consommé, and one or two added to each plate at time of serving; the soup should have strong tomato flavor with a suspicion of garlic.

CONSOMMÉ ANGLAISE—Plain consommé made with plenty of veal bones to give it a gelatinous taste; served with green peas and small squares of white chicken meat in each plate.

CONSOMMÉ BAGRATION—Make two separate consommés, one plain, the other with plenty of fish heads, when both are strained and seasoned, mix together, so that the fish flavor slightly predominates; when serving, a spoonful of the following mixture is placed in each plate of soup; small fish quenelles, tails of crayfish, flakes of small fish, and small cut vegetables of the season.

CONSOMMÉ BEAUVILLIERS—Soup of vegetable flavor, served with slices of stuffed cucumbers and small squares of toast. To stuff the cucumbers, cut off the ends, remove the seedy part with a column cutter, fill it with any forcemeat you have on hand, then simmer in milk and water till done, remove and drain, and when cold cut in thin slices.

CONSOMMÉ BOURDALOUE—A chicken-flavored soup served with small squares of cooked chicken breast, green peas, circular thin slices of rice that has been mixed with egg yolks and Montpelier butter, then steamed and allowed to become cold.

CONSOMMÉ BARIGOULE—A game-flavored soup seasoned with sherry wine, and served with slices of stuffed olives together with slices of button mushrooms.

CONSOMMÉ BRUNOISE—A vegetable-flavored soup served with green peas, very small squares of carrot, turnip (white and yellow) celery and artichokes.

CONSOMMÉ BOURGEOISE—To the consommé ingredients is added a couple of ham knuckles, thus giving the soup a slight ham flavor. It is served with shred cooked cabbage, leeks, very small balls of potatoes, and minute squares of carrot, turnip and celery.

CONSOMMÉ CARÊME—A plain consommé flavored with Madeira wine and served with small snippets of toast, together with small circular slices of cooked carrot, white and yellow turnip, finely shred lettuce, sorrel leaves and a sprinking of chopped chervil.

CONSOMMÉ CELESTINE—A plain consommé flavored with sherry wine, served with small sandwiches of the following: Make six French pancakes, spread three with forcemeat and grated cheese, place the other three on top, then stamp them with a medium-sized column cutter.

CONSOMMÉ CHATELAINE—A plain consommé served with green peas, shredded string beans and squares of custard, made of one pint of onion purée, 24 egg yolks, salt, red pepper, mixed and steamed.

CONSOMMÉ CHANTILLY—A bunch of fresh mint should be boiled with the consommé ingredients, the soup to be served with blanched rings of green onion tops, and small squares of a stiff purée of green peas.

CONSOMMÉ WITH CHOUX—A plain consommé served with green peas, slices of button mushrooms and small balls of choux-paste made like stoned olives, the centre filled with forcemeat and baked ten minutes.

CONSOMMÉ CHIFFONADE—A vegetable flavored soup with shredded cabbage and lettuce, thin strips of carrot and turnip, together with green peas.

CONSOMMÉ CLAREMONT—A plain consommé served with small rings of onions that have been dipped in milk, then flour, then fried crisp; together with Royal custards cut in squares or circles, made of ten yolks of eggs, two whole eggs, and half pint of cold consommé; mixed together, not beaten; slowly steamed till set.

CONSOMMÉ COLBERT—A plain consommé served with a freshly poached egg, and a spoonful of small cut vegetables of the season.

CONSOMMÉ WITH CELERY—Plenty of celery trimmings should be boiled with the consommé ingredients, the soup served with a spoonful of shredded cooked celery, thin strips of tongue, mushrooms and a little dry boiled rice.

CONSOMMÉ CUSSY—With the consommé ingredients should be boiled plenty of game trimmings to give the soup a game flavor. It is served with small blanched and peeled chestnuts, a small timbale of game forcemeat mixed with mushrooms, finished with a little Madeira wine.

CONSOMMÉ DUCHESSE—Strain off a plain consommé, then thicken it with corn starch mixed with water, simmer it till it is perfectly clear and gelatinous; it is then served with strips of white chicken meat; the soup to be of strong chicken flavor.

CONSOMMÉ WITH DARIOLES—A consommé of strong chicken flavor served with quarters of darioles made of a pound of lean grated ham, half a cupful of Soubise purée, half a cupful of tomato purée, two whole eggs, eight yolks of eggs, a wine glass of Madeira wine, same of cold consommé, with a dash of red pepper; make the whole into a paste, then rub it through a fine sieve, fill dariole molds, steam till set, cut in quarters when cold, and serve with the soup together with green peas.

CONSOMMÉ DESCLIGNAC—A plain consommé flavored with sherry wine, served with circular slices of Royal custards.

CONSOMMÉ DOUGLAS—A plain consommé served with shreds of cooked celery, red tongue, mushrooms and a little dry boiled rice.

CONSOMMÉ DUBORG—A plain consommé served with dry boiled rice and some fancy shapes of Royal custards.

CONSOMMÉ D'ORSAY—A strong chicken-flavored consommé served with an egg poached in consommé, together with very small cut vegetables of the season.

CONSOMMÉ DAUMONT—A sherry wine-flavored consommé served with small pieces of cooked chicken breast, sweetbread, red tongue and tops of button mushrooms.

CONSOMMÉ EPICURE—A strong consommé of game-flavor, seasoned with Madeira wine, and served with a freshly poached egg in each plate.

CONSOMMÉ OF GAME—The preceding, but in place of the egg, it is served with quenelles or raviolis made of uncooked partridge one part, cooked calf's brains one part, Parmesan cheese half part, yolks of eggs to bind, pounded, rubbed through a fine sieve, molded into quenelles and poached.

CONSOMMÉ GAMBETTA—A chicken-flavored consommé served with a poached yolk of egg, and three quenelles of veal, one of its natural color, the others being colored red and green respectively.

CONSOMMÉ INDIENNE—Same as "consommé Africaine" adding, however, strips of cooked chicken breast and a little dry boiled rice.

CONSOMMÉ IMPERATRICE—A strong chicken-flavored consommé served with a freshly poached egg in each plate.

CONSOMMÉ ITALIENNE—A plain consommé slightly flavored with tomatoes and a suspicion of garlic; served with green peas and small pieces of well washed macaroni.

CONSOMMÉ IMPERIAL—A chicken-flavored consommé served with green; peas, asparagus points and small quenelles of chicken forcemeat.

CONSOMMÉ JULIENNE—A vegetable-flavored consommé served with fine shreds of green stringless beans, carrot, turnip, cabbage, celery, leeks, spring onions, and green peas, the vegetables should be sautéed in butter first, before simmering them in the consommé.

CONSOMMÉ JOINVILLE—A strong consommé well flavored with fish heads, pounded lobster heads and shells; when strained off, seasoned with white wine, served with small pieces of lobster and croûtons soufflés.

CONSOMMÉ KURSEL—A vegetable-flavored consommé served with a spoonful of cooked green peas, asparagus tips, shred lettuce, cut stringless beans, flageolets and green onions.

CONSOMMÉ MARIE STUART—A mutton-flavored consommé served with a spoonful of well washed, cooked pearl barley, and small cut vegetables of the season.

CONSOMMÉ MACEDOINE—A chicken-flavored consommé served with a mixture of vari-colored vegetables cut in very small squares, or else use the canned macedoines.

CONSOMMÉ MAGENTA—A plain consommé slightly colored with tomato juice, to which is added a macedoine of vegetables and some chopped parsley and celery leaves.

CONSOMMÉ MASSENA—Made with plenty of hare or jack rabbit trimmings mixed with the consommé ingredients, when strained off, flavored with sherry wine, served with small quenelles of rabbit.

CONSOMMÉ WITH MACARONI—A roast poultry stock should be used to make the consommé; when strained off and seasoned, served with macaroni that has been boiled, washed, drained, and then cut into quarter-inch pieces.

CONSOMMÉ MILANAISE—The preceding made consommé served with the addition to the macaroni, one inch lengths of boiled smoked tongue; a butter chip full of Parmesan cheese should be served separately.

CONSOMMÉ MONTE CARLO—A rich chicken-flavored consommé served with slices of cooked vegetables stamped out with cutters representing clubs, spades, hearts and diamonds; also circular slices of chicken forcemeat that is dotted with truffles to represent dominoes; also circular slices of cooked beetroot, carrot and turnip representing poker chips.

CONSOMMÉ MEFICIS—A rich chicken-flavored consommé lightly thickened with corn starch; served with a freshly poached egg in each plate, together with a canapé or small patty of chicken forcemeat served separately.

CONSOMMÉ MONTMORENCY—A rich flavored chicken consommé served with noodles, small balls of chicken forcemeat, and some lettuce leaves spread with chicken forcemeat rolled up like cigarettes and braised.

CONSOMMÉ NAPOLITAINE—A game-flavored consommé to which is added Madeira wine, served with small cut and washed macaroni, cooked celery cut in small squares, and small croûtons of toast.

CONSOMMÉ WITH NOODLES—A rich chicken-flavored consommé served with finely shred noodles.

CONSOMMÉ NIVERNAISE—A plain consommé flavored with sherry wine; served with small quenelles of veal, together with fancy Italian paste, and a macedoine of vegetables.

CONSOMMÉ NAUDIER—A rich chicken-flavored consommé served with small quenelles of chicken forcemeat of different colors; to make which, take some chicken forcemeat and divide it into four parts; into the first work some finely chopped truffle peelings; the second finely minced red tongue; the third, chopped parsley; the fourth, minced yolks of hard boiled eggs.

CONSOMMÉ NILSSON—A rich chicken-flavored consommé served with small quenelles of chicken forcemeat in three colors shape of a pencil, an inch long; to make which, divide the forcemeat into three parts, leave one plain, color the others red and green respectively.

CONSOMMÉ ORGE—A plain consommé served with pearl barley, breast of cooked chicken cut in squares, carrots and turnips cut into small squares.

CONSOMMÉ WITH PEAS—A vegetable-flavored consommé served with green peas, together with black peas scooped out of truffles.

CONSOMMÉ POISSON—A plain consommé slightly flavored with fish stock, seasoned with sherry wine; served with green peas, dry boiled rice and small quenelles of lobster.

CONSOMMÉ PRINTANIÈRE—A vegetable-flavored consommé served with plenty of green peas, asparagus tips, and other spring vegetables cut small.

CONSOMMÉ PRINTANIÈRE ROYALE—Same as the preceding, with the addition of Royal custards, into which has been steamed a finely cut macedoine of vegetables.

CONSOMMÉ PAYSANNE—A vegetable-flavored consommé served with a jardiniere of vegetables, shred cabbage and lettuce.

CONSOMMÉ PRINCESSE—A rich chicken-flavored consommé served with green peas, asparagus tips, pearl barley, diced chicken breasts, and forcemeat quenelles.

CONSOMMÉ PATTI—A plain consommé served with rice, green peas, breast of chicken and truffles cut in small squares, together with some Parmesan cheese served separately.

CONSOMMÉ PÂTÉ D'ITALIE—A chicken-flavored consommé served with fancy Italian paste.

CONSOMMÉ PRINCE DE GALLES—A game flavored consommé, served with asparagus tips, Royal custards, breast of chicken and chicken forcemeat, all cut in diamond shapes.

CONSOMMÉ PALESTINE—A chicken-flavored consommé served with dry boiled rice, and thin slices of stewed Jerusalem artichokes. CONSOMMÉ WITH QUENELLES, ASPARAGUS TIPS, TURNIPS, RICE, CORN, PEAS, OR ANY OTHER SIMPLE THING, AS OFTEN SEEN ON BILLS OF FARE, IS SIMPLY A PLAIN CONSOMMÉ SERVED WITH THE ARTICLE NAMED.

CONSOMMÉ ROYALE—A plain consommé served with circular slices of Royal custards, and flavored with sherry wine.

CONSOMMÉ RACHAEL—A game-flavored consommé seasoned with Madeira wine, and served with small quenelles of game together with shreds of cooked red tongue and truffles.

CONSOMMÉ RENAISSANCE—A game-flavored consommé seasoned with Malaga wine; served with sliced mushrooms, dry boiled rice, green peas and croûtons.

CONSOMMÉ RIVOLI—A plain consommé but highly spiced; served with noodles, also Parmesan cheese served separately.

CONSOMMÉ SEMOULE—A plain consommé, when strained off has tapioca or semolina washed, then simmered till same is clear in the soup.

CONSOMMÉ SAGOU—Same as the preceding, but using sago instead of tapioca.

CONSOMMÉ DE STAEL—A chicken-flavored consommé served with lozenge-shaped pieces of fried bread, and small quenelles of chicken forcemeat.

CONSOMMÉ SEVEIGNE—A chicken-flavored consommé served with asparagus tips, cut stringless beans, green peas, and Royal custards mixed with forcemeat.

CONSOMMÉ SOLFERINO—A strong beef-flavored consommé; served with small quenelles of farina. Plenty of roast beef bones should be boiled in the stock.

CONSOMMÉ SUEDOISE—A rich chicken-flavored consommé served with a small croûstade in each plate filled with a mixture as follows: run a couple of carrots, turnips and a small cabbage through a mincing machine, braise them till done, then mix with them a can each of flageolet beans and green peas, also a little Parmesan cheese; season to taste.

CONSOMMÉ TROIS RACINES—A mutton-flavored consommé served with cubes of braised turnip, carrot and celery.

CONSOMMÉ TALMA—A chicken-flavored consommé served with grains of boiled rice, and shapes of Royal custards made of eggs and almond milk.

CONSOMMÉ ST. XAVIER—A vegetable-flavored consommé served with a Printanière of vegetables, shred cabbage and the following: Cook together four ounces of butter, six ounces of flour, two ounces of grated cheese, one cup of cream; season it with pepper, salt and nutmeg; remove from the fire when done, and beat into it two whole eggs, two yolks of eggs, some chopped parsley; then rub it through a colander into the simmering soup.

CONSOMMÉ VERMICELLI—Is simply a rich veal-flavored consommé served with vermicelli that has been boiled, and then well washed and drained.

CONSOMMÉ VOLAILLE—Is simply a rich chicken-flavored consommé served with strips of chicken meat.

COQ—The French word for "cock," hence they have "coq de Bruyere," which in English means black cock or heath fowl, "coq d'Inde" or turkey cock.

COQUILLE—Is the French word for shell, and we have many dishes served "en coquille" or in shell, generally in a scallop shell, either natural, or of metal or earthenware to imitate it.

CORBEILLE—Is the French word for basket that is used to hold a display of crystallized fruits or flowers, etc., etc.

CORDIALS—Or liqueurs as the French call them, enter into many ices and drinks that are served at banquets, of which the following is a list of those most used. "Absinthe, Alkermes, Benedictine, Chartreuse, Curaçoa, Kummel,

Shrub, Kirsch or Kirschwasser, Maraschino, Nectar, Negus, Noyeau, Punch, Ratafia and Vermouth.

CORIANDER—Name of an aromatic seed resembling whole peppers in size and shape, used by confectioners as a flavoring, also by the cook for seasoning green turtle soup.

CORIANDER—An ancient and increasingly popular spice, coriander (*Coriandrum sativum*) leaves are also known as Chinese parsley and cilantro. These leaves have a strong flavor that some find objectionable ("It tastes like soap"), but most enjoy enormously. Coriander has a special affinity for garlic and pepper. Although it has been used for centuries in Middle Eastern and Indian cooking, especially in its seed form, American cooks are beginning to use the leaves more and more as they learn to prepare Southeast Asian and Caribbean dishes, both of which feature coriander as a brilliantly flavorful garnish.

CORN—A most succulent and nutritious vegetable. In its green state it is generally boiled for about twenty minutes in boiling water containing milk and salt, and is served on the cob. The dried corn or maize (mais in French) is ground course or fine for making the dishes following.

CORN—How does one best cook corn? There seem to be as many ways as there are cooks, and each seems sure that his or her way is best. What everyone agrees about is that the best corn goes straight from the field into the pot. Although it is difficult to argue with this axiom, some of the new corn hybrids retain their sugar for days and taste almost as good after refrigeration as they did when they were strictly fresh. What has been overlooked, at least recently, is just how good corn—both fresh (and frozen) and ground into meal—is as an ingredient. Fellows's recipes are excellent.

CORN MEAL MUSH—One gallon of water, one ounce each of salt and butter. The seasoned water is brought to the boil, into which is then strewn and beaten one and a quarter pounds of corn meal; when boiled up again, it should be removed to the back of the range where it must simmer for three hours with a cover on; served with cream or milk and sugar.

FRIED CORN MUSH—A popular breakfast dish. The mush of the preceding when cooked is poured into a buttered pan, smoothed, the top then brushed with melted butter to prevent a hard skin forming, allowed to become cold, cut in blocks or slices, fried plain in butter, or breaded and fried; served with maple syrup.

CORN BATTER CAKES—For recipe see heading of BATTERS.

CORN GEMS OR MUFFINS—One and a half pounds of corn meal, three quarters of a pound of sifted wheat flour, three teaspoonfuls of baking powder, half a cup of granulated sugar, one teaspoonful salt, all mixed together dry; one and a half pints each of water and milk, six beaten eggs, half a cupful of melted butter mixed together, the dry and wet mixtures then thor-

CORN GEMS (MUFFINS)

·

Makes 6 to 8

Freshly baked corn muffins are terrific. This recipe is so easy that you will make them often.

³/₄ cup yellow cornmeal	*1 egg*
³/₄ cup all-purpose flour	*³/₄ cup milk*
¹/₄ cup sugar	*¹/₄ cup butter, melted*
1¹/₂ teaspoons baking powder	

Preheat the oven to 350°F.

In a large bowl, combine the dry ingredients. Beat the egg in a water glass and add the milk. Add to the dry ingredients along with the melted butter. Mix well and pour into buttered nonstick muffin tins or use paper muffin cups to prevent sticking. Fill to about ¹/₄ inch from the top.

Bake for about 25 minutes, until light brown and done in the center.

C.W.

oughly incorporated and poured into hot greased patty shells or muffin rings and baked; light and delicious.

CORN BREAD, JOHNNY CAKE OR CORN DODGER—The preceding mixture poured into greased hot shallow baking pans and baked well done with crisp corners.

CORN MEAL GRUEL—Well boiled corn meal mush two-thirds, slightly sweetened boiling milk one-third, mixed, then forced through a fine sieve or colander.

CORN WAFFLES—The mixture above given for "Corn Muffins," poured into hot waffle irons, baked and served dusted with powdered sugar.

CORN BLANC-MANGE—Equal quantities of white corn meal and corn starch mixed dry, beaten into boiling milk sweetened to taste, then allowed to simmer for an hour, removed, flavored, poured into decorated molds, turned out when set and cold; served with whipped cream, fruit syrups or stewed fruits.

CORN MEAL OR INDIAN PUDDING—Thick well boiled corn meal

mush allowed to partly cool, into which is then mixed seedless raisins, grated lemon rind, ginger, butter, a little molasses beaten with a very little baking soda, beaten eggs, then baked and served with a fruit syrup sauce.

POLENTA—The Italian name for our corn meal mush; they also make a polenta from chestnut flour.

POLENTA—Other types of flour are used by the Italians to make polenta, and there are many different ways to prepare and serve it.

HULLED CORN—Dried white corn soaked in weak lye for two days is then well washed, boiled tender and served plain with milk. In the larger cities there are people who prepare it and sell it ready for boiling.

HULLED CORN—Hulled corn is known as HOMINY. When ground, it is hominy grits, still a popular breakfast cereal in the South.

TORTILLAS, A CORN CAKE MADE BY THE MEXICANS—The tortilla is typical of old Mexico, and is encountered wherever the influence of the cactus republic has reached. It was found as the main article of food among the ancient Aztecs at the time of the Spanish conquests, more than three and a half centuries ago; and the little hand ground and palm-fashioned corn cake has well held its own down through the ages, being today as popular and in as general use as ever. Shelled corn intended for this use is first soaked over night in lime water until the outer husk of the kernels is loose enough to be removed by being rolled between the hands, and is then ready for grinding. This is done by the Mexican women of the lower classes, who often work in the doorways of their homes, bending over the historic stone hand mill, called in Mexico a Matate. The mill is simply a rough slab of stone supported by four stocky legs and is made of volcanic tufa, the coarse grain of which is best adapted for the grinding of the corn, beans, chilli seeds, cheese or whatever it may be desired to finely pulverize. The stone mill is an indispensable item in the culinary outfit of the tropical home. The accompanying handpiece, looking like a rude rolling pin, is also of stone, and is briskly worked up and down the incline of the rude stone table by the woman as she bends to her work with a steady swing of body, shoulders and arms. It is claimed that the flour for the tortillas can be perfectly milled only by their ancient methods, and when one sees the result of the grinding he is ready to admit that possibly they are right. As the moist windrows of the meal roll off the grinding board it is caught in a basin and is then ready for being formed into cakes for baking. When ready to bake, a woman takes a small lump of the heavy mixture and lays it in the palm of her hand; then with the other palm, she rolls it into a ball and begins to quickly pat it in to the desired thinness, deftly spreading the fingers to allow it to enlarge its size, and changing it from hand to hand until it is only an eighth of an inch in thickness and generally about six inches in diameter, although sometimes as large as a dinner plate. The plastic cakes are tossed, one after another, as completed, upon the stove called a Brasero, and as fast as delicately browned and turned they are placed in a steaming heap and enveloped in a cloth to keep them warm.

CORN FRITTERS—Canned corn, or cooked corn cut off the cob, pounded, mixed with a little flour, beaten eggs, salt, pepper and a little butter, dropped by spoonfuls into hot fat and fried brown; served as a garniture to chicken, Maryland style, or as a vegetable.

GRATED CORN PUDDING—Two quarts of cooked corn grated off the cob, eight yolks of eggs, cup of melted butter, pint of milk, salt, pepper and nutmeg, mixed, poured into buttered baking pans, baked; served with a sweet sauce.

GREEN CORN SAUTÉ—Boiled corn cut from the cob, melted butter in sauté pan, corn tossed and heated thoroughly in it, seasoned with salt, pepper and nutmeg; served very hot; after sautéeing, it may also be mixed with a cream or Béchamel sauce, and served as a vegetable.

GREEN CORN BATTER CAKES— Two quarts of cooked corn grated from the cob, twelve ounces of flour, salt, pepper, nutmeg, pint and a half of milk, four beaten eggs, thoroughly mixed, baked on a griddle; served with butter and sugar, or syrup.

CORN SOUP—Fresh green corn partly grated off the cob and placed aside; the rest on the cob boiled in chicken broth till tender, then strain it off on to the grated pulp, boil up, season with butter, salt, nutmeg and a little sugar, then pass it through a fine sieve into an equal quantity of Velouté sauce. Another way is to take canned corn, pound it, rub it through a sieve, boil it with milk, then mix it with Velouté sauce.

CORN AND TOMATO SOUP— Canned, or corn cut from the cob, passed through a mincing machine, then rubbed through a fine sieve, the purée thus obtained boiled in a Velouté sauce, then combined with an equal quantity of tomato purée.

ROAST CORN IN EAR—Young green corn with the thick outer husks removed, the inner leaves after removing the silk, tied at the top, slowly roasted till done; served with the green covering; cut top and bottom so as to be removed easily.

POP CORN—A variety of corn that is held in a wire basket over heat enough to burst or pop it; it can then be cemented together into balls with butter and syrup, etc.

POPCORN—Popcorn is a variety of corn with a hard kernel that contains a fair amount of moisture. When heated, the moisture turns to steam and explodes—"pops"—the kernel, turning it inside out.

ROAST GREEN CORN—Young green corn stripped and the silk removed, arranged in a buttered baking pan,

CORN FRITTERS

•

Makes about 2½ dozen

This dish belongs in this book because corn is an American food product. The fritters make a nice accompaniment to any meal.

2 tablespoons butter

1 tablespoon olive oil

1½ cups peeled and finely
chopped yellow onions

1 tablespoon finely
chopped parsley

2 (10-ounce) packages
frozen corn kernels,
thawed

1 egg, beaten

¼ cup milk

½ cup all-purpose flour

2 teaspoons baking powder

Peanut oil for frying

Heat a frying pan and add the butter, oil, onions, and parsley. Sauté until the onions are clear. Do not brown too much.

Chop the thawed corn coarsely and place in a mixing bowl. Add the sautéed onions and the remaining ingredients, except the oil for frying. Blend well.

These fritters can be deep-fried, but they are better pan-fried with just a little oil. Spoon the batter by tablespoons into an oiled nonstick frying pan. Fry a few minutes on both sides, until golden brown. If the fritters break apart when frying, you may need to add a bit more flour to the batter. Drain on paper towels. (An electric frying pan set at 375°F. is great for this.)

C.W.

seasoned with salt, white pepper and melted butter, slowly baked, basted and turned till done.

CORN STARCH—A preparation of the inner part of corn used in making blanc-manges, thickening soups, sauces, etc.

STEWED CORN, CREOLE STYLE— Canned corn, or corn cooked and cut from the cob, mixed with an equal quantity of peeled and cooked tomatoes, a grating of onion and garlic, salt, pepper and butter, boiled down thick; served as a vegetable.

CORN SALAD—Called "Doucette" by the French, is a herb used in mixing salads; sometimes made into a salad by itself; is good to mix with lettuce salad, giving it a slightly bitter taste; it resembles somewhat a cabbage lettuce in appearance and growth.

COURT-BOUILLON—Is the name of a highly seasoned broth used to boil fresh water fish, to impart a better flavor to them, and is made from carrot, onion, parsley, bay leaves, cloves, thyme, garlic, sliced lemon, chervil, salt and pepper, all tied in a muslin bag and boiled with a few fish heads in water containing white or red wine or vinegar; after the seasoning is extracted, it is strained and put away for use as required; it also enters into a few soups, sauces and garnitures, such as Havraise, Holstein, Normande and Venitienne sauces, Chambord and Genevoise garnitures, Bouillabaisse, eel, lobster and other fish soups and bisques.

CRABS—Are a delectable shellfish. In this country we use for food two kinds, the hard shell blue crab which periodically sheds its shell, thus giving us the "soft shell crab," and the oyster crab. The male crab has a long white, narrow tail turned round its under part, the female has a broad brownish, feathery tail. The centre of the body is filled with its liver, which is a soft yellow substance. The meat used is obtained from the inner top of the back, and the claws. Crab meat is tasty but comparatively poor in nutriment and very hard to digest. There is one firm in this country "McMenamin of Hampton, Virginia," who for years past have made a specialty of putting up fresh cooked crab meat in cans, supplying with each can a sufficient number of shells to hold the amount of meat. They are obtainable of leading grocers everywhere, and from personal experience of their use, the author can say that he has found their crab meat give perfect satisfaction to hotel patrons.

CRABS—Fresh-picked crabmeat, widely sold to restaurants and sometimes found in better fish markets, varies in quality. Only when it is truly fresh and perfectly clean is it worth the expense. Frozen, canned, or pasteurized "fresh" crabmeat are all markedly inferior.

Many fresh crabs—especially the ubiquitous blue (*Callinectes sapidus*, or the "beautiful swimmer")— are a good deal of work to eat and yield very little meat. There are exceptions, of course: the Pacific Dungeness (*Cancer magister*) is large and meaty and often found fresh on the West Coast; the stone crab of Florida has rock-hard shells but very meaty claws, which are usually pounded open with wooden hammers; and the Alaskan king crab can have three-foot- long claws but is rarely sold fresh in the lower forty-eight states. Even tiny oyster crabs, which are found in oysters and mussels, are edible, either raw or quickly sautéed or fried (although they are more often considered a nuisance).

Soft-shell crabs are delicious eaten whole and are one certain way to enjoy the blue crab with a minimum of fuss; they are best sautéed, deep-fried, or grilled, basted with a bit of butter spiked with hot sauce such as Tabasco.

As for nutrition, all crabs are low in fat and calories, and not especially high in cholesterol. They are also excellent sources of zinc.

CRAB CAKES—Cooked crab meat four parts, fresh breadcrumbs one part, mixed and seasoned with salt, nutmeg, red pepper, and chopped parsley, and bound with raw egg yolks; made into cakes like "codfish cakes" then breaded and fried; served with cream or Hollandaise sauces.

CRAB TOAST—Cooked crab meat sautéed with butter, seasoned with salt, nutmeg and red pepper; served piled high on slices of hot buttered toast.

BUTTERED CRAB—Cooked crab meat cut small, two parts; fresh breadcrumbs, one part; mixed and seasoned with a little chopped parsley, salt, red pepper, nutmeg, caper vinegar and melted butter, then packed into crab shells, sprinkled with breadcrumbs, then melted butter, browned in hot oven and served.

CRAB SAUSAGES—Cooked crab meat seasoned with chervil, a suspicion of garlic, salt, red pepper and minced chives, the whole pounded, rubbed through a sieve, bound with raw yolks of eggs, formed into shapes of sausages, rolled in flour, fried a delicate brown with butter; served with Tartar sauce.

CRAB FRITTERS—Cooked crab meat finely minced, mixed with a little minced fried onion, a suspicion of garlic, seasoned with salt, pepper, nutmeg, dry mustard, Worcestershire sauce and chopped parsley, all boiled down in a Velouté sauce till thick; then is worked in a few beaten egg yolks, removed and poured into a but-

tered pan and allowed to become cold; then cut in finger slices, dipped into a thin frying batter, fried; served with Tartar sauce.

CRAB CANAPÉS—Minced cooked crab meat mixed with a little finely minced fried shallots, seasoned with salt, red pepper and grated Parmesan cheese, boiled down thick with a rich Velouté sauce, allowed to cool, then spread on fancy shapes of toast, the meat then strewn with grated cheese, browned off in hot oven and served.

CRAB OMELET—The preceding mixture while still hot enclosed in centre of omelet; served with Velouté sauce poured around.

CRAB SALAD—Cooked crab meat cut fine, seasoned with oil, tarragon vinegar, salt and red pepper mixed with a little finely shred and minced white cabbage; served on a leaf of lettuce, garnished with shred lettuce, stuffed olives, and slices of hard boiled eggs.

CRAB STEW—Cooked crab meat seasoned with salt, pepper and nutmeg, made hot in a rich Béchamel sauce; served in cases of croûstades, the top sprinkled with parsley dust.

CRAB, QUEEN STYLE—Cold cooked crab meat in shreds three parts, finely shred hearts of celery one part, mixed, seasoned with tarragon vinegar, olive oil, salt and red pepper, filled into crab shells, masked with mayonnaise, decor-

CRAB CANAPÉS

•

Makes a few dozen, depending upon size of toast

These make perfect hors d'oeuvres for entertaining. Be careful with the cayenne pepper; you don't want to overpower the crabmeat.

2 tablespoons butter	Pinch of salt
3 tablespoons minced shallots	Pinch of cayenne pepper
1/2 tablespoon minced parsley	3/4 pound cooked crabmeat, flaked
2 tablespoons all-purpose flour	Plenty of toast rounds or good crackers
1 cup milk	Additional Parmesan cheese for topping
1 tablespoon grated Parmesan cheese	

Heat a medium-sized frying pan and sauté the butter, shallots, and parsley until the shallots are clear. Stir in the flour and cook a couple of minutes. Do not brown. Add the milk, Parmesan cheese, salt, and cayenne pepper. Using a wire whisk, whip, simmering a few minutes to make a smooth sauce. Remove from the heat. Stir in the crabmeat and cool.

Spread the crabmeat mixture onto bite-sized toast rounds and sprinkle with a little more Parmesan cheese. Broil until lightly browned on top. Serve hot.

C.W.

ated with small shapes of hard boiled eggs, lobster coral and sliced stuffed olives (called Crab à la Reine).

EMINCE OF CRAB—Shredded cooked crab meat seasoned with salt, red pepper, dash of Worcestershire sauce and caper vinegar, mixed with a little Parmesan cheese, tossed and thoroughly heated in a saútoir with butter; served on hot buttered toast, sprinkled with chopped parsley.

DEVILLED CRABS—Cooked crab meat mixed with minced whites of hard boiled eggs and the yolks rubbed through a sieve, seasoned with salt, red pepper, dry mustard, Worcestershire sauce and tarragon

SCALLOPED CRABS • 191

vinegar; made hot with a good allowance of melted butter, filled into shells, smoothed, strewn with sifted breadcrumbs, browned off in the oven and served very hot. Some cooks have a habit of mixing the crab meat with a highly seasoned sauce instead of the directions just given, with the result that if not all served at the one meal, they go flat when cold, and look unsightly and unserviceable when reheated.

SCALLOPED CRABS—The deviled crab mixture of the preceding moistened with Velouté sauce, filled into crab or scallop shells, or small oval deep dishes, strewn with grated cheese and melted butter, browned in hot oven and served.

BAKED CRABS—Minced shallots, thinly sliced mushrooms lightly fried together with butter, into which is then mixed cooked crab meat, truffle trimmings, chopped parsley, salt, red pepper and a little Velouté sauce; filled into large crab shells, strewn with fresh sifted breadcrumbs, browned in oven, served hot.

CRABS, CREOLE STYLE—Live hard shell crabs, fish-kettle with separate perforated bottom, under which is poured white wine vinegar seasoned with salt and red pepper; live crabs placed on the false bottom, lid of kettle placed on tightly, kettle put over a good fire; when crabs are of a bright red color, taken up and served at once with the under shell separated.

CROÛSTADE OF CRABS—Cooked crab meat sautéed with minced shallots in butter, seasoned with salt, red pepper and caper vinegar, moistened and heated with sauce Normande, filled into bread or paste croûstades; served very hot.

CRAB FORCEMEAT—Cooked crab meat finely minced with chervil, chives and a small clove of garlic, seasoned with salt, red pepper and caper vinegar, pounded, then rubbed through a fine sieve, bound with raw egg yolks. Set aside for use.

CRAB CROQUETTES—Crab forcemeat made into shapes, breaded, fried; served with sauce Joinville.

CRAB KROMESKIES—Cold crab forcemeat rolled into size and shape of a finger, bound with a thin slice of cold boiled bacon, pinned with a toothpick, dipped into a plain batter, fried, toothpick removed, served with Tartar sauce.

STUFFED CRAB—Cooked crab meat seasoned with tarragon vinegar, curry powder, salt and red pepper, slightly moistened with Velouté sauce, filled into shells, strewn with sifted breadcrumbs, baked; served very hot.

TOMATOES STUFFED WITH CRAB—Raw peeled tomatoes of an even size, hollowed out, seeds removed, the outside then covered with crab forcemeat, and the inside filled with devilled crab mixture, smoothed off, rolled in sifted breadcrumbs, baked and basted with butter; served very hot.

CRAB SAUCE—Cooked crab meat minced with a few mushrooms, seasoned with nutmeg, salt, red pepper and lemon juice, simmered in Béchamel sauce for a few minutes; chopped parsley may be added if desired.

CRAB GUMBO (SOUP)—Very small squares of raw lean ham fried a delicate brown with minced onion or shallots and crab meat, flour added to form a roux, moistened with equal parts of court-bouillon and chicken broth, brought to the boil, skimmed; shred green peppers, sliced okras and peeled and sliced tomatoes then added, simmered for an hour, seasoned with salt, red pepper, herbs and white wine, a spoonful of dry boiled rice placed in each plate at time of serving.

BISQUE OF CRABS—Live crabs blanched as for "Creole style," meat removed and lightly fried with minced shallots and a clove of garlic in butter, moistened with fish broth and white wine, brought to the boil, shells then added with some well washed rice; when rice is cooked, little roux added, the whole then rubbed through a tamis or purée sieve, brought to the boil again, skimmed, seasoned with salt, red pepper and sherry wine; served with small croûtons.

BISQUE OF CRABS, CREOLE STYLE—Boil half a pound of rice to each gallon of soup required, when done add its equal weight of cooked crab meat, pound to a paste, adding half a cupful of melted butter and a flavor of nutmeg, then rub it through a purée sieve; make the soup stock of thin Velouté sauce, add the rice and crab purée, bring to a simmer, then add sliced okras, minced red and green peppers, sliced peeled tomatoes, season with thyme, marjoram, red pepper and lemon juice, simmer slowly for one hour and serve.

BOILED SOFT SHELL CRABS—Live crabs with small claws and sand pouch removed, dropped into boiling salted water and simmered for ten minutes; served with Velouté or parsley sauces.

SOFT SHELL CRABS FRIED—Live crabs with sand pouch removed, seasoned with salt and pepper, dipped in milk, rolled in flour, then in beaten eggs and again breadcrumbs, fried in deep fat or slowly in butter; served with Tartar sauce, or with mayonnaise, garnished with parsley and lemon.

SOFT SHELL CRABS BROILED—Prepared and breaded as in the preceding, placed between a double hinged wire broiler, broiled and basted with butter; served with Tartar sauce, garnished with parsley and lemon.

CURRIED SOFT SHELL CRABS—Take the very small ones and boil them a few minutes, then sauté them with minced onion in butter, take up, and put into curry sauce, simmer a few minutes; served with a border of boiled rice in grains.

SOFT SHELL CRABS STEAMED—Live crabs with the small claws and sand pouch removed, placed on false bottom of fish kettle containing vinegar and water underneath; steamed ten minutes, served with Béchamel sauce.

OYSTER CRABS, SAUCE POULETTE—Well washed oyster crabs sautéed with butter, seasoned with salt and pepper, moistened with Hollandaise sauce sharp with lemon juice, add a little chopped parsley; take a small oval platter, pipe a border of potato croquette mixture around the edge, brush it with butter and brown it off in the oven or under a salamander; serve the oyster crabs in the centre.

OYSTER CRABS FRIED—Oyster crabs well washed and drained, seasoned with salt and pepper, tossed in flour, thrown into cold milk, then into sifted breadcrumbs, fried in hot deep grease like whitebait, taken up, drained, sprinkled with salt; served in cases or croûstades.

OYSTER CRAB PATTIES—Make the "oyster crabs, sauce Poulette" above, fill small puff paste patty shells with the mixture; serve with some Poulette sauce around the base.

OYSTER CRABS, NEWBURG—Well washed and drained oyster crabs sautéed in butter for five minutes with some truffle trimmings, then is added some Madeira wine, reduce to one half, then work in a liaison of egg yolks and cream, shuffle about till thick and creamy; serve either in a tureen or chafing dish.

CRAB APPLES—A small sour apple used as a preserve, crystalized, or in jams or jellies, also a medicinal cider.

CRANBERRIES—A small red fruit that when made into a sauce or jelly is relished by the majority as an accompaniment to roast turkey, etc.

CRANBERRIES—Unfortunately, the uses for cranberries have not grown measurably in the last eighty-five years; most people still sweeten them to serve as turkey condiments or buy them in cans. But this native American fruit—one of the few—is actually quite versatile.

The cranberry growers of Massachusetts, Wisconsin, and elsewhere concentrate on the largest cranberry (*Vaccinium macrocarpon*), but there are many others in this family, all related to the heathers (Ericaceae) of the Scottish countryside and to blueberries, cowberries, bearberries, huckleberries, and about a hundred more.

Cranberries were appreciated by Native Americans and by the first settlers for three reasons: First, they are high in vitamin C and thus useful in warding off scurvy (they were regularly included in the pemmican of the northeastern tribes); second, they keep better than any other fruit, up to eight months with just refrigeration (they contain benzoic acid, a natural preservative); and third, they taste good.

CRANBERRY PIE—Cranberries washed, then put to boil with sugar and a very little water; when done, allowed to become cold; pie plates lined with short paste, spread with the cranberries, strips of paste placed over the top, the paste brushed with egg wash, then baked.

CRANBERRY JAM OR SAUCE—is the preceding mixture boiled down with more sugar until thick enough to coat a spoon.

CRANBERRY JELLY—Well washed cranberries: to each gallon, half a gallon of water, put to boil and boiled for ten minutes, they are then mashed and squeezed through a flannel jelly bag, the juice then returned to the fire with four pounds of sugar to each original gallon of cranberries, this is then rapidly boiled from fifteen to twenty minutes, then poured into molds and set; served with turkey, or as a preserve.

CRANBERRY ROLL—Light biscuit dough sweetened and flavored, rolled out thin, spread with cranberry jam, rolled up, ends tucked in, placed in buttered French bread pans and baked; or steamed; or tied in a floured cloth, plunged into boiling water and boiled; served in slices with sweet sauce.

CRANBERRY TARTLETTES—Fancy sets of gem pans lined with puff paste trimmings, spread with cranberry jam, baked; served for dessert. THERE ARE TIMES WHEN THE STEWARD CAN BUY GOOD SOUND CRANBERRIES VERY CHEAP; HE SHOULD THEN DO SO, FOR THEY CAN BE KEPT SOUND FOR MONTHS IF FILLED INTO JARS AND KEPT IN A COOL PLACE, COVERED WITH WATER THAT IS OCCASIONALLY REPLENISHED.

CRAYFISH—Also called "crawfish" is a diminutive looking lobster, found plentifully in our rivers. In Europe they catch a sea crayfish and often sell it as a lobster; our river crayfish on account of its form and color brings it into use as an artistic garniture, while the flesh from the tail forms many delicate entrées, salads and sauces, also soups, that are much thought of on the European continent.

CRAYFISH—Perhaps not as plentiful in our rivers as they were in Fellows's time, crayfish are now being farmed in Louisiana and Florida, and are increasingly available nationally. Although most crayfish look like little LOBSTERS (the Tasmanian crayfish, which can weigh eight pounds, looks like a *big* lobster), they actually taste something like SHRIMP and can be used in some shrimp recipes. In fact, they are extremely mild-flavored.

There are hundreds of species of crayfish throughout the world, more than two hundred in the United States and about thirty in Louisiana, where they are most popular. The Scandinavians are the fanatics of Europe, devoting entire festivals to eating crayfish.

Stored or shipped fresh, crayfish keep for just three or four days. So unless you fish for them yourself or visit the South, chances are good that you will buy—or be served—previously frozen crayfish. You may want to look for those that already have been removed from their shells; once the romance of eating them fresh has eluded you, the work should be avoided as well.

CREAM—Spelled by the French "crème" it is the oleaginous part of milk, and forms the most delicate soups, sauces, custards, creams, ices, russes, soufflés, cheeses and pastries. In general hotel routine, the cook uses the word cream, when little or no cream at all is used and with the following recipes such "creams" will predominate.

CREAM—Cream has fallen into disfavor because of its high fat content. Yet the rich flavor and silken texture that cream contributes to dishes cannot be duplicated. In the United States cream is defined by its percentage of milk fat. Half-and-half contains 10 to 18 percent fat; light cream, 18 to 30 percent; whipping cream, 30 to 36 percent; heavy cream, greater than 36 percent.

More than ever cream bought directly from a dairy farm is far superior to that purchased in the supermarket. That is not always possible, of course. But look for cream that has not been ultrapasteurized; the extra-high heat adds shelf life but robs cream of much of its flavor and adds a discernible cooked taste.

CREAM SAUCE—Boiling milk, melted butter in a saucepan with as much flour as it will take up, stirred together, gradually moistened while stirring with the boiling milk, seasoned with salt, red pepper, nutmeg, and lastly, when removing from the fire, the juice of a lemon is added, strained through a fine strainer, and some pure cream then mixed in.

BÉCHAMEL SAUCE—Boiling chicken broth flavored with the liquor from canned mushrooms, flour and butter mixed, moistened gradually with the boiling liquor while stirring, seasoned with red pepper, salt, lemon juice and nutmeg, strained through a fine strainer, one fourth of its bulk of pure cream then added.

CREAM FRITTERS—Boiling milk with a small piece of butter, sweetened to taste, thickened with corn starch mixed with cream, allowed to boil up again, then further thickened with a liaison of egg yolks and cream, removed from the fire, flavored, turned into a wet pan, allowed to become cold and firm, then cut into shapes, double breaded, fried, served with the following cream sauce.

CREAM SAUCE—Two thirds milk and one third cream mixed and sweetened, brought to the boil, then thickened to the consistency of double cream with a little corn starch moistened with cream and egg yolks, strained, finished with a glass of Madeira wine.

CREAM PUFFS—Choux-paste (see recipe) piped into dome shapes on a baking sheet, baked, hole then made in side and filled with a cream, made as given for "cream fritters" above, but softer.

WHIPPED CREAM—Good, heavy cold cream whipped till it stands like beaten whites of eggs; used for beverages, desserts, as an accompaniment to shortcake, etc.

BAVARIAN CREAM—The whipped cream above, when firm is sweetened and flavored, then melted gelatine at the rate of two ounces to the gallon is worked in quickly, rapidly poured into molds, shook level, set in ice box till firm, turned out on a dish; served either plain, or with cake, fruit, compôtes, etc.

BAVARIAN CREAM—May also be made with an equal quantity of the "cream fritter" mixture above and the preceding recipe. The ends and sides of the molds may be previously decorated with fruits, and the ornamental top of the mold with plain sweetened cream flavored and colored, set with gelatine; also the cream before being poured into the molds may have candied peels, seedless raisins, pistachio nuts, almonds, marmalades, stewed and fresh fruits pieces of wine jelly, etc., stirred in. The flavorings used are different syrups, liqueurs, essences, etc; also coffee, tea and chocolate.

ICE CREAM—There are two ways of making it, the best being made of pure cream sweetened and flavored, then strained into a freezer and frozen. The other way is to boil milk and sugar, thicken it with a liaison of egg yolks and cream, or cornstarch, then with eggs, or milk and eggs, thus forming a frozen custard (but which is called ice cream); again, others thicken or stiffen boiling milk with gelatine, Irish moss, etc., then flavor and freeze. All the different kinds of ice cream seen on "bills of fare" have either of the foregoing as a basis, the flavors, colors, shapes, etc., given afterwards.

ICE CREAM—The dessert Fellows described first, frozen cream, is not available commercially, although it is a simple enough matter to make at home. Today most ice cream is of the frozen-custard type. Commercial ice cream may be "all-natural," in which case it contains the same custard ingredients but also a high proportion of air; or it may be artificially flavored and contain few honest ingredients aside from milk and sugar.

CREAM OF TARTAR—A most valuable ingredient of baking powders. It is also, for feverish people, one of the most perfect of blood coolers when made into a drink as follows: Grate the rinds of three lemons and add the juice of them to a cupful of granulated sugar and three dessert spoonfuls of cream of tartar; on this pour three quarts of boiling water, allow to cool, strain, and it is ready for drinking.

CREAM OF TARTAR—Perhaps cream of tartar is still good for cooling the blood, and it remains an essential ingredient in BAKING POWDER, but there are few other uses for it in today's kitchen. If you have it, mix it, three parts to one, with baking soda as an emergency substitute for baking powder. Or, since cream of tartar is tartaric acid, a pinch added to egg whites while beating will result in a higher and more stable foam.

CRÉCY—The name of a French city, celebrated for its carrots grown in the neighborhood. A soup is named after it, hence we have "Purée Crécy" which is pureé of carrots.

CREPES—The French word for a kind of pancake, much used on festival occasions by the Latin race.

CREPES—As almost everyone knows, crepes are thin, eggy wrappers that are used to contain a variety of fillings, sweet or savory. In their form and function they are therefore more closely related to tortillas or rice paper than they are to American breakfast pancakes.

CREPINETTES—Small, flat sausages of various delicate morsels, wrapped in pigs caul; it is a French term, caul being called "Crépine" in French.

CREPINETTES—By "various delicate morsels," Fellows meant typical sausage ingredients: pork and other meats, organ meats, fat, herbs, and spices. Crepinettes, by definition, use pig caul for wrapping, and are usually round and flat.

CRESS—Called by the French "cresson" hence, dishes seen on "bills of fare" with the attachment "au cresson" are garnished with cress, watercress being generally used. Besides being a handsome garniture, it makes a fine salad, eaten plain or with a sprinkling of salt, or with a little salt, pepper and tarragon vinegar. Watercress canapés are made of finely minced watercress worked into fresh butter, and then spread on thin slices of graham bread.

CROÛTE-AU-POT—Is literally crust in pot or soup. It is a broth containing slices of carrot turnip, cabbage, and pieces of toast, the broth is generally made from roast meat bones with a piece of bacon or ham knuckle thrown in.

CROÛTES-AU-POT—In short, croûtes-au-pot are CROÛTONS in broth.

CROÛTONS—As the word is used in a culinary sense, are pieces of bread cut in the size and shape of dice, fried in hot fat, or browned in the oven, to serve with soup; or slices of bread cut into block forms and fried, used to support small birds, etc.; or slices of bread cut into fancy shapes and fried, then used to garnish hashes, minces, etc.; also used in connection with shapes cut or stamped out of aspic jelly; used to garnish salads and cold decorated foods.

CROUTONS—Although most croutons are indeed "cut in the size and shape of dice," the word can be used appropriately for any piece of bread—especially the end—that is dried, by sautéing or baking, until hardened. Croutons were once carved into elaborate shapes ("to support large hot or cold joints in order to be able to display the various garnishes around them," as it says in *Larousse*) and were not meant to be eaten. Now, however, they are almost as important to a bowl of split pea soup as the liquid itself.

CUCUMBERS—Are a vegetable fruit that is favorably received by the majority of guests, eaten plain with a seasoning of salt, pepper, and a little grated onion to offset the bilious effects.

CUCUMBERS—The "bilious effects" of the cucumber (*Cucumis sativus*) remain well known, although gardeners can grow "burpless" cukes, and supermarkets now sell the long English cucumbers, also reported to have a milder effect upon the gastricly sensitive.

Cucumbers have been grown for four thousand years; they are thought to have originated in China and been brought to Europe in the thirteenth or fourteenth century. Appreciated in salads—alone or teamed with other fresh vegetables—and as pickles, they are not much used in cooking. This is a shame, as you will see if you try Charles Fellows's Curried Cucumbers. However, because cucumbers are low in calories—they are 96 percent water—they are often used in low-fat recipes.

CREAMED CUCUMBERS—Peeled, cut in slices ¼ inch thick, steamed for a few minutes, then put into a Béchamel sauce, simmered till done; served either as a garnish or vegetable.

GLAZED CUCUMBERS ON TOAST—Peeled, cut in slices ¼ inch thick, boiled till tender in salted water, taken up and drained, then dipped in hot glaze; served overlapping each other on a slice of buttered toast.

FRICASSÉE OF CUCUMBERS—Peeled, cut lengthwise in finger lengths, then simmered in clear broth with a little sugar till tender, taken up and drained, then placed into Hollandaise sauce sharp with either lemon juice or white wine vinegar, to which has been added a seasoning of Worcestershire sauce.

BLANQUETTE OF CUCUMBERS—Peeled, cut in slices ¼ inch thick; steamed; then placed in a rich Velouté sauce, simmered; served in the centre of a border of green peas.

STUFFED CUCUMBERS WITH FORCEMEAT—Peeled, cut in slices an inch thick, cored, steamed, dipped into Velouté sauce, arranged on hot toast, the tops sprinkled with parsley dust, the holes then filled from a forcing bag and

tube with a rich forcemeat of whatever is on hand.

CURRIED CUCUMBERS—Cucumbers peeled and cored, cut into two-inch lengths, stuffed with mutton forcemeat, rolled in flour, quickly fried in butter, then arranged in a saûtoir, covered with curry sauce, simmered till tender; served with grains of boiled rice.

FRIED CUCUMBERS WITH MARROW—Cucumbers peeled and cored; marrow bones sawn into two-inch lengths and the marrow removed; cucumbers cut into two-inch lengths; both are then steamed for a few minutes, marrow then rolled into minced chives, chervil, tarragon and shallots, and inserted into the cucumber, which is then breaded and fried; served with cucumber sauce.

PURÉE OF CUCUMBERS—Cucumbers peeled, then parboiled in boiling salted water, taken up and drained, seasoned with salt and pepper, rolled in flour, simmered in clarified butter, little more flour added to form a roux, moistened with boiling milk, boiled up, the whole then passed through a purée sieve; if to be used for soup, it is thinned to the desired consistency with equal parts of white stock and milk, and seasoned with nutmeg and sugar.

CUCUMBER SALAD—Sliced cucumbers steeped in salted water and ice for an hour, then drained, dished up alternately with slices of pickled beet and quartered hard boiled eggs, dressed with oil and vinegar, salt and pepper.

CUCUMBER AND ONION SALAD—Sliced cucumbers steeped in salted ice water for an hour, a few spring onions also sliced; cucumbers drained, then mixed with the onions; served with salad cream dressing.

CUCUMBERS, FRENCH STYLE—Slice the cucumbers very thin, steep them in salted water for several hours, then drain and mix with French dressing containing some chopped tarragon; serve on a crisp leaf of lettuce.

CUCUMBER KETCHUP—Large cucumbers peeled and cored, then grated; to each gallon of pulp after being drained, is mixed half a gallon of cider vinegar, two teaspoonfuls of red pepper, eight teaspoonfuls of salt, and one pint of fresh grated horseradish; when thoroughly incorporated it is bottled and sealed.

PICKLED CUCUMBERS—Small pickling cucumbers select and firm, well washed and wiped; take 400 of them and put them in crocks; make a boiling brine strong enough to float a potato the size of an egg, pour it over them at boiling point and let them stand for 24 hours, then remove, wipe, and put into clean crocks and cover with hot vinegar spiced with cloves, mace, onion, and a ¼ pound of mustard seed.

CUMIN—Name of a seed used in Europe as a flavoring for stews, in cheeses, and by the Germans in bread.

CUMIN—Cumin is also the principal seasoning in most chili powders and can be used in place of them much of the time. In its seed form cumin (*Cuminum cyminum*) looks like caraway seeds, and in fact the two are confused linguistically, although their flavors are totally different. Delicious by itself, exotically aromatic, cumin is usually combined with other spices; it is an essential part of many CURRY powders.

CURACOA—Name of a liqueur made from bitter orange peel; in cookery is used as a flavoring to sweet sauces, creams, jellies, and blanc-manges.

CURACOA—Another of Fellows's strange misspellings, this one should be Curaçao (with a cedilla under the second "c" to be pecise). It is the generic name given to orange liqueur.

CURD—Is the basis of cheese; the solid part of milk used by confectioners in producing cheese cakes, blanc-manges, curds and whey, curd pudding, curd puffs, etc.

CURRANTS—Are of three colors and flavors red, white and black; they all make good pies; the white and red are also cooked in syrup, bottled, and named "Bar-le-duc" jelly; the black make fine jams and jellies, wine, vinegar, gin.

DRIED CURRANTS—Are a different variety, a sort of small seedless grape that grows wild in parts of Greece; they are ripened on the vine, then picked and packed into barrels, forming a solid mass, and exported all over the world; they are used in puddings, mince-meat, sauces, pickles, dumplings, cakes, buns, pancakes, and also made into a cheap wine.

CURRY—Name of a yellow powder composed generally of turmeric, coriander seeds, cardamoms, cumin seeds, red pepper, ginger, garlic, chillies, cinnamon and black pepper; used in making mulligatawney soups, and in flavoring food sauces that are called curries.

CURRY—There are two important things to remember about curry powder, which falls under the general Indian heading of *masala,* or spice mixture. One is that there is no fixed recipe for curry powder; in India it varies from dish to dish, depending on what mixture of spices best complements the other flavors present. The second is that homemade curry powder is always superior to the store-bought variety, and it can be put together in a matter of minutes.

CURING—By a safe and simple method applicable to country hotels and small institutions, of hams and bacon. The conditions under which the curing of bacon may be conducted successfully is a uniform coolness in cellar, a uniform strength of pickle, thorough cleanliness, the cellar temperature should not exceed 50 degrees F. Bacon is cured by simply rubbing the sides with powdered salt to which has been added a little saltpetre, then placing on the cellar floor; they are then covered with salt to which has been added 5 per

cent. of saltpetre, and allowed to lie for a week. The salt is then removed, and the sides turned, rubbed again with salt, saltpetre and a little sugar, and allowed to lie covered with a fresh quantity of salt and saltpetre for another week; the salt is then all removed, and the sides are either hung up to dry, or allowed to lie in the cellar for another week, after which the bacon is ready in the "green state"; or it may then be smoked. The best smoking materials are oak dust, oak chips, peat, wheat straw, ash dust, or chips of other hard woods; the two of greatest value are the oak dust and peat, each imparting a characteristic flavor. The word sides is used allowing for whole halves of the bacon hog; but if bellies alone are required, the process is the same.

CUSTARD—Name applied to a mixture of eggs, milk and sugar, mixed together, then baked, steamed or boiled. The best proportion is: to each quart of milk, work in eight beaten eggs, six ounces of sugar, then flavor; or the milk may be boiled with a flavoring, then allowed to cool; the custard to be in perfect condition must only be allowed to reach the boiling or settling point, as if allowed to cook longer it will disintegrate and become watery.

CUTLETS—Are really rib chops of lamb, pork, mutton and veal, but the term is also applied to neatly trimmed slices of the same meats; also to a slice cut an inch thick right across the middle of a leg of mutton; the term is also applied to breasts of chicken, game and poultry; imitation cutlets are also made of croquette mixtures shaped into rib chop form.

CZARINA—Name of a Russian sauce often served in that country with boiled tongue. It is composed of a good Espagnole sauce containing minced gherkins, seedless raisins and lemon juice, simmered till the raisins are soft.

DAMSON—The name of a peculiar flavored small blue plum that if eaten raw would contract the jaws; it is therefore always served in a cooked condition, in which form it is rich and delicious; it makes a fine preserve, jam, jelly, wine, compôte, pudding, pie and tartlette.

DAMSON—Common in England, especially before World War II, damson plums (the name comes from *Prunus damascena*, or Damascus plum) are hardly known in this country. They have an intense, somewhat bitter flavor that takes some getting used to. But when cooked with sugar, they produce a rich jam known as Damson cheese.

DANDELION—Or as the French call it "dent-de-lion" dent meaning tooth, inasmuch as its peculiar shaped leaves resemble lions' teeth. It makes a very pleasant salad, either by itself or mixed with other salad leaves. The leaves should be gathered before the sun is strong enough to toughen them. The most simple way of serving and that mostly liked, is dandelion leaves with French dressing; dandelion leaves and sorrel in equal parts, the dandelion cooked half done before the sorrel leaves are added; is used as a vegetable by the French.

DANDELION—Since Fellows wrote his entry, the dandelion has fallen into disfavor, especially since the suburban boom following World War II. It was then that the dandelion—with its bold yellow flower, which pops up everywhere in early spring and is followed by its less-than-attractive puffball of seeds—became known as a noxious weed, one that was then boldly attacked by hand, hoe, and herbicide. Countless suburban-raised children have memories of their parents, implement of destruction in hand, desperately trying to get to the root of the evil green.

The dandelion's loyal following, then, rested in the hands of immigrants—especially Italians—who could be seen each spring at roadsides and in fields, picking bags and bags of the slender green leaves. They remembered what the rest of us forgot: that like arugula, dandelion (*Taraxacum officinale*) is a bitter, strong, but good-tasting green that can serve us in many ways. (It is also packed with nutrition; there is no naturally occurring food higher in vitamin A.)

Things are changing. Dandelion greens are sold in supermarkets, featured in salads in trendy restaurants, sautéed with garlic, steamed and topped with lemon juice. They are at their best when young and can be eaten raw; as they age, they must be cooked in one or two changes of water or they are unpalatably bitter.

The greens are not the only edible part of the dandelion. The unopened flower embryos, picked from the base of the plant, make a wonderful vegetable when sautéed briefly. In their youth the crown—the broad part of the plant that sits at ground level—and the long taproot also make good eating; they should be steamed.

There are other uses for dandelion too: honey (not bad), wine and tea (only if there are no alternatives), and coffee (similar to CHICORY, to which dandelion is related).

DARIOLES—The name of a small plain or fluted mold, these are lined with thin paste, then filled with a cheese cake mixture, sweet custard mixture or whipped cream, turned out when done, and served like a small charlotte russe.

DARIOLE—The dariole mold is most often cylindrical in shape; the cake, as Fellows wrote, is usually a lining of puff pastry filled with one of several sweet, creamy mixtures.

D'ARTOIS—Is the name given to a certain kind of cake made with puff paste and marmalade; also in meat cookery to a sheet of puff paste spread with a salpiçon of fish forcemeat, crayfish tails, eel livers, oysters and mushrooms, another sheet is laid on top, edges pinched together, brushed over with egg wash, baked; served in slices twice as long as wide, on a folded napkin.

DATES—The fruit of the palm tree; the fruit in its green state is like a soft green pulp; when the tree is in flower, the native Arabs bore into the stem and draw the sap, which they call palm milk, and ferment it into wine, much the same as we draw the syrup from the maple tree and convert it into sugar. Dates may be substituted for figs in cakes. They make a pretty show on the fruit stand with slices of angelica; also opened and the stone removed, and in its place a piece of walnut, the date then rolled in powdered sugar.

DATES—The late food writer Waverly Root quoted an unnamed French author thus: "Dates are to the people of the Sahara what wheat is to the French and rice to the Chinese." Indeed, in the Arab world dates are used for almost everything: sweet, savory, juice, syrup, and vinegar; their pits serve as fuel for the fire. And they are an excellent staple: easy to grow (date palms have been around as long as civilization) and high in sugar, protein, and iron.

We rarely eat fresh dates—which are smooth and plump—even though almost all of our dates come from California's Coachella Valley. Rather, we usually use dried dates as a sweet snack or as an ingredient in desserts. But they are frequently featured, sometimes with dried apricots and prunes, in sweet and savory Middle Eastern stews.

DATE PUDDING—One pound of chopped beef suet, ¾ pound of stoned dates, 14 ounces of grated bread, 1½ ounces of baking powder, 12 ounces of flour, one grated nutmeg, two eggs and enough milk to make a medium mixture, poured into molds, steamed three hours; served with wine sauce.

DAUBE—Name given to a strong meat seasoning of salt, powdered herbs, pepper and spices; used to roll strips of larding pork in prior to inserting. The meat larded and daubed is named "beef à la daube."

DAUBE—Today daube refers to many meat or poultry preparations, all of which are covered and braised over low heat for several hours.

DAUPHINE—A French term applied to a cake of the doughnut variety that has jelly in the centre; sometimes called "Berlin pancakes" or "brioche fritters"; "à la Dauphine" is used by some cooks when decorating food with dauphine cakes.

DAUPHINE—When something is served à la dauphine, it features a potato garnish such as the one described by Fellows.

DEMI-GLAZE—Is half glaze, or glaze mixed to form a bright jellied gravy.

DEVILS—Devilled fish, meat, bones, etc., such as pork spareribs, ham, lobster meat, sardines, kidneys, boned legs of cooked poultry, salmon steaks, etc., are the articles highly seasoned, or spread with a highly seasoned paste, then broiled and served with or without a pungent sauce appropriate to the food.

DIABLOTINS—The French term for small balls of sweetmeats generally composed of almond paste, rice paste, and grated orange peel, made into balls, fried in very hot lard, drained, then rolled in flavored powdered sugar; also balls of the mixture given for cheese straws with an egg yolk added, then floured and fried, taken up and rolled in grated cheese.

DIABLOTINS—Also (and more commonly, we think), a diablotin is a thinly sliced bread round topped with béchamel sauce and grated cheese, browned and served in soups.

DIAMOND BACK—Name of the terrapin that inhabits the salt marshes of the Chesapeake, and is generally sold by the inch, 7 to 8 inches being in the best of condition, and bringing the highest price, from $6 to $10 each.

DIAMOND BACK—Most turtles, including this one, are now protected by law.

DIGESTION — Is something that every cook should study. Foods cooked in different ways, digest in different times, the following table is medically correct [see next page].

DINDON—Is the French word for turkey; "dindonneaux" is the French word for the spring turkey used for broiling, weighing 4 to 6 pounds.

DOLMAS—A term applied to leaves of cabbage parboiled, containing balls of forcemeat, and served generally with rissoto. Take 50 cabbage leaves, boil them for ten minutes, drain, make 50 balls of forcemeat size of a walnut, place in centre of the leaf, wrap the leaf around, arrange them in a saûtoir, pour over some rich chicken stock and a little melted butter, place the cover on and reduce to a glaze, arrange a little rissoto at each end of the serving dish, place the dolmas in the centre and pour the glaze over.

DOLMAS—The word *dolma* first referred to stuffed grape (or other vine) leaves, but Fellows adapted it, deftly, to cabbage.

DOUGHBIRDS—Are plentiful on the coasts; they are about 1½ pounds in weight, when in prime condition, have a bill like a snipe, are delicious eating broiled, roasted or in a salmis.

DOUGHBIRDS—Like most North American shore birds once hunted and eaten freely—PLOVERS, sandpipers, snipes, for example—doughbirds are protected by law to prevent their extinction.

DUCKS AND DUCKLINGS—That is the domestic ones, are in season all the year round, the duckling being in its best form about June.

DUCKS AND DUCKLINGS—For cooking purposes there are two kinds of ducks, wild and domesticated. There are dozens of wild ducks, some delicious and others—especially some of those that spend most of their time afloat —virtually inedible. Farm-raised ducks (usually called Long Island ducklings) are descendants of the Asian Pekin duck. They contain a much higher percentage of fat than wild ducks and not as much flavor.

American cooks have not made much progress with ducks, at least compared to the cooks of two older civilizations. The French and Chinese, especially, have spent hundreds of years perfecting duck-cooking techniques—the French (who invented the duck press) frequently concentrating on the liver, and the Chinese on the skin, which is often treated separately from the rest of the bird in order to make it as crisp as possible.

Many people complain about the fattiness of ducks, which has led to a national habit of overcooking the birds in an attempt to render the fat. Unfortunately, this practice results in meat that is tough and dry. It is better to subject fatty birds, skins punctured, to a brief steaming to render excess fat before cooking (after steaming, they can be broiled, which gives a crisp, delicious skin, or sautéed, as in Fellows's Curried Duck with Rice); or to find the less fatty wild ducks; or to physically remove as much fat as possible before roasting, then cook the duck until its meat is no longer bloody but still pink. Any of these techniques yields a moist, delicious bird.

BOILED DUCK, PARSLEY SAUCE— Ducks singed and drawn, second

A TABLE SHOWING THE TIME
REQUIRED TO DIGEST THE DIFFERENT FOODS
WHEN COOKED IN DIFFERENT WAYS.

		Hrs.Min
Pork steak	broiled	3–15
Pork steak fat and lean	roasted	5–15
Pork steak recently salted	raw	3–00
Pork steak recently salted	stewed	3–00
Pork steak recently salted	broiled	3–15
Pork steak recently salted	fried	4–15
Pork steak recently salted	boiled	4–30
Turkey, wild	roasted	2–18
Turkey, tame	roasted	2–30
Turkey, tame	boiled	2–25
Goose	roasted	2–30
Chickens, full grown	fricasséed	2–45
Fowls, domestic	boiled	4–00
Fowls, domestic	roasted	4–00
Ducks, tame	roasted	4–00
Ducks, wild	roasted	4–30
Soup, barley	boiled	1–30
Soup, bean	boiled	3–00
Soup, chicken	boiled	3–30
Soup, mutton	boiled	3–30
Soup, oyster	boiled	3–30
Soup, beef, vegetables and bread	boiled	4–00
Soup, marrow bones	boiled	4–10
Pig's feet, soused	boiled	1–00
Tripe	boiled	1–00
Brains, animal	boiled	1–45
Spinal marrow, animal	boiled	2–40
Liver, (beef), fresh	broiled	2–00
Heart, (animal)	fried	4–00
Cartilage	boiled	4–15
Tendon	boiled	5–50
Hash, meat and vegetables	warmed	2–30
Sausage, fresh	broiled	3–20
Gelatine		2–30
Cheese, old, strong	raw	3–30
Green corn	boiled	3–45
Green beans	boiled	3–45
Beans, pod	boiled	2–30
Parsnips	boiled	2–30
Potatoes	roasted	2–30
Potatoes	baked	2–30
Potatoes	boiled	2–30
Cabbage	raw	2–30

		Hrs.Min
Cabbage with vinegar	raw	2–00
Cabbage	boiled	4–30
Carrots	boiled	3–13
Turnips, white	boiled	3–30
Beets	boiled	3–45
Bread, corn	baked	3–15
Bread, wheat, fresh	baked	3–30
Apples, sweet, mellow	raw	1–30
Apples, sour, mellow	raw	2–00
Apples, sour, hard	raw	2–50
Milk	boiled	2–00
Milk	raw	2–15
Eggs, fresh	raw	2–00
Eggs, fresh	whipped	1–30
Eggs, fresh	roasted	2–15
Eggs, fresh	soft boiled	3–00
Eggs, fresh	hard boiled	3–30
Eggs	fried	3–30
Custard	baked	2–45
Codfish, cured (dry)	boiled	2–00
Trout, salmon (fresh)	boiled	1–30
Trout, salmon (fresh)	fried	1–30
Bass striped (fresh)	broiled	3–00
Flounder (fresh)	fried	3–30
Catfish (fresh)	fried	3–30
Salmon, salted	boiled	4–00
Oysters, fresh	raw	2–55
Oysters, fresh	roasted	3–15
Oysters, fresh	stewed	3–30
Venison, steak	broiled	1–35
Pig (suckling)	roasted	2–30
Lamb, fresh	broiled	2–30
Beef, fresh, lean, (dry)	roasted	3–30
Beef (with mustard)	boiled	3–10
Beef (with salt only)	boiled	3–36
Beef (with salt only)	fried	4–00
Beef, fresh, lean, (rare)	roasted	3–00
Beef steak	broiled	3–00
Mutton, fresh	broiled	3–00
Mutton, fresh	boiled	3–00
Mutton, fresh	roasted	3–15
Veal, fresh	broiled	4–00
Veal, fresh	fried	4–30

joint of wings and feet removed, washed, filled with a stuffing of dry breadcrumbs mixed with salt, pepper, chopped parsley, nutmeg and grated lemon rind, trussed, then simmered till tender in seasoned white stock; served with parsley sauce.

BONED STUFFED DUCK WITH ASPIC——Two ducks singed, split down the backs, boned, laid out flat, skin side down, seasoned with salt, pepper and nutmeg, one of them spread with forcemeat, the meat of the other placed on top, skin then drawn together, sewn, then either roasted or braised till tender, taken up, pressed between two boards till cold, trimmed and glazed; served in slices with aspic.

ROAST DUCK, ORANGE SAUCE— Ducks singed and drawn; filled with a stuffing made of dry breadcrumbs, blanched minced onions, chopped parsley, salt, pepper, nutmeg and a sour apple grated; truss, steam till firm and plump (about half an hour) then roast and baste till brown and tender; served with sauce made of finely minced onion and bacon fried slowly till tender; add them to a rich poultry gravy containing port wine and the grated rind and juice of an orange.

ROAST DUCK WITH PEAS, HANOVER SAUCE—Ducks singed, drawn and washed, filled with a stuffing made of dry breadcrumbs, minced fried onions and bacon, also the heart and liver of the ducks, chopped parsley, salt, pepper and sage; truss, steam half an hour, then roast and baste till brown and tender; serve with green peas at one end of the dish and Hanover sauce at the other, made as follows: poultry livers boiled, then rubbed through a sieve, added to a Velouté or cream sauce, seasoned with lemon juice and cayenne pepper.

BROILED DUCKLING WITH DEVILLED BUTTER—Duckling singed, second joint of wing removed, split down the back, drawn, breastbone removed, laid out flat, seasoned with salt and pepper, slowly grilled till done and brown; served on a slice of toast, with devilled butter spread over the bird, garnish with cress and lemon. . . . Devilled butter; to each four ounces of butter work in a level teaspoonful of cayenne pepper and half a teaspoonful of black, $1/4$ of a teaspoonful each of ground ginger and curry powder, and a little finely chopped chervil or parsley.

SAUTÉ OF DUCK WITH OLIVES— Ducks singed, drawn, washed and steamed for half an hour, taken up, seasoned with salt and pepper, brushed with melted butter, then rolled in flour, quickly browned and basted in hot oven, taken up, cut into portions; little minced onion lightly fried in butter, flour added to form a roux, moistened with poultry stock, boiled up and skimmed, ducks then added, also halves of stoned olives, simmered till ducks are tender, sauce seasoned and finished with little orange juice and port wine; served garnished with croûtons.

STEWED DUCKS WITH GREEN PEAS—Ducks singed, drawn and washed, lightly but quickly browned in oven, taken up and cut in portions, small pieces of bacon fried with some small cut spring onions; when brown, flour added to form a roux, moistened with poultry stock, boiled up and skimmed, ducks then added, with a few sprigs of green mint, simmered till tender, mint removed, seasoned with salt and pepper; served with a croûton at ends of dish, green peas at sides.

BRAISED DUCK WITH VEGETABLES—Ducks singed, drawn and washed, brasiere lined with thin slices of fat bacon, on which is placed slices of onion and turnip, carrot and pieces of celery, a few cloves, bay leaves, whole peppers and some sage leaves; ducks arranged on top moistened with white stock and the juice of a lemon with its grated rind, lid put on, braised and basted in oven till brown and tender, ducks then taken up, the braise strained and skimmed, poured over the ducks in serving pan; Julienne vegetables sautéed and seasoned; served, portions of duck with sauce over, garnished with croûtons at ends of dish and the Julienne vegetables at the sides.

SALMIS OF DUCK IN CROÛSTADE—Neat shaped slices of cold duck made hot in a thick Madeira sauce, to which is added slices of mushrooms and collops of salt pork that have been fried together, the sauce to be seasoned with powdered sage and orange juice; served in paste croûstade cases, on lace paper.

SALMIS OF DUCK WITH FRIED HOMINY—Ducks singed, drawn and washed, seasoned with salt and

pepper, floured, roasted and basted till brown and frothy, taken up and cut into portions; in the meantime the trimmings of the birds are sautéed in olive oil with minced shallots, chives, thyme and bay leaves, then moistened with white wine and reduced; equal quantities of Bigarade and Espagnole sauce then added with a few minced mushrooms, the whole boiled up and skimmed; poured through a strainer over the ducks in another saûtoir, simmered till tender; served garnished with slices of fried hominy.

SAUTÉ OF DUCK WITH CHESTNUTS—Ducks singed, drawn and washed, steamed for half an hour, then cut into joints, seasoned with salt and pepper, powdered sage and thyme, rolled in flour, fried brown with bacon fat, taken up and drained, then put into a brown sauce together with the minced giblets and some roasted and peeled chestnuts, simmer till tender, finish with port wine; served garnished with the chestnuts and a fancy croûton.

SALPIÇON OF DUCK IN CASES—Cold braised duck and some of the sauce, the duck cut into small neat pieces with a few mushrooms, reheated in the sauce; served in fancy paper cases on lace paper.

CURRY OF DUCK WITH RICE—Ducks singed, drawn and washed, steamed for half an hour, taken up, jointed, rubbed with curry powder, rolled in flour; onions sliced and fried a light brown in butter, taken up, joints then fried in the same butter, onions then returned, flour

DUCK STEWED WITH CHESTNUTS

•

Serves 4

Originally, Mr. Fellows called this dish Duck Sautéed with Chestnuts. It is actually a very rich stew.

5 slices bacon

1 (4-pound) duck, cut into serving pieces

1 teaspoon dried thyme, whole

1 teaspoon ground sage

Salt and freshly ground black pepper to taste

2 cups all-purpose flour

1 medium yellow onion, peeled and sliced

2 tablespoons chopped parsley

2 cups Beef Stock (page 48)

1 cup dried chestnuts, soaked overnight and drained

¹/₂ cup port wine

In a frying pan, fry the bacon to render the fat. Chop the bacon and set aside, reserving the fat.

Season the duck with the thyme, sage, salt, and pepper. Dredge the duck in flour, pat off the excess flour.

In the frying pan with the reserved fat, brown the duck. Remove the duck pieces to a 6- to 8-quart pot. Add the onions, parsley, Beef Stock, reserved bacon, and drained chestnuts. Simmer, covered for 1¹/₂ hours. Add the wine. Simmer for 10 minutes more. Adjust the salt and pepper, if needed.

C.W.

added, shook together, moistened with poultry stock, seasoned with salt, pepper, curry powder, grated green apple, the juice and grated rind of an orange, simmered till tender, duck then taken up into another saucepan, the sauce strained over it; served garnished with small molds of dry boiled rice.

STEWED DUCK WITH TURNIPS— Ducks singed, drawn and washed, steamed for half an hour, taken up, rolled in flour, fried whole in butter, taken up and cut into portions; large balls of turnip fried in butter, taken up and placed with the duck; in the remaining butter is then fried some minced shallots with sage and thyme leaves, flour added to form a roux, moistened with poultry stock, boiled up and skimmed, strained over the ducks and turnips, which are then simmered till tender; served garnished with the turnips and croûtons.

BRAISED DUCK WITH SAUERKRAUT—Ducks singed, drawn and washed, then trussed, arranged in brasiere with carrots, onion stuck with cloves, celery and parsley, moistened with seasoned white stock, covered with buttered paper, lid put on, braised till tender and glazy, taken up, braise strained and skimmed, ducks cut into portions and the braise strained over them. Sauerkraut well washed, put in a saûtoir with a piece of bacon, a piece of small bologna, carrot, onion and parsley, moistened with some fat and broth from the stock pot, stewed slowly for two hours, then taken up and drained; vegetables thrown away, bacon and sausage cut in slices; served, portions of duck flanked with the kraut and garnished with the bacon and sausage.

FILLETS OF DUCKLING, MACEDOINE—Ducklings singed, drawn and washed, then steamed for ten minutes to plump them, taken up, cooled, cut into four fillets, the backbones then roasted with vegetables; when brown, moistened with Bigarade sauce, boiled up and strained over a cooked macedoine of vegetables, the fillets seasoned with salt, pepper, powdered sage and thyme, rolled in flour, arranged in buttered baking pan, roasted and basted till brown and frothy; served on a croûton garnished with the macedoine in sauce.

FRIED FILLETS OF DUCKLING, SAUCE BIGARADE—Ducklings prepared as in the preceding, but instead of roasting, fried a golden color with butter; served on toast with Bigarade sauce poured over, garnished with watercress.

ROAST SPRING DUCK, APPLE SAUCE—Young ducks singed, drawn, washed and trussed, steamed for five minutes, taken up, seasoned, rolled in flour, arranged in baking pan, roasted and basted till done; served in portions with unsweetened stewed apples that have been rubbed through a sieve.

STUFFED DUCKLING, ORANGE SAUCE—Ducklings singed, drawn, washed, filled with a stuffing composed of fresh grated breadcrumbs, grated apple and lemon rind, seasoned with salt, pepper, chopped parsley and a little sage, trussed, then steamed for ten minutes, arranged in a baking pan, dredged with flour, roasted and basted till done; served with a brown sauce made in the pan they were roasted in, flavored with grated sour orange rind and its juice.

SAUTÉ OF DUCK WITH NOODLES—Ducks singed, drawn, washed and trussed, steamed for half an hour, taken up and cut into portions, seasoned with salt, pepper and powdered sage, rolled in flour, fried in butter, placed in a saûtoir, dredged with flour, moistened with thin Bigarade sauce, simmered till tender; noodles boiled till done, taken up and drained, then mixed with a little minced chervil, and the ducks' giblets minced and sautéed; served, the duck in portions flanked with the noodles.

STEWED DUCK WITH STUFFED TO-MATOES—Ducks singed, drawn and washed, filled with a stuffing composed of grated breadcrumbs mixed with minced ham, mushrooms, anchovies, shallot, parsley, salt and pepper, trussed, steamed for ten minutes, arranged in saûtoir, moistened with stock and white wine, lid put on, simmered till done; served with the stuffing under each portion, garnished with stuffed small tomatoes, tomato sauce poured around.

STEWED DUCK WITH PURÉE OF PEAS—Ducks singed, drawn, washed and trussed, stewed till tender in white stock containing a few cloves, a clove of garlic, onion, thyme, parsley and bay leaves; when tender, taken up and cut into portions, the broth reduced to a half glaze with the addition of some Velouté sauce, dried green peas boiled with a few sprigs of mint and a little sugar; when done, rubbed through a sieve, then mixed to a stiff consistency with the reduced sauce; serve the duck in portions masked with the peas purée.

STUFFED DUCK, ITALIAN SAUCE—Ducks singed, drawn, washed, filled with a mixture of breadcrumbs with small pieces of fried liver and bacon, thyme, truffles, seasoned with salt, pepper and powdered sage, bound with egg yolks, trussed, steamed for half an hour, taken up, rolled in flour, arranged in buttered baking pan, roasted and basted till tender; served in portions with the stuffing under, and Italian sauce (brown) poured over.

SCALLOPED DUCKS' LIVERS—Livers sliced, seasoned with salt, pepper and mixed spices, sautéed in butter with a few minced shallots and mushrooms, chopped parsley and a minced clove of garlic, pour off the remaining butter, add a few grated breadcrumbs, moisten lightly with Bigarade sauce, fill into deep oval or scallop dishes or shells, sprinkle with sifted crumbs, baste with butter, brown off the top and serve.

BROCHETTE OF DUCKS' LIVERS—Livers sliced, seasoned with salt, pepper and mixed spices, lightly sautéed with butter, then run on a skewer alternately with thin slices of parboiled bacon; when skewer is full, rolled in melted butter, then in sifted breadcrumbs, broiled till done; served on a strip of toast with Hanover sauce at the sides, garnished with cress and lemon.

STEWED DUCKS' GIBLETS IN BORDER—Livers and hearts sliced and sautéed with butter, gizzards sliced and simmered in white seasoned stock till tender, then taken up and drained; hearts, livers and gizzards then mixed into a mushroom sauce; simmered till done; fancy border of mashed potatoes arranged on serving dish one inch from the edge, giblets placed in the centre, with green peas around the potatoes.

DUCKS' GIBLET SOUP—Made the same as chicken giblet soup (which see) substituting the ducks' giblets.

DUTCH SAUCE—Another name for Hollandaise sauce, which is made by taking half a cupful of white sauce and working into it a small piece of glace, half a cupful of melted butter, 6 yolks of eggs, bringing it slowly to a custard-like thickness over a medium fire, then seasoning it with salt, nutmeg and lemon juice.

D'UXELLES—Name of a very thick sauce generally used to coat cutlets before breading them, composed of $\frac{1}{4}$ each chopped parsley and minced fried shallots and $\frac{1}{2}$ minced sautéed mushrooms, all worked into a thick Velouté sauce; or instead of $\frac{1}{2}$ minced mushrooms, $\frac{1}{4}$ need only be used and the other $\frac{1}{4}$ be minced cooked ham or tongue.

ECARLATE—A French term often seen on bills of fare as "à l'ecarlate. It is used to signify that the food is red, and its natural color preserved.

ECLAIRS—A hollow form made of "choux-paste" that is filled with pastry cream, with the top generally coated with chocolate glaze.

EELS—Are of two kinds, the river or fresh water eel, and the sea or conger eel. The flesh of the river eel is sweet, fine grained and dainty; that of the sea eel is coarse grained and oily; they must always be skinned before using: to do which a little silver sand is used to hold the eel by the head. With a sharp knife make a circle round the neck, force down the skin an inch or so, and then with a steady pull the skin will strip off easily.

EELS—There are different types of eels, but the differences are regional and not, as Fellows thought, freshwater versus sea. (It could be that Fellows was referring to true eels as freshwater and the sea lamprey—not an eel but once considered one—as the ocean type.)

In fact, all eels spend part of their lives in the ocean and part in rivers and streams. Both European and northeastern American eels are born in the Sargasso sea, a part of the Atlantic south and west of Bermuda. For one to three years after their birth they drift toward either Europe or North America. During this period they are called elvers or glass eels, and are but a few inches long and completely transparent. They begin to take on color only when they reach their freshwater homes. There they live and grow until it is time to breed, when they begin the return voyage to the Sargasso sea.

In the United States elvers were once popular sautéed when they were in season each spring. Europeans still enjoy them, and *angulas*, as they are called (their Latin name is *Anguilla anguilla*), are something of a national dish in Spain. There they are baked in olive oil and garlic.

Mature eels, however, are still a part of this country's menu, especially at Christmastime, among Italians and other European immigrants. Because they are best sold live and skinned just before cooking (not an easy task), eels are not likely ever to become a mass-market food in the United States. But they are delicious and, like most fish, low in fat and high in protein.

STEWED EELS, LONDON STYLE—A most simple and dainty dish, made by cutting river eels into two-inch lengths, boiling them till done in a parsley butter sauce seasoned with salt, pepper and a little vinegar; served in soup plates with bread and butter.

GRILLED EELS, LONDON STYLE— River eels skinned, coiled round and kept in shape with a small skewer, dipped into beaten eggs then coated with a mixture of grated breadcrumbs, lemon rind, chopped parsley and thyme leaves, salt, pepper, nutmeg; broiled with a golden color and served with horseradish, with the option of Tartar sauce.

BAKED EELS, LONDON STYLE— River eels skinned, coiled round, pinned into shape with a skewer, coated with D'Uxelles sauce, rolled in breadcrumbs, arranged in a buttered baking pan, the inside of the coil filled with a piping of fish forcemeat; brushed with butter,

baked a golden brown; served with Admiral sauce.

BOILED EELS, MÂITRE D'HÔTEL— River eels cut into finger lengths, boiled fifteen minutes in salted water; served with a border of mashed potatoes, with some mâitre d'hôtel butter poured over the eels.

ROAST EELS, ANCHOVY BUT-TER——River skinned, coiled, fastened with skewers, seasoned with salt and pepper, wrapped in buttered paper, roasted in medium oven till done, taken up, paper removed, spread with anchovy butter; served very hot with a sprig of parsley and slice of lemon inside the coiled eel.

FRIED EELS, SHRIMP SAUCE— River eels skinned, cut into finger lengths; marinade them over night in a mixture of vinegar, grated lemon rind, salt, pepper and thyme, then taken up, drained, breaded, fried; served with shrimp sauce.

MATELOTE OF EELS—River eels skinned, cut into finger lengths, seasoned with salt and pepper, rolled in flour, lightly fried in butter, taken up, add to the butter they are fried in some white or red wine, thyme, marjoram, fish stock, red pepper, a few cloves and minced shallots, rapidly reduce; then is added Velouté sauce, boiled up, skimmed, strained over the eels in another saûtoir, finished by adding some button mushrooms, blanched oysters or mussels, and season with lemon juice; served garnished with fancy croûtons.

FRICASSÉE OF EELS—River eels skinned, cut into finger lengths, put to boil in fish stock with a little white wine, an onion stuck with cloves, a few minced shallots, bunch of herbs, salt and whole peppers; when done, taken up into a saûtoir, the liquor reduced, then strained into a thick Hollandaise sauce, containing chopped parsley; eels placed into the finished sauce; served with a garnish of fancy croûtons.

BROCHETTE OF EELS, TARTAR SAUCE—For recipe, see heading of BROCHETTE.

BRAISED EELS, ALLEMANDE SAUCE—River eels skinned and cut into finger lengths, sprinkled with salt, allowed to remain with the salt on for half an hour, then washed in cold water, drained, arranged in a saûtoir with a little butter, parsley, whole peppers, slices of lemon, minced shallots, salt, pepper, nutmeg and a few slices of bacon, moistened with a little fish stock and braised till done, taken up into another saûtoir, braise strained and skimmed, then mixed into Allemande sauce which is poured over the eels; served with them, garnished with croûtons.

BROILED BONED EELS—River eels skinned and cut into finger lengths, split down the back and the bone removed, seasoned with salt, pepper and nutmeg, dipped in beaten egg, then rolled in sifted breadcrumbs, seasoned with powdered herbs and pepper, broiled and basted till done; served on toast with anchovy butter, garnished with lemon.

ORLY OF EELS—Prepared and boned as in the preceding, but instead of breading they are dipped in batter, fried, and served with rings of crisp fried onions.

EEL SALAD—River eels skinned and boned, cut into short finger lengths, laid in salted water for an hour, then taken up and wiped dry, arranged in baking pan, sprinkled with salt, pepper and mixed ground spices, moistened with water and a little vinegar, adding a little dissolved gelatine, bake till done and glazy; served cold masked with Ravigote or Tartar sauce, garnished with slices of cucumber.

ROAST STUFFED CONGER EEL, ADMIRAL SAUCE—Portion cuts skinned and boned, laid for two hours in salted vinegar with chopped sweet herbs, taken up, filled with veal stuffing, tied round with string, rolled in flour; arranged in baking pan, roasted and basted till done; served with Admiral sauce.

BOILED CONGER EEL, ALLEMANDE SAUCE—Portion cuts skinned and boned, tied round with string, blanched, then placed in saûtoir with bay leaves, onions, parsley, whole peppers, little garlic, salt and vinegar; cover with water, simmered till done, taken up and drained; served with Allemande sauce, garnished with parsley and lemon.

FRIED CONGER EEL, TARTAR SAUCE—Portion cuts skinned and boned, steamed for ten minutes, then seasoned with salt and pepper, breaded, fried; served with

Tartar sauce, garnished with parsley and lemon.

CURRIED CONGER EEL WITH RICE—Portion cuts skinned and boned, marinaded for an hour in salt water and vinegar, taken up, rinsed in cold water, wiped dry, seasoned with salt and pepper, rolled in flour, fried with butter, removed into a saûtoir; minced onions, chives and a clove of garlic fried in the remaining butter, flour added to form a roux, moistened with fish stock, brought to the boil and skimmed, then simmered for half an hour; the eels sprinkled with curry powder, sauce strained over them, simmered till done, finished with cayenne pepper and lemon juice; served inside a border of dry boiled grains of rice.

EEL-POUT—Is a combination of eel, catfish and some other kind of fish; breeds its young alive instead of with eggs; is more often called the "Burbot." It is good boiled and served with oyster sauce.

EGGS—That is, hen's eggs as most generally used in cookery (other birds' eggs will be found under their respective headings) are very nutritious, easily digested, and are used in a multitude of ways, but the following recipes will be found to be those most applicable to ordinary hotel, restaurant and club patronage. [Inexperienced hotel butchers have spoiled much meat through their brine, by using the egg test for strength, the test being that when the brine will float an egg it is just right. If he used a potato the same size as an egg he would be more sure, for a new laid egg will sink to the bottom of a brine and stay there; while a bad egg will float and every day's age to the egg from the newly laid brings it more to the surface of the same strength of brine. MORAL: weigh and measure your salt, saltpetre and water] (See heading of BRINE.)

EGGS—All fresh eggs are good for food—the Romans adored the eggs of peafowl and, after all, CAVIAR is a form of egg—but Fellows is correct: When we say "egg," we mean hen's egg." Eggs rank with milk, as most of us heard throughout our childhood, as the cheapest and most efficient animal sources of nutrition on earth.

Eggs are incomparably delicious when featured in a dish and are unsurpassed in their usefulness in baking and sauce making. Their yolks and whites are often separated, the former supplying body, flavor, and suppleness, the latter providing loft and an airiness that can be duplicated by no other food.

Much has been made of the declining quality of eggs since the end of World War II, at which time supervising egg laying stopped being the occupation of local farmers and essentially became an industry. Indeed, if you compare a farm-fresh egg with one from the supermarket, you immediately will notice that the farm egg has a firmer white that supports the yolk—orange rather than yellow—in a way that can best be described as proudly. The white's firmness can be attributed to freshness; the yolk's color to differences in feed. But the most significant difference is in flavor; no mass-produced egg can compare to an old-fashioned egg from a farm. It is worth going out of your way to find, especially if you are going to fry it up for breakfast.

SHIRRED EGGS—Shirred egg dish buttered, eggs broken into it, two or three drops of clear melted butter dripped over the eggs, placed in oven till set.

SCRAMBLED EGGS—Four-fifths broken eggs (not beaten), one fifth cream, seasoned with salt and little melted butter, ladleful (made to hold three eggs) poured into hot buttered frying pan, stirred about or shook till softly set; served either plain or on buttered toast.

POACHED EGGS—Eggs removed from shell, dropped into simmering salted water containing a dash of vinegar; when set, taken up drained; served plain or on buttered toast.

CURRIED EGGS—Hard boiled eggs with their shells removed, reheated in a curry sauce made from poultry stock; bed of rice in centre of dish sprinkled with finely chopped parsley; with the back of a spoon indentures made to receive the eggs; served with the sauce poured around the base.

STUFFED EGGS—Hard boiled eggs with their shells removed, split lengthwise, yolks removed and pounded with anchovy meat and butter, filled back into the whites, smoothed over, decorated and served.

DEVILLED EGGS—Hard boiled eggs with their shells removed, split in halves lengthwise, dipped in beaten egg, then in oil, sprinkled with salt and red pepper, arranged in baking pan on a sheet of oiled paper, thoroughly heated; served on toast with sauce Diable poured over into which has been mixed some Bengal chutney.

MASKED EGGS, MADEIRA SAUCE—Hard boiled eggs with the shells removed, coated with chicken forcemeat, then dipped into beaten egg, baked; served with Madeira sauce poured over, garnished with fancy croûtons.

EGG RAREBIT—Hard boiled eggs with the shells removed, cut lengthwise in slices, arranged on serving platter, seasoned with salt and pepper, covered with a mixture of grated cheese mixed with butter, browned off in oven; served very hot.

MOLDED EGGS, PROVENÇALE SAUCE—Timbale molds brushed with butter, bottoms sprinkled with minced fried shallots, eggs then broken in, a little Creole garniture placed on top. Baked till set, turned out on serving dish; served with Provençale sauce poured over and around.

EGGS, AU GRATIN—Slices of hard boiled eggs in a gratin dish covered with white sauce, then sprinkled with cheese and sifted breadcrumbs, baked and served.

EGG PATTIES—Small squares of hard boiled eggs mixed into a rich Suprême sauce with a few mushrooms, filled into hot puff paste patty shells.

SALPIÇON OF EGGS—Yolks and whites of eggs steamed separately till set; when cold, cut in slices, then stamped out with column cutter together with tongue, truffles and mushrooms, the whole then mixed into a rich Velouté sauce; served garnished with fancy buttered toast.

EGGS, INDIAN STYLE—Into a Soubise sauce is worked enough curry powder to lightly color it, brought to a simmer, eggs poached in it; served on circular slices of toast with some sauce poured around.

EGGS BREADED, CREOLE SAUCE—Eggs boiled five minutes, shelled, dipped in thick Hollandaise sauce, then in breadcrumbs, then breaded and fried; served with Creole sauce or garniture.

EGGS WITH BROWN BUTTER—Eggs fried with plenty of butter that is hot enough to turn a nice brown color and froth up; when set, taken up on toast; to the frothing butter is then added a little tarragon vinegar, poured over the eggs and served immediately.

FRICASSÉE OF EGGS—Yolks and whites steamed separately till set; when cold scooped out with oval cutter, made hot in an onion cream sauce and served.

EGGS WITH CAVIARE—Slices of hard boiled eggs on buttered toast, the yolk covered with caviare forced through a bag and star tube.

EGGS IN CROÛSTADE—Whites and yolks of eggs steamed till set; when cold, cut in form of dice with equal quantities of ham, tongue and button mushrooms, reheated in Suprême sauce, filled into hot paste croûstades and served.

EGGS SCRAMBLED WITH TOMATOES—One cupful of minced onions, 12 medium sized tomatoes rubbed through a sieve, mixed, seasoned with salt, pepper and butter, simmered till onion is done, 12 eggs then broken into the simmering mixture, tossed about till set; served in cases.

SCRAMBLED EGGS IN CASES—Eggs beaten with minced green herbs, salt and pepper, scrambled with plenty of butter; served in fancy paper cases.

EGGS WITH ONION PURÉE—Slices of hot hard boiled eggs arranged around a centre of thick purée of onions in Velouté sauce.

OMELET WITH BACON—Plain or with Piquante sauce. Cut the bacon into small dice, fry fairly well done, pour off most of the fat, turn in the beaten eggs, mix and form.

OMELET WITH VEAL KIDNEYS—Roasted kidneys cut in dice, and made hot in a little demi-glaze and chopped parsley. Enclose the mixture within the omelet; serve with a Madeira sauce poured around.

OMELET WITH CÈPES—Cut the cèpes into dice; fry in butter for

EGGS WITH BROWN BUTTER

·

Serves 2

A quick recipe that will add a little excitement to your normal breakfast routine. Do not overcook the eggs!

4 eggs

5 tablespoons butter

1 tablespoon white wine
  vinegar

2 teaspoons chopped fresh
  tarragon

Salt and freshly ground
  black pepper to taste

In a frying pan, fry the eggs to your liking in butter (over easy is best). Remove the eggs to serving plates, leaving the butter in the pan.

Cook the butter in the pan until browned but not burned. This will take less than 1 minute. Add the vinegar, tarragon, salt, and pepper. Stir the sauce over the heat until a smooth glaze is formed.

Top the eggs with this browned butter sauce.

C.W.

---

two or three minutes, pour off the butter, and pour in the omelet mixture; form and serve.

OMELET WITH CHEESE—Mix grated cheese with the beaten eggs, in proportion of one-third cheese to two-thirds beaten eggs, form the omelet, when placed on the serving dish sprinkle a little grated cheese on top of the omelet and brown off very quickly in a hot oven.

OMELET WITH CHICKEN LIVERS—Blanch the livers, then cut them into dice, fry them lightly in butter for ten minutes with some minced shallots and mushrooms, season with salt and pepper and add a little chopped parsley, enclose a spoonful within the omelet, and serve a little Hanover sauce at both ends of the omelet.

OMELET WITH CHIPPED BEEF—Scald, drain, and mince the dried beef, mix it with the beaten eggs, and form the omelet, pour a little cream sauce around when serving.

OMELET WITH HAM—Cooked minced ham made hot in Madeira sauce enclosed within the omelet.

Raw minced ham with a little minced shallot and parsley fried till done, omelet mixture poured over it, formed and served.

Minced fried ham beaten up with the eggs, poured into an omelet pan, formed and served.

OMELET WITH LAMB KIDNEYS, AUMADÈRE—Cut the kidneys into small dice and fry them with minced shallots for three minutes, add a little Madeira sauce and chopped parsley, enclose a spoonful within the omelet and pour some of the sauce around.

OMELET WITH SWEETBREADS—Cooked sweetbreads, cut in dice, simmered in mushroom sauce, a spoonful enclosed within the omelet and a little sauce poured around.

OMELET WITH MUSHROOMS—If fresh mushrooms, peel, trim and cut into dice and fry. If canned, cut them in thin slices and fry; drain and mix them into Madeira sauce, enclose a spoonful in the omelet, serve with a spoonful of the mushrooms at each end of the dish.

OMELET WITH SHRIMPS, MEXICAN STYLE—Take fresh or canned shrimps, cut in halves, mix with some finely chopped green peppers, put it into a Velouté sauce containing some lobster butter, simmer for five minutes, enclose a spoonful within the omelet, turn on to the serving dish, place two whole shrimps on top, and pour some of the sauce around.

OMELET WITH FINE HERBS—Beat up with the eggs, some finely minced shallots, thyme, marjoram, chervil, chives and parsley, season with salt and pepper, form the omelet and serve.

SPANISH OMELET—Finely shred onions, minced green peppers, minced mushrooms, solid tomatoes cut in small pieces, the whole fried in butter for five minutes, then add some tomato sauce, season with salt and pepper, reduce till thick, enclose a spoonful within the omelet; when on the serving dish, place a spoonful of the mixture at each end of the omelet and garnish the top with fancy strips of pimentoes in oil.

OMELET WITH PARSLEY—Mix some finely chopped parsley, pepper and salt with the beaten eggs, form and serve.

OMELET WITH TOMATOES—Stew fresh or canned tomatoes with a little butter, sugar, salt and pepper to a thick pulp, enclose within the omelet, pour tomato sauce around.

OMELET WITH TOMATOED RICE—Take some boiled rice, and moisten it with reduced tomato sauce, enclose within the omelet, and pour tomato sauce around.

OMELET WITH OYSTERS—Scald the oysters, cut them in quarters, put them into a rich oyster sauce, enclose a spoonful within the omelet; when on the serving dish place three whole scalded oysters on top of the omelet, pour some oyster sauce over all, and sprinkle with parsley dust.

OMELET WITH FRENCH PEAS—Simmer some French peas in reduced Velouté sauce till thick; place a spoonful within the omelet and a spoonful at each end of the omelet on the serving dish, with cream sauce poured around.

OMELET WITH EGG PLANT—Cut the egg plant into dice, fry it in butter; when done add a little meat glaze, enclose within the omelet and pour some brown sauce around.

OMELET WITH SPINACH—Beat some purée of spinach with the eggs, season with salt and pepper, form and serve.

OMELET WITH SPRING VEGETABLES—Cut a jardiniere or macedoine of vegetables (or use canned macedoine), boil till tender, drain, moisten with a little demi-glaze or Suprême sauce, enclose within the omelet, and decorate the top of the omelet with the vegetables; pour some of the sauce used around.

OMELET WITH ASPARAGUS POINTS—Take cooked asparagus points, make them hot in Allemande sauce, enclose within the omelet and pour some of the sauce around.

OMELET WITH OLIVES—Take the olives, stone them, slice them into four slices, make them hot in Madeira sauce, enclose within the omelet, decorate the top of the omelet with slices of olives, and pour some Soubise sauce around.

OMELET WITH MINCED CHICKEN—Take minced cooked chicken, moisten it with Velouté sauce, make hot, enclose within the omelet, serve with Velouté sauce poured around.

CREOLE OMELET—Chopped green peppers, onions, garlic, okras and a little boiled rice, made hot in thick tomato sauce, enclosed within the omelet, and spoonfuls served at ends of the omelet on the dish.

EGGPLANT—A cousin of the tomato and fellow member of the nightshade family, eggplant (*Solanum melongena*) is no less valuable. There are dozens of varieties of eggplants, which the British call by their French name, *aubergine:* white (obviously the original); brilliant lavender; purple, almost black, striped with green; long, short, round, and stubby; large and small.

They are all good when they are young; when old they become bitter and excessively spongy. This has led to the practice of salting, which, in theory at least, removes the bitterness along with some of the vegetable's water. Salting is not in the least harmful, but if you buy very firm young eggplants and cook them before much time passes, it is unnecessary. In fact, young eggplants, which have thin skins, need not even be peeled.

Unlike the TOMATO, the eggplant has never become a favorite in the American kitchen, although it is widely appreciated in Italy, the Middle East, and India. But an eggplant is extremely unappetizing when raw and can hardly be quickly steamed and served, which, in the United States, makes for two strikes against it. This is a vegetable with which you must take some time; but your efforts will be rewarded.

EGG PLANT, TURKISH STYLE—Peeled egg plant in slices, sprinkled with salt; after having laid a few minutes, wiped dry, then fried a golden color with butter; cold rare roast beef minced fine with a very little onion, mixed with a few slices of peeled tomatoes, chopped parsley, salt and pepper; stewed down thick, gratin dishes buttered, bottom covered with the egg plant, mince next, this covered with more egg plant, moistened with rich roast beef gravy baked half an hour and served.

FRIED EGG PLANT—Egg plant peeled, cut in slices, sprinkled with salt and allowed to marinade for an hour, then wiped dry, rolled in flour, dipped into beaten eggs, fried and served.

BROILED EGG PLANT ON TOAST—Peeled egg plant cut in slices, sprinkled with salt and allowed to remain for an hour, then wiped dry, rolled in flour, then in melted butter, broiled and basted; served on buttered toast.

STUFFED EGG PLANT—Small egg plant not peeled, cut in halves lengthwise, part of centre scooped out, the halves then fried on the cut side; the scooped out part mixed with some cooked salt pork, button mushrooms, minced shallots, chopped chives and parsley, filled into the openings, piled high, smoothed over and baked.

EGG PLANT FRITTERS—Peeled egg plant cut in slices, laid for an hour well sprinkled with salt, then wiped dry, dipped in batter, slowly fried in hot fat; served plain as a vegetable or as an accompaniment to meat.

EGG PLANT WITH CHEESE—Make the "broiled egg plant on toast" mentioned above; when finished and on the toast, cover it with a slice of cheese, place in hot oven till cheese is melted and browned; served at once.

EGG PLANT STEWED—Peeled egg plant cut in pieces size of small eggs, cold roast beef or mutton cut in small pieces and mixed into a rich gravy with a minced onion and peeled tomatoes, brought to the boil, egg plant then put in, simmered till done, then served.

ENDIVE—Also called CHICORY. Is cooked as a vegetable same as spinach; also made into salads, using the white leaves; dressed with French dressing.

ESPAGNOLE—Name of a stock sauce, used as a basis to form many of the brown sauces; made by frying in a thick bottomed large saucepan till brown, ham, veal and beef in meat and bones; carrots, onions, turnips, celery and parsley; flour then added to form a roux, moistened gradually with good brown stock, seasoned with thyme, savory, marjoram, bay leaves, cloves, whole peppers, and whole allspice; when boiled up, skimmed, then is added a liberal quantity of tomatoes, together with one or two old fowls or roast poultry carcasses, simmered slowly for several hours, strained, skimmed, finished with sherry wine.

STUFFED EGGPLANT

•

Serves 6

Eggplant is an ancient vegetable. When it is baked with this wonderful filling, the results are sweet and delicious.

3 medium-sized eggplants, cut in half lengthwise and top stems removed

1/2 cup plus 2 tablespoons olive oil

1/4 pound salt pork, skin trimmed off and finely chopped

3 cloves garlic, peeled and chopped

1/2 cup chopped shallots

1 pound mushrooms, chopped

1/4 cup chopped parsley

6 green onions, chopped

Salt and freshly ground black pepper to taste

1/3 cup grated Parmesan cheese

1/4 pound butter, melted

Using a large metal spoon, dig out the inside of the eggplant halves, leaving about ¼ inch of meat in the shells. Coarsely chop the scooped-out eggplant and reserve.

Heat a large frying pan and, using the ½ cup of olive oil as necessary, brown the eggplant halves. Do this in a couple of batches.

Heat another large frying pan and add the remaining 2 tablespoons of olive oil, the salt pork, garlic, and shallots. Sauté until the salt pork is lightly browned. Add the mushrooms, reserved chopped eggplant meat, parsley, and green onions. Sauté just until the mushrooms are tender. Salt and pepper to taste.

Butter a large baking dish and arrange the eggplant halves in it, cut side up. Fill the halves with the eggplant mixture and smooth over. Sprinkle with Parmesan cheese and drizzle with butter. Place in a preheated 350°F. oven and bake for 45 minutes, until tender and nicely browned.

C.W.

EXTRACTS—Or flavorings used in the making of ice creams, jellies, cakes, puddings, sweet sauces, etc., can be made much cheaper than buying at the stores and paying for fancy labels and bottles; the point is to obtain good oils and pure alcohol.

EXTRACT OF CLOVES—2 ozs. oil of cloves, 1 pint of alcohol, mix and use.

EXTRACT OF ANISEED—1 oz. of oil of anise, 1 pint of alcohol, mix and use.

EXTRACT OF CINNAMON—1 oz. oil of cinnamon, 1 pint of alcohol, mix and use.

EXTRACT OF BITTER ALMOND—2 ozs. oil of bitter almond, 2 pint of alcohol, mix and use.

EXTRACT OF LEMON—2 ozs. oil of lemon, 1 pint of alcohol, mix and use.

EXTRACT OF WINTERGREEN—1 oz. oil of wintergreen, 1 quart of alcohol, mix and use.

EXTRACT OF WINTERGREEN—Essence of wintergreen was once taken from low-growing evergreen shrubs. Now it is made from certain birch trees or is chemically manufactured.

EXTRACT OF SARSAPARILLA—1 oz. each of oils of sassafras and wintergreen, 1 quart of alcohol, mix and use.

EXTRACT OF VANILLA—2 ozs. of vanilla beans, 6 ozs. of alcohol, 12 ozs. of water; cut the beans small and bruise them, put them in wide mouthed bottles, cover with the alcohol and water, steep for two weeks, shaking it up every two days.

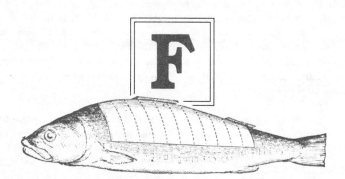

FARINA—A fine granular preparation made from wheat. Of two kinds, white and graham, the latter being used as a breakfast cereal, the former for puddings, quenelles and as a soup thickening.

FARINA—*Farina*, the Italian word for "flour," can also be used to refer to potato and other flours.

BAKED FARINA PUDDING—1 gallon of milk, 1 pound of farina, ¾ of a pound of sugar, ½ a pound of butter, 5 whole and 6 yolks of eggs; made by boiling the milk and sugar together, then sprinkling in the farina, stirring continually till smooth, simmered for ¾ of an hour, then is added the beaten eggs and butter; flavored to taste; poured into buttered pudding pans, baked till set; served with a sweet or wine sauce, preserved fruit, or compôte of stewed fruit.

BOILED FARINA PUDDING—Generally served cold with sweetened or flavored cream, whipped cream, stewed fruit or fruit marmalade; if after it is boiled it is poured into cups and set, they are called Farina cup custards. Made with ½ gallon of milk, ½ pound of sugar, ½ pound of farina, ¼ of a pound of butter and six yolks of eggs.

FARINA FRITTERS—The above mixture when boiled is poured into a shallow pan brushed with butter; when cold and firm cut into slices, double breaded, fried, taken up and rolled in powdered sugar; served with fruit sauce.

FENNEL—Name of a garden plant, esteemed as a flavoring to boiled salmon and mackerel; used in making "fennel sauce," which is the same as parsley sauce, simply substituting chopped fennel for parsley leaves.

FIGS—As seen in our markets are both fresh and dried; the fresh are used in compôtes and for preserves, the dried for cakes, puddings, ices, pastilles; also used as a dessert, either plain or rolled in powdered sugar.

FIGS—A fig is another of those foods that we have yet to appreciate fully. Dried figs have been in our markets as long as there have been markets—the Spaniards brought them here—but the succulent, sensual fresh fig is seen only occasionally. Even then it is usually a poor variety that has been bred with shipping in mind rather than flavor, as the number-one priority.

A pity, especially since the fig (*Ficus carica*) will grow almost anywhere it can gain a foothold in the soil. There are hundreds of varieties of figs, all different colors, sizes, and shapes, and all thought to be indigenous to the eastern Mediterranean (in any case, they are frequently mentioned in the Bible). All are better when tree-ripened and are fragile once picked. So it is not always easy to find good ones. The best places to look are in good California fruit markets and in small Italian fruiteries in the large cities of the Northeast, where ripe Italian figs are sometimes shipped in by air. They are relatively expensive but a justifiable luxury. If you have too many to eat plain—an unlikely but happy occasion—cook them in a pork stew or quarter them, dip them in batter, and fry them as fritters.

FINANCIÈRE—Name of both a sauce and garnish, much used; the sauce is composed as follows; one pint of sherry wine with a chopped truffle and a seasoning of red pepper is rapidly boiled down to half its volume, then is added one pint of Espagnole; boiled again for five minutes, then strained for use. For the garnish composition see heading of GARNISHES.

FINE HERBS—Called by the French "fines-herbes"; it is a combination of minced shallots, mushrooms and parsley. Fine herbs sauce is the ingredients mixed into some Espagnole or other brown sauce.

FINE HERBS—Fellows's definition was correct at the time of its writing, but it has become outdated. Today *fine herbs* means—or at least should mean—any combination of chopped *fresh* herbs, usually PARSLEY (which may itself be referred to as fine herbs), TARRAGON, CHERVIL, and CHIVES. Almost any fresh green herb can be added to the mixture, and shallots and mushrooms remain appropriate in certain dishes.

FINNAN HADDIE—Is the name commercially given to smoked haddocks (see HADDOCKS); they are imported to this country and sell generally at 10 cents per pound.

FINNAN HADDIE—Also known as finnan haddock, this smoked fish originated in Findon, a village near Aberdeen, Scotland. When fresh and properly cured—in a light brine with cold hardwood smoke, as it was a century ago—finnan haddie is golden, moist, and full of flavor. Unfortunately, the genuine article (which should be small, split, and have its backbone intact) has virtually disappeared. What is usually sold as finnan haddie is smoked cod; some of this is pretty good too, but some is not. Avoid pieces that are so dry that their texture is closer to that of jerky than to smoked fish.

Fellows's recipe for broiled finnan haddie is not only a classic but completely delicious. The Scottish tradition is to poach the fish in water and top it with a poached egg.

BROILED FINNAN HADDIE—Skinned, soaked in warm water for half an hour, taken up and wiped dry, the backbone removed from the bone side, seasoned with pepper, brushed with butter, broiled and basted; served very hot with a sauce composed of melted butter, containing lemon juice, mustard and chopped parsley.

BOILED FINNAN HADDIE—Prepared as in the preceding, put to boil in cold water (unless very thick three or four minutes boiling is sufficient), served with mâitre d'hôtel butter spread on the fish, garnished with parsley.

BAKED FINNAN HADDIE—Prepared as for broiling, arranged in baking pan, moistened with milk and melted butter, quickly baked and basted; served with the sauce given for broiled.

FINNAN HADDIE, DELMONICO STYLE—Prepared as for broiling, the fillets then arranged in a shallow saûtoir, moistened with cream, boiled for five minutes, little Madeira wine then added, boiled up again, then is stirred in a liaison of egg yolks and cream; when thickened like thin custard a little more Madeira wine added; served very hot in a chafing dish.

FLAGEOLETS—A green haricot bean put up in cans by the French and imported to this country; makes a very pleasing garnish, are cheap, the best being about $1.75 a dozen cans.

FLAGEOLETS—Unfortunately not nearly as inexpensive as they once were, flageolets are still French and quite delicious. Pale to medium green in color, the dry beans require only a brief soaking period before cooking and are delicious when seasoned with bay leaf, thyme, and cloves and finished with a scoop of crème fraîche or sour cream.

FLANNEL CAKES—A sort of pancake; for recipe see heading of BATTER.

FLOUNDERS—A flat fish of the halibut species but much smaller, in plentiful supply, very often filleted, in fact generally used in this country for fillets of soles; the name flounder seldom appears on our bills of fare, hence it will be found under that heading.

FLOUNDER—In today's U.S. market it is better to think of all types of flounder (there are several), as well as fish called SOLE, plaice, turbot, dab, and so on, as flatfish. All have eyes on top of their heads, all feed on the ocean bottom, and all camouflage themselves by changing color to match their surroundings. They are not interchangeable—European Dover sole is generally and rightfully considered to be the finest of the lot—but substitutions can be made. All of these fish are fine-grained, mild-flavored, and, when extremely fresh, delicious. (The

HALIBUT is also in this family but differs greatly in size: Those weighing seven hundred pounds have been caught.)

There are at least a dozen flatfish caught off our shores, with the following common names among them: Dover (Pacific), petrale, lemon, gray, English, rock, and sand sole; blackback (winter), fluke (summer), southern, starry, and yellowtail flounder; and dab, also called plaice. All yield thin, delicate fillets that must be cooked very quickly— by sautéing, broiling, baking, or poaching—and with care. Overcooking results in dry, flaky fish.

FOIE-GRAS—Literally fat liver, is made by taking the livers of fat geese, cooking them with sweet herbs, wine and bacon, then pounding it, rubbing it through a fine sieve, the paste thus obtained being put away in small jars, very often mixed with truffles; it is used for sandwiches, garnishes, in croûstades with aspic jelly; cut in pieces and mixed with button mushrooms in a rich sauce, then filled into scallop shells, gratinated, baked and served; also for lining game pies and patties; as a stuffing for small game birds, etc.

FOIE-GRAS—Fellows's description is for pâté de foie gras. Foie gras is the liver of a fattened goose (or duck). These days it is often quickly grilled as an appetizer, sprinkled with seasonings and port and baked into a creamy mousse, and used as a rich flavoring ingredient in sauces. Imaginative chefs, limited only by their customers' willingness to spend money, are finding other ways in which to use this luxury ingredient, which was once exclusively imported from France but is now produced in this country as

well. At its best, it is absolutely delicious.

FONDU—Is the name given by the French to a dish of eggs scrambled soft with grated cheese and butter; served very hot on toast, or filled into fancy paper cases, quickly browned on top and served.

FONDU—Or *fondue*. Fellows's definition is correct, as far as it goes. Fondue also is used to describe slow-cooked vegetables; a cheese sauce; or the familiar cheese, wine, or chocolate fondue, in which warm liquid is used, at the table, to cook or coat meat, bread, fruits, or other morsels of food.

CHICKEN FORCEMEAT—Raw breast of chicken with the skin removed, pounded, rubbed through a tamis mixed with a little cream and strained whites of raw eggs, seasoned with salt, red pepper, nutmeg and lemon juice.

VEAL FORCEMEAT OR GODIVEAU— Equal quantities of veal or beef kidney suet and lean veal minced, pounded, rubbed through a sieve with chopped chives, then is mixed in yolks of eggs at the rate of two to each pound of meat, then finished to the proper consistency with some strained cold Velouté sauce.

HAM AND LIVER FORCEMEAT— Light colored calf's liver and fat ham in equal quantities cut in small pieces, the liver laid in clear cold water long enough to extract the blood, so that the forcemeat will be whiter; after which it is drained and wiped, the ham sautéed over a quick fire, then the liver in the ham fat, of a golden color together with some chopped shallots, parsley and mushrooms, seasoned with red pepper, salt and a little mixed spices, the whole then chopped fine, pounded, rubbed through a sieve; it is then ready for use.

FRANGIPANE—Name given to a cooked custard cream used in filling puffs, eclairs, tartlettes, paper cases for soufflés, open pies as cream pies, etc. Made by boiling half a gallon of milk with ¾ of a pound of sugar, then pouring it to 12 yolks of eggs that have been beaten and mixed with ½ a pound of sifted flour and a little cream; it is then returned to the fire with 4 ounces of butter, brought just to a boil, removed, flavored and strained for use.

FRANKFORTS—Name of a pork sausage that is generally served with "sauerkraut." Made of equal quantities of lean and fat pork minced finely, seasoned with 3 ounces of mixed ground coriander seeds, salt, nutmeg and pepper to every 8 pounds, the sausage skins filled in the ordinary way, then hung in a dry cool place till wanted.

FRANKFORTS—Today's frankforts are known as hot dogs, wieners, frankfurters, or franks. The ingredient list of contemporary hot dogs (of which we eat some sixteen *billion* each year) begins with chicken, pork, turkey, or beef "parts," continues with corn syrup, and ends with chemicals. Most of the calories are from fat; most of the flavor from corn syrup. The kosher brands, with their intense garlic flavor and firm texture, inevitably win taste tests.

FRAPPÉ—A French word that signifies a liquor is half frozen.

FRENCH DRESSING—Four parts of olive oil to one part of vinegar, white or tarragon, a little onion juice, finely chopped parsley, salt and red pepper, the whole thoroughly mixed.

FRENCH DRESSING—Note that Fellows provided a recipe for vinaigrette, not for the syrupy-sweet orange stuff that too many American restaurants and manufacturers of processed foods call French dressing. Essentially, vinaigrette is a mixture of good oil and good vinegar with salt and pepper. Everything else—parsley, herbs, variations in the types of oils (usually olive) and vinegars, mustards, and spices—is optional and completely delicious.

FRIANTINE—French word sometimes used to designate a "bouchée" or small patty shell, hence a small patty of game may be called a friantine of game.

FRICADELLES, ALSO CALLED FRICANDELLES—Are made of three-fifths cold cooked meat, one-fifth raw meat, one-fifth breadcrumbs or boiled rice, the whole minced, seasoned with salt, pepper, parsley, herbs and lemon juice, bound with beaten eggs, made up into balls, pats, cutlet shapes, etc., fried in dripping, or breaded and fried, then served with a sauce or garniture appropriate to the meat used.

FRICANDEAU—Name applied to the whole buttock or cushion of veal, that is larded, braised, and served in broad slices with a sauce or garniture.

CANDIED PEEL FRITTERS—Candied orange, lemon and citron peel chopped fine and mixed into a stiff batter composed of 1 pound of flour moistened with two-thirds sweet wine and one-third brandy; after all mixed, the whipped whites of ten eggs are stirred in, the mixture is then placed in a forcing bag with large tube, and forced out into boiling fat, fried crisp and done through, taken up, drained, rolled in powdered sugar; served with wine sauce, fruit purée or marmalade. Deviations may be made by using the imported "fruits glacés" such as angelica, poires, cerises, etc.

FRUIT FRITTERS—Blackberries, raspberries, dewberries, strawberries, etc., mixed into a medium stiff batter without breaking the fruit, dropped by spoonfuls into very hot fat, fried, drained; served with a sauce made of the fruit used, the fritter being dusted with powdered sugar.

SPANISH PUFF FITTERS—Made by boiling together 7 ozs. of butter, 2 ozs. of sugar, and one pint of water; when boiling, 9 ozs. of sifted flour is thrown in all at once, and stirred till well cooked, about five minutes, then removed from the fire and ten eggs beaten in one at a time, each egg to be thoroughly incorporated before the next is put in; with the last egg is added a tablespoonful of vanilla extract;

dropped in small spoonsfuls in medium hot fat they will expand into hollow balls about the size of an orange; room must be allowed to allow of their expansion and for them to roll over; when done, drained; served dusted with powdered sugar, vanilla or wine sauce around.

QUEEN FRITTERS—Same as the preceding, but omitting the sugar and vanilla in the mixture; when done, they may be split in the side and filled with pastry cream.

CUSTARD FRITTERS—Boiling milk and sugar thickened stiff with corn starch, some beaten eggs then worked in, flavored with extract poured into shallow pan; when cold, cut into, diamond shapes, breaded, fried; served with custard sauce.

CHOCOLATE FRITTERS—Same as the preceding, but boiling some chocolate with the milk; served with vanilla cream sauce.

APPLE FRITTERS—Apples peeled, cored, leaving the stalk on, the core hole filled with stiff fruit marmalade; dipped into a stiff batter, slowly fried till done; served dusted with powdered sugar.

APPLE FRITTERS—Large good cooking apples peeled and cored, cut in slices, dipped in batter, fried; served with fruits, rum or wine sauce.

RICE FRITTERS—Well boiled rice drained and pounded, mixed with eggs, sugar and a little flour; flavored with grated lemon rind, made into flat round cakes with a depression in the centre, fried; served coated with powdered sugar, and the depression filled with marmalade or jelly.

GERMAN FRITTERS—Very light roll dough cut out in thin flats, little jam placed in centre of one, covered with another flat, allowed to rise, then fried, drained, rolled in powdered sugar and served; also called "Bismarks."

ORANGE FRITTERS—Quarters of skinned oranges with the seeds removed blanched in a thick syrup, taken up and drained, then dipped in batter and fried; served with orange sauce made from the syrup they were blanched in.

CONFITURE FRITTERS—Also called "beignets aux confitures." Fruit marmalade spread between two thin slices of plain cake, then dipped in batter and fried.

PEACH FRITTERS—Halves of peeled fresh fruit or canned ones drained, dipped in batter and fried; served with a thick syrup sauce into which has been worked some peach butter, the fritters dusted with sugar.

APRICOT FRITTERS—Same as the preceding but substituting apricots for peaches; another way is to form a half apricot from rice croquette mixture, and putting the half apricot with it, pinning with a toothpick, dipped in batter and fried,

toothpick then removed; served with sauce.

PINEAPPLE FRITTERS—Slices of cored canned pineapple drained, dipped in batter and fried; served with a wine syrup glacé sauce.

CORN FRITTERS—Cooked corn cut from the cob, or canned corn, pounded, mixed with flour, eggs and butter, seasoned with salt, dropped by spoonfuls in hot fat, fried; served either as a vegetable or garnish.

PARSNIP FRITTERS—The parsnips boiled, then mashed and mixed with flour, eggs and butter, seasoned with salt and white pepper (the mixture should be medium soft), dropped by spoonfuls in hot fat; when done, served as a vegetable or garnish.

FROGS—There are two kinds on the market, the small marsh frog, and the large bull frog; the bull is the most convenient for use and trade, giving the guest most satisfaction, and the cook least trouble in preparation.

FRIED FROGS, TARTAR SAUCE—The legs marinaded for an hour in lemon juice, salt and pepper, wiped, rolled in flour, then breaded and fried; served with Tartar sauce, garnished with lemon slices and parsley.

BROILED FROG LEGS—The legs marinaded for an hour in olive oil, lemon juice, salt and pepper, taken

PARSNIP FRITTERS

▪

Makes about 2 dozen

Parsnips are one of my favorite vegetables, and they were very popular during the winter months at the turn of the century. These fritters make a great side dish.

2 pounds parsnips

$^1/_2$ cup milk

$^3/_4$ cup all-purpose flour

2 eggs, plus 1 egg white

1 tablespoon chopped
    parsley

Salt and freshly ground
    black pepper to taste

Peanut oil for frying

Trim and peel the parsnips. Cut into large pieces and place in a saucepan. Add just enough water to cover. Bring to a boil, cover, and simmer for 10 to 15 minutes. When the parsnips are barely tender, drain well.

In a food processor, purée the parsnips with the remaining ingredients, except the oil.

Ladle about 1$^1/_2$ ounces of batter into a hot nonstick frying pan with a little oil. Spread out the batter to 3 inches in diameter and cook over medium heat. Fry a few minutes on each side until well browned. (An electric frying pan works great set at 375° F.)

Remove the little pancakes to drain on paper towels. Sprinkle with salt and serve.

C.W.

---

up, floured, broiled and basted with the marinade till done; served with maître d'hôtel butter, garnished with lemon and parsley.

STEWED FROG LEGS WITH PEAS—Frog legs blanched for a few minutes in salted vinegar water, then drained and put into a rich Velouté sauce, simmered till done;

served with a border of sautéed green peas,

FRICASSÉE OF FROG LEGS—Frog legs lightly sautéed with butter and minced shallots, taken up, the butter then lightly browned, flour added to form a roux, moistened with chicken stock, brought to the boil, skimmed, seasoned with salt, red pepper and sherry wine, legs put back into it and simmered till done.

FROG LEGS, SOUTHERN STYLE— Frog legs sautéed with butter and minced shallots, then taken up; to the butter and shallots is now added a little raw lean ham cut in small dice, together with a chopped green pepper; when ham is nearly done, add two quarts of chicken consommé, a quart can each of okra and tomatoes, brought to the boil, a cupful of well washed rice then added; when rice is nearly done, the frog legs are put in and simmered till tender. It should be a thick stew. Served, the legs in centre of dish with the vegetables around as a garnish.

FROG LEGS SAUTÉ, PROVEN-ÇALE—The legs seasoned with salt and pepper, then sautéed with butter, taken up into a saûtoir, covered with Provençale sauce, simmered till tender; served garnished with small stuffed onions and tomatoes.

FROG LEGS SAUTÉS, POULETTE— The legs seasoned with salt and pep-per, then sautéed with butter and minced shallots, taken up into a saû-toir, covered with sauce Poulette, simmered till tender; served with the sauce, garnished with flageolet beans and fancy croûtons.

FROG LEGS SAUTÉ, BORDE-LAISE—The legs sautéed with minced ham, garlic, shallots, thyme and butter, taken up, to the residue is then added sauce Espa-gnole with a glass of claret wine; this is then reduced to a demi-glaze and strained over the legs; served garnished with fried slices of beef marrow.

FROG OMELET, SOUTHERN STYLE— Shredded frog meat left over from ei-ther of the four preceding receipts, mixed into a sauce composed of one-third each of tomato, Espagnole and Creole sauce; a spoonful enclosed within a savory omelet; served with more of the frog meat down the sides.

FUMET—_Fumet_ describes any well-concentrated stock—chicken, vege-tables, fish, meat, mushroom, etc.— used to flavor sauces.

GALANTINE—A name applied to fowl, some game, fish and meat that may be boned, stuffed, boiled, braised or roasted, then pressed and cut into slices for service when cold, either plain or filled into molds with aspic jelly and decorated.

GALANTINE OF TURKEY OR CHICKEN—Two birds, the larger one to be singed, the smaller skinned, the birds' skin split down the back from the head to tail, the carcass removed without further breaking the skin; the large one laid out flat, skin downwards, seasoned with salt, pepper and powdered mixed herbs; the under fillets of the breast to be filled into the space which the breastbone occupied, the wing and leg meat drawn inwards and the sinews removed, the whole then spread with a force or sausage meat; two strips each of cooked tongue and fat salt pork arranged alternately down the centre, also some slices of truffles if at hand; the meat of the smaller bird then laid over the stuffing, the white meat covering the dark of the other bird, so that when cut, light and dark meat is served to each portion; the skin of the large bird is then drawn together and sewn closely, placed into a cloth which is again sewn and tied at the ends like a roly poly pudding, plunged into boiling seasoned white stock and simmered till done; taken up and while still hot, pressed into a mold with screw pressure or weight on top; when set and cold, the cloth removed, the bird wiped with a hot cloth to remove all grease and stains, it is then sliced for the table. If the birds are both young and juicy, instead of being boiled they may be braised or roasted (of course without being tied in a cloth), when done, taken up, pressed, trimmed and glazed.

GALANTINES—Generally served with aspic jelly, and the nicest way is to take the birds when pressed, wipe and trim, cut into even slices; galantine molds lined with aspic jelly, then decorated with cooked peas, macedoines, fancy shapes of white of eggs, beet, carrot and truffles, these decorations again coated with aspic to keep them in position, the slices of bird then laid into the mold EDGES DOWNWARDS not laid flat; limpid aspic run between each slice; when the mold is full, set, turned out, decorated and sent to table. I have seen galantines served at banquets where the slices of meat have been laid flat in the mold, with the result that the waiters could not procure a decent slice to serve; had the edges been placed downwards, the waiter or serving man would have been able to move each slice with the jelly adhering simply by the aid of a fork.

GAME—Name applied in a culinary sense to birds and animals fit for table use that are hunted by sportsmen, the animals and birds not being domesticated; these embrace woodcock, quail, snipe, partridge, wild ducks, geese and brant, prairie chickens, grouse, pheasant, reed birds, rail sora, ortolans, rice birds, sage hens, wheat ears, larks, capercailzie, plover, etc., squirrels, hares, venison, moose, caribou, black bear, elk, antelope, mountain sheep and goat; recipes will be found under each respective heading.

GARDEN PARTIES—Country club stewards and caterers are often called upon to prepare for and superintend garden parties, and as a rule the meal is served out of doors, under a marquée. When the steward or caterer has several through the summer season, invarably the same guests are to be found, he must therefore rack his brains to continually change the card. Solid food is NOT REQUIRED. The refreshments should be tea and coffee, various kinds of cups, delicate sandwiches of minced and creamed meat and fish, individual cakes, rolled bread and butter, ices, fruit; strawberries and cream are usually served from large silver bowls. The buffet should be well supplied with canapés, bouchées, timbales, darioles, individual galantines made in fancy gem pans—all things to be of an individual form as far as possible. Whatever wines are used should be of the light and sparkling variety, never anything heavy and heating.

GARFISH—Name of a fish with an elongated mouth resembling in body both mackerel and eel; they are prepared and served in all the ways applicable to eels.

GARFISH—The garfish (*Belone belone*) is rarely seen in this country; it is fished almost exclusively in the eastern Atlantic and is most popular in Scandinavia.

GARLIC—Name of a podded or cloved form of onion of very strong taste and flavor, always to be used sparingly; it enters into many soups, sauces and ragouts; in the recipes requiring it, the word clove, signifies one of the sections.

GARLIC—One could argue that garlic is the single most important flavoring in many cuisines, and that it is rarely used sparingly except with raw. *Allium sativum*, related not only to onions but also to lilies (take a look at a lily bulb sometime), comes in three basic types and sizes: white, which may be small or fairly large; purplish, usually rather large and sometimes called Italian garlic; and elephant garlic, which has a relatively mild flavor. The best bet is white or purple garlic in a medium to large size.

Like any bulb, garlic is seasonal. In the summer and fall, when it is fresh, it is rarely bitter. But as winter comes, green sprouts form inside each clove and bitterness results. At this stage garlic is especially harsh when raw.

To mince garlic, crush cloves with the side of a heavy knife, remove the skin, and mince.

GARNISHES—Name given to mixture of small tasty foods in sauce, used as a garnish and appropriate sauce to the main article served. Unhappily there are so many garnishes that the average cook has not the brain to retain but a limited number, and not one cook in a hundred could sit down and write the component parts of twenty garnitures right off the reel. It is the garnishes that stupefy the guests and make them order plain roast turkey; that covers the "bills of fare" with worse than mongrel French; that spoils many a good dish because the garnish used is not appropriate to the food served; that makes the country hotel keeper ask the cook what he wants this and that for; that makes the guest when he looks at the bill of fare exclaim: What in thunder is à la Montmorency! à la this and à la that. The following garnishes are the most principal in use, are put in a simple way to memorize, not only their ingredients; but that most important point that up to date no cook book has ever attempted to show. THE DISHES THAT THE GARNISHES ARE APPROPRIATE TO.

GARNISHES—Fellows's definition is the most comprehensive summary of pre–World War II fancy American garnishes we have ever seen. Experienced diners and cooks will recognize how much things have changed since Fellows wrote. Such elaborate—and expensive!—garnishes are rare these days. Still, these are interesting and stimulating.

ADMIRAL—Composed of shrimps, boiled crayfish tails, fried tufts of parsley, oysters or mussels blanched, drained, dipped in Villeroi sauce then breaded and fried; appropriate as a garnish to whole fish, the parts arranged in small groups around the fish with Admiral sauce served separately.

ALLEMANDE—For braised meat, is composed of stewed sauerkraut, prunes and potato cakes arranged around the meat, with Poivrade sauce poured under it.

ALLEMANDE—For boiled leg of pork; omit the stewed prunes and potato cakes, substituting glazed pieces of carrot, turnip and small onions.

ALLEMANDE—For boiled chicken; the garnish is quenelles of potatoes poached, then covered with fried breadcrumbs, arranged around the chicken with Allemande sauce poured under. This same is applied to most fowl and game served à l'Allemande.

ALLEMANDE—For braised fish such as carp or pike, the garnish is composed of small fish quenelles, button mushrooms, crayfish tails, and either small oysters or mussels, arranged around the fish with Allemande sauce in which has been worked some of the fish braise and anchovy butter.

ALLEMANDE—For roast or braised venison, the meat is garnished with prunes stewed in red wine, potato quenelles, and a sauce poured over the meat; made by taking equal parts of red currant jelly, Burgundy wine and Espagnole sauce, boiling them together with the rind and juice of an orange, and a piece of stick cinnamon, then strain.

ANDALOUSE—Small stuffed tomatoes and green peppers, with a small mold of dry boiled rice, arranged alternately around a dish of braised or roast meat or fowl, with Andalouse sauce poured under the meat.

AURORE OR AURORA—Composed of small fish quenelles, button mushrooms and blanched oysters or mussels, the whole mixed into Aurora sauce; appropriate to garnish cutlets of fish, such as salmon trout, pike, cod, snapper, halibut, etc.

ANGLAISE—For boiled beef is composed of neatly trimmed plain boiled carrots and turnips, arranged alternately around the meat with suet dumplings; Piquante sauce served separately.

ANGLAISE—For roast beef or fillet, is small browned potatoes at the side of the meat, with scraped horseradish at the ends.

ANGLAISE—For calf's head, is composed of a slice each of boiled bacon and glazed tongue, and served either with parsley or devil sauce.

ANGLAISE—For boiled chicken, is composed of tufts of boiled cauliflower, a thin slice of ham, and Béchamel sauce poured around.

ANGLAISE—For roast goose, is garnished with plain sage and onion stuffing, a brown gravy poured over, and apple sauce served separately.

ANGLAISE—For boiled leg of mutton, is garnished with a small mold of mashed white turnips, alternated with a trimmed boiled carrot, and served with caper sauce.

ANGLAISE—For boiled leg of salt pork, is garnished with trimmed boiled carrots and turnips, arranged alternately around the meat with a purée of split peas.

ANGLAISE—For roast pork, is garnished with sage and onion stuffing in spoonfuls alternately with a small baked apple; brown gravy or apple sauce served separately.

ANGLAISE—For boiled salmon, is garnished either with shrimp, mussel or parsley sauce.

ANGLAISE—For roast turkey, is composed of small pork sausages fried, a slice of boiled ham, bacon, or salt pork, stewed chestnuts, arranged alternately around the meat with stuffing under it, Poivrade sauce poured around. [The English Way of serving salmis of game is to simply garnish with button mushrooms and croûtons. Their roast venison is served plain with Yorkshire sauce.]

AFRICAINE—Composed of stewed okras, artichoke bottoms and pieces of egg plant mixed into an Espagnole sauce; appropriate to serve with braised veal and fowls.

AFRICAINE—Africaine sauce is a rich, dark, spicy sauce. Here, Fellows has lent its name to a ratatouille-like garnish.

AU JUS—Dishes so named are served with their natural juice or gravy.

BAYARD—Composed of circular slices of red tongue, truffles, mushrooms and artichokes, all boiled down with a little Madeira wine, then mixed into Espagnole sauce; appropriate to serve with sweetbreads, lamb fries and other white meat entrées, the ends of the dish being garnished with croûtons spread with foie-gras.

BORDELAISE—Composed of slices of parboiled ox marrow and Bordelaise sauce, or a sauce or butter composed of minced shallots, a suspicion of garlic, minced parsley and butter; served with broiled steaks.

BORDELAISE—For matelote of eels, is composed of very small onions stewed, button mushrooms and blanched sautéed oysters, the whole sprinkled with chopped parsley, arranged alternately round the matelote with fancy croûtons; no sauce.

BORDELAISE—For roast quails, is a garnish of slices of truffles and mushrooms mixed into a Bordelaise sauce.

BOURGIGNOTTE OR BOURGIGNONNE—Is composed of very small onions stewed, then glazed, with an equal quantity of button mushrooms and small quenelles of forcemeat all mixed into a Bourgignotte sauce; appropriate to serve with croûstade of quails, cutlets of sturgeon sautés, cutlets of mutton sautés, braised pigeon cutlets, salmis of small birds, etc.

BOUERGOISE—Consists of plain root vegetables glazed; appropriate for simple dishes, such as, glazed shortribs of beef, braised flank of beef, rolled breast of veal, etc.

BOUERGOISE GARNISHES—A misspelling by Fellows; the correct term is *bourgeoise*. His definition is appropriate, however: dishes à la bourgeoise are garnished with cooked carrots, onions, and bacon.

BOHEMIENNE—Composed of stoned olives, button mushrooms, small onions and balls of potatoes; appropriate to garnish braised and roast meat, under which is poured Poivrade sauce.

BRETONNE—A garnish chiefly used with braised leg of mutton; composed of boiled navy beans, drained, then moistened with Bretonne sauce, which is made of fried onions with a suspicion of garlic, moistened with brown sauce, seasoned, then rubbed through a tamis; small olive shapes of potatoes fried a light brown in butter, generally accompanies the beans in the garniture.

CARDINAL—Composed of small quenelles of lobster, small turned truffles and button mushrooms, all mixed into a Cardinal sauce; appropriate to serve with stuffed baked pike, carp, boiled salmon, turbot, halibut, fillets of sole, boudins of lobster, paupiettes of sole, fillets of trout, etc.

CHAMBORD—Composed of fish quenelles, truffles, button mushrooms, crayfish, small fish roes, moistened with Genevoise sauce for the one part. Crayfish tails, turned truffles, small fish roes moistened with Villeroi sauce for the second part; appropriate to garnish whole fish, such as salmon for a banquet table, the two colored garnishes being used alternately, intersticed with whole crayfish.

CHIPOLATA—Composed of small glazed onions, glazed balls of carrot and turnip, chestnuts, cocks combs and kernels or pieces of chicken, pieces of braised bacon, balls of veal or pork sausages and button mushrooms, the whole moistened with Financière sauce; appropriate to garnish small birds on toast, braised cutlets of mutton, roast pheasants, roast suckling pig, roast turkey, sauté of rabbit, braised prairie hen, partridge with cabbage, braised capon, cutlets of turkey, etc.

CHIVRY—Composed of blanched oysters coated with Villeroi sauce, then breaded and fried; small potato croquettes, small bouchées of oysters, and crayfish tails dipped in Villeroi sauce; appropriate garnish to whole fish.

DUCHESSE—Composed of strips of red tongue and cocks combs mixed in Velouté sauce; appropriate for white meat entrées.

DAUPHINE—Composed of Duchesse potatoes, fried tufts of parsley and Italian sauce; used for fried cutlets of chicken, veal cutlets, etc.

DURAND—Composed of trimmed slices of truffles, chicken livers, mushrooms, ham, sweetbreads, bacon, olives stuffed with truffle farce, cocks combs, gherkins, and hard boiled yolks of eggs cut in halves, the whole moistened with Espagnole sauce that is flavored with thyme; appropriate garnish to fricandeaus, roast or braised legs of mutton, cushions of veal, etc.

D'ARTOIS—A fish garnish composed of strips or circles of puff paste containing a salpiçon of cooked crayfish tails, oysters, mushrooms and white fleshed fish.

DUMAS—A garnish to be used with game; composed of ham, veal kidneys, cooked and cut into small sections, then moistened with Madeira sauce containing chopped parsley, tarragon and lemon juice.

ÉCARLETTE—Composed of pieces of red tongue, corned beef and mushrooms moistened with a Villeroi sauce; appropriate to garnish blanqettes, suprêmes, etc. Also consists of red tongue in tomato sauce; or lobster coral in a Velouté sauce; these latter two should be used when the meat or fish is red, so as to preserve the color.

FERMIÈRE—Composed of Parisienne fried potatoes, glazed balls of carrot, braised small lettuces and hearts of cabbages; appropriate to garnish braised or boiled beef, pot roasts, à la modes, etc.

FINANCIÈRE—Composed of button mushrooms, turned truffles, pieces of sweetbreads, cocks combs and kernels, small quenelles of forcemeat, the whole moistened with Financière sauce; appropriate to garnish fillets of beef, poultry, calf's head, sweetbreads, pigeons, salmis of plovers, braised turtle fins, black game, braised saddle of lamb, salmis of partridge and pheasant, fillets of rabbits, necks of veal, veal cutlets, roast loin of veal, etc.

FLAMANDE—Composed of small pieces of bacon and sausages, plenty of braised white cabbage, turned boiled carrots and turnips, glazed onions; or the dish served with Brussels sprouts in half glaze, or with Flemish sauce. Appropriate garnish to boiled beef, boiled or

roast ham, fillets of beef, large steaks, etc.

GODARD—Composed of turned and glazed truffles, diced sweetbreads, godiveau quenelles and button mushrooms (cocks combs and kernels, optional) moistened with Madeira sauce; appropriate garnish to braised sirloin of beef, larded capons, braised saddle of lamb, etc., also as a filling for timbales of macaroni which are subsequently served with Perigueux sauce.

GOURMET—Composed of neat-shaped pieces of ox palate, artichoke bottoms, turned truffles and button mushrooms, moistened with Madeira sauce; used for garnishing larded and braised fresh ox tongue.

GRECQUE—Composed of trimmed and blanched okras which are then simmered in a little Madeira sauce for ten minutes; used to garnish veal cutlets sautés, with a little Béarnaise sauce at ends of dish, also as a garnish to stewed veal.

HUSSARD—Composed of small circles of cooked red tongue, slices of mushrooms and small godiveau quenelles, the whole moistened with equal parts of Madeira sauce and tomato purée; used for garnishing braised white meat.

JOURNEAUX—Composed of slices of sautéed chicken livers, moistened with rich Madeira sauce; appropriate garnish to roast or braised chicken, and as a filling for timbales, patties, omelets, etc.

MACEDOINE—Composed of fancy shapes of cooked carrot, turnip, stringless beans, with green peas, moistened with Allemande, Suprême or Béchamel sauces, when served with white meat entrées; or mixed with Espagnole sauce for dark meat entrées. Appropriate garnish to fillet of beef, boiled capon, braised ducks, glazed fillets of ducklings, braised saddle of lamb, breaded mutton cutlets, glazed ox tongue, fricandeau of veal, roast fillet of veal, epigramme of lamb, fillets of capon, braised quails, larded sweetbreads, etc.

MARINIÈRE—Composed of blanched oysters, crayfish tails, turned truffles and small fish quenelles; used to garnish boiled fish.

MATELOTE—Composed of pieces of fish roe, very small onions sautéed in butter then drained, pieces of truffle, blanched mussels or small oysters and small fish quenelles, the whole moistened with a Matelote sauce; appropriate garnish to crimped codfish, eels, boiled salmon steaks, fillets of soles, baked stuffed bluefish, boiled carp, baked codfish, fried fillets of pike, boiled red snapper, braised trout, etc.

MILANAISE—Composed of inch pieces of boiled macaroni and red tongue, slices of mushrooms, a little boiled rice, chopped truffle peelings and Parmesan cheese, the whole moistened with equal parts of Madeira sauce and tomato purée (some raviolis optional); appropriate garnish to braised fillet of beef, boiled capon, boiled chicken, braised saddle of lamb, breaded mutton cutlets, fillets of chicken, stuffed breast of lamb, braised breast of veal, etc.

NAPOLITAINE—Composed of inch pieces of boiled macaroni dressed with Parmesan cheese; sultana raisins stewed in wine, and glazed raviolis, arranged alternately around the entrée with Napolitaine sauce poured under. Appropriate garnish to roast fillet of beef, suckling pig, braised capon, larded and glazed sweetbreads.

NIVERNAISE—Composed of Julienne vegetables sautéed in clarified butter with a little sugar, then drained, moistened with consommé, and when nearly done, rapidly boiled down to glaze; used in this way or mixed into a Hollandaise sauce. Appropriate garnish to breaded chicken cutlets, braised beef and mutton, braised ducks, haricot of mutton, mutton cutlets, etc.

PAYSANNE—Composed of slices of stuffed and braised cucumber, slices of braised carrot and small sausages, the whole then moistened with strained braise; appropriate garnish to black game, pheasant, haricot of mutton, haricot of ox tails, etc.

PERIGUEUX—Composed of scallops of fat bird livers and truffles braised in a mirepoix, to which is then added some quenelles of forcemeat, cocks combs and kernels with button mushrooms, the whole then moistened with Perigueux sauce, boiled up for a minute or two. Appropriate garnish to roast black game, large boudins of poultry, salmis of partridges, roast pheasant, roast stuffed turkey, roast stuffed suckling pig, broiled stuffed boneless pigs feet, braised quails on fried croûstades, fried quarters of young rabbit, veal chops sautés (these are first trimmed, seasoned, dipped in whipped egg whites, rolled in minced truffles, smoothed with a knife, sautéed slowly with butter a delicate brown about twenty minutes).

PARISIAN—Composed of equal quantities of turned truffles, button mushrooms and cocks kernels, moistened with Parisian sauce. Appropriate garnish to roast larded fillets of beef, fillets of chicken sautés, fillets of partridges breaded and sautéed, sautéed fillets of quails on toast, larded and braised sweetbreads. (For a club dish, the sweetbreads should be served three to the portion, one larded with strips of truffles, one with parsley stalks, the third with strips of red tongue, served on toast with the garnish around.) Fillets of soles stuffed and sautéed, (this is done by filleting the fish, spreading them with forcemeat, arranged on a baking sheet, moistened with a little white wine, covered with buttered paper, slowly baked till the fish is set, then allowed to cool, spread with a cold Allemande sauce, breaded, then gently sautéed a fine color with butter; served with the garnish.)

PROVENÇALE—Composed of small stuffed and baked tomatoes, small onions with the centres removed after being steamed, the whole then filled with forcemeat in which is worked a little cheese and a fla-

vor of garlic, they are then sautéed; the entrée when being served is surrounded alternately with the onions and tomatoes, also a sauce Provençale poured under the meat; appropriate garnish to braised fillet of beef, fried cutlets of chicken, braised ducks, leg of mutton boned, stuffed and braised, braised mutton cutlets, salmis of partridges, roast stuffed sucking pig, fried calf's brains in batter, salmis of all wild fowls.

REGENCY—Composed of small fish quenelles, cocks combs, button mushrooms, crayfish tails, truffles, and a little lobster coral, the whole moistened with some Regency sauce; appropriate garnish to whole boiled salmon, trout, pike, halibut, turbot and red snapper.

ROUENNAISE—Composed of turnips turned to an even small size, sautéed in butter with a little sugar till of a fine golden color, then moistened with some sauce Espagnole and simmered in it till tender; appropriate garnish to roast ducks, roast or braised pheasant, braised leg of mutton, capercailzie and black game.

ROUENNAISE—Is also the name of a useful fish garnish and is composed for this use with blanched oysters and shrimps with button mushrooms, each in equal quantities, also some lobster quenelles, the liquor form the blanched oysters and mushrooms reduced with a little white wine, then added to a Velouté sauce, finished with liaison of egg yolks and cream, lemon juice and chopped parsley, then is added the ragout.

RICHELIEU—Composed of small poultry quenelles which have some brown purée of onions in their composition, slices of braised poultry livers and cocks combs, the whole moistened with a brown onion purée sauce; appropriate garnish to entrées of game and poultry that are breaded and subsequently fried or broiled, also boneless pigs feet breaded, braised carbonade of mutton, crepinettes of partridge, etc.

ROYALE—Composed of a ragout of button mushrooms, cocks combs and kernels, small quenelles of chicken and turned truffles, the ragout to be moistened with the glazy strained braise from the meat. Appropriate garnish to braised loin of veal, breast of veal stuffed and braised, braised saddle of lamb, braised capon, braised rabbit, larded and braised fillets of chicken.

ROYALE—Garnish to be used for game, such as braised venison, hare, pheasant, partridge, etc., is composed of pieces of braised pork sausages, braised bacon, button mushrooms and green gherkins, the whole moistened with a Poivrade sauce.

ROYALE—This name is often applied to fish, but when so applied it has no garnish, but is meant to convey the form and style of cooking, which is the fish either filleted and fried, or boned, stuffed and stewed, then served with a white Ravigote sauce, sometimes garnished with fish quenelles.

ROYALE—This name when applied to soups and consommés, has a garnish or filling composed of fancy shapes or small timbales of custard; made with consommé and egg yolks, or court-bouillon and egg yolks, with some lobster roe, minced mushrooms, minced truffles, parsley, shallots, a green purée, etc., etc., mixed in according to fancy, the custard steamed slowly, the eggs simply mixed without much beating.

SOUBISE—Composed of small potato croquettes and a purée Soubise; made by sautéeing with butter some blanched onions, seasoning with nutmeg, red pepper and a pinch of sugar; when of a light color, moistened with white sauce; when done, the whole is rubbed through a tamis in conjunction with a boiled floury potato which keeps the purée firm. Appropriate garnish to braised black game, boudins of chicken, braised leg of mutton, larded neck of mutton, braised mutton cutlets, braised partridges, larded and braised pheasants, larded and braised pork cutlets, scallops of sweetbreads sauced, breaded and fried.

STANLEY—Garniture often served with steaks, composed of quartered fried bananas, small timbales of horseradish mixed with rice, minced shallots, cream and egg yolks; served with sauce Albert over or around the steaks.

SUPRÊME—Composed of a purée of white chicken meat and rice that has been boiled in chicken stock, the purée being mixed with a little rich cream; arranged on the serving dish as a border, decorated with fancy shapes of truffle, the meat in the centre being covered with a Suprême sauce, such as, breasts of chicken, sweetbreads, capon, quails and partridges.

TOULOUSE—Composed of slices of geese livers sautéed and glazed, button mushrooms blanched with lemon juice and butter, scallops of sweetbreads, turned truffles, cocks combs and kernels masked with Toulouse or Suprême sauce. Appropriate garnish to larded and sautéed fillets of chicken, fricandeau of veal, sweetbreads, capon, larded and sautéed ribs of veal.

TORTU—Composed of olive shaped pieces of truffle and green gherkins, stoned small olives, button mushrooms, scallops of blanched brains or sweetbreads, the whole moistened with a rich Madeira sauce; used to garnish calf's head, larded and braised turtle, stewed turtle fins.

GHERKINS—A small prickly cucumber used for pickling; to pickle them they are first washed and wiped, then placed in jars and covered with a boiling brine strong enough to float a potato the size of an egg; allowed to steep for 24 hours, then taken out, wiped, placed in clean jars and covered with hot vinegar spiced with an onion, whole cloves, mustard seed, bay leaves and mace; ready for use in two weeks.

GIBLETS—Are composed of the heart, liver, gizzard and neck of poultry, and as each take a different time to cook, they should be cooked in groups of each and afterwards amalgamated; all require blanching to remove the blood.

GIBLET SAUCE—Blanched and sautéed hearts, livers and gizzards, cut very small, then mixed into a thickened gravy from the roasted birds to be served with.

GIBLET PIE—Geese giblets blanched, stewed in stock till tender with some sherry wine, carrot, onion and parsley; when done, the vegetables removed, sauce made from the stock and seasoned with minced shallots, mushrooms, chopped parsley, red pepper, salt and a little sweet basil; the giblets then arranged in the pie dish together with some small pieces of tender sautéed beef, the sauce poured over all, covered with a short paste, egg washed and baked.

STEWED GIBLETS WITH GREEN PEAS—Poultry giblets prepared as in the preceding, but instead of mixing with beef and placing in pie dish, served as they are within a border of green peas.

RAGOUT OF GIBLETS WITH POTATO CROQUETTES—The giblets blanched, then sautéed with bacon, finished by stewing till tender in a brown sauce with balls of carrot and small onions, adding at the last some button mushrooms, season with sherry wine; served within a border of small potato croquettes.

GIBLET SOUP—The necks and second wing joints cut into inch pieces, the gizzards into thin slices, sauté them, boil the livers with some minced onions, split the blanched hearts and sauté them, mix all together and moisten with roast chicken gravy, let simmer till tender; meanwhile prepare a soup to the consistency of thin cream made from veal or chicken stock that has been flavored with celery, carrots, turnips and onions in equal proportions, bay leaf, thyme, basil, savory and mace; when ready, strain into the soup tureen, add the giblets in sauce, finish with sherry wine and serve.

GIBLET SOUP WITH RICE—The giblets prepared and sauced as in the preceding, the soup made of equal parts of Espagnole, tomato and Velouté sauces, thin to consistency with veal or chicken broth, brought to the boil, skimmed, rice added and simmered till tender, then poured to the giblets, finish with Madeira wine.

CLEAR GIBLET SOUP—Blanched giblets cut into neat size, simmered in white broth till tender, added to a chicken consommé together with some Julienne vegetables.

GLAZE—Or reduced meat juice, used to glaze or varnish cold meat, such as, boned roast fowls, tongues, hams, game birds, boars head, etc., to enrich soups and sauces; made by rapidly boiling down clarified stock, consommé or very clear broths; these should have had veal and beef bones, roast game and poultry carcasses boiled in them so as to give the glaze a rich flavor.

GODIVEAU—Name used for veal forcemeat, made from 2 lbs. of lean veal, 2 lbs. of beef suet, 1 lb. of cooked veal udder, the whole pounded till it is creamy, seasoned with red pepper, salt, nutmeg, 8 eggs and half a pound of fresh white grated breadcrumbs, when all smooth, it is rubbed through a tamis, and placed away for use. It is valuable in making forcemeat balls, as a lining for meat pies, etc., quenelles.

GOOSE—One of the domestic fowls much appreciated by hotel patrons if young. Stewards can tell this by the upper bill test, if the upper bill will bend or cave in the middle it is young, the firmer it is, the older the bird; it is not a very profitable bird to the proprietor unless purchased very low in price, because "when from a goose you've taken legs and breast, wipe lips, thank God, and give the poor the rest."

Spring or green geese about three months old are never stuffed for roasting: the best flavored geese are six to nine months old, and best from September to Christmas.

BOILED GOOSE WITH PICKLED PORK—The bird singed, drawn and washed, plunged into boiling salted water with an onion, simmered till tender; served in portions with a slice of boiled ham or leg of salt pork, accompanied with celery sauce.

ROAST GOOSE STUFFED WITH GODIVEAU—Young birds singed, washed, drawn, filled with godiveau, trussed, roasted; served with giblet sauce, accompanied with a garnish of sautéed green peas at one end of dish, and a mound of mashed potatoes at the other.

BRAISED GOOSE WITH SAUSAGES—The bird prepared, stuffed with pork sausage meat flavored with sage, braised with bacon and vegetables; served with a garnish of Parisienne potatoes, broiled sausages, and gravy made from the strained and skimmed braise.

ROAST GOOSE, APPLE SAUCE—The bird prepared and stuffed with a mixture of dry breadcrumbs moistened with chopped green apples, minced onion boiled with a little water and butter; seasoned with sage, salt and pepper, trussed, roasted; served with dressing under the meat, apple sauce served separately.

ROAST GOOSE STUFFED WITH CHESTNUTS—The birds prepared and stuffed with a mixture made of two-thirds chestnut purée mixed with one-third godiveau, trussed, roasted; served in portions; garnished with roasted and peeled chestnuts, brown gravy made in the roasting pan poured under the meat.

ROAST GOOSE WITH OYSTER STUFFING—The birds prepared and filled with a stuffing made of a quart each of oysters, breadcrumbs, and rolled oyster crackers, one-half a pound of soft butter, four eggs, salt and pepper, roasted; served with a brown oyster or brown celery sauce.

GOOSE WITH KRAUT, GERMAN STYLE—The goose prepared and trussed, arranged in a deep saûtoir with well washed and drained sauerkraut, bacon and small bologna sausage, an onion stuck with cloves, moistened with a little broth and some fat from the top of stock, fetched to the boil, then simmered till done; served in portions with a garnish of kraut, bacon and sausage.

STUFFED GOOSE WITH GLAZED TURNIPS—The bird prepared and stuffed with grated bread seasoned with sage and thyme leaves, parboiled minced onions, salt and pepper, placed in a saûtoir with an onion stuck with cloves, celery, parsley, little sherry wine and butter, lid placed on, then put into a hot oven, baked and basted till done and glazy; served with a brown sauce made in the saucepan it was cooked in, and garnished with columns of glazed turnips.

BRAISED GOOSE WITH VEGETABLES—Prepare, truss and braise the birds with bacon, herbs and vegetables; served with brown gravy, and garnished with even sized pieces of carrot and turnip glazed, intersected with Brussels sprouts.

STUFFED GOOSE WITH GLAZED APPLES—The birds prepared and filled with mashed potatoes mixed with minced and sautéed onions, trussed, roasted; served with brown gravy, garnished with small apples baked whole and glazy.

ROAST GREEN GOOSE, GOOSEBERRY SAUCE—The bird singed, drawn, washed, trussed, with the inside seasoned well with salt, pepper and powdered sage, roasted and basted; served with gooseberry sauce.

GOOSEBERRY SAUCE—Green gooseberries with a little sugar and just enough water to keep them from burning, in a saucepan, lid placed on, simmered till done, then rubbed through a sieve like cranberries; when passed through a little butter is added.

GORGONZOLA—Name of a prime cheese made in the North of Italy, somewhat resembling the English stilton; it is of yellow color with rich green veins, firm and creamy.

GORGONZOLA—Invented in the small village of Gorgonzola (near Milan) sometime before the twelfth century, the genuine form of this CHEESE is still produced only in Piedmont and Lombardy. When young, it is milder than either Stilton or Roquefort, the world's two other great blue cheeses. As it ages, Gorgonzola becomes stronger and stronger.

There are two factors to consider when buying Gorgonzola: Find a good brand and be sure it is of the age you prefer (young cheese can be well wrapped and aged in your refrigerator; there is, of course, no going back for older cheese). Serve Gorgonzola with fruit and nuts, or use it, mixed with butter and cream or tomato sauce, as a topping for PASTA.

GRAHAM FLOUR—Name given to unbolted flour by Sylvester Graham, who claims for it more nutritive properties, but it has, however, been proven to be less easy of digestion; it is made into bread, pancakes, waffles, muffins, mush and crackers.

GRAHAM FLOUR—This nutritious flour was widely heralded when it was first introduced; now, however, its distinctive flavor is rarely found outside of graham crackers.

GRAPES, FROSTED—Bunches of grapes dipped into whites of eggs whipped into a froth, then into powdered sugar, surplus sugar then shaken off, hung till set and dry, then served.

GRAPE JAM—Pulp the grapes, keeping the pulp and skins separate, pour the pulp into a porcelain lined kettle and bring it to boiling point, then press through a colander, add the skins and measure; to every quart allow a pound of sugar, mix, boil rapidly for 20 minutes, stirring occasionally, pour into tumblers or jars, seal. If green grapes allow one-half pound more sugar to the quart.

GRAPE JELLY—Use freshly gathered ripe Concord, Clinton or Isabella grapes, put them into stone crocks, place the crocks in the bain-marie of cold water, cover the tops and heat slowly till grapes are soft; now put a small quantity at a time into a jelly bag and squeeze out the juice; measure the juice and to each quart allow 2 lbs. of granulated sugar. Turn the juice into a porcelain lined kettle over a brisk fire, place the sugar in the oven to heat, boil the juice rapidly for 20 minutes; then quickly add the sugar, stirring till it is dissolved; dip the glasses into hot water, watch the liquid, and as soon as it comes to the boil, remove from the fire and fill the glasses.

GREEN GRAPE JELLY—Fox grapes are the best; put the stemmed grapes into a porcelain lined kettle, barely cover them with cold water, cover the kettle, and boil slowly till the grapes are very tender, then drain them through a flannel jelly bag; to every quart of the juice allow 2 lbs. of granulated sugar, put the juice into porcelain lined kettle, bring to the boil, then add the sugar, and boil rapidly till it jellies, about 20 minutes, skimming off the scum as it rises; as soon as it jellies, dip the glasses into boiling water and fill with the boiling liquid, stand aside till cold and firm, then seal the tops.

GRAPE FRUIT—Also called "shaddock" and "forbidden fruit" and the largest ones "pompoleons," a fruit of the orange species, plentifully grown in the West Indies and Florida, are of an agreeable acid grape flavor; served cut in halves across, with the sections loosened and the seeds removed; eaten with powdered sugar, a little sherry wine being a valuable addition.

GRAPEFRUIT—Shaddock (*Citrus grandis*), also called pomelo, is closely related to the grapefruit (*Citrus paradisi*)—it may even be an ancestor—but it is a distinctly different fruit. Pomelo, which is indigenous to Southeast Asia, became known to the Europeans in the seventeenth century; shortly thereafter it was planted in the West Indies. But no one saw a grapefruit (so named not for its flavor but for its habit of growing in bunches) until the mid-nineteenth century. It may have been a cross between the pomelo and the orange, or simply a mutant pomelo.

In any case some of the world's tastiest grapefruits have been grown in Florida since the turn of the century; with a bit of effort these fruits, superior to those from California, can be found almost anywhere in the country.

GRAYLING—A prime game fish of fine flavor weighing from 1 to 5 lbs.; cooked and served in all the ways applicable to brook trout.

GREENGAGE—Called by the French "Reine Claude," a species of plum that when ripe remains green; used as a table fruit, in compotes, pies, jellies, ices, and as a sweet entrée with rice.

GRENADINS—Name applied to the fricandeau of veal cut in half inch thick slices, then stamped circular with a biscuit cutter, these larded with seasoned strips of ham or bacon, arranged in a saûtoir, moistened with a light colored strong consommé, reduced to a half glaze and the larding is cooked; served overlapping each other with a garnish of green peas or glazed root vegetables in forms, or with gumbo and egg plant, or a chipolata garnish, or with small stuffed tomatoes and tomato sauce, or with a Financière garnish.

GRIDDLE CAKES—For recipes, see heading of "BATTER."

GROUPER—Name of one of our Southern fishes, found in three varieties, black, red and white; the shape is a cross between a carp and a bass, weighs from 5 to 10 lbs.; the flesh is firm but coarse; a second class fish.

GROUPER—There are some four hundred species of grouper, all members of the sea BASS family (Serranidae). They live in the world's warm waters, are found off the shores of Georgia, Florida, the Gulf States, and southern California, and may grow to be several hundred pounds.

Smaller fish, up to ten pounds or so, are commercially important. Although grouper does not have the big taste and firm texture of the best white-fleshed ocean fish such as RED SNAPPER and tilefish, deeming it second class seems a bit harsh. Filleted, it is firm enough to deep-fry; cubed, it can be kebabed or used in chowders or stews; steaked, it is well suited to the grill.

BOILED GROUPER, CAPER SAUCE— The fish prepared and boiled in salted water with a little vinegar (time to simmer about 40 minutes), taken up and drained; served with caper sauce and garnished with Hollandaise potatoes.

BOILED GROUPER, MATELOTE GARNISH—The fish prepared and scored, boiled whole in court-bouillon with a bunch of sweet herbs when done, drained; served in slices with a little lobster coral strewn over, garnished with a Matelote (see GARNISHES).

GROUPER STUFFED AND BAKED, TOMATO SAUCE—The fish scaled and washed, backbone and entrails removed, stuffed, put back in shape and tied with twine, baked whole with slices of salt pork; served in portions with a strip of the pork and tomato sauce poured around.

BAKED GROUPER, GULF STYLE— The fish scaled, head removed, split down the back and the backbone removed, laid out on greased pan, seasoned with mixed peppers and salt, placed in oven till heated through and set, then taken out, moistened with melted butter, returned to oven, baked with frequent basting till done and brown; served in portions with tomato purée around, and garnished with lemons.

GROUPER SAUTÉ, LOBSTER SAUCE —The fish prepared, cut in steaks, laid in seasoned olive oil, sautéed with it; when done and brown, served with lobster coral strewn over the portion and lobster sauce around.

BAKED RED GROUPER, SPANISH SAUCE—The fish cleaned and scored, arranged in baking pan, moistened with white stock and some fat from the stock pot, seasoned with salt, vegetables and a dash of vinegar, place in medium oven; when about a third done, remove the upper skin, then baste frequently till done and brown, (about one hour is required for a 7 lb. fish); served in portions with Spanish sauce poured around.

GROUSE—Under this heading comes the "spruce," "ruffled," "pintail," "moor fowl," "capercailzie," "prairie chicken," "ptarmigan," etc.

GROUSE—It is difficult if not impossible to find grouse in the markets or even by mail. Substitute the far less scarce partridge, game hen, or a small capon, if you choose to try any of Fellows's recipes.

STUFFED GROUSE, MUSHROOM SAUCE—The bird singed, drawn and washed, filled with a stuffing made from the liver, minced onions and mushrooms, breadcrumbs, butter, salt and pepper, strips of bacon tied over the breast, roasted; served with mushroom sauce flavored with sherry wine.

GLAZED GROUSE, SAUCE TRIANON—The birds trussed and roasted plain, taken up, quartered, skin removed, dipped into a game glaze; served on a fancy croûton with sauce Trianon poured around.

ROAST GROUSE, SCOTCH STYLE—The birds trussed and roasted plain, taken up, cut in quarters, served on toast with Bigarade sauce poured over, and garnished with slices of oranges.

SALMIS OF GROUSE—The birds trussed and roasted plain, taken up and cut into quarters, placed in a saûtoir, moistened with game sauce, fetched to the simmer, flavored with sherry wine; served with sauce over, garnished with fancy croûtons, the top of the bird sprinkled with grated orange rind and minced truffles.

ROAST GROUSE, HUNTERS STYLE—The bird trussed and roasted plain, taken up and cut into quarters; served on toast with sauce poured over, made of 2 parts of Espagnole and 1 part tomato sauces, seasoned with minced fried shallots, lemon juice, minced mushrooms and chopped parsley.

STEWED GROUSE WITH GREEN PEAS—Stuff and truss young birds, roll them in butter, quickly brown them in a very hot oven, take out and place in a deep saûtoir, moisten with game sauce, put on the saûtoir lid, let stew slowly till tender, take up and cut into portions, keeping them hot in a little sauce, the sauce they were stewed in then strained and skimmed, seasoned with sherry wine; served poured over the bird, garnished with green peas sauté.

BRAISED GROUSE WITH GLAZED CARROTS—Truss the birds, arrange in a braziere with slices of bacon, celery, onion stuck with cloves, bay leaves, slices of carrot and turnip, a bunch of sweet herbs and parsley, moisten with game gravy, slices of bacon placed on the birds and on the bacon a sheet of buttered paper, lid then put on, the birds braised till done and glazy, taken up, cut into portions, the braise strained and skimmed, then mixed with a rich brown sauce flavored with port wine; served with the sauce poured over and garnished with balls of sautéed and glazed carrots.

ROAST GROUSE, BREAD SAUCE—The breasts of the bird larded with seasoned strips of fat pork, trussed, seasoned with salt and pepper; rolled in melted butter, then in flour, roasted and basted till done; served with bread sauce at sides.

STUFFED FILLETS OF GROUSE WITH QUENELLES—Young birds trussed and roasted plain, taken up and filleted, the fillets spread with game forcemeat, arranged on a baking sheet, moistened and heated with game sauce; when to be served, dipped in a game glaze; served on a fancy croûton with game sauce and garnished with small game quenelles.

BROILED GROUSE WITH BACON—Young birds singed, split down the back, the back and breastbone removed, thigh bone snapped, laid for half an hour in olive oil, seasoned with salt and pepper, broiled till done; served on toast with strips of broiled bacon, maître d'hôtel butter, garnished with Julienne potatoes.

GROUSE CUTLETS BREADCRUMBED —Young birds singed, trussed and roasted, taken up and jointed, skin removed, dipped into a thick cooling rich game sauce, then in sifted breadcrumbs (not cracker dust), then breaded, and arranged on a baking sheet, sprinkled with melted butter, placed in oven, basted and browned; served garnished with Duchesse potatoes.

GRUYÈRE OR SWISS—Name of an imported cheese used both in cooking and for the table; is large, round, thick and flat in shape, has a peculiar nutty flavor and when cut is found to be full of small holes.

GRUYÈRE OR SWISS—Gruyère is a fairly hard CHEESE made in both Switzerland and France. "Swiss" cheese is the English name given to the original Emmental (or Emmentaler). Emmental is a bit softer and milder than Gruyère and has a nutty flavor (and, of course, holes). It is far superior to all other Swiss cheese.

GUAVA—Name of a Southern and West Indian fruit that is chiefly used in making preserves and jellies. Guava jelly is one of the best to serve with delicate flavored game.

GUAVA—Dense guava jam is often served, especially by Puerto Ricans, with fresh, mild white cheese as a dessert. And guava nectar can be found in almost any market frequented by Hispanics or Caribbean islanders.

Even though it is easily cultivated in warm climates throughout the world and is high in vitamin C, the guava (*Psidium guajava*) is rarely found fresh in this country outside of Florida and the Southwest, probably because it is fairly perishable and has a minuscule market. The many varieties of guava vary in shape, color, and flavor, but all have an intense aroma that will either attract or repel you.

GUINEA HEN—A domestic fowl smaller than the ordinary chicken, with darker flesh, often takes the place of partridge; is best to serve in the spring of the year when game is a bit scarce.

GUINEA HEN—These attractive, black-and-white speckled birds are a bit smaller than the average chicken (usually weighing in at about two pounds), their flavor is stronger and their meat moister.

ROAST LARDED GUINEA HEN—The bird singed and drawn, the legs and breast larded with seasoned strips of fat pork, rolled in buttered paper, baked till done and brown; served with a brown poultry gravy, garnished with watercress.

BROILED GUINEA HEN, WITH BACON—Young birds singed, split down the back, the breast and backbones removed, thigh bone snapped, seasoned with salt and pepper, rolled in flour, then in melted butter, broiled; served on toast with strips of bacon, maître d'hôtel butter, and garnished with Julienne potatoes and watercress.

ROAST GUINEA HEN, SAUCE BÉARNAISE—The birds singed and cleaned, trussed, slices of fat larding pork tied over the breast, roasted; when about done, the pork removed, then quickly browned; served in portions, garnished at ends of dish with fancy croûtons, and Béarnaise sauce at the sides.

BRAISED STUFFED GUINEA HEN—The birds singed and drawn, filled with a quenelle forcemeat, the breasts larded, arranged in a brazier with vegetables and spices, moistened with stock and white wine, covered with strips of bacon, braised and basted till done taken up, the braise strained and skimmed, then rapidly reduced to demi-glaze, which is then added to a Financière garnish, the bird served whole or in portions with the garnish around.

GUMBO—Another name for the vegetable okra; for recipes see OKRA.

GUMBO—Gumbo is the name of a Creole dish that often contains OKRA, seafood, meats, and rice. There are many different types.

H

HADDOCK—A fish of the cod species but smaller; when dried and
smoked is known as smoked haddock or Finnan Haddie, from the
village of Finnan near Aberdeen,
Scotland, which is as famous for its
curing haddocks as Yarmouth is for
its bloaters.

HADDOCK—Like COD, to which it is
closely related, haddock (*Melanogrammus aeglefinus*) has soft, mild-
flavored, stark-white flesh and is often sold skinned and filleted. Also
like cod, haddock has been over-
fished and so is not found in our fish
markets as reliably as it once was.
Those haddock that are caught are
usually much smaller than their ancestors, averaging five pounds or so
versus twenty just a few years ago.
Otherwise, there is little difference
(except, of course, today's fish is
more expensive). Industry represen-
tatives believe that supplies of haddock have always been cyclical, and
that the fish will become plentiful

again, possibly in the 1990s. See
FINNAN HADDIE.

BAKED STUFFED HADDOCK—The
fish scaled and cleaned, backbone
removed, filled with an oyster
stuffing, baked and basted till
done; served in portions with a
brown oyster sauce.

BOILED HADDOCK, OYSTER SAUCE—
The fish prepared and cut in portions, boiled till done in salted water with a dash of vinegar; served
with white oyster sauce and garnished with Hollandaise potatoes.
(With boiled haddock, egg, cream,
Béchamel, parsley, shrimp, lobster,
crab and Hollandaise sauces are
also appropriate.)

FILLETS OF HADDOCK, SAUTÉ—
The fish cleaned, boned, cut in fillets, seasoned with salt and pepper,

rolled in flour, sautéed in butter, taken up, gravy made in the pan, strained, the fish served sprinkled with parsley dust, gravy at the sides, garnished with Parisienne potatoes.

FILLETS OF HADDOCK, BREADCRUMBED, DUTCH SAUCE—Prepared and cut into fillets as in the preceding, seasoned with salt and pepper, dipped in beaten egg, then in sifted breadcrumbs, fried; served with Dutch sauce at the sides, garnished with cress and lemon.

BROILED FRESH HADDOCK, ANCHOVY BUTTER—Prepared and cut in fillets, rolled in flour, broiled and basted with butter; served spread with anchovy butter, garnished with Saratoga chips, watercress and lemon slices.

CREAMED HADDOCK WITH OYSTERS—Cold boiled haddock in flakes without skin, heated in Hollandaise sauce with an equal quantity of blanched and drained oysters; served piled high on toast, sprinkled with parsley dust.

BAKED FINNAN HADDIE, BUTTER SAUCE—The fish trimmed and skinned, arranged in a baking pan with a little water, placed in oven till set, water then poured off, seasoned with pepper, moistened with butter sauce, baked; served with the sauce, garnished with parsley and croûtons.

FINNAN HADDIE SAUTÉ, PARSLEY SAUCE—The fish skinned and trimmed, laid in warm water for a few minutes, then sautéed with butter; served on toast with parsley butter sauce poured over, garnish with watercress.

FINNAN HADDIE BOILED, CREAM SAUCE—The fish skinned and trimmed, laid in warm water for an hour, washed, then put to boil in cold water; served with cream sauce poured over, garnished with Hollandaise potatoes.

FINNAN HADDIE BAKED WITH TOMATOES—The fish skinned and trimmed, laid in warm water for an hour, washed, blanched, cut in portions, arranged in baking pan with sliced peeled tomatoes, minced fried shallots and chopped parsley, baked; served on toast with the tomatoes around.

FINNAN HADDIE BROILED, LOBSTER BUTTER—The fish skinned, trimmed, blanched, dried, seasoned with pepper, rolled in olive oil, broiled, served on toast, spread with lobster butter, garnished with watercress.

FINNAN HADDIE BAKED, ABERDEEN STYLE—The fish skinned and trimmed, baked with milk and butter; served with a sauce made of mustard, butter and lemon juice mixed together so that it is soft enough to melt when laid on the hot fish.

HAGGIS—Name of a Scotch national dish prepared by cutting into small pieces the heart, liver, milt and skirt, together with the lungs of a freshly killed sheep; after first blanching and boiling till tender each separate part, to each set of haslets as above is mixed one pound of finely chopped beef suet, one half pint each of minced onion and oatmeal, seasoned with salt, red and black pepper, nutmeg and lemon juice, the whole thoroughly mixed and moistened with a little beef gravy, the mixture is then filled into a well cleansed sheep paunch, sewn up, pricked with a fork to allow air escape, plunged into boiling salted water, and kept simmering till done, about two and a half hours; served without any garnish.

HALIBUT—A large flatfish of the flounder species, the young and medium sized ones being the best, and known as "Chicken halibut."

HALIBUT—By far the largest of the flatfish and generally a terrific eating fish, Atlantic halibut (*Hippoglossus hippoglossus*) is another of those fish the population of which is in decline and so has become harder to find and more expensive. Pacific halibut is also of high quality and remains plentiful; other fish sold as halibut (Greenland halibut, black halibut, etc.) are usually inferior.

Halibut season, such as it exists, is springtime. Look for the fish then, usually sold in steaks, and occasionally in fillets. Its white flesh is firm, tight-grained, and flavorful, making it ideal for sautéing and grilling.

BOILED HALIBUT STEAK, CREAM SAUCE—The fish scaled and trimmed, cut into steaks, simmered in boiling salted water containing a dash of vinegar; served sprinkled with parsley dust, cream sauce at the sides.

BROILED HALIBUT STEAK—The steaks seasoned with salt and pepper, rolled in flour, then in olive oil, broiled; served with maître d'hôtel butter, garnished with watercress and lemon, sometimes with a strip of broiled bacon.

BOILED HALIBUT—The fish scaled and trimmed, cut into portions, boiled in salted water with a dash of vinegar; served with either lobster, clam, cream or Hollandaise sauces.

BAKED HALIBUT, EGG SAUCE—The fish scaled and trimmed, cut into portions, arranged in baking pan, seasoned with salt and pepper, moistened with milk and butter, baked and basted till done; served with egg sauce, garnished with slices of hard boiled eggs.

FRIED HALIBUT STEAK, WITH BACON—Slices of bacon blanched, then fried, the steaks seasoned with salt and pepper, rolled in flour, then dipped into beaten eggs, fried a golden brown in the bacon fat; served with strips of bacon.

HALIBUT STEAK SAUTÉ, TOMATO SAUCE—The steaks seasoned with salt and ·pepper, rolled in flour, slowly sautéed a golden color with butter; served with a sauce composed of equal parts of tomato purée and tomato catsup.

CREAMED HALIBUT WITH MUSHROOMS—Flakes of cold boiled halibut mixed with slices of sautéed button mushrooms, moistened with Béchamel sauce, filled into

HALIBUT FRIED WITH BACON

·

Serves 4

Serving fresh fish from the oceans to a patron in the Midwest was difficult in 1904. The railroads in the early 1900s made it possible, but it was a long journey for the fish. Pan-frying halibut in bacon fat may have been the cook's way of masking any off-flavor in the fish. Actually, I think the two go very well together.

8 strips bacon, diced	*1 cup all-purpose flour*
4 halibut steaks	**Garnish**
Freshly ground black pepper to taste	*Chopped parsley*

In a large frying pan, fry the bacon to render its fat. Remove the bacon to drain on paper towels, leaving the fat in the pan.

Season the halibut with pepper and dredge in the flour. Pat off the excess flour from the fish.

In the frying pan with the reserved fat, pan-fry the halibut. Do not overcook and do not burn the bacon fat.

Serve with diced bacon and chopped parsley.

C.W.

---

deep oval or scallop dishes, sprinkled with breadcrumbs and melted butter, baked a delicate brown and served.

HAM—A leg of pork salted and smoked. Hams to be boiled, steamed or baked, should be soaked overnight in cold water, thoroughly scrubbed in the morning, and when cooking should be allowed 20 minutes time for each pound in weight. If to be kept for serving when cold, they should be allowed to cool in the water they were boiled in, as that keeps them moist down to the last cutting, even for a week or more.

HAM—Many supermarket hams, quick-cured, artificially smoked, and full of water, may be acceptable when cooked with other foods, but they do not have much character when served on their own. There are three major categories of ham.

Fresh: Although the word *ham* usually refers to cured meat, it also describes the rear leg of a pig (the Old English word for "thigh" is *hamm*). Fresh ham is a great treat, and can be baked or braised.

Dry, Salt-cured: These are the great hams from all over the world—Smithfield, Virginia, and other country hams from the American South; prosciutto di Parma (Italy); York (England); Westphalian (Germany); Bayonne (France); Serrano (Spain); and so on (China reportedly produces some of the world's best salt-cured hams). Heavily salted, usually smoked, and hung to dry for months or years, these strong-flavored hams are eaten in small amounts as an appetizer or snack, or used as a flavor-enhancing ingredient in a variety of dishes. They need not be cooked before eating, although many are in order to remove excess salt.

Brine-cured: These are the mild-tasting hams that are most often sold in supermarkets. They are soaked in or injected with brine and smoked, and vary enormously in quality. Those ordered by mail may be more flavorful than the national brands sold everywhere, but there is no guarantee.

STEWED HAM WITH SPINACH—The ham prepared and steamed as directed above, taken up, skinned; served in slices on a bed of spinach with brown sauce at sides.

BOILED HAM WITH LIMA BEANS—Soaked overnight, scrubbed, boiled for 20 minutes to the pound; served in slices with a garnish of fresh lima beans in brown sauce.

ROAST HAM, CHAMPAGNE SAUCE—The ham prepared, then steamed two-thirds of its cooking time, taken up and skinned, placed in baking pan in medium oven, baked and basted till done; but five minutes before taking up, sprinkle with sugar to nicely glaze it; serve with Champagne sauce at sides.

ROAST STUFFED HAM—The ham prepared, then boned, the bone holes filled with pork forcemeat, drawn together and tied with string then sewn in a cloth, steamed two-thirds of its cooking time, then finished in medium oven after removing cloth and skin; served with celery sauce or sauce flavored with celery salt.

BRAISED HAM WITH VEGETABLES—Prepared, boned and stuffed as in the preceding, tied in a cloth and boiled till within half an hour of its cooking time, then taken up, cloth and skin removed, placed in a brazier with a pint of Madeira wine, rapidly braised and basted till done and the wine reduced, taken up, Espagnole sauce added to the braise with a little currant jelly, boiled up, strained and skimmed; the ham served in slices with the sauce over or under, garnished with glazed root vegetables.

CROQUETTES OF HAM WITH GREEN PEAS—Cold cooked ham finely cut two-thirds, mixed with one-third of fresh mashed potatoes and a few egg yolks, seasoned with nutmeg and pepper, rolled into the desired shape, breaded, fried; served surrounded with green peas in Velouté sauce.

MINCED HAM WITH EGG—Cold ham trimmings minced, mixed with a seasoning of minced and fried shallots, parsley, cayenne and a little horseradish mustard, moistened with a little sauce or gravy, thoroughly heated; served heaped high on buttered toast, with a poached egg on top, or garnished with slices of hot hard boiled eggs. Creamed young carrots, Parisienne vegetables, jardinière, and asparagus tips also make a desirable garnish for this dish.

HAMBURGER—Or Hamburg steaks are minced beef with a little onion, a suspicion of garlic, salt and pepper seasoning, fried or broiled, and served either plain or with any of the sauces appropriate to steaks.

HAMBURGER—If you follow Fellows's recipe, using good beef—minced not ground—with his simple combination of ingredients, you will recall (or, if you are very young, you will learn) just how delicious the American hamburger once tasted.

TOMATOED HAMBURGER—The same as above but freely mixed with raw tomato meat freed from skin and seeds; should be served with tomato sauce.

HARE—Practically the dark fleshed rabbit which attains a larger size than the common or white fleshed one, and which is also of superior flavor. We commonly call it the "Jack rabbit." The steward should watch to buy young ones only; an old or soft limp one is beyond the chef's ingenuity to prepare for table service and give the patronage satisfaction; the young ones are EASILY told by tearing the ears with the thumb and finger, IF THEY DO NOT TEAR EASILY, LEAVE THEM ALONE.

STUFFED SADDLE OF HARE WITH JELLY—The saddle from the shoulders to the legs, cut in halves across making two portions, boned, stuffed with game or other forcemeat, tied round with twine, arranged in baking pan, each piece covered with a slice of fat pork, roasted and basted till done, taken up, little brown sauce added to the pan, boiled up, strained and skimmed, then poured to the hare; served with red currant jelly and garnished with fancy croûtons.

FILLETS OF HARE, POIVRADE SAUCE—The legs and saddles marinaded for two hours in a little white wine with slices of carrot and onion, salt, pepper and nutmeg, the whole then placed in a saûtoir with a little fat pork, lid put on, placed in hot oven, roasted and basted till done, about 45 minutes, taken up, poivrade sauce added to the residue, boiled up, strained and skimmed; served with the fillets, garnished with croûtons.

BRAISED HARE WITH GAME CROQUETTES—The legs and saddles prepared as in the preceding, the fore quarters of the hare used to make the croquettes; served, the fillets on a fancy bed of mashed potatoes, the sauce around, garnished with the croquettes.

CIVET OF HARE, HUNTER'S STYLE—The shoulders are the best for this dish, slices of bacon blanched, then cut into even sized small pieces and fried, the hare rolled in flour and fried lightly in the bacon fat, both then put into a saûtoir; to the remaining fat flour is added to form a roux, moistened with stock and red wine, boiled up, skimmed, then strained over the meat, to which is added a bunch of sweet herbs, parsley, onions, salt, pepper and a few whole cloves, simmered till done, hare and bacon then taken up into the serving pan, the sauce further thickened with the liver made into a paste, and the blood (it must not be boiled after the blood is in) then strained over the meat; served, garnished with fried button mushrooms and small onions that have been blanched, then fried.

FILLETS OF HARE, SAUTÉS—The legs and saddles trimmed, then fried with butter, or bacon fat, taken up into a saûtoir, moistened with Bourgignotte sauce, simmered till tender; served garnished with croûtons and slices of truffles on the hare.

FRIED FILLETS OF HARE—The legs and saddles trimmed, then fried with butter, taken up into a saû-toir, moistened with game gravy, simmered a little while; served garnished with small poached quenelles made from the forequarters.

LARDED SADDLES OF HARE—The saddles boned and trimmed, tied into shape with twine, larded with seasoned strips of pork, rolled in buttered paper, roasted till done, taken up, paper removed, rolled in game glaze; served on fancy shaped toast with Poivrade sauce poured around.

JUGGED HARE—The hare cut into fillets and boned, the bones and head pounded, then boiled with vegetables in stock and red wine, the fillets lightly fried in bacon fat; stone crock lined with bacon, the fillets put in, the bone liquor thickened, strained over the meat, baked slowly till tender (about three hours); when done, grease skimmed off; served. It may also be made in individual dishes and served in the one it was baked in.

FILLETS OF HARE, TOMATO SAUCE—The legs and saddles larded and braised; when done, the braise strained and skimmed, added to a rich tomato sauce; served with the meat, garnished with croûtons.

CUTLETS OF HARE, PIQUANTE SAUCE—The legs fried in butter, then simmered in game gravy till tender, taken up and cooled, then breaded and fried, Piquante sauce made from the gravy they were simmered in; served with the cutlets, garnished with slices of stoned olives.

SCALLOPS OF HARE WITH FINE HERBS—Fillets of hare cut into scallops, flattened, trimmed, sautéed in clear butter, taken up into a fines-herbes sauce to which is added button mushrooms, simmered till done; served piled high in centre of dish, garnished with small cone shaped croquettes made from the inferior parts.

SCALLOPS OF HARE WITH TONGUE, SAUCE PERIGUEUX—Prepared and sautéed as in the preceding recipe, taken up into a Perigueux sauce; served piled high in centre of dish with circles of tongue overlapping each other around the base, garnished with small croquettes as in the preceding.

HERRING—The Lake Superior herring is the best for filleting, as its fillets are boneless; the fresh water herring of the lower lakes is not so! The blue backs or sea herrings are packed into barrels and shipped all over the States when in season, which is a very short one.

HERRING—The Clupeidae family, of which herring are a member, also includes SHAD, alewife, sardine, sprat, and pilchard. Some live in fresh water, some the ocean, some part of their lives in each. The population of Atlantic herring (which Fellows calls the sea herring) spans the entire North Atlantic from Gibraltar to North Carolina and as far north as the Arctic Sea (where the Atlantic herring migrates to Alaskan and Siberian shores).

Every country that borders the North Atlantic save one—the United States—has long relished this fish fresh and enjoyed it in a variety of ways. Here, only the immature herring are used, canned as sardines in Maine and California. But elsewhere, the fat flesh of the herring has been salted, pickled, baked, grilled, sautéed, boiled, marinated, smoked, and potted. Kippers are herring, as are matjes, schmaltz, and BLOATERS. They traditionally have been the plentiful fish of the European working classes, flavorful and inexpensive.

Unfortunately, like so many other fish, the herring population is in decline, so this cheap, enjoyable staple of years gone by has become a luxury. But herring are still cheap enough to enjoy, pickled, with raw onions, on the end of a toothpick, on many Amsterdam street corners, or creamed in sour cream.

BOILED FRESH HERRING, SHRIMP SAUCE—Prepare by cutting off the head and fins, then scale, draw, wash and score the sides, put into boiling salted water and simmer for 15 minutes, take up, drain; serve with shrimp sauce.

BROILED FRESH HERRING, MUSTARD SAUCE—Prepared herrings marinaded for an hour in olive oil seasoned with salt and pepper, taken up, broiled; serve with a good anchovy sauce finished with mustard and lemon juice.

FRIED FRESH HERRINGS, MUSTARD BUTTER—Prepared herrings seasoned, rolled in flour, fried in clarified butter, served spread with melted butter mixed with mustard, garnished with parsley and lemon.

BOILED FRESH HERRINGS, CREAM SAUCE—Prepared herrings boiled in salted water slowly for 15 minutes, taken up, drained; served with cream sauce poured over.

BAKED FRESH HERRINGS, FENNEL SAUCE—Prepared herrings arranged in baking pan with a few bay leaves, moisten slightly with equal parts of fish broth and vinegar, baked and basted till done, taken up; served with a spoonful of the liquor over them, fennel sauce at the sides.

BAKED STUFFED HERRING—Prepared herrings filleted and boned; spread with fish forcemeat, the two sides then again put together as if the fish was sandwiched with farce, arranged in buttered baking pan, baked and basted; served with a maître d'hôtel sauce.

CURRIED FRESH HERRINGS, WITH EGGS—Boneless sides of herrings sautéed in clarified butter, taken up into a curry sauce made from fish broth, simmered a few minutes, taken up, coated with sauce; served on a long strip of toast, garnished with slices of hot hard boiled eggs. (Good dish for Fridays.)

BONED FRESH HERRING ON TOAST—Split, boned, sprinkled with pepper, salt, thyme, rolled from tail to head, tied with twine or tape, baked in court-bouillon with a dash of tarragon vinegar; served on circles of toast with lemon parsley sauce.

SOUSED HERRINGS—Scale and draw the fish, cut off the heads, wash and drain, arrange in porcelain lined baking pans, seasoned with salt and pepper, ground allspice, a few bay leaves and shallots, moisten to two-thirds of their height with white wine vinegar, cover with another pan, place in oven and bake very slowly for an hour; served cold, wiped dry, garnished with watercress.

HICKORY—Name of one of the common nuts, also called Pecans; used in cake making, decorating, flavoring, etc.

HICKORY—Pecan is a variety of hickory; there are other hickory nuts as well, almost all of them edible, and all related to the walnut. Hickory is an important wood in smoking meats and fish, especially in the South.

HOE CAKES—Name of a Southern pancake made of ground maize, salt and water.

HOMINY—Is hulled maize, marketed in different grades as to size; the large is generally known as "hulled corn," is boiled like rice and served with milk; or boiled very soft, turned out into a buttered pan, when cold, cut into strips rolled in flour (never bread it), fried a delicate brown and served either as a garnish, or for breakfast with maple syrup. When boiling hominy which is to be fried, always add towards the finish, some flour, as that will hold it together and stop it from breaking and spitting when being fried.

HOMINY—Hominy is dried corn kernels that are most often soaked in a solution of lye. The purpose of this treatment is to remove the germs and hulls. This staple of the South with the bastardized Algonquin name (originally *rockahominy*) is also known as *pozole* in the Southwest and *nixtamal* in Mexico—where it is used to make masa, the meal that forms the basis of tortillas. Hominy (with the germ removed) is usually ground into grits, which is in turn made into cooked breakfast cereal. Except for in that very specific use, cornmeal may be substituted for grits in any recipe. Hominy is featured in stews in the Southwest and occasionally in casseroles in the Deep South.

BOILED HOMINY—A breakfast cereal: fine hominy soaked overnight, boiled for two hours in a farina kettle; served with cream and sugar.

HORSERADISH BUTTER

·

Makes about 1¼ pounds

Flavored butters in cooking have become quite popular in our time. The concept is nothing new, however, as this is an old recipe. It is very versatile and convenient to use.

1 pound salted butter, softened	2 teaspoons Worcestershire sauce
½ cup prepared horseradish (you want hot stuff!)	2 tablespoons chopped parsley

In a mixing bowl, beat all the ingredients together well. (An electric mixer works best.)

Place a few large sheets of plastic wrap overlapping each other on the counter. Place the butter in a line on the plastic so you can form a log about 12 inches long and 2 inches in diameter. Fold the plastic over and work the butter into the desired shape with your hands. Place the log in the freezer until ready to use.

To serve, cut off a slice of butter ⅛ inch thick and top just about any grilled food. This compound butter will melt on the freshly grilled food as you serve it. Great on steaks! The butter will keep in the freezer a long time.

C.W.

HOMINY CROQUETTES—The preceding when boiled mixed with a little grated cheese and flour, beaten egg yolks, salt and red pepper, poured into buttered pan, when cold, made into form, breaded and fried.

HORSERADISH—Name of a pungent root, grated fine and used as a table condiment, and in flavoring sauces; as a condiment is best as follows: One pint of grated horseradish, one-half a pint of white wine vinegar, salt, little sugar, mix and use.

HORSERADISH—More and more you can buy fresh horseradish (*Armoracia rusticana*), a long, ugly-looking root, and grate it yourself. But beware: Tears will come to your eyes, and you will be surprised at how quickly the essential oils evaporate and this superhot substance becomes tame. That is why it is usually dried or preserved as in Fellows's preparation.

Dried horseradish, which is reconstituted with water before use, actually retains more fierceness than horseradish stored any other way. Wasabi, the green "mustard" served with sushi, is a type of re-

HOT POT OR HOTCH POTCH

•

Serves 8 to 10

This thick soup can have just about anything in it. It is rich in flavor due to the combination of vegetables. Mr. Fellows's recipe firmly states, "No spices." You may want to break the rules, since this is, after all, a Hotch Potch!

3/4 pound bulk pork sausage

1 1/2 pounds beef stew meat, cut into 1-inch pieces

1 1/2 cups peeled and diced carrots

1 medium yellow onion, peeled and sliced

1 cup cored and diced green sweet bell pepper

2 cups green cabbage, cut like coleslaw

2 cups chopped ripe tomatoes

6 cups water

1/2 cup long-grain rice

1 1/2 cups peeled, seeded, and chopped cucumber

1/2 pound asparagus, cut into 1-inch pieces

1 cup frozen peas, thawed

Salt and freshly ground black pepper to taste

Preheat the oven to 275° F.

Form the sausage into 1/2-inch balls. In a nonstick frying pan, brown the sausage balls for 3 to 4 minutes. Drain the fat.

In a 6- to 8-quart pot, combine the browned sausage balls, beef, carrots, onions, green peppers, cabbage, and tomatoes. Add the water and bring to a boil. Cover and bake for 2 hours.

Stir in the rice and cucumbers. Continue to bake, covered, for 15 minutes more. Add the asparagus and peas and bake, covered, for 5 minutes more. Remove from the oven. Salt and pepper to taste. If the rice is not tender yet, simmer on the stove top until done.

C.W.

constituted dried horseradish (fresh wasabi is almost never seen in this country).

For a quick horseradish sauce to serve with meats or fish, add prepared or dried horseradish, to taste, to mayonnaise and/or sour cream.

HORSERADISH BUTTER—Equal parts of grated horseradish and butter well pounded together with a seasoning of salt and lemon juice, then rubbed through a fine sieve; served spread over broiled steaks.

HOT POT OR HOTCH POTCH—A soup stew made and baked in a pot as follows: take a large earthern crock, into it put four lbs. of lean beef trimmings cut into inch pieces, one lb. of small balls of pork sausage meat, one-half a cupful of sliced onions, one cupful each of sliced and peeled cucumbers, carrots and asparagus points, one pint each of green peas and skinned tomatoes, a handful of washed rice, one cupful of chopped green peppers and a small heart of cabbage shredded, season with salt and pepper (NO SPICES), add four gallons of cold water, place on the crock cover, put in a moderate oven at 6 a.m. and it will be ready for 12 o'clock dinner.

Another hot pot is made with scrags of mutton instead of the beef and pork, substituting leeks and barley for the peppers and rice.

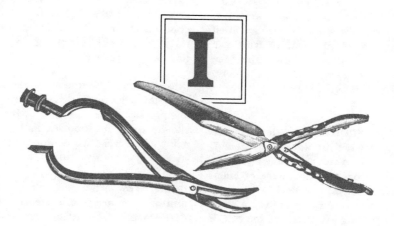

ICE CREAM—See CREAM.

ICES—These include sherbets, cream ices, water ices, etc., in infinite varieties.

CUP ICES—Small fluted cups or glasses filled with fruit syrups and placed in a large tub or tray, with pounded ice and salt around them; when frozen a sufficient thickness, the remaining liquor poured out, the cups then replaced so as to solidify the part where the liquid remained, the cups then turned out, filled with any form of ice different in color to the cup.

ORANGE ICES—Oranges with a slice cut to form a lid, the interior and pith scooped out, the skins then soaked in water for an hour, then dried and filled with orange water ice mixed with French fruits

glacés that have been soaked in a liqueur; they are then frozen and served.

IMPERIAL ICES—Ice cups made as above, then filled with Strawberry Water Ice flavored with Champagne, Pineapple Water Ice flavored with Santa Cruz rum, Cherry Water Ice flavored with Noyeaux, etc.

FANCY WATER ICES—Freeze solidly all forms of water ices in equal quantities, such as Nut Cream Ice, Madeira Ice, Claret Ice, Pistachio Cream, Raspberry and Strawberry Water Ices, Curaçao Cream Ice, Orange and Lemon Ices, Cherry Water Ice, Caramel Cream Ice, etc., then fill individual forms in shapes of fruit and flowers, close the molds, pack, freeze, turn out and serve.

The same to be done with all kinds of ice creams such as Vanilla, Cherry, Chocolate, Tea, Coffee, Currant, Grape, Chestnut, Almond, Pistachio, Noyeaux, filled into individual forms of fruit and flowers, vegetables, etc., the idea being to have variegated colors, flavors and shapes.

ICED SNOWBALLS—Rice boiled very tender, in water, sweetened, flavored with orange or lemon juice, frozen in the shape of balls, then taken out, rolled in whipped cream, served if possible in a shallow green glass dish, the top of the ball sparingly spotted with green pistachio gratings.

NEAPOLITAN BRICKS—Brick molds filled in three colors of ice cream or one of them may be water ice, so as when cut to show three distinct layers, frozen solid, turned out, cut in slices.

ICE FROTHS—Fancy shaped glasses filled with whipped cream piled high, sweetened, frozen; served in the same glasses.

IRISH MOSS—An edible seaweed, gelatinous, reddish brown in color, good for those with delicate digestions in blanc-mange, creams, flawns, farinas, etc.

IRISH MOSS—Also known as carrageen, this seaweed is currently used to produce carrageenan, which gives a thick, gelatinous quality to many commercial ice creams.

IRISH STEW—The neck chops of mutton that are under the shoulder, trimmed, gristle removed, boiled with the shanks from the legs and shoulders and other mutton trimmings till half done, taken up and stewed with potatoes and onions till tender in the strained and skimmed stock from the boiling, seasoned with salt and pepper, lightly thickened; served sprinkled with chopped parsley.

ISINGLASS—A form of gelatine prepared from the swim bladder of the sturgeon; more expensive than gelatine without any appreciable better results.

JELLY—A clarified, gelatinous combination of sugar, water, spices and colorings, flavored with wine, fruit juices, etc.; also made from calf's feet (see CALF). To make the stock jelly use 2 qts. of water or fruit juices, 3 ozs. of dissolved gelatine, the grated rind and juice of 4 lemons, 1 lb. of granulated sugar, the broken whites and shells of 6 eggs, mix well, bring to the simmer; after it coagulates, allow the scum to assume a grey color, so as to perfectly clarify, then strain through a flannel bag three times and use for the following recipes.

FRUIT JELLY—Stock jelly flavored with sherry wine, fancy molds filled an inch deep, allowed to set, then fruit arranged as a border; if currants or grapes arranged in bunches; molds then gradually filled with limpid jelly and set.

FRUIT JELLY—Fellows's old-fashioned fruit jelly recipes have little in common with the way most of us make jams and jellies today. But stock jelly, once a staple, produces a rich, flavorful jam that has real body.

WEST INDIAN JELLY—Stock jelly strongly flavored with Jamaica rum, fancy molds filled an inch deep and allowed to set, slices of bananas and sections of seeded oranges then arranged as a border, jellied and set, the mold then filled with limpid jelly, set, turned out and served.

RIBBON JELLY—Stock jelly in three parts, one colored with strawberry juice, one with caramel and flavored with brandy, the third whipped to a froth on ice, and flavored with benedictine, arranged in molds with six layers, each to be set before the other is put in, commence with the red, then the whipped, and lastly the caramel. These three colors and flavors look well in three triangles as follows: hold the mold so that you form a triangle shape of red jelly, set that, then reverse the side and form a triangle with the caramel, that leaves a wedge shape from the tip to the base, then fill up with the whipped jelly.

PINEAPPLE JELLY—Stock jelly flavored with Noyeaux, the mold filled with it and pieces of pine-apple.

STRAWBERRY JELLY—Stock jelly flavored with strawberry juice, the mold filled with it and whole straw-berries.

RASPBERRY JELLY—Stock jelly flavored with red raspberry juice, the mold filled with it and whole raspberries.

BLACKBERRY JELLY—For this use a border mold, and when turned out, fill the centre with whipped cream.

APRICOT JELLY—Stock jelly flavored with maraschino, the mold filled with it and halves of peeled apricots.

MACEDOINE JELLY—Stock jelly flavored with maraschino, the mold filled with it and small whole fruits.

RUSSIAN JELLY—Stock jelly flavored with liqueur, then whipped

to a froth on ice, filled into molds and set.

PISTACHIO JELLY—Stock jelly flavored with Dantzic brandy, mold filled half an inch deep, shredded pistachios then strewn in, the mold then filled in with layers of jelly strewn with pistachios.

ORANGE JELLY—When making the stock jelly add the grated rinds of oranges and a little cochineal to give it the orange tint; when done and strained, fill into molds.

LEMON JELLY—Made the same as orange jelly except use grated lemon rinds, and omit the cochineal.

JERUSALEM ARTICHOKES—Although the tuber of this native American sunflower has become increasingly popular in cooking, the name remains confusing. It makes perfect sense in Latin (*Helianthus tuberosus*); the Indians also had a logical name for it: sunroot. But Jerusalem artichoke, for reasons that remain unclear (despite hundreds of attempts at demystification), is the name that has stuck. The tuber's more aggressive marketers have tried sunchoke, and those who like mystery choose *topinambour,* the name of a Brazilian tribe that arrived in Paris at the same time as the, er, *Helianthus tuberosus,* which resembles a knob of ginger. In any case the Jerusalem artichoke is not even remotely related to the ARTI-CHOKE, although the taste, texture, and grayish color of its flesh are reminiscent of the edible thistle.

Nomenclature aside, the Jerusalem artichoke is one of the most delicious of our underutilized vegetables. It shines in most potato recipes (including potato pancakes) and often outdoes its more popular cousin, with its subtle, nutty flavor and superb, luxurious creaminess. For simple preparations wash or peel the tubers, parboil for a couple of minutes, slice thinly, then sauté in olive oil with garlic until nicely browned or layer with a bit of butter, top with grated Parmesan cheese, and run under the broiler until golden.

JULIENNE—Name applied to a garnish of shredded root vegetables, also to shredded potatoes.

JUNIPER—Name of a blue berry used for flavoring gin; also adds a nice flavor to corned meat when a muslin bagful of crushed berries is added to the brine.

JUNIPER—A spice that should be featured more often in strong-flavored marinades, juniper berries (of which *Juniperus communis* is the most widely picked) grow on several varieties of evergreen trees throughout the Northern Hemisphere. It is the dominant flavor in gin and is traditionally used in game dishes (in fact, its exotic flavor is often described as "gamy").

KALE—A vegetable in appearance like endive, and in taste like green cabbage, cooked the same as spinach.

KALE—Kale (*Brassica oleracea acephala*) is darker than ENDIVE, far stronger tasting than CABBAGE, and requires more cooking time than spinach. Quite bitter except when very young (or when harvested after a frost), kale is extremely high in calcium, iron, and vitamins A and C, and tolerates an almost unbelievably wide range of temperatures. It can survive frost and thrives in southern heat; it has long been a staple food in the South. In fact, countless European peasants relied upon kale for much-needed nutrition through hard winter months in centuries gone by.

Kale is one of the oldest of cabbages and is closely related not only to collards and mustard but to BROCCOLI and CAULIFLOWER. Home gardeners can include kale leaves in salads when the leaves are very young and tiny. When older, the leaves should be steamed, boiled, or sautéed as any other green. Kale is excellent when prepared as collards are in the South.

Kale also makes an excellent soup green and is a good addition to stir-fries (cut it into small pieces first). Finally, kale can be stir-fried on its own: Wash the leaves and dry them quickly, roll them up, and cut through the roll. Then stir-fry in a bit of oil with some garlic and soy sauce or red pepper; if you use more oil, the dish becomes a fast, nutritious topping for pasta.

KHULASH OR GOULASH—Name of a ragout much esteemed by the Hungarians; made by taking pieces of beef and sautéing them with onions in butter, seasoning with salt and paprika, moistened with brown sauce, simmered till tender;

served garnished with Hollandaise or Parisienne potatoes.

KIDNEYS—Recipes will be found under the name of the animal to which it belongs.

KINGFISH—Name of a Southern fish, exquisite in flavor, and of a nice size for restaurant and club service.

KINGFISH—More formally known as king mackerel (*Scomberomorus cavalla*), kingfish has dark-gray, almost blue flesh that is strong, sweet, and fine-grained. The fish, which is found along the Atlantic coast south of North Carolina, is sleek and large and usually weighs over twenty pounds. It is frequently cut into steaks and, although it can be grilled or broiled with no further adornment, it is best when marinated in lime juice, garlic, and a sprinkling of red pepper for an hour or two first. Kingfish can also be cooked successfully by following any recipe for MACKEREL.

BOILED KINGFISH, SAUCE NORMANDE—The fish prepared, boiled in salted water with a dash of vinegar, when done, drained; served with Normande sauce, garnished with Hollandaise potatoes.

KINGFISH WITH FINE HERBS—Prepared and trimmed, arranged in buttered baking pan, baked and basted with butter; served with fines-herbes sauce, garnished with Julienne potatoes.

BROILED KINGFISH, LEMON BUTTER—Prepared and trimmed, split down the front, laid open and the backbone removed, seasoned with salt and pepper, rolled in flour, brushed with butter, broiled and basted till done; served spread with maître d'hôtel butter, garnished with chip potatoes, lemon and parsley.

KINGFISH SAUTÉ, SAUCE COLBERT—Boneless sides of the fish seasoned with salt and pepper, rolled in flour, sautéed with butter a delicate brown; served with Colbert sauce and garnished with Colbert potatoes.

FRIED FILLETS OF KINGFISH, BREADCRUMBED—Boneless sides of the fish seasoned with salt and pepper, rolled in flour, dipped in beaten eggs, then breadcrumbs, fried; served with maître d'hôtel butter, garnished with lemon and parsley.

KIRSCHWASSER—Name of a liqueur made from cherry juice; obtained by crushing the fruit, stones and kernels, then fermenting; used as a flavoring to sherbets, cakes, icings, ices and confectionery.

KOHL-RABI—Name of the cabbage turnip; may be peeled, boiled, mashed and seasoned same as turnip; or, as is best, peeled, cut in quarters, boiled in salted water till done, drained, then simmered in butter sauce a few minutes before serving.

KOHLRABI—Another member of the enormous Brassica family, kohlrabi (*Brassica oleracea gonglylodes*) closely resembles a turnip in flavor, although it is sweeter and can be eaten raw.

Many people who see kohlrabi in either its green or purple form may admire its looks but haven't a clue as to how to cook it. The Germans use it, as do Eastern Europeans, Middle Easterners, and Asians, but it has never made much of an impact in the West.

Kohlrabi is actually quite good. Cut off the leaves—which can be cooked separately if they are young and healthy looking—and peel it, then steam it, and serve it as you would cauliflower.

KOUMISS—A milk preparation tasting like buttermilk, used as a health beverage; made by filling quart champagne bottles up to the neck with pure milk to which is added a syrup made by dissolving two tablespoonfuls of white sugar in one of water, also ¼ of a 2-cent cake of yeast; corked and tied securely, shaken well, stood for six hours in a warm room, then cooled overnight by placing in ice box.

KOUMISS—This digestible beverage originated in what is now Mongolia and reportedly was drunk by Genghis Khan (in those days it was made from mare's milk). It is mildly alcoholic.

KROMESKIES—Name applied to any form of croquette mixture made into form of corks, finger lengths, wrapped in a thin shaving of cold boiled bacon, dipped in batter and fried.

KROMESKIES—See CROMESKIES.

KUMMEL—Name of a liqueur prepared from cumin and caraway seeds in sweetened spirit.

KUMMEL—Kummel is also the German word for "caraway."

LAKE SUPERIOR HERRING—See CISCO.

LAMB—Young lamb is mild, succulent, tender, and juicy. It frequently can (and should) be cooked as rare as a fine piece of beef. Many people consider lamb the best domesticated meat there is. However, too many Americans have sampled only older lamb, further insulted by overcooking and a mint jelly garnish.

For the record: The term *spring lamb* is virtually meaningless. The official definition, written by the U.S. Department of Agriculture, allows "only" those lambs marketed between the first Monday in March and the second Monday in October to be sold as spring lamb, as if spring were seven months long.

"Genuine" lamb—under one year old—is available year-round. But the best widely sold lamb is probably that found in supermarkets in late spring and early summer. The smallest legs may come from lambs

as young as four months, and are worth looking for. This lamb is still ancient by European standards, where age is measured in weeks rather than months, but it is young enough to be perceptibly milder and more tender than that sold in the winter months.

All of this is contrary to what was thought during Fellows's time. Then, any lamb fewer than two years old was considered flavorless, and good MUTTON—as mature sheep meat is called—could be five years old. Such meat *is* good, especially when stewed; lamb, like any animal meat, becomes tougher yet more flavorful with age.

The other extreme is milk-fed lamb, slaughtered at three or four weeks, weighing a mere ten pounds or so, and the rough equivalent of a suckling pig. Called *agnelet* in France and *abbacchio* in Italy, it is usually roasted while being basted with a strong sauce; in fact, milk-fed lamb is not especially flavorful.

CUTS OF LAMB
and where they come from

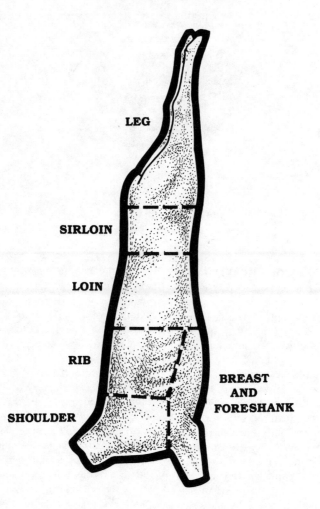

LEG

SIRLOIN

LOIN

RIB

SHOULDER

BREAST
AND
FORESHANK

All in all young lamb is preferable for most purposes. In addition to the more popular cuts, try lamb riblets, every bit as good as pork ribs; ground lamb, which makes a tasty burger; shanks, which are inexpensive and wonderful when braised; and lamb stew, which may be cooked with an infinite variety of spices.

ROAST LAMB—Any joint roasted a quarter of an hour to each pound in weight in a medium oven; must be frequently basted; about 10 minutes before taking up, should be dredged with flour and basted with melted butter, so as to take on a delicate color; served either with mint sauce or currant jelly in separate dishes, with a spoonful of gravy under the meat.

BRAISED LAMB—The shoulder lifted off and boned, leaving the shank for a handle, lay it out flat, season with salt and pepper, spread with forcemeat, roll up, tie in neat shape, braise it with vegetables; served with the strained and skimmed braise, or with a garnish of turned vegetables—green peas, glazed columns of turnips, stuffed egg plant and okras, Brussels sprouts, Milanaise garnish, asparagus, larded lamb's sweetbreads, etc.

BOILED LAMB—The legs simmered in white stock with a bunch of sweet herbs till done, allowing 12 minutes to the pound; served with cream sauce, caper sauce, spinach purée, sorrel purée, haricots verts, shred wax or stringless beans, macedoine of vegetables, asparagus tips.

SAUTÉ OF LAMB—The shoulder boned and cut into neat pieces, sautéed with minced onions and a flavoring of garlic in butter, raw skinned tomatoes cut in halves, and lightly fried with butter, taken up and added to the lamb, the whole then cooked for 20 minutes; served garnished with fancy croûtons.

BLANQUETTE OF LAMB—The breast or boned shoulder cut in neat pieces, seasoned with salt and white pepper, rolled in flour, quickly without coloring, sauté them with butter and a few minced shallots, take up into a saûtoir, make a cream sauce in the butter, etc., they were sautéed in, strain over the lamb, simmer till done, adding some button mushrooms and a little chopped parsley; serve in a casserole, or with a border of fancy mashed potatoes.

EPIGRAMME OF LAMB—Breasts of lamb simmered in seasoned white stock till the bones are easily removed (keeping the little rib bones), press the breasts; when cold, trim and cut into cutlet shapes, point the rib bones and insert into the pieces of lamb, bread and fry one-half of them, roll in flour and sauté with butter the other half; served at the side of a croûstade filled with garnish, and a sauce at the sides; the sautéed one should be brushed with light colored glaze; the croûstade may be filled with Toulouse garnish, sautéed lamb fries, macédoine of vegetables, green peas, asparagus tips, button mushrooms, diced lamb sweetbreads or brains, etc.

FRICASSÉE OF LAMB—Breast of lamb cut into neat pieces, seasoned with salt and pepper, rolled in flour, sautéed lightly with butter, taken up into a saûtoir, moistened with thin white sauce, simmered till done, skimmed, sauce then thickened with a liaison of egg yolks and cream, seasoned with nutmeg and cayenne; served with a garnish of green peas, inverted molds of dry boiled rice, macedoine of vegetables.

CURRIED LAMB—Cold roast lamb cut into neat pieces with the skin removed; curry sauce made from lamb or mutton stock, simmered in it till thoroughly heated; served within a border of dry boiled rice.

CURRIED LAMB—Rack of lamb cut into chops, trimmed, sautéed with minced shallots, taken up into a saûtoir, sprinkled with flour and curry powder, seasoned with salt, lemon juice and a dash of cayenne, moistened with white stock, simmered with a sprig of green mint till done, mint then removed; served within a border of rice, potatoes, green peas, button mushrooms, etc.

STEWED LAMB—Scrag of lamb and the chops from under the shoulder cut in neat pieces, simmered in white stock till done, sauce made of the broth; served with a sprinkling of parsley and a garnish of vegetables.

CUTLETS OF LAMB—The rack of lamb cut into chops and trimmed, then either breaded after seasoning, sautéed; spread on one side after lightly broiling with forcemeat or D'Uxelles dressing, then finished in oven; served with a garnish of green peas, or any of the following: asparagus points, macedoine, button mushrooms in sauce, maître d'hôtel butter, Printanière, Villeroi sauce, Godard garnish, slices of stuffed cucumber, Toulouse or Financière garnish, small new potatoes, purée of mint, stuffed tomatoes, purée of peas and Béchamel sauce, green peas and caper sauce, peas and asparagus points in Béchamel, Julienne vegetables in Madeira sauce, sauté of small new carrots cooked whole and seasoned with lemon juice, sugar and chopped parsley, purée of peas and the sautéed cutlets dipped in glaze, the cutlets larded, dipped in Perigord sauce, then breaded and fried; served with truffle sauce, Italian style *i.e.* sautéed in butter just enough to set them, dipped in Italian sauce thickened with Parmesan cheese, when cooled, breaded and fried; served with Italian sauce; they may also be first set by lightly sautéing, then dipping into appropriate lamb sauces, cooling, breading, frying and serving with a sauce the same as they were coated with.

EMINCE OF LAMB—Cold leg or shoulder of lamb cut in thin slices, then again into circles with a large column cutter, reheated with butter over a quick fire, seasoned with salt, pepper and powdered mint, then drained; into the butter is then placed some minced shallots; when lightly browned, flour added to form a roux, moistened with mutton broth, seasoned with salt, nutmeg, pepper, herbs and a dash of Worcestershire sauce, boiled five minutes, then strained over the lamb, which simmer for fifteen minutes; served on toast.

HASHED LAMB WITH POACHED EGG—Roast lamb trimmings chopped fine and seasoned with salt, pepper and finely chopped green mint, moistened with thickened roast lamb gravy, fetched to the simmering point; served on a slice of toast, garnished with triangles of buttered toast on which is a trimmed poached egg.

RAGOUT OF LAMB—The breast, chops under the shoulder, and the scrag, neatly cut and trimmed, fried a light color with butter, taken up, very small whole onions then fried in the butter, taken up and added to the lamb, flour then added to the butter to form a roux, moistened with white stock, seasoned with salt, pepper, pot herbs and a crushed clove of garlic, boiled, skimmed, strained over the lamb and onions, simmer till done; served with a border of fancy vegetables, macedoine, mushroom sautés, green peas, flageolets, new lima beans, Parisienne potatoes, small stuffed tomatoes, etc.

STEWED LAMB, GARNISHED—Preferably use the centre cuts of the breasts, boil them with a bunch of green mint in seasoned white stock; when done, taken up and the bones removed, placed in a colander and washed with hot water to remove any scum; white sauce made from the broth, seasoned with salt, red pepper, lemon juice and nutmeg; when done, strained over the washed lamb in a saûtoir, simmer, skim; serve sprinkled with parsley dust and garnished with small new potatoes of even size, green peas, asparagus points, mushrooms sautés, small stuffed tomatoes, small rice timbales, forcemeat balls, a jardinière of vegetables, mixed haricots, potato croquettes, French beans, etc.

LAMB'S FRIES—The testicles blanched and trimmed, cut in halves, skinned, seasoned with salt, pepper, nutmeg and lemon juice, rolled in flour, then breaded and fried; served with tomato, Bearnaise, remoulade and trianon sauces, or on a bed of mashed potatoes and flanked with peas, flageolets, etc. May also be broiled and served on toast with maître d'hôtel butter, Tartar or Bearnaise sauces, also fricasséed and served with a garnish suitable to sweetbreads.

SCALLOPS OF LAMB WITH RICE—Take cold lamb and cut into pieces the size of half dollars, simmer them in Velouté sauce seasoned with a little nutmeg. To serve: arrange some hot boiled rice grains around the edge of a platter, place the lamb in the centre and sprinkle with parsley dust, garnish the rice with scallops of red tongue reheated with a little butter.

LAMB SWEETBREADS IN CASES—Cooked lamb sweetbreads cut in dice two-thirds, diced mushrooms one-third, mixed, simmered in thick Velouté sauce, filled into buttered paper cases or croûstades, sprinkle with breadcrumbs, browned in a quick oven and served.

LASAGNES—Name of an Italian paste in the form of yellow ribbon, often used as noodles in soups, garnishes, etc.

LASAGNE—See PASTA.

LEEK—A plant of the onion species having a non-bulbous root and flat broad leaves; in flavor a cross between the onion and garlic; very valuable as a soup stock flavoring.

LEEK—Leeks (*Allium porrum*) are the sweetest and mildest members of the onion family. Here and in England they are usually grown until they are quite large (there are competitions at English fairs), and are used almost exclusively to make vichyssoise (cold leek and potato soup). The leek is also a national symbol of Wales. But in many European countries they are considered a prime vegetable and are eaten when they are small, tender, tastier, and less gritty (all leeks must be washed thoroughly before using). Then they are baked, served like asparagus, used in pies, quiches, tarts, and puddings, sautéed with mushrooms, and, of course, used in soups and stews.

BOILED LEEKS—Young leeks trimmed and washed, tied in small bundles like asparagus, cooked till tender in boiling salted water, taken up and drained; served on toast with melted butter, Béchamel sauce or meat gravy.

LEEK SOUP, SCOTCH STYLE—Leeks trimmed and washed, cut into pieces an inch and a half long, boiled in equal parts of chicken broth and beef stock, oatmeal added, seasoned with salt and pepper, simmered till done, skimmed, finished with a liaison of egg yolks and cream.

LEMONS—This country consumes in a year about 500,000,000 lemons, or about six and a half lemons for each man, woman and child. The California lemons are very good ones, and only experts can tell them from the Mediterranean crop. For culinary purposes the lemons of Sicily, i.e. from Messina and Palermo, are to be preferred as they possess a much better flavor. A box of lemons averages about 300 each. From 1,500,000 to 2,000,000 boxes are sold in a year here. It is predicted that the California crop will soon average 1,000,000 boxes. It will be interesting to note whether they will drive out any or all of the foreign lemons. They are used by the catering fraternity in large quantities for flavoring and garnishing soups, sauces, salads, meats, fish, pies, puddings, cakes, jellies, extracts, confectionery, mixing with drinks, ices, sorbets, creams, etc.

LEMONS—Undoubtedly Asian in origin—India seems the most likely place—lemons (*Citrus limon*) are now grown in temperate climates (but not tropical ones, as are LIMES) worldwide. They are arguably the most important citrus fruit, at least in cooking. Once, as an anti-scorbutic (taken, as they said in Fellows's time, "to cleanse the blood of scurvy"), limes, lemons, or both were critically important to health (they are high in vitamin C), especially in late winter, when fresh meat, fruit, and vegetables were scarce, and for sailors on long ocean voyages.

The lemon is an ingredient—like garlic and olive oil—the absence of which from the kitchen would be painful. It is essential in many marinades, is pleasant in salad dressings, complements and even enhances the flavor of most vegetables (where, these days, it frequently fills in for butter as a quick topping) and sweet fruits (which it also preserves: Rub the surfaces of cut fruit with lemon and they will not brown; add lemon juice to fruit salad and colors will remain vivid). Around the world lemon juice is used in sauces (including avgolemono, the Greek egg-lemon sauce), to "cook" fish (as in seviche), with meats (especially in North African dishes), fish, and countless desserts.

LEMON MARMALADE—Three dozen lemons, their equal weight in granulated sugar, lemons halved and their juice extracted and strained, the rinds boiled till tender in plenty of water, then drained, pith scooped out, the skin then finely shred, the juice and sugar then boiled to a syrup, after which is added the shredded skins, boiling continued till reduced to the marmalade consistency; used for steamed roly-poly puddings, tartlettes, layer cakes, etc., etc.

LEMON MINCEMEAT—Useful for mince pies in temperance hotels and other temperance functions. Made of 2 lbs. of lemons, 4 lbs. of sour apples, 2 lbs. of beef suet, 4 lbs. of currants, 2 lbs. granulated sugar, ½ lb. each of candied citron and lemon peel, 1½ ozs. grated nutmeg, ½ oz. of mace. The apples cored and minced, the candied peels finely shred, the suet finely chopped, the currants washed, picked and drained, the lemons pared and the juice extracted, the

rinds boiled tender, then minced, the whole then thoroughly mixed, allowed to stand a week before using; brandy and port wine may be added if used for other than temperance people.

LEMON CREAM—Two quarts of milk brought to the boil with a pound and a half of sugar; grated rinds of four lemons mixed with six ounces of sifted flour, then made into a smooth thickening with milk; when smooth, poured to the boiling milk and stirred till creamy, then is added three ounces of butter, juice of the lemons and the yolks of 12 beaten eggs, continue stirring till of a custard consistency; then remove and use for filling puffs, eclairs, lemon cream pies, tartlettes, spreading layer cakes, etc.

LEMON SOUP—A rich cream of chicken soup nicely flavored with the grated rinds and juice of lemons.

LEMON SAUCE—Lemons with seeds removed finely minced or passed through a mincing machine, enough of it worked into a Velouté sauce to give a pronounced flavor; used for boiled capons, chickens, turkey and fish.

LEMON TRIFLE—Small glasses with a piece of sponge cake at bottom, spread with lemon marmalade, the glass then filled up high with whipped cream that is sweetened and flavored with nutmeg, and the grated rinds and juice of lemons.

LEMON DUMPLINGS—4 lbs. of grated breadcrumbs, 2 lbs. of finely

LEMON MARMALADE

.

Makes about 3 pints

You will love this tart jelly on your toast in the morning. But please remember that preparing sugar syrups to make jams and jellies can be dangerous; they are extremely hot. Be careful not to burn yourself or anyone else.

8 lemons, quartered
lengthwise

$1^1/_2$ quarts cold water
$1^3/_4$ pounds sugar

Remove the seeds from the lemon quarters. Place the lemon quarters in a 4- to 6-quart pot and add the cold water. Leave the lemons in the water overnight on the counter.

The next day, bring the pot of soaked lemons to a boil. Cover and simmer for 1 hour. Drain, reserving the liquid. Allow the lemons to cool. Using a tablespoon, dig out the pulp and pith and discard. Slice the peel into very fine shreds. Return the reserved liquid to the pot and add the sugar. Simmer gently, uncovered, for 40 minutes. Add the lemon peel and simmer gently for 15 minutes more. Watch the pot closely to prevent its boiling over. Do not brown the syrup. Allow to cool.

Use immediately or pack into jars.

C.W.

chopped beef suet, 2 lbs. of powdered sugar, grated rinds and juice of eight lemons; rinds, crumbs, suet and sugar mixed together dry, the whole then bound with the lemon juice mixed with 18 beaten yolks of eggs; form into dumpling shapes, boil in a cloth, or steam till done (steaming is best); serve with a sweet lemon flavored cream sauce.

LENTILS—Name of a brownish red, flatted small pea, cultivated on the European continent and Asia as a food; it is a most nourishing article, containing about twice as much nourishment as meat.

LENTILS—The dull-brown seed to which Fellows referred is indeed the most familiar lentil (*Lens culinaris*). But there are many others, including the small, dark green, and pricey *lentilles vert du Puy* of France and the lovely orange lentil frequently used to make the dal of Indian cooking. Few of the world's

LEMON TRIFLE

▪

Serves 6 to 8

This is a classic Old World dessert of British origin. It is also known as tipsy cake due to the generous amount of sherry and brandy tasted within. Normally we don't use prepared foods or powder mixes in recipes, but in this case it will save a lot of time, and you'll still have a delicious trifle.

2 (10³/₄-ounce) pound
    cakes (if frozen, thaw)
¹/₂ cup dry sherry
¹/₂ cup brandy
1 recipe Lemon
    Marmalade (page
    286)

2 envelopes Bird's
    Imported English
    Dessert Mix (prepared
    as instructed on the
    box) (found in most
    supermarkets)
2 pints heavy cream
3 tablespoons sugar
1 tablespoon grated lemon
    rind
1 teaspoon vanilla

Break the pound cakes into pieces. Place a layer of cake in the bottom of a large glass bowl. Mix the sherry with the brandy and drizzle half of it over the cake in the bowl. Spread a layer of marmalade over the cake. Spread a layer of custard dessert mix on top of the marmalade. Whip the cream with the remaining ingredients until stiff. Add a layer of whipped cream over the custard. Repeat the layering, finishing with whipped cream. Cover with plastic wrap and refrigerate a few hours.

C.W

cuisines do not have at least one or two recipes for lentils.

Like most BEANS, lentils are a staple rather than a luxury, although they can be dressed up elegantly, especially when used as a flavorful bed for grilled meat or fish. They are among the fastest beans to cook; they require no soaking and most swell and soften within an hour. Be careful when cooking, since lentils will quickly absorb three times their volume in water and will burn if left unattended.

lightly thickened with roux, seasoned with salt, pepper, tomato catsup; served with croûtons.

LENTIL SOUP—Lentils boiled till tender in white stock, with leeks, celery, parsley and a piece of salt pork; when done, pork removed, the soup lightly thickened, then rubbed through the tamis; served with croûtons.

CREAM OF LENTILS—The preceding purée mixed with an equal quantity of Velouté sauce; served with croûtons.

LETTUCE—One of the best of salad plants; seen on our markets in three shapes, called the cabbage lettuce, Cos lettuce and Romaine lettuce.

LETTUCE—Cabbage lettuce, I imagine, is the now-common iceberg; cos (originally from the Mediterranean island of Kos) is the same as romaine. But there are many other salad greens known as lettuce that we can add to this short list: oak leaf, buttercrunch, corn salad (mâche), green-leaf, and red-leaf, for example. In addition, there are a dozen other greens that can—and should—be used in salads: watercress, arugula, spinach, SORREL, PARSLEY, and other herbs, and the young greens of many vegetables.

But lettuce need not be limited to its "highest and best use," which is undoubtedly as a salad green. It makes a decent soup, a good braised vegetable, and is suited for use as a rolled-up holder for other foods, like a tortilla.

LETTUCE SALAD—Well washed, wiped and shred lettuce leaves sprinkled and tossed with French dressing.

LETTUCE AND ONION SALAD—Same as the preceding, adding very finely shred spring onions.

LETTUCE SALAD—Hearts of cabbage lettuces washed and wiped dry, sprinkled with chopped chives, chervil and tarragon leaves, then dashed with a dressing of oil, vinegar, salt and pepper.

LETTUCE AND TOMATO SALAD—Well washed, wiped and shred lettuce tossed with French dressing, garnished with peeled and sliced tomatoes having a drop of Ravigote sauce on each.

LETTUCE AND TOMATO SALAD—Well washed, wiped and shred lettuce tossed lightly with Remoulade sauce, add minced capers, garnish with sliced peeled tomatoes sprinkled with French dressing.

LETTUCE AND CUCUMBER SALAD—Well washed, wiped and broken lettuce leaves tossed and glistened with a dressing composed of 2 tablespoons of olive oil well beaten with 3 whole eggs, then add a dessert spoonful of rich cream and one of tarragon vinegar; served garnished with very thin slices of cucumber sprinkled with French dressing.

BAKED STUFFED LETTUCE—Trimmed, washed and drained lettuces, parboiled a few minutes, the insides then filled with sausage meat, the heads tied, arranged in a shallow saûtoir, moistened with white stock and Madeira sauce, seasoned with salt and pepper, covered with buttered paper, placed in oven and cooked till done, about 20 minutes; served with the string removed and the sauce poured over.

LIMES—A small kind of lemon, used in the bars for Rickeys and other drinks; served with oysters in preference to lemons, also with veal cutlets, fried soles, smelts and bass. At Montserrat the limes are cut in halves, the juice extracted and bottled, then supplied to most ships at sea as a preventive of scurvy, British ships using it by law, so that an English ship is known amongst sailors as a "Lime-juicer."

LIMES—An English sailor was also called a Limey. Somewhat less important than LEMONS in European cooking, the lime (*Citrus aurantifolia*) is indispensable in the cuisines of the tropics, where it originated. Generally limes are a bit more sour and strong-tasting than lemons, and sometimes substitute for each other.

LIVER—For the following recipes either sheep's, lamb's, calf's, pig's or ox liver will do.

RAGOUT OF LIVER—Wash and dry a liver, steam it till quite tender, then cut it in slices, add it to a rich brown sauce or gravy, stew it till thoroughly heated through; served garnished with slices of lemon and hard boiled eggs.

FRIED LIVER WITH ONIONS—Liver washed and wiped dry, cut in slices, seasoned with salt and pepper, rolled in flour, fried in bacon fat; served with sliced onions that have been fried, drained and lightly moistened with brown sauce.

SAUTÉ OF LIVER—Thin slices of liver and bacon, the bacon fried not crisp, the liver seasoned with salt and pepper, rolled in flour and lightly fried in the bacon fat, then taken up and placed with the bacon in a saûtoir; lightly fry then a little minced onion in the bacon fat, add flour, stir, moisten with stock, boil up, skim, pour it to the liver and bacon, simmer till done; served sprinkled with chopped parsley, garnished with croûtons.

LIVER AND SALT PORK—Same as the preceding, substituting salt pork for the bacon.

LIVER PUDDING—Liver and bacon cut in squares, stewed in brown gravy, seasoned with salt and pepper, then filled into pudding molds lined with paste, covered, cloth tied over, boiled or steamed for an hour and a half; serve.

CURRIED LIVER WITH FORCE-MEAT—Equal quantities of udder and liver minced, then pounded and rubbed through a sieve, seasoned with salt, pepper, sweet herbs and a little sifted breadcrumbs, add an egg or two; when thoroughly mixed, form into balls, rolled into sifted breadcrumbs, fried brown, then simmered in curry sauce till done through; served with the sauce and garnished with slices of broiled liver dipped in maître d'hôtel sauce.

LOBSTER—There is rock lobster, spiny lobster, Spanish lobster, langouste ... and then there is *Homarus americanus*, typically called Maine lobster (but more formally known as American lobster) and found off the coast of New England and Canada's Maritime Provinces. The *homard* of France and northern Europe (*Homarus vulgaris*) is similar—if smaller—but has been in such short supply for decades that most lobster in the European capitals is, in fact, imported from North America.

Our supply of lobster is relatively stable, but it is nothing like it was two hundred years ago, when many colonists considered the plentiful lobster a pest; even one hundred years ago it was used as a baitfish to catch the then more desirable COD. Those were the days when thirty- and forty-pound lobsters were common, and anything under three pounds was barely worth picking up. Now, a three-pound lobster is considered good size, and those over six or seven pounds are scarce. One-pound to one-and-a-half-pound lobsters are the norm these days, but lobster meat does not necessarily become tougher as the crustacean grows, so larger lobsters are often a good buy; they are certainly fun to wrestle with (once they are cooked!).

The best lobsters are boiled lobsters, and they are better still if boiled in seawater or, best yet, lobster stock made from the scraps of a previous lobster feast. But grilled lobster is also enjoyable, as long as care is taken to avoid overcooking.

Lobster coral, the dark, almost black eggs found in gravid females, turns bright red when cooked and may be used to color sauces, although it is delicious on its own. Salted, as it sometimes is in Maine, it can be preserved as lobster caviar.

LOBSTER SALAD—Lobster meat with lettuce or celery and mayonnaise, arranged on a dish and decorated with shapes of beet root, capers, pickles, whites of eggs and quartered hard boiled eggs.

MIROTON OF LOBSTER—Slices of lobster meat, half of them dipped in cold white sauce, the other half in a cold cardinal sauce, served on a bed of shred lettuce with mayonnaise down the centre.

MAYONNAISE OF LOBSTER—Lobsters (hens) boiled in court-bouillon, when cold, the tail and claw meat sliced into a dish, the creamy part of the head with the coral mixed with yolks of eggs, mustard, oil and lemon juice, then worked to form a mayonnaise, when done, mixed with the lobster meat; served garnished with shred lettuce.

LOBSTER IN ASPIC CREAM—Also called "Mazarins of Lobster." Lobster meat in slices, molds thinly lined with aspic and decorated with coral, truffles and egg whites. Aspic cream made by taking a pint of light colored aspic jelly, melt it and place in a bowl surrounded with broken ice, add to it a short half cup of white wine vinegar, two tablespoons of granulated sugar, a level teaspoon of dry mustard, two teaspoons of salt and a seasoning of red pepper, beat with a whisk, and as soon as it thickens add oil and vinegar alternately, a little at a time till of a mayonnaise consistency, finish with a dash of lemon juice; when ready, add the lobster meat, fill into the decorated molds, and when finally set, wipe the mold with a hot cloth, turn out on the dish, decorate with green stuff and serve.

LOBSTER CHEESE—Same as the preceding, but the molds not decorated (larger molds); when serving, the meat cut in slices like head cheese.

DEVILLED LOBSTER—The lobster boiled, cooled, split in halves, all meat taken from the shells without breaking them, the inside of shell then brushed with olive oil or butter. Fry some minced shallots with the brown meat of the claws in butter, add little white sauce, season with salt, red pepper and Bengal chutney; when thick, add the lobster meat cut in small squares, then fill the shells, sprinkle with breadcrumbs and melted butter, brown off in a brisk oven and serve garnished with cress.

SCALLOPED LOBSTER—Also called "Lobster au gratin." Equal quantities of lobster meat and button mushrooms cut in small squares, added to a reduced Béchamel sauce, with lobster coral or lobster butter and a little glaze, fill into lobster shells as in the preceding, finish off and serve as above.

LOBSTER CROQUETTES—Lobster meat and button mushrooms in equal quantities cut into very small dice, measure them, and for each pint, allow a pint of Velouté sauce; boil the sauce till reduced one third, then work in some lobster

butter and a liaison of egg yolks and cream, then add the lobster meat and mushrooms, stir thoroughly, turn out into a buttered pan, cover with a sheet of oiled paper; when cold and firm, shape into croquettes, bread, fry; serve with Perigueux, Poivrade or tomato sauces.

LOBSTER CUTLETS—Same as the preceding, forming them into shape to imitate a mutton chop, using the small claws to imitate bone handle.

RISSOLES OF LOBSTER—Same preparation as for croquettes, but instead of breading them, they are rolled into paste and fried.

LOBSTER PATTIES—Lobster meat cut in dice, mixed into a lobster sauce, patty shells filled with it, top placed on; served on ornamented dish paper.

BOUCHÉES OF LOBSTER—Same as the preceding but smaller (bouchée means mouthful).

STUFFED LOBSTER—The croquette preparation filled into lobster shells, covered with sifted crumbs, basted with butter, baked brown and served.

STEWED LOBSTER—Lobster meat simmered in a flour and butter sauce, seasoned with vinegar, mustard and red pepper, finished with a glass of sherry wine; served on very hot toast, garnished with lemon slices.

BROCHETTE OF LOBSTER—Slices of lobster meat from the tail, and very thin slices of parboiled bacon, arranged alternately on a skewer, rolled in a mixture of melted butter, seasoned with Worcestershire sauce, salt, pepper and nutmeg, broil, carefully turning them; served on a slice of very hot toast, with a little maître d'hôtel butter.

BROILED LIVE LOBSTER—At least that is what it is called, but the lobster is dead immediately the head is split, even though the flesh may quiver. The lobster split, the uneatable parts removed, seasoned with salt and pepper, placed within a wire hinged broiler, brushed with butter, broiled; served with melted butter and lemons.

CURRIED LOBSTER—Lobster meat made hot in a good curry sauce lightly flavored with anchovy essence; served within a border of dry boiled rice.

LOBSTER SANDWICH—Mash some cheese and lobster coral, add mustard, pepper and salt to taste, mix into a smooth paste with tomato catsup, place between thin buttered bread, cut on the bias and serve on a lettuce leaf.

LOBSTER TOAST—Minced lobster meat seasoned with salt and red pepper, then moistened with rich cream, made thoroughly hot and served on buttered toast.

LOBSTER, BORDELAISE—Lobster meat sautéed with a little minced onion, moistened with equal quantities of Madeira and Chablis wines, reduce to half glaze, then add equal parts of Espagnole and tomato sauces, bring to the boil, finish with chopped parsley and cayenne; serve in chafing dish.

LOBSTER NEWBURG—Meat of two lobsters cut in inch pieces with some sliced truffles, sauté in butter for five minutes, then add a half cup of Madeira wine and reduce to one half; beat a cupful of cream with five egg yolks, add it to the lobster, shuffle about till thick; serve in a chafing dish.

SALPICON OF LOBSTER—Diced lobster meat, truffles and mushrooms added to a reduced Béchamel sauce; served either in paper cases or fancy croûstades.

BAKED LOBSTER IN SHELL—Lobster meat cut into very small dice, seasoned with salt, red pepper, mustard, onion juice, Worcestershire sauce, chopped parsley and Béchamel sauce, filled into lobster shells, covered with breadcrumbs, basted with butter, baked brown and served.

LOBSTER WITH TOMATOES—Small pieces of lobster in Béchamel sauce, small tomatoes stuffed with it, placed inverted in patty pans, steamed; served hot with lobster sauce or cold with aspic jelly, or masked with aspic mayonnaise.

LOBSTER OMELET—Lobster meat in lobster sauce, enclosed within an omelet; served with Aurora sauce down the sides.

ESCALLOPED LOBSTER—Lobster meat cut in dice made hot in either Normande or Hollandaise sauces, filled into scallop shells or oval dishes, strewn with breadcrumbs and melted butter, browned off and served.

FRICASSÉE OF LOBSTER—Lobster meat cut in slices, made hot in a rich Velouté sauce, finished with a liaison of egg yolks and a dash of lemon juice; served garnished with strips of buttered toast or toasted crackers.

LOBSTER AND OYSTER PIE—Individual pies for restaurants and clubs; blanched oysters and lobster meat in equal quantities, a thick lobster sauce thinned a little with the oyster liquor, individual pie dishes with the lobster and oysters, moistened with the sauce, strewn with chopped parsley, covered with puff paste, egg washed and baked (A RATTLING GOOD SELLING DISH).

LOBSTER SOUP—Equal parts of fish broth and white stock thickened with roux, boiled up and skimmed, seasoned with salt, red pepper and Harvey sauce, into the soup tureen place lobster meat cut in dice together with the claws and upper shell of the lobsters that have been pounded and rubbed through a fine sieve, add the strained soup with a glass of sherry wine; serve with croûtons.

LOBSTER SOUP, CREOLE STYLE—Court-bouillon mixed with an equal quantity of Creole sauce, boiled and skimmed, the soup tureen to contain diced lobster meat, boiled rice, and a little chopped green mint, add the soup and serve.

LOBSTER SOUP, MARINER'S STYLE—Court-bouillon seasoned with carrot, turnip, onion, celery and anchovy essence, thickened with corn starch, simmered till clear, soup tureen to contain lobster meat, lobster butter, small claws, small boiled onions, soup poured to it with a little sherry wine and served.

LOBSTER MULLIGATAWNEY—Make a mulligatawney soup from court-bouillon, soup tureen to contain lobster meat and a little dry boiled rice, soup poured to it and served.

BISQUE OF LOBSTER—Meat of fresh boiled lobsters cut in dice, the tough parts with the shells and claws boiled for 20 minutes, the coral dried in a slow oven, little rice boiled in fish broth, make a thin Béchamel sauce from fish broth, add the liquor from the shells, then the rice and coral, rub the whole through a tamis, bring to the boil again and skim, then pour it to the diced lobster meat; serve with lobster quenelles in each plate.

BISQUE OF LOBSTER—Pieces of ham, salt pork, parsley, sweet herbs, onions, lobster meat and shells fried together with butter, little flour then added, moistened with fish broth, boiled an hour, then rice added and boiled till tender, the whole then rubbed through a tamis, seasoned, finished with sherry wine; served with croûtons.

LOCUSTS—A curious sight in the market place of Fez is the daily arrival of wagon loads of locusts. With the Moors who inhabit this part of North Africa, locusts form a regular article of food; they are eaten in almost every style, pickled, salted, dried or smoked, but never raw. The Negroes on the northern coast of Africa show a great partiality for locusts and eat from 200 to 300 at a sitting. They remove head, wings and legs, and boil them for half an hour in water, take out and drain, season with salt and pepper, then fry with vinegar.

MACARONI—Name of a preparation of wheat flour and water, that which is of home manufacture being equally as good in grades as the imported.

MACARONI—See PASTA.

MACARONI, ITALIAN STYLE—Macaroni broken into three-inch lengths and put to boil with a seasoning of salt and a pat or two of butter; when done, turned into a colander and drained dry; meantime heat some tomato sauce and work into it a little butter and glaze. Into a buttered pan place a layer of the macaroni, moisten it with the sauce, then strew with Parmesan cheese, renew this operation till pan is full, strew the top plentifully with cheese, bake for half an hour in medium oven and serve hot.

MACARONI AND CHEESE (PLAIN)—Break the macaroni and boil in salted water with a pat of butter till done, then drain, place back into the saûtoir and add to it a cupful each of melted butter, Parmesan cheese, grated Swiss cheese, and cream, toss it well over a quick fire; serve garnished with fancy croûtons.

BAKED MACARONI AND CHEESE—Also called "macaroni au gratin"; the preceding when prepared, turned into a buttered pan, strewn with equal parts of grated cheese and breadcrumbs, sprinkled with melted butter, baked a delicate brown and served.

MACARONI (AS THE MONKS LIKE IT)—Macaroni broken, boiled and drained, then mixed with a rich purée of pounded anchovies and mushrooms.

MACARONI AND CHEESE (FRENCH STYLE)—Broken lengths of macaroni boiled 20 minutes, drained, turned into a buttered pan; mix into each pound half a cup of melted butter and a cupful of coarsely chopped cheese, to this add a quart of liaison made of water, 4 eggs and a little flour, place in a medium oven for ten minutes, then pour over all, without stirring, a pint and half of Béchamel parsley sauce, bake brown and serve.

MACARONI AND TOMATOES—Macaroni broken, boiled and drained; returned to saûtoir, and to each pound of macaroni add half a pint each of minced cheese, brown sauce, and roast meat gravy, also a pint of thick stewed tomatoes; when thoroughly reheated it is ready to serve; or it may be turned into a buttered pan, sprinkled with cheese and simmered for half an hour in a medium oven.

MACARONI AND OYSTERS, MILAN STYLE—Macaroni broken, boiled and drained, placed in layers in buttered pan, the top of each layer covered with drained raw oysters, a sprinkling of melted butter, pepper and salt; when full, the whole moistened with a thin cream sauce, baked till set. Cooked and served in individual dishes this is a good seller in clubs and restaurants.

MACARONI, CREOLE STYLE—A pound of macaroni broken, boiled and drained, one large onion minced with two cloves of garlic and fried in oil; when of a pale brown, add two minced red peppers and a quart of tomato sauce, then add the macaroni, simmer and serve.

MACARONI, GENOISE STYLE—Macaroni broken, boiled and drained,

then kept hot. Equal parts of tomato and Espagnole sauces mixed and fetched to the boil; served, sauce in bottom of shallow dish, macaroni on it, this then strewn with Parmesan cheese.

TIMBALES OF MACARONI—Macaroni boiled and drained, then cut into inch lengths, seasoned with Parmesan cheese, pepper and salt; to each pound of the macaroni is then added a half pint each of sliced button mushrooms, braised chicken livers and smoked tongue, a truffle or two, the whole mixed and slightly moistened with Italian sauce. Timbale molds buttered, coated with cracker meal, filled with the mixture, brushed with butter, baked brown, turned out; served, a little Spanish sauce on dish, timbale in centre, the top piled high with Parmesan cheese.

MACARONI WITH LOBSTER BUTTER—Macaroni broken, boiled and drained, a deep pan buttered, layer of macaroni, on it is spread lobster butter, that again strewn with Parmesan, then a little Béchamel sauce, repeat till pan is full, then place in oven and thoroughly heat without browning; served in portions decorated with slices of lobster meat alternated with slices of truffle.

BUTTERED MACARONI—Macaroni broken, boiled and drained; while still hot, each portion served by putting a spoonful of melted butter in oval dish, then the macaroni, tossed in the butter and strewn while tossing with Parmesan cheese.

MACARONI WITH FISH FLAKES— Proceed as in recipe given for mac-

MACARONI WITH OYSTERS, MILAN STYLE

▪

Serves 6 as a pasta course

I suppose that Mr. Fellows named this dish after Milan simply because it is a city in Italy. The Italians are known for their wonderful pastas, but Milan is specially known for its risottos (rice dishes), not pasta. The name of this dish makes no sense, but the flavor does!

3/4 pound small pasta shells

2 tablespoons butter

6 tablespoons all-purpose flour

1 cup Chicken Stock (page 153)

1/4 cup dry white wine

2 cups half-and-half

2 tablespoons chopped parsley

1 1/2 tablespoons Worcestershire sauce

Juice of 1 lemon

1/2 teaspoon Tabasco sauce

Pinch of cayenne pepper

Salt to taste

2 1/2 cups medium-sized shucked raw oysters with their liquor

Cook the pasta in water until *al dente*. Drain and rinse with cold water. Drain well.

In a large frying pan, melt the butter. Add the flour and cook to form a roux. Add the Chicken Stock and wine. Using a wire whisk, whip until smooth. Simmer a couple of minutes and add the remaining ingredients, except the oysters. Stir until smooth. Allow to cool a bit.

In a large mixing bowl, combine the cooked pasta, cooled sauce, and the oysters. Pour into a 9-inch by 4-inch round casserole dish and cover with aluminum foil. Bake at 375°F. for 40 minutes, until hot throughout and the oysters have poached. Adjust salt, if needed.

C.W.

aroni and oysters; substituting either flakes of boiled fresh codfish, redsnapper, salmon, salmon trout, whitefish or pike for the oysters.

MACARONI WITH LAMB KIDNEYS—Macaroni broken, boiled and drained; lamb kidneys sliced and sautéed with butter; buttered pan, layer of macaroni, on it, a layer of the kidneys, moisten with tomato sauce, repeat till pan is full, the top then covered with slices of hard boiled eggs, these thickly strewn with Parmesan cheese, placed in oven till of a delicate brown, then served.

MACARONI WITH SPINACH PURÉE—Macaroni broken, boiled and drained; spinach well washed, boiled, drained, rubbed through sieve, moistened with rich roast veal gravy; buttered pan, layer of macaroni, then spinach; strew with Parmesan, repeat till full, then bake half an hour in a medium oven, and serve.

TIMBALE OF MACARONI AND FORCEMEAT—Macaroni boiled in full lengths, drained; buttered mold, macaroni coiled close all round the inside, filled with a forcemeat of chicken, then steamed till firmly set, turned out; served with white Italian sauce poured over.

MACARONI WITH SAUSAGES—Macaroni broken, boiled and drained; pork sausages boiled, skinned and cut into slices; buttered pan, layer of macaroni, then sausages, strewn with grated cheese, repeat till full, then a rich veal gravy poured over, baked half an hour in a medium oven, then served.

MACARONI CROQUETTES—Macaroni boiled and drained, cut in small pieces, returned to saûtoir, to which is then added grated ham and tongue, minced mushrooms and truffles, Parmesan cheese and a little thick Velouté sauce; reheat thoroughly, turn into a buttered pan 2 or 3 inches deep, cover with buttered paper and allow to set firm; then stamp out with the largest sized column cutter, the columns then rolled in Parmesan cheese, then breaded, fried and served with Trianon sauce composed of equal parts of Bearnaise and reduced tomato sauces, carefully mixed together.

MACARONI PUDDING—Macaroni broken, boiled with sweetened milk, grated lemon rind and a stick of cinnamon; when done drained, the milk returned to the fire, brought to the boil, thickened with a liaison of egg yolks, cream and a little corn starch; when to custard thickness, removed, seasoned with nutmeg; macaroni in deep buttered pan spread with preserves or marmalade, the custard poured over, baked and served.

MACARONI WITH HAM—Take cold ham trimmings, put through a mincing machine, use it instead of cheese, and bake, au gratin.

MACARONI CREAMED WITH EGGS—Macaroni broken, boiled and drained, then tossed over a quick fire with butter; meantime make some scrambled eggs with cream, equal the amount of eggs with Parmesan cheese, add both to the hot macaroni, keep hot and serve as called (do not let it boil).

MACARONI WITH TOMATO PURÉE—Macaroni broken, boiled and drained; tomato purée thick, containing a little grated ham and a slight flavor of garlic, layers of each strewn with Parmesan in buttered pan till full, bake and serve.

MACARONI SOUP—Macaroni broken, boiled and drained, add to a

rich beef broth, or in tomato soup, or chicken broth, etc. When turning the soup into the tureen on steam table, place some Parmesan cheese in the bottom, or else serve a butter chip full with each portion (club or restaurant service).

CREAMED MACARONI—Macaroni broken, boiled and drained, returned to saûtoir, moistened with Velouté sauce; served strewn with Parmesan and garnished with puff paste croûtons (made in leaf shape from trimmings).

MACE—The inner shell that covers the nutmeg; used in its blade form as a flavoring to soups and sauces; in its ground or powdered form, as a flavoring to sweet sauces, puddings, mincemeats, cakes, etc.

MACKEREL—A fine salt water fish enjoyed by most people; it should not be washed, wipe it dry with a clean cloth, cut off the fillets, season with salt and pepper, score the skin lightly, squeeze a little lemon juice on the flesh, broil it skin side down first, serve it with maître d'hôtel butter, garnish with Julienne potatoes, and you have the dish of an epicure.

MACKEREL—Mackerel is a fish that has the undeserved reputation of being too strong-flavored. In fact, very fresh mackerel is, if anything, almost tasteless. But it is an oily fish and one in which flavor develops rapidly as it ages. Unfortunately, Americans often have been subject to mackerel that has been stored for too long, at which stage its oiliness is overpowering.

This could change: Mackerel (Scomber scombrus) and the related Spanish mackerel, wahoo, Pacific sierra, and KINGFISH are among the few fish off American shores that remain plentiful and so relatively inexpensive. Mackerel run in size from less than a pound (tinker mackerel) to two pounds or so; related species are usually larger. Mackerel is excellent when smoked (the English prefer it this way), pickled (as it is in Japan and France), and dried (it is treated thusly in the eastern Mediterranean).

When fresh, mackerel is a perfect fish to grill, since its high oil content keeps it moist and prevents sticking. Finally, because of its round shape and regular bone structure, mackerel is a good fish on which to learn the fine art of filleting.

BOILED MACKEREL—Draw and wipe the fish, boil it plain in salted water; serve with melted butter separate, garnish with Hollandaise potatoes and half a lemon.

BOILED MACKEREL—Head removed, cut in halves across, drawn, wiped, boiled in seasoned fish broth containing an onion, bunch of parsley and a little Chablis wine; when done (about 12 minutes) serve either with parsley, caper, olive, drawn butter or Ravigote sauces.

BUTTERED MACKEREL—Fillets of mackerel wiped dry, placed into a sauce made of melted butter seasoned with anchovy essence, a little mustard, lemon juice, ground mace and red pepper, stew slowly for twenty minutes, then serve.

BROILED STUFFED MACKEREL— Draw the fish and wipe dry; make the stuffing of cold butter with a very little fresh grated bread-crumbs, chopped chives and shallots, lemon juice, salt and pepper, stuff the opening where drawn, roll in buttered paper, tie the ends, broil slowly till done, remove the paper; serve at once garnished with green stuff and lemon.

BAKED FILLETS OF MACKEREL— The fish wiped and filleted, the fillets baked and basted with maître d'hôtel butter; served with a brown fish sauce containing chopped chervil, tarragon, minced truffle peelings and a flavoring of port wine.

FRIED MACKEREL, BUTTER SAUCE —Fillets of mackerel wiped, seasoned with lemon juice, salt and red pepper, dipped in flour, then into beaten eggs, fried in hot fat; served with lemon butter sauce, garnished with Parisienne potatoes.

FILLETS OF MACKEREL, SAUTÉS— The fillets wiped seasoned with salt, red pepper and lemon juice, rolled in flour, sautéed with butter; served with a brown fish sauce at the sides, garnished with green stuff and lemon.

SOUSED MACKEREL—Heads and tails removed, the fish drawn and wiped, arranged in pan with whole peppers, allspice, bay leaves and cloves, cover them with equal quantities of white wine vinegar and water, bake slowly for one hour, serve cold, either plain or with Ravigote sauce.

BAKED STUFFED FILLETS OF MACKEREL—Split, bone and wipe the fish, season with salt and pepper, quickly set the cut side by lightly frying in butter; make the stuffing of fresh grated bread-crumbs moistened with Allemande sauce and seasoned with minced fried shallots, chopped parsley, anchovy essence and Harvey's sauce; spread it on the fried side, smooth, arrange on buttered baking sheet, bake; serve garnished with potato croquettes and lemon.

BOILED SALT MACKEREL—No. 1 mess are the best; soak them overnight in cold water, then rinse in clear running water, then lay them for an hour in milk, put to boil in cold water, when done, serve with melted butter, maître d'hôtel, mustard, or parsley sauces.

BROILED SALT MACKEREL—Extract the salt as in the preceding, then wipe dry after taking them out of the milk, season with pepper, brush with butter, broil; serve with melted butter, garnished with parsley and lemon.

MADEIRA—Name of a wine. Sauces, cakes, ices and jellies so named are supposed to contain some of it, which rarely happens, sherry and Marsala usually being substituted.

MADEIRA—A fortified wine that fell into disfavor in the last century, Madeira has one unique characteristic: its acidic, smoky taste. It can be quite enjoyable, either as an aperitif or an after-dinner drink.

Madeira is named after the island on which it was first made, a fifteenth-century Portuguese colony some five hundred miles west of North Africa. Following its discovery, the green island was defoliated by a fire that burned for years; when the island was covered with ash, vines were planted. For some reason the strong, smoky wine made from Madeiran grapes improved as barrels of it were first aged in the equatorial sun and later shipped around the world. Most wine is delicate and suffers during long voyages; this one only got better, and one-hundred-year-old Madeira is not only drinkable but wonderful. "As far as anyone knows," wrote Hugh Johnson, the British wine writer, "it is immortal."

Today only the sweet Malmsey Madeira is aged in the sun; the rest are heated in stoves. Sercial is the driest Madeira, and Verdelho just a bit sweeter; Rainwater is, in theory at least, a blend of the two. Any of these three makes a good aperitif. Malmsey and Boal Madeira, dark and sweet, can be served in place of port after a meal.

MADELINES—Name given to small cakes baked in fancy patty pans, made of a pound mixture, viz: a pound each of butter, sugar, sifted flour, eggs (ten) and a wine glass of cognac; some also add sultana raisins, currants and candied peels.

MADELINES—The correct spelling of this small shell-shaped sponge cake made famous by the French writer Marcel Proust is *madeleine*.

MAÎTRE D'HÔTEL—Name applied to a sauce and a garnish (the literal meaning of the name is a steward). The sauce is composed of melted butter, chopped parsley and lemon juice, and is used chiefly with broiled meat and fish; quartered boiled potatoes in the sauce is the garnish for boiled fish; and quartered lemons with the meat is the garnish.

MAÎTRE D'HÔTEL—Although Fellows believed that "seasoned butter" is the more important definition of this term, it is now most often used to refer to the person in charge of a restaurant dining room.

MALLARD—Name of our best and largest wild duck.

MALLARD—One can no longer legally buy wild mallard in this country; you can eat the bird only if you hunt or know a hunter. This is a shame, since the dark-purple meat of the wild mallard is full flavored, delicious, and unforgettable. There is, however, farm-raised mallard, which gives a good idea of what the wild DUCK tastes like.

ROAST MALLARD, AMERICAN STYLE—The birds plucked, singed, drawn and trussed, then roasted rare 30 to 40 minutes, jointed, the joints kept hot; the carcasses stewed down with herbs and seasonings, sauce made from it, finished with currant jelly and port wine, served with the joints.

MALLARD, PROVENÇALE STYLE—The birds plucked, singed, drawn, stuffed, trussed, roasted and served in portions with the gravy from the birds mixed with shallot sauce.

BROILED MALLARD, MAÎTRE D'HÔTEL—The birds plucked,

singed, split down the back; back and breastbones removed, laid skin downwards in a pan, seasoned with salt, pepper and olive oil, marinaded in this for 15 minutes, then broiled rare; served with maître d'hôtel butter and garnished with watercress.

FRIED MALLARD, ORANGE SAUCE—The birds prepared, split down the back, back and breastbones removed, thigh bone snapped, marinaded for an hour in olive oil with a few chopped onions, parsley and mushroom ketchup, taken up, fried rare with a little olive oil; served with Bigarade sauce.

FILLETS OF MALLARD, GAME SAUCE—Prepare and roast as for American style above; when done, take off the fillets, stew down the carcasses in game sauce with a few shallots, port wine and a piece of game glaze, strain through a fine chinee cap, finish with cayenne and lemon juice; served with the portions.

SALMIS OF MALLARD—The birds plainly roasted very rare, jointed, the joints skinned; carcasses and skins then boiled down with herbs, cloves, whole peppers, bay leaves and fried shallots; when reduced, made into a sauce, strained and skimmed, finished with a little glaze and port wine, joints then put in and simmered for 15 minutes, afterwards kept hot but not allowed to boil; served garnished with croûtons.

MANGO—Name of a most superb torrid climate fruit, about the size of a large lemon, the interior of a pulpy nature attached to a stone in size like that of a large peach stone. On account of its perishability in transport, we obtain it chiefly as a pickle, jelly, chutney or preserve.

MANGO—Perhaps the reason that mangoes are not as popular in this country as they should be (they are among the most delicious fruits) is that they are messy. Most of the flesh seems to stick to the huge central pit and must be sucked and licked off. To some people, it's worth the trouble. Others prefer the mango (*Mangifera indica*) in shakes, sorbets, and chutneys.

MARASCHINO—A very fine liqueur of Italian origin, obtained from the Marasca cherry, plum and peach kernels; used both as a drink and a flavoring to jellies, ices, sauces, puddings, meringues, etc., etc.

MARINADE—A pickling mixture made of oil, vinegar, lemon juice; salt, pepper, herbs, Worcestershire sauce, anchovy essence, onions, bay leaves, whole peppers, whole cloves, and parsley, the different ingredients above being variously added to the oil; vinegar or lemon juice according to the fish, flesh or fowl to be marinaded, the article being steeped for an hour or so prior to being cooked so as to either enrich or bring out the flavor in cooking.

MARINADE—Although Fellows's list of marinade ingredients may be on the dogmatic side, his description of the goal of marinating food is on the mark. Currently dozens of "experts" recommend long marinating times in order to tenderize meat. But this depends on the kind of meat and the cut.

Although, as Fellows wrote, they serve to "enrich or bring out the flavor" of the foods being soaked, there are two points to remember: Soaking times of more than an hour usually do not do much to increase the effectiveness of the marinade. And don't rely on marinades to turn a piece of chuck into filet.

MARJORAM—Name of a garden herb used as a flavoring to soups, sauces and stuffing for fish and fowl.

MARJORAM—Marjoram (*Origanum majorana*) is more subtle and sweet-tasting than oregano, to which it is related.

MARMALADE—Another name for jam, marmalade being the word mostly used in this country. Recipes for its making are found under the fruit headings which can be used.

MARMALADE—Today the word *marmalade* is more frequently used for jams made from citrus fruits than for those made from berries or stone fruits.

MARRONS—French name for chestnuts. The French take the large nuts and preserve them by candying, then export them either in cans with syrup, or crystalized.

MARROW—The contents of leg of beef bones, especially the bone of the buttock, which runs between the thick flank, top side and silver side, the buttock generally being termed the round. The top side of the buttock makes very fine steaks indeed, and in England fetches 25¢ per pound; the silver side of the buttock being used for boiling either fresh or salt, and fetches 16¢ per pound. The marrow bone should be sawn in three pieces, the marrow taken out, blanched in boiling milk and water for a minute, cooled, then cut in slices to lay on a steak, over which may be poured fines-herbes sauce, or it may be cut in pieces and mixed with chopped mushrooms, onion and parsley, and filled into paper cases that have been buttered and lined with breadcrumbs, then baked and served; or into fancy paste croûstades; or it may be cut into small dice, seasoned, mixed with cream and beaten eggs, filled into patty pans lined with puff paste and baked; or again simmered in white Italian sauce and used as a bouchée or small patty filling; again cut into long pieces, dipped in a frying batter, fried and served with a tomato purée; made into quenelles by adding an equal quantity of breadcrumbs, a little flour, salt, pepper and egg yolks, pound, rub through a sieve, form with spoons, then poach.

MARROW—The soft tissue filling the cavities of long bone is most commonly enjoyed these days in osso-buco, the Italian dish of braised veal shanks.

MARZIPAN—Name given to an almond paste used by confectioners; made of 14 ozs. of sweet almonds, two of bitter, one pound of powdered sugar, a flavoring either of orange flower or rose water; the almonds are blanched, dried, pounded with the sugar and flavoring to a paste, then put into a preserving pan and stirred over the fire till it clings in a mass to the spatula, it is then formed into rolls, cut in slices and baked in a very cool oven till of a light brown color, or forced through a bag and tube into ring shapes, dusted with sugar and baked.

MASTIC—An aromatic resin used for flavoring chewing gum.

MAYONNAISE—Name of a salad dressing, also as a decorative sauce for cold fish. Made with a pint of olive oil, half a pint of white vinegar, juice of two lemons, five raw egg yolks, one ounce of dry mustard, salt and red pepper to taste; place the cold yolks and mustard in a cold bowl, thoroughly mix, then drop by drop stir in one-fourth of the oil, when like butter gradually thin with some of the liquid, then add the salt, when it will be found to have thickened right up again; then finish stirring in the remaining oil and liquid at alternate intervals, finish with the red pepper (some add a little powdered sugar with the pepper). When finished it should be thick enough to mask a fish or salad without running off.

MAYONNAISE—Fellows's proportions are on the grand side: You can make mayonnaise (in a blender, if you like) with a single egg, a dash of mustard, salt, black pepper, and cayenne pepper, and a tablespoon or two of vinegar or lemon juice, with a cup of oil added gradually to this mixture. Mayonnaise is a sauce that is easily made in the home.

ASPIC MAYONNAISE—Equal parts of mayonnaise and bright aspic jelly barely melted, beaten together, used to set mazarins.

MAZARINS—Molds of decorated fillets of fowl, game or fish, set with aspic mayonnaise, turned out when cold and firm, decorated and sent to table.

MEDALLIONS—Name given to medal size and shaped pieces of savory foods, such as foie-gras, potted tongue, ham, etc., jellied meats. They are always nicely decorated and generally used as an appetizer or hors d'oeuvre.

MEDALLIONS—The term can also be used to refer to rounds of beef, veal, lamb, pork tenderloin, lobster, monkfish, and so on.

MELONS—Name of a fruit largely contained of water; the watermelon and the different varieties of canteloupe; the latter being used generally as a breakfast appetizer, and the former as a dinner dessert; preserved watermelon rind makes a fine preserve for the summer tea.

MELONS—See CANTALOUPE.

MELON PRESERVE—Cut the watermelon rind into small pieces, place 20 lbs. into a tub, sprinkle it well with a pint of salt, just cover it with cold water and allow it to marinade for five hours, then drain, and again cover it with cold water and soak for two hours, changing the water three times, then drain, put on the fire in a preserving pan, cover with boiling water, bring to

boiling point, then drain again; make a syrup of ten pounds of sugar and six quarts of boiling water, boil and skim, then add the melon rind, and slowly simmer till tender; skim out the rind, place it on draining sieves for two hours in a warm place to set; when hardened place into cold crocks; boil up the syrup again with the sliced peel and juice of eight lemons and two ounces of sliced ginger, boil ten minutes, then strain over the fruit in the crocks.

MENU—French term for "bill of fare." Why should the word MENU head our American dinner bills? Why should the progressive American ape dying France? Why should the American culinary student detest the kitchen because he cannot twist his tongue around the French culinary à la this and that? Is not the American flag dear to the American? Then why not the American language? Does not the farmer, mechanic, layman and every American who patronizes hotel, restaurant and club life know the meaning of the term "bill of fare"? Then why put the French word "MENU" at the head, and the generally mongrel Frenchy terms throughout the bill of fare? When in Rome do as the Romans do; then when in America do as the Americans do. Let those from France, or the French scholars, read the plain homelike American language on our bills of fare, the same as the traveling American has to read the menus in the languages of Europe. They do not print the menus in France in the American language; then why should we print our American bills of fare in French, or as is generally the case in half French and half American? For ex-ample: "Veal cutlet a la Francaise," or "Small patties de volaille," why not put "Small patties of chicken"? Everyone knows what chicken is and will order it, but all do not know that volaille translated means fowl.

One of my first thoughts in writing this handbook was to abstain from French terms. I said to myself, I WILL WRITE AN AMERICAN CULINARY HANDBOOK FOR AMERICANS. I have heard it frequently stated that the terms for the bill of fare could not be properly represented in the American language. I SAY IT CAN, and as a proof positive you have it here. There are no French terms used for the receipts of this book, and the headings as given are what should in my opinion be placed on the bill of fare, as perfectly adequate in describing the dish.

MERINGUE—Name given to a mixture made by whipping whites of eggs to a stiff froth, then working in sugar, and sometimes flavorings and colors; used as a covering to cup custards, puddings, cream pies, shortcakes, florentines, etc., as an icing for cakes; also when of a firm mixture forced through a bag and tube into shapes, then baked dry without much color, the insides are then scooped out and used as a receptacle for ices, ice creams, creams, etc.

MILANAISE—Name of a garnish composed of strips of white chicken meat, red ham, black truffles and pipe macaroni worked into a Velouté sauce, finished with a little Parmesan cheese.

MILT—Name of the soft roe of fish.

MILT—Milt—actually the male roe, or testes—is rarely used these days. It is usually softer than female roe, from which CAVIAR is made. Do not eat the roe of any fish unless you are certain it is, in fact, edible. Some is poisonous. See SHAD ROE.

MINCEMEAT—Ten pounds of sound cooking apples chopped fine, ten pounds of raisins seeded and chopped, five pounds of currants thoroughly cleaned and freed from grit, ³/₄ pound each of orange and lemon candied peel, two pounds of citron all shredded, ten pounds of granulated sugar, a mixture of ground spice (made of five grated nutmegs, a dessert spoonful each of cloves, mace, allspice, cinnamon and black pepper), seven and a half pounds each of beef suet and boiled lean beef chopped, half a cup of salt, mix well, then moisten with the juice of ten oranges, a quart each of good brandy and Jamaica rum and enough old cider to form a stiff consistency.

MINT—A garden herb, used as a soup and sauce flavoring; mint sauce for lamb made by finely chopping fresh green mint, then place it in a tureen adding to it the grated rind and juice of a lemon; bring to the boil with enough sugar to be palatable, one pint of good vinegar, pour it to the mint, let cool and serve.

MINT—There are a couple of dozen mints in the world—all with square stems—with spearmint being the most frequently used in cooking and in tea (peppermint is usually reserved for candy). It is an ancient flavoring, used only sparingly in most European cuisines but still essential to certain dishes in the Middle East and India.

MOLASSES—A thick liquid obtained from sugar in its process of refining; used for cakes, puddings, candy, etc.

MOLASSES—An ingredient now used only for a few specific recipes (such as gingerbread), molasses—also known as treacle—was once an important sweetener in this country.

MULLET—A small sea fish of the Southern coasts, seldom seen at table, as the gray is too common, and the red too scarce. The red should be just wiped, the entrails drawn, leaving the liver and trail in the fish, roll them in olive oil, sprinkle with parsley, broil them in paper cases and serve with Italian, Ravigote or fine herb sauce. The gray mullet may be treated in any of the forms applicable to herrings.

MULLET—The problem with mullet is that its shelf life—the time it stays fresh once out of the water—is among the shortest of any saltwater fish. When mullet is eaten in Louisiana, Texas, or the Florida panhandle—where it is usually dipped in cornmeal and deep-fried—it is thoroughly enjoyable, a full-flavored fish with firm texture. By the time it is shipped north or anywhere else, however, it spoils; the fish tastes oily and mushy. Freezing helps, but not much; the fish is simply too delicate. Smoked mullet, however, does store fairly well.

The roe of almost the entire catch of Gulf Coast mullet, incidentally, is shipped to Japan, where it is considered a delicacy.

MUSCALLONGE—A large fish of the pike species found in the great lakes; may be cooked and served in all the ways for pike (which see).

MUSCALLONGE—More often spelled *muskellunge* (*Esox masquinongy*), this is a sport fish of the northern lakes. It is rarely, if ever, seen in markets.

MUSHROOMS—An edible fungi, umbrella shaped, dark gills, with easily removable skin; if those sold you have white gills and the skin will not strip easily, but breaks off in bits, discard them, they will probably be found to be toadstools. At least 70 per cent of the mushrooms used in culinary preparations are canned button mushrooms and morels. Fresh mushrooms are seldom used in sauces on account of their color. The recipes following will use canned, except where stated.

MUSHROOMS—Canned mushrooms are far inferior to fresh, dried, or frozen mushrooms. And cultivated mushrooms, while fine for some purposes, lack the intensity of flavor found in CÈPES and other wild mushrooms (also known as porcini, boletes, and steinpilze).

One way to bring more flavor to any dish that features mushrooms is to combine a small amount—even a half ounce will do the trick—of dried wild mushrooms, reconstituted, with the cultivated mushrooms. The flavor of the wild mushrooms will permeate the entire preparation.

Remember that the term *edible fungi* includes tree ears, white fungus, and other fungi used in Chinese cooking.

PURÉE OF MUSHROOMS—Canned button mushrooms minced, sautéed with butter for five minutes, moistened with Velouté sauce, reduce quickly, then add some thick cream and lemon juice, reduce five minutes more, then rub through a tamis for use.

MUSHROOM GARNISH—Canned mushrooms drained, the liquor reduced, the mushrooms boiled down with a seasoning of salt, lemon juice, butter and a little white stock, when nearly dry, the liquor added, the whole then put into a thick Allemande sauce and used to garnish white entrées, or put into a rich Espagnole sauce to garnish brown entrées.

STUFFED MUSHROOMS, ITALIAN SAUCE—Large fresh mushrooms skinned, stalk removed, placed skin side downward in a buttered baking pan, filled with the following: Mince the stalks with some shallots, parsley, fat bacon, lean ham and thyme leaves, sauté them in olive oil for five minutes, then work in some egg yolks, season with salt and pepper; when filled, sprinkle with breadcrumbs and melted butter, bake till nicely browned (about 20 minutes); serve with brown Italian sauce poured around, garnish with fancy croûtons.

BAKED MUSHROOMS ON TOAST—Medium sized fresh mushrooms skinned and the stalks removed, wash in cold water containing a dash of vinegar, drain, arrange in a buttered baking pan skin side downward; into each then place half a pat of butter, bake till done (about 20 minutes) basting with the butter once or twice; serve on buttered toast garnished with tufts of fried parsley.

BROILED MUSHROOMS—Large fresh mushrooms skinned and the stalks removed, dipped in melted butter, seasoned with salt and pepper, placed in wire hinged broiler, broiled till done; meantime slice the stalks very thin and sauté them with butter and a little chopped parsley; serve the mushrooms on toast, or as an accompaniment to steaks, cutlets, etc., adding the sautéed stalks.

MUSHROOMS IN CROÛSTADES— Small fresh button mushrooms peeled, washed, drained, sautéed with butter, chopped chives and parsley, seasoned with salt and pepper, just moistened with Allemande sauce and a dash of lemon juice filled into fancy paste, or fried bread croûstades and served.

SAUTÉ OF MUSHROOMS—Medium sized fresh mushrooms peeled, washed and drained, sautéed with butter and minced shallots, seasoned with salt, pepper and nutmeg, moistened slightly with chicken broth, then reduce; serve on toast, or on platter garnished with strips of buttered toast, or as a garnish.

STUFFED MUSHROOMS, CREOLE STYLE—Medium sized fresh mushrooms peeled and washed, stalks removed and minced with a little celery and green peppers, sauté the mince in olive oil, then moisten with chicken liquor, reduce, then thicken with fresh grated breadcrumbs, remove from fire and add strips of truffle peelings, chopped parsley, salt and paprika, fill the mushrooms, smooth, brush with beaten eggs, press on some breadcrumbs, arrange in a shallow saûtoir, sauté on both sides, when nicely browned, take up and serve on toast with Creole sauce separate.

STEWED MUSHROOMS—Canned mushrooms drained, the liquor reduced, the mushrooms fried light brown with butter, seasoned with salt and pepper, when brown add a little flour, shake, moisten with the liquor, juice of lemons, Espagnole sauce and sherry wine, simmer and skim; when bright, use as a garnish to larded fillet of beef, etc.

FRICASSÉE OF MUSHROOMS— Canned button mushrooms drained, the liquor reduced, the mushrooms fried a light brown with butter and minced shallots; when colored, drained, and placed with the reduced liquor into a rich Poulette sauce, season with nutmeg, salt, cayenne and lemon juice; served on toast, in cases, croûstades, or as a garnish to white entrées.

MUSHROOM SAUCE—Canned mushrooms drained, the liquor reduced, the mushrooms sautéed lightly with butter, then added to a Velouté sauce with the reduced liquor, season with cayenne and lemon juice for white entrées, or use Madeira or Espagnole sauces for brown entrées.

CREAMED FRESH MUSHROOMS—Fresh button mushrooms peeled, washed and drained, thick pure cream fetched to the boil, mushrooms cooked in it till done (about 7 minutes), season with salt and cayenne; serve in chafing dish.

MUSHROOM CATSUP—Fresh mushrooms wiped (not washed) and placed into crocks in layers till full, each layer being well sprinkled with salt; when full, cover with a folded cloth and stand in a warm place for 24 hours, then mash and strain through a very coarse towel or a sack; to each gallon of the liquor thus obtained add a quarter of a pound of whole peppers and simmer for half an hour, then add one ounce of whole cloves, one ounce of whole allspice, two ounces of bruised ginger and half an ounce of whole mace, simmer for another half hour, then remove from fire; when cold, strain through a jelly bag, bottle, cork and seal.

STUFFED MUSHROOMS ON TOAST—Fresh mushrooms, the stalks minced and sautéed with a few shallots and parsley, added then to a little minced chicken in sauce Suprême, the mushrooms stuffed with it and baked; served on circles of buttered toast.

FRICASSÉE OF MUSHROOMS—Fresh mushrooms peeled, broiled on outside till brown, simmered in thin Béchamel sauce till done; served with fancy croûtons.

MUSHROOM RISSOLES—A quart of minced fresh mushrooms, two minced medium sized onions, pepper, salt, a pinch of ground mixed herbs, simmered in thick sauce till the onion is done, a spoonful then placed in rounds of pastry, edges folded over, pinched round, sprinkled with breadcrumbs and fried in oil.

MUSHROOM OMELET—Use either canned or fresh mushrooms, sauté till tender with a few minced shallots, drain, add them to a Madeira sauce, simmer, make the omelet, enclose the mushrooms, pour the sauce around it and send to table.

MUSSELS—A large almond shaped shellfish found along the coasts, equally as good as oysters, but on account of their cheapness not so much used; are eaten raw the same as oysters, but generally first blanched, the usual way being to thoroughly wash the shells, then to ⅔ fill a saucepan with them, adding just a little water, put on the lid, then steam till they open their shells, when the fish is removed, they may then be used.

MUSSELS—Mussels, which are usually bluish-black but may be amber and even bright green, are among our most inexpensive and underrated shellfish. The blue mussel (*Mytilus edulis*) is common on all American shores and is being farmed in increasing numbers in Maine, Massachusetts, and California. These mussels, which are usually grown on ropes, can be preferable to some harvested in the wild, which are often gritty. But wild mussels from smooth-bottomed waters contain little or no grit and are plumper and meatier than any farmed specimens.

Today mussels are almost never eaten raw, and the practice of blanching them to clean the shells before actually cooking them isn't done either. Simply rinse the mussels well in cold water and trim off their fuzzy beards. They are then ready for use in any recipe. When Fellows calls for blanched mussels in the recipes, he is referring to ones that have been steamed open.

SCALLOPED MUSSELS—Large fat mussels raw, simmered till plump in a little fish broth with bay leaf, thyme and parsley; taken up, drained, added to a thick Béchamel sauce, filled into scallop shells, smoothed over, sprinkled with breadcrumbs and grated cheese, browned off and served.

BROCHETTE OF MUSSELS— Blanched mussels threaded on skewers, dipped in melted butter and breadcrumbs twice, then broiled, or may be dipped in butter and fried in deep fat.

FRIED MUSSELS—Raw mussels drained, rolled in flour, then in beaten eggs, fried a golden brown in a little very hot fat in a frying pan.

FRICASSÉE OF MUSSELS— Blanched mussels in Hollandaise sauce; served on toast sprinkled with parsley dust.

STEAMED MUSSELS, LEMON BUTTER SAUCE—Blanched mussels simmered in maître d'hôtel butter;

served on strips of hot toast, sauce poured over them.

STEWED MUSSELS—Blanched mussels, boiling milk ²/₃, mussel liquor strained ¹/₃, butter, salt, red pepper; same as oyster stew.

STEWED MUSSELS—Blanched mussels, thin white sauce made of ²/₃ milk and ¹/₃ strained mussel liquor, mussels added with chopped parsley, salt and red pepper; served with oyster crackers or thin brown bread.

MUSSELS BREADED, VILLEROI SAUCE—Blanched mussels dipped into cooling Villeroi sauce; when set, dipped into sifted breadcrumbs, then egg and breadcrumbs, fried in dripping a golden color; served garnished with tufts of fried parsley, and lemon.

MUSSELS SAUTÉS WITH FINE HERBS—Blanched mussels sautéed with butter, minced chives, parsley, garlic and sifted breadcrumbs, seasoned with salt and pepper; served in cases.

MUSSEL SAUCE—Blanched mussels in sauce Normande.

CREAMED MUSSELS—Raw mussels dropped into hot butter and sautéed till plump, Béchamel sauce then added, simmered; served on toast with sauce poured over.

MUSSELS, ITALIAN STYLE—Raw mussels sautéed in butter with minced onions; when onions are

SCALLOPED MUSSELS

.

Serves 8 to 10 as an appetizer

This dish can be a bit time consuming to prepare. However, it does make a first-class appetizer when served in individual baking shells.

4 pounds mussels (small
  Penn Coves are best)

2 tablespoons olive oil

2 cloves garlic, peeled and
  minced

2 tablespoons chopped
  parsley

1/4 teaspoon dried thyme,
  whole

1/2 cup dry white wine

6 tablespoons butter

6 tablespoons all-purpose
  flour

1/4 cup heavy cream

3/4 cup bread crumbs

1 1/2 tablespoons finely
  chopped parsley

Cut off the fuzzy beards from the mussels and discard. Rinse the mussels in cold water.

Heat a large pot (about 8 quarts) and add the oil and garlic. Cook a moment and then add the mussels, parsley, thyme, and wine. Stir, cover, and bring to a boil. Reduce the heat and simmer, covered, for 10 to 12 minutes, until the mussels open. Drain, reserving the "nectar." When cool enough to handle, remove the mussel meat from the shells and discard the shells. Place the mussel meat in a small bowl and set aside.

In a medium-sized frying pan, melt 4 tablespoons of the butter. Add the flour and cook a few minutes to form a roux. Do not brown! Add the reserved nectar along with any liquid that has collected in the bowl of mussels. Using a wire whisk, whip this smooth so there are no lumps. Stir in the cream. Simmer, uncovered, about 10 minutes to make a thick sauce. Set aside to cool to room temperature.

Stir the reserved mussels into the sauce.

In a small pan, melt the remaining 2 tablespoons of butter. Add the bread crumbs and parsley and mix well.

Fill a shallow baking dish, small ramekins, or baking shells with the mussel mixture. Top with the bread-crumb mixture. Bake at 375°F. for 20 to 25 minutes, until bubbly and nicely browned.

NOTE: If using baking shells, cooking time may be reduced.

C.W.

slightly brown, the oysters taken up into a saûtoir, tomatoes added and reduced till thick, then added to the mussels with white sauce and chopped parsley; seasoned with salt, pepper, butter and a dash of anchovy essence; served in scallop dishes garnished with sippets of toast.

MUSSELS, FISHERMEN STYLE— Raw mussels dried between cloths, butter fried to a nut brown, mussels then added and fried till plump, taken up; light brown sauce then made with the butter, flour, salt, pepper and fish broth, mussels arranged on toast, sauce poured over and served.

PAN ROAST OF MUSSELS—Raw mussels dropped into frothing butter and fried till plump, seasoned with salt and cayenne; served on strips of toast with enough of the liquor to moisten it, sprinkled with parsley dust and garnished with cress and lemon.

MUSTARD—A yellow flour produced by finely grinding the seeds of the mustard plant; prepared for table as a condiment by simply mixing to a thick cream with cold water and a taste of salt. The French prepare mustard for table use by boiling together equal quantities of tarragon and cider vinegars, pouring it to the mustard flour and when thickened, simmered a few minutes, meanwhile adding a flavoring composed of white wine which has had soaked in it in a warm place for an hour or so some celery seeds, whole spices and a clove of crushed garlic, salt and a taste of sugar.

MUSTARD—Making mustard at home is an almost ridiculously easy process, as anyone who tries Fellows's recipes will see.

MUSTARD AND CRESS—These are the first sproutings of the cress seed and the mustard seed, used in equal proportions mixed, after being thoroughly washed and drained. To form sandwiches between brown bread and butter simply sprinkled with salt, or used as a breakfast salad by lightly tossing with a sprinkling of salt, olive oil and lemon juice.

MUTTON—What a tremendous difference there is in mutton, brought about by its different pastures and breeds. The steward should always buy WETHER mutton, leaving the EWES entirely alone, unless they are MAIDENS. The best cutting sheep are from sixty to seventy pounds in weight. The skin should be dry. Leave the oily skinned ones alone as they will eat TOUGH. See that they are moderately lean by noting the shoulder meat showing through the skin, and also that the meat of the leg outwards can be seen through the skin extending well down towards the loin. Cheaper to buy the whole sheep and use all its parts (except the head) than to keep on buying racks, racks, racks. The butcher is going to cut those racks LONG, and you have to cut off two or three inches, before you can send them to the broiler, and the chops then come very expensive. The loin chops which are infinitely the best should be used with the neck chop, one of each, thus making the pair of chops usually called for, the trimmed bone of the neck one carrying the frill and a croquette tip stuck into the loin one. In cutting up the sheep, split it straight through the spinal column, then separate the quarters, cut off the legs close to the pin bone. The loin will yield three half pound trimmed chump chops, and ten six ounce trimmed loin chops. With the forequarter, lift off the shoulder, cut off the breast, then cut off the scrag with the first two bones of the rack adhering; you now have eleven neck chops to each quarter, or forty-eight chops to the sheep, two legs and two shoulders for joints, the breasts and scrags for the mulitude of entrées and the helps hall.

MUTTON—Mutton, or sheep, is rarely seen anymore in this country because of our evident preference for LAMB. You can sometimes find mutton in ethnic markets.

BOILED LEG OF MUTTON—Cut off the shank bone, put to boil in cold water with salt, whole carrots and white turnips; when done, take up, cut the vegetables into finger sizes; make a white sauce from the stock, adding capers and caper vinegar; serve in portions with the sauce at ends of dish, using the vegetables as a garnish.

ROAST LEG OF MUTTON—Cut off the shank bone, rub with salt and pepper, dredge with flour, roast till done with frequent basting, take up, pour off surplus fat from the pan, add a little flour to the remaining gravy, moisten with stock to make a sauce, strain, add capers and caper vinegar, or let it remain plain and serve with each portion some red currant jelly separate.

BRAISED LEG OF MUTTON—Cut off the shank bone, put the leg into a brasiere with some fat bacon trimmings, onions, carrots, bay leaves, bunch of sweet herbs, whole peppers and allspice, moisten with mutton stock, place on the lid, then put the whole into a hot oven, cook till done and glazy, take up, then reduce the braise to half glaze, strain, skim; serve with the portions and red currant jelly separate; or you may garnish it with glazed balls of carrot and turnip, also some glazed small onions.

BRAISED STUFFED LEG OF MUTTON—Bone the leg, and where the bone was, insert a filling composed of minced mushrooms, parsley, shallots, grated ham, little grated lemon rind, seasoning of salt, pepper and nutmeg, mix these well, then work in some forcemeat, sew up the openings, place the stuffed leg into a brasiere with carrots, turnips, celery, clove of crushed garlic, whole cloves and mace, moisten with stock, braise and glaze; when done, take up, and reduce the braise, strain and skim it, add it to a Velouté sauce containing capers; serve with a stuffed tomato at ends of dish, with the sauce poured around.

BRAISED LARDED LEG OF MUTTON—Bone and stuff the leg of mutton as in the preceding recipe, then lard the outside with seasoned strips of bacon, place in brasiere with carrot, turnip, onion, celery, bunch of sweet herbs, cloves and mace, moisten with stock, braise and glaze, take up when done, reduce the remaining braise, strain and skim it; serve with onion purée at one end of the dish, potato croquette at the other, and send the sauce to table separate.

BRAISED LEG OF MUTTON, WITH BEANS—Cut off the shank, insert six cloves of garlic into the leg at different places, braise with vegetables and spices, take up when done, then reduce, strain and skim the braise. Meanwhile boil some navy beans; when done, drain, and mix them into a sauce of brown onion purée; serve the portions of mutton on top of a spoonful of the sauced beans, pour a little of the braise around and garnish with a few Parisienne potatoes.

BRAISED LEG OF MUTTON WITH VEGETABLES—Bone the leg, season it inside with salt, pepper, nutmeg and thyme, sew up, braise with vegetables and spices, take up when done, reduce, strain and skim the braise; serve garnished with glazed young carrots, small whole new turnips, flowerets of cauliflower, green peas, points of asparagus, small new potatoes, quartered artichoke bottoms, a macedoine or jardinière, stringless French beans (haricots verts), flageolet beans, new lima beans, stuffed cucumber, baked tomatoes, etc., etc. If when using any of the moistened garnishes by themselves, place it on the bill of fare as Braised Leg of Mutton with such and such garnish.

ROLLED SHOULDER OF MUTTON, OYSTER SAUCE—Bone the shoulder; where the bone was, spread with oyster croquette mixture, roll up tight, tie closely with string, place in a steamer and steam till done; serve in portions with white oyster sauce; or if after it has been steamed two-thirds done, take it up and finish cooking in a sharp oven, take out when a deep fawn color and serve with brown oyster sauce.

BOILED MUTTON WITH TURNIPS—Use either the leg or the shoulder, boil it medium done in salted water with a few root vegetables; serve portions on a bed of mashed turnips, with caper sauce around the base.

STUFFED BREAST OF MUTTON, SAUCE ROBERT—Lean breast of mutton, pocket made the entire length between the meat and rib bones, filled with a stuffing made of sausage meat mixed with minced onions, parsley, mushrooms and a few fresh breadcrumbs, sew up the opening, steam till done; serve in portions with sauce Robert.

BREAST OF MUTTON WITH TURNIPS—Lean breasts of mutton boiled tender in seasoned broth; when done, bones removed, pressed till cold and firm, then cut in strips, breaded, fried; served on a bed of mashed turnips with gravy round the base.

ROLLED STUFFED BREAST OF MUTTON—Broad cut lean breasts of mutton, boned, spread with veal or chicken forcemeat, rolled, tied with twine, baked slowly in roast mutton gravy; served garnished with a jardinière of vegetables.

BRAISED BREAST OF MUTTON, ITALIAN SAUCE—Breasts of mutton simmered in seasoned broth till the bones are easily removed, then press till cold, cut in triangular pieces, braise them in the reduced stock they were simmered in, then take up and strain the braise into a brown Italian sauce, which serve with the portions.

GLAZED BREAST OF MUTTON—
Lean breasts of mutton boiled till tender in seasoned broth, taken up and boned, then pressed till cold, cut in pieces, seasoned with salt and pepper, sauté in butter, then place in hot demi-glaze; serve garnished with small glazed onions.

FRIED BREAST OF MUTTON—
Breasts of mutton boiled tender in seasoned stock, taken up, boned, pressed, cut in shapes, dipped in beaten egg, rolled in fresh breadcrumbs, arranged in a buttered baking pan, sprinkle with melted butter, browned and frothed in a sharp oven; served surrounded with tomato sauce.

BROILED BREASTS OF MUTTON
—Lean breasts of mutton steamed long enough to draw the bones, taken up, skin scored, a seasoning of powdered thyme, salt and pepper then rubbed in, dipped in beaten egg, then in fresh breadcrumbs; placed two whole breasts at a time in wire hinged broiler, broiled, basted with butter; when nicely browned, served in two-inch wide strips with Piquante sauce under the meat. This dish is well appreciated at breakfast or luncheon.

HARICOT OF MUTTON—Lean breasts of mutton in strips seasoned with salt and pepper, fried

quickly a light brown, taken up into a saûtoir, sprinkled well with flour, shaken together, moistened with seasoned broth, brought to the boil and skimmed; column cut slices of root vegetables fried in butter with a little sugar, drained, added to the meat, the whole then simmered till half an hour before done, small balls of raw potatoes then added with small sautéed onions, finish cooking, season with salt and paprika; served with the vegetables as a garnish.

CURRY OF MUTTON WITH RICE—
Lean breasts of mutton in strips seasoned with salt, rubbed with curry powder, sautéed with butter a light brown color; taken up into a saûtoir, sprinkled and well shook with flour and little more curry powder, moistened with seasoned white broth, brought to the boil, skimmed, rings of sautéed onions then added, simmered and skimmed till done; serve within a border of dry boiled rice.

IRISH STEW—Lean breasts of mutton cut in strips, blanched, rinsed, put back into a clean saûtoir with balls or column cut slices of root vegetables, moisten with white stock, simmer and skim; when nearly done, balls of raw potatoes added; finish cooking, thicken with flour and butter, season with salt and pepper; serve sprinkled with chopped parsley.

RAGOUT OF MUTTON WITH TOMATOES—Lean breasts of mutton in strips, fried a light brown with butter and shallots, taken up into a saûtoir, sprinkled and shook well with flour, moistened with mutton gravy, simmered and skimmed, seasoned with salt, pepper and paprika; served garnished with a stuffed tomato at one end, and balls of glazed turnips at the other.

RISSOLES OF MUTTON, SAUCE HOLLANDAISE—Cold pieces of stewed mutton free of bones, minced finely, seasoned with salt chopped parsley, paprika, thyme and mace, mixed into one-third of its bulk of fresh mashed potatoes; when thoroughly mixed, allow to become quite cold, then form into finger lengths like sausages, double bread, fry; serve with Hollandaise sauce.

CASSEROLES OF MUTTON—Make a stiff potato croquette mixture, shape pieces of it like a patty, double bread and fry; now cut a lid scoop out the inside, thus leaving a case, fill the interior with mutton mince of the preceding recipe (heated), put on the lid, keep them hot; with the potatoes you scooped out, form into Duchesse potatoes and use as a garnish.

HASHED MUTTON WITH PEPPERS —Cold breasts of mutton from any of the foregoing recipes, cut small in dice shape, sautéed with minced onion, moistened with some Espagnole sauce. Green peppers, tops cut off, insides scooped out, double blanched, drained, filled with the mince, gratinated, slowly baked and basted till of a nice brown color; served with a rich tomato sauce poured around.

BREADED MUTTON CHOP WITH BEANS PURÉE—Best neck chops seasoned with salt and pepper, dipped in beaten egg, then breadcrumbs, fried medium done with butter; navy beans boiled, drained, rubbed through a tamis, little Béchamel sauce added, used as a bed on which to lay the chops; served with a demi-glaze around the base.

MUTTON CHOPS SAUTÉS, SAUCE SOÛBISE—Best neck chops trimmed, seasoned with salt and paprika, sautéed with butter and minced shallot; served on a bed of onion purée mixed with Velouté sauce, garnished with fancy croûtons.

MUTTON CHOP WITH POTATO BORDER—Best neck chops trimmed, fried a golden brown in butter, fresh mashed potatoes mixed with a little chopped parsley forced through a bag and tube around the dish, chop in centre with maître d'hôtel butter spread on it.

BREADED MUTTON CHOP WITH MUSHROOM PURÉE—Best neck chops trimmed, seasoned with salt and paprika, breaded, fried with butter; mushrooms stewed in Velouté sauce till soft, then rubbed through sieve; chop served resting on fancy shape of buttered toast with the purée around.

MUTTON CHOPS, PROVENCE STYLE —Trimmed neck chops sautéed half done with butter, equal parts of onion and mushroom purées with a flavor of garlic and a little chopped parsley, brought to the boil, thickened with egg yolks, stirred till of a thick paste; this spread on one side of the chop, ar-

LAMB CHOPS WITH MUSHROOM PURÉE

Serves 4

The original recipe calls for mutton chops. If you can find them, invite me over for dinner. If you can't, use lamb and invite me over anyway. This dish provides a great combination.

Purée

2 tablespoons olive oil

3 cloves garlic, peeled and chopped

1 cup peeled and sliced yellow onions

$^1/_3$ cup dry white wine

$^3/_4$ pound mushrooms, sliced

$1^1/_2$ tablespoons chopped parsley

2 tablespoons butter

4 tablespoons all-purpose flour

$1^1/_2$ cups Chicken Stock (page 153)

2 teaspoons Worcestershire sauce

Salt and freshly ground black pepper to taste

Heat a large frying pan and sauté the oil, garlic, and onions until almost clear. Add the wine, mushrooms, and parsley. Cover and simmer until the onions are very tender. Purée in a food processor and set aside.

In a 2-quart saucepan, melt the butter. Add the flour and cook to form a roux or paste. Do not brown. Using a wire whisk, whip in the Chicken Stock and simmer until smooth. Stir in the mushroom purée, Worcestershire sauce, and salt and pepper to taste. Keep warm until the meat is ready.

Meat

8 lamb chops, cut 1 inch thick

Paprika to taste

Salt to taste

2 cups all-purpose flour

1 egg, beaten with 1 tablespoon water

2 cups bread crumbs

$^1/_4$ cup olive oil

Garnish

Parsley sprigs

Season the lamb chops with paprika and salt. Dredge the chops in flour. Pat off the excess flour and coat with the egg mixture and then the bread crumbs.

In a large frying pan, heat the oil. Add the lamb chops and fry for about 2 minutes on each side. Do not overcook, as you want these tender and juicy.

To serve, put a pool of the warm mushroom purée on a plate and float the breaded chops in the sauce. Garnish with parsley.

C.W.

ranged in a buttered baking pan, sprinkled with Parmesan cheese, finished in a quick oven; served with a brown sauce poured around.

MUTTON CHOP WITH GLAZED NEW CARROTS—

Best neck chops trimmed, seasoned and broiled medium done; new carrots trimmed, blanched, then sautéed till tender with butter and a little sugar, taken up, drained, then tossed in maitre d'hôtel sauce; served as a garnish to the chop. (Plain broiled chop as in the recipe here given may be served with a garnish of either Bretonne purée, stuffed egg plant, stewed okras, haricots verts, macedoine or jardinière of vegetables, flageolets, green peas, vegetable purée, fried parsley, spinach purée, mashed potatoes, sautéed balls of turnip, and simply named on the bill of fare as Mutton Chop with such or such garnish, as prepared.)

MUTTON CHOP WITH TRUFFLES—

Loin chops trimmed, seasoned, broiled; served with a Madeira sauce containing plenty of sliced truffles.

COATED CUTLETS OF MUTTON

—Trimmed loin chops, quickly sautéed with butter half done, dipped into a thick sauce containing minced ham and mushrooms, they are then breaded and slowly fried till done; served resting on a fancy croûton, or they may be coated with an onion purée and served with a Soûbise sauce.

MUTTON CHOP, SOUTHERN STYLE

—Loin chops trimmed, seasoned, sautéed till done with butter and minced shallot; served on a fancy croûton garnished with a mold of dry boiled rice, a stuffed baked tomato and some stewed okras.

MUTTON CHOP WITH PEAS PURÉE

—Loin chops trimmed and partly sautéed, then dipped into a thick yellow parsley sauce, breaded, fried; served on a bed of peas purée and surrounded with Velouté sauce.

BAKED MUTTON CUTLETS WITH APPLES—

Take the chops of the neck under the shoulder, place them in a buttered pan with some sliced apples and onions, season with salt and pepper, just cover with a nice clear gravy, place another pan over as a lid, bake about 45 minutes, remove when glazy; serve the chop in centre of dish with apples at one side and onions at the other side, garnishing the ends of dish with fancy croûtons.

MUTTON CHOPS FRIED, ITALIAN SAUCE—

Best neck chops trimmed, spread with a sauce containing minced onions, little garlic, Parmesan cheese and hard boiled egg yolks rubbed through a sieve; when set, double breaded, fried and served with a brown Italian sauce.

BREADED MUTTON CHOP, SAUCE PERIGUEUX—

Best neck chops trimmed, spread with a thick truffle sauce; when set, double breaded, fried; served with Perigueux sauce.

MUTTON CUTLETS FRIED, REFORME GARNISH—

Loin chops trimmed, seasoned with salt and pepper, dipped in beaten eggs, then in grated ham, again in eggs, then in a mixture of grated ham and fresh breadcrumbs, arranged in buttered baking pan, placed in a medium oven, browned and basted with butter; served with a garnish of shredded ham, slices of carrots and truffles, also rings of whites of hard boiled eggs in a sauce Suprême.

MUTTON STEW WITH VEGETABLES—Scrags and lean breasts of mutton cut in neat pieces, seasoned with salt and pepper, sautéed a golden color in butter with a few small onions, flour then added to form a roux, moisten with boiling stock, then boil up and skim, season to taste with salt, pepper, nutmeg and a clove of garlic; when half done, cubes of carrot and turnip then added, also some lima beans, simmer till done; serve. (Varieties of stew as above may be made by garnishing with rice timbales and small stuffed tomatoes instead of the vegetables; also instead of the vegetables, use stewed tomatoes and an extra clove of garlic; or using a plain garnish of either green peas, flageolets, stringless beans, butter beans, haricot beans, glazed new carrots, braised stalks of celery, fried egg plant, rice and okras; small white turnips hollowed out, steamed, then filled with a macedoine, jardinière; green peas, flageolets, etc., potato croquettes, slices of stuffed cucumber, stuffed artichoke bottoms, etc., and named accordingly.) REMEMBER ALWAYS THAT IT IS THE STEWS WHICH KEEP DOWN THE KITCHEN EXPENSES, AND ARE ALWAYS IN STRONG DEMAND BY THE PATRONS, IF WELL COOKED, SEASONED, AND VERY NEATLY GARNISHED; IT THEN APPEALS TO THE EYE AND ITS SAVORINESS TO THE PALATE. DO NOT LET YOUR VEGETABLE OR FRY COOK JUST DISH IT OUT ON TO THE PLATTER WITH A LADLE SIMPLY BECAUSE IT IS A STEW; PLACE THE MEAT NEATLY ON A DISH, THEN GARNISH IT WITH CARE.

HASHED MUTTON IN PEPPERS—Four lbs. of cold cooked mutton cut in small dice, four medium sized onions minced and lightly fried with butter, then added to the mutton, mix, then moisten with a little Espagnole sauce, season to taste, then bring to a simmer. Two dozen medium sized green peppers, tops cut off, seeded, double blanched, then filled with the hash; gratinate the tops, bake in a slow oven to a delicate brown; served with tomato sauce poured around.

CROÛSTADES OF MUTTON WITH POACHED EGG—Cold roast mutton cut in small dice, then placed in a saûtoir and moistened with a light consommé and a pint of demi-glaze to each four lbs. of meat. Reduce it to about half over a medium fire; half a dozen each of green peppers and shallots minced and lightly fried with butter then added to the hash, mix; fill into fancy croûstades to order, placing on top of each a freshly cooked and trimmed poached egg, garnish with watercress.

MUTTON CHOPS WITH BUTTERED CORN—Take a rack of mutton, remove the meat from the bone in one piece, trim, cut it up into four ounce cutlets, season with salt and pepper, broil between a wire hinged broiler a golden brown; meanwhile cut corn from hot cooked cobs, season with salt and cream, fill into oval dishes, cover the top with breadcrumbs and sprinkle with melted butter, bake brown quickly; when done, place a chop on the corn, a few Julienne potatoes around the edge, and send to table.

MUTTON CUTLET SAUTÉ WITH FINE HERBS—Trimmed chump chops fried with butter, fried minced shallots, parsley and mushrooms, sprinkled over when sending to table.

MUTTON PIE, ENGLISH STYLE—Middle neck chops trimmed and shortened, arranged in a deep pie dish around the sides, the centre filled with balls of potatoes or small new ones; make a rich white sauce from strong mutton stock, season with pepper and salt, chopped parsley and capers, cover the mutton and potatoes with it plentifully, place on a short crust, egg wash, bake one hour in a medium oven.

BRAISED BONED LOIN OF MUTTON—Take a loin of mutton and remove the chine bone (this can be done without injuring the meat by loosening the tenderloin first); where the bone was, fill with a stiff forcemeat, roll over the flap and tie with twine; arrange in a brasiere with vegetables and spices, moisten with stock enough to just cover the mutton, braise and baste till done and glazy; serve in portions with a garnish either of green peas, macedoine, jardinière, asparagus tips, new carrots, stringless beans, small glazed turnips, stuffed and glazed cucumbers, flowerets of cauliflower, etc. It should be noted that glaze should be over and around slightly the meat portion, and the vegetable garnish should be moistened with either a Velouté, Béchamel or Allemande sauce.

BRAISED MUTTON CHOPS, GARNISHED—Racks of mutton trimmed, chine bone loosened and the yellow gristle that runs the full length of the chine removed, arranged in the brasiere with carrot, onion, celery, parsley, whole cloves and mace, moistened with stock just enough to cover, braised and basted till done and glazy, taken up, the braise strained and skimmed; served in chops, each chop rolled in the glaze; served garnished with small stuffed tomatoes, Brussels sprouts, glazed small onions, flageolets, green peas, asparagus tips, sauerkraut, new carrots or turnips, potato quenelles and stewed prunes (German style), potato croquettes, Soûbise purée, jardinière or a macedoine of vegetables.

BROILED MUTTON CHOPS, GARNISHED—Racks of mutton trimmed, chine bone and gristle removed, cut into cutlets, seasoned with salt and pepper, dipped into melted butter, broiled medium done of a golden color; served on a triangle of toast, garnished with either brown Italian, tomato, Provençale, Poivrade, piquante, shallot or fines-herbes sauces, or with mashed potatoes in shapes, mashed turnips, spinach purée, endive purée, Soûbise purée, Bretonne beans purée, jardinière, macedoine, asparagus tips, Brussels sprouts sautées, green peas, Julienne vegetables in Allemande sauce, small new potatoes boiled, then moistened with maître d'hôtel butter, purée of artichoke, chipolata garnish, French beans (haricots verts), new lima beans, button mushrooms sautées, stuffed olives.

NASTURTIUM—Name of a plant whose seeds are extensively used as a substitute for pickled capers.

NASTURTIUM—The edible leaves and flowers of nasturtiums (*Tropaeolum majus*) have a slight peppery flavor, and have had some recent popularity as a salad ingredient and colorful garnish.

NAVARIN—A French word given to a brown mutton stew with vegetables, the same as our "haricot of mutton."

NESSELRODE—Name given to an iced pudding, named after a Russian statesman, composed of a purée of chestnuts, whipped cream, glazed fruits, a flavoring of maraschino, mixed and frozen.

NESSELRODE—Nesselrode pudding, like most cream-and-egg desserts, is not as popular as it once was. In its most recent incarnation, however, it was made with eggs, sugar, cream, ladyfingers, and—sometimes—fruit. Chestnut purée distinguished it from other puddings. It was chilled, not frozen.

NEUFCHÂTEL—Name of a cream curd cheese imported from Switzerland. But most of that used in hotel life is made in our own dairies and equally as good as the imported.

NEUFCHÂTEL—Closely related to cream cheese, Neufchâtel is a bit richer.

NIVERNAISE—Name given to a garnish of Julienne vegetables mixed in Allemande sauce.

NOISETTE—French name for nut. Sometimes seen on "bills of fare" as "Noisettes of mutton," "Noisettes d'agneau (nuts of lamb)," "Noisettes de veau (nuts of veal)." To prepare this dish I will quote Leon Cieux, a Parisian chef:

"NOISETTES OF LAMB, À LA MAINTENON—Take the two fillets and small fillets (filets mignons) from a saddle of lamb, take out the nerves, trim them, and divide each fillet into six parts and the small fillets into three parts, beat them, season with salt and pepper, sauté them quickly on both sides with clear butter; as soon as sautéed, put in a good Perigorde sauce, this stops the wasting and prevents the meat from giving up its gravy. Place each noisette of lamb on a crust of breadcrumb passed through butter and the shape of the noisette; arrange in a crown on the dish, cover each noisette with a Soûbise a la Béchamel. Powder with grated Parmesan cheese, moistened with melted butter, glazed in a hot oven; pour in the middle of the dish some Perigord sauce, put on each noisette a fine slice of truffle and serve hot, the cooking must be quick. This recipe is for twelve persons."

I will here quote the author of the *Epicurean*, Charles Ranhofer.

"NOISETTES OF MUTTON, AU MADERE—Cut eight chops of four ounces each from two racks of mutton. Remove the noix (centre of chop), beat them lightly, trim all to the same size, season with salt and pepper. Heat four ounces of butter in a frying pan, when it is very hot add to it the noix, sauté them over a quick fire, taking care to turn them when they have a good color, let them cook several minutes more, arrange them on croûtons of bread fried in butter and of the same size as the noix. Dry out the butter from the pan, add half a gill of Madeira, cook it down, add a little brown sauce, cook it down again until it is a light sauce, pass through the strainer and pour on the noix."

NOODLES—A stiff paste made with sifted flour and yolks of eggs, then rolled out very thin in sheets, place several sheets one on another, then with a sharp knife cut in strips; for soups or to be used for all purposes in place of macaroni; for all the recipes given for macaroni, noodles may be substituted; from the sheets may be stamped out fancy shapes for decorating raised pies, etc.

NOODLES—See PASTA.

NOYEAU—Name of a very fine liqueur prepared from the kernels of fruit stones, almonds, brandy, gin, flavoring extracts and syrup.

NUTMEG—The kernel of the fruit of the nutmeg tree. The fruit itself is in size and shape that of a small pear, which on ripening, bursts, exposing its kernel covered with a netting; this netting is known as mace, the kernel itself as nutmeg; it is used as a flavoring to soups, sauces, puddings, custards, etc. The nutmegs from Penang are considered of most commercial value.

NUTMEG—Curiously, the nutmeg tree (*Myristica fragrans*), which grows to be sixty feet high in the Moluccas (once known as the Spice

Islands) and Grenada, the only two places in the world where it flourishes, *does* provide us with mace as well as nutmeg. Mace, which is used mostly in sweet-and-spicy desserts, is usually described as having a hot, rather coarse nutmeg flavor. It is no longer a widely used spice.

Nutmeg, on the other hand, was so popular in seventeenth- and eighteenth-century Europe that one French poet wrote, "Do you like nutmeg? It's in everything." English men and women carried small silver nutmeg graters with them so they could add their favorite spice to dishes at the table, despite the fact that the food undoubtedly had been cooked with it and other spices. This is perhaps understandable: Until the "discovery" of nutmeg and the other "noble" spices, European food was bland. The highly competitive—and sometimes violent— spice trade enlivened cooking to an excess (and made for interesting geopolitical arrangements as well!).

Now few people would argue that nutmeg is a spice of major importance; like mace, it is primarily reserved for use in desserts. But anyone who has ever grated a bit of fresh nutmeg onto a bowl of steaming spinach recognizes the status of this spice and realizes that it has the power to transform many dishes.

OATMEAL—As the word implies it is the meal of oats; the oat grains are skinned, dried, then ground in a mill and placed into commerce as coarse and fine oatmeal. This is then used to make in conjunction with wheat flour, cakes, biscuits, bread, gruel, drinks, mush, puddings, thickening soups, etc., etc. A mistake is therefore made when writing "bills of fare" to say "oatmeal porridge" unless you use the meal; and seldom is the meal used. It is customary nowadays to use rolled oats, flaked oats, and the different names given by manufacturers, such as H. O., Quaker Oats, etc., which are all rolled and not meal. Groats is the proper name for the dried out grains which are neither crushed or ground.

OATMEAL—The *Larousse Gastronomique* plainly states, "Roast oat grains have a smell which strongly resembles that of vanilla." This smell obviously has escaped most of us, who treat oats as a second-rate grain at best. It is close to useless for bread (no gluten develops during kneading), and its taste is bitter. Consequently it has few devotees, and its uses are extremely limited.

Our aversion to oats is nothing new. Samuel Johnson, in his *Dictionary of the English Language*, says that this is a grain that "in England is generally given to horses but in Scotland supports the people." Because they grow farther north than wheat or any other grain except BUCKWHEAT, oats have long been a staple in Scotland, Scandinavia, and northern Europe east to Siberia (but in those areas where wheat can be grown, oats usually are not).

Oats do produce a wonderful porridge (using whole grain and a technique similar to that employed in making POLENTA) and a good breakfast cereal (using rolled oats, which are steamed before rolling, a process that significantly prolongs their shelf life). But few of us eat either dish without plenty of butter, cream, or milk, and sugar, honey, or maple syrup.

OKRA—Name of an American vegetable chiefly grown in the South; of a seed pod shape like the long pepper. It is preserved and canned, this being generally used in making gumbo soups when the fresh is not obtainable. The fresh is trimmed at both ends, boiled in salted boiling water till tender, taken up and drained, seasoned with salt, pepper and melted butter and served as a vegetable, or used as a garnish, or in conjunction with other vegetables as a garnish. The Creoles like it slippery, and after trimming it they place it in a saûtoir with just enough water to moisten, cover with oiled paper, place on the lid and stew it till tender and mucilaginous, then it is further seasoned with olive oil, salt, pepper and a little minced green or red peppers. Okras are esteemed stewed with tomatoes, keeping the okras whole; also by taking peeled raw tomatoes and okras, cutting them both into quarters, then stewing with butter, pepper and salt; also the whole okras trimmed, then stewed tender in a rich tomato sauce; also tipped at both ends, breaded and fried, like egg plant.

OKRA—African or Asian in origin, okra was brought to the New World along with the slaves. The tomato-and-okra preparations mentioned by Fellows are still made in the South, as is fried okra. It plays a role as a thickener in some Creole gumbo (the word *gumbo* once meant "okra") recipes and also in dozens of dishes throughout the Third World.

Okra has a clean, light flavor, but it has a mucilaginous, almost slimy quality that offends many people (a 1974 Department of Agriculture survey of Americans found okra to be among the three least-liked vegetables.)

Actually, okra is a delicious vegetable, and when cooked long enough, it loses the "slimy" characteristic that most people claim it has. Try it fried.

OKRA SALAD—Okras trimmed and boiled in boiling salted water, then drained and cooled; stripped endive washed and crisp arranged on dish, the okras quartered and laid on top, the whole sprinkled with a French salad dressing containing chopped chives.

OLIVES—The fruit of the olive tree, picked green, prepared and salted, then packed into barrels, kegs, etc., also put up in glass jars. Our own California olives have been brought to such perfection, that they are now found to be superior to the imported European, French, Spanish and Italian. Olive oil is prepared from the ripe fruit. Olives are used as an appetizer, either plain or stoned and stuffed; as a decorative to salads, as a flavoring to sauces, as an addition to garnitures, etc.

OLIVES—California olives may be a marvel of size, uniformity, and packaging, but they not among the world's best when it comes to flavor (there are, fortunately, increasing numbers of Californians who are interested in growing and producing good olives). For good quality, look to the Mediterranean, where the intensely bitter fruit—it is essentially inedible until soaked and then brined or salted—originated, where it still grows wild, where it exerted its most powerful influence on great cuisines, and where the best olive groves are found. Some groves are literally a thousand years old, and there are living trees, say the locals, that were planted at the time of Christ.

The olive (*Olea europaea*) is green when immature and black (or sometimes purple) when ripe. Although green olives are sometimes stuffed with red pepper or anchovies, the most intriguing specimens from Greece, Spain, Italy, and France are varied enough to make such treatment superfluous. Increasingly, olives from these four countries can be found in our markets. The Greek kalamátas are widely available (look, too, for the excellent green náfplion), as are the French niçoise and the oil-cured black olives from Italy. The Italian barese olives, for example, are almost forest green, fresh, and sweet. Olives are almost as varied as breads, and equally worthy of attention.

Now, olive oil. Like olives, the most worthy olive oils are from Spain, Italy, France, and Greece. Unlike olives, olive oil has become a trendy, precious food. All you need to know about olive oils is that extra-virgin oils are from the first, most gentle pressing, have few impurities, and are expensive. This doesn't make them best for all purposes. Many extra-virgin oils from northern Italy are too delicate for cooking.

The lesser grades of olive oil are great for cooking. Use the extra-virgin oil in preparations when you want to enjoy its rich flavor, such as to dress salads and vegetables and sprinkled on bread.

OLLA PODRIDA—One of the national dishes of Spain; a rich soup stew, made in the style of a pepperpot. A large earthenware pot into a which is placed tomatoes, garlic, long peppers, chick peas, pieces of root vegetables, chopped cabbage and endive, a piece of flank of beef, a fowl, a piece of streaky bacon and sausages. The sausages are made of equal quantities of minced lean and fat pork, seasoned with garlic and red pepper; when mixed it is macerated in dry sherry wine for four days till it has absorbed all it can, it is then filled into sausage casings, tied in links, hung till dry in a cool air. The contents of the pot are seasoned with salt and pepper, moistened with water, placed in medium oven and cooked till tender. It is served as a family dish by placing the vegetables at the bottom of a platter as a garnish to the three meats, the sausages on top of the vegetables, and the broth poured over the whole.

OMELET—Slightly beaten eggs seasoned with salt and a little melted butter so as to prevent it from sticking to the pan in cooking; see that the pan is free from any sticky substance on the inside, bottom and flange; place in a little melted butter, let it get hot (not burnt), pour in a ladle of eggs, shuffle around till nearly set, then take the handle in the left hand, depress the pan, then with the right hand knock the handle near the pan, and the omelet will roll up from the furthest end, thus forming a roll with pointed ends, hold to the fire for a moment and the centre will puff up, turn on to a platter, garnish one end with a sprig of crisp cress or parsley and send the plain omelet to the table at once. I HAVE SAID

POUR A LADLE OF EGGS, BECAUSE I HAVE FOUND THAT THE ORDERS ARE SERVED MORE EQUAL BY ITS USE. HAVE A LADLE MADE THAT WILL HOLD EQUAL TO THREE LIGHTLY BEATEN EGGS. ONE LADLEFUL WILL BE FOUND THE RIGHT QUANTITY PER PERSON.

OMELET WITH BACON—(Plain or with Piquante sauce). Cut the bacon into small dice, fry fairly well done, pour off the fat, pour in a ladle of eggs, mix and form; served with sprig of green, or with Piquante sauce at the ends.

OMELET WITH VEAL KIDNEYS— Roasted kidneys cut in dice and made hot in a little demi-glaze with chopped parsley, enclose the mixture within the omelet; serve with a Madeira sauce poured around.

OMELET WITH CÈPES—Cut the cèpes into dice, fry in butter for a few minutes, pour off the butter, add a ladle of eggs, form and serve with a little Italian sauce at the sides.

OMELET WITH CHEESE—Mix grated cheese with the beaten eggs in proportion of one-third cheese to two-thirds eggs, form the omelet; when placed on the serving dish sprinkle a little grated cheese on top of the omelet and brown off quickly in oven or under a salamander.

OMELET WITH CHICKEN LIVERS— Blanch the livers, then cut in dice, fry them lightly with butter, minced shallots and mushrooms for ten minutes, season with salt, pepper and chopped parsley, enclose a spoonful within the omelet while forming; served with Hanover sauce at the sides.

OMELET WITH CHIPPED BEEF— Scald, drain and mince the dried beef, mix it with the eggs, form the omelet; serve with cream sauce poured around.

OMELET WITH HAM—Cooked minced ham moistened with Madeira sauce enclosed within the omelet.

Raw minced ham with a little minced shallot and parsley fried till done, ladle of eggs poured in, formed and served.

Minced fried ham beaten up with the eggs, poured into the omelet pan, formed and served.

OMELET WITH LAMB KIDNEYS —Cut the kidneys into small dice and fry them with minced shallots in butter for three minutes, add a little Madeira sauce and chopped parsley, enclose a spoonful within the omelet while forming; serve with Madeira sauce poured around.

Stew the kidneys in a sherry wine flavored brown sauce, season well with red pepper or a minced red pepper; when done, strain the sauce on to some unsweetened apple sauce passed through a fine sieve; into the beaten eggs put some finely chopped green mint, enclose a spoonful of kidneys within the omelet while forming; serve with plenty of the sauce poured around.

OMELET WITH SWEETBREADS— Cooked sweetbreads cut in dice,

simmered in mushroom sauce, a spoonful enclosed within the omelet while forming; served with mushroom sauce poured around.

OMELET WITH MUSHROOMS—If fresh mushrooms, peel them, trim, cut into dice and fry with butter; if canned, cut them in thin slices and fry, drain, then mix them into Madeira sauce; enclose a spoonful within the omelet; serve with a spoonful of mushrooms in sauce at the ends of the omelet.

OMELET WITH SHRIMPS, MEXICAN STYLE—Take fresh cooked or canned shrimps, cut in halves, mix with some finely chopped green peppers, put them into a Velouté sauce containing some lobster butter, simmer for five minutes, enclose a spoonful within the omelet, turn on the serving dish, place two whole shrimps on top, and pour some of the sauce around.

OMELET WITH FINE HERBS—Beat up with the eggs some finely minced shallots, thyme, marjoram, chervil, chives and parsley, season with salt and pepper, form the omelet, and serve plain or with fine herbs sauce poured around.

SPANISH OMELET—Finely shred onions, minced green peppers, minced mushrooms, solid tomatoes with the juice and seeds expressed, cut in small pieces, the whole fried with butter for five minutes, then add tomato sauce, season with salt and pepper, reduce till thick, enclose a spoonful within the omelet, turn on to the serving dish, garnish the top with fancy

strips of pimentoes and place a spoonful of the mixture at each end of the omelet.

OMELET WITH SPINACH—Beat some purée of spinach with the eggs, season with salt and pepper, form and serve.

OMELET WITH PARSLEY—Mix some finely chopped parsley with the beaten eggs, season with salt and pepper, form and serve plain or with Velouté sauce at the sides.

OMELET WITH TOMATOES—Stew fresh or canned tomatoes with a little butter, sugar, salt and pepper till of a thick pulp, enclose a spoonful within the omelet; serve with tomato sauce poured around.

OMELET WITH TOMATOED RICE— Take some boiled rice grains and moisten them with a good tomato purée, enclose some within the omelet; serve with tomato purée poured around.

OMELET WITH OYSTERS—Scald the oysters, cut them in quarters, place them into a rich thick oyster sauce, enclose a spoonful within the omelet, turn on to the serving dish, place three whole scalded oysters on top, pour some oyster sauce over the whole and sprinkle with parsley dust.

OMELET WITH FRENCH OR SMALL GREEN PEAS—Simmer some peas in reduced Velouté sauce with a little minced green mint, till thick, enclose some within the omelet, turn on to the serving dish, garnish each end with more of the peas and the sides with cream sauce.

OMELET WITH EGG PLANT—Cut the egg plant into dice, fry it with butter, when done, add a little meat glaze, enclose within the omelet; serve with a good brown sauce at the sides.

OMELET WITH SPRING VEGETABLES—Cut a jardinière of macedoine of vegetables (or use canned ones), boil till tender, drain, moisten with a little demi-glaze or sauce Suprême, enclose within the omelet, turn on to the serving dish, decorate the top of omelet with more of the vegetables and pour some of the sauce around.

OMELET WITH ASPARAGUS POINTS —Take cooked asparagus tips, reheat them in Allemande sauce, enclose within the omelet, turn on to serving dish, decorate the top with more tips, and serve with Allemande sauce at the sides.

OMELET WITH OLIVES—Stuffed olives sliced, heated in a rich Madeira sauce, enclosed within the omelet, turned on to serving dish, the top of omelet decorated with slices of stuffed olives; served with Madeira sauce at the sides.

OMELET WITH ONIONS—Fry some thin slices of onions with a clove of garlic in butter, enclose within the omelet; serve with Soûbise sauce at the sides.

OMELET WITH MINCED CHICKEN —Take minced cooked chicken, moisten it with Velouté sauce, make hot, enclose within the omelet; serve with Velouté sauce at the sides.

CREOLE OMELET—Chopped green peppers, onions, garlic, okras and a little boiled rice, made hot in a thick tomato sauce, enclosed within the omelet; served with a spoonful of the mixture at the sides.

ALGERIENNE OMELET—Rissoto moistened and reheated with tomato purée, enclosed within the omelet; served with tomato purée at the sides.

OMELET WITH TRUFFLES—Slices of truffles moistened with truffle sauce, enclosed within the omelet; served with truffle sauce at the sides.

OMELET WITH PURÉE OF GAME—A rich game purée is enclosed within the omelet; served with game sauce at the sides.

INDIAN OMELET—Minced onion lightly fried then mixed with the beaten eggs, adding a seasoning of curry powder and a spoonful of thick cream, boiled rice enclosed within the omelet; served with curry sauce at the sides.

OMELET WITH CHICKEN PURÉE—A rich puré of chicken enclosed within the omelet; served with Velouté sauce at the sides.

MILANAISE OMELET—Boiled macaroni chopped fine, mixed with Parmesan cheese and a spoonful of tomato purée, enclosed within the omelet; served with Milanaise sauce at the sides.

OMELET WITH SHRIMP PASTE—Omelet spread with shrimp paste just before forming; served with shrimp sauce at the sides.

SHRIMP OMELET—Chopped shrimps in Aurora sauce enclosed within the omelet, turned on to the serving dish, the top decorated with coiled shrimps, served with Aurora sauce at the sides.

OMELET WITH SCALLOPS—Scallops blanched then fried with butter, cut in dice, moistened with Béchamel sauce, enclosed within the omelet; served with the top decorated with a whole fried scallop, Béchamel sauce at the sides.

OMELET FINANCIÈRE—A spoonful of Financière garnish enclosed within the omelet; served with some more of the garnish at the sides.

OMELET WITH CALF'S HEAD—Useful to use up the remains of entrée "Calf's head, turtle style." Cut the meat small, enclose within the omelet; served with more of the garnish at the sides.

OMELET WITH CAPON—Cold capon cut in dice and moistened with Velouté sauce, enclosed within the omelet; served with Suprême sauce at the sides.

OMELET WITH CALF'S BRAINS—Scalded and trimmed calf's brains cut in dice and moistened with Hollandaise sauce, enclosed within the omelet; served with some Hollandaise sauce at the sides.

OMELET WITH TURKEY LIVERS—Braised turkey livers cut in scallops and moistened with fine herbs sauce, enclosed within the omelet; served with more of the sauce at the sides.

OMELET WITH ANCHOVIES—Filleted anchovies cut in shreds, moistened with Aurora or Genevoise sauces, enclosed within the omelet; served with the sauce used at the sides, the top of the omelet to be garnished with strips of the anchovies in lattice work form.

OMELET WITH FOIE-GRAS—Foie-gras cut in dice with a little chopped truffle peelings, moistened with Madeira sauce, enclosed within the omelet; served with Madeira sauce at the sides, the top of the omelet to be decorated with a slice each of the foie-gras and truffle.

OMELET CHIPOLATA—A spoonful of chipolata garnish (see GARNISHES), enclosed within the omelet; served with Madeira sauce at the sides, the ends of the omelet to be garnished with Parisienne potatoes.

OMELET WITH JELLY—With the omelet mixture add a spoonful of cream and a very little sugar; before starting to roll the omelet, spread with jelly, then roll it up; when turned on the serving dish, dust with powdered sugar, mark the top in lattice work style with a red hot wire, place a little more jelly at the sides and serve.

OMELET WITH MERINGUE—Little cream and sugar mixed with the beaten eggs, before rolling, spread with jam, then form; when on the serving dish, spread with meringue, decorate the meringue with point of knife, place in oven till of a delicate fawn color and serve at once.

OMELET WITH CUSTARD CREAM —Little cream and sugar mixed with the beaten eggs, a spoonful of rich custard cream enclosed within the omelet, turned on to the serving dish; served with a little apricot purée at the sides.

OMELET WITH MARMALADE—Little cream and sugar mixed with the beaten eggs; before rolling, spread with fruit marmalade, form, place on serving dish, dust with powdered sugar, then place in hot oven to glaze, or glaze with a salamander.

OMELET WITH RUM—Little cream and sugar mixed with the beaten eggs, omelet formed, turned on to the serving dish, dusted with powdered sugar, marked with a red hot wire, rum made warm and poured around the omelet; then set on fire, either at the entrance to the dining room or on the table at the request of the guest.

OMELET SOUFFLÉ—One teaspoonful of sugar to each egg, yolks and whites whipped separately, the sugar and a teaspoonful of cream with the yolks, then all stirred together, poured into oval dish or pan, baked partly on top of the range, then finished in oven; when nicely puffed, dust with powdered sugar, and glaze with a salamander; the omelet mixture may be flavored with most any liqueur or cordial.

ONIONS—Quite possibly the world's most important vegetable, the onion (*Allium cepa*) is prehistoric. Although it probably originated in Asia, it long has been ubiquitous, and few cuisines could do without it. Nor is great flavor the onion's only asset; when briefly cured above ground, it has the ability to keep from fall until spring, when new, green onions can be harvested.

Like GARLIC, the onion is a lily and, like garlic, most species stink when raw and are mild and sweet when cooked. This has not stopped people from eating onions raw: Ernest Hemingway was partial to peanut-butter-and-onion sandwiches— an uniquely American creation if ever there was one—and many salads are given a boost by a sprinkling of chopped or sliced onions. Oftentimes the sweeter types (Walla Walla, Vidalia, or Bermuda) are used here.

Clearly, however, the onion's most important role is in cooking. It can be stuffed as a main course, and is enormously useful as a vegetable and a sauce, and its aromatic flavor enormously improves countless dishes.

ONIONS FRIED—Large sized onions peeled, cut in fairly thick slices, the rings then separated, seasoned with salt, dipped in milk, then shaken up with flour till coated, fried till done in very hot deep fat like French fried potatoes; when done, drained, sprinkled with salt; served plain or as a garnish.

ONIONS FRIED—Thinly sliced onions fried with butter, bacon fat, beef dripping, etc., till well done and brown, surplus fat then poured off; used as a garnish to steaks.

ONIONS IN CREAM SAUCE—Small onions peeled, boiled in salted water till tender, taken up and drained, then put into cream sauce; used as a vegetable.

BOILED ONIONS—Medium sized onions peeled, boiled well done in salted water, taken up and well drained, kept very hot; served with a spoonful of melted butter poured over them; used as vegetable.

CREAMED ONIONS—Small button onions peeled, steamed till tender, drained, then put into a Poulette sauce; served as a garnish or vegetable.

BAKED ONIONS STUFFED—Large onions peeled, steamed till nearly done, centres removed in ONE PIECE which can be used the following day for the recipe preceding, the aperture filled with sausage meat, baked and basted till brown and glazy; served with a little meat gravy poured around.

ONIONS ON TOAST—Onions steamed till very well done, then mashed through a colander or tamis, seasoned, simmered with meat gravy; fancy cut slices of toast then spread thickly with the onions and served very hot (a good thing for a cold on the chest).

STEWED ONIONS—Onions cut in quarters, steamed till half done, then simmered in a parsley butter sauce till done; served as a vegetable.

BRAISED ONIONS—Medium sized onions peeled, blanched, drained, arranged in a pan or brasiere, baked and basted with slices of bacon and its fat till brown and glazy; served as a garnish or vegetable.

ONION SAUCE—Well boiled onions mashed through a tamis, slightly moistened with sauce made from mutton stock; to be served with boiled mutton.

ONION SAUCE—Onions peeled and parboiled, then cut up small and blanched again, then allowed to simmer in a white sauce if to be served with boiled meat, and in a brown sauce if to be served with roast or braised meat.

GLAZED ONIONS—Peeled onions of a uniform size arranged in a shallow sautoir, seasoned with salt, pepper and sugar, slightly moistened with stock, covered with a sheet of buttered paper, simmered till done and brown, and the liquor to a glaze.

ONION PURÉE—Onions peeled, blanched, drained, chopped, placed in a saûtoir with butter and lightly fried without color, flour then added to form a roux, moisten with white or brown stock according to whether it is to be served with boiled or roast meat, simmer till very tender, season with salt and a little sugar, then rub the whole though a tamis.

PICKLED ONIONS—Small button onions peeled, placed in crocks, boiled brine poured over them, allowed to stand for 24 hours, brine then drained off onions then covered with scalding hot (not boiling) cider vinegar spiced to taste with mace, chilies, whole peppers and a little horseradish.

ONION VINEGAR—Two quarts of white wine vinegar, one dessert spoonful of salt, two dessert spoonfuls of granulated sugar, two pounds of peeled Spanish onions; grate the onions, mix them with the sugar and salt, allow to macerate for three hours, then pour over the vinegar; fill fruit jars 2/3 full, screw the lid on, shake well every day for a couple of weeks, then strain off through cheese cloth, fill into bottles and cork tight; this is very useful when a delicate onion flavor is desired with mayonnaise, salads, etc.

ONION SALAD—Take either the Bermuda or Spanish onion, peel, slice in rings 1/4 of an inch thick, steam till half cooked, let become very cold; serve on lettuce leaves with Ravigote sauce.

ONION SOUP WITH CRUSTS—Make a thin cream of chicken soup, thinly slice half a pound of onions to each gallon of soup, fry them with butter to a golden color, then add them to the soup and simmer for ten minutes; served with a small unsweetened rusk to each plate.

PURÉE OF BERMUDA ONIONS—Bermuda onions lightly fried with butter and little sugar, flour added to form a roux, moistened with chicken stock, simmered till done, the whole then rubbed through a tamis, and added to 1/3 of its bulk of cream or cream sauce; serve with croûtons.

A variation of the above recipe is, after it is passed through the tamis, place it back on the range, bring to the boil, then add a rich liaison of egg yolks and cream, finish with a little very finely chopped parsley.

ONION SOUP WITH CHEESE CANAPÉS—A cream soup made of white stock with plenty of minced onions boiled in it till very tender, adding a little chopped parsley; fancy cut slices of toast spread with cheese and melted on in the oven, one in each plate, the soup poured over it and sent to table.

BROWN ONION PURÉE—Fried onions, flour added to form a roux and browned, moistened with roast veal gravy and stock, the whole then rubbed through a tamis; served with croûtons.

ONION PURÉE WITH FISH QUENELLES—Make the white "Purée of Bermuda onions" of a preceding recipe, and serve with quenelles of fish that may be on hand.

BUTTON ONION SOUP WITH PEAS —A cream of chicken soup with plenty of very small button onions boiled in it, also fresh or canned green peas.

OPOSSUM—A Southern animal found in hollow trees, hunted for by trained dogs, is killed, scalded, scraped, split, skin scored like a suckling pig, arranged in a pan surrounded with peeled and split sweet potatoes, roasted and basted till done; served with the potatoes and corn bread.

OPOSSUM—Good southern cooks still favor opossum, although it is rarely obtainable from anyone other than hunters.

ORANGES—One of the world's oldest fruits, oranges were planted in Florida almost as soon as the first Spaniard set foot ashore, and the Sunshine State still produces the hemisphere's juiciest, tastiest, and sweetest crops. (Unfortunately, Floridians keep the best for themselves and ship the rest elsewhere.) We think of oranges as a winter fruit, and rightfully so: Few varieties ripen until December and many remain on the tree until early spring.

Like many fruits, the orange—in all its forms, which include kumquat, bitter orange, tangerine, mandarin, and the more common tight-skinned sweet oranges (*Citrus sinensis*)—is native to Asia, specifically, China. It is now grown in temperate and tropical zones throughout the world and, according to John McPhee, who wrote a detailed book about the fruit's history, the orange moved around the Old World, from India to Spain, with the conquering Muslim armies of the sixth and seventh centuries.

Americans "eat" most of their oranges in the form of juice and pay little attention to the variety of fresh oranges they buy. Navel is the most popular, but the blood orange, a small, late-season variety, is usually the sweetest. Oranges should have tight skins and no blemishes; color is of secondary importance, but they should feel heavy for their size, an indication of an abundance of juice.

ORANGE JAM—Four pounds of oranges, one pound of lemons, four pounds of sugar, one pound of butter, 32 yolks and 4 whole eggs. The fruit grated, the juice extracted, the juice, sugar and grated rinds then boiled together, butter melted and beaten up with the yolks and eggs, added to the boiling juice, constantly stirring till of a jam consistency; used for pie filling, layer cake spreading, filling darioles, cheesecakes, patty-pan tarts, etc.

BAKED ORANGE PUDDING—Two pounds of stale sponge cake; juice of 8, and grated rinds of 2 oranges, 1 cup of sugar, 2 tablespoons of melted butter, 6 beaten eggs, 1 pint of milk. Boil the milk, pour it to the sponge cake, whip it, add the juice, grated rinds and other ingredients, fill into molds, bake; serve with orange sauce.

ORANGE FRITTERS—Large oranges peeled, pith removed, pulled into quarters, simmered for five minutes in boiling syrup, drained, dipped in frying batter (see BATTERS), fried in hot deep fat, taken up, dusted with powdered sugar; served with claret sauce.

COMPOTE OF ORANGES—Small oranges (the seedless variety) peeled, pith removed, blanched, drained, blanched again, then simmered in the left over syrup of the preceding recipe, the peel of the oranges boiled tender in two or three waters, then finely shredded and added to the syrup; when done, allow to become cold; served, an orange decorated on top with the shredded peel, the syrup poured around.

CANAPÉ OF ORANGES—Oranges peeled and the pith removed, pulled apart in sections, the sections boiled for a few minutes in syrup, taken up and arranged on fancy shapes of bread that have been fried a golden brown with butter.

ORANGE PIE—One dozen sound oranges cut into thin slices, seeds and cores removed, covered with six quarts of water, allowed to soak for 24 hours, then put all on to boil; boil slowly for three hours, then add seven pounds of granulated sugar, and boil till clear, pour off into a crock, allow to set, and you then have the filling. Line pie plates with puff paste trimmings, making a raised edge, spread well with the filling, bake; when done, spread with an orange flavored custard, on it pipe a fancy meringue, brown quickly; serve. This is one of the most delicious pies it is possible to make.

ORANGE MARMALADE—24 oranges, 8 lemons; oranges peeled and the pith removed, the peel then boiled till tender, about three hours, changing the water three times, the first time it is put on in cold water, the changing time in boiling water; when tender, drain, shred very fine; meanwhile extract every drop of juice from all the oranges and lemons, measure it, then add one-fourth of its bulk of clear water, measure it again, and to every pint, add one and a half pounds of granulated sugar, then the shredded rinds, bring to the boil, skim, then continue boiling till thick enough to set.

JELLIED ORANGES—Oranges with the stem end cut to form a lid, emptied of their contents with a spoon, the shells then soaked overnight, they are then drained, then half filled with a colored fruit jelly and allowed to set, then filled with another colored fruit jelly, closed, set away in ice till firm; served by cutting in halves or quarters, and arranging on serving dish with the colors alternating.

ORANGE SAUCE—Roast duck carcasses boiled down with some Espagnole sauce, then strained, orange juice then added to taste for the quantity made, finely shredded and boiled rinds then added. (The natural sauce for roast domestic ducks.)

ORANGES WITH RICE—Quartered and peeled oranges with the pith and seeds removed, boiled in syrup till tender, the syrup then thickened with corn starch and allowed to simmer till clear; when done, add a little maraschino; to serve, dry boiled rice grains arranged as a border on an oval platter, the rice sprinkled with finely chopped pistachio nuts, the oranges and sauce in the centre (this is always an acceptable sweet entrée).

ORANGE TRIFLE—Slice of orange-flavored sponge cake spread with marmalade, this spread with custard, the custard piped with whipped cream, the edges sprinkled with finely chopped pistachio nuts.

ORTOLAN—A very small game bird, a native of Southern Europe. Our rice bird does duty for it here generally.

ORTOLAN—Ortolan are tiny birds, usually eaten whole, and occasionally offered on menus in the expensive restaurants of Western Europe. The American equivalent is the reedbird, or bobolink, a finchlike bird of the South.

ORTOLANS IN CROÛSTADE—The bird plucked and singed, neck and gizzard only of the inside removed, season with nutmeg, salt and pepper; large truffles hollowed out, the bird placed in the truffle, arranged in a saûtoir, with bacon over the breasts, moistened with a mirepoix and some Madeira wine, cooked about twenty minutes, taken up and placed in a fancy bread croûstade; reduce the sauce in saûtoir to a demi-glaze, remove the bacon, mask with the glaze; serve surrounded with watercress.

ORTOLANS IN CASES—Make (or use the bought ones) a fancy paste croûstade case, line it with foiegras; ortolans plucked and singed, feet, beak and skin of head removed, truss, season with salt, pepper and nutmeg, place one in each lined case, cover with a strip of fat bacon, roast in moderate oven about 20 minutes, remove the

bacon; serve with a spoonful of Madeira sauce over the bird.

BROILED ORTOLANS—Pluck and singe the birds, wipe with a damp cloth, remove beak and feet, truss, but do not draw, season with salt, pepper and nutmeg, wrap in a buttered paper case, broil over a raked clean space of the grill, in ten minutes the bird will be done; serve with the paper, surrounded with watercress, paper to be removed by waiter at the guest's request, just as about to be eaten.

ROAST ORTOLANS—The birds plucked and singed, wiped, slit made in the side and the gizzard removed, cut off beak and feet, skin the head, which place inside where the gizzard was, season with salt, pepper and nutmeg, wrap around each a thin slice of bacon, or wrap each in a vine leaf if procurable, roast about ten minutes; serve on a fancy cut slice of bread fried a delicate brown with butter, pour round a rich Madeira sauce.

BROCHETTE OF ORTOLANS—Pluck, singe and wipe the birds, remove the gizzard, rub the body with lemon, then roll each one in soft maître d'hôtel butter, then in grated breadcrumbs (not cracker dust), then thread them on a skewer, broil; serve on toast buttered with the drippings from the broiling, garnish with lemon and watercress.

FRIED ORTOLANS—The birds plucked and singed, feet and beak removed, gizzards drawn, head skinned and placed where gizzard was, rubbed with lemon, dipped in maître d'hôtel butter, then in grated breadcrumbs, then in beaten eggs and again in the crumbs, plunged in boiling hot fat, fried ten minutes; served with a rich brown Italian sauce.

TRUFFLED ORTOLANS—Pluck and singe the birds, remove beak, feet and gizzard, skin the head and place where gizzard was, arrange them in a serving casserole, moisten with a rich truffle sauce containing plenty of sliced truffles, bake for ten minutes in a quick oven; serve in the casserole.

OXTAILS—Most "ox-tails" bought today are, in fact, beef tails and are to be used in any oxtail recipe.

OX-TAIL SOUP—Saw the tails into neat pieces half inch thick, soak over night in salted water; with a large sized column cutter stamp out slices of white and yellow turnip, carrot; drain and wipe the pieces of ox-tail, then sauté them with the vegetables, add them to a rich brown stock flavored with sweet herbs and celery, simmer till tails are tender and gelatinous, then thicken the soup with roux, season with salt and pepper, port wine and mushroom catsup.

CLEAR OX-TAIL SOUP—A consommé of rich brown stock made with roast meat, poultry and a flavor of ham, in which is slices of ox-tail and vegetables as in the preceding recipe, finish with a flavoring of port wine.

HARICOT OF OX-TAILS—Tails separated in their natural joints, the large end split, placed in a deep saûtoir with fat from the stock toppings and some sliced onions, fry a nice brown, stock then added to well cover, stewed for about three hours, then taken up, the stock strained and freed from grease, the tails placed in another saûtoir with slices of braised carrot and turnip, sauce made from the strained stock, then poured over the tails and vegetables, season with salt, pepper, mushroom catsup and port wine; served within a border of mashed potatoes, sprinkling the tails with finely chopped parsley.

CURRY OF OX-TAILS—Tails separated in their natural joints, the large end split, lightly fried with onion, then taken up into a saûtoir, covered with a rich curry sauce, simmered till tender; serve within a border of boiled grains of rice.

SAUTÉ OF OX-TAILS—Tails separated in their natural joints, the large end split, seasoned with powdered mixed herbs, rolled in flour, sautéed a light brown with butter, taken up into a saûtoir, covered with sauce Robert, simmered till tender; served garnished with a braised jardinière of vegetables.

OX-TONGUE BOILED—Salted ox-tongue, put to boil in cold water and cooked till tender, according to size, but generally about three hours, then take up and skin, remove the bones from the root and trim off the waste fat, then keep hot in seasoned broth; to serve, cut in thin slices, place them overlapping each other down the centre of the dish, first dipping each slice into a jellied gravy or demi-glaze, then garnish the sides with either a purée of spinach, flageolet beans, a macedoine or jardinière of vegetables, Brussels sprouts, pieces of cauliflower, stringless green beans or asparagus points.

BRAISED FRESH OX-TONGUE—Blanch and trim a good sized tongue, then place it in a braisiere with slices of carrot, turnip, celery, onions, a few cloves, bay leaf, mace, salt, pepper and a glass of cooking brandy, cover with good stock, then braise slowly till tender; when done, taken up and placed in a saûtoir, the braise then strained and skimmed, then mixed with some Madeira sauce and reduced to half glaze, this is then poured over the tongue and kept hot in it; served in thin slices overlapping each other down the centre of dish, covered with the glaze, and garnished with small quenelles or croquettes of potatoes.

SMOKED OX-TONGUE, GERMAN STYLE—Smoked tongue soaked over night in cold water, then scrubbed, parboiled for half an hour, taken up and trimmed, then placed in a saûtoir with well washed sauer-kraut, onion stuck with cloves, carrots and a bunch of soup herbs; moisten with stock, lay slices of fat salt pork over the top, put on the lid and place in a medium oven, cook till tongue is tender, about two hours, take up; serve in thin slices with Poivrade sauce, flanked with the sauerkraut.

BOILED SMOKED TONGUE, SAUCE PIQUANTE—Smoked tongue soaked overnight in cold water, then scrubbed, put to boil in cold water, cooked till tender, taken up, skinned and trimmed; served in slices with Piquante sauce, garnished with gherkins.

BRAISED FRESH TONGUE, SAUCE ITALIAN—Fresh ox-tongue put to boil in cold water, boiled one hour, taken up, skinned and trimmed, then larded with seasoned strips of fat pork and lean strips of ham, arranged in braisiere with sliced vegetables, herbs, spices and pieces of fat bacon, moistened with stock, braised till tender, taken up, the braise reduced, strained and skimmed, then added to a thick rich brown Italian sauce, the tongue served in slices with the sauce and garnished with sautéed button mushrooms.

OYSTERS—The best oysters on the North American continent come from Cape Cod, Maine, Canada, and the Pacific Northwest.

There are only four types of oysters generally consumed in this country—there are three hundred worldwide—although they masquerade under a huge variety of names. Therein lies the confusion. The most common oyster, the indigenous Atlantic (*Crassostrea virginica*), is the worst offender: It is called Bluepoint, Wellfleet, Apalachicola, Malpêque, Pemaquid, Cotuit, Chincoteague, and so on. All of these are the names of the areas in which the oysters are raised, and they are important (again, those from the North are usually tastier). But they are all the same creature.

Also indigenous are the European flat oysters (*Ostrea edulis*), commonly called the belon but more correctly, in this country at least, known as the Westcott European flat (belons, strictly speaking, are from France). These are large flat oysters raised in the Northeast; they make great eating and may be confused, harmlessly, with northern Atlantic oysters.

The tiny Olympia (*Ostrea lurida*) is related to the European flat but is much smaller. It is the only oyster native to our Pacific coast, and is beloved for its crisp, slightly metallic flavor. Finally, there is the Pacific oyster (*Crassostrea gigas*), originally from Japan and best when grown in the Pacific Northwest. Common names include Yakima Bay, Golden Mantle, Kumamoto, Penn Cove, and more.

All good oysters are delicious when eaten raw, and should be consumed immediately after being shucked. The technique is tricky—please use a towel or glove to protect your naked hand, especially when learning—but can be mastered, at least well enough to open a dozen oysters for yourself and a loved one. When cooking with oysters, preshucked oysters will work just fine, although when broiling, smoking, or baking on the half shell, freshly shucked oysters are best.

OYSTER STEW—Bulk oysters (Selects) for hotels, when served for dinners, breakfasts, suppers, luncheons, and catering parties. Counts for restaurant orders, club and European plan orders. The oysters scaled in their own liquor, taken up, the liquor skimmed and poured back to the oysters, milk brought to the boil; bowl or serving dish containing a piece of GOOD butter, salt, dash of red pepper; oysters and liquor poured to it, then filled up with boiling milk; served with oyster crackers: a dish of finely shred cabbage is sometimes served with it—but why?

CREAM STEW—Prepared as above, using cream instead of milk.

PLAIN STEW—Same as oyster stew above, using more oyster liquor and no milk.

DRY STEW—Same as preceding, no milk and but little oyster liquor.

BOX STEW—Dry stew of the very largest oysters placed on a slice of buttered toast, then boiling cream with a little butter poured over the whole.

BOSTON STEW—Simply a milk stew of count oysters, but the oysters on toast as in box stew.

INDIAN STEW—Box stew, but using equal parts of chicken curry sauce with the cream.

PHILADELPHIA STEW—Very large oysters in their shells placed on a very hot grill; meantime scald and skim some oyster liquor, season it with salt, red pepper and butter; when the oysters are broiled, remove them from their shells, place them in the boiling liquor; serve in soup plate, garnished with strips of buttered toast.

BROILED SHELL OYSTERS—Scrub the shells clean, lay them on a very hot grill, when they open their shells, take them up and remove the flat shell, also loosen the oyster from the deep shell, place a few drops of melted butter or mâitre d'hôtel butter on each oyster, then serve very hot.

BROILED OYSTERS—Very large oysters wiped dry, seasoned with salt and pepper, dipped in flour, arranged between a wire hinged broiler, brush with melted butter, broil till done, basting with butter while broiling; serve overlapping each other on buttered toast, garnish with cress and quartered lemons.

BROILED OYSTERS BREADCRUMBED —Same way as the preceding, but after dipping in flour, they are dipped in beaten eggs, then rolled in bread (not cracker) crumbs.

DEVILLED OYSTERS—Oysters scalded, drained, cut in squares, the liquor with a little cream made into a thick butter sauce with an added egg yolk or two; season with salt, red pepper and chopped parsley, then add the oysters, fill into large deep oyster shells, then strew the top with breadcrumbs and melted butter, bake off a delicate brown and serve very hot.

PANNED OYSTERS—Another form of dry stew; oysters washed and drained, very hot frying pan with a little melted butter, oysters thrown in and shuffled about till they sizzle, turned out into a small hot soup plate, season with salt and cayenne.

ROAST SHELL OYSTERS—The shells scrubbed clean, arranged in a baking pan, placed in a very hot oven; when they open, remove the flat shell and loosen the oyster from the deep shell, place a little melted butter in each, serve quickly with strip of hot buttered toast aside.

SCALLOPED OYSTERS—Baking pan inch and a half deep, brushed with butter, oyster crackers rolled fine with rolling pin, the buttered pan well lined with them, oysters drained, laid all over the rolled crackers, seasoned lightly with salt and pepper (mixed), then well covered with more of the crackers, this then sprinkled well with a mixture of oyster liquor, milk and melted butter, then another layer of oysters, season as before, cover with the rolled crackers, moisten well with the mixed liquors, bake quickly well done, but a delicate brown; cut out in squares; serve very hot, garnish with cress and lemon. (For individual orders in scallop shells, they should be prepared the same way.)

STEAMED OYSTERS—Shell oysters well scrubbed, placed in a steamer, turn on full steam, time three minutes; meantime take a small deep soup plate, in it have melted butter, salt and a dash of red pepper, open out the oysters and their liquor into it; serve very hot with strips of buttered toast.

GLAZED OYSTERS ON TOAST— Large oysters wiped dry, sautéed quickly with butter, take up, pour the liquor from the sautéeing into a rich Madeira sauce, adding a piece of glaze, reduce this rapidly to half glaze; have the serving platter hot with strip of buttered toast down the centre, dip the oysters into the half glaze and arrange them overlapping each other on the toast, garnish with cress and lemon.

BACON COATED OYSTERS, FRIED— Large oysters wiped dry, very thin slices of parboiled bacon rolled round the oysters and pinned with a toothpick, dipped in batter, fried, toothpick withdrawn; served with tomato sauce.

SAUCE COATED OYSTERS, FRIED— Large oysters wiped dry, dipped into a thick Villeroi sauce, allowed to set, then dipped into beaten eggs, rolled well in sifted bread-crumbs, fried a golden brown; served garnished with quartered lemon.

OYSTERS STUFFED AND BROILED—One pint of egg yolks stirred without much beating, poured into a buttered pan and steamed till set firm, allowed to cool, then grate them; one pound of cooked fat salt pork minced very fine, added to the grated yolks with some chopped parsley; season to taste with salt and pepper; five dozen large oysters wiped dry, slit made in their sides, stuffed with the mixture, rolled in sifted bread-crumbs, then rolled in melted but-ter and again in the crumbs, arrange between a wire hinged broiler, broil a golden brown, bast-ing with butter; serve garnished with quartered lemon and fried parsley.

BROCHETTE OF OYSTERS—Mince some thyme, parsley and shallots very fine, add a little salt and pep-per; wipe large oysters dry, roll them in the herbs, then dip in beaten eggs, then in sifted bread-crumbs, then arrange them alter-nately on a skewer with pieces of sweetbread and bacon, fry; serve on toast with maître d'hôtel butter and quartered lemon.

CROÛSTADE OF OYSTERS—Oysters scalded in their own liquor, taken up, the liquor then added to equal quantities of Velouté and anchovy sauces, reduce till thick, then add the oysters, fill into fancy croûs-tades, sprinkle over the tops a mix-ture of grated Parmesan cheese and breadcrumbs, bake a delicate brown in a quick oven and serve on hot plate with paper doily.

OYSTERS BAKED WITH MUSH-ROOMS—Fricassée the oysters and mushrooms, having the sauce thick, fill into individual molds or shells, sprinkle the top with mixed cheese and breadcrumbs, bake a delicate brown; serve very hot.

FRICASSÉE OF OYSTERS—Oysters scalded till plump in boiling milk, taken up, butter melted in saûtoir and allowed to frizzle without be-coming colored, flour then added to form a roux, made into thick sauce with the milk, seasoned with salt, red pepper, lemon juice and a dash of Harvey sauce, finished with a liaison of egg yolks and cream. Hot serving platter, buttered toast down the centre, oysters dipped in the sauce, placed overlapping each other down the toast; served with more of the sauce at the sides.

BAKED OYSTERS WITH CHEESE— Oysters wiped dry, then rolled in sifted breadcrumbs that are mixed with Parmesan cheese and chopped parsley, seasoned with salt and pepper, moistened with little white wine; arrange in scallop shell, strew with more cheese, bake a delicate brown and serve very hot.

FRIED OYSTERS—Count oysters rolled in cracker dust or yellow corn meal, then in beaten eggs, then in the meal again, fried; served with quartered lemon.

FANCY FRY—Count oysters wiped dry, seasoned with mixed salt and red pepper, dipped in flour, then in mixed beaten eggs and whipped cream, then in sifted breadcrumbs, pressed slightly between the hands, fried a golden brown with butter; served with quartered lemon and garnished with green stuff.

OYSTERS BAKED WITH POTATOES—Large oysters wiped dry, seasoned with salt and pepper. Duchesse potato mixture rolled out thin, cut out in diamond shapes, oysters laid in the centre, edges folded over and pinched into shape, arranged in a buttered baking pan, brushed over with beaten egg, baked a golden brown; served very hot.

OYSTER LOAF—Small French rolls, insides hollowed out, the loaf shell then fried a golden brown with butter, the interior then filled with a fricassée of oysters.

CURRIED OYSTERS—Oysters scalded and drained, curry sauce made from the liquor, finished with a liaison of egg yolks and cream. Rice boiled in some scalded oyster liquor; served as a border to the curried oysters in the centre.

BAKED OYSTERS, ITALIAN STYLE—Macaroni boiled in one inch lengths in oyster liquor from the scalded oysters. Fricassée sauce made of the liquor after the macaroni is drained. Buttered baking pan, alternate layers of the macaroni and oysters, the top strewn with mixed grated cheese and breadcrumbs, dashed with melted butter, sauce then poured over, baked till set; served very hot.

OYSTERS IN CASSEROLE—Line the casserole with Duchesse potato mixture, fill the interior with oysters in a rich Poulette sauce, bake lightly and serve.

CREAMED OYSTERS ON TOAST—Scalded oysters placed into a rich cream sauce, then arranged on buttered toast; served with the sauce poured over.

OYSTERS WITH CELERY—To each portion of oysters allow a tablespoonful of minced white celery and the same of sherry wine, sauté all together with butter, season with salt and red pepper; serve on toast with the liquor poured over.

OYSTER TOAST—Oysters scalded and drained, then pounded to a paste with cream, seasoned with lemon juice and red pepper, spread on circles of brown bread toast.

OYSTER OMELET—Scald the oysters, add the liquor to a sauce Normande, reduce, put the oysters into the omelet, dip two of them into the sauce and place on top, then pour the sauce around the omelet.

SUPRÊME OF OYSTERS—Oysters scalded and drained, the liquor strained through muslin and added to a rich Velouté sauce, brought to the boil, piece of chicken glaze then added, then finish by adding a little thick cream and the juice of a lemon, add the oysters; serve on toast.

OYSTER PIE—Diamond shaped pieces of puff pastry ¾ of an inch thick when baked, split, the under side laid on the serving platter, the Suprême above laid on it, the upper part of the pastry laid on; served immediately. Another way, take the Suprême of oysters, add some chopped hard boiled eggs and parsley, fill in to a pie dish, cover with a puff paste, bake off quickly without letting the oysters come to the boil in the pie.

COD AND OYSTER PIE—The Suprême above with the addition of flakes of fresh boiled codfish, prepared and served in the ways given for oyster pie.

OYSTER PATTIES—The Suprême above filled into puff paste patty shells.

OYSTER POT PIE—The Suprême above, keeping out the oysters till the pie is finished, i.e., prepare the sauce, put it into the saucepan, bring to the boil, drop light dumplings all over it close together, place on the lid, and cook till dumplings are done, then remove the centre one, place in the oysters, replace the dumpling, keep very hot, but do not let it boil again; this method keeps the oysters plump and tender; serve with a sprinkling of chopped parsley. Cod and oyster pot pie may be prepared the same way, and is useful when oysters are few and you have some cod that wants using up, such as the shoulders that cannot be cut into nice steaks.

EPIGRAMME OF OYSTERS—A rich Suprême as above, having the sauce thick enough to stay on the oyster when lifted out; arrange them down the centre of the serving dish, flanked with neatly fried oysters; serve garnished with triangle shaped pieces of buttered toast, the point dipped into the sauce, then into lobster coral.

OYSTER SAUCE—Oysters blanched and drained, liquor strained through muslin, brought to the boil, a butter and flour roux moistened with the boiling liquor, seasoned with salt, red pepper and lemon juice, finished with some boiling cream; this is used for white foods.

OYSTER SAUCE—For brown foods such as steaks, fried fish, meat pies, oyster pies, roast turkey, roast capon, etc., is prepared same as the preceding, but substituting a good brown sauce for the boiling cream.

STEAK AND OYSTER PIE—Tender pieces of beef cut into small neat pieces, seasoned with pepper and salt, quickly sautéed a nice color with butter, taken up and placed into the pie dish, oysters scalded and drained. Into the pan the beef was sautéed in add a little more butter, then flour to form a roux, moisten with the strained boiling liquor, boil, skim, strain over the meat and let simmer till meat is nearly done, then add the oysters, some good brown sauce, a seasoning of salt, pepper, lemon juice and Harvey sauce, cover with puff paste, bake quickly; serve hot.

OYSTER CROQUETTES—Two quarts of Selects or Standard oysters, one can of mushrooms, the liquor of the mushrooms poured to the oysters, which are then scalded and drained, the scalded liquor then strained through muslin; mushrooms minced and sautéed a golden color with butter, taken up, flour then added to form a roux, thick sauce then made with the boiling liquor, adding a little cream and a seasoning of salt, pepper, lemon juice, anchovy and Harvey sauces, the chopped oysters and mushrooms then added, boiled, finished to proper thickness with a liaison of egg yolks and cream; turned into a buttered shallow pan, smoothed, covered with a sheet of oiled paper, allowed to become firm and cold, then formed into shape of sausages, breaded, fried; served with brown oyster sauce.

OYSTER CUTLETS MINCED—The croquette preparation made into the shape of rib chops, breaded, fried; served with brown oyster sauce.

OYSTER RISSOLES—Crimped circles of puff paste, the centre containing some oyster croquette mixture, edges then folded over and pinched, brushed with egg wash, baked.

OYSTER STUFFING—For fish and poultry: oysters blanched and drained, cut in quarters, or if using Standards, leave them whole. Moist stale bread grated one part, rolled oyster crackers one part, the third part of oysters, the whole mixed together and seasoned with salt, pepper and chopped parsley, the liquor brought to the boil with an addition of butter, poured to the dry mixture, stirred, then ready for use.

OYSTER SOUP—Scald the oysters, drain, strain the liquor through muslin, bring to the boil, season with salt, red pepper, mace, Harvey and anchovy sauces, flour and butter roux, moistened with the strained liquor, boiled up, skimmed, then poured to an equal quantity of Béchamel sauce, add the scalded oysters; serve with oyster crackers.

OYSTER SOUP—Oysters and their liquor scalded in strong fish broth, taken up and drained, the liquor strained; a can of mushrooms opened, liquor poured to the broth, the mushrooms minced with some shallots, fried with plenty of butter, then taken up and added to the scalded oysters; flour added to the frying butter to form a roux, this then thinned to soup consistency with the boiling broth, season to taste, oysters, etc., then added with some chopped parsley and a glass of white wine; serve with oyster crackers.

OYSTER GUMBO—Minced onions, green peppers and ham fried with plenty of butter, then taken up, oysters scalded in their own liquor and fish broth, taken up and drained, half a gallon can of tomatoes rubbed through a fine sieve then added to the strained liquor and boiled, skimmed, flour added to the butter to form a roux, moistened to soup consistency with the boiling liquor and tomatoes, seasoned, two cans of okra then added with a little boiled rice, then the oysters and other fried ingredients; served with oyster crackers.

OYSTER SANDWICH—Three or four dozen oysters dried with a cloth, melted butter in a frying pan, drop in the oysters and sauté them brown, take up, chop fine, season with salt and pepper, spread on hot thin buttered toast, sprinkle with chili sauce, cover with another slice of toast, trim the edges, cut across and serve.

BREADED OYSTERS, CELERY SAUCE—Large oysters wiped dry, seasoned with salt and pepper, dipped in melted butter, then in fresh grated breadcrumbs, place between a wire hinged broiler, broil rapidly a delicate brown, then place on a narrow strip of hot fresh buttered toast; serve with celery cream sauce poured around.

OYSTER BOUCHÉES—For two dozen, blanch four dozen oysters in their own liquor, take up and place two in each bouchée, strain the liquor through muslin, add its equal volume of rich tomato purée, then season with butter and tabasco sauce, bring to the boil, keep the bouchées hot, and when serving, fill up with the boiling sauce.

OYSTER PLANT—Officially known as salsify (and even more officially as *Tragopogon porrifolius*), this poor white taproot is supposed to taste like an oyster. Almost no one thinks that it does (food writer Elizabeth Schneider describes it as having "the flavor and consistency of a soft-cooked artichoke heart with a touch of coconut," and that rings closer to the truth). This has led to disappointment, and perhaps explains salsify's lack of popularity in this country.

It is, along with the related scorzonera, or black salsify, an excellent root vegetable, popular in Europe since the Middle Ages and cooked in much the same way as carrots or parsnips. Try any of Fellows's recipes or boil oyster plants until done, then serve at room temperature, dressed with a mild vinaigrette.

OYSTER PLANT, FRIED—Scraped clean and laid in cold water containing salt and a little white vinegar; when to be cooked, first boil tender, then take up and drain, dip into frying batter, plunge into hot fat, fry a delicate brown, take up, sprinkle with salt and serve as a vegetable.

OYSTER PLANT, BOILED—Prepare as above, then boil tender, take up and drain, place in vegetable steamer, cover with cream sauce; serve as a vegetable.

OYSTER PLANT, SAUCE POULETTE—Scrape clean, cut in small pieces, lay in acidulated water for an hour, then boil till tender in boiling water containing salt and a little white vinegar; when done, taken up, turned into hot Poulette sauce and served.

OYSTER PLANT FRITTERS—Prepared and boiled as above, when drained, mashed thoroughly, then seasoned and stiffened with salt, pepper, yolk of egg and flour, spoonfuls then fried in hot fat, taken up, sprinkled with salt and served.

STEWED OYSTER PLANT—The plant prepared and boiled as above, then stewed in a rich meat gravy sauce; served on hot buttered toast.

OYSTER PLANT SAUTÉ—The plant prepared, boiled, drained, then rolled in flour, sautéed a golden brown with butter; served on toast with hot maître d'hôtel sauce poured over.

P

PANCAKES—Known to us in every household as "batter cakes." For recipes, see heading of BATTER.

PARMESAN—Name of an Italian cheese; see heading of CHEESE.

PARSLEY—A garden herb used as a garnish; to ornament dishes, chopped and mixed in sauces, stews, soups, salads, etc.

PARSLEY—The all-American habit of using a sprig of parsley only as a garnish has fallen into some disfavor. Parsley (*Petroselinum crispum*) has begun to secure for itself a place as an important herb, one that is available fresh at a reasonable price year-round in almost every supermarket. Although parsley is rarely an essential ingredient, the inclusion of a handful of the herb, minced, enlivens many dishes.

There are many types of parsley, including that grown for its edible root (a relative of the carrot) and even one that is grown for its stalks. But usually we see the curly (northern) and flat (Italian) varieties. When buying, choose the freshest and greenest you can find.

Parsley can also be used to replace a small part of the basil in any pesto recipe; the resulting sauce will be lighter and somewhat less intense.

PARSNIP—A root vegetable, peeled, cut in finger lengths, boiled in salted water, taken up and drained; served as an accompaniment to boiled salt leg of pork.

PARSNIP—Closely related to CARROTS, parsnips (*Pastinaca sativa*) are a winter vegetable best harvested after a frost and keep very well in a cold spot. Parsnips are not as dense as carrots and require less cooking time.

PARSNIPS, CREAM SAUCE—Boiled in finger lengths, drained, placed in cream sauce; served as a vegetable.

PARSNIPS FRIED IN BATTER—Boiled in finger lengths in salted water, taken up and drained, dipped in batter, fried in hot lard, taken up, sprinkled with salt and served.

PARSNIP FRITTERS—Boiled and mashed, seasoned and stiffened with salt, pepper, yolks of eggs and flour, fried by spoonfuls in hot lard, taken up, sprinkled with salt, served.

PARSNIP SAUTÉES—Boiled tender in finger lengths, drained, seasoned with salt and pepper, rolled in flour, sautéed a delicate brown with butter, taken up, sprinkled with chopped parsley and served.

MASHED PARSNIPS—Boiled tender, mashed, seasoned with salt and pepper, milk and butter; served as a vegetable.

BAKED PARSNIPS—Peeled, quartered, steamed till nearly done, taken up and arranged in a buttered baking pan, seasoned with salt and pepper, moistened with rich gravy and butter, baked tender and brown.

PARTRIDGE—Partridge are smaller than PHEASANT, more strongly flavored, and raised in much the same way. Look for wild birds from Scotland in the fall and farm-raised birds year-round. Partridge, which have tender leg muscles and a large proportion of meat concentrated in their breasts, are delicious and easy to cook; most weigh less than a pound.

PARTRIDGE BROILED—Young birds split down the back, breastbone removed, trussed, seasoned with salt and pepper, brushed with olive oil, broiled and basted well done; served on buttered toast with maitre d'hôtel butter, garnished with jelly and parsley; may also be garnished with slices of fresh hominy or bacon, or after broiling, served with either Colbert, Italian or Madeira sauces.

ROAST PARTRIDGE—Young birds singed and drawn, wiped with towel, trussed with a slice of fat bacon tied over the breast, roasted about half an hour; served with game sauce and red currant jelly.

BOILED PARTRIDGE—Singed, drawn, wiped and trussed, boiled in white stock till tender; served with a rich cream sauce.

BOILED PARTRIDGE, GARNISHED—Partridges singed, drawn, wiped and trussed, put to boil with cabbage, bacon, pork sausages, frankforts, parsley, white stock and a little sherry wine; when tender, taken up, the meats also, parsley thrown away, cabbage pressed dry, then chopped, the remaining liquor strained into a rich game sauce. To serve, place a spoonful of cabbage in centre of dish, portion of bird on it, flanked with a piece of bacon, sausage, frankfort (skinned), sauce poured over.

PARTRIDGE SAUTÉ—Young birds singed, drawn, wiped, jointed, seasoned with salt and pepper, sautéed with butter a delicate brown, taken up, minced shallots then added to the butter with button mushrooms and fried; when browned, surplus butter poured off, partridge put back, covered with Espagnole, boiled up and skimmed, seasoned with Madeira wine, simmered till tender, served garnished with fancy croûtons.

SALMI OF PARTRIDGE—The birds singed, drawn, wiped, trussed, roasted, cooled, quartered, the back and breastbones with other trimmings then placed in some Espagnole with bacon, minced onion, bay leaf, thyme and crushed peppers, brought to the boil and rapidly reduced, skimmed, strained over the birds in another saûtoir, seasoned with sherry wine, simmered a few minutes; served garnished with croûtons.

PARTRIDGE LARDED AND BRAISED—The birds singed, drawn and wiped, the breasts larded, trussed, arranged in brasiere with slices of root vegetables and sweet herbs; place a few slices of bacon on top, moisten with a little stock, cover with a sheet of buttered paper, place on the lid and put in a slow oven to cook in its own steam for about two hours; when done, taken up, add a game sauce to the liquor in the brasiere, reduce, strain, flavor with sherry wine, glaze the birds; serve with the sauce.

PARTRIDGE SAUTÉ WITH RISSOTO—Young birds singed, drawn, wiped, jointed, seasoned with salt and pepper, fried lightly with butter, taken up; into the butter they were fried in, add flour to form a roux, moisten with game stock made from the backbones and trimmings, add the juice and a little of the grated rind of a sour orange, put in the fried birds, simmer slowly till tender; served with a border of rissoto.

BREAST OF PARTRIDGE, LARDED AND FRIED—Take the breasts, trim and lard them, season with salt, pepper and powdered thyme, dip in beaten egg, then roll in freshly grated breadcrumbs, arrange in a saûtoir, pour over melted butter, placed in a moderate oven and brown nicely on both sides; serve on a fancy croûton with a little Richelieu or Sultana sauce poured around.

EPIGRAMME OF PARTRIDGE WITH MUSHROOMS—Take young birds, remove the breasts, lard them, bread and fry as preceding one half of them, slowly broil the remaining half (so that you have one plain and one breaded), dish up one of each, points crossing each other, garnish with fried mushrooms in a Fumet sauce.

BREAST OF PARTRIDGE, SAUCE COLBERT—Take the breasts of young birds, lard them, slowly broil them till done; served on buttered toast with sauce Colbert poured around.

BREAST OF PARTRIDGE, GLAZED VEGETABLES—Take the breasts of young birds, lard and roast them.

With a half inch sized column cutter, cut inch lengths of carrot and turnip, braise and glaze them together with button onions, use them as a garnish to the breasts, and pour game sauce around.

PARTRIDGE BRAISED WITH CABBAGE—Take old birds, braise them with sliced vegetables and sweet herbs till three parts done, take up into a saûtoir, add cut cabbage, pour over the strained liquor they were braised in, add some thin slices of bacon (if not enough liquor add some white stock), simmer till done, lightly thicken the liquor with flour and butter; serve portion of bird with slice of bacon on top, cabbage around, and a little game sauce over the bird.

PARTRIDGE BREADCRUMBED AND BROILED—Truss the bird out like a frog, season with salt and pepper, dip twice in beaten eggs and fresh grated breadcrumbs, broil slowly till done over a clear fire; serve on toast with Italian sauce.

FILLETS OF PARTRIDGE WITH CRAYFISH—Take the upper and lower fillets from the breasts, trim and lard them, arrange them in a saûtoir with slices of bacon, moistened with little stock and white wine, cover with a sheet of buttered paper, place on the lid, braise in the oven; when done, glaze them, strain and skim the braise, then add it to an Allemande sauce. To serve: place a ragout of crayfish tails in centre of dish, large fillet of partridge at each end with points meeting over the ragout, small fillets at each side, points upwards,

sprinkle over all a little lobster coral, and pour the sauce around.

FILLETS OF PARTRIDGE, PARISIAN STYLE—Take the fillets and coat them with Allemande sauce, then in beaten eggs and sifted breadcrumbs, then sprinkle with melted butter and press on a little more of the crumbs, sauté them of a golden color with clear butter, when done, take up and drain; meanwhile, prepare a ragout of crayfish tails, button mushrooms, cocks kernels and small truffles, moisten with a little game glaze, Allemande sauce, crayfish butter and lemon juice. To serve: place the ragout in centre of dish, the fillets around it, decorate the base with scallops of tongue, and serve some more of the sauce from the ragout separate.

PARTRIDGE WITH BACON, CELERY SAUCE—Take old birds and boil them with salt pork, carrots, onions and turnips in white stock till tender; serve in portions with a slice of the pork at the sides, and a purée of celery in a white game sauce poured over.

PARTRIDGE RISSOLES, SAUCE RICHELIEU—Make a croquette mixture with cold cooked partridge and game sauce, stamp out crimped circles of thin puff paste, place a little of the mixture in the centres, fold over the edges and pinch close, fry or bake them of a golden color, and serve with a Richelieu sauce.

EMINCE OF PARTRIDGE—Take cold roast partridge, cut in broad thin slices, simmer it in equal parts of white game and Godard sauces;

serve on toast, garnished with sautéed fresh button mushrooms.

SALPICON OF PARTRIDGE—Take cold cooked partridge, cut the meat in small dice, also some truffles, red tongue and button mushrooms, cut same size as the bird, mix, moisten with either game, Béchamel or Suprême sauces; serve garnished with small potato croquettes.

CROÛSTADES OF PARTRIDGE—Take cold cooked partridge, cut the meat in small squares, simmer it in a rich game sauce, then add a ragout of mushrooms, cocks combs and sweetbreads; serve in paste croûstades, garnish with fancy croûtons.

HASHED PARTRIDGE WITH EGG—Take cold cooked partridge, cut the meat in small squares, lightly fry it with butter, add flour to form a roux, moisten with game stock, simmer for fifteen minutes; serve on toast with a trimmed and drained poached egg on top, then garnish the ends with fancy croûtons.

PARTRIDGE CROQUETTES, SAUCE PERIGUEUX—Cold cooked partridge minced, thick game sauce heated, partridge worked in, stirred till it boils, two or three whipped yolks of egg may be worked in, turn into buttered pan, smooth, let it become thoroughly cold, form into shapes of corks, bread, fry; serve with Perigueux sauce.

PARTRIDGE PATTIES—Prepare the mixture as given for "croûstades of partridge," fill either into patty or vol-au-vent cases and serve.

STEWED PARTRIDGE—Old birds, lard them, place them in a saûtoir with a piece of fat bacon, sweet herbs, vegetables, moisten with white white and stock, let them stew slowly till tender, then take up and cut into quarters, strain the liquor they were stewed in, skim off the fat, reduce it, then add it and the birds to a chipolata garnish (see GARNISHES), serve the bird with the garnish around.

PARTRIDGE SALAD—Cold roast birds skinned, trimmed into neat pieces, moistened with one part of tarragon vinegar to two of olive oil, add a little chopped chervil and chives, season with salt and cayenne, mix all together with an equal quantity of Julienne cut celery (like matches); serve on a bed of curly endive, garnish with rings of hard boiled eggs and filleted anchovies.

PASTA—Charles Fellows could never have imagined how important pasta would become (after all, in his time it was a fairly obscure Italian specialty). But twenty years ago neither could we.

Whether flour-and-water or -egg dough was first rolled, boiled, and sauced in Asia or in Sicily is a moot point (as you can guess, the Italians and the Chinese both claim it). The important thing to know is that there are essentially two areas of that world that have given us great noodles: East Asia, including China, Japan, and Southeast Asia; and Italy. Although we may consider ourselves experts on the subject of Italian noodles, we still have a great deal to learn. And we have just begun to scratch the surface when it comes to Asian noodles.

In Italy pasta is rarely sold "fresh" unless it is stuffed, and the popularity of fresh pasta—which is relatively difficult to cook—is in fact waning in this country. Dried pasta is made from nothing more than flour made from hard wheat (typically durum, most of which is grown in the Great Plains of the United States and Canada) and water; fresh pasta may or may not contain eggs. There are infinite pasta shapes, and pasta may be stuffed with almost any filling.

Italians visiting the United States complain of two mistakes Americans commonly make when cooking pasta. First, even those of us who are aware of the need to make pasta *al dente* overcook it (there should be a core of uncooked starch in the pasta when it is removed from the water to ensure that it will not be at all mushy when it arrives at the table). Second, we oversauce our pasta: It is not, they say, sauce served with a bit of pasta, but the other way around.

If Italian pasta is a complex galaxy worth a lifetime of exploration, Asian pasta (most food writers now use the Italian word *pasta* generically) is a vast universe with hardly a beginning or an end. Pasta is usually made with wheat flour—frequently sold fresh, even in this country—but also quite commonly with rice flour, mung bean starch, buckwheat flour, and occasionally with potato starch, breadfruit flour, chestnut flour, and acorn flour. Noodles are often soaked or steamed before boiling, stir-frying, deep-frying, or sautéing; they may be served in broth and are frequently eaten cold. As in Italy, sheets of noodles are also stuffed and formed into shapes before cooking.

PEACH—One of our choice fruits, the two varieties chiefly used in hotel life being the "freestone" for dessert, and the "clingstone" for cooking purposes.

PEACH—The most important distinction among the literally thousands of varieties of peaches (*Prunus persica,* so named because they traveled from China to Europe via Persia) is not whether they are freestone or clingstone but whether their flesh is white or yellow. Freestone varieties, as anyone who has ever visited a peach orchard knows, are generally juicier and sweeter than their golden-fleshed cousins. They are also more perishable, which explains why our markets stock only yellow peaches.

Even the yellow clingstones do not tolerate shipping when fully ripe; they are picked when firm and, although they soften at home, do not become perceptibly sweeter. Like so many fruits, the best peaches are those that come from nearby orchards rather than from across the country (or, increasingly in these days of the year-round season, from across the ocean).

Nectarines are *not* a cross of peach and plum (although all three are related), but rather a smooth-skinned variety of peach with a somewhat more pronounced flavor. Their flesh, too, comes in pale and deep colors.

PEACHES WITH CREAM—Freestone peaches skinned, cut in slices, sprinkled with powdered sugar,

covered with thick cream and served.

COMPOTE OF PEACHES—Halves of peaches skinned, simmered in syrup till tender; served cold with a small pitcher of cream separate—may also be served hot as a sweet entrée. An improvement to the syrup is to take the kernels from the stones, blanch and skin them, then boil in the syrup.

PEACH AMBROSIA—Peaches peeled and sliced, simmered in the above syrup till tender, taken up, arranged in centre of dish flanked with slices of peeled and pipped oranges, then cover the peaches with some of the syrup, and pipe a fancy centre over them with whipped cream.

PEACHES WITH RICE—Rice boiled in sweetened milk with a vanilla bean till dry in grains; served as a border to the compote of peaches as above.

PEACHES WITH RICE CROQUETTES—Rice boiled very tender in sweetened and flavored milk, then taken up and whisked till creamy, set with the addition of egg yolks; when cold, made up into two forms of croquettes, one like a small egg nest, the other like a small pyramid; bread them lightly, fry a golden color, depress the centre of the egg nest shape, and place in half a peach from compote, pipe the edge with peach marmalade, garnish with the pyramids, decorating the point with whipped cream and chopped pistachio nuts, pour syrup from the compote flavored

with Madeira wine around the base, then serve.

PEACH MARMALADE—Peaches wiped but not pared, halved, stoned, weighed; to each pound of fruit allow half a pound of sugar; take a porcelain lined kettle, pour in just enough water to cover the bottom, then put in the peaches, place on the lid and heat slowly to boiling point; then stir and mash the fruit till fine; then add the sugar and a few blanched and pounded kernels, boil up again and continue stirring for fifteen minutes, then draw to a cooler part of the range and let simmer for twenty minutes with an occasional stir; place in stone crocks and use as wanted.

PEACH BUTTER—Yellow mellow peaches peeled and stoned, weighed; to each pound of fruit allow three-quarters of a pound of sugar, put peaches with just a little water in the preserving kettle, cover, heat slowly to boiling point, whisk till thoroughly mashed, then rub through a fine sieve, then add the sugar, boil up, boil and stir thoroughly for fifteen minutes, fill into small jars; when cold, tie over with air-proof paper.

PEACH JELLY—Two gallons of pared and sliced peaches, one pint of water, two dozen of the kernels blanched and pounded and mixed with the fruit, put all into a stone crock, stand in the bain-marie, cover closely and let boil for an hour, stirring till the fruit is well broken, then turn into a jelly bag and let drip thoroughly; to each quart of juice add the juice of two lemons and two pounds of sugar, bring quickly to the boil, then boil fast for twenty minutes, skim as the scum rises, roll the glasses in boiling water, fill with the boiling jelly, let cool for 24 hours, then cover with air-proof papers; keep in a cool place.

SPICED PEACHES—Twenty-eight pounds of peaches, sixteen pounds of granulated sugar, two quarts of white wine vinegar, two ounces of bruised ginger, ounce of ground cloves, two ounces each of ground allspice and cinnamon and half an ounce of ground mace, mix all the spices together and fill into two muslin bags, tie tight, bring the sugar and vinegar to the boil, put in the spices, then the peaches peeled but left whole, when they come to the boil again, remove from the fire and carefully place them in a stone crock, allow to cool overnight, then pour off the liquid into a preserving kettle, gradually bring to the boil, then pour back over the fruit, repeat this with the liquor every day for ten days and on the last day reduce the liquor till there is only just enough to cover the peaches, then place the crock in the bain-marie and bring to boiling point, fill into fruit jars and use as wanted.

BRANDY PEACHES—Large firm freestone peaches placed in a preserving kettle and covered with boiling water, lid then put on and allowed to remain till the water becomes cold, then drain off the water and repeat with another scalding and cooling, then take each peach out of the cold water and allow to drain and dry between two towels, then put the fruit into small stone crocks and cover with brandy; cover with air-proof paper and allow to macerate for a week; at the week end take out and weigh the fruit; to each pound of peaches make syrup of one pound of sugar and a cupful of water, bring to the boil and skim, then put in the fruit and simmer, when tender, take out and drain, put into fruit jars, allow the syrup to cool; when cold, make a mixture of equal quantities of the syrup and brandy, pour over the fruit in the jars, seal up, keep in a cool dark place, use as wanted.

BOTTLED PEACHES—Ripe, large juicy peaches peeled and halved, then weighed; to each pound, allow one pound of sugar. Take a stone crock, fill it with alternate layers of peaches and sugar, let macerate for 24 hours, then turn all carefully into preserving kettle with some of the kernels blanched and skinned, bring rapidly to the boil, then simmer till the fruit is tender and the syrup clear, take up gently and fill into fruit jars without breaking the halves, allow the syrup to become cold, then pour over the peaches, screw on the covers, use as wanted.

PEACH COBBLER—Shallow buttered baking pan lined with a good short paste, halves of peeled peaches filled into it, covered with powdered sugar, upper crust of short paste placed on and pinched down at edges, egg washed and baked in a medium oven for half an hour; served cut in squares dusted with powdered sugar and a small pitcher of cream served separately.

PEACH SHORTCAKE—Ripe freestone peaches peeled and chopped,

mixed with sugar to taste, short-cake baked, split, the peaches then spread between and on top, the top layer then piped with whipped cream; served cut in squares, with or without a separate pitcher of cream.

PEACH CHARLOTTE—Buttered baking pan, slices of an evenly trimmed stale loaf dipped in melted butter and arranged around the sides and bottom of the pan leaving no cracks, peach marmalade then put in half an inch thick, covered with more slices of the bread, brushed with beaten egg, then well sprinkled with granulated sugar, baked brown and glazy; served with or without sauce.

PEACH CROÛTONS WITH GLAZED FRUITS—Sponge cakes baked in a long round mold; when one day old, cut into slices inch and a half thick. Compote of peaches, the syrup flavored with Kirschenwasser, after peaches are done, removed, and into the syrup is put pieces of angelica with other "fruits glaces." To serve: dip the slice of cake in the syrup, on it place the fruit, then decorate with the "fruits glaces" finish with a little of the syrup poured over.

PEACH CHARTREUSE—Ornamental jelly molds, fancy slices of "fruits glaces" peach butter stiffened with gelatine. Line the molds with a thin layer of stiff Madeira wine jelly, dip each slice of fruit in some more of it and decorate the sides of the mold in a pretty design, then pour in some more jelly to set the design, then fill up with the stiffened peach butter, put away in ice box to set firm, turn out on a fancy glass dish, pipe a fancy border with whipped cream, sprinkle it with very finely chopped pistachio nuts and serve.

PEACH TARTLETTES—Fancy patty pans lined with puff paste, halves of preserved peaches placed into each, baked, then a piping of meringue round the edges sprinkled with chopped pistachio nuts, returned to oven till the meringue takes on a delicate fawn color; when serving, pipe the centre fancifully with whipped cream.

PEACH FRITTERS—Freestone peaches peeled and halved, coated with frying batter, plunged into hot lard, fried a golden brown, taken up and drained; served with wine sauce.

PEACH DUMPLINGS—Large peaches peeled and stoned, enclosed with short paste, steamed till done; served with any pudding sauce.

PEACH PIE—Peaches peeled and cut in slices, and made up same as apple pie.

PEACH TRIFLE—A sheet of sponge cake moistened with sherry wine, this spread with a purée of peaches, the peaches with whipped cream, cut orders in a diamond shape, and serve with whipped cream piped around the edges.

PEACH ICE—Purée of peaches flavored with ratafia mixed with water

PEACH ICE

.

Serves 6 as dessert, 12 to 16 as sorbet

This ice makes a very elegant *intermezzo*, or palate cleanser, for your fancy dinner parties. You may also serve this in larger portions for dessert.

2 pounds very ripe peaches	*3 tablespoons sugar*
1 teaspoon Fruit-Fresh, to prevent browning (find in any good supermarket)	*¹/₃ cup Grand Marnier*
	Garnish
	Fresh mint leaves

Blanch the peaches in boiling water for 1 minute. Drain, cool, and remove the peel with your fingers. Remove the fruit from the pit and discard the pit. In a food processor, purée the peaches with the Fruit-Fresh.

In a small saucepan, dissolve the sugar in the Grand Marnier over low heat. Simmer gently for 1 minute and stir into the purée. Pour the mixture into a stainless-steel bowl, cover tightly, and refrigerate overnight.

If you have a Donvier ice-cream maker, it is simple to turn this mixture into an ice. If not, place the stainless-steel bowl, uncovered, in the freezer and allow the mixture to begin freezing. Stir the mixture regularly, until it turns to an ice. Spoon into frosted glasses and keep in the freezer until ready to serve.

C.W.

and sugar to taste, frozen; served in ice cups.

ICED PEACHES—Large freestone peaches peeled, halved; stone removed; where the stone was, filled with the peach ice above; place the halves together, then coat the outside of the peach with more of the ice, place in refrigerating box till firm, then serve with whipped cream piped around the base.

PEANUT—One of the most nutritive of foods, is the peanut kernel, as they contain 7.85% of water, 2.77% of ash, 29.47% of protein, 4.29% of fiber, 14.27% of nitrogen free extract, 49.29% of fat, 4.67% of nitrogen. *** In describing the uses of peanuts it is scarcely necessary to more than refer to that use which fully three-fourths of the American raised crop is devoted. The nut is sorted in the factory into four grades, the first, second and third being sold to vendors of the roasted peanut, either directly or through jobbing houses. The fourth grade, after passing through a sheller, is sold to confectioners, to be used in the making of "burnt almonds," peanut candy and cheaper grades of chocolates. The extent of the use of the peanuts by the American people will be more fully appreciated when it is remembered that they use 4,000,000 bushels of nuts yearly (at a cost to the consumers of $10,000,000) which do not form a part of the regular articles of food, but are eaten at odd times.

PEANUT—More than half the peanuts eaten in this country are consumed in the form of peanut butter. Although the protein and mineral values of peanuts are undeniably high, so is their fat content, and they are no longer considered "one of the most nutritive of foods." Still, peanuts (Arachis hypogaea) are an important part of our heritage, indigenous to South America but planted in the southeastern United States since early colonial times. They are most frequently used in cooking in West Africa, although peanut butter is contained in several sauces, such as saté, from Indonesia and elsewhere in Southeast Asia.

PEAR—A delicious fruit, produced at its best in California. The Bartlett is the best for serving plain or in the fruit stands. May be used in almost all the ways just previously described for peaches.

PEAR—One of the great losses of American eating is that we have never considered the pear to be the equal of the apple. (In most of France the pear is seen as the apple's superior.) There are several thousand varieties of pears (mostly Pyrus communis) and, although some are gritty and others only barely sweet, the vast majority are—during their sometimes fleeting moments of ripeness—exquisite, with a soft, juicy, almost liquid texture and a uniquely rich flavor.

Pears are almost never ripened on trees, even in home orchards. To ripen hard pears at home, wrap them in a paper bag and check them daily. When they are almost ripe—the narrow stem end will yield to light pressure—check them even more frequently. When they are fully ripe, eat them or put them in the refrigerator.

PRICKLY PEAR—The fruit of a cactus named Opuntia, is peeled, sliced, moistened with brandy and the juice of an orange, then served with powdered sugar.

PRICKLY PEAR—One of those "new and exotic" foods that has in fact been around for a while, the prickly pear—also called cactus pear, Indian fig, and a host of other names (including Opuntia ficus-indica)—is actually a berry that grows in the Southwest, Mexico, the entire Mediterranean perimeter, and elsewhere. Once you get past their scary exterior you will find that cactus pears vary widely in color —from pale to yellow to watermelon red—and in flavor, from insipid and barely sweet to quite lush.

Even when the spines have been mechanically removed, as is usually the case with cactus pears sold in supermarkets, these fruits must be carefully cleaned, as the remnants of the prickers are irritating to the skin. Hold them with tongs or a fork, or use gloves, and rinse them carefully, then slit the skin from end to end and "unwrap" it from the fruit.

PEAS—Garden peas shelled and washed, the toppings removed from the water, put to boil in boiling water with salt, little sugar and a small bunch of green mint, boil rapidly without a cover till tender, about ten to fifteen minutes, take up and drain, remove the mint; serve plain as a vegetable or garnish, or mix with cream or gravy, or butter sauce. The dried green peas of commerce may, after soaking in cold water over night, be treated the same as fresh garden peas.

PEAS—The distinction Fellows makes between garden peas and "the dried peas of commerce"—also known as field peas—is a legitimate one. They are in fact different species (*Pisum sativum* versus *Pisum arvense*). And although you can treat dried peas in the same manner as garden peas, the difference in taste is astronomical. Fresh peas (there are hundreds of varieties available to gardeners), straight from the garden, are even more fragile than CORN. Since their sweetness dissipates with every passing minute, frozen peas are often preferable to "fresh" peas in supermarkets.

Dried peas, of course, have great keeping qualities, although they are best used within a year or so of harvest. They are green or yellow, whole or split. Split peas can be treated in the same manner as LENTILS and need not be soaked before cooking. See BEANS.

GREEN PEA SOUP—Garden peas shelled and washed, boiled till tender in good chicken broth, seasoned to taste, then is added some shredded chervil and lettuce.

GREEN PEA SOUP—Peas shelled and washed, boiled in white stock till tender, slightly thickened with roux, then rubbed through a tamis, seasoned; served with croûtons. To the purée may also be added finely cut chervil, chives, spring onions, asparagus points, stringless beans . . . also may be mixed in for a change, two or three cans of macedoines . . . or a Julienne of vegetables . . . royal custards . . . rice grains . . . flageolet beans . . . etc.

PURÉE OF PEAS—Dried green peas soaked over night, put to boil in white stock with a ham knuckle, mint, onion, carrot, spring onions and chives; when tender, remove the ham, rub the rest through a tamis, season to taste, bring to the boil again and slightly thicken with roux, to avoid settling; cut the ham in small dice and add to the soup; serve with croûtons.

PURÉE OF PEAS—Dried green peas put to boil with salt pork and a bunch of pot herbs in veal broth, boil till soft and pork is done, then remove pork, thicken a little with roux to prevent settling, then rub through tamis, bring to boil again, season to taste, cut the pork in

dice, add to the soup; serve with croûtons.

SPLIT PEA SOUP—Split peas soaked over night, put to boil in white stock with onion, celery, carrot and salt pork; when done, thicken lightly with roux to prevent settling, remove the pork, rub the rest through a tamis, bring to boil again, season to taste, add the pork cut in small dice; serve with croûtons.

PEAS PUDDING—An English dish used with boiled salt pork, salt beef, etc. Split peas soaked over night, then put into a cloth allowing room to swell, put to boil in cold water with salt and a small piece of common washing soda, boiled till soft, taken up, the cloth hung to allow all water to drain out, then untied, turned on to a dish and served with the accompanying meat.

PEPPER—Black, White and Mignonette, the berry of the pepper vine. The Black is the unripe berry dried; Mignonette is the black crushed (not ground) used in seasoning foods or stocks, etc., that will be strained; White is the kernel of the ripe berry.

PEPPER—Here we are talking only about black and white pepper (for chiles, see CAPSICUMS), which come from the same plant, *Piper nigrum*. Black peppercorns, being unripe, are green when picked. They darken as they dry. If they are canned rather than dried, they remain green and soft, and are sold as green peppercorns.

RED PEPPER—is the ground seeds and pods of the small capsicum; also called cayenne pepper.

PEPPERMINT—Name of a combination plant of pepper and mint, one of the mint species; a volatile oil is extracted from it which is used for medicinal purposes, also as a flavoring to many things in the confectioners' trade.

PEPPER POT—Name of the national soup stew of the West Indies; composed of pieces of beef, veal, ham, chicken, game, all sorts of vegetables, chopped green marjoram, savory, basil, parsley, small potatoes and dumplings, finished and seasoned with sauce Cassareep and chili pepper.

PERCH—A delicate dainty flavored small fish abundant all summer in our fresh water lakes, rivers and streams. As the skin is hard they should be skinned by first running a sharp knife down either side of the back fins, lifting the fin out, then with a sharp jerk pull off the skin from the sides, empty the entrails, cut off the other fins, season with salt and pepper, roll in flour, then in beaten eggs, then breadcrumbs, fry a golden brown; serve with lemon, garnish with parsley, and you have a dish acceptable to all. . . . Or, after preparing, season, roll in flour, broil and baste till done; serve garnished with chip potatoes and a little maître d'hôtel butter, . . . prepare and boil in salted water with a bunch of parsley, take up and drain; serve with Allemande, parsley butter or anchovy cream sauce, . . . prepare, season with salt and pepper, roll in flour, sauté in butter; serve with a strip of bacon and a little anchovy butter spread on it ... prepare, season, roll in flour, bake with a little bacon fat till done and delicate brown in color; serve with Allemande sauce.

PERCH—Most of the perch found in our markets are one of the saltwater varieties, of which there are several. But the freshwater fish, from our inland lakes, is rather small, yet delicious.

PERIGUEUX—Name given to a sauce made by frying a delicate brown sauce together some minced shallots, onion and ham, then moisten with a glass of white wine and allow to simmer till half reduced, then add an equal quantity of brown roux and good meat gravy, also some truffle peelings and a piece of meat glaze, simmer the whole for ten minutes, then pass through the china cap, add plenty of thinly sliced truffles and set in bain-marie for use.

PERSIMMON—Name of a fruit resembling in appearance a smooth tomato, in color between the red and yellow sorts; best when having caught the frost; has a flavor from its pulpy interior like a mixture of a rough banana and tamarinds; its taste must be cultivated to be liked as a fruit. It is prepared in the Southern states as a beer, cider and wine. Also its pulp is rubbed through a sieve, mixed with corn meal instead of water and made into a sweet corn bread.

PERSIMMON—One of our indigenous fruits, the persimmon (*Diospyros virginiana*) is bitter until fully ripe. We can assume that Fellows, who believed persimmon to be an acquired taste, did not let his ripen fully—a common mistake. When allowed to ripen until mushy, the persimmon is a sweet, luscious, instantly likable fruit. Asian persimmons (*Diospyros kaki*) need not ripen as long, but are never as sweet.

PHEASANT—A fine game bird; should be hung by the tail for at least a week or till its gamy flavor is pronounced, then pluck, draw, singe, wipe and truss, plunge him into boiling salted water with an onion and some celery stalks; when he is tender take out, serve in portions with a good combined celery purée sauce containing an equal quantity of rich oyster sauce.

PHEASANT—Pheasant live in fields and take off like a rocket when threatened, a maneuver that requires powerful lower legs. This makes those limbs tough to eat, and many chefs disregard them, reserving them for stock and cooking only the tender breasts. This is a shame: The legs are flavorful, and the thighs, especially if cooked slowly, make for wonderful eating (the tendons in the lower leg are annoying, but the meat makes the effort worth it).

Only hunters hang pheasant nowadays, but we have plenty of choices when it comes to buying this best-known of game birds. There are at least three kinds of pheasant available: small (one-pound) wild birds from Scotland; fully domesticated birds, the biggest producers of which are in Connecticut, Pennsylvania, and California; and "free-range" birds, grown under nets, available from small producers in

New Jersey, California, and elsewhere.

The two- to three-pound domesticated birds are quite mild in flavor, rather like guinea hens or true free-range chickens. Free-range pheasant, which cost about the same per pound but are a bit smaller, have darker, more flavorful meat and are a better choice. The powerfully flavored wild birds are a bit more expensive, but they are a real treat. Since their flavors dissipate when frozen, they are best sampled in the fall, when distributors have a fresh supply.

BROILED PHEASANT—Take the very young birds, and after hanging, pluck, singe, split down the back, remove back and breast bones; season with salt and pepper, brush well with olive oil, place in a wire hinged broiler, broil over a cleared space of the charcoal till tender; serve with a brown game sauce.

ROAST PHEASANT—Hung birds plucked, singed, drawn, wiped, trussed, breasts larded, bacon tied over the larded breasts, roasted and basted till done; served in portions with bread sauce.

BRAISED PHEASANT—Hung birds plucked, singed, drawn, wiped, stuffed with a Financière ragout mixed with grated stale bread and a little grated lemon rind, trussed, braised with bacon, sweet herbs and a little game stock; when done, taken up, the braise strained and skimmed, then poured to a game sauce, reduced, finished with a glass of port wine; served in portions with some of the ragout under, the sauce over. . . . May also be braised without being stuffed, and served with a purée Soûbise . . . also braised with cabbage lettuces and pork sausages; served garnished with the sausages and a game sauce poured over . . . also braised, served garnished with glazed sweetbreads, and a Financière ragout. PHEASANT MAY BE USED TO PRODUCE ALMOST ALL THE ENTRÉES GIVEN WITH PARTRIDGE, AND NAMED ACCORDINGLY.

PICALLILI—Cut the following vegetables rather fine, crush the garlic, then add, pack all into stone crocks and cover with slightly salted water, and stand in a cool place for one day and night, then drain on sieve and press with cloths till dry; then place back into the crocks, cover with the boiling vinegar and spices, hermetically seal on the crock covers while contents are at boiling heat—100 small cucumbers, 3 small white cabbages, 18 small heads of celery, 6 medium cauliflowers, 6 quarts of stringless beans, 9 each of medium sized green and red peppers, 4 cloves of garlic, 6 ozs. of mustard seed, 2 level teaspoonfuls each of ground allspice, mace and ginger, 2 heaping teaspoonfuls of ground black pepper, enough cider vinegar to well cover.

PICKLES—When making any pickles from the receipts given under their respective headings, always use the best cider vinegar, scald to boiling point but do not let it boil, prepare always in either granite or porcelain lined kettles, use wooden spoons or paddles. A piece of horseradish root in the jars will prevent the vinegar from becoming moldy. They should always be kept in stone or glass, and in a dry dark place.

PICKLE—Aromatic salt pickle (German): Take seven and half gallons of water, one pound of Indian cane sugar, half pound of pulverized cleaned saltpetre, three ounces of coriander seeds, half a dozen bay leaves, three cloves of garlic. Boil all for five minutes, let it cool, strain into brine tub through a fine strainer, throw away the refuse. This brine will keep all summer, and can be used for every kind of meat. All meat from this pickle will have a fine red color and a pleasant taste.

PICKLE PUMPS—There is perhaps no process so important in the curing of meat as pumping. Meat is liable to very quick decomposition unless it is immediately brought in contact with a preservative of some kind, such as salt, borax, etc. In ordinary course if these preservatives were laid on the surface of the meat, they would mingle with the meat juices, dissolve and percolate slowly through the tissues; but this process is slow and under many conditions of temperature, dangerous. Hence the necessity of an appliance which brings the preservatives at once into operation. The salt brine or pickle is filtered so that it runs clear, and is then injected by the pickle pump into the meat to be cured.

PICKLING BEEF AND HAMS—To 100 pounds of beef or hams, use 7 pounds of rock salt, 5 pounds of brown sugar, 2 ounces of saltpetre, half an ounce of salaratus, mix to-gether and boil in four gallons of water, skim while boiling and pour on to the meat hot. For hams to cure well, they should remain in the pickle for six weeks.

PIG PRODUCTS—Under the name of fresh pork is comprised generally all the lean and fresh parts of the pig destined to be roasted or broiled, particularly the cutlets, the loin and small fillet. The loin is the fleshy part between the cutlets and the ham; it furnishes an excellent roast. The "filet mignon" as the French call it, is the long and narrow fleshy part under the kidney along the dorsal spine known to us as the pork tenderloin. It is the most delicate morsel of pork and weighs from half to a pound in weight.

PIG PRODUCTS—See PORK.

HAMS—Nearly always entire hams are salted (cured); sometimes they are used for cooking after several days curing; sometimes for smoking or preserving a longer or shorter time; sometimes they are boned and used for the manufacture of different kinds of sausages.

SHOULDERS—These are used to make rolled or boned hams; sometimes they are cured and smoked, and are then called fore hams or California hams; most often they are used for the manufacture of sausages.

CAUL—The caul is mostly used for wrapping around different stuffed pieces such as truffled feet, stuffed

CUTS OF PORK
and where they come from

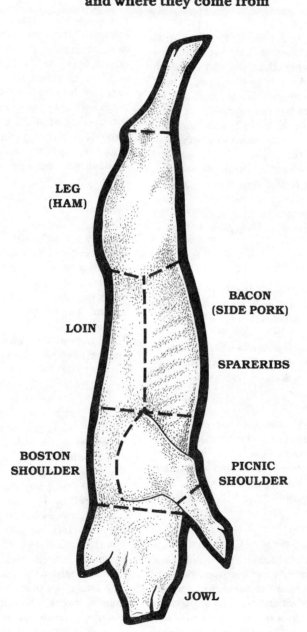

LEG
(HAM)

BACON
(SIDE PORK)

LOIN

SPARERIBS

BOSTON
SHOULDER

PICNIC
SHOULDER

JOWL

cutlets, flat sausages, broiled livers, etc.

FRESH LARD-BACK FAT-LARDING PORK—Fresh lard or back fat. The fat between the skin and the flesh is called fresh lard or simply lard. There are two kinds, melting fat and hard fat; the first, or that nearest the flesh, is easily known by the touch; it yields to a moderate pressure of the fingers, and is used for making lard. The other, or hard fat, adheres to the skin and is not easy to melt; it is used for larding and in the preparation of a great number of products in the pork butchers' trade.

KIDNEY FAT—Is the fat that covers the kidney and tenderloin; it is used for fine forcemeats and in black puddings, to which it gives a delicate taste. From this fat also is obtained a very fine white lard superior to ordinary melted lard.

GUT FAT—The fat that adheres to the intestines. If melted alone, lard of second quality is produced; more often it is melted with other lard so as to produce lard of ordinary quality.

LUNGS, LIVER, HEART, KIDNEYS, BRAIN, SPLEEN—The lungs and liver form part of the ingredients of various kinds of sausages, liver pates, broiled and fried liver, etc. The heart, kidneys and brain are prepared by the culinary processes which are used for other similar pieces of butchers' meat. The spleen is generally used in sausages of an inferior quality.

STOMACH—Comprises the small intestines, the coecum, the colon and the rectum. The small intestine is used as a casing for different kinds of sausages, black pudding (boudin noir), etc. The coecum, called also the bag or pocket, is used, as also the colon and the rectum and fat end for the packing of different sausages to keep, and for the making of stuffed chitterlings. The stomach or paunch requires long cooking, after which it is used in common sausages and chitterlings.

TONGUE, EARS, SNOUT, FEET, HAMS AND TAIL—All these different pieces can be cooked alone, or with vegetables without any special preparation being necessary. Very often they are put for some days in a brine. The tongue, ears and snout are used also for head cheese, collared brawn, etc. The tongue can also be used for converting into savory tongue.

PIGS' FEET—The handling of which, so as to produce a profitable return requires scientific method and absolute cleanliness. The feet should be used fresh as cut from the pig. The front feet are always used first as they are the best for turning into edible delicacies, and the hind feet contain more bone. The toes are pulled off and the hair clean shaved; the feet should then be well washed and scraped, taking care not to cut them, as this causes them to break when cooking; after cleaning, fresh water should be kept running on them until they are to be cooked. The constantly changing of the water removes the blood and makes them more inviting and whiter when cooked.

SKIN—The skin of the pig can be easily tanned. It furnishes a leather superior to that of the ox. It forms an important element in the making of jellies. Skin left on salt meat preserves it from the ravages of insects, and from the effects produced by the air.

BLOOD—The blood of the pig is very valuable for the manufacture of blood puddings. It is used in cooking to thicken sauces; and it clarifies jellies and gives them a beautiful golden tint.

HAIR—The hair or bristles are used extensively in brush making. The bristles on the back serve as needles for hand sewn boot and shoe manufacturers.

HOOFS—Pulverized hoofs make a very rich manure. They are also used in the manufacture of glue and Prussian blue.

BONES—The bones are used in the making of soups and jellies. After being cooked they may be pulverised and used for manure.

BLADDERS—The bladders after being well washed, blown and dried, are used for wrapping round sausages, and for filling with lard, also for hermetically sealing pots of preserves.

GALL—The liquid contained in the gall bladder is very good for taking out grease stains without taking out the color of even the most delicate stuffs. Hence the products of the pig are, taken together, of immense value.

BRINE FOR HAM, PICKLES, ETC.—Before proceeding with the subject of pork I will draw the "hotel butcher's" attention to the subject of his pickling, and as in some parts of the country the hotel keepers raise their own pigs and desire their cooks to use up every part of it to advantage I will give the receipts of ham pickles.

Many butchers prepare their brines in a way as simple as it is DEFECTIVE. They are content to dissolve a certain quantity of salt and saltpetre in cold water. THIS BRINE DOES NOT PRESERVE, and must not be used for delicate meats.

Put into a boiler and let boil for ten minutes 6 gallons of water, 21 pounds of salt, 6 pounds of sugar, 2 pounds of saltpetre, stir well during cooking, then empty out the brine and all that remains undissolved, allow to become quite cold, then add a quarter of a pound of mixed whole spices; rub the meat with powdered saltpetre and salt, place in the brine tub, pour over the brine. This brine is excellent and can be used for all kinds of meat, and notably for meat where special brines are not indicated.

Boil as in the preceding 5 gallons of water, 8 pounds of white salt, 2 pounds of gray salt, 2½ pounds of sugar, 2½ pounds of saltpetre; allow to cool, flavor with ¼ pound of whole spices.

Boil and cook as above 10 gallons of water, 50 pounds of white salt, 4 pounds of gray salt, 4½ pounds of saltpetre, 5 pounds of sugar, flavor with ½ pound of spices.

In some Italian provinces an excellent brine is prepared, composed of 1¼ gallons each of Barola wine and water, 8 pounds of white salt, ½ pound of gray salt, ¼ pound of saltpetre, flavored with thyme, bay leaves, basil, savory, and juniper.

In Westphalia the hams are pickled with brine made with, 2½ gallons of water, 8 pounds of salt, 2 pounds of sugar, ½ pound of saltpetre, 2 ounces of spices tied in a muslin bag.

For Bayonne hams, the following brine is used, 1¼ gallons each of good red wine and cold water, 8 pounds of white salt, 2 pounds of gray salt, 2 ounces of saltpetre, and a flavoring of sage, rosemary and lavender.

There are two principal processes for salting meats; the wet process and the dry. Both have their merits, and their combined use offers advantages. THE WET PROCESS consists in steeping meats in a brine for some time, according to the thickness of the pieces of meats; it is carried out by the big packing companies, where the system of curing has reached a most perfect condition. THE DRY PROCESS: place the meats on the salting table, powder them with fine saltpetre, rub well into the meat, rub afterwards with gray salt (sea salt). Arrange them one beside the other in such a way that they will not get out of shape, then cover evenly with white salt; this operation is renewed every two or three days until the salt has been well soaked into the inside of the flesh, a result which is obtained in from one to four weeks, according to the size of the pieces. This process is generally carried on by salt meat exporters.

By the wet process the necessary salt flavor is obtained, inasmuch as they are immersed in brine more or less salted. With the dry process, on the contrary, the meats coming into immediate contact with the salt are impregnated too strongly.

This difference in result is easily explained through the action of the salt. In both methods this condiment clears out the aqueous portions of the blood in the tissues and thus preserves the meat from taint. With dry salting it is pure salt which saturates the meats. In the wet process the brine, which acts like salt, being a solution of it, impregnates in a much less degree the flesh, as it is so much weaker being in solution. If the wet process is used, nothing must be done until after the meats are thoroughly chilled, which is not often complete (according to temperature) before twelve to eighteen hours. If this precaution is neglected, and the warm meats were heaped into a brine tub, not only would they become unshapely, but they would become hot and ferment, the inevitable consequence of which would be their corruption and that of the brine.

With the dry process the meats can be salted immediately after slaughter, which is favorable to the success of the operation. In fact, it is known by the reason of its chemical composition, meat tends to decomposition as soon as the animal ceases to live, and it is therefore apparent that the less advanced is the tainting, the greater is the success of the salting.

PICKLING OF ROLLED HAMS— Choose hams that are not very fat, bone and trim them, pickle in brine for two weeks, wash in fresh water for an hour or so, brush the hams, beat with a mallet so as to make them round and uniform, tie with string, dry them in the air, then smoke them. When these hams are dry they can be served raw, but usually they are served cooked.

FORE HAMS OR CALIFORNIA SHOULDERS—Trim the shoulders, cut them round, put through the dry process (as above) for three days, then through the wet process for ten days, take out of the brine, wash, scrub, dry, smoke, and finish like ordinary hams.

PICKLING OF OX TONGUES—Cut away the dead flesh, the gristle, and the fat which is found at the root. Make on each side of the root slight incisions to facilitate the salting. Wash the tongues in running water, brushing them well, dry with a cloth, rub them with saltpetre, then with a mixture of 9 parts salt and 1 part sugar, and put them in a good brine for 12 days. Ox tongues, like those of pigs, calves and sheep, have on their thick side a slimy liquid, which easily taints the brine. This is why it is important to well wash and dry them before putting into the brine. For the same reason tongues should always be pickled alone in a special brine tub in which only the necessary quantity of brine should be put.

PIGS HEAD STUFFED—More often called "Boars Head (glazed)." Select a perfect head with good ears; the head must be cut off full, that is with two or three joints of the neck bone left on; carefully bone it; the head is then well washed in cold water to remove all blood, and put into a spiced pickle for six days; it is then well washed and stuffed tightly with pork sausage meat, a piece of rind being stitched on back of head to keep the stuffing in. The head is then placed on a thin board and another piece placed alongside each cheek and tied in position to keep head in shape; the whole is now tied up in a cloth, and cooked gently, so as not to break the ears, but long enough to cook thoroughly; allow to cool, taking care to place in position, so that it cools to a good shape with ears erect; when cool insert glass eyes, and, if available, a pair of tusks, then glaze and decorate.

PIGEONS—The young ones called squabs, are best split down the back, breastbone removed, trussed, seasoned with salt and pepper, rolled in melted butter, broiled; served on toast with maître d'hôtel or Piquante sauces.

PIGEONS—Pigeons are almost never sold in this country. But squab—defined as pigeons not old enough to fly—are fairly easy to find, although they are expensive. Their meat is rich, flavorful, and succulent.

ROAST PIGEON—Young birds plucked, singed, drawn, wiped, trussed with bacon over the breast, roasted; served with their own gravy, garnish with cress.

BREASTS OF PIGEON—Breasts of young birds, seasoned, breaded, and broiled, or fried; or coated with sauce then breaded and fried; or the breasts sautéed then breaded and fried; served with any garnish appropriate to dark fleshed birds or game.

STEWED PIGEON WITH MUSH-ROOMS—Separated into four joints, sautéed with butter, taken up into a saûtoir to which is added little lean ham, button mushrooms sautéed, bunch of pot herbs, seasoning, little red wine and stock, the whole simmered till tender; served with the mushrooms as a border.

PIGEON PIE—Into a deep pie dish place on the bottom some thin slices of beef, then halves of young pigeons, slices of bacon, some forcemeat balls, mushrooms, and yolks of hard boiled eggs, little chopped parsley, moisten with seasoned gravy, cover with a short paste, brush the top with egg wash, and bake gently till done, about an hour and a half.

POTTED PIGEON—Young birds plucked, singed, drawn, wiped, stuffed with a mixture of grated bread, chopped parsley, chopped suet, grated hard boiled egg yolks, salt, pepper, and nutmeg, trussed, placed into a crock with celery, thyme, parsley, an onion stuck with cloves, glass of Madeira and a little stock, cover, place in oven, and cook gently till tender; served with the strained gravy, garnished with cress and lemon.

COMPOTE OF PIGEON—Practically the same as above, generally garnished with sautéed button mushrooms.

PIGEON CROÛSTADE—Young birds prepared and trussed, arranged in a saûtoir with slices of bacon, moistened with chicken broth, stewed till tender, taken up and placed in a toasted fancy bread croûstade; served with Financière garnish poured around.

CURRIED PIGEONS—Small young birds, one to the portion, prepared and trussed, placed in oven with bacon fat and quickly browned and basted, taken up into a curry sauce made of chicken and game stock, to which is added a grated green apple, simmered till tender; served garnished with timbales of rice and rissoto.

CURRIED PIGEONS WITH RICE—Split the birds in halves, take out the breast bone, season with salt and pepper, roll them in curry powder and then in flour, mince some onions and a clove of garlic, fry them without much color in oil of butter, take up the onions; then fry the pigeons, moisten with stock, return the onions, add a grated sour apple, also a spoonful each of tamarinds and Bengal chutney with a little preserved ginger, simmer slowly till done, take up the birds, skim off any grease from the curry, strain it over the birds; make a border of dry boiled rice around the serving dish, place two halves of birds in the centre with some of the sauce poured over them.

STUFFED PIGEON WITH POTATOES—Draw the bird as for roast, take out the breast bone, stuff with a mixture of breadcrumbs, parsley, its own liver and heart minced with a little bacon, grated lemon rind, salt and pepper. Arrange them in a saûtoir, cover with stock and simmer slowly till tender. Make a mound of mashed potatoes on the serving dish, place a pigeon on top, pour over some of the gravy made from the stock the birds were simmered in.

STUFFED PIGEON WITH VEGETABLES—Prepare the birds and cook as in the preceding recipe; when tender, take up the birds, then boil some Julienne cut vegetables in the stock the birds were simmered in, season, place the bird on a slice of toast, pour the gravy over it, and garnish with the drained vegetables.

LARDED PIGEONS, GARNISHED —Lard the breast of the birds with bacon, arrange them in a saûtoir, moisten with chicken stock and simmer till tender, take up, reduce the gravy to a glaze, roll the birds in it, and serve each one on a fancy croûstade, pour over a little Financière sauce, and garnish the base with a ragout of truffles, mushrooms, cocks combs and quenelles of chicken.

SALMIS OF PIGEONS—Take cold cooked birds, split in halves, arrange in a saûtoir, moisten with a game sauce, add a glass of sherry wine, serve the birds on a fancy croûton, pour over a little of the sauce and garnish with stoned olives.

BRAISED PIGEON WITH FLAGEOLETS—Prepare and stuff the birds as for "Stuffed pigeons with potatoes," braise them slowly till tender, take up, add a good brown sauce to the contents of the brasiere, reduce, then strain it over the pigeons; serve the bird on toast

with a spoonful of the sauce poured over; garnish with some flageolets that have been sautéed in butter.

FRICASSÉE OF PIGEONS—Draw the birds as for roasting, take out the breast bone, stuff the aperture with a veal forcemeat, tie up, blanch, arrange in a saûtoir, cover with a Velouté sauce, put on the cover and simmer slowly till tender; serve with green peas, and a fancy croûton at each end of the dish.

BRAISED PIGEON, GARNISHED —Braise the birds till tender, split them in halves, arrange neatly on toast, pour over some of the strained and skimmed braise, garnish with stoned olives, button mushrooms, small quenelles, olive shaped pieces of carrot and turnip that have all been simmered in chicken or veal stock till done.

ROAST PIGEON WITH TOMATOES—Take young birds and stuff them with breadcrumbs seasoned with salt, pepper, butter, minced parsley and onions parboiled in broth, add an egg to bind, cover the breasts with broad thin slices of bacon, roast, take up, add to the pan they were roasted in some Espagnole sauce, and a seasoning of Worcestershire sauce, boil up and strain, then add to it a little tarragon vinegar and chopped parsley; serve a spoonful over each bird, and garnish with sautéed tomatoes.

SAUTÉ OF PIGEON—Split the birds down the back, remove the breast bone, flatten with the cleaver, season with salt and pepper, roll in flour, fry in butter; when done, take up and add flour to the butter they were fried in, moisten with stock, boil up and strain over the birds, add some chopped estragon leaves and a spoonful of tarragon vinegar, simmer a little while, then serve.

SQUABS, SAUCE CRAPAUDINE— Draw the birds as for roasting, then without detaching the parts, cut the breast from the tip to the wing joint, turn the two ends so as to look like a frog, flatten with a blow of the cleaver, dip in melted butter, then in fresh grated breadcrumbs, broil slowly till done; serve with sauce Crapaudine.

PINTAIL—Name of one of our common wild ducks, is good stuffed and roasted, and in a salmi.

PIQUANTE—Name of a sauce made with an equal number of chopped shallots and green gherkins, boiled till shallots are done in caper vinegar, then is added some capers, bay leaf and a few sprigs of thyme, boiled again till vinegar is reduced to one third of its original volume; remove the bay leaf and thyme, add enough good Espagnole sauce and a little chicken broth, till of the proper sauce consistency.

PISTACHIO—Name of a pea green nut of almond flavor, used by pastry cooks and confectioners.

PISTACHIO—So widespread is the notion that pistachio tastes like almond that the pistachio's alternative name—green almond—was once widely used. Yet a pistachio is a distinctly different species (*Pistacia vera*) with a distinctly different flavor.

Pistachios grow in hot places —the Middle East, North Africa, southern Europe, southern California—in clusters that resemble olive clusters. The nuts are dried in the sun, during which time most of the shells open naturally. They make a terrific snack but are little used in cooking (although real pistachio ice cream is one of the world's great treats).

PLANTAIN—The plantain is part of the BANANA family (Musa paradisiaca), but it is far more versatile than the yellow bananas we usually eat as a raw fruit.

When green, the plantain—the flesh can be ivory, yellow, or even pink—is frequently made into tostones, crisp, pan-fried morsels to be sprinkled with salt and lime. But plantains can also be baked, boiled, mashed, deep-fried as chips . . . in short, used in any of the ways in which Americans have traditionally cooked potatoes.

PLOVER—Plovers, which are shorebirds similar to sandpipers, were so delicious that they were eaten by the thousands, almost to extinction. Their eggs, which featured bright orange yolks, were especially favored. Now it is illegal to hunt plovers (or to gather their eggs) in the United States. Use Fellows's recipes to cook other small game birds, such as quail.

BROILED PLOVER ON TOAST—Wipe the birds but do not draw them, broil over a clear fire, basting often with butter; serve on toast, garnish with a croûton spread with currant jelly.

ROAST PLOVER—Wipe the birds but do not draw them, spread a thin piece of fat bacon over the breast, roast quickly till done; serve on a fancy croûstade with a little game sauce poured over.

BREAST OF PLOVER, EN SALMI—Wipe but do not draw the birds, roast, take off the breasts and simmer them in a game sauce containing minced mushrooms, take the trail of the birds, spread it on fancy croûtons; serve the breasts on a Duchesse potato, pour the sauce around, and garnish with the croûtons.

BREASTS OF PLOVER WITH SWEETBREADS—Roast the birds, then remove the breasts and place them in a saûtoir with a little demi-glaze and some stoned olives. Take small sweetbreads lard and braise them; serve one of each with the sauce poured over them.

PLUMS—As there are so many varieties grown, and all good for dessert, compotes, etc., I will simply here append a few ways of taking care of them when they are to be had very cheap.

PLUMS—Almost all plums (*Prunus domestica*) sold in this country (90 percent of which are from California) are shipped—and bought—before they are ripe. They can be refrigerated before ripening if longer keeping is desired, but they must be ripened at room temperature.

The ripening process of most plum varieties can be hastened by enclosing the plum in a paper bag for a few days. Ethylene gas (the same gas that is sometimes used by distributors to artificially ripen certain fruits) is released naturally through the plum's skin and speeds the ripening or metabolic process that changes starch to sugar within the fruit.

We have come to think of black and dark red plums, especially those with red flesh, as the most succulent, but there are those who insist that green and yellow plums add a certain complexity of flavor to the sweet-and-sour taste of the simpler varieties. Don't take this opinion lightly until you try a ripe green gage (which is sometimes considered to be a different species altogether).

Prunes are simply dried plums and have an undeservedly bad reputation. Try them in meat stews, in fruit pies, and swirled through ice cream.

PLUM MARMALADE—Rub the plums but do not pare them, cut in halves and remove the stones, weigh them, and allow half a pound of sugar to each pound of fruit. Put the fruit into a preserving kettle, add sufficient water to cover the bottom, cover, and bring slowly to the boiling point, then stir and mash the fruit until fine, add then the sugar and some of the kernels blanched and minced, boil and stir continually for fifteen minutes, then draw to one side and allow to simmer for twenty minutes more; pack away in stone crocks.

PLUM BUTTER—Select mellow fruit, peel and remove stones, weigh the fruit then, and to each pound allow three quarters of a pound of sugar, place the fruit in preserving kettle, heat slowly to boiling point, then mash till smooth, then rub through a fine sieve into another kettle; add the sugar and boil for fifteen minutes, stirring continually; pack away in small jars.

PLUM JELLY—Take common blue plums, wash in cold water, place in preserving kettle, adding two quarts of water to each bushel of fruit, cover the kettle and heat slowly until the fruit is soft and tender, then turn into flannel jelly bag and let drip till fruit is dry. To every pint of this juice allow one pound of granulated sugar, put the juice into preserving kettle and bring it quickly to the boil, add then the sugar and stir till dissolved, then boil rapidly till it jellies, about twenty-five minutes; remove scum as it rises; as soon as it jellies, take jelly tumblers, roll them in boiling water, fill with the boiling liquid, stand aside for 24 hours, then screw on the covers.

PLUM PUDDING—As each and every pastry cook has his own favorite recipe for this dish, which is usually associated with Christmas, I will simply append one that has always given satisfaction to the best of critics:

Pound and a half of raisins stoned and freed from stalks . . . Pound and a half of currants, rubbed and freed from stones . . . Pound mixed of citron, orange and lemon candied peels . . . Two and a half pounds of finely chopped beef suet . . . Two pounds of sifted flour . . . One and a half pounds of brown sugar freed from lumps . . . Eight eggs . . . One and a half pints of rich milk . . . The grated rind and juices of two lemons and two oranges . . . One ounce of mixed ground nutmeg, cloves and cinnamon . . . Half a pint of Cognac and a teaspoonful of salt.

Mix overnight before to be boiled in the morning; fill into molds or into a buttered and floured cloth; boil steadily for five hours; serve with hard and brandy sauces.

PLUM CAKE—The finest wedding cake as made by a late employer of mine:

Pound and a half of sifted flour . . . Pound and a half of pure butter . . . Pound of powdered sugar . . . Pound of French cherries cut in halves (cerises glacées) . . . Pound and a half of seeded raisins and cleaned currants (three-quarters of each) . . . Half a pound each of shredded citron, orange and lemon candied peels . . . Half a pound of finely chopped almonds . . . Eight whole eggs . . . Grated rind and juice of four oranges . . . Half an ounce of mixed ground cinnamon, cloves and nutmeg . . . Half a pint of Cognac and a teaspoonful of salt.

POLENTA—See CORN.

POMPANO—A most delicious nutty flavored fish of the Southern waters, broiled whole, or, if large, filletted and broiled; served with maître d'hôtel sauce, or melted butter and Tartar sauce aside, garnished with lemon and fancy potatoes. . . . Broiled fillets of Pompano served spread with Montpelier butter and garnished with Julienne potatoes. . . . Filleted Pompano sautéed with strips of bacon, served with it and fancy potatoes. . . . Small Pompano fried a delicate brown with butter, butter oil then poured off into another pan, browned, then is added lemon juice and chopped parsley; served over the fish, garnished with Saratoga chips.

POMPANO—It is the Florida pompano (*Trachinotus carolinus*) to which Fellows referred, a slim, silvery fish that glistens in the sun as it rides the waves toward shore. Like most dark-fleshed fish, pompano does not keep well, so it is best appreciated where caught (occasionally as far north as Massachusetts, but usually from the mid-Atlantic states south to Florida) or where it has been just delivered. Rarely seen in large quantities—it is a sport fish rather than a commercial fish—pompano is never inexpensive, but it is meaty and sweet—a true delicacy.

POPCORN—See CORN.

PORGIE—Name of a small fish plentiful in the Eastern States markets; served in every way applicable to perch.

PORGY—There are a dozen or so fish known generically as porgy found throughout the world, but mostly in the warmer waters of the Atlantic and the Mediterranean. In addition to porgy, they are called bream; jolthead; pink, white, or silver snapper; scup; sheepshead; and whitebone. They are mild but delicious white-fleshed fish, with a good, firm texture. But because they are bony and difficult to fillet, they never have been extremely popular in the United States.

PORK—Most pork today is leaner and lighter-tasting than it has been at any time in the past. Cuts from the loin and other naturally tender areas should be cooked quickly, and even those tougher but fattier cuts—which were once simmered or baked all day—should not be overcooked.

There has been another change in pork: It is now only rarely affected by the trichina parasite that can cause trichinosis in humans. Even the conservative United States Department of Agriculture now recommends cooking pork to 160°F., down from 180° ten years ago. (Many chefs insist that pork is perfectly safe even at 135°.) Since the temperature of most roasts rises by 15 degrees or so after the meat is removed from the oven, we recommend cooking pork to a temperature of about 145°. After a 10-minute rest, it will have risen to the recommended temperature, but still be quite juicy. If you cook it to 160°, the meat's texture is liable to be terribly dry.

Although consumption of pork has fallen steadily over the last two decades, it remains a delicious meat. No one needs to be sold on ribs, of course, but pork can be quite elegant too.

PORK TENDERLOIN WITH SWEET POTATOES—Season the meat with salt, pepper and sage, roll in flour, then in melted roast pork drippings, arrange in baking pan with small whole, or halved, peeled sweet potatoes, bake till done with plenty of basting, about three-quarters of an hour; serve with gravy made in the pan they were cooked in.

STUFFED PORK TENDERLOIN—The meat split and stuffed with sage and onion dressing, tied with twine (which is afterwards removed), baked and served as the preceding.

PORK TENDERLOIN WITH SWEET POTATOES

.

Serves 6

An unusual dish that yields a succulent pan gravy. This is the kind of food that I think of when I think of Diamond Jim Brady and his eating habits.

3 strips bacon

2¹/₂ pounds whole pork tenderloins

Salt and freshly ground black pepper to taste

¹/₂ cup all-purpose flour

2 tablespoons olive oil

3 cloves garlic, peeled and chopped

1 medium yellow onion, peeled and sliced

2 tablespoons chopped parsley

1³/₄ pounds sweet potatoes, peeled and cut in ¹/₂-inch slices

1 cup Chicken Stock (page 153)

¹/₂ cup dry white wine

Heat a large frying pan and cook the bacon to render its fat. Remove the bacon, leaving the fat in the pan. Drain the bacon on paper towels. Chop and set aside.

Season the pork tenderloins with salt and pepper. Dredge in flour and pat off the excess flour. In the pan of bacon grease, brown the pork. Do not burn the grease. Remove the pork to a 13-inch by 9-inch baking pan. To the frying pan, add the oil, garlic, and onions and sauté for a couple minutes, until the onions are tender. Add the parsley, sweet potatoes, and reserved bacon; brown the potatoes lightly. Add the Chicken Stock and wine and simmer for 1 minute. Pour all on top of the pork, cover with aluminum foil, and bake at 375°F. for 1 hour.

Slice the pork and serve with the sweet potatoes and the pan gravy that has formed in the dish.

C.W.

BROILED PORK TENDERLOIN—Split, seasoned with salt, pepper and sage, rolled in flour, broiled well done, basting with butter; served with apple sauce, sauce Soûbise or sauce Robert.

BRAISED PORK TENDERLOIN—
Braised with vegetables and bacon;
when done, the braise strained and
skimmed, then added to a sauce
Robert or Lyonnaise, the tenderloin dipped in the sauce, then laid
on a neat centre of purée of sweet
potatoes, little more of the sauce
poured around the base.

CURRIED PORK TENDERLOIN—
Take any unused tenderloins of the
preceding receipt, cut them in neat
scallops quarter inch thick, reheat
them in a good curry sauce; served
garnished with small glazed onions
at the sides and a small mold of
rice at the ends.

CORNED PORK TENDERLOINS—
Use tenderloins that have been in a
good brine for three days, wash,
boil slowly for three-quarters of an
hour, take up and drain, then split
in halves, season with pepper and
powdered sage, roll in flour, arrange in baking pan, bake a delicate brown, basting with sausage
drippings, serve garnished with Julienne vegetables in a cream sauce.

ROAST LOIN OF PORK—With a bon-
ing knife separate the joints on the
chine bone of the loin of pork (better than chopping it), season with
salt, pepper and sage, score the
rind, arrange on a meat rest in baking pan, with sage and onion dressing under the meat, bake in a
medium oven well done and brown;
serve in chops on a spoonful of the
dressing, gravy at the sides, and
apple sauce served in a separate
dish; also roasted without dressing,
and served with Remoulade sauce.

ROAST LEG OF PORK—Legs 10 to
12 pounds in weight are of best
quality and most economical. Remove the foot, score the rinds into
dice shape, roast in a medium oven
well done two and a half to three
hours; serve with sage and onion
dressing, gravy, and apple sauce
separate; or with tomato sauce, or
Robert, or Piquante sauce, or with
baked apples.

STUFFED LEG OF PORK—For serving cold. Lay the leg on table skin
side down, remove the aitchbone,
then cut along the leg bone to the
knuckle joint, remove the leg bone
leaving the knuckle bone in, fill the
cavity with a stuffing composed of
fresh mashed potatoes, minced and
sautéed onion, salt, pepper, sage,
pork sausage meat and one whole
egg to each leg of pork, draw the
meat together close, tie tightly,
score the rind, bake slowly with a
few apples in the pan, till done,
basting with the apple juice and
gravy; then take up and allow to get
thoroughly cold; serve for luncheon or supper, in slices garnished either with small pickled
onions, sliced gherkins, Tartar
sauce, Remoulade sauce, purée of
cranberries or purée of apples.
After you have got the guests (especially in a family hotel) to try this
dish, you will have to keep two or
three on hand all the time to keep
up the demand.

BONED BOILED SALT LEG OF
PORK—For serving cold. Use a 12
pound leg, get it fresh, remove the
foot, rub with salt, wash it, pump it
with brine; then lay it in brine for
four days, take up, drain, remove
the bones as in the preceding recipe, draw the meat together, letting
the thin side come right over the
thick, tie tightly with twine, put to

boil in cold water with a few bay leaves and an onion stuck with cloves, boil slowly for one hour and a quarter, then allow it to become thoroughly cold in the water it was boiled in; serve in slices with a garnish of horseradish mustard and a few pickles, or sliced tomatoes with Tartar sauce, or German potato salad.

COLD ROLLED BELLY OF PORK (STUFFED OLIVES)—Nice lean bellies of pickled pork, may be boned, rolled, tied, then wrapped in a cloth and tied again like a roly poly pudding, boiled till tender, taken up and allowed to become cold in the cloth it was boiled in, the cloth then removed, the pork wiped with a hot wet cloth; served in slices garnished as above.

BROILED PORK CHOPS—Remove the rind, cut the chops to an even thickness, trim off any superfluous fat, season with salt and pepper, roll in butter then in breadcrumbs and broil a golden brown, or broil them plain, and serve plain or with apple sauce, or with Robert, Tartare, anchovy, curry, Bretonne, Soûbise or Lyonnaise sauces, or serve plain and garnished with fried sweet potatoes or fried apples.

FRIED PORK CHOPS—Remove the rind or leave it on (some like it on), season with salt and pepper, roll in flour, fry with pork fat a golden brown; serve plain or with tomato, Robert, Piquante, curry, Soûbise or sage sauces, or with fried apples.

PORK CHOPS SAUTÉES—Trim the chops, season with salt and pepper,

fry them a golden brown with butter. Make a stiff purée of split peas, place a heaping spoonful in centre of dish, place chop on it, and pour a little gherkin sauce over.

PORK CROQUETTES, ANCHOVY SAUCE—Make the pork croquette mixture from cold roast pork trimmings, season it with a little sage, adding to stiffen it some pork sausage meat; serve with a brown thick roast pork gravy flavored with anchovy essence.

EMINCE OF PORK WITH FRIED APPLES—Take the lean of cold roast leg of pork and cut in circular slices size of half dollars, dust them with salt, pepper and powdered sage, reheat them in sauce Robert; serve on toast; garnished with slices of fried apples.

SALT PORK WITH PARSNIPS—Lean pickled belly of pork, boil it with whole parsnips for half an hour, take up and drain, then slice the pork and quarter the parsnips, now fry the pork a golden brown, then the parsnips in the pork fat; serve two slices of each.

MINCED PORK WITH FRIED APPLES—Lean minced fresh pork three parts; white bread soaked in milk, then squeezed dry one part; season with salt, pepper and powdered sage, add a few beaten eggs, mix all thoroughly; place it in a buttered baking pan, cover with a sheet of buttered paper and bake in a medium oven for an hour and a half, cut out in squares or diamond shape when done and served with fried apples.

MINCED PORK WITH FRIED APPLES

•

Serves 6 to 8

Pork and apples go great together. Try this dish; it is inexpensive and very flavorful.

¹/₂ pound white bread slices

1 cup milk

2 pounds boneless pork butt, ground coarsely

2 eggs, beaten

1 teaspoon ground sage

2 cloves garlic, peeled and crushed

2 teaspoons salt

Freshly ground black pepper to taste

3 tablespoons butter

2 Red Delicious apples, peeled, cored, and cut in wedges

1 teaspoon sugar

Pinch of ground cinnamon

Pinch of ground nutmeg

¹/₄ cup dry sherry

Garnish

Parsley

Remove the crusts from the bread. Tear the bread into pieces and place in a large bowl. Add the milk and toss so that the bread is saturated. Set aside for 10 minutes.

Place the pork in a large bowl and add the eggs, sage, garlic, salt, and pepper.

Squeeze the milk out of the bread and add the bread to the pork. Mix very well, until the bread is thoroughly incorporated.

Grease an 8-inch by 3¹/₂-inch round casserole dish with 1 tablespoon of the butter. Add the pork mixture and smooth out evenly. Cover with aluminum foil and bake at 375°F. for 1¹/₄ hours.

Heat a large frying pan and add the remaining 2 tablespoons of butter. Add the apples, sugar, cinnamon, and nutmeg and sauté for 5 minutes over medium heat, until the apples are just tender and lightly browned. Deglaze the pan with the sherry and toss about. Add a pinch of salt, if needed.

While still hot, cut the pork casserole into wedges and serve with a bit of the fried apples. Garnish with a parsley sprig.

C.W.

FRIED SALT PORK WITH APPLES —Take the cold rolled belly of pork of a preceding recipe, slice it in quarter inch thicknesses, roll the slices in corn meal. Take sour cooking apples, core them, slice in half inch thicknesses, then arrange the pork and apples alternately in a baking pan, brown off of an even color in a quick oven and serve.

FRIED PORK KIDNEYS—Take the kidneys and split them, remove the white centres, soak them in salted water containing a little vinegar for an hour; then wipe dry, season with salt, pepper and powdered sage, roll in flour, fry a golden brown with butter; serve on toast, garnish with Brussels sprouts and pour over the kidneys a spoonful of maître d'hôtel butter.

PORK SAUSAGES—These may be made in various ways according to the price per day or meal of the hotel or restaurant. They are rarely made of the pure meat, as when so made they are too rich and unpalateable. If, however, a large proportion of the meat used be lean the richness will to a great extent disappear. It is in all cases, however, advisable to have present some cracker meal, bread or granulated rice, even if added only in small quantities, as by that means only FIRMNESS can be obtained. The hotel butcher or cook should make all the sausages used for every purpose, and not have them purchased from the meat purveyor. In the case of the sausages that are smoked, etc., and served as a relish, that part of it can be always done by the people from whom your hams are purchased for a mere trifle. Further, it is my very firm conviction, that, the ordinary hotel butcher knows but little about sausage making. He should know! and I shall here devote several pages of this book to that

teaching, with the hope that it will enable the hotel butcher to become of much more value to his employer, by economy, and also to become a man proper to use the title of butcher. Butchering is not merely cutting roasts, chops, steaks, hams, bacon, and doing general "garde mange" work; it consists of a knowledge of what to do with meat in its every use, and how to utilize every particle to advantage, hence, as you have read so far in this book, I have been profuse in explanations of the uses of meat and how to properly take care of it; as the butcher's bill is always the heaviest one for the proprietor to meet for the back part of the house.

PORK SAUSAGES—The sausage recipes in this book are a fine survey of the state of sausage making in the United States at the turn of the century. And many of those recipes can hold their own today.

Sausage making consists not so much of a body of recipes as a basic set of rules about the proportions of meat, fat, spices, and, occasionally, fillers that are needed to make a good-tasting sausage. Simply put, you start with a third each of meat, fat, and "everything else," and take it from there. These days, the proportion of meat to fat is usually higher, and the amount of "everything else"—spices, fillers, marinating or flavoring liquids, and herbs—is reduced. But the principles remain about the same.

"It could be said," writes the English food writer Jane Grigson, "that European civilization—and Chinese civilization too—has been founded on the pig." Certainly sausage making was founded on the pig, a completely useful animal with loads of sweet, easily rendered fat. When pig-slaughtering time came in the pre-refrigeration era, relatively little meat was eaten fresh, while much was brined, salted, and smoked and made into sausages, loaves, and terrines.

The art of charcuterie—from *chair cuit,* or "cooked meat"—goes back at least to Roman times, when the Latin word *salsus* ("salted") was first coined. After the hams and bacons were taken off to be brined and smoked, after the people had had their fill of fresh meat, the rest of the pig, along with a good deal of its fat, was salted and mixed with various herbs, spices, and saltpeter (potassium nitrate, an all-important preservative). The mixture was stuffed into pieces of cleaned intestine, then dried and smoked. Thus treated it would keep for months.

In fact, none of this is necessary now: Almost no individuals raise and slaughter pigs, and we can buy all the fresh pork we want and freeze it if there is too much to consume at once. But the products of charcuterie are delicious; the combination of tasty meat, juicy fat, and accenting spices remains irresistible. This is one ancient tradition that lives on.

DANISH SMOKED SAUSAGE—The following recipes have been obtained from the largest and best sausage factory of Copenhagen, Denmark.

For this recipe, use 25 pounds each of lean beef and pork, 12 pounds of fat cut fine and 8 pounds of fat cut into small dice, two and a half pounds of salt. 30 gram. powdered saltpetre, 70 gram. powdered sugar, 85 gram. ground white pepper. Remove all sinews, then chop the beef and pork to-

gether; when about half chopped, add the 12 pounds of fat and finish by chopping all fine, adding the seasonings toward the finish; then work in thoroughly the 8 pounds of fat cut in small dice. When well mixed the whole mass should be packed tightly in a wooden trough for 24 hours so as to allow the saltpeter to effect its color and also render the mass more firm. The meat is then placed into the sausage filler, and filled into beef casings as TIGHTLY AS POSSIBLE. The tighter the skin is filled, the better the sausage will be for cutting when dried. When the casings are filled, they should be laid in a pickling tub and lightly covered with coarse salt, place a board on top and let them remain till the salt has turned into pickle, then lift them out and hang in the air until ALL moisture has run off them. When dry, they should be smoked in cold smoke until they are a rich dark brown in color. The sausage is then ready for eating, and will keep for several months. Length, about eighteen inches.

CERVELATPOLSE OR DANISH BEEF AND PORK SAUSAGE—For this recipe, use 25 pounds each of beef and pork, twelve and a half pounds of pork fat cut in small dice, one and a half pounds of salt, 30 gram. powdered saltpetre, 50 gram. ground white pepper, 50 gram. powdered sugar, 13 gram. each of ground ginger and nutmeg. Remove all sinews, then chop the beef and pork together quite fine, adding the seasonings towards the finish, then add the diced fat and thoroughly mix. When mixed placed into the filler and fill TIGHTLY into beef casings, tying into 18-inch lengths; hang in the air for 24 hours, then smoke in very warm smoke till the skins are brown; then boil them until the sausage is as elastic as an indiarubber ball and will bounce if dropped on the table. This is a sure proof that the sausage is thoroughly cooked. When done, dry them and glaze the skins. Serve as in the first recipe, in slices, as an appetizer, or hors d'oeuvre.

KNOCKPOLSE OR HARD SMOKED DANISH SAUSAGE—For this recipe, use 21 pounds of beef, 12 pounds each of veal and pork and 5 pounds of pork fat cut into small dice, one and a quarter pounds of salt, 30 gram. powdered saltpetre, 15 gram. ground nutmeg, 20 gram. each of ground cinnamon and ginger, 60 gram. ground white pepper, 4 garlic cloves and 4 small shallots finely grated. First chop beef and veal together half fine, then add the pork and finish chopping till fine, adding the seasonings towards the finish; then thoroughly work in the pork fat cut in small dice. Place the meat in the sausage filler and fill into hog casings, tying in six inch lengths, meat NOT to be filled too tightly. When filled, hang to dry for a day and smoke in warm smoke. Boil for eating hot or cold.

WEINERPOLSE OR BAVARIAN SAUSAGE—For this recipe, use 25 pounds of pork, 12 pounds of veal, 12 pounds of pork fat, 20 ounces of salt, 30 gram. powdered saltpetre, 30 gram. ground coriander, 50 gram. powdered sugar, 60 gram. ground white pepper, 2 garlic cloves and 4 shallots grated fine. Use only the best meat and CAREFULLY remove all sinews. Mince the pork and veal together first then mince the fat, then thoroughly mix all together, adding the seasonings. Place into the sausage filler and fill into sheep or lamb casings, tying into five inch links. Let them hang for 24 hours, then smoke in warm smoke until of a bright brown color; boil five to eight minutes, when they are ready for the table.

LEVERPOLSE OR LIVER SAUSAGE— For this recipe, use 1 large pig's liver, 10 pounds of veal (from the neck), 10 pounds of belly of pork, 8 pounds of pork fat, 3 pounds of salt, 40 gram. powdered thyme, 50 gram. each of ground nutmeg and ginger, 60 gram. of powdered marjoram, 140 gram. ground white pepper, 5 pounds of lean pork, 4 small onions in winter, NONE in summer, as they easily cause acidity. Remove sinews and gristle from the pork and veal, boil them and mince together. The fat to be cut into small dice, the liver to be skinned, and the thick veins removed and to be boiled in the boiling broth for five minutes; then chop it a little, add a little salt, and mince quite fine. Now throw the minced veal and pork, diced fat and liver into the mixer along with the five pounds of minced RAW lean pork, add the spices and a cupful of the fat and water from the broth and mix altogether thoroughly. Place the meat into the sausage filler and fill into hog casings NOT too tight, tying into 18-inch lengths. Then boil the sausages in boiling water 20 minutes, take up, wash them and lay them on a table to cool. They are then ready for the table, cut in slices cold. Are also used fried in slices warm. This sausage can be smoked in cold smoke in winter, and keeps well.

LEVERPOSTEJ, LIVERWURST OR DANISH LIVER SAUSAGE—10 pounds of pigs' flare, 3 or 4 pig's livers according to size, 4 to 5 pounds of minced lean pork, 10 eggs, 6 to 12 anchovies according to size. Add pepper, salt, nutmeg and cinnamon to season according to taste. Fill into beef casings, boil two hours. These are well liked by most people.

BEEF SAUSAGE—A good article for the "help's hall." Take 20 pounds of flank of beef freed from skin and bones, cut it up into inch pieces and mix thoroughly into it 10 ounces of salt, 4 ounces of pepper, half an ounce of ground nutmeg, and 2 ounces of rubbed sage, then mince through the machine; meanwhile soak 4 loaves of bread (eight pounds) squeeze it dry and amalgamate with the meat, then add DRY, three pounds of sifted cracker meal; then place the whole into the sausage filler and fill into sheep casings, link them; then separate the links, arrange in baking pan, and bake till done and brown, about 15 minutes.

BLOOD SAUSAGE—Use cheek meat, heart, lungs, and pork rinds in any quantity that is convenient. Cut the pork rinds into small pieces, boil in clean water until three parts cooked, saving the broth and the rinds. Cut the balance of the meat together quite fine, and boil it slowly with the pork rinds and broth, allowing the broth to cover the meat. Remove the fat that comes to the surface, cook until it is well done. Take one gallon of calf's or pig's fresh blood immediately after killing. Stir it in a vessel 10 to 15 minutes until it will retain its fluid condition. Then pass through a fine sieve to break up any lumps. Mix 15 pounds of the cooked meat as above with one gallon of blood and season to taste. Pour through a funnel into beef middle casings, filling three parts full, the end being tied. Tie the open end, and place the sausage in the broth and allow it to boil. The blood, in cooking, will expand and fill out the remaining part of the casing. Stir continually, or the blood will all collect in the lower side of the casing. When cooked, the sausage will rise to the surface, owing to the expansion of the air. Where ever air collects, pierce with a fork or fat will fill these places. When of a good appearance, remove and wash in clean cold water and allow it to remain there till cold. The sausage may be improved by smoking cold over a low fire of shavings and sawdust. A hot fire will cause it to sweat and spoil its appearance.

BLOOD SAUSAGE (NORTH GERMANY)—Boil fat pork till not quite cooked and then cut it into small dice. To every 10 pounds boil 2 pounds of well dried pork rinds, and a calf's or pig's lungs, or, instead of that, a corresponding quantity of pork trimmings. When these are boiled tender, put the rinds and lungs or trimmings through the mincing machine, scald the pork dice, and add enough well beaten pig's blood to make the whole moderately liquid, then get the exact weight (reckon 12 pounds to the gallon). To every gallon add 6 ounces of salt, 1 ounce of white pepper, ¼ ounce each of ground cloves and marjoram. Stir all well together and fill into casings. Boil about an hour and a half until no blood oozes out on the sausages being pricked. On coming out of the boiler, wash in warm water, and lay on a table to cool, and afterwards smoke for a few days in cold smoke. (To every 10 pounds of sausage meat, reckon about one and a half pounds of blood.)

BLOOD SAUSAGE (FRENCH)—Take equal quantities of lean and fat pork and boil it till tender; then cut the fat into small dice and the lean meat into small pieces. Meanwhile have some onions, leeks and shallots steamed soft, added to the above meat. To every 10 pounds of this sausage meat add 2 pounds of pig's blood, 5 ounces of salt, ½ ounce of white pepper and one tenth of an ounce each of ground mace and thyme. Stir all well together and fill into narrow hog casings. Boil until no blood exudes on being pricked. Then remove and wash in warm water, and let it cool on a table.

BOLOGNA SAUSAGE—Use lean fresh meat, trimmings and cheek meat. Chop together very fine; while chopping add spices and seasoning, and from 25 to 30 ounces of salt to every 100 pounds of meat. To every 100 pounds of beef add 5 pounds of pure fat, either fresh or salted pork. When the beef is nearly chopped add from one to one and a half pounds of farina and sufficient water to suit; mix thoroughly. Stuff into beef middle casings. Tie the ends together into rings 24 inches long. Smoke with hickory wood and hickory sawdust, remove when well colored, cook in boiling water. When the bologna is sufficiently cooked it will rise to the top. Pepper and coriander are the spices used for bolognas.

BOLOGNA SAUSAGE (ITALIAN)— Take 27 pounds each of raw lean pork, cooked pickled pork and raw veal, 5 pounds of anchovies finely chopped together. Then add 14 pounds of raw fat pork cut in small dice; season with 18 ounces of salt, 11 ounces of white pepper, 4 ounces of ground caper, 21 ounces of peeled pistachio nuts cooked in wine. After carefully mixing the meat and spices, distribute amongst it six pickled and cooked tongues cut in slices. Then fill into beef middle casings or bungs. Wrap each sausage in a clean cloth, tie round with twine, then boil one hour, take up, lay them out in a cool place for 24 hours, remove the cloth, wipe with a warm cloth, pour over them either colored or uncolored fat, then decorate.

BRUNSWICK, CERVELAT SAUSAGE —For every block of fifty pounds take 28 pounds of lean pork, 10 pounds of lean beef freed from sinews, 12 pounds of bacon fat cut in shreds, 2 pounds of salt, 3 ounces of coarse ground white pepper, 1 ounce of powdered saltpetre, 2½ ounces of powdered sugar. First mince the beef very fine, then add the pork and mince and mix the two together till the pork is about the size of peas; then add the pork fat which must be mixed until it shows amongst the rest in pieces the size of beans; then add the mixed spices and salt, mixing well. After a thorough mixing, place into the filler and stuff tightly into small middle beef gut casings. They must now be hung in a well ventilated room of 60 degrees temperature for two weeks until they begin to look red under the skins; then smoke them in cold dry smoke until they take on a cherry red color;

then keep in a well aired room for use or sale.

SARDINE AND LIVER SAUSAGE— For this recipe, use 8 pounds of pigs liver, 7 pounds of lean and 4 pounds of fat fresh pork, 6 pounds of fresh bacon and ½ pound of sardines, 12 ounces of salt, 1¼ ounces of white pepper, ½ an ounce each of ground ginger and marjoram, and ⅓ of an ounce of ground thyme. Cut the liver into strips, wash it, then blanch it; drain dry, then chop it. Boil the lean pork for half an hour, then chop with the liver; blanch the fat pork and add it with the bacon and seasoning and sardines, mincing all fine and thoroughly mixing. Fill this into skins nine inches long, not too tightly, boil for half an hour without pricking them, then take them up into cold running water, letting the water run till they are cold and firm.

MOSAIC SAUSAGE—Take an 18 pound leg of pork, bone it out and remove all skin and sinews, this will leave 15 pounds of meat; cut this up, put into a stone crock after first rubbing into it 12 ounces of salt, 1 ounce of cane sugar, and ½ an ounce of powdered saltpetre; put on the cover and allow to macerate for 24 hours, then take it from the crock and mince it with 5 pounds of lean veal, adding during the mincing 1 ounce of white pepper, ⅓ of an ounce each of mace and ginger and one-sixth of an ounce of cardamons. Then fill into skins 6 inches thick and 8 inches long, three parts full. To make the mosaic work use long inch square pieces of red cooked tongue each wrapped neatly with a thin shred of

bacon fat, also a column each of blood sausage, Frankfort sausage and liver sausage, each wrapped like the tongue. To insert these columns, take a stick a little thicker than the column, dip it into cold water, push it into the sausage, withdraw it, then slip in the mosaics at equal distances, then tie the sausage, hang up in smoke for one hour, then boil very gently for an hour and three-quarters, then smoke again lightly. [N.B. Both while smoking and simmering, keep the sausage in an upright position so that the inlaying may be kept straight.]

CAMBRIDGE SAUSAGE—This makes a nice breakfast sausage: Take 12 pounds of lean and 6 pounds of fat pork, cut it into small pieces and rub well into it 9 ounces of prepared sausage seasoning, pass through the mincing machine, then mix into it 3 pounds of scalded rice, 2 pounds of cracker meal. Place the whole then into the filler, fill into sheep casings, link up and use.

COBLENZ SAUSAGE—A good seller for restaurants: Take 10 pounds each of veal and pork, cut it up and allow to macerate for 24 hours after being rubbed with 12 ounces of salt and ½ an ounce of powdered saltpetre. First chop the veal very fine, then add the pork and chop all together, adding 1 ounce of white pepper, ⅓ of an ounce each of ground ginger and peppermint, three shallots and three cloves of garlic. Mince till the fat shows through the rest like pin heads, then add water as much as the meat will take, leaving it very stiff; place then into the filler, fill into sheep casings, link them up into 6 to the pound; hang up for some hours to dry: then smoke with mixed sawdust at a temperature of 100° Fahr, till they are a beautiful dark orange color, about 1 hour. To serve, simmer them for 10 minutes.

EPPING SAUSAGE—23 pounds of lean beef, 7 pounds of fat pork, 8 pounds of bread, soaked and pressed dry, 4 ounces of white pepper, 13 ounces of salt, ¼ of an ounce each of ground nutmeg and ginger, ¼ of an ounce of rubbed marjoram. Mix the seasonings with the meat, mince fine, then work in the bread; place into the filler, fill into sheep casings, link them, and use by frying and broiling.

EPPING SAUSAGE—30 pounds of pork fat and lean, 8 pounds of bread soaked and pressed dry, 4 ounces of white pepper, 13 ounces of salt, ¼ of an ounce each of mace and rubbed sage. Prepare and use as above.

FRANKFORT SAUSAGES (WEINERWURST)—9 pounds of veal, 36 pounds of lean pork and 5 pounds of fat pork. Chop finely, adding a seasoning of 1 pound of salt, 6 ounces of white pepper, and one head of garlic; when ready place into the filler and fill into sheep casings, linking them at about four to the pound. Smoke for 48 hours, boil for 5 minutes before serving plain or with sauerkraut, etc.

CHICKEN HAM AND TONGUE SAUSAGE—10 pounds of lean pork, 4 pounds of fat pork, 4 pounds of veal, 2 pounds of ox tongue, 4 pounds of granulated rice scalded, 2 pounds of cracker meal, the meat from one fowl and six hard boiled eggs, 9 ounces of salt, 3 ounces of pepper, ½ an ounce each of ground mace and finely chopped parsley, and ¼ of an ounce of powdered thyme. Cut the meats into pieces, add the seasoning and rice, mince altogether till fine, then the eggs minced, and the meal, fill into weasand casings, simmer slowly for an hour, use cold in slices.

TRUFFLED LIVER SAUSAGE—Take 5 pounds of pig's liver and 3 pounds of fat pork. Mince these together very fine, and add a ¼ of a pound of truffles cut into narrow strips and cooked in wine. Add a seasoning of salt and pepper and knead together. Fill into narrow hog casings, simmer for about half an hour, wash well in cold water and hang up to dry. If to be kept any time, smoke for a day. Take care to use no spices, otherwise the flavor of the truffles will be spoiled.

GOOSE LIVER SAUSAGE, TRUFFLED—Take 2 pounds of well blanched calf's liver cut in pieces the size of small nuts, 4 pounds each of lean and fat firm fresh pork both minced very fine. Next add 4 shallots sliced and fried with butter to a golden color. Season with 5 ounces of salt, ½ an ounce of white pepper, one-fifth of an ounce each of ground ginger and mace. Then cut from a fine red cooked tongue half a pound, cut in very small dice also a quarter of a pound of truffles; mix all well. Then take 5 pounds of geese livers blanched and sliced. Fill into the filler alternately the truffled meat and the sliced geese livers. Then press into

EPPING SAUSAGE

·

Makes about 3½ pounds

I imagine that this sausage originated in Epping, England. It certainly tastes English. Try serving it with Eggs with Brown Butter (page 221).

*1 pound fresh sliced white
    bread*

1½ cups milk

*2 pounds beef, finely
    ground*

*¾ pound pork butt, finely
    ground*

1 teaspoon ground nutmeg

1 teaspoon ground ginger

*2 teaspoons dried
    marjoram whole*

1 tablespoon salt

*1 teaspoon freshly ground
    white pepper*

Remove the crusts from the bread. Tear up the bread and soak it in the milk for 10 minutes. Drain and squeeze the excess milk out of the bread. Place the bread in a bowl with the remaining ingredients and mix very well. Stuff the mixture into sausage casings or form it into rolls with your hands. Grill, pan-fry, or broil.

This is a good breakfast sausage with eggs. You can make meatballs as well.

C.W.

very wide pig skins not more than 12 inches long. Boil them gently one hour in fresh clear water. When done, take up into cold running water, which will make them beautifully white.

LIVER SAUSAGE—To every two hog's livers add one calf's liver; cut in thin slices. Scald well with hot water until the livers look white and clean. Chop well, adding one-eighth the amount of pure pork fat, boiling the fat for half an hour before mixing. Mix and chop together

very fine, adding four ounces of fat pork to every five pounds of the balance. Then boil for half an hour, adding the following spices to each 100 pounds: 7 ounces salt, 2 ounces pepper, 1 ounce ground marjoram, ½ ounce each of ground sage, basil and thyme, 2 minced onions and a small head of garlic. Stuff from stuffer into narrow hog casings 13 to 18 inches long (not filling very full) tying the ends with twine. When filled and tied, they are cooked in water just below the boiling point for thirty minutes (to give the white appearance) continually stirring them. Care must be taken to prick the air places, or they will fill with fat. After cooling, hang for three days in the open air, then smoke for six days over a slow fire.

SARDINE LIVER SAUSAGE—Use 40 pounds boiled pigs' livers, 7½ pounds boned and trimmed sardines, 15 pounds cooked veal, 7½ pounds cooked lean pork, 20 pounds cooked fat pork, 10 pounds raw fat pork. Chop together very fine, and add 14 ounces salt, 10 ounces white pepper, 1 ounce each ground thyme and marjoram. Stuff into beef middle casings. Cook and smoke the same as the liver sausage of the preceding recipe.

LYONS SAUSAGE—(German recipe). The Lyons sausage (Saucisse de Lyon) was introduced into Germany in the year 1852 by Lill on his return from his tour in France. Sausage makers throughout Germany then tried to make it, because of his success with it, but no one else succeeded. It can only be manufactured to keep by taking the greatest of care. When it is well made and well dried, it would pass for Cervelat sausage. It is prepared in the following manner: For a quantity of 40 pounds take 25 pounds of well fed pork, 10 pounds beef from a young bullock, which should be chopped up when warm and then pounded in mortar, 5 pounds pork fat, cut into dice the size of peas and then cooked for a little in boiling water, 12 ounces salt, 2 ounces Indian cane sugar, 1 ounce powdered saltpetre. Mix the two lean meats, then mix the salt, saltpetre and sugar. Rub them into the meats, and let it stand for 48 hours in a cool room in summer, and a warm room in winter. Now chop up the meat fine, then mix the seasonings and add them. They are 2 ounces white pepper, ½ ounce each of ground white ginger and nutmeg, 2 shallots salted and grated. Before the pork fat is put amongst the rest, the spices should be well mixed up amongst the other things and a little water worked into the mass. Now mix in lightly and quickly the pea diced pork fat. Put the meat into medium wide beef runners, 15 inches long, pressing it in very tight. Now DRY the sausages WELL before smoking. When they are smoked a fine red color, put them at once into a saucepan, and cook for half an hour at a heat of 203° Fahr. When the sausages are cool, there are usually some wrinkles in the skin; this can be remedied by putting them in pairs into boiling water not more than fifteen seconds. After they are cool again, they should be smoked in cold smoke for eight hours; they are then ready.

OBERLAND LIVER SAUSAGE—Take a shoulder of pork and remove the bones and skin. Boil it well with three pounds of bacon cut in dice. Then mince the shoulder with half its weight of raw liver and a large onion chopped very fine; add the diced bacon and season with salt, pepper and grated nutmeg, and mix in a little fat if the paste is too stiff. Stuff into ox skins and boil gently for 40 minutes. Then take up into cold running water, and keep them in it until quite stiff.

POLISH SAUSAGE—This is the national sausage of Poland, liked by rich and poor: Take 25 pounds of pork, ⅔ lean, and ⅓ fat, which has been salted for a few days with 1 pound salt and a little sugar. Grate finely three large cloves of garlic, salt them, stir in amongst them a quart of water. Then add the meat which has been chopped into dice size. Now add 1½ ounces pepper, ½ ounce grated nutmeg. Mix well and put into narrow pig skins very full. When filled, tie into fifteen inch lengths; hang to dry for a day; then smoke them with beech wood at a heat of 133° Fahr., and let them hang till they are thoroughly cooked inside merely with the hot smoking.

PORK SAUSAGES (FIRST CLASS)— Take 15 pounds of lean and 6 pounds of fat pork, cut it up into two inch pieces and mix with it 14 ounces of pork sausage seasoning (from recipe below); chop together fine, or run through meat cutting machine with a fine plate; then thoroughly incorporate with it 3 pounds of crumb bread soaked and pressed. When mixed, further work in one pound of sifted cracker dust. Place the mass then into the sausage filler, and run into pig casings, linking them at six to the pound.

PORK SAUSAGES (GOOD ORDINARY SAUSAGE)—Take 15 pounds lean and fat pork and pork trimmings, cut it up into two-inch pieces and mix with it 11 ounces of pork sausage seasoning; chop fine, then thoroughly incorporate with it 4 pounds of crumb bread soaked and pressed. When mixed, further work in 4 pounds of sifted cracker dust, adding cold water to it as it becomes too stiff. When of the proper sausage consistency, place into the filler, and fill into pork casings, linking them six to the pound.

PORK SAUSAGE SEASONING— Thoroughly mix together, then keep in tight covered tins, 9 pounds table salt, 6 pounds pure ground white pepper, ½ pound each of ground mace, ground nutmeg, and rubbed sage leaves, 1 ounce each of ground cloves, ginger and rubbed basil, and ½ an ounce of cayenne pepper.

SALAMI—Use 50 pounds of beef free from fibre, 25 pounds each of lean and fat pork, chop very fine and add 18½ ounces of salt, 4½ ounces ground white pepper, 1½ ounces ground saltpetre, with 8 glasses of Rhine wine, in which previously has been soaked one pound of garlic. (In place of Rhine wine, rum may be used.) Stuff into calf's bladders. Let them hang in the open air for two or three weeks, then smoke for 12 days.

VERONA SALAMI (SALAMI DE VERONA)—Use 18 pounds of cleaned beef, 18 pounds of lean pork, 14 pounds of back fat, 2 pounds of salt, 1 ounce of powdered saltpetre, 3 ounces each of ground white pepper and cane sugar, 1 gill of old French cognac. First mince the meat, then chop the fat in amongst it the size of pecan nuts; then mix in the spices, and chop until the fat is the size of peas. Wipe the knives often while mincing. Three sticks of garlic finely grated may be added. Use skins for holding this, and bind with pretty thick string all the way over. For the rest, prepare like "Cervelat sausage" but do not smoke; only let the salami hang for four or five weeks to dry.

SMOKED SAUSAGE OR KNACKWURST—Take 60 pounds of lean

pork, 14 pounds of lean beef and 26 pounds of fat pork. Chop very fine, then add 1 pound salt, 5½ ounces ground pepper, 1½ ounces ground saltpetre, 2½ ounces whole caraway seeds, a small quantity of grated garlic. Stuff in beef rounds or hog casings. Hang in the air for 8 days, then smoke for 6 days, they may then be preserved in a cool dry place.

TENDERLOIN SAUSAGE—Take the pork tenderloins and trim them as near the shape of a sausage as possible; rub with hot salt, and place for two weeks in a vessel containing a solution of 17 ounces of salt boiled in 5 pints of water. Remove, wash, and stuff tightly in beef bungs. Smoke for two weeks.

THURINGIAN RED SAUSAGE—14 pounds thick streaky pork off the belly part (half tenderly cooked) cut in quarter inch dice, 3 pounds of boiled pigs rinds, 4 pounds raw liver and lungs finely minced. This may be varied by substituting boiled tongue or salted boiled heart, cut into pieces of equal size. Now put 8 pounds of blood in a tin dish, and then into a big pot, and stir CONSTANTLY until hot. Add first the rind, liver and lungs, and stir well, and then the pork. Season with 24 ounces of table salt, 3 ounces ground white pepper, 1 ounce ground marjoram, ⅓ of an ounce each of ground caraway seeds and ground cloves. Work all thoroughly together, and as quickly as possible fill the hot meat into the widest pigskins you have. Give plenty of room, and then put at once into water which is BOILING HARD; stir constantly. Prick this sausage often, and cook at a temperature of 212° Fahr. It is ready when, on pricking, the fat which exudes is perfectly clear. Smoke in cold smoke, with some juniper berries in the sawdust.

TOMATO SAUSAGES—Lean mutton 6 pounds, mutton fat 8 pounds, canned tomatoes 3 pounds, sifted cracker dust 1½ pounds, scaled granulated rice 1 pound, 10 ounces sausage seasoning. Cut the meat up fine in the machine, take out into a mixer, and add the rice and tomatoes, then the seasoning and the cracker dust. Place in the filler, fill into sheep casings, and link them 6 to the pound. (When cheap enough, use fresh tomatoes.)

VEAL SAUSAGES—Chop together 22 pounds of veal freed from sinew and 11 pounds of bacon, and make very fine; season with 12 ounces of salt, 1½ ounces ground white pepper, 3 nutmegs grated and ½ ounce of ground mace. Knead all together, adding a pint of milk. Fill into narrow skins.

WESTPHALIAN SAUSAGE—Take three parts of lean and one part of fat pork, and cut into pieces like small dice; then season with salt, pepper and cloves, so that it tastes mildly of the spices, and knead all together. Stuff into long narrow casings, and let dry out of doors for several days; then smoke yellow. NOTE: The above sausage is made almost exactly like the SASTER SAUSAGE of the country people of Scotland, only the Scotch omit the smoking, and the "sasters" are dried by hanging from a string attached to the ceiling in the kitchen. The Scotch sausages are usually kept for several months before being used.

POTATOES—Are much improved if peeled and laid in cold water overnight. It saves time in the morning, and they are nicer and whiter in consequence.

POTATOES—For certain dishes, such as potatoes Anna, in which excess starch can be beneficially done away with, Fellows's tip is a good one. But it is neither necessary nor desirable in most cases.

Potatoes have been this country's most popular vegetable throughout the twentieth century; their popularity waxes and wanes (increased consumption of PASTA put a dent in potato sales), but nothing else really comes close. And they are almost as popular elsewhere in the world. Indigenous to Peru, the potato (*Solanum tuberosum*) is now grown almost everywhere. There are many varieties, differing in taste, color, and texture. Unfortunately, very few are grown commercially, but if you try a Mayfair pink or a golden wonder, for example, you might quickly devote yourself to potato gardening.

When it comes to store-bought potatoes, the major difference from one type to the next is starchiness: waxy, low-starch potatoes are best for boiling, potato salad, stews, and the like. High-starch potatoes (such as Idaho) make the mealiest baked and mashed potatoes. Our most popular variety now is the russet, a medium-starch variety that is sold as *all-purpose,* but it is not necessarily ideal for all preparations.

"New" potatoes are early-developing varieties that are harvested in mid-summer; they are, generally speaking, thinner skinned than potatoes from the fall crop and do not keep well. Late potatoes, stored in a cool, dark, dry place, should maintain their shape, texture, flavor, and nutrients for many months. (This is especially true if they are purchased unwashed; washed potatoes, whether because they have lost the protection afforded by dirt or because they are slightly damaged by the high-pressure hoses used for cleaning, do not keep as well.)

IN STEAMING POTATOES—Put a cloth over them before placing on the steamer lid, they will then take less time to cook and be much more mealy than when steamed without the cloth.

TO EXTRACT FROST FROM POTATOES—After paring, put them in cold water for an hour, boil them with a small piece of saltpetre and the sweet taste will be removed.

POTATOES BAKED IN THEIR SKINS—Will always come out more dry and mealy, if a small piece be cut off ONE end, to allow steam to escape in cooking.

POTATOES WHEN BOILING—Are sometimes allowed too much water, so that it boils over on to the range, producing a very disagreeable smell. A little baking soda thrown on to any burning overflow of this nature will immediately drive away all odors.

FRENCH FRIED POTATOES—Raw peeled potatoes cut in strips about the size of the little finger, fried in hot fat till done, taken up and drained, sprinkled with salt, then served.

SCALLOPED POTATOES

·

Serves 6 to 8

This is a classic potato dish that few seem to serve in our time, though it has been popular for a hundred years, at least. Plenty of onions is the key to the flavor in this recipe. Serve this dish with anything, and everyone will love it.

4 tablespoons butter

3 cloves garlic, peeled and minced

2 medium yellow onions, peeled and thinly sliced

1/2 cup dry sherry

3 cups half-and-half

2 1/2 teaspoons salt

1/2 teaspoon freshly ground white pepper

3 pounds russet potatoes, peeled and cut in 1/8-inch slices

Garnish

Freshly ground black pepper to taste

Chopped parsley

Heat a medium-sized frying pan and add the butter, garlic, and onions. Sauté until the onions start to turn limp. Do not brown. Delgaze the pan with the sherry and set aside.

In a small saucepan, heat the half-and-half, salt, and white pepper to scalding. Set aside.

Grease a 13-inch by 9-inch by 2-inch baking pan with a bit of butter or oil. Starting with some of the onions in the bottom of the pan, layer the onions and potatoes. Pour over the scalded half-and-half. Bake in a preheated 375° F. oven for 50 minutes. After the first 30 minutes of cooking, lightly stir the potatoes so that the sauce is coating everything. Finish baking.

Garnish with plenty of freshly ground black pepper and chopped parsley before serving.

C.W.

PARISIENNE POTATOES—Balls about the size of small cherries scooped out of raw potatoes; cooked and served the same as French fried.

LYONNAISE—Cold boiled potatoes, either minced or sliced thinly, seasoned with salt and pepper, mixed with a little chopped parsley and minced fried onions; fried with butter in the form of an omelet.

SAUTÉ—Also called Home Fried, Cottage Fried, German Fried, are thinly sliced cold boiled potatoes, seasoned with salt and pepper, browned on both sides in a fry pan containing butter. For restaurant service they should be served in the form of an omelet, nicely browned.

STEWED IN CREAM—Raw potatoes cut in very small dice, boiled till perfectly done, drained, put in a stew pan with a piece of good butter, seasoned with salt, covered with cream, simmered for two or three minutes, then served.

HASHED IN CREAM—Same as the preceding, but having the potatoes minced after whole boiling, instead of cut in dice.

SCALLOPED POTATOES—Same as stewed in cream above; when ready to serve, put into scallop or vegetable dishes, sprinkle with grated cheese and breadcrumbs, brown off quickly in the oven or under a salamander.

HASHED BROWNED—Same as the minced Lyonnaise, but omitting the parsley and onion.

JULIENNE—Raw peeled potatoes cut in shreds like matches, fried a delicate brown in very hot lard, taken up and drained, sprinkled with salt and fine parsley dust.

STEWED WITH BACON—Bacon cut in small dice, fried well done, drained, mixed in with potatoes stewed in cream.

POTATOES REITZ—Shapes of the parallelogram, or long square (about two inches long and an inch square) cut with a ribbed scallop knife, steamed two-thirds done, then plunged into hot fat and finished like French fried.

POTATOES VILLAGEOISE—Cold boiled potatoes, minced and simmered in Béchamel sauce.

SARATOGA CHIPS—Very thin shavings of peeled potatoes cut with a machine, steeped in ice water to draw out the starch and become crisp; fry a few at a time in very hot lard.

POTATOES BROILED—Either plain or sweet potatoes, cold boiled, cut lengthwise one-fourth of an inch thick, seasoned with salt, dipped in melted butter, then in flour, broiled between a a wire hinged broiler; served with maître d'hôtel butter over them.

STUFFED POTATOES—Whole peeled potatoes, made hollow with a column cutter, ends levelled, the both then steamed, the column pieces mashed, and mixed with one-third of its bulk of grated Parmesan cheese; seasoned with salt and pepper, grated nutmeg and bound with some whipped eggs; stuff the potatoes with the mixture, arrange in a baking pan with butter and brown off quickly.

STUFFED POTATOES—Large oval shaped potatoes, peeled, hollowed out as above, filled with any kind of forcemeat, placed in a well buttered pan, and baked a delicate brown.

POTATO CROQUETTES—Steamed potatoes mashed dry, seasoned with salt, butter and a few raw egg yolks, formed into shapes like corks, breadcrumbed and fried. Also shaped like olives with two tea spoons, dipped in batter and fried.

STUFFED POTATO CROQUETTES —Small croquettes in the form of cones, breaded and fried, drained; inside then partly hollowed out, and replaced with a salpiçon; served upright.

POTATOES DUCHESSE—Potato croquette mixture, only a little softer, with butter and yolks of eggs, forced from a bag with a star shaped tube, on a buttered pan, brushed over with egg wash and baked.

POTATO FRITTERS—The croquette mixture with some beaten whites of eggs worked in, shaped, breaded, fried; served with parsley sauce poured over.

POTATOES ORSINI—One part croquette mixture, one part well cooked rice, one part grated tongue, the whole mixed, formed into small balls, breaded, fried and served.

POTATO CASSEROLES—The croquette mixture shaped liked a small nest, brushed over with beaten egg, baked a delicate brown; used to receive salpiçons.

POTATO PATTIES—Very small casseroles, filled with a salpiçon of game or fowl.

POTATOES CREOLE—Like the patties preceding, but filled with a Creole garniture; these make fine entrée garnishes.

STEWED PARISIENNE POTATOES— Scoop out small balls from raw potatoes, put them into a saûtoir with butter and a seasoning of salt, put the lid on and stew gently till done; served sprinkled with parsley dust.

CURRIED POTATOES—Same as the preceding, adding a spoonful of curry powder while stewing.

POTATO RAGOUT—Same as the stewed Parisienne, but when nearly done, taken up and drained, then placed into a good Espagnole sauce, and simmered till done.

POTATO QUENELLES—The croquette mixture rolled into very small balls, dipped in beaten eggs, then in flour, fried very quickly (else they burst) in very hot lard.

POTATO PUFFS—Cut out with a large column cutter the inside of large raw potatoes, level the ends, then cut into four pieces each column, lengthwise. Have two French friers on the range half full of lard, one hotter than the other; fry the potatoes five minutes in the one, then take up, and plunge into the very hot one; they will then puff out quickly.

POTATOES BERNHARDT—Twirled out like a curl with a cutter, fried in hot lard, taken up and drained, sprinkled with salt and parsley dust.

POTATOES VICTORIA—The croquette mixture shaped like walnuts, breaded and fried.

GLAZED POTATOES—Very large balls scooped out of steamed potatoes, seasoned with salt, dipped in beaten eggs, browned quickly in a hot oven.

POTATOES NAVARRAISE—Cut with a scallop knife very large dice from peeled raw potatoes, steam them till barely done, finish of a fine color in boiling oil.

POTATOES MAÎTRE D'HÔTEL—Raw potatoes peeled, cut in sections like a section of an orange, steamed till barely done, then simmered till done in a thin Velouté sauce containing chopped parsley, lemon juice, and a grating of nutmeg.

POTATOES INDIENNE—Marinade for three hours some minced onions and hot green chillies in lemon juice, add a little French mustard at the finish. Mix all into some light dry mashed potatoes, season with salt, use as a border to a curry, with, or instead of, boiled rice or rissoto.

POTATOES IN CASES—Very thin slices of cold boiled potatoes and onions, mixed together with a little minced parsley, filled into fancy paste cases, with a little butter, sprinkle with Parmesan cheese, and bake till browned and heated through.

POTATOES HOLLANDAISE—Cut like sections of garlic, steamed; served with maître d'hôtel sauce over them.

POTATOES MARIE—Steamed potatoes, mashed, made soft and rich with cream and butter.

POTATOES GASTRONOME—(1) Raw, cut with column cutter, size and shapes of corks, steamed barely done, then fried with butter till done and of a golden color; served sprinkled with salt and parsley dust. (2) Cut same as No. 1, parboiled in water containing a little vinegar, drain, then sauté with butter till done, take up and serve with Perigueux sauce.

POTATOES MAIRE—Cut with a large column cutter tubes of raw potatoes, cut these into slices six to the inch, boil till barely done, then simmer till done in reduced cream.

POTATOES MONACO—Slices same as Maire, cooked same as Gastronome No. 1.

POTATOES GENEVOISE—Take small fancy patty pans, butter them well, then coat the inside with grated cheese, fill with mashed potatoes, sprinkle with grated cheese, bake half an hour in a medium oven.

POTATOES CONDÉ—Scoop out balls of raw potatoes with a large scoop, steam barely done, then fry till done and brown in clarified butter, serve sprinkled with salt and parsley dust.

POTATOES COLBERT—Cold boiled and peeled potatoes, cut in large dice, simmered in Colbert sauce; when serving, sprinkle with parsley dust.

POTATOES CHATEAU—Olive shapes of potatoes turned out with an oval scoop, blanched, drained, fried a light color in clarified butter.

POTATOES BARIGOULE—Take small round new potatoes, steam till barely done, then plunge into boiling oil till brown; serve sprinkled with salt, pepper and tarragon vinegar.

POTATOES BRETONNE—Cut cold boiled potatoes in squares with a scallop knife, sauté with a little chopped parsley, then simmer in Bretonne sauce.

POTATOES BRABANT—Cut like for Bretonne, sautéed with minced shallot and parsley.

POTATOES BIGNONNE—Scoop balls out of raw potatoes with largest sized scoop, take the centre out with a column cutter, blanch, drain, fill centres with forcemeat, then bake till done and brown with butter.

POTATOES BRABANCONNE—Dry mash some steamed peeled potatoes, mix in some minced parboiled onions, a little chopped parsley and Parmesan cheese, with a little cream sauce, bake in paper cases.

POTATOES ANGLAISE—(1) Scoop balls out of raw potatoes with a very large scoop, parboil with a little salt and vinegar in the water, take out, drain, then fry till done and brown in roast meat drippings. (2) Raw potatoes peeled, trimmed, quartered, steamed; served with maître d'hôtel sauce over them.

POTATO SOUP—One pound of mashed potatoes rubbed through the tamis, added to one gallon of very thin cream sauce, season with salt, pepper and nutmeg, finish with a sprinkling of chopped chervil; serve with croûtons.

POTATO SOUP—One pound of mashed potatoes rubbed through the tamis, added to one gallon of thin creamy soup made from white stock, in which has been cooked onion, carrot, celery, salt pork and a ham knuckle; season with salt, pepper and nutmeg, finish with a sprinkling of chopped parsley; serve with croûtons.

POTATO SOUP—One pound of mashed potatoes rubbed through the tamis (they should have been boiled in water that hams have been boiled in); use this water in conjunction with veal stock, to make a thin creamy soup, then add the purée of potatoes, finish with a liaison of egg yolks and cream, remove from the fire, and pour the soup over a braised Julienne of vegetables.

POTATO SOUP—Three pounds of peeled potatoes sliced with a Saratoga cutter, one large onion peeled and sliced and one head of celery sliced, the whole put into a saûtoir with a cupful of melted butter, a seasoning of salt, pepper and nutmeg, put on the lid, and let simmer with an occasional stir till quite done, then rub the whole through the tamis; add this purée to a gallon of chicken consommé, boil up, skim, then add a pint of good cream; serve with croûtons.

POTATO SOUP—Prepare the purée as given in the preceding, add to it the consommé, then finish it with asparagus points, and green stringless beans cut in diamond shapes.

POTATO SALADS—See SALADS.

POULETTE—The French name for a hen chicken, hence Poulette sauce is made from chicken broth, as follows: Half a cup of melted butter, flour added to form a roux, moistened with one quart of good chicken broth (strained), seasoned with salt, red pepper and nutmeg, brought to the boil and skimmed; then is worked in a liaison of egg yolks and cream, finished with a little lemon juice and chopped parsley.

PRAIRIE CHICKEN—Is best cooked in three ways, ROASTED, BROILED and in a SALMIS. To roast it, first pluck, singe, draw and wipe clean, truss it with slices of bacon tied over the breast, roast it rare; serve with the gravy from the roasting strained into a sauce Bigarade; serve garnished with watercress. . . . To broil it, pluck and singe YOUNG birds, split down the back, remove the breast bone, truss out flat, season with olive oil, salt and pepper, place between a wire hinged broiler; broil rare done; serve on toast with maître d'hôtel sauce poured over, garnish with cress. . . . For salmis, simmer the cooked joints in Madeira sauce; serve garnished with mushrooms, stoned olives and fancy croûtons. Or simmer in Bigarade sauce; serve with sliced oranges and fancy croûtons. In HUNTER'S STYLE is to roast the birds rare, cut in joints, then simmer in sauce Chasseur; serve garnished with fancy croûtons. . . . Another nice way to serve the bird is to take cold roast birds, joint them, trim the joints to a wing shape, dip in sauce Richelieu, roll in fresh grated breadcrumbs, then dip in beaten egg and again roll in the breadcrumbs, arrange them in a well buttered pan, sprinkle the tops with melted butter, place in oven, and let come to a nice brown color, with the butter frothing on them; serve at once with sauce Richelieu.

PRAIRIE CHICKEN—A type of grouse also known as the prairie hen (*Tympanuchus cupido pinnatus*), this bird was once found throughout the western Plains states. It has virtually disappeared from everywhere except Texas.

PROVENÇALE—Name of a splendid sauce; also applied to the Southern French style of cooking. For the sauce (see SAUCES).

PROVENÇAL—There is one ingredient almost always associated with the cooking of Provence: garlic. That explains its popularity.

PUFFS—Forms of hollow pastry (see FRITTERS).

PUMPKIN—Name of a large vegetable fruit of the melon species, grows on vines, the young shoot leaves of which make a most splendid substitute for spinach in the summer months.

PUMPKIN—Pumpkin (*Cucurbita pepo*) is, after all, a squash, and can be used in any squash recipe. Despite the fact that it is an all-American vegetable, we have done very little with pumpkin.

Limiting pumpkin to pie and jack-o'-lanterns seems a bit unfair. There is a great pumpkin soup, roast pumpkin, fried pumpkin, pumpkin gratin, baked pumpkin, and so on. Since this is one of our few indigenous foods, it seems as though we might put it to better use.

BAKED PUMPKIN—Slices of peeled pumpkin arranged in buttered pan, seasoned with salt, moistened with roast meat gravy, baked and basted till done, served as a vegetable. . . . Also not peeled, but baked plain in slices and served like baked potatoes. . . . Also slices of peeled pumpkin, steamed for ten minutes, then placed in buttered pan, seasoned with salt and pepper, sprinkled with Parmesan cheese, baked till done and glazy, then served at once.

PUMPKIN PURÉE—Slices of peeled pumpkin, steamed till done, then rubbed through the tamis, seasoned with salt and nutmeg, finished with a little cream and butter; served as a vegetable.

PUMPKIN PIE—The pumpkin sliced, peeled, steamed and rubbed through the tamis, mixed with a rich custard, flavored with cinnamon and rose water, baked in custard pie pans lined with puff paste.

PRESERVED PUMPKIN RIND—The thick cut rind of the pumpkin may be preserved in exactly the same way as melon rind (see MELON).

PURÉE—Name applied in cookery to vegetables, etc., first cooked then rubbed through a fine sieve; used as a basis to soups, also as a garnish to entrées. I will here append the principal purées in general use.

PURÉE—The food processor, which was supposed to change the way we cooked, hasn't quite done so. But it has made purées easier to make than they were ninety years ago. To make one of almost any vegetable, cook it until soft, then process it with salt, pepper, a bit of butter or olive oil, and, as Fellows would say, a suspicion of garlic. Beets make a lovely purée, and the combination of potatoes and turnips is more delicious than either of the two alone. When making fruit purées, add sugar and lemon juice to taste.

PURÉE OF ARTICHOKES—Peel and slice Jerusalem artichokes, place them in a saûtoir with butter and a seasoning of pepper, salt and nutmeg, moisten with a little white stock, boil till done and the broth reduced, then add some cream, reduce and mash till like mashed potatoes, add a pat of butter, then rub through the tamis. PURÉE OF POTATOES made exactly the same way, substituting potatoes for artichokes.

PURÉE OF CARROTS—Young carrots peeled and sliced with a Saratoga cutter, place them in a saûtoir with butter and a seasoning of salt, nutmeg and sugar, place on the lid and let simmer to a light brown color, then add a little good white stock, and simmer down to a glaze, rub through the tamis and use as required.

PURÉE OF CELERY—Celery cut up small, blanched for five minutes, drained, placed in saûtoir with butter, season with salt, sugar and nutmeg, moisten with a little white stock, and simmer till soft; when soft and the stock reduced, add a little Béchamel sauce, rub the whole through a tamis and use as required.

PURÉE OF PEAS—Shelled green peas with a bunch each of mint and parsley and a few spring onions boiled tender, drained, pounded,

taken up into a saûtoir, seasoned with salt and a little thick white sauce, then rub through the tamis for use.

PURÉE OF CHESTNUTS—Slit large chestnuts and steam them for twenty minutes, then remove the husks and brown skin, put the cleaned nuts in a saûtoir and moisten with a little consommé and simmer till soft and the consommé reduced to glaze, then pound them; season with salt, nutmeg and sugar, add a little cream sauce, then rub through the tamis for use.

PURÉE OF SPINACH—Wash the spinach free from sand, blanch it, then take up and let it drain well, now chop it very fine, then pound it; place in a saûtoir, season with salt, sugar and nutmeg, add a little white sauce, reduce rapidly to preserve its color, add a little butter and a piece of glaze, then rub through the tamis for use.

PURÉE OF ASPARAGUS—Take the green parts of asparagus, wash free from sand, place in a saûtoir with some spring onions and a bunch of parsley, boil in salted water till asparagus is tender, then drain all, return to another saûtoir, season with salt, sugar and nutmeg, add a little butter and some white sauce, also some white grated breadcrumbs, reduce rapidly, finish with a little green coloring paste and a small piece of glaze, then rub through the tamis for use.

PURÉE OF TOMATOES—Into a saûtoir put some butter, lean raw ham, minced shallots, a few whole peppers, mace and cloves, two or three bay leaves and a few sprigs of thyme, fry together to a golden color, then add either fresh or canned tomatoes with a little Velouté sauce, reduce rapidly till thick, add a seasoning of salt and sugar, with a piece of glaze and a pat of butter, then rub through the tamis for use.

PURÉE OF ONIONS—Sliced onions blanched for five minutes then drained, placed in a saûtoir with butter, seasoned with salt, sugar and nutmeg, moistened with a very little white stock, simmered till soft and the broth reduced to glaze, then add some thick white sauce, reduce rapidly, then rub through the tamis for use.

PURÉE OF SEAKALE—Seakale cut small and blanched, then drained, placed in a saûtoir with butter and a little white stock, season with salt, sugar and nutmeg. Simmer till soft, then add some thick white sauce, reduce rapidly till thick, then rub through the tamis for use.

PURÉE OF MUSHROOMS—Canned button mushrooms drained, chopped fine, placed in a saûtoir with butter and allowed to fry to a light straw color, then is added the juice of a lemon, and a good cream sauce made with cream and the liquor from the canned mushrooms; seasoned with salt, pepper and nutmeg, reduce rapidly, then rub through the tamis for use.

PURÉE OF LIMA BEANS—Fresh green lima beans boiled for a few minutes with some spring onions and a bunch of parsley, also a few sprigs of chives, drained, placed in a saûtoir with butter and a small bunch of savory, seasoned with salt, sugar and a little white sauce, simmered till very tender, then add a piece of glaze and a little green coloring paste, rub through the tamis for use.

QUAHAUG—Or quahog. One of the clam species, the tender part only should be used; in every way of cooking applicable to oysters and clams.

QUAHAUG—*Quahog* is the spelling preferred in New England, where a quahog means a very large—three inches across or more—hard-shell CLAM, one that is definitely too big and tough to be eaten raw. Such clams are best used in chowders and other similar recipes.

QUAIL—Pluck and singe the quail, split down the back, remove the breast bone, season with salt, brush with butter, broil done to a golden brown; spread the trail on buttered toast, pop it in the oven a few minutes during the broiling, place the bird on the toast, brush over with butter, garnish with a little cress and send to table.

QUAIL—Tiny birds of about four ounces each, quail are extremely lean and easily can be overcooked if grilled, sautéed, or roasted. You might try braising: The result is a moist, tender bird that retains its flavor. Quail are often sold in butcher shops and specialty stores in vacuum-packed packages of four.

ROAST QUAIL—Pluck and singe the bird, draw it, return the liver, truss; run half a dozen on a long steel skewer; place across a baking pan, letting the ends of the skewer rest on the edge of the pan; sprinkle with salt, dredge with melted butter, roast; serve on toast garnished with a little cress. Sauce Perigueux, or a Financière garnish may be served with it, but is far from being essential.

QUINCE—Although the quince (*Cydonia oblonga*) is related to apples and pears, it is difficult to find and rarely eaten raw because of its sourness. (There are apparently quinces that become sweet when properly ripened; I have never encountered one.) Because it is high in pectin, the quince is often included in jams and jellies; because it has a lovely, enticing aroma, it is sometimes cooked with meats.

QUINCE HONEY—Five large quinces grated, one pint of water, five pounds of granulated sugar, boil the sugar and water, add the grated quinces, boil fifteen minutes, pour into glasses, allow to cool before covering.

QUINCE JELLY—Wipe, but do not peel, the fruit; slice it, and remove all seeds. Put them in a porcelain lined kettle and barely cover with cold water, put on the lid, and boil slowly till very tender, then pour all into a flannel jelly bag and let drain without squeezing. To each pint of juice allow one pound of sugar, put the juice into the kettle, bring to the boil, add the sugar, stir till it is dissolved, then boil rapidly (skimming the while) till it jellies (about twenty five minutes), then roll the jelly glasses in boiling water, and pour in the boiling jelly. Stand aside for twenty-four hours until set firm, then screw on the lids. Keep in a cool dark place.

QUINCE MARMALADE—Peel, core and slice the fruit, boil with just enough water to cover them, stirring and mashing them till soft; when reduced to a paste, allow eleven ounces of granulated sugar to each pound of fruit, boil twelve minutes, stirring constantly; remove from fire, allow to cool, then fill into jars for use.

RABBIT—Even if you have never eaten rabbit, you have heard this famous disclaimer: "It tastes like chicken." Actually, domesticated rabbit is as mild-flavored as chicken, although it is also a little leaner and finer textured (wild rabbit, or hare, is a different story altogether). You can cook rabbit using almost any chicken recipe—note that Fellows's recipes resemble chicken recipes more than a little bit—and the chances are good that you will enjoy it.

STEWED RABBIT, GERMAN STYLE —Young rabbits cut in six pieces, the two legs, breasts and shoulders, and the back cut in halves; wash well, drain, then steep them for a few hours in vinegar containing thyme, carrots and onions sliced; when ready, take the pieces, roll them in flour and fry lightly in butter, put them in a sautoir when fried; now fry some pieces of salt pork in the remaining butter, add them to the rabbit, with some flour, shake together, moisten with stock, simmer and skim; then add some button onions, a little thyme and enough of the vinegar they were steeped in to give a sharp flavor, simmer till tender and serve.

FRICASSÉE OF RABBIT—Legs, backs and shoulders of young rabbits, washed and wiped dry, then lightly fry with butter till the flesh is firm; take up into a saûtoir, add some flour, moisten with white stock, simmer and skim; when about half done, add some button onions and mushrooms, also a glass of white wine; when about finished, thicken the sauce with a liaison of egg yolks and cream, season with nutmeg, salt, red pepper and the juice of a lemon.

POTTED RABBIT—Legs, shoulders and backs of young rabbits, remove

FRICASSÉE OF RABBIT

.

Serves 4 to 6

Do not be afraid to serve rabbit. It was very popular at the turn of the century because the meat is light and delicate when cooked. However, you can also try this dish with chicken.

2 (2½-pound) rabbits, cut into serving pieces	2 medium yellow onions, peeled and sliced
Salt and freshly ground black pepper	2 tablespoons chopped parsley
1 cup all-purpose flour	1 pound mushrooms, sliced
4 tablespoons butter	1 cup dry white wine
2 tablespoons olive oil	2 cups Chicken Stock (page 153)
2 cloves garlic, peeled and chopped	1 cup half-and-half

Season the rabbit pieces with salt and pepper. Dredge in flour and pat off the excess flour, reserving the flour.

In a large frying pan, brown the rabbit lightly in the butter. Do this in batches, using a bit of the butter each time. Remove the meat to a heavy enameled baking dish (about 14 inches by 10 inches). In the same frying pan, add the oil, garlic, and onions. Sauté until the onions are almost tender. Add the parsley and mushrooms and sauté until the mushrooms are tender. Stir in 2 tablespoons of the reserved flour and cook a couple of minutes until smooth. Add the remaining ingredients, simmer, and stir until smooth.

Transfer the mixture to the heavy baking dish and bring all to a simmer on the stove. Remove from the heat. Cover with aluminum foil and bake in a preheated 350°F. oven for 1¾ hours. Adjust salt and pepper, if needed.

Serve with rice.

C.W.

the bones from each joint, then place the pieces in individual jars (like bean jars) with diced bacon and mushrooms. Take the bones and head, pound them, boil them with carrot, celery, onions and a little thyme, thicken it slightly, strain, and cover the meat in the jars with it, put on the lids, and bake slowly till tender; serve in the jars.

BRAISED RABBIT WITH TOMATO SAUCE—Legs and backs of young rabbits, lard them with seasoned strips of bacon, place in a brasiere with bacon, onions, carrots and a bunch of thyme, moisten with white stock and a glass of white wine, braise till tender and then remove to another saûtoir; strain the braise, boil up, skim, then add it to a thick tomato sauce; serve it over the rabbit, garnished with fancy croûtons.

BROILED SADDLE OF RABBIT—Take the whole of the back of the rabbit, soak it in warm salted water for an hour, then take it up and wipe dry, season with salt and pepper, roll in melted butter, dredge with flour, place between a wire hinged broiler and broil it well done over a clear fire, basting with butter during cooking; serve on toast with maître d'hôtel butter in which has been incorporated a little red currant jelly.

SAUTÉ OF RABBIT—Take the legs and saddles of the rabbits, soak in warm salted water for an hour, then drain and wipe each piece dry, season with salt and pepper, roll in flour, fry a golden color with butter, make the sauce in the same pan, boil up and skim, put back the rabbit, add some sliced mushrooms, simmer till tender, finish with the addition of a little sherry wine.

SMOTHERED RABBIT WITH ONIONS—Take the legs and saddles, blanch and drain them, then arrange them in a saûtoir, cover with a light brown sauce and let simmer for half an hour; meanwhile fry lightly plenty of onions (the small button ones), add them to the rabbit, simmer till tender; serve garnished with the onions and a fancy croûton.

RABBIT PIE—Take the legs and saddles, cut into inch pieces, make them into a sauté; take the hearts, livers and brains, and with the addition of a little grated bacon, breadcrumbs, chopped parsley and a flavoring of thyme make forcemeat balls; lay the rabbit in the pie dish, add the forcemeat balls and some diced bacon, pour over the sauce, cover with a good short crust and bake for one hour. May also be done in individual pie dishes for restaurant and club service, where it is a good seller.

RABBIT CUTLETS, TOMATO SAUCE —Take the legs, roll them first in a mixture of salt, pepper and poultry seasoning, then in flour, dip in beaten eggs, then grated breadcrumbs, place in a buttered baking pan, sprinkle with melted butter, bake slowly for half an hour; serve with tomato sauce.

EPIGRAMME OF RABBIT—Take the legs and lard them with seasoned strips of bacon, fry one half of them slowly till tender, and braise the other half; when serving, place a line of mashed potatoes down the centre of the dish; on one side place a braised leg dipped in a brown Italian sauce, on the other side place the fried leg dipped in a white Italian sauce, garnish the ends with fancy shaped quenelles made of the hearts, liver and brains.

DEVILLED RABBIT—Take the legs and saddles, boil them for fifteen minutes, let cool, then score them slantwise in three or four places to the bone; make a mixture of melted butter, cayenne, Worcestershire sauce, mustard and tarragon vinegar, thoroughly rub into the cuts with the mixture, then slowly broil them of a light color; serve garnished with croûtons and a little of the devil mixture made hot and poured over.

BLANQUETTE OF RABBIT—Legs and saddles of rabbits blanched, then lightly fried with butter, taken up into a saûtoir, covered with Velouté sauce, simmered till tender; served garnished with button mushrooms that have been sautéed with butter.

FRIED RABBIT CUTLETS—Legs of young rabbits, bones removed and their place filled with forcemeat, steam them for ten minutes, then take up and spread a little of the forcemeat on the outside, then bread them; arrange in a buttered pan, sprinkle with melted butter, brown off in the oven; serve with a sauce made from the inferior parts.

STEWED RABBIT WITH VEGETABLES—Prepare the blanquette of rabbit of a preceding recipe; serve garnished with balls of carrot and turnip, green peas and small onions.

BROILED RABBIT—Young rabbits, the legs and saddle cut in one piece, like frogs are cut, seasoned with salt and pepper, broiled well done; served with bacon and maître d'hôtel sauce.

RAGOUT OF RABBIT—Legs, saddles and shoulders of rabbits, cut into even sized pieces, seasoned with salt and pepper and sautéed with butter to a golden color, then add some chopped truffle, mushrooms, parsley and shallot, simmer all in the butter for ten minutes, then pour off the waste, moisten with some good Espagnole, boil up and skim, then add a piece of chicken glace, juice of a lemon, and a grating of nutmeg, let simmer till nearly done, then add some forcemeat balls prepared from the inferior parts; serve garnished with the quenelles and fancy croûtons.

RABBIT FILLETS GARNISHED, SAUCE PERIGUEUX—Legs and saddles of young rabbits seasoned with salt, pepper and nutmeg, sautéed with butter to a golden color, taken up and drained, placed into a rich Perigueux sauce, simmered in it till done; served with the sauce poured over and garnished with small quenelles of rabbits made from the inferior parts, alternately with button mushrooms sautées.

SALPICON OF RABBIT—Take the whole rabbit and roast it of a light color, well basting it to keep it moist; take up and allow to cool, then cut in small dice, the meat only, add also a few mushrooms, and truffles, a little tongue and sweetbread all cut in small dice, moisten the whole with a rich Velouté sauce; serve in fancy croûstade cases.

MINCED RABBIT ON TOAST—Cold cooked rabbit, the meat cut into very small dice, moistened with a brown Italian sauce; served on toast with or without a trimmed poached egg.

CURRIED RABBIT WITH RICE— Legs, saddles and shoulders of rabbits lightly fried with minced onions in butter, then taken up into a saûtoir, sprinkled with curry powder and flour, moistened with white stock, simmered till done; served with rice.

RASPBERRIES—A delicious fruit used chiefly as a table fruit, being picked over, then served with cream. Made into puddings, charlottes, ices, creams, meringues, tarts, jellies, trifles, etc., by the pastry cooks; into syrup for flavoring; also used as a drink in summer for cooling the blood known as raspberry vinegar; made by taking equal measurement of raspberries and vinegar, and steeping them for a week, then straining off the liquor, allowing a pound of granulated sugar to each pint of juice; it is boiled, skimmed and bottled for use.

RASPBERRIES—Raspberry vinegar is also one of the more valuable cooking vinegars; a bit added to sauce reductions, especially when cooking game, organ, or other rich meats, gives wonderful flavor and enriches the sauce. It is also superb in vinaigrettes and is sweet enough to use plain on greens, without any oil at all.

Raspberries themselves are northern fruits, and many experts say that the farther north you go—within limits, of course—the better they are (raspberries grow in Alaska, Labrador, and Greenland,

although these are not the best). We think of most fruits as being delicate and better off the vine, bush, or tree than in stores, but raspberries are extreme. Not only do they taste better in the field, they seem to rot almost immediately upon picking, and so are not only expensive in stores—because they must be shipped so quickly—but rarely very good.

It is difficult to improve upon fresh raspberries served with a bit of cream. But a cold ice is extremely refreshing on a hot August night, when, if you're lucky enough, you may have had your fill of unadulterated raspberries.

RATAFIA—Almost any infusion of fruit or fruit juice in strong brandy was once called a ratafia. All also contained some bitter ALMONDS, or the similar flavor of peach or apricot pits. Certain macaroons, especially those with an especially strong bitter-almond flavor, such as the Italian amaretti, are also called ratafia.

RAVIOLES—Are essentially poached rissoles or rissolettes; they are made up from any kind of croquette mixture, rolled up the size and shape of an egg, then slightly flattened, and laid on a small square piece of noodle or short paste, the four ends brought over the top to a centre and slightly pressed together; they are then poached in white stock for six or seven minutes, drained, placed on the serving dish; an appropriate sauce to the croquette mixture is poured over them, then sprinkled with grated Parmesan cheese.

RAVIOLI—See PASTA.

RAVIGOTE—Name given to a sauce, made with plenty of melted butter, flour to form a roux, moistened with good white stock, seasoned with salt, pepper and nutmeg, and containing plenty of chopped chives, chervil, tarragon, burnet cand parsley.... Also a cold sauce, which is mayonnaise containing finely minced chives, shallot, tarragon, parsley and chervil.

RED SNAPPER—There are lots of snappers—15 off of our coasts, 250 worldwide—all of them good. Red snapper (*Lutjanus campechanus*) has meaty, firm, white flesh and is very common throughout the country. But its greatest asset becomes apparent when the fish is cooked whole, whether steamed, pan-fried, grilled, baked, or broiled. Then it remains moist and succulent, yet still pulls off the bone easily.

RED SNAPPER, BOILED—Clean and scale the fish, place in the fish kettle, cover it with hot water, adding salt and a little vinegar, simmer till done (from half to one hour according to size), then raise and drain; serve in portions garnished with Hollandaise potatoes and either caper, Matelote, Allemande, Admiral, Diplomate or Venitienne sauces.

RED SNAPPER, BAKED—Clean and scale the fish, split it down the back and lift off the two sides free from bones; lay these skin side down in a buttered pan, season with salt and pepper, place in oven till set, then brush liberally with melted butter; bake done and brown, basting well with butter during the cooking; serve in portions with a quarter of a lemon, and a rich tomato sauce made with court-bouillon.

RED SNAPPER, SAUTÉ—Prepare the fillets as in the preceding recipe, then cut them in portion pieces, season with salt and pepper, roll in flour, sauté them a delicate brown color with plenty of melted butter; when done, take up and drain, sprinkle the surface with finely minced parsley; serve with Parisienne potatoes and either lobster, Genoise, Aurora, Cardinal, Chambord, or Normande sauces.

RED SNAPPER, BROILED—Clean and scale the fish, split down the back and remove the sides free from bones, season with salt and pepper, brush with melted butter, pass it through flour, place between the wire hinged broiler, broil till done, well basting with butter during cooking; serve garnished with chip or Julienne potatoes, and either maitre d'hôtel, Genoise, Bearnaise, Eschalote, or Nantaise sauces.

RED SNAPPER, STUFFED—Clean, trim and scale the fish; cut from the belly part deep enough at sides of bone so as to withdraw it without cutting the skin of the back; stuff with a fish forcemeat, then sew the opening; score the sides, bake with slices of salt pork; serve in portions garnished with Duchesse potatoes and tomato sauce.

RHUBARB—Rhubarb (*Rheum rhaponticum*) originated in Siberia and can be as stringy as celery and nearly as acidic as vinegar. It does have a fair number of culinary uses—especially when it is young and pink—as Fellows indicates. It also can be puréed and served as a tart vegetable, teamed with other fruits and spices and used in tarts or puddings, cooked with meats (it has an affinity for ginger), or even made into soup.

RHUBARB COMPOTE—Young rhubarb cut in finger lengths, placed in enameled pan covered with cold water, slowly brought to the scalding (not boiling) point, then drain. Measure the scalded water, and add to it a pound of sugar to each pint, boil together till of a thin syrupy nature, then pour over the rhubarb.

RHUBARB PIE—Line the sides of pie dish with short paste, cut the rhubarb into half inch thick pieces, sprinkle well with sugar, a little grated nutmeg and lemon rind, just a little water, cover with short paste, egg wash the top, bake and serve.

RHUBARB WITH CUSTARD—Cut the rhubarb into finger lengths, place it in an enameled pan, adding sugar and a few strips of candied lemon peel, a little water, place the pan in a slow oven and let simmer till done without breaking the fruit; serve with a spoonful to each portion of thin boiled custard, flavored with vanilla.

RHUBARB JAM—Wash the young rhubarb and cut into pieces about an inch long, do not peel it, weigh, and to each pound allow three-quarters of a pound of granulated sugar, boil in a porcelain lined kettle, bringing slowly to the boil, then boil and stir continually for forty-five minutes, fill into Mason jars, screwing the lids on tight.

RHUBARB JELLY—Wash the young rhubarb and cut it into inch lengths, put the cut fruit into a stone crock, put on the lid, stand it in the bain-marie, and heat slowly till the fruit is soft; now put a small quantity at a time into your jelly bag, and squeeze out all the juice. Measure the juice, and to each pint allow one pound of granulated sugar. Turn the juice into a porcelain lined kettle, and stand over a brisk fire. Put the sugar into earthen dishes and stand in the oven to heat. Boil the juice rapidly and continuously for twenty minutes, then turn in the sugar quickly, stirring all the while till the sugar is dissolved. Dip jelly tumblers into hot water, watch the liquid carefully, and as soon as it comes to the boil, take it from the fire and fill the glasses.

RHUBARB FRITTERS—Take pieces of the rhubarb from the compote of a preceding recipe, dip in frying batter, fry in deep, hot lard, drain, dust powdered sugar over; serve with rum sauce.

RHUBARB MERINGUE—Wash young rhubarb, then cut it into inch lengths; fill a pie dish with the rhubarb, sugared alternately with slices of stale sponge cake; bake in a moderate oven about half an hour, then cover with a meringue sprinkled with colored sugar; return to oven and bake till of a light fawn color.

RICE—To boil it properly so as to have it in grains when cooked instead of pasty: Take a large saucepan containing plenty of boiling water with a little salt, then sprinkle in the rice, let it boil up, then shift it to a cooler part of the range where it will just simmer, do not stir it, but let it swell itself tender, then turn it into a colander, place the colander in the saucepan, take it to the sink and thoroughly wash it clear with running cold water, then allow to drain dry, then put the drained rice into a receptacle of the bain-marie, put on the cover, and let the boiling water surrounding it reheat the rice. . . . Rice cooked as above is good to serve with curries, compotes, as a breakfast cereal with cream and sugar, etc. . . . Also mixed with a little butter, plenty of tomato sauce and Parmesan cheese it forms Rissoto. . . . Added to consommés it does not cloud the soup. . . . Mixed with wheat flour, baking powder, sugar and milk for making rice muffins.

RICE—In this country, the most common way to cook rice is to add 1½ cups of water to every 1 cup of rice, bring the water to a boil, lower the heat, cover, and cook for precisely 17 minutes (some say 15, some say 20, but all believe they have discovered the magic time).

But this is hardly the only way to do it. Fellows's method will work. Or you can cover any quantity of rice with about an inch of water, bring it to a boil, lower the heat, cover it, and cook it until the water is absorbed. And there are many other ways to cook long-grain rice, including beginning with a brief sauté in oil or butter—the pilaf style—until the rice is translucent.

Cooking rice like pasta—in a large quantity of boiling water, tasting it until it is *al dente*—gives the best results. Although this method takes a bit more effort since you have to boil more water and drain the rice before serving, it does allow for the differences in the amount of water absorbed by each batch of rice.

Our newfound love of rice began with Americans' introduction to sushi and continued with RISOTTO. And the future probably lies with the newly developed—or recently discovered—aromatic rices, with bouquets and flavors far more pronounced than those of standard rices. It was the thin, long-grain, cream-colored basmati strain that suddenly made even simple, unadorned rice enormously appetizing.

Nearly 80 percent of the rice cooked in this country is, like basmati, long grain. Most of us think that long-grain rice, most of which cooks in separate, firm, dry kernels (at least if you cook it right) is "correct" rice. But this near-obsession with separate grains is a cultural prejudice.

Most of the rest of the world relies on short-grain rice: Soft, sticky, and moist, the outer layer of these rices softens readily and absorbs the flavors of the cooking medium more than any other commonly cooked carbohydrate.

There are literally thousands of different rices. In India alone there are about one thousand varieties grown, four hundred of which are sold routinely. Indian food writer Julie Sahni says that any good market has twenty varieties—long and short grain, brown and white, young and old, cheap and expensive. This is not unusual in Asia, but it is in Europe, where only Italy takes rice seriously.

If it had been India, Italy, China, or Japan, where the word for rice is the same as that for meal, that was our strongest and earliest culinary influence, we would have learned about rice sooner. But the French taught us to despise rice. Their uses for it are limited and unimaginative. (As English food writer Elizabeth David observed, "The French have never found out how to cook rice.")

In their defense, the French have known rice for only seven hundred years—the Asians have cooked it nearly ten times as long—and have ignored it much of that time (probably because they were busy perfecting bread). Americans are only just beginning to know rice, but at least we have fewer prejudices against it. It will become increasingly popular as we learn more ways to cook it.

RICE CROQUETTES—Well washed rice boiled till soft in milk with a seasoning of sugar, a stick of cinnamon, and the peel of a lemon; when done remove the lemon and spice, add a piece of butter, then work in a liaison of egg yolks; turn out into a buttered pan, allow to become cold, then form into cakes with a depressed centre, bread and fry them, drain, sprinkle with powdered sugar; when sending to table fill the depression with preserve, and pour a vanilla or wine sauce around the base.

CROÛSTADES OF RICE—Well washed rice boiled till soft in white stock; when done, season with salt, butter and nutmeg, then whip it creamy, adding some Parmesan cheese. Now turn it out into a buttered pan, smooth it well, place a sheet of buttered paper over it, on that a board with a weight; when thoroughly cold, stamp out with a biscuit cutter, dou-

ble bread, then fry them, drain, scoop out the centres and use the shell for the reception of salpicons, macedoines of fruit or vegetables, etc.

RICHILIEU—Name of a garnish (see GARNISHES**).**

**RISOTTO—Risotto is an Italian rice dish using a starchy, short-grain rice called arborio. The rice is usually cooked in oil or fat and simmered, adding stock a bit at a time. Once cooked, risotto can also be set into molds. Very popular in the northern part of Italy, it often replaces a pasta course.

ROE—The eggs of fish, those chiefly used being taken from the shad, codfish, carp and mullet. Recipes will be found under their respective headings.

ROE—The egg sack of a female fish and other aquatic life. It is worth noting that the best-quality CAVIAR is sturgeon roe, specially treated to keep for a long period of time. Salmon and lumpfish roe are also good.

ROLY POLY—Name applied to puddings made from a sweet biscuit dough, rolled out thin, then spread with chopped fruit, currants, sultanas, etc., then rolled up, tied in a cloth, plunged into boiling water, and boiled; or else placed in a cake or bread tin and steamed till done; served in slices with sauce appropriate.

ROMAN PUNCH—To lemon water ice when nearly frozen is added Jamaica rum, brandy, and sherry

wine in equal parts, and enough meringue to whiten it, then finish the freezing; served in punch glasses with the dinner.

ROQUEFORT—Name of a French cheese (see CHEESE).

ROUX—The name given to an equal mixture of butter and flour, used to thicken sauces and soups. Take the saûtoir, place in the butter; when melted, add the flour and stir till thoroughly smooth and heated, then moisten with the stock, milk, etc. If for a brown sauce or soup, allow the roux to brown before moistening.

ROUX—In Creole cooking roux is often made with oil or margarine rather than butter and then browned for flavor. The ultimate purpose is the same—to thicken and flavor sauces.

ROYAL CUSTARDS—Name applied to a combination of eggs and a liquid either plain or in conjunction with a solid; used to decorate soups, and also with garnishes; also for garnishing galantines, etc. Yolks and whites of eggs separated, stirred to amal-gamate (must not be beaten light) with a little milk or stock, then poured into a buttered basin or tin, covered with a sheet of oiled paper, and placed in the steamer where they must be gradually steamed till set; they are then removed and allowed to become cold; they may then be cut in slices and afterwards into all sorts of fancy shapes for the purpose required. Into the eggs may also be mixed a macedoine of vegetables, chopped truffles, chopped mushrooms, forcemeat, lobster coral, green peas, chopped chervil, parsley, chives, tarragon, etc.; and when required for garnishing whole pieces they, after being mixed with whatever solid is used, should be filled into small timbale molds so that they can be turned out and used whole.

RYE—Name of a cereal, used in distilling for whisky, ground into flour for making rye bread, muffins, batter cakes, mush, etc.

RYE—Like OATS, rye is more tolerant of cold than wheat. And, like oats, it is not as versatile a grain as wheat. However, it works wonderfully with wheat to produce one of the world's great breads.

SALADS

ALLIGATOR PEAR—It is either eaten raw with salt and pepper; or sliced and dressed with French dressing; served on a bed of shredded endive.

ANCHOVY SALAD—(1) Shredded fillets of salted anchovies, garnished with small white pickled onions, capers, and sliced hard boiled eggs; sprinkle a little tarragon vinegar over the anchovies ... (2) Shredded lettuce and shredded anchovies, a few minced shallots, all mixed together dry; then moistened with equal quantities of olive oil and caper vinegar thoroughly beaten together.

ARTICHOKE SALAD—(1) Artichoke bottoms and medium sized onions both cooked and cooled, then sliced and dished alternately; garnished with small balls of cooked beetroot and carrots; served sprinkled with either French or a cream dressing ... (2) Cooked artichoke bottoms, skinned raw tomatoes; slice both and arrange alternately on the serving dish, sprinkle with finely chopped chervil, then with a French dressing ... (3) Hearts of lettuce finely shred; artichoke bottoms cooked and cooled, then shred; mixed, then moistened with French dressing and served.

ASPARAGUS SALAD—(1) Two-inch lengths of cooked asparagus with the head; served on lettuce leaves, the points piped with cream dressing or mayonnaise ... (2) Cooked asparagus heads; raw, skinned, sliced tomatoes. Place the asparagus in the centre of the dish, garnish with the tomatoes; serve with mayonnaise ... (3) Flowerets of cooked cauliflower in centre of dish masked with cream dressing; garnished with asparagus points moistened with French dressing, decorate with capers ... (4) Flakes of cooked salmon dipped in a thin Ravigote sauce, placed overlapping each other down centre of the dish; garnished with asparagus points, the tips of which should be piped with mayonnaise ... (5) Canned salmon drained; a spoonful in centre of dish masked with a mayonnaise and decorated with capers; garnished with asparagus points dipped in French dressing.

BEAN SALAD—Take the French beans, bought in cans and called "Haricots Verts." Wash and drain them, then moisten with French dressing and send to table in one of the numerous shaped croûstade cases, placed on a leaf of lettuce ... (2) Fresh green lima beans boiled tender, drained, mixed with cream dressing; served garnished with cress.

BEETROOT AND POTATO SALAD— Cut out of cold boiled beetroots small balls; the same size balls also to be cut out of raw peeled potatoes; then steamed till done; when cooled, place the potatoes in a Ravigote sauce, the beet balls in tarragon vinegar; dish them up alternately.

BEET AND EGG SALAD—Large beetroots boiled and cooled, then with the largest sized column cutter stamp out cork-like pieces; these slice, also do the same with steamed whites and yolks of eggs. Place some grated horseradish down the centre of the dish, on it place alternately a small white pickled onion and a caper; surround the horseradish with the yellow slices, and those with the alternate slices of beet and white egg; serve with cream dressing aside.

CABBAGE SALAD—Cut some bacon into dice, fry; when done, add a cup of vinegar, a cup of water, season with salt and pepper, bring all to the boil, pour over very finely shred cabbage, set away to get cold, then serve ... (2) Finely shred white cabbage, seasoned with salt, pepper, oil, vinegar and a little sugar ... (3) Take a firm green and a firm red cabbage, quarter them, soak in salted water for an hour, then steam them till tender, take out and cool; when cold, shred them very finely, arrange them on the serving dish alternately, two rows of each, placing between each centre row some salad cream dressing containing chopped chervil and shallots.

CAULIFLOWER SALAD—(1) Cooked cauliflower in flowerets in centre of dish, masked with mayonnaise, garnished with a macedoine of cooked vegetables dressed with French dressing ... (2) Flowerets of cooked cauliflower in centre of dish masked with a sauce Remoulade; garnished with fancy cut strips of cooked and pickled beetroot.

CELERY SALAD—(1) Cut the white celery in two-inch lengths like matches or macaroni; serve dressed with mayonnaise ... (2) White celery cut in dice, mixed with Livornaise sauce; served garnished with slices of stuffed olives.

CHICORY SALAD—Shred chicory (endive), two parts, shred celery, one part, mixed, dressed and served with French dressing.

CODFISH SALAD—Salt cod well soaked and boiled in two separate waters, cooled, flakes taken free from bones; cold boiled potatoes sliced and mixed with the cod; seasoned with cream dressing, the salad then placed down the centre of dish; garnish the sides with finely shred lettuce seasoned with French dressing, the top of the salad to be garnished with shredded and filleted salted anchovies.

CHICKEN SALAD—(1) Make round chicken croquettes of white chicken, tongue, mushrooms and truffles; bread, fry, let become cold, cut in halves and set around a bed of fine shred lettuce and endive . . . (2) Equal parts of chicken and white celery cut in dice, seasoned with salt, pepper, oil and vinegar, dressed with sliced eggs and mayonnaise . . . (3) Take two parts of mayonnaise and one part of cold limpid aspic jelly and beat them together; decorate and line individual patty pans with the beaten mixture, allow them to set, then fill up with slices of chicken dressed with Remoulade sauce, a few capers and slices of stoned olives, cover with more of the beaten mixture, let set till firm, turn out on to a bed of shredded lettuce, garnish with shredded anchovies and shredded gherkins.

CHICKEN, MAYONNAISE OF—Cold roast chickens, cut into joints, marinaded in a mixture of olive oil, tarragon vinegar, salt and pepper; taken up, drained, skinned, dipped in a mayonnaise; when well coated, lain on a bed of shredded lettuce, garnish with quartered eggs, balls of pickled beetroot and stoned, stuffed olives . . . (2) Boned and roasted chicken, pressed, sliced, coated with mayonnaise; served garnished with green peas and asparagus points sprinkled with French dressing, and cubes of savory chicken aspic.

CRAB SALAD—Fresh crab meat, to which is added one-fourth of its bulk in minced cold boiled cabbage; season with dry mustard, a dash of Worcestershire sauce and cream salad dressing. Fill the crab shells with the salad, place the shell on a curved lettuce leaf; decorate the salad in the shell with two rows of egg, chopped whites and yolks alternately . . . (2) Fresh crab meat cut in small dice, dressed with tarragon vinegar, salt, olive oil and cayenne pepper; served within a border of shredded lettuce; garnish with slices of stuffed olives and hard boiled eggs . . . (3) Make from fresh crabmeat, some forcemeat balls the size of walnuts; when poached and cooled, coat them with a Remoulade sauce; serve them within a border of cold slaw, garnish with quartered hard boiled eggs and fancy strips of pickled beetroot.

CUCUMBER SALAD—Cucumbers peeled, sliced thin, steeped in salted ice water for two or three hours, taken up into a salad basket and swung dry; then place in a bowl and anoint them with French dressing containing chopped tarragon and parsley . . . (2) Peeled cucumbers thinly sliced and steeped in salted ice water for an hour, then taken up into a salad basket and swung dry; then anoint them with a spray of tarragon vinegar, place in centre of dish, and garnish them with a few spring onions sliced and moistened with cream salad dressing . . . (3) Peeled cucumbers thinly sliced, steeped in salted ice water for an hour, taken up into a salad basket and swung dry; then anoint them with salt, pepper and a spray of caper vinegar; dish them up alternately with slices of hard boiled eggs and pickled beetroot.

DANDELION SALAD—Fresh gathered young dandelion leaves (gathered before the sun shines on them in the morning too strongly), wiped clean WITHOUT BEING WASHED, seasoned with French dressing; served garnished with fancy slices of pickled beetroot.

CRESS SALAD—Arrange well washed, picked over and drained watercress on the serving dish, garnish with sliced eggs and filleted anchovies.

EGG SALAD—Hard boiled eggs, the yolks rubbed through a sieve, mixed with their equal weight of grated Parmesan cheese, seasoned with chopped chervil, salt, pepper and enough melted butter to moisten; fill the whites with the mixture, and lay them on a bed of shredded lettuce; garnish with peeled and sliced tomatoes, piped with Remoulade sauce.

EEL SALAD—Raw eels skinned and marinaded, then boiled and the bone removed; when cold, masked with mayonnaise, arranged in centre of dish garnished with sliced eggs and tufts of parsley.

EGG PLANT SALAD—Cold well boiled egg plant, cut in small dice and well seasoned with lemon juice and olive oil; served on a curled leaf of lettuce.

ENDIVE SALAD—Shred the leaves and cores of well washed endive, and serve it with French dressing made with tarragon vinegar, containing a suspicion of garlic.

FRENCH SALAD—Cold roast meat (veal for preference), cut in small dice, mixed with shredded lettuce and endive, seasoned with French dressing, garnished with chopped whites of hard boiled egg.

GARDENER'S SALAD—Fine strips of vegetables of various colors cooked and cooled, with green peas and cut stringless beans, all mixed together and dressed with salt, pepper, olive oil and vinegar, or with a thin mayonnaise.

GERMAN SALAD—Pickled red cabbage, blanched sauerkraut, small pickled onions, grated horseradish, chopped shallots, gherkins, dill pickles and capers with sliced cold frankfurters, all mixed together, seasoned with Rhine wine, salad oil, pepper and tarragon vinegar.

GERMAN POTATO SALAD—Sliced cold boiled potatoes, minced parsley, fried diced bacon (with its fat

GARDENER'S SALAD

·

Serves 6

This is a very colorful salad. Even though the recipe is one hundred years old, the dish is very up to the minute in terms of today's tastes.

1 cup peeled and julienned carrots	**Dressing**
1 cup julienned green beans	2 tablespoons chopped parsley
1/2 cup frozen peas	3/4 cup olive oil
1 cup julienned green zucchini	2 tablespoons white wine vinegar
1 cup julienned yellow zucchini	Juice of 1 lemon
1/2 cup chopped white onion	Salt and freshly ground black pepper to taste
1/2 cup cored and julienned red sweet bell pepper	Lettuce cups for serving

In a large pot of simmering water, blanch the carrots, beans, and peas for a few minutes and drain.

In a large bowl, toss the blanched vegetables with the zucchini, onions, and red peppers. Mix together the ingredients for the dressing, add to the vegetables, and toss well. Refrigerate.

Serve in lettuce cups.

C.W.

---

thrown over the potatoes), pepper, salt, the whole well mixed with cream salad dressing.

GAME SALAD—Any kind of cold roast game skinned and cut into dice, mixed with shredded lettuce, shredded cooked carrots and a few raw minced shallots, season the whole with Tartare sauce; serve garnished with slices of pickled beetroot, chopped eggs and small balls of butter and pounded watercress ... (2) Cold roast game skinned and sliced, moistened with French dressing and allowed to marinade for three hours, arrange them on the serving platter, garnished with shredded lettuce, the whole then sprinkled over with chopped whites of egg and the yolks that have been rubbed through a sieve.

HERRING SALAD—Shredded boneless salted herrings and sardelles, mixed with thin sliced cold boiled potatoes, sliced dill pickles and gherkins, capers, chopped chives and shredded lettuce; placed on the serving platter and masked with a thin mayonnaise; garnish with filleted anchovies and slices or strips of pickled beetroot . . . (2) Blanched smoked herring, skinned, split, boned, cut up small, mixed with chopped eggs, minced onion, thin sliced cold boiled potatoes and chopped parsley, seasoned with French dressing, garnished with pickled beetroot and capers.

ITALIAN SALAD—Diced fowl mixed in cream salad dressing; served within a border of picked watercress and hearts of lettuce; garnish with slices of eggs, yolks removed, its place filled with a slice of beetroot.

ITALIAN SALAD—Cooked green peas two-fifths, small diced cooked carrot one-fifth, diced cooked white turnip one-fifth, small cut cooked stringless beans one-fifth, all mixed together. Then into a French dressing mix some chopped chervil, tarragon and chives; moisten the vegetables with this mixture, and serve garnished with slices of cold boiled potatoes and pickled beetroot.

KALE SALAD—The small inside leaves of kale four-fifths, picked and washed watercress one-fifth,

mixed and served with French dressing.

LETTUCE SALAD—Broad shred lettuce leaves, sprinkled with salt and pepper, then sprayed with mixed olive oil and tarragon vinegar . . . (2) Well washed and drained lettuce leaves finely shred and served with French dressing . . . (3) Broad shred lettuce leaves and finely shred spring onions, sprinkled with salt and pepper, then sprayed with mixed olive oil and tarragon vinegar . . . (4) Finely shred lettuce seasoned with French dressing and garnished with peeled, sliced tomatoes, piped with a Remoulade sauce . . . (5) Shred lettuce tossed with Remoulade sauce and minced capers; served garnished with peeled and sliced tomatoes sprayed with French dressing.

LIMA BEAN SALAD—Fresh green lima beans boiled, drained, cooled, moistened with a cream salad dressing; served garnished with watercress sprayed with caper vinegar.

LOBSTER SALAD—Two parts of diced lobster meat to one part of fine cut celery, seasoned with salt, pepper and tarragon vinegar, placed on platter and masked with mayonnaise; garnished with slices of hard boiled eggs and shredded lettuce . . . (2) Equal parts of diced lobster meat and diced cold boiled potatoes, mixed with cream salad dressing; served with cubes of steamed whites and yolks of eggs alternately as a garnish . . . (3) Slices of lobster meat dipped in Montpelier butter arranged down the centre of platter; served garnished with alternate tufts of watercress; sliced egg with yolk removed and its place filled with lobster coral; sliced cucumber, and small rings of onion, the interior of the ring filled with caviare ... (4) Shredded lettuce and lobster meat, seasoned with oil, salt, pepper and tarragon vinegar, placed on platter and masked with mayonnaise, decorated with capers, sliced stuffed olives, lobster coral, quartered eggs, and watercress (also the small claws).

MACEDOINE SALAD—Out of slices of cooked carrot, white and yellow turnip, and bottoms of artichokes, stamp fancy shapes, add to them cooked green peas and asparagus tips, also finely cut stringless beans, mix all together; serve on lettuce leaves, with French dressing and a few capers.

OYSTER SALAD—Oysters scaled and washed, cooled, served on lettuce leaf with Tartar sauce ... (2) Equal quantities of white celery and cabbage minced together and blanched, then cooled; oysters scalded with their own liquor, to which is added a little vinegar and salt, then drained and cooled; season the celery and cabbage with a little oil and white vinegar, place it in centre of dish, dip the oysters in mayonnaise and surround the centre.

ONION SALAD—Take either the Bermuda or Spanish onion, peel them, slice in rings one-quarter inch thick, steam them till half done, then let them become very cold; serve on lettuce leaves, with Ravigote sauce.

OYSTER PLANT SALAD—Cold boiled oyster plant, cut in finger lengths; when very cold, season them with salt and pepper, dip the ends in Ravigote sauce, arrange on fancy strips of cooled toast (like asparagus) and garnish with aspic jelly.

OKRA SALAD—Okras blanched, drained and quartered; served on a bed of shredded endive; pour over French dressing containing chopped chives and chervil.

PARTRIDGE SALAD—Cold trimmed joints of roast partridge, marinaded in tarragon vinegar and olive oil. (One in two add salt, pepper, minced chives and chervil); serve on a bed of shredded lettuce, pour the marinade over, garnish with sliced eggs, capers and gherkins ... (2) Cold roast partridge cut in dice, marinaded for two hours in French dressing, drain it, then mix the partridge with an equal amount of diced white celery; place the salad on a leaf of lettuce, mask with a mayonnaise, garnish with minced pickle and chopped capers.

POTATO SALAD—Cold boiled potatoes sliced, little minced onion and chopped parsley, mixed and seasoned with salt, pepper, oil and vinegar ... (2) Slices of cold boiled potatoes, shredded salt anchovies, chopped parsley, pepper, salt, French mustard, tarragon vinegar and cream salad dressing, all mixed together and served on lettuce ... (3) Sliced thin cold boiled potatoes, thoroughly mixed with French dressing, adding a little more vinegar ... (4) Sliced cold boiled potatoes, sliced onion, chopped parsley, fried bacon in dice with its fat, salt, pepper and cream salad dressing, all mixed together and served on lettuce . . . (5) Balls of potatoes scooped from peeled raw ones, steamed till done, then cooled, moistened with Hollandaise sauce; served on lettuce and sprinkled with finely chopped chives and chervil.

ROMAINE SALAD—Broad shredded Romaine lettuce leaves, sprinkled with salt, pepper, oil and tarragon vinegar.

RUSSIAN SALAD—Cooked salad of carrots, parsnips and beetroots cut in shapes; pieces of fowl and shredded anchovies, mixed together and seasoned with combined oil, vinegar and French mustard; served garnished with olives and caviar . . . (2) Cooked ham, smoked tongue, roast beef, chicken and mutton cut in dice, shredded salt anchovies; season and mix with Tartar sauce; serve within a border of shredded lettuce.

RADISH SALAD—Take round red and white radishes, thoroughly clean them, then cut in halves, arrange the halves alternately, skin side up, on a bed of shredded lettuce, sprinkle with French dressing and garnish with stuffed olives.

SARDINE SALAD—Hard boiled eggs and boiled onions in slices, sardines in fillets, dished up in alternate layers, sprinkled with French dressing containing chopped parsley, chives and chervil.

SALMON SALAD—Equal quantities of cooked beet and raw celery minced, then mixed together; boiled salmon in flakes added; season with salt and pepper to taste, then moisten with one part of vinegar to three parts of olive oil; serve on a bed of shredded lettuce and garnish with eggs.

SALSIFY SALAD—Cold boiled salsify, mixed with French dressing, in centre of dish, garnished with small balls of steamed potatoes moistened with cream dressing.

SCOTCH SALAD—Two parts of diced celery to one part of flakes of cooked salmon; season with oil, salt and vinegar; serve on lettuce, mask with mayonnaise, garnish with sliced egg and stuffed olives.

SHRIMP SALAD—Shrimps marinaded in oil and vinegar, drained, mixed with shredded celery in inch lengths, dressed with mayonnaise, garnished with stoned olives, capers, hard boiled eggs and coiled shrimps.

SPANISH SALAD—Peeled tomatoes sliced and arranged on dish with pickled small white onions, mayonnaise in centre . . . (2) Shredded endive garnished with quartered peeled tomatoes and quartered eggs, yolk removed and its place filled with shrimp paste. The endive to be sprinkled with minced sweet peppers and shallots, oil, salt, pepper and vinegar.

SOUTHERN SALAD—Take tender okras, trim the ends, boil till tender, drain, let become very cold.

SALMON SALAD

·

Serves 4 to 6 as a salad course

We love our salmon in the Pacific northwest. Normally, one would not pair salmon with cooked beets, but such a marriage was very common in earlier times. This is a very tasty salad.

2¹/₄ pounds fresh salmon steaks (thick steaks are best)

Salt and freshly ground black pepper to taste

2 tablespoons chopped fresh dill

1 cup thinly sliced celery

¹/₂ cup peeled and thinly sliced white onions

1 cup canned beets, well drained and cut in ¹/₈-inch dice (buy beets packed in glass with water, not pickled!)

³/₄ cup olive oil

3 tablespoons lemon juice

1 tablespoon white wine vinegar

Lettuce leaves for serving

Garnish

3 hard-boiled eggs, sliced

Preheat the oven to 350°F.

Season the salmon with salt and pepper (easy on the salt). Place the salmon in a 13-inch by 9-inch baking dish and cover with aluminum foil. Bake for 25 minutes. Remove the foil, cool, and debone the salmon. Tear the salmon into large flakes, but do not shred it. Discard the bones and skin.

Combine the cooked salmon, dill, celery, onions, and drained beets in a large bowl.

In another bowl, mix the oil, lemon juice, and vinegar.

Add to the salmon mixture and fold it in gently. Try not to break up the salmon too much.

Serve in lettuce leaves with sliced-egg garnish.

C.W.

Dip some sweet peppers in hot fat and take off the skins, then finely shred them like matches, mix them with the okras and serve with mayonnaise . . . (2) Boil till done some green peppers, let them become very cold, then shred them like matches and serve with French dressing.

SWEDISH SALAD—Cut into dice an equal quantity of cold meat, boiled potatoes, green apples, pickled herring and salted anchovies, mix into it some chopped gherkins, capers and hard boiled eggs, mix all; serve on lettuce with French dressing and garnish with stoned olives.

SWEETBREAD SALAD—Slices of cooked sweetbread dipped in flour, fried with butter, then cooled and trimmed; shredded lettuce in centre of dish with salad cream dressing; sweetbreads masked with mayonnaise, arranged around the lettuce; garnish with slices of radishes and beetroot.

TARTARE SALAD—Shredded lettuce, pickled cucumbers, pickled onions and pickled herring; slice the cucumbers and cut the herring in dice, mix together, season with a little oil and vinegar, and finish with Tartare sauce; serve on lettuce.

TOMATO SALAD—Sliced peeled tomatoes marinaded in French dressing, drained, sprinkled with salt and pepper . . . (2) Sliced peeled tomatoes sprinkled with Parmesan cheese moistened with Rhine wine and olive oil.

VEAL SALAD—Equal quantities of cooked veal and boiled potatoes cut in dice with some white celery; seasoned with salt, pepper and

cream salad dressing; served on lettuce, garnished with eggs.

WATERCRESS SALAD—Crisp, cleaned and picked watercress, seasoned with salt, pepper and vinegar.

COMBINATION SALADS—Slices of cold boiled potatoes, Brussels sprouts boiled and cooled, flowerets of boiled cauliflower, and shredded celery, arranged neatly in salad bowl with French dressing . . . (2) Shred lettuce, endive, sliced tomatoes, spring onions and radishes, tossed lightly together with French dressing . . . (3) Slices of potatoes even in size, slices of truffles and minced shallots, dressed with oil and caper vinegar . . . (4) Yolks of eggs rubbed through a sieve, chopped egg whites, gherkins, chervil and soy, mixed with a little dressing composed of French mustard, essence of anchovies, pepper and white wine vinegar, garnished with sliced potatoes, beetroot and celery.

FRENCH DRESSING—Four parts of olive oil to one part of vinegar, white or tarragon, a little onion juice, finely chopped parsley, salt and pepper.

CREAM DRESSING—One cup each of white vinegar and melted butter, one dessert spoon of dry mustard, one teaspoon of paprika, eight yolks of eggs, one quart of whipping cream. Boil the vinegar, butter and seasonings together; pour it then to the beaten yolks, stir over the range till like custard, remove and cool, then whip the cream and beat it into the dressing.

HOLLANDAISE DRESSING—One pint of white vinegar, one quart of milk, one cup of oil or melted butter, one basting spoonful of dry mustard, one teaspoon of red pepper, one tablespoonful of paprika, twelve eggs, salt to taste. Boil the vinegar with the seasonings; meanwhile separate the yolks and whites, and beat them separately; bring the milk to the boil and pour it to the yolks, then add the boiling vinegar, stir on the range till it just thickens like custard (do not let it boil or it will curdle). When of the custard consistency, remove from the fire and beat in the whipped whites with the melted butter or oil, then put away to cool for use.

SALLY LUNN—Name applied to a light sweet yeast raised tea cake; served split and buttered, fresh and hot.

SALMON—Many eighteen-century domestic servants demanded contracts that stipulated that they not be served salmon more than twice a day. That gives a good indication of just how common this gorgeous, free-swimming fish was in our rivers and streams. Now, although wild Atlantic salmon (*Salmo salar*) is recovering from the devastation of the early and middle part of this century, it remains a protected species. We have, therefore, two sources of salmon: Pacific and farm-raised.

There are five major species of Pacific salmon, all *Oncorhynchus*—chinook (also called king), chum (dog), coho (silver), pink (humpback), and sockeye (red or blueback)—of which king, coho, and sockeye are considered the best for fresh eating. Seasons vary, but fresh salmon from the Alaska runs is usually available from late spring to early fall. Prime salmon has deep orange, almost-red flesh and a full, fatty flavor.

Fish farms raising Atlantic salmon have spread from Norway to the rest of the world, including numerous locations in North and South America. The early efforts by the Norwegians resulted in a nice-looking fish, but it was overly lean and not very flavorful. Currently, however, farm-raised Atlantic salmon from Maine and the Maritime Provinces—especially New Brunswick—from the Pacific Northwest, and from Chile are all consistently excellent. We are convinced the best salmon is from the Pacific Northwest and Alaska.

Poached salmon is, of course, a classic preparation. But grilled salmon is also superb. Brush steaks with almost any marinade and grill over a fairly high flame and enjoy.

SALMON, BOILED—If small, boil whole; if large cut in two or three. Put to boil in boiling salted water, laying the fish on a drainer, boil a minute, raise the drainer, let the water boil very rapidly, then plunge fish and drainer in again, then repeat the operation and allow to boil till done. By this method the albumen of the fish coagulates and the flesh eats much better. Serve with plain melted butter, Hollandaise, Allemande, caper, Béchamel, fennel, cream or butter parsley sauce.

SALMON, BAKED—The fish should be small. Scale, trim, wash and dry it, turn the thin flap of the belly inwards and tie it with thin twine; cover the fish then with a fish forcemeat; bake and baste till done; serve in portions with Genoise or Perigueux sauces.

SALMON, BROILED—Scale, trim, wash and dry the fish, then cut in equally thick slices, season with cayenne pepper and salt, dip in olive oil, roll up in oiled paper, tuck in the ends and pin with a toothpick, plunge into hot fat and cook for 7 to 10 minutes according to the thickness, then raise the frying basket, let it drain for a minute; then put the cutlet, still in the paper, on the broiler, broil till nicely marked, remove the paper, place on dish; serve with Tartar, Genevoise, fine-herbs or maître d'hôtel sauces or with anchovy or Montpelier butter.

SALMON STEAKS OR CUTLETS—Boil them in boiling seasoned white fish stock till done and serve with lobster, oyster, cucumber or suprême sauces. Sauté them with clear butter a delicate brown and serve with Aurora, Milanaise, Velouté, gherkin, Piquante, or Ravigote sauces.

SALMON (COLD, BOILED)—May be served with sliced cucumbers, Tartar, Ravigote or mayonnaise sauces.

SALMON CROQUETTES—Take flakes of cold boiled salmon and shred them, season with red pepper and salt, also a dash each of anchovy and Harvey sauces. Then mix the fish with one-third of its bulk of fresh mashed potatoes; turn on to a dish, smooth it over, allow to become cold, then shape pieces of the mixture into small flat cutlets like a cutlet from the tail of the fish; bread and fry them and serve with cream or fennel sauces, garnish with Hollandaise potatoes.

SALMON, SMOKED—May be boiled and served with cream sauce . . . Broiled and served with devil or drawn butter sauce . . . Fried in oil and served with lemon sauce . . . Toasted and served with maître d'hôtel sauce.

SALMON, MAYONNAISE OF—Take the center cut of a salmon, curl the flaps under and tie with twine, boil in seasoned fish stock till done, remove and skin, then allow to become cold (retaining its shape), place on dish, mask well with mayonnaise, decorate the mayonnaise with lobster coral, garnish with watercress; serve.

SALMON TROUT—See TROUT.

SALSIFY—For recipes, see OYSTER PLANT.

SALT COD—In the days before refrigeration, when COD was plentiful, the fish was often salted for long keeping; its extremely lean flesh is particularly well suited to this treatment. And, just as we still crave the taste of bacon long after curing became unnecessary, our taste for salt cod mandates the continuation of this tradition. In fact, many fish retailers in this country complain that fresh cod is scarce because the Spanish, French, Portuguese, and Italians buy so much of it for salting.

Salt cod must be soaked before using: Immerse it in water in a nonmetal container for at least 12 hours (as long as two days may be needed, depending on the fish), changing the water occasionally. The cod is then ready for cooking.

SARDINE—*Sardine* includes a number of members of the herring family (most often *Sardinia pilchardus* and *Sprattus sprattus*), which are usually canned in oil. Like other herring, however, these are fine fish to cook when fresh.

SASSAFRAS—A flavoring or perfumed obtained from the bark of the North American sassafras tree.

SAUCES AND THEIR USES

ADMIRAL SAUCE—Into a good butter sauce made with white seasoned fish stock, work some pounded anchovies, minced fried shallots, chopped capers, and a little grated lemon rind . . . Serve with bluefish sauté . . . boiled pickerel . . . pike or muskallonge . . . boiled sheephead . . . boiled weakfish . . . Mackinaw trout.

ADMIRAL SAUCE—As you might guess from the name, admiral refers to sauces (or garnishes) served with fish; most contain fish.

ALBERT SAUCE—Into a good butter sauce made from veal or other white stock, work some grated horseradish, minced fried shallots, chopped parsley, tarragon vinegar; boil up again, then strain, then finish with a liaison of egg yolks, a pinch of mustard and chopped parsley. Serve with braised fillet of beef, any braised beef. . . . It is also used to poach eggs in when an addition of curry is given to it for "Eggs Indienne style." See EGGS.

ALBERT SAUCE—The dominant presence in Albert sauce is horseradish (it is also called horseradish sauce). Serve Albert sauce with any braised or roast beef.

ALLEMANDE SAUCE—Into a good Velouté sauce, work some lemon juice, a little mushroom catsup, cayenne, butter, yolks of eggs, a grating of nutmeg, then strain. It should be yellow, and smooth as velvet. Serve with boiled pigs' feet . . . braised eels . . . fried carp . . . paupiettes of sole . . . boiled codfish . . . fried haddock . . . fried fillets of mackerel . . . baked perch . . . baked shad . . . baked trout . . . boiled chicken . . . boiled pheasant . . . fried pike. It is also the foundation of many other sauces, fish especially.

ALLEMANDE SAUCE—So named not for its German origin, but because, in most variations, it is light (as opposed to the dark espagnole), the basic allemande is an egg-and-cream–based velouté (white) sauce. Fellows's version is a little more elaborate than basic white sauce.

ALMOND SAUCE—A sweet custard sauce containing pounded and shredded almonds, also a dash of ratafia. Served with fig fritters . . . almond custard fritters, etc.

ANCHOVY SAUCE—Anchovy butter worked into a good Espagnole sauce. Used for broiled steaks, baked fish, and as a filler for steak and oyster pie.

ANCHOVY SAUCE—Into a well made butter sauce work in the juice of a lemon, a dash of cayenne pepper, some pounded anchovies or anchovy essence. Used for boiled fish such as:

boiled bass, cod, plaice, haddock, halibut, herring, kingfish, pike, rockfish, weakfish, and shad roe.

ANDALUSIAN SAUCE—Into a rich tomato sauce, work some grated lean cooked ham, and a little minced (fried) garlic. Used with braised meats, such as larded tenderloin of beef, fricandeau of veal, legs or saddles of mutton, and haunch of venison.

ANDALUSIAN SAUCE—All andalusian sauces are based upon tomatoes; some combine tomatoes and mayonnaise. In addition to Fellows's suggestions, andalusian sauce has often been served with chicken.

APRICOT SAUCE—A syrup sauce containing apricot marmalade and a flavoring of Catawba wine. Used for timbale of apples, charlotte of apples, apple puddings, apple fritters.

AVIGNON SAUCE—Equal quantities of a Soûbise purée and a good Béchamel sauce combined together with the addition of a little crushed garlic, Parmesan cheese and olive oil; bring it to the boil, then thicken with a liaison of egg yolks, strain and use for boiled legs of mutton, boiled fowls and capons, stewed partridge, boiled pheasant, boiled salt leg of pork, fried sweetbreads, chicken croquettes, sweetbread croquettes.

AURORA SAUCE—Into some reduced Espagnole sauce work enough lobster butter to give the sauce an orange color . . . Or work lobster butter into a Béchamel sauce . . . Or take two parts Béchamel and one part tomato sauce, adding also a little mushroom catsup and lobster butter. In either of these combinations add the juice of a lemon, a dash of cayenne pepper and tarragon vinegar. Used for baked carp, boiled cod steak, baked fillets of soles, halibut steak sauté, salmon steak sauté, fillets of trout sauté, boiled trout; also used in preparing "eggs a l'Aurore" (see EGGS).

AURORA SAUCE—The most commonly made aurore sauce (another misspelling) is a combination of velouté sauce and tomato purée. In addition to fish, it can be served with roast or poached chicken.

BAVARIAN SAUCE—Boil some vinegar to half its original volume with some butter, a little horseradish, salt and grated nutmeg; beat some yolks of eggs, then pour the boiling mixture to it to make like mayonnaise, strain, then beat in a little more butter, and some lobster roe, beat till creamy and frothy, then use for cold fish, and fish salads.

BÉCHAMEL SAUCE—Into some reduced chicken broth, add some mushroom essence or purée, an equal quantity of rich milk or cream, a seasoning of mace; bring to the boil, then thicken with roux (flour and butter), strain. Used for boiled chicken, scalloped codfish, scalloped halibut, scalloped turbot, scalloped sweetbreads; chicken, turkey and sweetbread croquettes; also for mixing with green peas, asparagus points, macedoine of vegetables, etc., when used for garnishing.

BASIC WHITE SAUCE

.

Makes 2¹/₂ cups

This cream sauce is basic to any kitchen. It is used in soups, sauces, and several other dishes. While it appears to be very rich for our time, it was absolutely common in the 1904 kitchen.

2 cups milk

3 tablespoons peeled and
    chopped yellow onions

1 bay leaf

Pinch of cayenne pepper to
    taste

4 tablespoons butter

3 tablespoons all-purpose
    flour

Salt to taste

In a saucepan, bring the milk to a simmer. Add the onions, bay leaf, and cayenne pepper. Simmer for a few minutes. Strain the milk stock, discarding the vegetables. Return the milk to the stove.

In another pan, melt the butter and stir in the flour to form a roux. Whisk the roux into the milk. Bring the milk to a simmer, stirring until thick, about 10 minutes. Add salt to taste.

VARIATION: Try adding a dash or two of dry sherry to this sauce. It is great on vegetables. I stir cooked onions into this sauce, spoon it over my favorite vegetable, and eat the whole dish by myself!

J.S.

BÉARNAISE SAUCE—Braise some shallots with a little tarragon vinegar, add some rich, thin Velouté sauce, simmer, then add some beaten yolks of eggs; when like custard, remove from the fire, then beat in melted butter at the rate of three tablespoons to the pint, work in the juice of a lemon, a little cayenne pepper, then strain and finish with some finely chopped parsley and tarragon. Used for broiled steaks, roast fillet of beef, broiled sweetbreads, lamb fries, veal and lamb cutlets.

BEYROUT SAUCE—Fetch to the boil one and a half pounds of butter with two minced medium sized onions, a basting spoonful of tarragon vinegar and the same of common vinegar, a half pint of Espagnole, a half cupful each of mushroom catsup and Harvey sauce; simmer, skim, then boil till creamy, remove from the fire, finish with a little sugar and anchovy essence. Used with cold fish and fish salads.

BIGARADE SAUCE—Take equal quantities of game and Espagnole

BAVARIAN SAUCE

•

Makes about 1¾ cups

This sauce is known as an emulsion, meaning that there is butter or oil suspended within it. The key here is not to boil the final product or it will curdle and separate. Serve with fish or poached eggs.

¹/₂ cup white wine vinegar

¹/₂ cup (1 stick) butter

2 teaspoons anchovy paste

2 tablespoons dry sherry

5 egg yolks, at room temperature

¹/₂ cup half-and-half

1 tablespoons finely chopped parsley

Pinch of cayenne pepper to taste

In a small saucepan, simmer the vinegar, butter, anchovy paste, and sherry. Reduce the liquid by half.

In a mixing bowl, using a wire whisk, whip the egg yolks and half-and-half until frothy, about 5 minutes. Whip the reduced vinegar mixture into the egg mixture.

Return to the saucepan, and cook over the low heat, whipping the entire time. Do not boil this sauce as you risk curdling it. As soon as the sauce thickens to a creamy consistency, remove from the heat and add the parsley and cayenne.

Serve immediately or pour into a sauceboat to stop the cooking.

C.W.

---

sauces, and work in the juice and grated rind of Seville or other bitter orange. Used for braised fillet of beef, stewed duck, fried duckling, roast duck.

BOHEMIAN SAUCE—Make some panada with chicken or veal broth, and work into it some grated horseradish and a little butter. (A white bread sauce, used with roast partridge.)

BOHEMIAN SAUCE—As described by Escoffier, Bohemian sauce is an egg-enriched BÉCHAMEL spiked with tarragon vinegar and dry mustard.

BOURGEOISE SAUCE—Into a pint of thin Espagnole, work a spoonful each of chopped parsley, chervil, tarragon, meat glaze, French mustard and sugar, bring it to a simmer, then add the juice of a lemon. Used with forcemeat balls; in garnishing fricandeaus of veal, carbonades of mutton, roulade of veal, sauté of pigs feet (boneless), and braised ox heart.

BOURGUIGNOTTE SAUCE—Into some Espagnole, work some minced fried onions, sliced truffles and mushrooms, finish with some Burgundy wine. Used with braised small game birds, braised carp, whole carp stewed in red wine, fried cutlets of sturgeon, mutton cutlets sautés, fillets of pigeons sautés.

BORDELAISE SAUCE, WHITE—Into a rich butter sauce work some minced fried shallots, chopped parsley and white wine. Used with matelote of eels, paupiettes of soles, boiled mackerel, crimped cutlets of pike, boiled halibut, turbot.

BORDELAISE SAUCE, BROWN—Into some Espagnole, work some minced fried shallots, and garlic, red wine, cayenne pepper, chopped parsley, lemon juice and slices of beef marrow. Used with broiled steaks and almost any braised red meat . . . Omit the marrow and add fillets of anchovies and a little anchovy essence, it is then used with braised fish, also baked and broiled fish.

BORDELAISE SAUCE BROWN—The Bordelaise live in Bordeaux, where great red (and good white) wine is made, and most bordelaise sauces have red wine at their base, although in Fellows's time the white bordelaise was obviously enjoyed.

BRESSOISE SAUCE—Into some Madeira sauce, work a purée made of chicken livers, panada, fried minced shallots, grated rind and juice of an orange. Used with roast chicken, chicken croquettes, roast capon, omelet of chicken livers, and quenelles of turkey.

BRETONNE SAUCE, HOT—Into some Espagnole, work a purée of fried onions, finish with chopped parsley. Used with roast mutton, braised saddle of mutton, cutlets of mutton, braised ox cheek, and grenadins of pork.

BRETONNE SAUCE, COLD—A spoonful each of mustard and sugar, with two spoonfuls of grated horseradish, worked into a half pint of tarragon vinegar. Used with cold roast or braised mutton, beef, ox tongue, roast pork, etc.

CAPER SAUCE—Into a good butter or Velouté sauce, work in some whole capers and a little tarragon vinegar. Used with boiled mutton, boiled fresh ox tongue and boiled pigs' feet.

CAPER SAUCE FOR FISH—Make a white roux, moisten it with a light consommé, season it with cayenne, grated nutmeg, essence of anchovies, lemon juice, and capers, with a dash of caper vinegar. Used with broiled salmon steak, broiled carp, baked codfish, boiled red mullet, boiled pike, boiled sheephead, boiled red snapper, boiled shad, and braised salmon trout.

CARROT SAUCE—Into some Velouté sauce work a purée of young carrots. Very good for boiled beef.

CARROT SAUCE

·

Makes about 1 quart

Puréed vegetable sauces were popular in the nouvelle cuisine trend. This sauce has a clean, bright flavor, and it certainly predates current cooking styles.

*1 1/2 pounds carrots,
   trimmed and peeled*

*2 cloves garlic, peeled and
   chopped*

1 teaspoon salt

1/4 cup half-and-half

*1 1/2 cups Velouté Sauce
   (page 448)*

1/2 cup dry white wine

Slice the carrots 1/4 inch thick and place in a small pot. Add the garlic, salt, and add just enough water to cover the carrots. Bring to a boil, cover, and simmer for 20 minutes.

Drain and, in a food processor, purée the carrots. Add the half-and-half and blend until very smooth.

Return the purée to the pot and add the Velouté Sauce and wine. Simmer for 5 minutes. Adjust the salt, if needed.

This is a very versatile sauce that is especially good with roasted chicken or pork.

C.W.

CARDINAL SAUCE—Into a good Velouté sauce work some lobster butter, a little anchovy essence, lemon juice, cayenne, essence of mushrooms, and lobster roe, or shrimps, rubbed through a tamis. Used with boiled chicken and capon, boudins of lobster, paupiettes of soles, ragout of mullets, fillets of perch, stuffed and braised carp and pike, boiled salmon, fillets of turbot and halibut, fillets of soles and boiled sturgeon.

CAULIFLOWER SAUCE—Into a good butter sauce work some small flowerets of white cauliflower. Very good for boiled poultry.

CELERY SAUCE, WHITE—Into some light Allemande sauce work a purée of celery. Good with boiled turkey and white entrées of turkey wings.

CELERY SAUCE, BROWN—Into a good thickened roast poultry gravy work in some finely cut celery and simmer it till done. Very good with roast poultry, and dry, brown entrées of poultry.

CHASSEUR SAUCE—Into equal parts of Espagnole and tomato sauces, work some minced fried onions, sliced mushrooms, chopped parsley and lemon juice. Used with mutton cutlets sautés, sauté of partridge, veal cutlets, roast prairie chicken, roast black game, braised small game birds, venison steak, cutlets of roebuck, roast young rabbit, legs of rabbit sauté, fillets of hare or jackrabbit, and braised larded ribs of beef.

CHASSEUR SAUCE—Common to almost all recipes for chasseur sauce are mushrooms and tomatoes; serve this sauce with any full-flavored meat.

CHANTAUSEN SAUCE—A syrup sauce flavored with cloves, cinnamon, bay leaves and Chantausen wine. Used for puddings and sweet entrées.

CHANTAUSEN SAUCE—You will never find Chantausen wine in any store, so if Fellows's recipe intrigues you, substitute a decent Auslese from the Moselle region of Germany.

CHATEAUBRIAND SAUCE—One pint of Espagnole, a half pint of meat glaze, a half pint of white wine, simmer, strain, then beat in a half pint of maître d'hôtel sauce. Used with broiled steaks, fillets of beef.

CHAMBORD SAUCE—Into a pint of Velouté, work a half pint of white mushroom purée, a piece of chicken glaze, a glass of Sauterne, and a spoonful of lobster butter. Used with fillets of bass, baked bass, pike, carp, fish croquettes.

CHAMPAGNE SAUCE—Into a pint of Espagnole, simmer a half pint each of sherry wine and vinegar with a little sugar. Good with roast ham.

CHADEAU SAUCE—A foaming sauce of eight yolks and two whites of eggs, juice of a lemon, half a pound of sugar, a quart of Chablis, whipped over a slow fire to boiling point. Used for sweet entrées.

CHADEAU SAUCE—Although no one refers to chadeau sauce anymore, Fellows's recipe makes it clear that this is essentially a zabaglione, a well-known dessert sauce that combines egg yolks, sugar, and dry white wine.

CHAUD-FROID SAUCE—Take some carcasses of roast game or poultry and a bunch of mixed garden herbs, cover with good stock, simmer for several hours, strain, skim, boil up again and add enough gelatine to make a brown jellied gravy. Used with roast poultry.

CHERRY SAUCE—Sweet, butter sauce, containing cherries that have been stewed with port wine and sugar, then rubbed through a sieve. Used for sweet entrées.

CHEVREUIL SAUCE—Into one-third part Espagnole sauce, one-third tomato sauce and one-third stock, add a little thyme, a bunch of parsley, two or three bay leaves, some minced fried shallots, a spoonful of white pepper, some tarragon vinegar and butter; reduce it to one-half of its original bulk, strain, finish with currant jelly, Harvey sauce and port wine. Used with roebuck and venison, roasted, filleted, braised, etc.

CHILI SAUCE

•

Makes about 6 cups

A tasty sauce to be used as a condiment. Serve on the side with omelets or with roasted or grilled meats.

3 fresh green Anaheim
   peppers (found in
   most supermarkets)

2 green sweet bell peppers

1 red sweet bell pepper

1 fresh jalepeño pepper

2 tablespoons chopped
   parsley

3 cloves garlic, peeled and
   chopped

2 cups Chicken Stock
   (page 153)

2 tablespoons
   Worcestershire sauce

$^{1}/_{2}$ cup dry red wine

1 tablespoon tomato paste

$^{1}/_{2}$ teaspoon salt

$^{1}/_{4}$ teaspoon freshly ground
   black pepper

Pinch of cayenne pepper

Core and coarsely chop the peppers.

In a 4- to 6-quart pot, add the peppers along with the parsley, garlic, and Chicken Stock. Simmer, covered, $1^{3}/_{4}$ hours. Pour the mixture into a food processor and purée. Return the purée to the pot. Add the remaining ingredients and simmer, covered, for 1 hour longer.

C.W.

CHILI SAUCE—Chop together six tomatoes, four green peppers, one onion, add them to a pint of white wine vinegar, with one teaspoon of sugar and a little salt, simmer for one hour, strain, bottle. Used as a table condiment.

CHILI SAUCE—Into a good Béchamel sauce, work some minced red peppers, tomatoes, shallots and minced parsley, finish with melted butter, catawba wine and lime juice. Good with veal cutlets, pork tenderloins, boneless pigs' feet, stewed catfish, lamb fries, fricadelles, broiled beef palates, pickled lamb tongues.

CLAREMONT SAUCE—Minced onions fried in oil, drained, then added to a thick veal gravy. Good with roast veal.

CLARET SAUCE—A foaming sauce of grated lemon rind, powdered

cinnamon, eggs, sugar and claret, whipped over a slow fire to boiling point. Used with puddings and sweet entrées.

COLBERT SAUCE—Into a pint of Espagnole, work in a spoonful of meat glaze, a little cayenne, lemon juice and chopped parsley, make very hot, but do not boil, then very gradually beat in a cupful of melted butter. Used with broiled meats, and most cutlets.

COURT-BOUILLON SAUCE—Into a butter sauce that has been made from the stock of boiled fish, add some rings of boiled onions and chopped parsley. Used with boiled codfish, boiled haddock, braised eels, boiled rockfish, boiled plaice, boiled weakfish, boiled red snapper, and boiled salmon trout.

CRAPAUDINE SAUCE—Take equal quantities of Espagnole and tomato sauces, combine them, then add some minced gherkins, shallots, chives, olives and capers, a little mustard, tarragon vinegar, minced mushrooms and a glass of sherry wine. Used with braised brisket of beef, broiled pork chops, frog legs, boiled calf's head, broiled pigeons, fried saddles of rabbit, calf's liver sauté, braised fillets of hare, broiled opossum, braised turtle fins, and venison.

CREOLE SAUCE—Into a good tomato sauce, work in some chopped blanched sweet peppers, minced fried shallots, a little Madeira sauce and Madeira wine. Used with scallops of fillet of beef, ragout of beef, chicken sauté, pork rissoles,

honeycomb tripe cut in finger lengths and stewed down rich in it, catfish steak sauté, tomatoes stuffed with crab meat, fried oysters, timbales of spaghetti, boiled spaghetti with minced ham made hot in it, broiled pork kidneys and lamb fries, pork tenderloins, fried spareribs, veal chops sautées, timbale of calf brains, croquettes of beef, beef sweetbreads sautées, minced mutton cutlets.

CREVETTE SAUCE—Into a cardinal sauce work some pieces of shrimps and anchovies. Used with boiled crimped codfish, boiled plaice and flounders, fillets of Spanish mackerel, boiled trout and whitefish, fried soles.

CUCUMBER SAUCE—Into a good butter sauce work a purée of cucumbers or some slices of cucumber fried with butter. Good for boiled salmon and trout.

CURRY SAUCE—Into a Velouté sauce, boil a ham knuckle for an hour, then remove and work in a liaison of egg yolks beaten with curry powder; simmer, strain. Used with pork chops, pork tenderloin, fried veal chops and cutlets, and tripe.

CZARINA SAUCE—Into some Espagnole work the juice of a lemon, some minced gherkins and seedless raisins, boil till the fruit is soft, then serve with boiled ox tongue.

CURACOA SAUCE—A butter syrup sauce containing curaçoa. Used

with puddings and some sweet entrées in the fritter line.

CUSTARD SAUCE—Boiling milk or cream poured to and whipped into half a pound of sugar and six beaten eggs to each quart of milk; flavored as desired, but generally with nutmeg or vanilla. Used with puddings and sweet entrées.

CRANBERRY SAUCE—Cranberries stewed with sugar till soft, then rubbed through a sieve. Used with roast turkey.

DIABLE SAUCE—Three tablespoonfuls of melted butter, three of meat glaze, one of sugar, half a cupful of mushroom catsup, and the same of white wine, juice of a lemon, and enough cayenne pepper to make it as hot as its name implies; thoroughly incorporate while making it hot, but do not allow it to boil. Used with broiled steaks, broiled kidneys, broiled ham steaks, broiled live lobster, broiled pork chops and spareribs.

DIABLE SAUCE—Another way of making is to take one-third stock and two-thirds of good Espagnole, and work into them some Worcestershire sauce, cayenne pepper and made mustard, then simmer and strain.

DIPLOMATE SAUCE—Into a good Béchamel sauce, work some crayfish butter and a little court-bouillon. Good for most boiled white fleshed fish.

DUCHESSE SAUCE—Into a pint of tomato sauce work in half a pint of lean cooked ham in small dice, half a cupful of white wine, a little glaze, bring to the boil, remove from the fire, and then beat in a half pint of Hollandaise sauce. Used with pork, veal and mutton chops, plain macaroni, Vienna steaks, pork tenderloin and spareribs, ham croquettes, fried tripe, epigramme of sweetbreads, braised breast of veal, roulade of mutton, fried boneless pigs' feet breaded, rechauffe of mutton, fried chicken.

D'UXELLES SAUCE—Into a Velouté sauce, work some white wine, minced mushrooms, grated tongue and chopped parsley . . . Or else use Béchamel sauce and work in minced parsley, shallots, mushrooms and grated ham. It is used for coating cutlets prior to their being breaded and fried.

EGG SAUCE—Into a butter sauce, work in some chopped hard boiled eggs and the juice of a lemon. Useful for all kinds of plain boiled fish.

ESPAGNOLE SAUCE—Two pounds of good cooking butter placed in the bottom of a large saûtoir; into it then place, chopped in good sized pieces, two ham knuckles, three shins of veal, a shin of beef, and let them fry brown; then add slices of carrots, onions, turnips, celery, parsley, thyme, marjoram, savory, bay leaves, cloves, allspice, peppers; when browned, add sufficient flour to form a roux. Let the flour brown also. Then moisten gradually with a rich clear brown stock; boil up and skim, then add plenty of tomatoes; boil and skim again, then add two or three chickens (old ones, useful for salad afterward) or roast fowl carcasses; simmer slowly for several hours, then strain off into a clean saûtoir; then add a gallon of consommé, and reduce rapidly till of a good consistency; strain off again and finish with good sherry wine. This is one of the grand stock sauces which form the basis of most of the brown sauces used. YOU CANNOT BE TOO PARTICULAR IN ITS PREPARATION, FOR IF THE FIRST PROCESS IS NOT SUCCESSFULLY EFFECTED, NO SUBSEQUENT CARE WILL REMEDY THE MISCHIEF.

FINE HERBS SAUCE—Sauté together with butter some minced parsley, shallots and mushrooms, season with a little pepper and nutmeg; after about five minutes, pour off the waste butter, and add a ladle of good Espagnole if for brown, or a ladle of good Velouté sauce if for white. Used with scallops of mutton, scallops of hare and rabbit, fried reed and rice birds, sauté of soles, brook trout baked in cases of paper spread with the sauce, roulade of beef, stuffed calf's heart, roulade of veal, veal chops and cutlets, broiled steaks, brains, sweetbreads, lamb fries.

FENNEL SAUCE—Into a good butter sauce, work a spoonful of chopped fennel leaves. Looks like parsley sauce. Used with boiled mackerel and boiled salmon.

FINANCIÈRE SAUCE—Into a quart of good Espagnole, work a little meat glaze, cayenne, a half pint of Madeira wine, a half pint of mushroom liquor or mushroom catsup, and a few minced mushrooms and

truffles. Used with roast or braised black game and grouse . . . boudins of game . . . sautéed fillets of fowls . . . larded and braised legs of fowls . . . boned, stuffed and braised saddle of lamb . . . paupiettes of ox palates . . . for heating a salmis of partridge . . . for a filling to raised pies of game, rabbits and quails . . . roast pheasant . . . boned, stuffed and braised quails . . . larded and braised fillets of rabbits . . . braised sweetbreads . . . turkey stuffed with veal forcemeat and roasted . . . veal chops larded and braised . . . larded and braised fricandeau of veal . . . larded and braised woodcocks.

FLEMISH SAUCE—(1) Into a butter sauce, work a little grated nutmeg, chopped parsley, tarragon vinegar, and a liaison of yolk of eggs with a little mustard. (2) Make a quart of vegetable cream sauce, then take a cupful of the red part of carrot, mince it, boil till done, add it to the sauce, together with some chopped cucumber, pickles, parsley and grated horse radish. Used with boiled beef.

FUMET SAUCE—Into a good Espagnole, boil some game carcasses, strain and finish with port wine. Used with roast game.

GENEVOISE SAUCE—Into a good Espagnole, add a little grated ham, carrots, minced onions, a few bay leaves, cloves, a clove of garlic, some thyme and parsley, boil fifteen minutes, add some claret wine, strain, and finish by beating in anchovy essence and butter to taste. Used with braised eels, baked pike, broiled salmon, broiled red snapper, fricandeau of sturgeon, baked trout, baked whitefish, brook trout, braised sheephead, baked pickerel, baked Spanish mackerel, baked and stuffed bluefish, blackfish sauté.

GÉNOISE SAUCE—Equal quantities of Espagnole and court-bouillon sauces boiled together for ten minutes with the addition of some port wine, ground mace, essence of anchovies and walnut catsup, then strain, finish with a little chopped parsley. Used with larded and braised eels, fillets of bluefish, roast carp, baked cod steak, roast eels, baked haddock, baked Spanish mackerel, baked mullet, braised pike and pickerel, baked salmon, braised sheephead, broiled fillets of red snapper, baked sturgeon, baked trout, baked or braised carp, boiled char, matelote of eels, broiled mackerel, boiled salmon steak, roast turbot and halibut.

GERMAN SAUCE—A foaming sauce, made of twelve eggs beaten fifteen minutes. Now place into a saûtoir half a pound of powdered sugar and a pint of Marsala wine, make hot, but do not boil, then beat in the eggs with the juice of a couple of lemons, whip till thick and frothy without boiling. A rich pudding sauce.

GIBLET SAUCE—The trimmed and finely shred gizzards, livers and hearts of poultry stewed tender and added to the thickened and strained gravy of roast poultry and served with it.

GODARD SAUCE—Fry some slices of ham, carrots and onions in butter till brown, then add a quart of good cider, simmer for half an hour, then add a can of mushrooms minced, and their liquor, reduce for ten minutes, then strain it into a quart of good Espagnole, and boil till creamy. Used with braised fowls, braised capons, braised turkey, roast ham, boned, stuffed and braised saddle of lamb, braised leg of mutton, carbonade of mutton.

GOLDEN SAUCE (SAUCE DOREÉ)—Half a pound of butter beaten till very creamy; into it dissolve half a pound of powdered sugar, now beat in the yolks of two eggs over the fire; when thick, work in half a pint of brandy and a grating of nutmeg. A good pudding sauce.

GOOSEBERRY SAUCE—Into Velouté sauce, work a purée of stewed green gooseberries. It is liked by many with boiled mackerel.

HAM SAUCE—Into a Madeira sauce, work some minced shallots and grated ham that have been fried together, finish with the juice of a lemon. Used with roast veal.

HANOVER SAUCE—Take chicken livers and boil them, then rub through the tamis, add cream sauce, lemon juice and a dash of cayenne, little salt, make hot but do not boil. Used with roast poultry.

HARROGATE SAUCE—After roasting veal and poultry, take the roasting pan, add some minced shallots and grated lemon rind, bake till shallots are brown, then add some flour and stir it with the residue in the pan from the roasting, moisten with stock to the proper consistency of sauce, then add some mushroom catsup, cayenne, claret wine and lemon juice, boil up, strain and skim. Used with roast veal and poultry.

HARD SAUCE—One pound of powdered sugar and eleven ounces of good butter worked together till creamy. Some add grated nutmeg. Used with plum pudding.

HARD SAUCE—Usually, hard sauce is refrigerated before using.

HAVRAISE SAUCE—Make a good butter sauce with strong broth from boiled fish, then beat in a liaison of egg yolks and cream. Good for all plain fish boiled.

HOLLANDAISE SAUCE—One cupful each of white vinegar and butter, a half cup of lemon juice, two cupfuls of chicken stock, little salt and cayenne, boil, then pour it, beating all the while, to a liaison of egg yolks till thick like custard. Used with boiled sea bass, boiled codfish and haddock, fillets of codfish, boiled eels, boiled plaice and flounders, boiled halibut, boiled kingfish, boiled perch, boiled rockfish, boiled salmon, boiled sheephead, boiled weakfish, boiled sturgeon, boiled whitefish, cauliflower, asparagus.

HORSERADISH SAUCE—Fresh grated horseradish boiled in white stock, seasoned with pepper and nutmeg, then is worked in a liaison of egg yolks and tarragon vinegar. MUST NOT BOIL after liaison is added. Used with boiled beef, broiled steaks . . . Another form for

roast beef is to add the grated root to thickened and strained roast beef gravy, adding a little Worcestershire sauce . . . Again, for cold roast beef, simply grated horseradish seasoned with salt and white vinegar. Some add to this a little cream sauce.

INDIENNE SAUCE—Braise together some ham trimmings, a few anchovies, onions, green apples, thyme and whole peppers, then add curry powder to taste, fill up with Velouté sauce, boil, add the juice of a lemon and a few beaten yolks, beat till creamy, then strain for use with pork chops, pork tenderloin, fried veal chops and cutlets, fried tripe, fried chicken, roast veal, fried calf's head, fried sweetbreads and lamb fries, cannelons of ox palates, fried pigs' feet, fried saddles of rabbit.

ITALIAN SAUCE, WHITE—Into a Velouté sauce, work some minced and fried shallots and mushrooms, chopped parsley and white wine. For ITALIAN SAUCE, BROWN, substitute Espagnole for Velouté, and Madeira for the white wine. Used with calf's head, boiled calf's tongue, broiled calf's liver, fried pigs' feet, attereaux of rabbit, broiled tripe, stuffed turkey legs, sautéed artichokes, braised black game and grouse, fried calf's feet, capilotade of chicken, boiled chicken, boudins of salmon, sautéed fillets of haddock, fried larks, rice and reed birds, roast pheasant, croquettes of rabbit, chicken and turkey, fried skate, boiled trout, fillets of turbot and halibut, scallops of veal and ham, breaded pork tenderloin.

JARDINIÈRE SAUCE—Take a small column cutter and cut out columns of carrots, white and yellow turnips; slice them quarter inch thick, add some very small button onions; fry all in butter with a little sugar; when brown, add a little stock and simmer till done, then drain them; when drained, place them into a rich Espagnole sauce, adding some cooked green peas, finely cut stringless beans and very small pieces of cauliflower. Used with braised beef, boudins of partridge, braised calf's liver, braised capon, braised duck, braised neck of mutton, larded and roast leg of lamb, boned and braised leg of mutton, braised ox cheek, boiled salted ox tongue, fricandeau of veal, roast breast of veal, boned, stuffed and braised breast of veal.

JOLIE-FILLE SAUCE—Half a pint of panada, two small onions sliced, two yolks of hard boiled eggs, one pound of veal or poultry meat, all boiled with one quart of Velouté sauce; when done, rub through the tamis, and bring to the sauce consistency with boiling milk; finish with a little chopped parsley. Used with boiled chicken, boiled capon, boiled turkey, sweetbreads, croquettes of veal, fowl, turkey, sweetbreads, lamb, and boudins of white meat.

LIVOURNAISE SAUCE—Into a mayonnaise work some pounded anchovies and chopped parsley. Used with cold fish.

LIVERNAISE SAUCE—Out of carrots, white and yellow turnips, scoop very small balls, steam them till barely done, then drain, and fry with a little butter and sugar to glaze them; then add them to equal parts of Espagnole and tomato sauces; simmer till done. Used with sautéed cutlets of veal, mutton, fricandeaus of veal, braised legs and saddles of mutton, fillets of beef, braised fowls and capon.

LYONNAISE SAUCE—Into a combined sauce of two-thirds tomato and one-third Espagnole, add rings of onions that have been lightly fried with butter and then drained. Used with sautéed fillets of fowls, broiled pork cutlets, roast leg or sparerib of pork, sautéed legs or saddles of rabbit.

LOBSTER SAUCE—Into a butter sauce work some lobster roe, pieces of lobster meat, lemon juice and a dash of cayenne. Used with croquettes of lobster, boiled haddock, cod, pike, whitefish, pickerel, plaice, sauté of red snapper, lobster cutlets, croquettes of shad roe.

MADEIRA SAUCE—Powdered sugar, Madeira wine, yolks of eggs and grated lemon rind beaten together over fire till thick. Used with puddings and sweet entrées.

MADEIRA SAUCE—Equal quantities of Espagnole and tomato sauces well flavored with Madeira wine. Used with steaks, cutlets, tenderloin of beef, broiled liver, fried chicken, broiled calf kidneys, braised fillets of hare, partridge, roast pigeon, roast prairie chicken, brochette or epigramme of rabbit, cutlets, croquettes and rissoles of rabbit, glazed sweetbreads, broiled turtle steaks, braised turtle fins, broiled veal cutlets, kromeskies of veal, broiled venison steak.

MAÎTRE D'HÔTEL SAUCE—Into melted butter add lemon juice, chopped parsley and a little grated nutmeg. Used with broiled steaks, fried calf brains, broiled boneless pigs' feet, broiled snipe, broiled sweetbreads, brochette of fowl and turkey, broiled woodcock and partridge, artichoke bottoms, broiled soft shell crabs, broiled frog legs, broiled lobster, broiled fresh mushrooms, broiled oysters; broiled fish such as sea bass, blackfish, fillets of striped bass, bluefish, cisco, haddock, finnan haddie, halibut, herring, kingfish, Spanish mackerel, fresh mackerel, salt mackerel, gray mullet, fillets of pike and pickerel, smelts, salmon trout, brook trout and whitefish, shad.

MATELOTE SAUCE—Into a butter sauce work some boiled button onions, scalded mussels and oysters, a flavor of garlic, essence of anchovies, lemon juice and a dash of cayenne. Used with boiled carp, crimped codfish, conger eel, skate, sturgeon, bluefish, baked codfish and boiled red snapper.

MATELOTE SAUCE—Equal quantities of veal broth and white wine, some tarragon, parsley, bay leaves, pepper and salt; boil ten minutes, add a little Velouté sauce and strain. Used with veal entrées, roast veal and boiled calf brains.

MAINTENON SAUCE—Braise some ham trimmings, chopped shallots, parsley and mushrooms with a little sugar and lemon juice; take out the ham, add some Velouté sauce, reduce, finish with a liaison of egg yolks, then strain. Used with croquettes of white fleshed meats and fowls, boudins of white meat, etc., and for heating pieces of cooked white meat, etc., for developing into entrées.

MAYONNAISE SAUCE—Take raw yolks of eggs, beat in a little olive oil; when it becomes like butter, add some salt, then a little more oil, then dry mustard and cayenne; then alternately oil, vinegar and lemon juice, till thick enough to spread. Used with salads, cold fish, and with aspic jelly to make aspic mayonnaise.

MILANAISE SAUCE—Into equal quantities of Velouté and Suprême sauces, work some Parmesan cheese. Used with boiled capon, calf's sweetbreads, boiled chicken, boiled leg of lamb, breaded mutton and veal cutlets, quenelles and boudins.

MINT SAUCE—Finely chopped green mint and a little grated orange rind placed in a tureen, vinegar brought to the boil with enough sugar to take off the rawness; poured to the chopped mint, etc.; served with roast lamb.

MUSHROOM SAUCE, WHITE—Into a Velouté or Béchamel sauce work a purée of mushrooms, and some sliced button mushrooms that have been lightly fried with butter; season with lemon juice and cayenne. Used with boiled chicken, capon, pheasant, partridge, sweetbreads, legs and saddles of rabbits, turkey wings, croquettes and rissoles of poultry, sweetbreads, veal, etc.

MUSHROOM SAUCE, BROWN—Into equal quantities of Espagnole and tomato sauces, work in some mushroom purée and sliced button mushrooms that have been fried with butter; a little chopped parsley, lemon juice and Madeira wine. Used with roast fillet of beef, braised sirloin of beef, broiled steaks, braised ox and calf tongues, scallops of calf's liver, braised veal, braised fowls, broiled pigeons and young rabbits, cromeskies of sweetbreads, broiled sweetbreads, broiled tripe, braised turkey legs, roulade of veal, stuffed shoulder of veal, fricandeau of veal, venison chops, broiled veal chops and cutlets, broiled chicken, Hamburger and Vienna steaks, braised ox heart, stuffed calf's and sheep hearts.

NANTAISE SAUCE—Into a white Ravigote sauce, work in some pounded lobster and coral. Used with fillets of fish such as soles, pompano, kingfish, bass, pickerel, red snapper, trout, whitefish, also with carp and shad roes.

NAPOLITAINE SAUCE—Into some Espagnole, work a little currant jelly, seedless raisins and port wine. Used with braised capon, braised sweetbreads, braised fresh ox tongue, braised venison, braised turtle fins.

NEAPOLITAN SAUCE—Braise some vegetables and bacon with garden herbs; when done, add equal quantities of Espagnole and tomato sauces, some game glaze and Madeira wine, simmer twenty minutes and then strain. Used with braised game chiefly.

NEAPOLITAN SAUCE—Into a good Espagnole, work some currant jelly, grated horseradish, grated ham, port wine and Harvey sauce. Used with braised meat.

NIÇEOISE SAUCE—Into some cold Velouté sauce work a liaison of hard boiled yolks of eggs rubbed through a sieve and mixed with oil vinegar, mustard, chopped chives and parsley. This is a good cold sauce for cold meats.

NIÇEOISE SAUCE—Things Niçoise should smack of the Mediterranean; Nice, after all, was once part of a separate kingdom that included parts of Italy. Use olive oil to lend authenticity to Fellows's sauce.

NORMANDE SAUCE—Equal quantities of court-bouillon and scalded oyster liquor thickened lightly with roux, then with a liaison of egg yolks and cream. Use with eels, filleted sole, plaice, trout, pike, pickerel, whitefish, halibut.

NONPAREIL SAUCE—Into a Hollandaise sauce work some sliced fried button mushrooms, minced truffles, lobster coral, lobster butter and some slices of hard boiled whites of eggs. Used with boiled white flesh fish.

ONION SAUCE, WHITE AND BROWN—Into a Béchamel sauce simmer minced onions till tender. Into equal quantities of Madeira and Espagnole sauces simmer till tender some minced fried onions. The white is generally used with boiled mutton, and the brown with roast and braised mutton.

ORANGE SAUCE—Into a brown poultry thickened and strained gravy, simmer till tender some shredded orange peel and finish with the juice of an orange. Used with roast and braised ducks.

OYSTER SAUCE—Into a sauce Poulette, work some scalded and cut up oysters, also some of the scalded and strained oyster liquor. Used with boiled white flesh fish, boiled capon, boiled chicken and boiled turkey.

PARSLEY SAUCE—Into a butter sauce, work some chopped parsley. Used with plain boiled fish, boiled chicken, calf's head; dipping cutlets of meat and fowl in before breading; also for mixing in with foods in preparing various entrées.

PARSLEY SAUCE—Alternatively, cream 2 or 3 tablespoons of minced fresh parsley into a stick of butter and refrigerate. This compound butter is a simple way to give a nice, glazed appearance to broiled or grilled meats and poultry.

PASCALINE SAUCE—Take some thin white Italian sauce and raw egg yolks with the juice of a lemon, simmer till creamy, strain, add some chopped and blanched parsley. Used with boiled poultry, sweetbreads, for reheating entrées of the same, calf's head, calf brains, pigs' feet, turkey wings, grenadins of veal.

PERIGUEUX SAUCE—Into a Madeira sauce work some minced and fried shallots, a little meat glaze, anchovy butter, sliced truffles and Madeira wine. Used with fillets of beef, sweetbreads, croquettes of

poultry and game, stuffed pheasant legs, quenelles of turtle, cromeskies of veal, braised small game birds, roast black game, boudins of poultry, carp stewed in wine and drained, fried fillets of hare and rabbit, roast turkey, roast pheasant, larded and roasted pork, veal cutlets, filleted woodcock.

PIQUANTE SAUCE—Minced pickles, shallots, olives, capers, a spoonful each of lemon juice and caper vinegar, mixed into a Madeira sauce, simmered for a few minutes and served with boiled beef, pigs' feet, calf's head, boiled tongue, calf's liver, carbonade of mutton, fried or broiled young pigeons, pork chops and pork tenderloin, braised venison, venison rissoles, broiled and fried tripe, antelope, bear, venison and buffalo steaks.

PORTUGUESE SAUCE—Reduce with half a pint of sherry wine, a bay leaf, thyme, mace, peppercorns, cloves, for ten minutes, then add half a pint of Espagnole and half that quantity of consommé; let the whole boil slowly till of the required consistency, skim, then strain and use with braised fillet of beef.

POIVRADE SAUCE—Fry together with butter of a light brown color a diced carrot, diced onion and a head of celery, a slice of lean ham diced, some thyme, parsley, blade of mace, bay leaf, and a few bruised peppercorns; then moisten with half a pint of sherry and the same of white vinegar. Reduce to half its volume, then add a ladle of Espagnole and a little consommé; boil up, skim, strain, and use with braised mutton, braised roebuck, cannelons of ox palates, sauté of rabbits and hares, roast young rabbit, broiled legs and saddles of rabbit; legs and saddles of cooked rabbit, cooled, then breaded and fried; larded fillets of venison, venison chops and braised venison.

Another way of making Poivrade sauce is to take equal quantities of Espagnole and tomato sauces, work in some minced shallots, a bunch of parsley, bay leaves, a tablespoon of white pepper to each quart, along with two ounces of butter and two tablespoonfuls of vinegar; reduce to half its volume, strain, then finish with a little Harvey sauce, port wine and red currant jelly.

POLONAISE SAUCE—Make a sauce with veal broth and boil in it some grated horseradish, juice of a lemon, chopped fennel or parsley leaves and a little sugar; season with salt and nutmeg, strain and use with roast veal.

PAPILLOTE SAUCE—Fry together for five minutes slowly a slice of bacon scraped, two scraped onions and two cloves of garlic, and some minced mushrooms, then moisten with a quart of Madeira sauce, boil up, finish with chopped parsley. Used with cutlets of food that are first sautéed, cooled, dipped in sauce, then placed in cutlet papers and slowly broiled, such as salmon cutlets, mutton cutlets, partridge cutlets, halves of boned squabs, cutlets of veal.

POULETTE SAUCE—Make a white sauce with strong chicken broth, then work in a liaison of egg yolks and cream; strain, finish with the juice of a lemon and some chopped parsley. Used with artichoke bottoms, blanquette of lamb fries and lamb sweetbreads, boudins of poultry, boiled capon, boiled chicken, boiled turkey, entrée of calf or lamb tails, inch lengths of stewed cucumbers, eels that have been stewed with a little wine, lamb's feet simmered in white broth till tender, scallops of sweetbreads, scallops of veal, boiled calf's head, stewed pigs' feet, stewed turtle fins, stewed breast of veal, lamb and mutton.

PROVENÇALE SAUCE—Four hard boiled egg yolks, four anchovies, a spoonful of capers, a little chopped tarragon, parsley, chervil, a clove of garlic, a seasoning of salt, pepper, a wine glass of olive oil and half of vinegar. Pound the whole, then rub through a tamis; finish with a little chopped parsley and lemon juice. Used with broiled eels, but mostly with fish salads.

PROVENÇALE SAUCE—Stew together for five minutes, four bruised cloves of garlic, some thyme, parsley stalks, spoonful of capers, bay leaf, and the pulp of a lemon with a little olive oil; then moisten with a ladle of Espagnole, add a pinch of pepper and a piece of glaze. Let the whole simmer for a quarter of an hour, then rub through the tamis; finish with a little anchovy butter. Used with roast fillet of beef, calf's brains fried in batter, carp stewed in white wine, braised ducks, braised leg of mutton; braised cutlets of mutton, cooled, then spread with a stuffing on one side only, reheated and served; braised boned ox cheek, salmis of partridge, scallops of sweetbreads, scallops of veal.

PROVENÇALE SAUCE—Into some Espagnole work some minced fried

POIVRADE SAUCE

·

Makes about 3 cups

This unusual sauce is slightly sweet and sour. It is very versatile and can be served with all types of meat. Make no substitutes for the Beef Stock called for in this delicious sauce.

1 tablespoon olive oil

$^1/_2$ cup peeled and diced carrots

2 cloves garlic, peeled and sliced

$^1/_2$ cup peeled and diced yellow onions

$^1/_2$ cup diced celery

$^1/_3$ cup diced good ham

$^1/_2$ teaspoon dried thyme, whole

1 tablespoon chopped parsley

Pinch of ground mace

1 bay leaf

$^1/_4$ teaspoon freshly ground black pepper

1 cup dry sherry

$^1/_2$ cup distilled white vinegar

4 cups Beef Stock (page 48)

1 tablespoon tomato paste

Freshly ground black pepper to taste

Heat a 4-quart pot, add the oil, and sauté the carrots, garlic, onions, celery, and ham. Cook until the onions are almost clear. Add the remaining ingredients, except the Beef Stock and tomato paste. Cook and reduce by half. Add the Beef Stock and tomato paste and simmer gently, uncovered, for 45 minutes. Stir occasionally. The sauce should reduce and thicken nicely. Season with additional freshly ground black pepper to taste. Pour through a fine strainer before serving.

C.W.

mushrooms, onions, tomatoes and a clove of garlic. Used with braised beef.

RAVIGOTE SAUCE—Into a Velouté sauce work a purée of parsley and tarragon leaves, some minced fried shallots and a little white vinegar. Used with calf brains, ox piths fried in batter, roast partridge, skinned perch boiled in white wine, fillets of turbot, fillets of halibut and other white fleshed fish.

RAVIGOTE SAUCE—Into a mayonnaise work a purée of chives, chervil, parsley, tarragon and shallots. Used with cold meat and meat salads.

RAVIGOTE SAUCE—Take a small teacup and put in a third each of tarragon vinegar, chili vinegar and Harvey sauce; pour the cupful thus obtained into a small saûtoir and boil it down to half the quantity, then add half a pint of butter sauce and a ladlespoon of mixed chopped chives, chervil, parsley and tarragon. Used with boiled poultry and fillets of fish.

REGENCY SAUCE—Braise some ham trimmings, shallots and onions, then add equal quantities of chicken glaze, Espagnole and tomato sauces, boil slowly for twenty minutes then strain and use with braised meat, game and poultry.

REGENCY SAUCE—Cut an eel of a pound weight into thin slices and boil gently with a pint of claret, adding cloves, mace, thyme, bay leaf, carrot, mushrooms, an onion and a little salt, for half an hour, then rub the whole through a tamis. Put the essence then into a saûtoir and add a ladleful of Espagnole; boil, skim, finish by working in some essence of truffles, anchovy butter, nutmeg, lemon juice and a knob of sugar. This sauce is admirably adapted for every sort of colored fleshed fish.

RAIFORT SAUCE—Into a Velouté sauce work some grated horseradish and a little white vinegar. Used with fresh boiled beef, salt beef and fresh boiled ox tongues; also some like it with steaks.

RAIFORT SAUCE—Raifort is the French word for "horseradish."

REMOULADE SAUCE—Pounded hard boiled yolks of eggs rubbed through a sieve, mixed with olive oil, vinegar, dry mustard, minced garlic, chopped parsley and parsley juice. Used with frog legs, cold meat and meat salads.

REFORM SAUCE—Another form or name of Poivrade sauce (which see).

RICHELIEU SAUCE—Into a white game sauce, work some minced fried onions and a little white wine. Used with game birds.

ROE SAUCE—Into a butter sauce, work a purée of fish roes, using the soft roe or milt. Used with plain boiled fish.

ROYAL SAUCE—Into a Velouté sauce, work a purée of chicken and bread panada; finish with a liaison of egg yolks and cream. Used with boiled capon, boiled chicken, sweetbreads, boiled turkey, boiled partridge, pheasant, cushion of veal.

ROBERT SAUCE—Minced fried onions, dry mustard, a little meat glaze and white wine mixed into Espagnole or other brown sauce. Used with roast pork, broiled or fried pork tenderloins, pork chops, and many entrées of pork.

RUSSIAN SAUCE—(1) Into a Velouté sauce work some grated horseradish and vinegar, then work in a liaison of egg yolks and cream. (2) Into a Velouté sauce work some grated horseradish, vinegar, sugar, white wine, then some lightly fried grated ham, minced shallots and garden herbs. Used with boiled beef and tongues. (3) Made mustard, tarragon vinegar, salt, pepper, sugar, and grated horseradish stirred together. Used with cold meat.

RUSSIAN SAUCE—In the third of these sauces you can see the antecedent of today's Russian dressing, a mixture of mayonnaise and ketchup.

SAGE SAUCE—Good for roast pork and goose. Make a brown gravy in the pan with the residue of the roasting, add some chopped sage leaves, simmer for 15 minutes, then strain and skim.

STE MENEHOULD SAUCE—Make a cream sauce and boil in it some minced onions till tender, strain, then add some chopped parsley and minced mushrooms, simmer for ten minutes, skim, then use with boiled pigs' feet, boiled calf's head and feet, calf's brains and ears, salt pigs' head, ox piths and ox palates.

SCALLOP SAUCE—Into a good butter sauce, work some cut cooked scallops and their strained and skimmed liquor. Used with plain boiled fish.

SHALLOT SAUCE—Into a sauce made from the residue of roasting poultry, game or suckling pig, work some butter and minced shallots that have been stewed in sherry wine, and use with the meats mentioned.

SICILIAN SAUCE—Take some veal stock and boil in it a ham knuckle, a head of celery, a clove of crushed garlic, the peel of a lemon, a few cloves and crushed coriander seeds with a bay leaf; reduce to one half, add a little roux and white wine, strain, skim, and use with roast or boiled poultry.

SHRIMP SAUCE—Into a good butter sauce, work some cut shrimps, lemon juice, cayenne pepper and anchovy essence. Used with boiled fish, fish croquettes, and many fish entrées.

SORREL SAUCE—Into a Velouté sauce work a purée of sorrel. Used with boiled beef.

SOÛBISE SAUCE—Boiled onion pulp worked into a Suprême sauce. Used with boiled mutton . . . roast and braised black game and grouse . . . boudins of poultry . . . braised legs and necks of mutton . . . larded and braised pheasants and partridges . . . larded and roast neck of pork . . . larded and braised sweetbreads.

SUPRÊME SAUCE—Make a rich Velouté sauce with reduced chicken liquor, then finish with pure cream. Used with delicate entrées such as boudins of breasts of chicken, lamb sweetbreads, and delicate white fleshed fish . . . sautéed fillets of chicken, garnished with scallops of tongue . . . boiled capon . . . boiled prairie hen . . . sweetbread and chicken patties, and vol-au-vents.

SULTANA SAUCE—Into a good game sauce, work some seedless raisins, simmer till tender, finish with port wine and use with roast game in general.

TARTARE SAUCE—Into a mayonnaise sauce work some finely chopped parsley, gherkins, chives, capers and shallots. Used with breaded and fried fillets of chicken and capon . . . frog legs . . . sweetbreads . . . eels cut in finger lengths . . . broiled salmon steak . . . fried calf brains . . . fried tripe . . . fried butter fish.

TOULOUSE SAUCE—One pint of Hollandaise sauce, half cup of white wine, half cup of minced mushrooms, little chicken glaze, mix together, then bring to the simmer, without breaking or curdling. Used with boiled and stewed poultry . . . sweetbreads.

TOMATO SAUCE—Take equal quantities of good stock and tomatoes, a veal and a ham shank, a few herbs, sliced vegetables, and bay leaves; two or three cloves of garlic are optional; boil all till vegetables are done, thicken with roux, strain, add a little sugar. Used with broiled steaks, chops, veal and pork chops, pork tenderloin . . . fried sweetbreads and lamb fries . . . broiled calf kidneys . . . fried chicken breaded or in batter . . . epigramme of sweetbreads . . . quenelles of turkey . . . grenadins of veal . . . fried or broiled tripe . . . hamburger steaks . . . fried or broiled pigs' feet . . . fried ciscoes . . . codfish steaks . . . fried haddock and halibut . . . filleted pike and muskalonge . . . fried smelts . . . broiled weakfish, whitefish and trout . . . broiled and fried oysters . . . venison chops and steaks, etc. etc., and is used in conjunction with other sauces.

TORTUE OR TURTLE SAUCE—Equal parts of tomato and Espagnole sauces, into which work some sliced mushrooms, garden herbs and sherry wine, the grated rind and juice of a lemon, and a few minced shallots. Used with calf's head.

TRIANON SAUCE—Equal parts of Bearnaise and reduced tomato sauces carefully blended together. Used with broiled steaks, sweetbreads, calf brains, etc.

VELOUTÉ SAUCE—Into some strong chicken and veal broth boil a small piece of pickled pork, a small bunch of garden herbs, a few carrots and onions, a little salt, sugar and pepper, simmer slowly till the pork and vegetables are done, then thicken with white roux; simmer gently, taking off the fat and scum as it rises till of a smooth velvet appearance; then strain through a hair sieve. It is used as a basis for other sauces.

VENITIENNE SAUCE—Court-bouillon thickened with white roux, simmered and skimmed; add chopped parsley and lemon juice; finish with a liaison of egg yolks and cream. Used with boiled fish.

TOMATO SAUCE

•

Makes about 2½ quarts

Fellows went so far as to simmer fresh pork hocks in his tomato sauce. The result is a sauce rich in flavor and useful in the kitchen for many recipes, including over pasta. This would have been in his restaurant refrigerator at all times. It works well.

1½ pounds fresh pork hock, sawed into 1-inch pieces

2 stalks celery, finely chopped

2 medium yellow onions, peeled and finely chopped

3 cloves garlic, peeled and crushed

¼ cup chopped parsley

4 cups Chicken Stock (page 153)

5 pounds very ripe tomatoes, cored and coarsely chopped

½ cup dry red wine

1 teaspoon dried basil, whole

1 tablespoon tomato paste

Salt and freshly ground black pepper to taste

In an 8-quart pot, combine the pork, celery, onions, garlic, parsley, and Chicken Stock. Bring to a boil and simmer, covered, for 2 hours. Remove the pork and save the meat for another use. Add the remaining ingredients, except the salt and pepper, to the pot. Simmer, covered, for 1 hour. Uncover and simmer for 30 minutes more, stirring occasionally, to desired consistency. Salt and pepper to taste.

C.W.

VERJUICE SAUCE—Boil some green grapes in Espagnole till soft, then strain. Used with roast ducks.

VERTE-PRE SAUCE—Into a Velouté or white Ravigote sauce work a purée of chives, spinach and tarragon leaves. Used with boiled eels.

VINAIGRETTE SAUCE—Minced shallots, chopped parsley, oil, vinegar and a little salt and cayenne carefully blended together and used with cold pigs' feet and pickled lamb tongues.

YORKSHIRE SAUCE—Into some Espagnole, work a little currant jelly, port wine, orange juice and finely shredded boiled orange peel. Used with roast ham.

SAUERKRAUT—A preparation of cabbage (see CABBAGE).

VELOUTÉ SAUCE

•

Makes 6 cups

This basic sauce is used in many recipes. It is also used in the preparation of other, more complex sauces. Do not be put off by its French name. It is simply chicken sauce.

6 tablespoons butter

$^1/_2$ cup all-purpose flour

6 cups Chicken Stock
(page 153)

Salt and freshly ground
white pepper to taste

In a small frying pan, melt the butter. Stir in the flour and cook over low heat to form a roux, or thick paste. Do not brown.

In a saucepan, bring the Chicken Stock to a boil. Using a wire whisk, whip in the roux, until lump free. Cover and simmer gently for 30 minutes, stirring occasionally. Salt and white pepper to taste.

C.W.

SCALLOPS—A broad flat shelled fish, white in color, with pink gills. Used in many ways as oysters; such as "sautéed," "scalloped," "fried in batter," "breaded and fried," "baked and served on the half shell," "stewed" and in soup.

SCALLOPS—Creamy and almost translucent, the best scallops offer the most complex flavors and enjoyable textures of any mollusk. When they are perfectly fresh—which is really the only time to eat them—they should be treated gently and served in delicate, subtle preparations.

Four types of scallops are available in this country: The sea scallop, or giant scallop (Pecten magellanicus), which can live for twenty years and grow to be the size of a dinner plate, is the largest, averaging ten to thirty per pound. It is fished off the northeastern coast, from Labrador to the mid-Atlantic states. Briny, sweet, and tender, sea scallops are available year-round.

The bay scallop (Pecten irradians) is much more rare. Cork-shaped and fairly small (up to one hundred per pound), they are the sweetest, richest, and most flavorful scallops you can buy and, when strictly fresh, are excellent raw. The fishing ground for bay scallops is small, ranging from Long Island (where there are few left) to Cape Cod, and the season is limited to mid-winter.

Calico scallops (Aequipecten gibbus) are the familiar, eraser-sized scallops usually sold in supermarkets; it takes as many as 250 of these to make a pound. Fished off the Atlantic coast and farmed throughout the world, these are not bad tasting, but their diminutive size makes them easy to overcook. And, once overcooked, their texture is rubbery.

The pink scallop (*Chylmis hericius*), also called singing scallop, is a relatively rare mollusk taken from the Puget Sound. Pink scallops are usually sold in their pearly shells and steamed like clams or mussels. They are rarely seen outside of the Pacific Northwest.

SCRAPPLE—Generally termed "Philadelphia scrapple" is pigs' head brawn with corn meal boiled together, then set in blocks; afterwards cut in slices and fried for breakfast or supper.

SCRAPPLE—You can make scrapple with just about any meat, and it is an interesting alternative to sausage because it is far more "filler"—in this case, cornmeal—than it is meat. To make it, scraps of meat are mixed with cooked cornmeal and seasonings and poured into a loaf pan. Once the mixture has become firm, it is sliced and sautéed. Remember that any pieces of meat, including leftovers, can be used (turkey scrapple is a great post-Thanksgiving dish).

SEA KALE—A vegetable resembling in appearance a head of celery. It is cooked in lengths like asparagus, boiled and served with butter, Hollandaise or Espagnole sauces; also after being boiled and cooled, is cut up and mixed with endive and lettuce and used as a salad with French dressing.

SEA KALE—Once popular in Northern Europe, sea kale (*Crambe maritima*) is rarely seen anywhere anymore, a victim of worldwide coastal development. It is similar to Swiss chard and bok choy in appearance and use.

SEMOLINA—Name given to a preparation of wheatlike farina. It is used in the making of puddings; as a soup and sauce thickening; also mixed with pressed bread in the preparation of sausages, as it takes up more fat and water.

SEMOLINA—Like flour, semolina is made from the endosperm of grains (usually wheat). The difference is in its texture: Flour is a powder, and semolina (which is sometimes called farina) is more of a meal. Cornmeal is, in effect, corn semolina. When cooked, semolina is lighter and less pasty. Semolina can be used alone or in combination with flour in pasta, gnocchi (pasta made with potato flour), pizza, and bread; it is featured in several Indian and Middle Eastern desserts.

SHAD—Name of one of our best fish. To be broiled it should be split, back and rib bones removed, seasoned with olive oil, salt and pepper, then placed between the wire hinged broiler, cooked over a medium fire, served with maître d'hôtel butter, and garnished with parsley and quartered lemon.

SHAD—Do not try Fellows's maneuver unless you have an expert handy, for shad is among the most difficult fish to fillet. In fact, some shad filleters in New England jealously guard their techniques, passing them down from generation to generation.

There are several fish called shad, although *Alosa sapidissima*—the second word means "most delicious"—is the best known. These days shad is more appreciated for its ROE than its meat, but these members of the herring family were an eastern staple before the arrival of Europeans. (Shad was introduced to western rivers in the late nineteenth century, where it remains a popular sporting fish.) Like SALMON, the population of shad declined as inland waters became polluted, but shad is a hardier fish and was never actually endangered.

Shad have rich, buttery flesh and countless tiny bones. When they are not filleted, shad are often cooked for hours over low heat, during which time many of the bones actually dissolve. The French stuff shad with SORREL, which contains such a high percentage of oxalic acid that it, too, does away with many bones. Fillets are traditionally cooked by planking—nailing the meat to a wooden board and standing it in front of a hot fire. Broiling, not quite so exciting, also works well.

PLANKED SHAD—The fish cleaned, split, bones removed, made fast to the plank, cooked under a salamander or in a quick oven; served on the plank, with maître d'hôtel butter.

BAKED SHAD—Take a full sized shad, clean trim, score the sides, wipe dry, then season with salt; place them in a buttered pan and cover the fish with small pieces of butter; put in a medium oven and cook for fifteen minutes, then pour over the fish a small ladle of stock, some tabasco sauce and a cupful of cream; return to oven and bake till nicely done; then lift the fish on to the serving platter, garnish with maître d'hôtel potatoes, pour the strained and skimmed sauce over the fish and serve.

BOILED SHAD—Clean, trim and score the sides of the fish, place on the drainer of fish kettle, cover the fish with boiling water, add a little salt, simmer till done (about thirty minutes), lift, drain; serve with either caper or lobster sauce, and garnish with small boiled potatoes.

FRIED SHAD—Fillet the fish into serving portions, season with salt and pepper, dip into beaten eggs containing flour enough to make a soft batter, then fry a delicate golden color in deep fat; drain; serve with chips and lemon.

BAKED STUFFED SHAD—Scale and trim the fish, split down the belly and withdraw the bones; season with salt and pepper; stuff with forcemeat made of a pound of whitefish pounded in the mortar with half a pound of soaked and squeezed dry bread, quarter pound of butter, four yolks of raw eggs, juice of a lemon, chopped parsley, salt and pepper to taste. When stuffed, sew up the opening, score the sides, place in buttered pan, brush over with melted butter, bake till done; serve whole or in portions with maître d'hôtel sauce and a garnish of fancy potatoes.

SHADDOCK—A dessert fruit from the West Indies (see GRAPE FRUIT).

SHAD ROE—Keep the roes whole, lay them in cold water for an hour, trim, wipe dry; then season with salt and pepper, roll in flour, fry in lard; serve with chip potatoes, a slice of bacon, and quartered lemon . . . Also boiled and served with cream sauce and garnished with Hollandaise potatoes . . . Breaded whole if small, or blanched, split, then breaded and fried; served with Parisienne potatoes, lemon and parsley . . . Broiled and served with bacon, garnished with Julienne potatoes and lemon . . . Made into croquettes and served with lobster sauce . . . Also blanched, mixed with Hollandaise sauce and scalloped.

SHAD ROE—The key in cooking shad roe is in keeping the heat low and the cooking time short; overcooking results in tough, dry, individual eggs. Shad roe carefully poached in butter, however, is a luxuriously rich dish (so rich, in fact, that it's more a once-a-year treat). Shad roe can also be broiled with shad (though for a shorter time than the fish itself); complete that dish with a few slices of bacon. Traditional cooking methods call for 3 to 5 minutes of poaching in water, followed by brisk browning in butter.

SHALLOT—Name of a small onion, very mild in flavor. Used in the preparation of delicate sauces and soups.

SHALLOT—Countless French dishes, including the incomparable BÉARNAISE sauce, cannot be made without shallots, and many people—Americans too—argue that the perfect vinaigrette must include them. The shallot is a mature onion, (not a green one as some cookbooks suggest), lavender, gray, or, less frequently, yellow in color. It is used raw or gently cooked, never browned, for intense heat spoils its sweet, piercing, and wonderful flavor. We think the flavor of a shallot is a cross between garlic and onion.

SHEEPSHEAD—Name of one of our seafish, so called on account of the shape of its mouth being like that of a sheep; also its having two similar rows of teeth. It is boiled and served with caper sauce and garnished with Hollandaise potatoes . . . Baked and served with Piquante sauce, garnished with Parisienne potatoes . . . Broiled and served with Venitienne butter, garnished with Saratoga chips . . . Sautéed and served with brown Italian sauce, garnished with Duchesse potatoes . . . Braised and served with Creole sauce, garnished with small potato croquettes.

SHEEPSHEAD—See PORGY.

SHERRY—Name of a Spanish wine. Used with dinner service, in making cobblers, jellies, sauces, etc.

SHERRY—Though most Americans think of this fortified Spanish wine as universally sweet, sherry runs the gamut, from the bone-dry fino to the thick Pedro Ximénez (PX), which some have likened (favorably) to prune juice.

Sherry is produced in three Andalusian towns: Jerez (pronounced "heh-RETH," which somehow became "sherry" in English), Sanlúcar de Barrameda, and Puerto de Santa Maria. The soil in this area is light and chalky, the sun is strong, and the sea air moderating; the combination is excellent for the Palomino grape, which is used, alone, to produce dry to moderately sweet sherry. With the sweet PX grape, it makes the extremely sweet cream sherries.

Sherry is a blended wine; small amounts of liquid from many different barrels at different stages of development are combined to produce a consistent product (this is known as the *solera* system). Thus vintages are not only unimportant, they are nonexistent, and most producers' wines taste pretty much the same from year to year.

As to the characteristics of the different sherries: Finos, as mentioned, are light and delicate. They are best served chilled, in small amounts (their alcohol content may be as high as 17 percent), as an aperitif. Manzanilla, also dry, are even lighter, and it is said that they taste of the sea breezes of Sanlúcar.

Amontillados are softer, richer wines that contain a bit more alcohol and are traditionally older blends (visitors to the *bodegas* of Jerez are often treated to a glass of 80-year-old amontillado). These and the slightly sweet, fuller-bodied olorosos are best served just below room temperature.

Sweet cream sherries are traditionally served at tea, in the morning, or on the rocks before dinner.

SHORTBREAD—A name given to a sort of cake, much used by the Scotch people.

SHRIMP—Name of a thin shelled fish, used generally after being boiled, trimmed and shelled; always to be had in cans. The Barataria shrimp in cans are as good as can be purchased. Made into salads, sauces, omelets, patties, bouchées, croquettes, in the preparation of appetizers, etc.

SHRIMP—Thousands of species of shrimps are caught and grown all over the world, in both fresh and salt water. Some are tiny—two hundred to the pound—while others are huge, weighing one half pound each. Americans favor those that fall in the middle, and a couple of dozen varieties grace our shores in numbers substantial enough to warrant commercial fishing. The species, for our purposes, are more or less interchangeable; we rarely notice the differences.

Most shrimps sold in supermarkets and fish stores come from the vast Gulf of Mexico fishery or, increasingly, from the Asian Pacific. They are caught and flash-frozen on huge ships and sold thawed; as long as the crustaceans have been well handled, their quality should be excellent. Smell them and poke them: If they smell good and are fairly firm, buy them.

Shrimps are highly perishable—as are most crustaceans—but fresh product can be found from time to time. In New England, for example, there are increasing quantities of Maine shrimps, a small, soft variety with outstanding flavor. They are best used for soups and sauces—they are too delicate for broiling or grilling—and can be sautéed.)

Shrimps need not be deveined before eating, and fewer and fewer people are bothering with this troublesome task, which has only cosmetic benefits. When it comes to cooking this versatile creature, no matter which method you choose, take care not to overcook it. For all but the largest shrimp, 3 minutes is usually enough time and 5 minutes is pushing it (shrimps with the shells on take a minute or two longer).

SMELT—Name of a small delicate fish which has the flavor of cucumbers. To be cooked is drawn from the gills, seasoned with salt, rolled in flour and sautéed with butter, or breaded and fried . . . Broiled; or run on skewers and broiled.

SMELT—We have several varieties of smelts in the United States; they are all small and some—such as those known as whitebait—are downright tiny. You eat them head, tail, skeleton, and all; they are full-flavored and fatty (one variety is so fatty that the Chinook Indians dried it for use as candles).

SNIPE—A small game bird; may be roasted, broiled, fried, made into boudins, pies, galantines, salmis.

SOLES—Name of a delicate flat fish. As there are few to be had in the United States the flounder and plaice is substituted.

SORREL—Name of a vegetable. Used in soups, sauces; served plain or mixed with spinach as a vegetable; puréed as spinach, and used as an accompaniment to veal, pork, fried sweetbreads, brains, etc.

SORREL—Cultivated sorrel (mostly *Rumex scutatus*) is an amazingly bright-tasting herb that is sometimes used as a vegetable. Although it should not be eaten in enormous quantities because of its high oxalic-acid content, sorrel makes an agreeable replacement for spinach in omelets and soups (some say it tastes like spinach with lemon juice), and for parsley in green sauces. Sorrel risotto is also excellent.

SOUBISE PURÉE—This can be made by incorporating sautéed and puréed onions into a Bechamel sauce or by mixing sautéed onions and cooked rice together before puréeing. It is served with meats.

SOUFFLÉ—Name given to a very light pasty preparation of meats, or sweets; of the omelet order.

SOUPS—See heading of any meat, etc., wanted; also CONSOMMÉS.

SPAGHETTI—An Italian solid paste like macaroni. Used in every way like macaroni; for recipes of which, see MACARONI.

SPINACH—A vegetable good for the stomach, because not only its own properties are absorbed but the life sustaining qualities of that with which it is prepared; for spinach from Greenwhich plain boiled and eaten as a greens may be all right; but to those who live at hotels, clubs, etc., it is prepared as a purée, richly endowed with cream, butter, gravies, etc., well seasoned with salt, pepper and nutmeg; and when used either as a vegetable, garniture, in an omelet, or as an accompaniment to roast or boiled ham, it is good.

SQUAB—Name given to a young pigeon. For recipes, see PIGEON.

SQUASH—A vegetable of the melon order, peeled, cut in pieces, plain boiled or mashed, then served as a vegetable; cut in slices and baked or steamed, then the pulp removed, mashed and used instead of pumpkin for pies.

SPINACH AND SAUSAGE TIMBALES

.

Serves 6

This recipe is similar to the dressing that I have enjoyed at every Thanksgiving dinner. Here I have added some egg so that the timbales set properly. This is a terrific side dish.

1 pound lean bulk pork
    sausage

1 tablespoon olive oil

1 tablespoon butter

2 cloves garlic, peeled and
    crushed

1 stalk celery, minced

1 medium yellow onion,
    peeled and minced

1 (10-ounce) package
    chopped frozen
    spinach, thawed

1/2 cup plain bread crumbs

2 eggs

Salt and freshly ground
    black pepper to taste

In a medium-sized frying pan, brown the sausage until crumbly. Drain the sausage of the fat, reserving the sausage, and return the pan to the burner. Add the oil, butter, garlic, celery, and onions. Sauté until the onions are clear.

Place the browned sausage in a mixing bowl. If the sausage is not crumbly enough, break it up with your hands. Squeeze the defrosted spinach dry with your hands and add to the sausage, along with the sautéed vegetables, the bread crumbs, and eggs. Using your hands, mix very well. Taste for salt and pepper.

Grease the insides of 6 timbale molds (approximately 2½ inches by 2 inches). Lightly pack the molds with the mixture. Place the timbales in a baking dish and fill with hot water a quarter of the way up the sides of the molds. Bake at 375°F for 30 to 35 minutes. Remove and cool slightly.

Run a knife around the inside edges of the molds and invert onto plates.

C.W.

SQUASH—The genus *Cucurbita* includes pumpkins, gourds, winter and summer squashes, cucumbers, melons, and a few other members, all of which have large, mostly white seeds and all of which grow in warm or moderate climates. They are popular garden vegetables, and some are popular in the kitchen as well. The most familiar squashes are zucchini (known as *courgettes* in France), summer squash (the English marrow), and a variety of winter squashes including acorn, butternut, Hubbard, pattypan, and so on. Summer squashes are best sautéed or grilled, although they are also excellent in sauces; winter squashes are usually baked.

SQUIRREL—Either the red, gray or black, may be practically used in all the ways of spring chickens; and are relished too.

STILTON—Name of a prime English cheese (see CHEESE).

STRAWBERRIES—One of the choice table fruits eaten with cream and sugar; crushed and mixed into ices; made into tarts and pies, jellies, shortcakes, meringues, charlottes, etc.

STRAWBERRIES—Anyone who has ever had the experience of finding wild strawberries in a springtime meadow is never again satisfied with even the finest representative of the cultivated variety. ("Doubtless God could have made a better berry," wrote William Butler in the seventeenth century, "but doubtless God never did.")

Unfortunately, encountering a field of wild berries is not something to depend on, so most of us make do with the garden-grown varieties. These vary widely in quality: There are those you can pick yourself at local nurseries and orchards, and there are the cotton-textured ones shipped from California to the rest of the country every spring. Deep

red color is sometimes, but not always, an indication of flavor, and size rarely lends a clue; you must taste a representative strawberry to know whether to buy (or pick) a pint or a bushel.

There are several varieties of strawberries in the world, all of which grow in extreme latitudes, as far north, in fact, as 70 degrees, which is inside the Arctic Circle. Although they can be grown in much warmer climes—the large commercial crops in this country are from southern California and Florida—the plants are susceptible to attack by fungus when the weather is warm and humid (most Florida strawberries, especially, are routinely doused with fungicides).

STURGEON—Name of a large fish that is sold skinned as catfish are. Used baked and served with Remoulade sauce . . . larded as a fricandeau and served with bacon and mushroom sauce . . . braised with herbs and vegetables and served with the strained and skimmed braise . . . broiled in steaks and served with Piquante sauce . . . stuffed, baked and served with Bourgignotte sauce . . . boiled and served with Genevoise and Hollandaise sauces.

STURGEON—Like a SALMON, a stur- geon—whose eggs make the best CAVIAR—is anadromous in nature, born in rivers but living most of its life in the open sea. Although it is meaty, fatty, and fairly strong-flavored (it is frequently compared to veal), sturgeon is in fact a rather delicate creature, and its numbers have dwindled as human numbers have increased.

Increasingly, sturgeons are farmed, both for their eggs and

their meat. The fish are raised in tanks, primarily in California, to sizes of thirty pounds or more (wild beluga sturgeons grow to hundreds of pounds), with most of the fish harvested at half that weight.

Sturgeon is wonderful smoked or baked whole; steaks can be grilled with success. Many chefs cut small, thin, cross sections (paillards) and use the fish in veal scaloppine recipes.

STERLET—Name given to the young sturgeon.

SUCCOTASH—Name given to a combination of cooked corn and lima beans. Used as a vegetable.

SWEETBREADS—The name given to two succulent pieces of flesh of the calf, ox and sheep, that adhere to the throat and heart. Before using in the preparation of dishes, they must first be blanched, trimmed and skinned.

SWEETBREADS—True sweetbreads are the thymus glands—not pancreas, testes, or any other glands—of young calves (although those of oxen and sheep qualify, you will never see them). Adult cattle have no sweetbreads; the thymus shrivels and virtually vanishes with age.

Sweetbreads are not strong-flavored and their texture is superb—creamy and firm and unlike that of any other meat. They are usually parboiled and trimmed before cooking.

SWEETBREADS WITH SPINACH—Lard the sweetbreads with sea-

soned strips of pork, arrange them in a brasiere with bacon, herbs, vegetables and stock; when done, take out; serve on a bed of spinach purée, with the strained and skimmed braise poured over them.

SCALLOPED SWEETBREADS—Sweetbreads and button mushrooms cut into dice, sautéed with butter, surplus butter then poured off, moistened with Velouté sauce, filled into scallop shells or dishes; sifted breadcrumbs and a little Parmesan cheese strewn on top; baked a delicate brown and served.

FRICASSÉE OF SWEETBREADS—Sweetbreads cut in even sized pieces; button mushrooms sautéed, added to the sweetbreads; moistened with Velouté sauce, simmered; served within a fancy piped border of mashed potatoes.

FRIED SWEETBREADS, COLBERT SAUCE—The sweetbreads split, seasoned with salt and pepper, dipped in butter, then in beaten eggs and sifted breadcrumbs, fried a delicate brown with butter; served on fancy toast with Colbert sauce.

BRAISED SWEETBREADS WITH VEGETABLES—The sweetbreads larded, braised with herbs, vegetables and stock, taken up when done, the braise strained and skimmed; then used to moisten a macedoine or jardiniere of vegetables; served, the sweetbreads on fancy toast, the vegetables around.

FRIED STUFFED SWEETBREADS—Split the sweetbreads, then spread it on both sides with a D'Uxelles sauce containing minced mushrooms and onions, then double bread and fry; serve with a rich brown sauce containing sherry wine.

CASSEROLE OF SWEETBREADS— Line the casserole with boiled rice, arrange the interior with lamb sweetbreads in fricassée, bake and serve in the casserole.

CROÛSTADES OF SWEETBREADS— Into the fancy croûstade cases (now to be purchased by the dozen or barrel), serve the fricassée of sweetbreads above.

BLANQUETTE OF SWEETBREADS— Slice the sweetbreads into even slices with corresponding slices of truffles, moisten with a Suprême sauce; served within a border of well cooked rice grains.

EPIGRAMME OF SWEETBREADS— Lard, braise and glaze one half of the quantity of sweetbreads required, the other half to be breaded and fried a golden color; place one of each against fancy toast; serve with tomato sauce.

CURRY OF SWEETBREADS—Beef sweetbreads are as good as any for this. Take the breads, soak for two hours in warm water, boil till tender, clean and trim them, then press between plates till cold; slice them and fry with butter a golden color; then fry sliced onions, add flour to form a roux, moisten with the strained and skimmed stock the sweetbreads were boiled in, add

curry powder to taste, simmer, skim; serve within a border of well boiled grains of rice.

SWEETBREADS WITH KIDNEYS— Take large veal sweetbreads, blanch, cool, press and trim them, then lard them with strips of truffles. Beat to a froth the whites of three eggs, into it then mix some finely chopped pistachio nuts; roll the truffled sweetbreads in the egg, then insert in buttered paper cases, bake till of a nice color, remove the paper, place the sweetbread on a circle of buttered toast, then flank it with broiled lamb or sheep kidneys, and serve with port wine sauce.

MEDALLIONS OF SWEETBREAD— Take smooth skinned tomatoes, cut them in halves, place cut side down in baking pan and dry them down in a medium oven; then place a slice of sweetbread in each half, put the two halves together, pin them with a toothpick, then bread and fry them, drain, remove the pick; serve on circles of toast and Suprême sauce.

LARDED SWEETBREADS, TOULOUSE GARNISH—Take veal sweetbreads, lard them with seasoned strips of bacon, braise till done and glazy with herbs, vegetables and stock; serve on circles of toast with Toulouse garnish around (see GARNISHES).

CROQUETTES OF SWEETBREADS— Take the trimmings of sweetbreads and some boiled sweetbreads from the ox, cut them up very fine, adding some minced mushrooms and shallots, then boil them down thick with Velouté sauce (a little chopped parsley may be added if desired), turn out into a buttered pan, smooth, cover with a sheet of buttered paper and set away to get thoroughly cold; then make up into croquettes, or form into small cutlets, bread, fry and serve with a white Italian sauce, or garnish with peas in a Velouté sauce, or with some flageolet beans in a Madeira sauce.

KROMESKIES OF SWEETBREADS are made of the croquette mixture shaped like a core, then rolled round with thin slices of boiled bacon, dipped in batter and fried.

RISSOLES OF SWEETBREADS are made from the croquette mixture shaped like a finger, then enclosed with a thin piece of pie paste and fried.

BROILED SWEETBREADS—Prepare and trim the sweetbreads, then season with salt and pepper, roll in melted butter, then in flour, and broil a delicate brown; serve on toast with or without a strip of bacon and some maître d'hôtel sauce.

ROAST SWEETBREADS—Prepare and trim veal sweetbreads, season with salt and pepper, roll in melted butter, then in flour, place in a buttered baking pan, roast gently till of a delicate color, then serve on a circle of buttered toast with Suprême or Madeira sauces.

PATTIES OF SWEETBREADS—Take the prepared veal sweetbreads and cut them into small dice, adding a small quantity of iced and fried button mushrooms, moisten them with either Velouté, Italian or Ma-

deira sauces, simmer, then fill into patty cases.

VOL-AU-VENTS are the same thing but much larger.

BOUCHÉES are the same thing but smaller than the patty case.

SALPICON OF SWEETBREADS—Take the prepared veal sweetbreads and cut them into medium-sized dice, adding also the tops of small button mushrooms, small diced pieces of cooked red tongue, and some small diced truffles; moisten the whole with a white Italian sauce, simmer, then serve in fancy cases.

BROCHETTE OF SWEETBREADS—Take the prepared veal sweetbreads and slice them into squares or circles with an equal number of slices of parboiled bacon, run them on a skewer alternately, with a button mushroom; season with salt, pepper and the juice of a lemon, then dip in beaten eggs, then roll in sifted breadcrumbs, and fry a delicate brown in butter; serve with Italian sauce.

FRIED SWEETBREADS—Take the prepared veal sweetbreads and cut them into slices, season with salt and pepper, roll in flour, then fry a delicate brown with butter; take up and moisten with a little Madeira sauce, just enough to keep them hot in the bain-marie; place within a border of veal forcemeat piped on the dish with a bag and tube, then pour Perigueux sauce over the sweetbreads and serve.

SCRAMBLED SWEETBREADS WITH EGGS—Take all the trimmings of

the sweetbreads which may have accumulated from the two or three previous days, cut them into small neat pieces, then scramble them with eggs, afterward moistening them with white Italian sauce; serve on buttered toast.

SWEETBREADS WITH BROWN BUTTER—Slices of the prepared veal sweetbreads fried a golden brown with plenty of good butter; taken up and laid on toast, the butter then frothed up and seasoned with lemon juice, or tarragon vinegar, browned well, and poured over the sweetbreads.

SWEETBREAD SOUP—Mince some ham and onions, blanch and slice some sweetbreads, add a bunch of herbs and sauté the whole gently with butter for an hour, add flour to form a paste, then rub the whole through the tamis, make hot again and bring to the soup consistency with a combined veal and chicken broth, season with salt, white pepper, a little sugar; serve with croûtons.

TAPIOCA—A form of starch obtained from the root of a plant; used in the making of puddings and jellies; also in soups and custards.

TAPIOCA—Tapioca is made from yucca (*Manihot esculenta*, also known as cassava and manioc), a root native to Brazil and an important starch throughout the Third World.

TARRAGON—An aromatic herb; used in soups, sauces, and as a flavoring to vinegar.

TARRAGON—Tarragon's Latin name—*Artemisia dracunculus*—means "little dragon." Although that name is often thought to be a reference to its medicinal uses (tarragon was once considered effective in treating snakebites), it may have to do with the tendency of the plant's roots to grow around one another—as a dragon's tail curls about its body—often to the detriment of its own health.

The powerful scent of tarragon has been described as a combination of anise and vanilla; not far off. Fresh tarragon is superior to dried, but not so much so that dried is useless. Tarragon is an essential ingredient in the combination known as FINES HERBES and is especially well known for its inclusion in egg and chicken dishes, and in vinegars.

TARTARIC ACID—A powder obtained from cream of tartar; used in conjunction with it to form baking powder.

TEAL—Name of the duck next best to the canvas back; delicious when broiled, roasted or in a salmis.

TERRAPIN—Name of the most costly of the tortoise family, having to be purchased by the inch, the diamond back being the best. To kill it, plunge into boiling water and let it remain there with the lid on for fifteen minutes, then take it out and peel the skin off the back and remove the nails from the claws; remove the under shell by cutting with a sharp knife where it joins the upper one, then remove the sand bag and gall bladder; save the blood, and remove all the meat and eggs; cut off the head and use it and the shell for soups; keep the meat, eggs and the green fat found at the shoulders in water till wanted for use.

BAKED TERRAPIN—Take the terrapin meat, eggs and fat, put into the upper shell, moisten with a little Madeira sauce, add the juice of a lemon, season with salt, pepper, butter, a glass of Madeira wine; cover with a sheet of buttered paper, bake till done and serve in the shell.

TERRAPIN, MARYLAND STYLE—Terrapin meat simmered in butter with the liquor obtained from the cutting up; flour added to form a roux, then moistened with boiling cream, till like a fricassée; seasoned with salt, pepper and mace; finish by adding the eggs, simmer, then add sherry wine.

TOMATOES—One of the best of the vegetable fruits. Used in making pies, preserves, soups, sauces, salads, as a vegetable, baked and stuffed as a garnish; used as an accompaniment to steaks when broiled, as a pickle, and in the preparation of piccalili, as an ingredient to chutney; and used by the cook in more ways than any other fruit vegetable known.

TOMATOES—The tomato (*Lycopersicon esculentum*) is probably indigenous to Peru. Although the Spaniards introduced them to Europe in the sixteenth century, tomatoes were not taken seriously until the eighteenth century. Not until very late in that century did an Italian combine tomatoes with pasta, and it was the mid-nineteenth century before tomatoes gained a serious foothold in North America. Now it is our most popular garden vegetable, even if it is actually a fruit.

TORTILLAS—See CORN.

TRIFLE—Name given to a combination of sponge cake, sherry wine, preserves, custard, and whipped cream.

TRIPE—The first stomach of the ox. Used after being prepared by the butchers. It is easily digested, contains good nutrients. It may be broiled and served with melted butter . . . Fried either after breading, or dipping in fritter batter, and served with fried onions or with a purée of onions in either brown or white sauce . . . Stewed plain with onions in white sauce . . . Stewed with tomatoes, a clove of garlic, red peppers, olive oil, Worcestershire sauce, sliced onions and meat gravy. This is called "in creole style" . . . Stewed in Espagnole sauce with an addition of fried onions . . . Stewed down rich in tomato sauce . . . Stewed in a sauce Poulette and served with toast . . . Baked in a rich white onion sauce . . . Grilled and served with Tartar sauce . . . Curried and served with fancy croûtons . . . Made into a fricassée by stewing in a sauce Velouté . . . Laid out in lengths, the inside spread with sausage meat, rolled up into cannelons, baked and basted with tomato sauce; served with some of the sauce and garnished with sausage balls . . . Sautéed and served with Bordelaise sauce . . . Simmered down till nearly dry with a little white broth, chopped parsley, and strips of lean ham, then moistened with a sauce Toulouse, finished with a few gherkins finely minced.

TRIPE—Tripe sold in our markets is from the cow rather than from the ox (sheep and pig stomachs are also referred to as tripe). The simple statement "used after being prepared by the butchers" belies the amount of work that goes into such preparation. Before it is sold, tripe is cut up, washed and scalded repeatedly.

TROUT—One of the most delicate flavored fish, lake trout, salmon trout and the brook trout. The delicate brook trout is either broiled or fried, and served with a maitre d'hôtel sauce . . . The lake and salmon trout may be cut in steaks and broiled; served with a Hollandaise sauce . . . Cut in steaks and fried, served with a slice of bacon; garnish with fancy potatoes . . . Boiled and served with anchovy sauce . . . Baked and served with Italian sauce.

TROUT—None of the several varieties of trout—brook, lake, rainbow, brown (which is also known as salmon trout or char), and so on—can be legally caught and sold. And the farm-raised fish, which is most often from Idaho, cannot compare to fresh wild trout. So why all the fuss? Because trout, which is related to SALMON, remains an enormously popular game fish, and because it is incomparably delicious when it is cooked immediately after it is caught.

BAKED SALMON TROUT—Scale and cleanse the fish, score the sides where the portion is to be cut, rub the scores with mixed salt, pepper and ground herbs, lay in buttered pan, bake and baste with butter and court-bouillon; when done, lift off gently on to the steam table; serve in portions with either Genevoise or Espagnole sauces, garnish with small potato croquettes.

SALMON TROUT SAUTÉ—Cut the fish into steaks, season with salt and pepper. Fry some slices of bacon a delicate brown, then roll the fish in flour and fry in the bacon fat till of a golden brown; take up, add flour to the pan, stir, moisten with boiling fish broth, add the juice of a lemon, and a little tomato catchup, strain over the fish in a clean saûtoir, simmer for a few minutes, then serve with some of the sauce and a strip of the bacon on the top.

BAKED STUFFED TROUT—Take the lake trout, trim and scale it, stuff with a fish forcemeat, sew up the belly, score the sides in portion cuts, season with salt and pepper, brush with butter, dredge with flour, place in a buttered pan, bake and baste till done; serve with an anchovied Espagnole sauce, garnish with Duchesse potatoes.

BROILED SALMON TROUT—Take the whole sides freed from bones, moisten with olive oil, season with salt and pepper, dredge with flour, broil well done over a clear fire; serve in portions with maitre d'hôtel butter, garnish with Parisenne potatoes, lemon and parsley.

SALMON TROUT BAKED WITH TOMATOES—Take the sides of fish freed from bones, season with salt and pepper, dust with paprika, dredge with flour, arrange in a buttered baking pan, cover with canned tomatoes, add a minced green pepper, bake and baste till done; serve with the tomatoes, and garnish with Victoria potatoes.

FILLETED TROUT FRIED, WITH BACON—Take the sides of salmon trout freed from bone, cut them into portion pieces, season with salt and pepper, have ready some frying oil, very hot. Make a batter of beaten eggs and a very little flour, dip the fillets in the batter, fry in the oil; serve with a strip of bacon on the fish, garnish with Saratoga chips, lemon and parsley.

TROUT STEAK, SAUCE TRIANON—Take the centre cut steaks of salmon trout, season with salt and pepper, moisten with olive oil, dredge with flour, broil over a clear fire, basting with butter; serve with a sauce Trianon poured around.

LAKE TROUT FRIED, TOMATO SAUCE—Scale and trim the trout, cut in steaks, season with salt and pepper, dredge with flour, fry in bacon fat to a golden color; serve with tomato sauce poured around.

Or may be served with a strip of bacon, garnished with Reitz potatoes.

BOILED TROUT, SHRIMP SAUCE—Lake or Salmon trout, scaled and trimmed, scored in portion cuts, placed on the drainer of fish kettle, covered with cold water containing a bunch of garden herbs, a little salt and vinegar, brought to the boil, skimmed, simmered till done, lifted up and drained; served with shrimp sauce, garnished with Hollandaise potatoes.

BAKED TROUT STEAKS—Take the lake trout, scale and trim, cut in steaks, arrange in buttered pan, cover with Allemande sauce, bake gently till done; serve garnished with Villageoise potatoes.

BRAISED TROUT, MATELOTE—Scale and trim the fish, score the sides in portion cuts, braise with bacon, herbs, and fish broth; when done, take up, strain and skim the braise, glaze the portions with it; serve garnished with a Matelote.

BROOK TROUT WITH QUENELLES—Clean and trim the fish, stuff with a fish farce, arrange in a well buttered pan, season with salt and pepper, add a few mixed herbs and a glass of white wine with a little fish broth; bake about fifteen minutes, well basting with the liquor; then take up, strain the residue into some Espagnole sauce, boil up and skim; then add sliced truffles and mushroom, some blanched oysters and a little lobster coral; serve with the oysters as a garnish and the sauce poured over.

BROILED BROOK TROUT—Scale and trim the fish; draw it through the gills, then stuff it through the mouth with butter mixed with finely minced sweet herbs, slightly score the sides, season with salt and pepper, pass the fish through either melted butter or olive oil; broil gently without breaking the skin; serve with Poivrade sauce.

TRUFFLES—Name of an aromatic tuber. On the European continent are served baked, boiled, gratinated, broiled, stewed in wine, etc. But on account of their very high price in this country, the cook uses them in sauces, forcemeats, omelets, salads and turkey stuffing.

TUNNY "THON MARINE"—As it generally appears on the bill of fare, under the heading of hors d'ouevres or appetizers, is the name of a fish of the appearance and flavor of Spanish mackerel. It is generally imported in tins, prepared in olive oil.

TUNNY "THON MARINE"—Tunny "Thon Marine" is, of course, tuna, the fish (in its fresh form) that was "discovered" by Americans only ten years ago. Prior to that, it was generally consumed in the canned form.

Tuna—primarily yellowfin (*Thunnus albacares*), bluefin (*Thunnus thynnus*), and albacore (*Thunnus alalunga*)—is in season from spring through fall and is fairly plentiful (it's expensive because the Japanese are willing to pay so much for it). The fish is related to MACKEREL and is among the most impressive creatures on earth: It is warm-blooded, a rare feature among fish, and capable of swimming as fast as fifty-five

miles an hour. This enables it to outsprint nearly all of its enemies (mako sharks and killer whales can catch it) and to catch any prey.

Tuna swim constantly; the majestic bluefin covers about seventy-five thousand miles a year. This fish, which may live for thirty years or more and weigh a ton, eats as much as 10 percent of its weight each day in order to maintain its high-pressured circulatory system, which feeds its body's main feature, muscle.

It is this muscle that makes such good eating. Most tuna is butchered by quartering, and one of these cuts off the central bone taken from even a small fish weighs ten pounds or so. Loin cuts could be made into roasts if one so desired, but they're usually cut into thick steaks. Twice that thickness makes a lovely steak for grilling too, and a skilled knife wielder can cut quarter-inch-thick slices to use as cutlets.

Tuna is so flavorful that it is best prepared simply: Like good steak, adorning tuna with complicated sauces is overkill. Sashimi-grade tuna may be cut into chunks and dipped in flavored soy sauce (add sesame oil, fresh ginger, and/or garlic) before eating as an appetizer. One eighth to one quarter of a pound per person suffices for this simplified sashimi.

TURKEY—One of the native American poultry birds found wild in Mexico. And the wild bird is as superior to the domestic one as the canvas back duck is to the domestic duck.

TURKEY—It is difficult to be a fan of wild turkey (*Meleagris gallopavo*); most of what we buy in specialty stores is lean, tough, hardly tastier than the supermarket birds, and three times as expensive. Stick with the domesticated type.

The great thing that has happened during the past few years is what we might call the chickenization of the bird: It is being cut into parts, so we no longer have to face a ten-pound bird every time we want a bite of turkey. The wings and legs are good braised, and the whole breast makes a fine small roast (and you needn't overcook it, as you must when baking it with the legs).

Cutlets are terrific too. More flavorful than chicken, more tender than veal, you can use them in recipes that call for either.

BROILED SPRING TURKEY—Plump young birds, singed, split down the back, breast and back bones removed, thigh bone snapped, the sides then cut in halves; season with salt and pepper, brush with butter or olive oil, broil a golden brown; serve on slices of buttered toast and garnish with two roast mushrooms on the bird, flanked with slices of tomatoes breaded and fried, a little maitre d'hôtel butter sprinkled over the whole.

STEWED SPRING TURKEY, SOUTHERN STYLE—Take young plump birds singed, drawn and washed, cut into joints, leaving the leg and wing bone a little exposed. Place the pieces in a baking pan, season with chili pepper and salt, sprinkle with melted butter and roast slowly till brown; then take up into a saûtoir, add flour, shake together, moisten with chicken or turkey stock, bring to the boil, skim, then add the grated rind and juice of an orange, simmer till the bird is tender. Take one pound of raw ham and one medium sized onion, cut in small squares, fry them lightly with plenty of butter in the saûtoir, then add a pound of well washed rice, moisten with half a gallon of chicken or turkey stock, place on the cover and let simmer till rice is well done. To serve: place the rice neatly on serving platter, the portion of bird on the rice with a croquette frill on it; or on the wing or leg bone; pour some of the gravy over the whole and flank the rice with small roasted potatoes.

BOILED TURKEY, OYSTER SAUCE—Take very large plump birds, singe, draw, wash, truss them with the legs forced well into the body, then boil them with a piece of salt pork, carrots, onions and celery, for about three hours; take up, and serve portions with plenty of oyster sauce poured over. A well made celery sauce is also very appropriate.

ROAST SPRING TURKEY, OYSTER SAUCE—Take young plump birds, singed, drawn, washed and trussed (not stuffed). Roast about an hour, well basting with butter. Serve in portions with a good brown oyster sauce (see SAUCES).

ROAST TURKEY, STUFFED—Take plump young birds, singe, draw, wash, stuff with a mixture of white bread soaked and squeezed dry, seasoned with salt, pepper, mixed herbs, melted butter and yolks of eggs. Truss with the legs well into the body; season the bird with pepper and salt, roast for about two hours, well basting during roasting; serve portions with the stuffing under the meat, and a dish of cranberry sauce or jelly separate . . . The turkey may also be stuffed with mashed sweet potatoes . . . Again with veal forcemeat containing a liberal quantity of peeled boiled chestnuts, then served with chestnut sauce; that is, with boiled chestnuts peeled, rubbed through the tamis, and the purée thus obtained mixed into the turkey gravy . . . They may also be stuffed with an oyster dressing and served with a brown oyster sauce . . . They may also be stuffed with stewed truffles and served with Perigueux sauce, and garnished with quenelles of poultry . . . Also stuffed with pork sausage meat in which has been mixed some boiled and peeled chestnuts, and served with a Chipolata garnish (see GARNISHES) . . . Also stuffed with veal forcemeat and served with a Financière garnish. In England the common way of the people is to stuff the turkey with ordinary dressing as given above, and to serve it with roast pork sausages, and a slice of boiled salt leg of pork, always handing round sticks of fine white celery.

BOILED STUFFED TURKEY—Take young plump birds, singe, draw, wash, stuff with veal forcemeat; trussed with the legs well into the body; boil it till tender with a carrot, onion, celery, and a salted ox tongue; serve with a couple of slices of the tongue on the bird, the stuffing underneath, and a sauce made from the liquor it was boiled in poured around . . . It may also be stuffed with grated breadcrumbs mixed with minced and boiled celery, raw eggs, salt, pepper and butter, and served with Hollandaise sauce . . . Or with egg sauce, Ve-

louté sauce, parsley sauce . . . Also garnished with a slice of boiled ham and a spoonful of spinach purée.

BONED TURKEY—This dish is always served cold, either plain or with aspic or in a galantine. It is a favorite with ball parties, and other luncheon or supper gatherings. Take two birds, one smaller than the other. Remove the head, feet and wings, then split the skin down the spinal column; remove the flesh without breaking through the skin, and leave the carcass with entrails entire. Lay the birds out on the table skin side down. On the larger one place a column of pork sausage or veal forcemeat down the breast centre; on that, lay a column of cooked tongue, and on either side of it a smaller column of pickled belly of cooked pork. Season with salt, pepper and thyme. Remove the flesh from the skin of the smaller bird and place the white meat over the dark of the stuffed bird, and the dark over the white meat. Then draw the two sides together, sew it up into a good shape; then sew it into a cloth and boil till tender (about two hours). Take up and drain, then place it between two boards; put a weight on top and let become thoroughly cold; then remove the cloth, trim the bird, wipe clean with a hot wet cloth, glaze it and cut portions to order. If to place on a table whole, then decorate the glazing with fancy piped butter, and take off the first slice . . . It may also be roasted instead of being in a cloth and boiled . . . To make a GALANTINE OF TURKEY, take the bird when the cloth is removed, have a galantine mold nicely decorated with aspic jelly and fancy forms of green peas, white and yolk of hard boiled egg, macedoine of vegetables; then fill the mold with slices of the boned bird, placing the edges downwards (not one on top of the other), then fill up with limpid aspic jelly, allowing the jelly to get between each slice of turkey, so that in serving there is no cutting to be done, simply removing the slice with the jelly adhering. When serving, place at either end of the dish a small quantity of aspic and currant jelly.

BLANQUETTE OF TURKEY—Slices of cold cooked turkey freed from skin, a can of good button mushrooms also sliced. Put the two into a rich Velouté sauce, bring to the simmer, skim, add juice of a lemon; served within a border of green peas, or grains of rice, or finely shred noodles.

BRAISED TURKEY—Singe and truss the bird without stuffing as for roasting; then roast, quickly basting with butter to get on a nice brown color. Take up as soon as browned, and place it into a deep saûtoir with a few slices of veal at the bottom; cover the bird with slices of fat bacon, then fill up with good white stock; add a bunch of sweet herbs, a little salt, then simmer till done; take up the bird, reduce the stock to half glaze, skim, strain and serve with the bird. Garnish with small potato croquettes.

STUFFED YOUNG TURKEY LEGS— Cut off the leg and thigh, thus making four portions from each bird. You can stuff the other part of the bird and roast in the usual way, as everybody wants a slice of the breast . . . Remove the bone from the leg cuts, season them with salt and pepper, then stuff the opening with a white forcemeat in which is incorporated minced ham, truffles and mushrooms; roll them into shape, sew the ends, wrap each one in a piece of bacon, then boil gently in white stock till tender; take up and cool; then remove the sewing; meantime reduce the stock till of a sauce consistency; place the legs in again, to reheat, then take up and roll in fresh grated breadcrumbs; place in a buttered pan, sprinkle with butter, place in oven and get on a good color; serve on a bed of boiled rice with the sauce poured around.

CREAMED COLLOPS OF TURKEY— Slices of cold cooked turkey freed from skin, cut into neat thin slices; then place into a Suprême sauce and simmer for ten minutes; serve on a slice of toast, sprinkle the top with finely minced truffles and lean ham mixed together; garnish the sides with fancy croûtons spread with foie-gras or liver paste.

HASHED TURKEY WITH EGG—For this dish, buy a big old gobbler weighing twenty pounds or so, truss as for boiling, then steam it till tender; when cooled, remove the skin, and take off every particle of meat, cut it into very small dice, moisten it with Velouté sauce, bring it to the simmer; serve on buttered toast with a poached egg on top.

TURKEY CROQUETTES—Take the preceding recipe, and when brought to the simmer, work in some well boiled rice, so as to thor-

TURKEY HASH WITH POACHED EGGS

Serves 4, with 2 eggs per person

Jeff and I both hate overcooked turkey. In this wonderful turkey hash recipe I have used poached turkey, far superior to leftover dried turkey, but we must recognize that the kitchen of 1904 wasted very little—thus turkey hash from the leftover and rather dried bird. This version is just delicious, but you must not overpoach the eggs.

2 turkey hindquarters (about 3³/₄ pounds total) (if frozen, thaw)	2 cups russet peeled and diced potatoes
1 tablespoon olive oil	2 tablespoons chopped parsley
2 tablespoons butter	Salt and freshly ground black pepper to taste
²/₃ cup peeled and chopped yellow onions	8 poached eggs

In an 8-quart pot, place the turkey and add enough cold water to cover. Bring to a boil, cover, and simmer for 15 minutes. Turn off the heat and leave, covered, directly on the burner you are using for 1¹/₄ hours.

Remove the turkey and cool, skin, and debone it. Reserve the turkey broth. Dice the turkey meat and remove to a plate. (This should yield about 2 pounds of cooked meat.) Cover the meat so that it does not dry out.

Heat a large frying pan and add the oil, butter, and onions. Sauté until the onions are tender, and stir in the potatoes. Turn the heat to low and cover. Cook about 10 minutes to "sweat" down the onions and potatoes. Stir a few times during cooking (a little browning is okay). Add the turkey, parsley, ¹/₂ cup of reserved broth, and salt and pepper to taste. Simmer a couple of minutes until the liquid is absorbed.

Serve topped with poached eggs.

VARIATION: Bind the cooked hash together with a small amount of bread crumbs and beaten eggs. You may need to adjust the salt and pepper. Form the mixture into patties and fry in butter until golden brown on both sides. Top each patty with a poached egg. *Serves 8*

C.W.

oughly stiffen it; then pour into a buttered pan, cover with oiled paper and let become cold, then shape it into the shape desired; bread, fry and serve with a white Italian sauce.

TURKEY PATTIES AND VOL-AU-VENTS—Take the cold white meat of cooked turkey, cut it into small dice, season with salt and nutmeg, then moisten it with a rich cream sauce (made with cream); fill into patty or vol-au-vent cases and serve.

SALPIÇON OF TURKEY—Take cold cooked turkey freed from skin, three-fifths; lean cooked ham, one-fifth; truffles and mushrooms in equal parts to make the last fifth; cut the whole into neat small dice, moisten with a Suprême sauce, simmer for ten minutes, then serve in fancy paper cases.

CROÛSTADES OF TURKEY—Take the salpiçon of the preceding recipe and fill into fancy croûstade cases and serve.

FRICASSÉE OF TURKEY WINGS— Take the middle joints of the wings, pick out all the dark feathers, trim the edges, singe them, boil them very slowly with a heart of celery, salt and a few blades of mace; when tender take up; make a good white sauce from the boiling liquor, skim and strain it over the wings in another saûtoir, then add some good button mushrooms cut into slices, bring all to the simmer and serve. TURKEY SALADS AND SOUPS ARE MADE THE SAME AS THE RECIPES GIVEN WITH CHICKEN.

TURNIPS—A nutritious vegetable both white and yellow; used plain boiled or boiled and mashed; cut into shapes and used as a garnish; or stewed in a cream sauce and used either as a garniture or as a vegetable; they are very useful in soups. The young green turnip tops also make a most excellent vegetable. Young white turnips of an even size may be peeled, the inside scooped out, steamed till done, then used as a receptacle for green peas, etc., and served as a vegetable, the parts scooped out being used next day as a vegetable; also the turnip can be used for a nice entrée by taking white turnips all of an even size, peel them, cut off a lid, scoop out the inside, fill the space with minced mutton (thus using up your mutton trimmings), replace the lid, arrange in a shallow saûtoir, moisten with white stock and simmer till tender; serve with a good gravy poured over them.

TURNIPS—There was a time when most American houses had root cellars, and turnips—the most easily grown edible root—helped keep people fed through the winter. Progress has made available to us a wider variety of vegetables during the cold months. But turnips remain firm and tasty throughout the winter—even in primitive supermarket conditions—and their benefits should be exploited.

Root vegetables were among the first foods eaten by humans, and the white turnip is probably the oldest vegetable known. The rutabaga is younger, the result of a seventeenth-century cross between the turnip and the cabbage; its nickname swede comes from its popularity in northern Europe. Generally speaking, rutabagas are cheaper than white or purple-topped turnips, but their flavor is not as fine. Both, though, are among the most underrated vegetables.

A turnip purée—add butter—is an incomparable side dish. Even better: half turnips, half potatoes, some butter, perhaps some heavy cream, salt, and pepper, puréed. This is among the simplest and most elegant purées that you can make. In fact, turnips have an affinity for potatoes and substitute well for them in many instances; try using them, for example, in potato pancakes.

TURTLE—To kill it, hang it up by the hind fins, cut off the head and let it bleed overnight into a bucket; then lay it on its back, cut off the fins, then the under shell, remove the entrails and gall; save the eggs and green fat, the white flesh, and the red meat, and the fins. The shell is then sawn into pieces and boiled with the head to make the stock for turtle soup; the green fat is served with the soups, the white and dark meat used for entrées and steaks, etc. The white meat may be used in all the ways given in the recipes for veal. The red meat in all the ways given for beef. The fins are generally stewed in any of the ways applicable to fowl.

GREEN TURTLE SOUP—Place in a large and deep saûtoir half a pound of butter, three pounds of sliced raw ham, the meat from three shins of beef and three knuckles of veal, two old fowls, a dozen cloves, four blades of mace, a handful of parsley roots, a bouquet of parsley tied up with shallots, thyme, green onions and two bay leaves, a pint of Madeira wine and a gallon of good stock; boil this down sharply to a half glaze, then fill up with stock, adding the turtle head, fins, shell and the coarse meat, turnips, carrots, onions and a head of celery; simmer for six hours, then work in a roux to the consistency of thin sauce, boil and skim till smooth and velvety, then strain off into another saûtoir . . . Make a purée of herbs by boiling together in a quart of consommé, one-third of sweet basil, and the other two-thirds of herbs to be used are equal quantities of savory, thyme and marjoram, a good handful of parsley, a small bunch each of spring onions and shallots, and some mushroom trimmings; boil for one hour, then rub all through the tamis; add the purée to the soup with a pint of Madeira wine; some of the turtle eggs, some forcemeat balls made from the white turtle meat, the cooked green fat cut in pieces, and the juice of one lemon to each gallon of soup. For clear turtle soup, proceed and finish in the same way, but instead of adding a roux to the stock, let it cool and clarify it into a consommé. A good sherry wine may be used instead of Madèira.

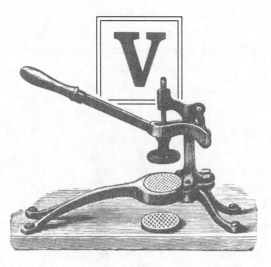

VANILLA—The fruit or pod of the vanilla plant; used as a flavoring to sauces, ices, puddings, blanc-manges, fritters, creams, liqueurs, soufflés, eclairs, syrups, caramels, etc.

VANILLA—The vanilla beans, which are picked unripe from a tropical orchid (*Vanilla planifolia*), are packed into a box and "sweated" to develop their powerful aroma and flavor. During that time crystals sometimes appear on the long black beans.

Vanilla can be used in several ways: by soaking pieces of the bean in warm liquid that later will be mixed with other ingredients; by scraping the tiny seeds from inside the bean into any mixture; or by allowing the bean to sit in a jarful of sugar and using the sugar in any recipe that requires the flavor of vanilla. True vanilla flavor is also provided by the alcoholic extract of vanilla, sold in bottles in all food stores.

Vanillin is a synthetic vanilla flavoring that is much used in commercial food making. Although it is much less expensive than pure vanilla, it is rarely used by serious cooks because its flavor and aroma are far less complex than those of real vanilla.

VEAL—Twenty-five years ago a combination of clever economics and aggressive marketing made super-tender, mild, white-fleshed veal—"milk-fed" veal—synonymous with prime veal. But such has not always been the case, nor will it necessarily remain the case. There has been no small uproar about the poor treatment given to "crate-raised" veal, which is how animal-rights activists think of milk-fed veal, and it has raised demand for "natural" veal, veal taken from calves that either graze with their mothers or at least have free access to barn and corral.

There are differences between the two meats. Milk-fed veal is

CUTS OF VEAL
and where they come from

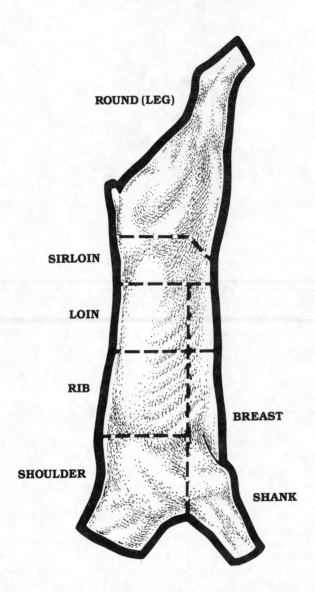

grayish pink when raw and nearly white when cooked, and naturally raised veal is rosy pink when raw and pink when cooked. Milk-fed veal is mushy and often dry in comparison to natural veal, which is also more flavorful and juicy than meat taken from calves raised in confinement.

In the future we will see more and more naturally raised veal, and, especially when it comes from the European breeds that traditionally have been raised for this purpose, it will be of better and better quality.

VEAL ROLL WITH TONGUE—This is a delightful cold dish for luncheons, suppers, etc. Take a large breast of veal, bone it, then place in the brine tub for two days; prick it and punch the air out if it has been blown, remove from brine and wipe dry, then spread thick with a layer of seasoned pork sausage meat; on that place down the centre four cooked pickled pigs' tongues, cover them with more of the sausage meat, draw the sides together and sew up with twine, then tie it in a cloth like a roly poly pudding; boil for two hours in white stock, take up and let cool in the cloth, then remove the cloth, wipe with a hot cloth, glaze and serve in slices.

VEAL CUTLETS, GARNISHED—Take the rib chops, remove the chine bone and gristle, trim the bone so as to leave a handle for a frill to be placed on when serving, lard the flesh with strips of bacon, ham, tongue, truffle, or sweetbread and truffle according to desire; then place in a brasiere on a bed of sliced root vegetables, parsley, spring onions, cloves, mace and whole peppers, cover with slices of fat bacon, moisten to the height of the cutlets with stock and a glass of sherry wine, braise till done (about an hour) then serve with a brown Italian sauce . . . mushroom sauce . . . Financière, Toulouse or Perigueux garniture. These cutlets after being braised, may be cooled, trimmed, masked with sauce, then breadcrumbed and fried, and served with Allemande sauce containing scallops of tongue and button mushrooms . . . Or with tomato sauce.

VEAL CUTLETS SAUTÉED—Take the rib chops and trim as in the preceding recipe. Season with salt and pepper, fry a delicate brown on both sides with clarified butter; when nearly done take up and in the butter fry some shallots, mushrooms and parsley, then add some Espagnole sauce, boil up and skim off the fat, add the cutlets and simmer till done; serve garnished with thin scallops of fried ham.

FRICANDEAU OF VEAL WITH VEGETABLES—Take the leg of veal and remove the thick flank, lard it with seasoned strips of bacon, braise with carrot, celery, onions, parsley, green onions and slices of bacon with mace, cloves and peppers in the usual way, for about two and a half hours; when done, take up, strain, boil and skim the braise, add some sherry or Madeira wine; use it as a sauce to the fricandeau; serve garnished with any vegetable garnish or purée described in this work. It may also be garnished with either Chipolata, Financière or Toulouse garniture.

GRENADINS OF VEAL WITH SPIN-ACH—After removing the thick flank for fricandeau from a leg of veal, you have the buttock and aitchbone left. Bone out the aitch on the leg; remove the marrow bone, split the buttock in the natural seam, then slice the two sections into cutlets or grenadins, lard and braise them; serve on a bed of purée of spinach . . . purée of celery . . . purée of green peas . . . purée of red haricot beans, etc.

BLANQUETTE OF VEAL—Take cold roast or braised veal, remove the brown skin, and then cut into neat scallops, add some button mushrooms, or scallops of truffle or tongue, moisten the whole with Allemande sauce, simmer; serve garnished with small croquettes of rice . . . or potatoes . . . or veal forcemeat.

SCALLOPS OF VEAL, ITALIAN SAUCE—For this dish use up the thick end of the loin, neck, aitchbone, or leg; cut them into neat shaped scallops; also about one-third of the amount similar cut scallops of raw ham; fry them all of a delicate brown color with clarified butter; then pour off the surplus, add some button mushrooms, and brown Italian sauce, simmer till done; serve with the sauce, and garnish with the mushrooms . . . Or they may be served with either tomato or an Espagnole sauce and garnished with quenelles of veal forcemeat.

EMINCE OF VEAL—For this dish use the shin taken from the shoulder, also the leg and the trimmings from the neck and scrag; boil it in seasoned stock till done, then allow to become cold; cut it up into small dice with some mushrooms, ham, tongue and truffles, then moisten the whole with just enough Béchamel sauce to keep it together; serve heaped on a slice of toast; place a neatly poached and drained egg on top.

CROQUETTES OF VEAL—Take the parts of the preceding recipe, but instead of cutting them all into dice, run them through the mincing machine, moisten with enough Velouté sauce, and stir over the fire till thoroughly heated and stiff; then pour into a buttered pan, smooth with a knife, cover with oiled paper, put away to become cold, then form into croquettes or cutlet shapes, bread, fry and serve with either mushroom, tomato, Italian or Perigueux sauces.

VEAL AND OYSTER PIE—For this dish use the scrag end of the neck and the middle neck under the shoulder, boil in one piece in seasoned white stock; when done, take up and cool, then cut into neat shaped pieces, place into the pie dish with a liberal quantity of scalded oysters, make a good white sauce from the stock and oyster liquor, season with salt and nutmeg, add a little chopped parsley; pour over the contents of the pie dish, cover with a good short paste, glaze with egg wash, bake and serve.

ROAST LOIN OR NECK OF VEAL—Take the loin or neck of veal, allowing the tops to be long, remove the bones and gristle, season with salt and pepper, roll up and tie with twine, roast gently without drying the skin into strings; serve with Béchamel sauce and garnish with small potato croquettes.

CROÛSTADE OF VEAL—Take the blanquette of veal of a preceding recipe but cutting the meat into large dice, and serve in croûstade cases.

SALPIÇON OF VEAL—Take the emince of veal of a preceding recipe and serve it in croûstade cases, paper cases, or steamed and hollowed out white turnips.

BOUDINS OF VEAL OR TIMBALES OF VEAL—Take the remains of cold veal, trim off the skin, run it through the mincing machine with some cooked bacon and button mushrooms, then moisten with a very little sauce, thoroughly stir over the fire till thick; butter some timbale or boudin molds, line them with browned bread crumbs, fill in the mince, steam them for about twenty minutes, then turn out and serve with mushroom, tomato, white Italian, brown Italian, Perigueux or Velouté sauces. They may also be garnished with finely shred noodles, green peas, macedoine or Jardinière of vegetables, button mushrooms, etc.

BROILED VEAL CHOPS—Use either the loin or rib chops, trim, season with salt, pepper and nutmeg, brush with butter, broil and baste to a golden color; serve with maitre d'hôtel, Colbert, tomato, or Madeira sauces.

CURRY OF VEAL—For this dish use up the breasts, cut them into even sized pieces, removing the thick bones, season with salt and pepper, fry a very light color with clarified butter; take up and into the butter then fry a liberal amount of thinly sliced onions, add flour to form a roux, then the curry powder to taste, bring to the boil and skim; simmer for half an hour till the onions are well cooked, then rub through the tamis on to the pieces of breast; simmer then till the meat is done; serve within a border of rice, rissoto, macaroni, spaghetti or noodles.

GALANTINE OF VEAL—Take a large breast of veal and remove the bones, prick it and punch out the air if it has been blown, season with salt, pepper, nutmeg and a little powdered thyme all mixed together, then spread it with a layer of veal forcemeat; on it lay a thinly beaten out and skinned sheet of pigs' flare, down the centre place a column of red cooked tongue, on either side of it a smaller column of cooked boiled salt pork, then sprinkle over a mixture of chopped whites and yolks of eggs with minced pickled gherkins, cover with another layer of veal forcemeat, draw the sides together and sew into a neat roll with twine, then tie in a cloth and boil in white stock for two and a half hours, take up and press till cold in the cloth between two boards, then remove the cloth, wipe clean, glaze; serve in slices with croûtons of bright aspic jelly.

STEWED BREAST OF VEAL—Take the breast of veal and boil it whole till tender enough to take out the bones, then let become cold, cut into even sized pieces

VEAL (OR PORK) TIMBALES

·

Makes 6

This dish is a very elegant way to serve leftover cooked meats. We must admit that even in the midst of the overconsumption common at the turn of the century, the kitchens wasted very little. Very frugal!

1 slice bacon

3 tablespoons butter

½ cup minced shallots

⅓ pound mushrooms, coarsely chopped

1 tablespoon chopped parsley

½ cup Beef Stock (page 48)

¾ pound veal or pork roast, cooked and finely chopped

Salt and freshly ground black pepper to taste

2 eggs, beaten

In a medium-sized frying pan, fry the bacon. Remove the bacon and drain on paper towels. Chop the bacon fine and set aside.

Discard the bacon grease and return the pan to the burner. Add 2 tablespoons of the butter and the shallots. Sauté until the shallots are tender. Add the mushrooms, reserved bacon, parsley, and Beef Stock. Sauté until the mushrooms are tender and the excess liquid is evaporated. Add the veal and toss about. Salt and pepper to taste. Remove the pan from the heat and allow to cool a bit, about 5 minutes. Mix in the beaten eggs.

Grease 6 timbale molds with the remaining 1 tablespoon of butter. Fill the molds with the veal mixture. Even out the tops and place in a baking pan. Add enough hot water to the pan so that the water comes a quarter of the way up the sides of the molds. Bake in a preheated 375° F. oven for 30 minutes.

To serve, run a knife around the inside edges of the molds. Invert onto a plate.

Serve with Tomato Sauce (page 447).

C.W.

and stew it in a sauce made from the liquor it was boiled in; serve with a garnish of green peas, lima beans, Chipolata garniture, glazed carrots, mushrooms, forcemeat balls, fried oysters, cauliflower, small white turnips, rice, mushrooms.

VENISON—The flesh of the deer. The leg and saddle are usually roasted. To roast the leg, season it with salt and pepper, brush it all over with melted butter, then enclose it with a crust made of plain flour and water, bake it about an hour, then take up and remove the crust, place it in another baking pan on a stand, pour in a melted mixture of a half pint each of melted butter, red currant jelly, and boiling water; with the residue of the first pan it was baked in, if any, finish roasting and basting till done; serve with the gravy from the pan . . . The saddle or double loin, is generally encased with buttered paper instead of the crust . . . The rib and loin chops, are generally broiled and served with a jelly, Piquant, Colbert, Poivrade, Financière, Portugaise or Bigarade sauces, or fried, or sautéed and served with the same sauces or with a chestnut purée . . . The scrag and breasts are generally formed into a stew or a "Civet of Venison." Made the same way as jugged hare (which see) . . . The shoulder or the whole forequarter may be roasted and served with Poivrade sauce, and red currant jelly sent to table separately. The cold cooked parts left over may be made into croquettes and cutlets and served with a game sauce made from the bones stewed down with herbs, and a little jelly and Madeira wine. The rougher parts may also be made into pies, and the cutlets made into a good VENISON PIE or patties or vol-au-vents. A good soup is made from the shanks, shins and head, boiled down rich, finished with a little Espagnole sauce, Madeira wine, lemon, cayenne pepper; served with game forcemeat balls and croûtons.

VERMICELLI—A fine form of Italian paste used in most of the ways applicable to macaroni and spaghetti (which see).

VERMOUTH—A form of liquor cordial; used in making mixed drinks especially.

VINEGAR—A distilled acid liquor of the wine formation; used as a flavoring and a condiment.

VINEGAR—The mystique surrounding vinegar has increased with the popularity of balsamic vinegar, the aged-in-wood red wine vinegar that has been made for nearly one thousand years in the area of Modena, Italy. But, contrary to reigning "wisdom," balsamic is neither the only vinegar worth buying nor the only vinegar aged in wood.

Traditionally balsamic vinegar—or *aceto balsamico*—was made only in Modena, Italy, from liquid pressed from the Trebbiano grape. The liquid is cooked until thick, at which point it is called must, and then aged in a series of wooden casks—oak, cherry, chestnut, ash, mulberry, and others in exact and proprietary proportions—for a minimum of ten years. The result is a thick, slightly sweet vinegar (unaged must was once used for sweetening), the unusual flavor of which not only has inspired chefs to serve it atop strawberries but has helped to popularize it in the United States.

Balsamic vinegar has led the way, but there are other well-made vinegars, which is not surprising because vinegar has been produced for at least five thousand years. Most vinegars are wine vinegars (*vinaigre* means "sour wine"), chiefly red, white, sherry, and Champagne vinegars. (Cider vinegar, of course, is made from apples, and other vinegars are made from grain, beets, potatoes, or anything else that can be fermented to produce alcohol, which is converted by bacteria to acid.)

Like balsamic vinegar and SHERRY, sherry vinegar is the product of a *solera* system in which the contents of a number of casks are combined over the years to produce a final product. At their best, both of these vinegars are mellow and flavorful, despite their relatively high acid content. And wood-aging makes them extremely complex. Unless advised otherwise, you can assume that other wine vinegars are made and aged in stainless-steel tanks and have simpler flavors.

The other major category of vinegars is the infused or aromatized vinegars, in which a basic vinegar—most often made from wine—is flavored with herbs, spices, fruits, nuts, or vegetables. Popular examples of this include raspberry and tarragon vinegars; less well known are lime, walnut, and garlic vinegars. Most specialty vinegars are imported from France, Italy, and Spain, but several infused vinegars are made in this country; domestic producers often begin with imported wine vinegar.

WAFFLES—A form of batter cake pastry baked in waffle irons and eaten generally with powdered sugar or syrup.

WALNUT—A hard shelled nut, the interior of which is used for dessert, candies, etc. When plucked green they are used as a pickle after going through the pickling process.

WHITEFISH—A delicious fish obtained in our lakes. It may be cooked and served in all the ways applicable to our lake trout.

WHITEFISH—Members of the salmon and trout family (Salmonidae), whitefish are usually taken from the freshwater lakes of the Far North. They are rarely seen fresh in the United States, but may be found smoked, in urban markets, especially in cities with a substantial Jewish population. See CISCO.

WOODCOCK—A delicious game bird; cooked and served in all the ways of small game birds described in this work.

WOODCOCK—With the related snipe, the woodcock (*Scolopax rusticola*) is considered to be the finest-tasting game bird. Since its sale is prohibited in the United States—due to overhunting earlier in the century—most of us will never have a chance to find out, unless we have the opportunity to eat it in restaurants in England or France.

INDEX

Index entries in **boldface** refer to recipes adapted or created by Jeff Smith and Craig Wollam

A

Almond(s), 13
  marzipan, 303–304
  sauce, 425
Anchovy(ies), 13–16
  bluefish with, 64
  bouchée of, 66
  butter, 15, 78
  canapés, 14, 15, 100
  omelet with, 16, 331
  salad, 15, 413
  sauce, 15, 425
Apple(s), 17–21
  Anglaise garnish, 240
  fried, minced pork with, 379
  fritters, 232, 233
  mincemeat, 306
  roly-poly, 19, **20**
Apricot(s), 21–22
  fritters, 233
  sauce, 22, 426
Artichoke(s), 22–25
  africaine garnish, 241
  bayard garnish, 241
  chicken broth with, 155
  creamed brains with, 70
  salad, 24, 25, 413
  tenderloin of beef with, 45
Artichokes, Jerusalem, 272–273
  purée of, 399
Asparagus, 25–26
  purée of, 399
  salad, 26, 413–414
Asparagus points (tips):
  carrot salad with, 110
  chicken broth with, 155
  fillets of chicken with, 142
  omelet with, 223, 330
Aspic jelly, 26
  potted calf's liver with, 94

B

Bacon, 27–28
  brain cakes with, 68–69
  calf's liver with, 92, 93
  coated oysters, fried, 342
  curing of, 200
  devilled chicken legs with, 142
  fried blackfish with, 62
  fried cabbage with, 82
  garnishes, 240, 241, 242–243

Bacon (*cont.*)
   halibut fried with, 260
   haricot beans with, 37
   omelet with, 221
Bananas, 29
   stanley garnish, 246
Basic white sauce, 427
Bavarian cream, 195
Bavarian sauce, 426, **428**
Bavaroise:
   apple, 17
   apricot, 21
Bayard garnish, 241
Bean(s), 34–37
   flageolets, 35, 229
   French, glazed calf's
      sweetbreads with, 96–97
   salad, 414
   string, chartreuse of chicken
      with, 141–142
   string, fillets of beef with, 45
   see also kidney beans; lima
      bean(s)
Béarnaise sauce, 37–38, 427
Béchamel sauce, 38, 195, 426
Beef, 38–57
   bologna sausage, 384
   brains, 68–71
   chateaubriand, 122
   chipped, omelet with, 221
   cuts of, 38–40
   filets with oysters, 54
   hamburger, 262
   hot pot or hotch potch, 267
   marrow, 66, 303
   mincemeat, 306
   sausage, 383; *see also* sausages
   soup, English style, 46, **47**
   steak and oyster pie, 344–345
   stock, 48
   tenderloin steak, 45–46, 122
   tongue, 54; *see also* tongue(s)
Beet(s), 57
   and egg salad, 57, 414
Beetroot and potato salad, 414
Biscuits, cheese, 126
Blanc mange, 62–63
   chocolate, 159
   corn, 184
Blood sausage, 383–384

Brains, 68–71
   calf's, 68–71, 75, 87, 331
Brandy(ied), 71
   cherries, 129
   peaches, 356
Breads, 71–72
   cheese biscuits, 126
   cheese straws, 125, **126**
   corn gems (muffins),
      183–184, **184**
   tortillas, 185–186
   see also sandwiches
Broth:
   beef, 46
   chicken, with custards, 155,
      156
   clam, 163
   consommé, 175–182
   court-bouillon, 188
   see also soup
Buckwheat cakes, 33
Butter, 77–79
   anchovy, 15, 78
   brown, eggs with, 220, **221**
   horseradish, 78–79, **266**

C

Cabbage, 81–85
   baked with cheese, 83
   cole slaw, 84, **85**
   consommé St. Xavier, 182
   dolmas, 206
   fermière garnish, 243
   flamande garnish, 243
   hot slaw, 85
   kohlrabi, 276
   salad, 414
   see also sauerkraut
Cake(s):
   apple, 17
   apple shortcake, 19
   blackberry shortcake, 60
   butter, 77–79
   chocolate, 159
   citron, 163
   madelines, 301
   plum, 374
   see also trifle
Calf, 86–99

brains, 68–71, 75, 87, 331
tongue, 69, 87, 88, 94
Canapés, 100–102
anchovy, 14, 15, 100
of caviar, 101, 115
crab, 100, 189, **190**
of oranges, 336
Candied peel fritters, 232
Caper(s), 104
sauce, 429
Carrot(s), 109–110
garnishes, 240, 242, 243
purée of, 399
sauce, 429, **430**
Catsup (ketchup):
anchovy, 15
cucumber, 199
mushroom, 309
Cauliflower, 112–113
anglaise garnish, 240
and asparagus salad, 26
boiled, hollandaise sauce,
112–113
boiled capon with tongue and,
106
pickled, 113, **114**
salad, 113, 414
sauces, 113, 430
Caviar, 113–115
canapés of, 101, 115
Celery, 115–118
purée of, 399
salad, 414–415
sauces, 430
Cèpes, 118
omelet with, 220–221
tenderloin of beef with, 45
on toast, 118
Chantilly soup, 120, **121**
Charlotte, 121
apple, 17
apricot, 21
blackberry, 60
cherry, 130
peach, 357
Cheese, 122–128
asparagus with, 26
baked celery with, 117
biscuits, 126
cabbage baked with, 82, **83**

Camembert, 100, 124
canapés, 102
eggplant with, 224
flans, 127
golden buck, 125
Gorgonzola, 250
Gruyère, 254
macaroni and, 295–296
omelet with, 221
straws, 125, **126**
Swiss, 254
Cheesecakes, apple, 17
Cherry(ies), 129–131
sauce, 431
Chestnuts, 131–132
purée of, 399
stewed duck with, 209, **210**
Chicken, 133–157
bouchée of, 65
boudin of, 67
broth with custards, 155,
156
canapés of, 101
chipolata garnish, 242
consommé naudier, 180
forcemeat, 142, 143, 146,
230
fricassée of, 134, **404**
galantine of, 144, 237
giblet and potato pie, 149,
150
gumbo, 152, **154**
ham and tongue sausage, 386
omelet with, 223, 330
prairie, 397–398
salad, 157, 415
soufflé, 146, 147
stock, 153
suprême garnish, 246–247
Chicken livers, 150–152
brochette of, 74
canapés of, 100–101
durand garnish, 242
journeaux garnish, 243
omelet with, 221
Chicory, fricandeau of
sweetbreads with, 97
Chiles (capsicums), 106–107
Chili sauce, 432, 432
Chipolata garnish, 242

Chipolata garnish (*cont.*)
  braised capon with, 105
  calf's head with, 86
  omelet, 331
Chocolate, 158–161
  cup custards, 159, **160,**
    160–161
  fritters, 232
Chowder:
  clam, 163–164, **165**
  codfish, 173–174
Chutney, 161
  apple, 17–18
Clam(s), 163–166
  chowder, 163–164, **165**
  cocktails, 169–170
Cobbler, 167
  apple, 19
  apricot, 21
  cherry, 130
Coconut, 167–168
  banana salad, 29
Cod(fish), 170–174
  and oyster pie, 344
  salad, 415
Cole slaw, 84
  hot, 85
Compote, fruit:
  apple, 19
  apricot, 21
  banana, 29
  blackberry, 60
  cherry, 129
  of oranges, 336
  of peaches, 355
  rhubarb, 409
Corn, 183–188
  fritters, 144, 186, **187,** 233
  gems (muffins), 183–184,
    184
  griddle cakes, 33
Corned beef, 40–41
  hash, 52
Court-bouillon, 188
  sauce, 433
Crab(s), 188–193
  bisque, 58, 192
  canapés, 100, 189, **190**
  salad, 189, 415

Cranberry(ies), 193–194
  sauce, 434
Crayfish, 194
  admiral garnish, 239
  bisque of, 58
  bouchée of, 66
  butter, 78
  tails, brochette of, 76
Cream, 195–196
  chocolate, 159
Creole sauce, 433
Croquettes:
  apple, 18
  bass, 32
  beef, with peas, 49–50
  beef with, 42, 43
  brain, with peas, 68
  calf's kidneys, 91–92
  calf's sweetbreads, with peas,
    95
  chicken, 134
  clam, 164
  crab, 191
  ham, 261
  hominy, 266
  lobster, 291
  macaroni, 298
  oyster, 345
  partridge, 353
  potato, 42, 99, 151, 394
  rice, 43, 411
  salmon, 424
  sweetbreads, 95, 457–458
  turkey, 468
Croûtons, 197
  anchovy, 14
Cucumber(s), 197–199
  consommé beauvilliers, 176
  paysanne garnish, 244
  salad, 199, 415–416
  sauce, 433
Curry(ied), 200
  beef with rice, 51
  calf's head, with rice, 88
  calf's sweetbreads, croûstade of,
    97
  carrots, with rice, 110
  chicken, 139, 142
  codfish, 171

conger eel with rice, 218
cucumbers, 198
of duck with rice, 209–210
eggs, 219
lamb, 282
liver, 289
lobster, 292
mutton, 315
of ox tails, 56–57, 338
oysters, 343
pigeon, 370
rabbit with rice, 407
sauce, 433
soft shell crabs, 192
of sweetbreads, 457
Custard(s), 200
apple, 18
cheese, 127
chicken broth with, 155, **156**
chocolate cup, 159, **160,**
160–161
cream, omelet with, 332
frangipane, 231
fritters, 232
rhubarb with, 409
royal, 412
royale garnish, 246
sauce, 434
tenderloin of beef with, 44–45

D

Dandelion, 203–204
salad, 416
Duck(ling), 79, 206–212
brochette of, 73
livers, 73, 212
mallard, 301–302
stewed with chestnuts, 209,
210
Dumplings:
apple, 18
lemon, 285–286
peach, 357

E

Eel(s), 215–218
brochette of, 74

salad, 217, 416
Egg(s), 218–223
anchovy baskets, 14
artichokes with, 24
beef cakes with, 50
and beet salad, 57, 414
with brown butter, 220, **220**
cabbage with, 84
with caviar, 115
chicken panada with, on toast,
148
golden buck, 125
macaroni creamed with, 298
minced beef with, 51
poached, hashed lamb with,
283
poached, minced chicken with,
148
poached, turkey hash with,
469
salad, 416
sauce, 434
scrambled beef with, 41
scrambled salt cod on toast, 173
scrambled sweetbreads with,
459
see also omelet(s)
Eggplant, 223–225
africaine garnish, 241
omelet with, 223, 330
stuffed, 224, **225**
Epping sausage, 386, **386**
Espagnole sauce, 224, 434–435

F

Fennel sauce, 435
Fish:
bass, 31–32
blackfish, 62
bloaters, 63
bluefish, 63–65
carp, 108–109
cisco, 162
codfish, see cod(fish)
eels, see eel(s)
finnan haddie, 228–229
grouper, 251–252
haddock, see haddock

Fish (*cont.*)
　halibut, *see* halibut
　herring, *see* herring
　kingfish, 276
　mackerel, 299–300
　mullet, 306
　perch, 361–362
　pompano, 374–375
　red snapper, 408
　salmon, *see* salmon
　salt cod, 173, 424
　shad, 450–451
　smelt, *see* smelt(s)
　trout, 463–465
　see also shellfish
Fish roe:
　carp, 109
　caviar, 113–115
　chambord garnish, 242
　cod, 173
　matelote garnish, 244
　sauce, 444
　shad, 451
Flageolets, 35, 229
Flans, cheese, 127
Foie gras, 230
　artichoke bottoms with, 23
　bouchée of, 65
　omelet with, 331
Forcemeat, 230–231
　artichoke bottoms with, 23,
　　24
　brain, 68
　canapés of, 101
　chicken, 142, 143, 146, 151,
　　230
　clam, 166
　crab, 191
　ham, 151, 230–231
　liver, 230–231
　liver, balls, 93
　veal, 230
Fowl:
　blackbirds, 60–61
　black cock, 61
　capon, 104–106
　chicken, *see* chicken
　duck, *see* duck(ling)
　goose, 248–250; *see also* goose
　　liver

grouse, *see* grouse
guinea hen, 254–255
heath, salmis of, 61
ortolans, 337–338
partridge, *see* partridge
pheasant, 362–363
pigeon, 369–372
plover, *see* plover(s)
prairie chicken, 397–398
quail, 401
turkey, *see* turkey
Fricassée:
　of chicken, 134, **404**
　of lamb, 282
　of lobster, 293
　of mushrooms, 308, 309
　of mussels, 310
　of rabbit, 403, **404**
　of turkey wings, 470
Fritters, 232–233
　anchovy, 14, 15–16
　apricot, 22
　artichoke, 23
　banana, 29
　candied peel, 232
　celery, 117
　cheese, 127
　cherry, 131
　chocolate cream, 159
　clam, 164
　corn, 144, 186, **187,** 233
　crab, 189
　cream, 195
　eggplant, 224
　orange, 335
　oyster plant, 347
　parsnip, 233, **234**
　rice, 21, 232–233
Fruits:
　batter for frying, 32
　see also specific fruits
Frying, batter for, 32

G

Game, 238
　birds, anchovy stuffing for, 15
　bouchée of, 65, 66
　boulettes of, 67
　salad, 417

Gardener's salad, 416, **417**
Garlic, 238–239
  butter, 78
Garnishes, 239–247
  beets for, 57
  mushroom, 307
Giblet(s), 247–248
  chicken, 149–151
  duck, 212
  and potato pie, 149, **150**
  sauce, 151, 436
Godard garnish, 243
Golden buck, 125
Gooseberry sauce, 250, 436
Goose liver:
  brochette of, 74
  sausage, 387
  toulouse garnish, 247
Goulash, 275–276
Griddle cakes, 33
  butter, 77–78
  French pancakes, 32, 33
  green corn, 186
Grouse, 253–254
  braised black, 61
  prairie chicken, 397–398
Gumbo, 255
  chicken, 152, **154**
  crab, 192
  oyster, 345–346

H

Haddock, 257–258
  finnan haddie, 228–229
Halibut, 259–260
  fried with bacon, 260
Ham, 260–262
  baked cabbage with, 82
  curing of, 200
  forcemeat, 151, 230–231
  garnishes, 240, 241, 242, 243
  hashed chicken and, with rice,
    149
  omelet with, 221–222
  potted, canapés of, 101
  sauce, 436
Hare, 262–263
  boudin of, 67
  see also rabbit

Haricot beans, 35–37
  flageolets, 35, 229
  glazed calf's sweetbreads with,
    96–97
Hash:
  corned beef, 52
  **turkey, with poached eggs,
    469**
Heart:
  beef, 56
  calf's, 90–91
Heath fowl, salmis of, 61
Herbs, fine, 228
Herring, 263–265
  bisque of, 58
  bloaters, 63
  salad, 418
Hollandaise sauce, 437
Horseradish, 266–268
  anglaise garnish, 240, 241
  boiled beef heart with, 56
  braised sirloin with, 44
  butter, 78–79, **266**
  sauce, 437
Hot pot or hotch potch, 267
Hot slaw, 85

I

Ice cream, 196
  banana, 29
  chocolate, 159
  coffee, 175
Ices, *see* water ices
Icing, chocolate, 159
Indian pudding, 184

J

Jams and jellies, 271–272
  apricot, 22
  blackberry, 60
  calf's feet, 90
  cherry, 130
  cranberry, 194
  grape, 250–251
  orange, 335
  peach, 355
  plum, 373–374
  quince, 402

Jams and jellies (*cont.*)
  rhubarb, 409
  see also aspic jelly; marmalade
Jelly, omelet with, 332
Jerusalem artichokes, 272–273
  purée of, 399

K

Ketchup, *see* catsup
Kidney(s):
  beef, 56
  and beef steak pie, 51
  calf's, 91–92
  lamb, brochette of, 73
  lamb, macaroni with, 297–298
  pork, 380
  omelet with, 220, 222
Kidney beans, 35
  braised ox tails with, 56
  creamed brains with, 70
  French style, 35, **36**
  stewed calf's sweetbreads with,
    98
Knackwurst, 389–390

L

Lamb, 279–283
  brains, 68–71
  brochette of, 73
  **chops with mushroom
    purée, 317**
  fricassée of, 282
  fries, brochette of, 75
  kidneys, brochette of, 73
  noisettes of, 322
Leeks, 284
  chicken soup with rice and, 153
  cockie-leekie soup, 168–169
Lemon, 284–287
  marmalade, 285, **286**
  trifle, 285, **287**
Lettuce, 288–289
  fermière garnish, 243
  salad, 288, 416
Lima bean(s), 34–35
  purée of, 400
  salad, 35, 418

Liqueur:
  absinthe, 11
  kirschwasser, 276
  kummel, 277
  maraschino, 302
Liver(s), 289
  brochettes of, 73–74
  calf's, 92–93
  chicken, *see* chicken livers
  curried, 289–290
  duck, 73, 212
  forcemeat, 230–231
  fried, 289
  goose, *see* goose liver
  sausage, 382–383, 385,
    387–388
  turkey, brochette of, 74
  turkey, omelet with, 331
  see also foie gras
Liverwurst, 383
Lobster, 290–293
  bisque of, 58
  bouchée of, 65–66
  brochette of, 75, 292
  butter, 78
  salad, 418–419
  sauce, 438

M

Macaroni, 295–299
  chicken dishes with, 138,
    140–141
  glazed ribs of beef with, 42
  milanaise garnish, 244
  napolitaine garnish, 244
  with oysters, Milan style,
    296, **297**
Macedoine garnish, 244
Maître d'hôtel sauce, 301, 439
Mallard, 301–302
Margarine, 79
Marmalade, 303
  apple, 19
  apricot, 22
  cherry, 130
  lemon, 285, **286**
  omelet with, 332
  orange, 336
  peach, 355

plum, 373
quince, 402
see also jams and jellies
Marrow, 303
celery with, 117
fried cucumbers with, 198
Mayonnaise, 304
sauce, 439
Meat:
scrapple, 449
stuffed cabbage, 82
see also specific kinds of meats
Meringue, 305
apple, 18
cherry, 131
omelet with, 332
rhubarb, 409
Minced pork with fried apples, 379
Mincemeat, 306
lemon, 285
Mint, 306
sauce, 439
Mock turtle soup, 88–89
Muffins, corn gems, 183–184, 184
Mushroom(s), 307–309
beef dishes with, 43, 44, 46, 50, 51
bouchée with, 66
brain dishes with, 69
broiled, 308
calf's meats dishes with, 90, 91, 93, 98
chicken dishes with, 137, 138, 141, 143, 151
garnishes, 240, 241, 242, 243
omelet with, 222
purée, lamb chops with, 317
purée of, 400
sauces, 308–309, 439–440
stuffed, 309
vol-au-vent of sweetbreads and, 96
see also cèpes
Mussels, 309–312
admiral garnish, 239
brochette of, 74
scalloped, 311

Mutton, 312–320
brochette of, 74
noisettes of, 322
tomato sausages, 390

N

Noodles:
chicken soup with, 157
roast capons with, 104–105
see also pasta

O

Okra, 326
africaine garnish, 241
grecque garnish, 243
see also gumbo
Olive(s), 326–327
anchovies with, 15
anchovy stuffing for, 15
calf's head with, tomato sauce, 87, 88
canapés of, 101
caviar on toast with, 115
omelet with, 223, 330
tournedos of beef with, 52
Omelet(s), 220–223, 327–332
with anchovies, 16, 331
apricot, 22
artichoke, 24
asparagus, 25
with Brussels sprouts, 76
with calf's head, 88
calf's kidneys, 92
with cèpes, 118
cheese, 128
of chicken livers, 151
crab, 189
frog, Southern style, 235
lobster, 292
mushroom, 309
with oysters, 222, 329
savory, of calf's brains, 70
souffle, 332
Onion(s), 332–335
artichoke bottoms with, 24
and artichoke salad, 24
bean purée with, 37
boiled celery with, 117

Onion(s) (*cont.*)
  and cucumber salad, 199
  fried, spring chicken in batter
    with, 146
  garnishes, 240, 241, 242
  hamburg steak with, 46
  liver with, 92, 93, 289
  omelet with, 330
  purée, 220, 334, 400
  salad, 334, 419
  sauces, 440
Orange(s), 335–337
  banana salad, 29
  bouchée of, 67
  fritters, 233
  sauce, 440–441
Ox, 338–339
  palate garnish, 243
  palates, bouchée with, 66
Ox tails, 56
Oxtail soup, 47–49, **49,** 338
Oyster(s), 339–347
  admiral garnish, 239
  baked, 242, 343
  baked codfish stuffed with, 170
  beef filets with, 53
  and beef steak pie, 51
  bisque of, 58
  bouchée of, 65, 346
  brochette of, 73, 342
  canapés of, 101
  chicken sauté with 149
  cocktails, 169–170
  devilled beef with, 51
  and lobster pie, 293
  macaroni with, Milan style,
    296, **297**
  omelet with, 222, 329
  pie, 293, 344–345, 476
  salad, 419
  sauce, 441
  scalloped beef with, 51
  small fillets of beef with, 53

P

Pancakes, *see* griddle cakes
Parisian garnish, 245
Parsley, 349
  sauces, 441

Parsnip(s), 350
  fritters, 233, **234**
Partridge, 350–353
  bisque of, 59
  salad, 353, 419
Pasta, 353–354
  curried ox tails with spaghetti,
    56–57
  ravioles, 407
  see also macaroni; noodles
Pea(s), 360–361
  chicken dishes with, 142, 144,
    145, 157
  croquettes with, 49–50, 68,
    91–92, 95, 261
  émince of beef with, 52
  French, omelet with, 222–223
  purée of, 399
  soup, 360
  stewed carrots with, 110
Peach(es), 354–358
  bouchée of, 67
  fritters, 233
  ice, 357–358, **358**
Pepper(s), bell:
  butter, 78
  chicken dishes with, 140, 148
  stuffed, tenderloin of beef with,
    45
  tenderloin steak sautéed with,
    45
Peppers, capsicum, 106–107
Pickled:
  beets, 57
  cabbage, 84
  cauliflower, 113, **114**
  cucumbers, 199
  onions, 334
Pickling, 363–364, 367–369
  of ox tongues, 369
  of rolled hams, 368–369
  of vegetables, 161
Pies, dessert:
  apple, 18
  blackberry, 60
  cherry, 130
  orange, 336
  pumpkin, 398
  rhubarb, 409
Pies, savory:
  beef, 50–51

blackbird, 61
chicken, 134–135
cod and oyster, 174
giblet, 149
giblet and potato, 149, **150**
goose giblet, 247
lobster and oyster, 293
mutton, 320
oyster, 293, 344–345, 476
pigeon, 370
rabbit, 405
veal and oyster, 476
Plover(s), 372–373
bisque of, 59
Plums, 373–374
bouchée of, 67
damson, 203
Poivrade sauce, 441–442, **443**
Polish sausage, 388–389
Popcorn, 186–187
Pork, 375–390
brains, 68–71
cuts of, 364–366
kidneys, 74, 380
**minced, with fried apples,
379**
salt, see salt pork
sausages, 380–390; see also
sausages
**tenderloin with sweet
potatoes, 376**
timbales, 477
see also ham
Potato(es), 391–397
balls, chicken sauté with,
147–148
and beet salad, 57
blackbirds in, 61
calf's tongue with, mushroom
sauce, 94
croquettes, 42, 99, 151, 394
garnishes, 239–240, 242, 243,
246
and giblet pie, 149, **150**
salad, 419
salpicon of chicken with, 142
sausage cakes with, 57
scalloped, 392
stuffed, 43–44, 394
**Potatoes, sweet, pork
tenderloin with, 376**

Poultry, see fowl
Prawns, bisque of, 58
Preserve(s):
bottled peaches, 356
melon, 304–305
see also pickling
Provençale garnish, 245
Provençale sauces, 398, 442–443
Pudding, dessert:
apple, 19
apple roly-poly, 19, **20**
baked orange, 335
blackberry, 59–60
cherry, 130
chocolate, 160
corn meal (Indian), 184–185
date, 205
farina, 227
macaroni, 298
plum, 374
see also blanc mange; roly-poly
Pudding, savory:
boudin, 67
cheese, 127
grated corn, 186
liver, 289
macaroni, 298
meats, 67
peas, 361
veal, 477

R

Rabbit, 403–407
bisque of, 59
boudin of, 67
brochette of, 75
fricassée of, 403, **404**
hare, 262–263
Radish salad, 420
Rarebit, Welsh, 124
egg, 219
golden buck, 125
Reed bird(s):
bouchée of, 66
brochette of, 75–76
Regency sauce, 444
Ribbon jelly, 271–272
Rice, 409–411
andalouse garnish, 240

Rice (*cont.*)
   chicken dishes with, 135, 136,
      139, 142, 145, 147, 149,
      153
   croquettes, 43, 411
   fritters, 21, 232–233
   griddle cakes, 33
Roe, *see* fish roe
Roly-poly, 411
   apple, 19, **20**
   cherry, 130

S

Sage sauce, 445
Salad dressings:
   cream, 422
   French, 231, 422
   hollandaise, 423
   mayonnaise, 304
Salads, 413–422
   anchovy, 15, 413
   artichoke, 24, 25, 413
   asparagus, 26, 413–414
   banana, 29
   beet and egg, 57, 414
   beet and potato, 57
   carrot, with asparagus tips, 110
   cauliflower, 113, 414
   chicken, 157, 415
   cole slaw, 84, **85**
   crab, 189, 415
   cucumber, 199, 415–416
   eel, 217, 416
   gardener's, 416, **417**
   hot slaw, 85
   lettuce, 288, 416
   lima bean, 35, 418
   onion, 334, 419
   partridge, 353, 419
   salmon, 421
   sweetbread, 99, 422
Salami, 389
Salmon, 423–424
   and asparagus salad, 26
   bisque of, 58–59
   bouchée of, 66–67
   salad, 421
   smoked, canapés, 100
   trout, 463–465

Salt cod, 173, 424
Salt pork, 378, 379
   boiled capon with, 105
   boiled chicken with, parsley
      sauce, 137
Sandwiches:
   anchovy, 14
   lobster, 292
   oyster, 346
   potted beef for, 52
   potted chicken for, 148
   smoked beef, 41
Sardine(s):
   bouchée of, 66
   canapés, 101
   liver sausage, 385, 388
   salad, 420
Sauces, 425–447
   anchovy, 15, 425
   apricot, 22, 425
   basic white, 427
   Bavarian, 426, **428**
   Béarnaise, 37–38, 427
   Béchamel, 38, 195, 426
   brandy, 71
   butter, 77–79
   carrot, 429, **430**
   cauliflower, 113, 430
   chili, 432, **432**
   crab, 192
   cream, 195
   D'uxelles, 213, 434
   Espagnole, 224, 434–435
   giblet, 151, 436
   gooseberry, 250, 436
   lemon, 285
   maître d'hôtel, 301, 439
   mushroom, 308–309, 439–440
   onion, 333, 440
   orange, 336, 440–441
   oyster, 344, 441
   Perigueux, 362, 441
   poivrade, 441–442, **443**
   Provencale, 398, 442–443
   tomato, 446, **447**
   Velouté, 446, **448**
Sauerkraut, 85, 447
   allemande garnish, 239
   smoked tongue with, 53–54,
      55

Sausages, 380–390
  anglaise garnish, 241
  beef, 57
  chipolata garnish, 242
  crab, 189
  Epping, 386, **387**
  frankforts, 231, 386
  hot pot or hotch potch, 267
  macaroni with, 298
  mutton, 390
  pork, 380–390
  and spinach timbales, 454
  stewed red cabbage with, 84
  stuffed cabbage, 82
  tomato, 390
  veal, 390
Scalloped:
  mussels, 310, **311**
  potatoes, 392
Scallop(s):
  brochette of, 75
  omelet with, 331
  sauce, 445
Shallot(s), 451
  sauce, 445
Sheep:
  brains, 68–70
  see also lamb; mutton
Shellfish:
  garnishes, 239, 240, 241,
        242–243, 244, 245–246
  see also clam(s); crab(s); lobster;
        mussels; oyster(s); shrimp(s)
Sherbet:
  apricot, 22
  cherry, 130
Shortcake:
  apple, 19
  blackberry, 60
  peach, 356–357
Shrimp(s), 452
  admiral garnish, 239
  bisque of, 58
  butter, 78
  canapés of, 100
  omelet with, 222, 331
  salad, 420
  sauce, 445
Smelt(s), 453
  brochette of, 75

smoked tongue with
        sauerkraut, 53–54, **55**
Snapper, red, 408
Sole, 453
  bouchée of, 66
Sorrel, 453
  brains with, sauce ravigote, 70
  braised calf's sweetbreads with,
        98
  chicken broth with, 156–157
  sauce, 445
Soubise garnish, 246
Soup:
  apple, 19
  artichoke, 24
  asparagus, 25–26
  beef, 46–47
  beef, English style, 46, **47**
  beef kidney, 56
  bisques, 58–59
  bouillabaisse, 68
  button onion, with peas, 335
  calf's head, 88–89
  carrot, 110–111
  celery, 116–117
  Chantilly, 120, **121**
  chestnut, 132
  chicken, 151–157
  chicken gumbo, 152, **154**
  clam, 166
  clam chowder, 163–164, **165**
  cockie-leekie, 168–169
  codfish chowder, 173–174
  colbert, 175
  consommé, 175–182
  corn, 186
  crab gumbo, 192
  giblet, 151–152, 248
  haricot, family style, 37
  hot pot or hotch potch, 267
  leek, Scotch style, 284
  lemon, 285
  lobster, 293
  macaroni, 298–299
  olla podrida, 327
  oxtail, 47–49, **49,** 338
  oyster, 345, 346
  pea, green, 360
  potato, 396–397
  sweetbread, 99, 459
  see also broth; stock

Spaghetti, curried ox tails with,
    56–57
Spinach, 453
    calf's liver and bacon with, 93
    omelet with, 223
    purée of, 298, 399
    and sausage timbales, 454
    smoked beef with, 41
    sweetbreads with, 456
    tongue with, 54–56
Squab, 372
Steak:
    beef tenderloin, 45–46
    chateaubriand, 122
    and oyster pie, 344–345
    salisbury, 45–46
    see also beef
Stew:
    clam, 164
    crab, 189
    hot pot or hotch potch, 267
    Irish, 270, 315
    mutton, with vegetables, 319
    olla podrida, 327
    oyster, 340
Stock:
    beef, 48
    chicken, 153
Stuffed eggplant, 224, 225
Sweetbread(s), 456–459
    bouchée of, 65
    brochette of, 74–75, 458
    calf's, 94–99
    durand garnish, 242
    financière garnish, 243
    lamb, in cases, 283
    omelet with, 222
    salad, 99, 422
**Sweet potatoes, pork
    tenderloin with, 376**

T

Tartlettes:
    apricot, 22
    blackberry, 60
    cranberry, 194
    peach, 357
Tarts:
    apple, 18–19

cherry, 130
Timbale(s):
    apple, 19–20
    of macaroni, 296, 298
    spinach and sausage, 454
    veal or pork, 477
Tomato(es), 462
    andalouse garnish, 240
    and artichoke salad, 24–25
    baked, sauté of calf's
        sweetbreads with, 98
    baked bluefish with, 64
    braised beef tongue with, 53
    braised capons with rice, 105
    and corn soup, 186
    grilled, Salisbury steak with, 46
    hamburg steak with, 46
    and lettuce salads, 288
    lobster with, 292
    macaroni and, 296
    omelet with, 222
    purée of, 399–400
    sausages, 390
    stewed chicken with, 135
Tomatoes, stuffed:
    braised brains with, 69
    braised sirloin with, 44
    with crab, 191
Tomato sauce, 446, 447
    rabbit with, 405
    calf's meats dishes with, 88, 89,
        94
    chicken dishes with, 137, 138,
        146
    fried cod steak, 171
Tongue(s):
    beef, 53
    boiled capon with cauliflower
        and, 106
    calf's, 69, 87, 88, 94
    codfish, 172, 174
    ox, 338, 339
    potted, canapés of, 101
    **smoked, with sauerkraut,
        53–54, 55**
    veal roll with, 475
Tortillas, 185–186
Trifle, 462
    cherry, 130–131
    lemon, 285, 287

peach, 357
Truffle(s), 465
  blanquette of chicken with, 139
  braised sirloin of beef with, 43
  calf's ears with, sauce trianon,
      89
  liver sausage, 387
  omelet with, 330
  sauce, sauté of beef, 53
  sweetbreads and, in shell,
      97–98
Turkey, 465–470
  boudin of, 67
  brochette of, 75
  galantine of, 237
  **hash with poached eggs,
      469**
  livers, brochette of, 74
  livers, omelet with, 331
Turtle, tortoise, 471
  bisque of terrapin, 59
  diamond back, 205
  soup, green, 471
  soup, mock, 88–89

V

Veal, 473–478
  boudin of, 67
  brains, 68–70
  brochette of, 73
  chipolata garnish, 242
  cuts of, 474
  forcemeat, 230
  quenelles, braised calf's head
      with, 87
  sausages, 390

  stewed, 477–478
  timbales, 477
Vegetables:
  batter for frying, 32
  see also specific vegetables
Velouté sauce, 446, **448**
Vinegar, 479–480
  onion, 334

W

Water ices, 269–270
  apple, 18
  cherry, 131
  orange, 269
  peach, 357–358, **358**
  Roman punch, 411–412
Weinerwurst (frankforts), 231,
      386
Welsh rarebit, see rarebit, Welsh
Westphalian sausage, 390
Whipped cream, 195
Wines:
  Burgundy, 77
  Chablis, 119
  champagne, 119–120
  Chianti, 132
  claret, 166–167
  Madeira, 300–301
  sherry, 451–452
Woodcock, 481
  bouchée of, 66

Y

Yorkshire pudding, 33